C0-ARX-018

THIRD EDITION

BUSINESS CYCLES

and

FORECASTING

By

CARL A. DAUTEN

Professor of Finance
Washington University
St. Louis, Missouri

LLOYD M. VALENTINE

Professor of Economics
University of Cincinnati
Cincinnati, Ohio

Published by

SOUTH-WESTERN PUBLISHING COMPANY

Cincinnati   Chicago   Burlingame, Calif.   Dallas   New Rochelle, N.Y.

H51   [1968]

PREFACE

Our economy, like that of every industrialized nation, is characterized by fluctuations in economic activity that affect the operations of business, the welfare of labor, the policies of government, and the everyday life of all of us as consumers and as citizens. Every citizen should understand the nature of these fluctuations and the factors which produce them. He should be able to analyze plans that are proposed to mitigate the effects of these fluctuations or to eliminate them.

The analysis of current and prospective levels of national income is one of the major concerns of the economist. He is being called upon more and more frequently to recommend policies that will promote economic growth and stability. He can recommend appropriate action only if he thoroughly understands the factors that promote growth as well as those which lead to fluctuations in the level of economic activity. The economist is also being called on with increasing frequency to forecast the future state of economic activity, so as to provide the economic background for developing governmental, business, and labor policies.

The businessman has a special interest in business fluctuations. The level of economic activity affects his volume of business and his ability to operate profitably. He must make the best possible projections of future sales when he buys goods for inventory, when he hires labor, and when he expands his plant. In fact, modern business planning is based on a forecast of business conditions in the immediate future and for longer periods of time.

This book provides the background which is needed by individuals, economists, and businessmen to understand the factors which contribute to economic growth and stability and to the level of national income. It also surveys the techniques which may be used to analyze current economic conditions and to forecast future levels of activity. The authors believe that the factors which affect the level of economic activity and national income and the techniques of forecasting them should be studied as a unit. Prediction of future events in any field of knowledge is possible only when the causal factors that produce changes are fully understood. The factors at work to produce changes in economic activity and in the level of national income are not fully understood in all of their ramifications, but many of the basic factors at work are clear. The business cycle is no longer a completely unsolved riddle, and a large measure of understanding exists of the factors that promote economic growth and determine the level of national income. As the knowledge of the causal factors at work is steadily increased, forecasting will increase in accuracy.

This book is intended for senior or graduate courses in the field of business cycles or national income analysis and in forecasting. These courses do not have uniform content nor titles, but are given under such titles as *Business Cycles* or *Business Cycles and Forecasting, Business Conditions Analysis, National Income Analysis,* or *Forecasting.*

The earlier editions of this book studied the factors which led to economic growth and to fluctuations in such growth and used this material as a background for forecasting. This third edition has continued this integration of the knowledge in this field and has carried it further. The introductory section discusses those factors which affect economic development and summarizes the major characteristics of American economic development. Part II has been completely rewritten with major emphasis on national income analysis. Business cycle theory has been used as a background for developing an understanding of the factors which affect the level of national income. Business cycle analysis and national income analysis have developed, in part at least, along separate paths but both are dealing with the same basic factors. The integration of business cycle analysis and national income analysis is one of the major features of this edition.

The section on the behavior of inventories has also been rewritten in keeping with this approach. It is now organized around the impact on the economy of the various factors which are used by businessmen to determine the level of inventories. This also has been done in other areas such as the discussion of hog and cattle cycles. The discussion of the role of monetary and fiscal policies in the 1929–33 depression has been revised to take account of recent theoretical developments and research in this field.

The chapter on projecting the trend of economic activity also has been reorganized in line with the general approach used in the text. It is now developed around the supply of the factors of production and the demand for them. The chapters on short-run forecasting contain new data on the latest group of leading indicators and on experience with econometric models based on national income analysis. The last section on promoting economic growth and stability has been largely rewritten with major emphasis on the relationship of policies and programs in this area to the factors which determine levels of national income.

The authors wish to express their appreciation to their colleagues and to their friends in business and government. Without their help in discussing what is being done and can be done to analyze and forecast national income and business conditions, this book could not have been written. Professors Merle Welshans, Jack Wolff, Henry Guithes, Arthur Vieth, Robert Virgil, and others have offered valuable suggestions based on classroom use of the earlier editions of this book. Professors David G. Davies, of Duke University, and John M. Kuhlman, of the University of Missouri, also kindly read and discussed sections of the manuscript.

Carl A. Dauten

Lloyd M. Valentine

CONTENTS

PART I

INTRODUCTION

This book concerns itself with fluctuations in economic activity. Changes are continually taking place in prices, in wages, in the level of employment, and in other economic factors; and these changes affect the fortunes of all of us not only in our country but in the world. The early pioneers on the frontiers of civilization could largely ignore economic changes since they built their own homes from native timber, raised their own food, and made their own clothes. In an economy of interdependence in which almost everyone works for a living and uses the money he receives to buy the goods and services he needs, however, the state of economic activity is of primary concern to all.

Periods of depressed economic activity, which have occurred from time to time, have caused untold deprivation and suffering for many people. In fact, the argument has been made with some appeal that the free-enterprise system is unacceptable because of such suffering during major periods of depressed economic activity. Those who favor a controlled economy have promised an end to periods of economic depression. Thus, one of the challenges for our society is to cure this problem within the framework of a free society and, at the same time, to continue to raise the standard of living of our people.

The struggle for power in our modern world is in part a struggle between two competing economic systems, each claiming that it can raise the standard of living of its people and of those of the rest of the world more rapidly than the other.

This introductory part presents the background for the study of business fluctuations and of procedures for forecasting them and for striving to stabilize economic activity. The first chapter describes the nature of economic fluctuations and of forecasting. It identifies the major types of fluctuations in economic activity in a preliminary way. This is followed by a preliminary discussion of the nature of forecasting of economic fluctuations. The second chapter discusses the major characteristics of American economic development. Consideration is first directed to the record of growth in the American economy and then to the characteristics of major cyclical variations in such growth.

1 *Nature of Economic Fluctuations and Forecasting*

The volume of economic activity in America has been increasing since early colonial days. This has been true not only because population has been increasing but also because our productivity has been increasing as methods have been developed to turn out more and more goods with a given amount of labor. This growth of economic activity has not taken place, however, at a steady rate. It was very rapid during World War II and the postwar years and much slower in the 1930's. Nor has growth taken place without interruption. There have been several periods of minor decreases in economic activity even in the prosperous years since the end of World War II. From time to time there have been much more serious and protracted interruptions in the forward push of economic progress. This happened from 1929 to 1933 and in several other periods in our history.

NATURE AND SIGNIFICANCE OF ECONOMIC FLUCTUATIONS

Severe fluctuations in production, employment, prices, and other phases of economic activity are of primary importance as economic, social, and political factors. They not only affect the economy and society at large but also the lives of individuals of all ages and in all walks of life.

Depression Periods in Economic Activity

It is difficult to comprehend the full effect on the lives of individuals of periods of severe depression in economic activity. Those who are unable to find employment in a period of depressed activity are forced to curtail consumption of goods and services to such an extent that real want and privation often exist. The psychological impact on their lives is more difficult to measure, but it is certainly great. The effect on the attitudes of young people who are just entering the labor force and cannot find employment is highly detrimental to the social framework of the nation. Older workers who lose their jobs during the decline in business activity on the down-swing of the cycle may find it almost impossible to get gainful employment again on a regular basis. Depression periods have also been periods of declines in the general level of prices, that is, of deflation.

In a period of deflation debtors find their loans and interest payments on them more difficult to repay since it takes more purchasing power to do so than it did at the time the loan was made. This creates problems for businessmen and farmers who mortgaged their property in a period of high prices and must pay off mortgages and meet interest payments in a period of falling prices. The same is true for individuals buying a house on which they have a substantial mortgage. Not only does it take additional real income to repay the loan and interest on it, but problems arise when an individual is forced to move. He may find that he owes more dollars than the house will bring on the market and, as a result, he has debts after he sells and no down payment for a new home.

Business fluctuations also create problems for the total economy and for society at large. From the economic standpoint there is the loss of goods that might have been produced during the period of less than full employment. This will amount to billions of dollars even in relatively minor downturns and is staggering in major depressions. There is also a loss of capital equipment which deteriorates faster than it is replaced. As a result, it is more difficult to achieve high levels of production in the ensuing prosperity period, and the nation is permanently poorer than it would have been if capital had been replaced and expanded at more normal levels.

Business failures increase rapidly during periods of depressed business activity, especially in major depressions. This not only involves losses for the owners, but generally also for creditors. Such losses to creditors have been substantial even in minor downturns. Business failures also have an adverse effect on the employees of the concerns that fail and on the communities in which they are located.

Depressions also create social problems that become especially severe during protracted periods of large-scale unemployment. The crime rate increases, especially among the younger people who have not been firmly established in their jobs and homes or who are just entering the labor force and find it impossible to get jobs. Marriages are postponed and birth rates drop with resulting social problems.

This also intensifies the depression since demand for housing and consumer goods related to homemaking and rearing a family is further reduced.

The political repercussions of business fluctuations are also of great importance. When large numbers of people are unemployed, they are easily swayed by demagogs who promise them food and shelter in exchange for their freedom. At least part of the rise of communism and fascism, especially the latter, can be traced to such situations in periods of greatly depressed business activity. In democratic nations there is tremendous pressure on the government during times of subnormal business activity to do something about unemployment and its problems with the result that the trend toward government regulation and public ownership of business is greatly accelerated.

Boom Periods in Economic Activity

Problems of a severe nature also occur when demands are made on the economy that are beyond its ability to supply them. Increasing output of itself creates no economic problems, but the effect of demand in excess of the ability to supply it leads to an increase in the general level of prices. Prices do not change uniformly but do so at different rates in different sectors of the economy, and this creates problems. It leads to inequities between individuals and groups and so to a less than optimum allocation of resources.

Inflation creates serious problems for the individual. His debts become easier to pay off, but he has problems in planning insurance, investment, and retirement programs. The face value of life insurance policies remains unchanged, but the proceeds buy less. The same is true of pension programs guaranteeing a fixed dollar amount as most of them do. Investment also becomes a problem since bonds and savings and loan shares lose value as prices go up, and the average individual does not have the necessary analytical ability to invest in common stocks so as to keep ahead of inflation.

Many groups in society suffer a loss in real income in inflation and try to use political pressure to stop it. The pay of government workers, teachers, employees in regulated industries, and others lags behind the rise in prices; and this makes it difficult to recruit and hold good workers. The teaching profession is likely to be hard hit since, when income fails to keep up with prices, fewer students, especially the good ones, plan to become teachers and, therefore, a shortage exists for several years.

There is also constant pressure to raise social security payments since purchasing power has been reduced. This makes it more difficult to plan social security tax payments to meet the needs at retirement. It also leads to tax increases which adversely affect some groups of workers that have not kept pace with the inflationary spiral.

In the American economy the desire to avoid the undesirable consequences of economic fluctuations led to the enactment of the Full Employment Act of 1946, which stated that it was the policy of the federal government to plan its activities that affected the economy so as to promote full employment. The government is also under continuing pressure to use its powers and influences to control inflation as well as deflation. Government programs in agriculture have been directed toward stabilizing agricultural income and in housing toward stabilizing overall economic activity.

TYPES OF VARIATIONS IN ECONOMIC ACTIVITY

Economists recognize different types of variations in economic activity. These are the trend, business cycles, seasonal fluctuations, and irregular and random fluctuations in economic series.

Trend

Even though economic activity does not proceed smoothly but is interrupted by periods of decline followed by increased activity, there is an underlying long-run tendency for economic activity to increase that is referred to as the trend. *Trend* is the persistent underlying movement that takes place in economic activity in general or in a sector of the economy over a period of years. It is the basic growth or decline that would exist if there were no periods of boom or depression or of less pronounced variations in economic activity.

The trend in total economic activity is a linear one; that is, activity has grown at a more or less constant rate over a period of years. This trend in the United States has been upward due to many factors. The development of a new continent was a major factor until around 1900. Also significant have been the rapid increase in population, the increasing stock of capital goods, technological progress, the increased education and skills of the labor force, increased managerial skills, and the discovery of new sources of raw materials.

The trend of total economic activity is the combined result of the trends of individual industries and businesses. A successful new industry usually grows rapidly in its early stages. Growth then levels off to a more gradual rate, and after a time the industry becomes integrated with the economy and its growth is largely governed by the growth in the general economy. The trend of growth of such a new industry is a curvilinear one; that is, it resembles an elongated S. As the demand for goods and services changes, some industries may pass their peak and decline. This may be a gradual downward movement, as in the case of coal furnaces, or a rapid decline, as in the case of a product, such as wagon wheels, which has become obsolete.

Business Cycles

Changes in the level of economic activity caused by the trend are overshadowed by continually recurring variations in total economic activity. Several years of expansion in total economic activity are followed by a period of slower growth or of contraction in such activity. These fluctuations occur in total economic activity, not just in a particular industry or sector of the economy. Such expansions and contractions in the level of activity occur at about the same time in most sectors of the economy. This sequence of fluctuations is a recurring one, but it is not periodic; that is, such variations do not occur at regular time intervals and do not last for the same periods of time. The amplitude of movement from the low point of activity to the high point of activity is not the same. These fluctuations have become known as *business cycles*. Any connotation of regularity, however, which the term "cycles" may give does not exist in data on total economic activity, production, employment, prices, or any other major economic series.

Seasonal Fluctuations

Seasonal fluctuations are changes in economic activity during the course of a year that occur in a more or less regular pattern from year to year. Such changes are related to the changing seasons of the year or to holidays or the calendar. The canning or freezing of fruit, for example, must take place during that season of the year when the fresh fruit is available and, therefore, this economic activity follows a seasonal pattern. Other seasonal patterns are related to customs in our society, such as sales arising out of Christmas gift exchanges and the Easter parade. The changing date of Easter leads to a changing seasonal pattern in those sectors of economic activity which are affected. Other seasonal variations occur because of the unequal number of days in the month in our calendar and the unequal distribution of holidays that are generally observed.

Irregular and Random Fluctuations

Economic activity in various sectors of the economy, and to some degree in the total economy, is also affected from time to time by such exogenous factors as a widespread drought, a major flood, or a political disturbance. It may also be affected by a major strike. Some minor variations in economic activity are due to more or less unpredictable factors, such as unusual absenteeism due to an epidemic of flu. Others may be due to purely random factors, such as the bunching of large orders from several major customers in one month or quarter. These various factors are known as *irregular and random fluctuations.*

PRICE LEVEL CHANGES

The changes in economic activity involved in the trend, the business cycle, seasonal factors, and irregular and random fluctuations affect the general level of prices. For example, there is some tendency for prices to rise in the upswing of a business cycle as demand for goods and services grows faster than the ability of the economy to provide goods and services and some tendency for prices to decline on the downswing of the cycle. Changes in the price level from time to time may also be primarily related to changes in the money supply or the money standard, rather than to real changes in the level of economic activity. For example, during World War II the money supply was increased greatly by the methods used to finance the war and the base was laid for an increase in the price level. When price controls were abandoned at the end of the war, prices rose until the supplies of money and of goods were in balance. At other times the basic movement of prices has been downward. This was true in the 1870's and 1880's because economic activity was expanding and the money supply was more or less fixed.

FORECASTING AND ECONOMIC FLUCTUATIONS

When making decisions about the future course of a business, management must take into consideration all of the factors that are likely to affect it, both external and internal. Business fluctuations are among the major external factors that affect a business and are therefore of prime importance in making management decisions.

The Relationship of Economic Changes to Business Management

The primary function of management in a business is to determine the objectives of the business in the long run and short run. Then management must make plans to carry out these objectives, organize human and material resources to put the plans into action, implement the plans, and control the activities of the business to be sure that all is going according to plan. Economic analysis and forecasting are involved in all of these steps in management, but primarily in determining objectives and in developing long-range and short-range plans to carry out these objectives.

In determining its objectives each business must decide on the good or service it plans to produce and sell, the price range of its product or service, the geographic region in which it plans to sell, the potential market for the product, the share of this market it can realistically hope to get, the prospective return on capital it can expect, and the like. Such objectives can only be realistic and well balanced if management has analyzed trends in the economy and has forecast the demand for its product both in the long run and short run, the price at which it will sell, the cost of the factors of production, and the like. Thus, an analysis of trends and current developments in the economy and a forecast of such trends and current developments is basic to establishing sound business objectives and in developing long-range and short-range plans to carry out such objectives.

The Need for Forecasting in Business

Some businessmen and economists still feel that forecasting is impossible in their businesses or at best is so indefinite as to be hazardous as a basis for business decisions. The statement is frequently made that forecasting may have succeeded well for others but "our business is different." The fact remains, however, that in any business in which raw materials must be purchased before orders are received or in which substantial capital equipment is used, some form of forecasting is being done, even if unwittingly.

If a business plans to continue to operate at present levels, the forecast implicitly made is that present levels of business are predicted for the future. For most businesses this is not true for any period of time since they are continually affected by changing business conditions. Another frequent basis for business decisions is that past trends will continue. If, for example, business has been increasing at a rate of about 5 percent a year, that rate of increase is expected to continue for the next year or several years. This can be a hazardous assumption because growth does not continue at the same rate for an indefinite period of time in a dynamic economy.

In many concerns in which the top officials feel that forecasting cannot be done, someone is actually doing the forecasting. For example, a manufacturer of appliances used in home construction felt that the level of his business could not be forecast successfully. He believed that current orders were the only real guide to follow in planning production. Since orders usually were received several weeks ahead of the requested delivery date and since the appliances could be assembled in several days, this looked like a reasonable procedure. Some of the raw materials, however, had to be ordered as much as five months ahead of time to allow for delivery and fabrication. Since no one would venture a forecast, not even the purchasing agent, the clerk who did the ordering had to decide when to order materials. He tried to follow production but, of course, got behind on an upswing on account of the time required to obtain materials. As pressure was placed on him for raw materials when business increased, he ordered faster. As business turned down, he received large stocks when they were no longer needed.

What was happening in effect was that the order clerk was forecasting. He knew little about the prospects of the business and acted in response to pressure from superiors to obtain materials in a hurry or to reduce his excess stocks. The manufacturer finally called in outside consultants for advice on reorganizing the purchasing department and was surprised when told that top management was to blame because no forecast existed.

Nature of Forecasting

Business has no alternative to some type of forecasting, since aimless drifting is unthinkable in a well-managed organization. The basic question really concerns the approach that is to be used in forecasting. It can be done in a mechanical way, as, for example, predicting a 5 percent increase in sales since this has been the average experience over the last few years. Or it can be done by relying on one or several series that have generally led business in the past, such as using changes in stock prices to predict changes in business activity. On a somewhat more sophisticated level it can be done by studying the economic and business situation and then more or less intuitively deciding what will happen.

The scientific approach in this field is the same as in any field. It involves, first of all, a knowledge and understanding of what has happened in the past, what is currently happening in the economy, and why it is happening. Only when phenomena are understood is it possible to predict accurately what will happen and take action in the light of such predictions.

Our knowledge of the causal factors at work in business fluctuations is not comprehensive enough to make it possible to forecast with complete accuracy. But it is advanced enough to make possible more reliable indicators of future events than can be done with unscientific approaches. The forecasts which can be made more than justify the time and money spent on them. And as knowledge increases in this field, better and better results will be forthcoming.

Benefits from a Forecasting Program

The only thing certain about any specific forecast is that it will be wrong, at least to a degree or in some particular. With the present knowledge of business fluctuations, it is impossible to gauge all variables exactly. As a rule, however, it should be possible in most businesses to forecast total sales for a quarter of a year ahead within a range of 5 percent above and below the actual figure, and for a year ahead within a range of 10 percent. Such results are usually accurate enough to be of real aid in managing a business, even if sales and production forecasts of individual products are off somewhat more. Such forecasting is a valuable managerial tool for business planning.

Consideration of Every Contingency. A forecasting program should help a business to meet any eventuality. A good forecast considers all factors that might influence a business, including remote possibilities. If management studies the forecasts carefully, it will at least not be caught unawares when the unexpected happens.

It is impracticable to prepare in advance for every contingency, but knowing what can happen and spotting unusual situations early will go a long way in preventing serious difficulties.

Study of Past Record. Forecasting forces a business to study its past record carefully. This must be done to determine past trends and the most likely pattern in the future. A study of the past is also necessary to determine if any regular seasonal pattern exists. Furthermore, an analysis of past cyclical movements should be made in developing data for future forecasting. The determination of the trend, cycle, and seasonal pattern requires the recognition of all sporadic or unusual factors. An analysis of these compared with a study of the past policies of the business will often reveal both good and bad courses taken by management. Such study can provide the basis for avoiding the same mistakes in the future, and for continuing the policies that have proved successful.

Study of Outside Factors. Another important benefit of forecasting is that it forces management to look at all the outside factors affecting the business. In this way executives are kept up to date on the governmental and social environment in which they make decisions. Favorable trends may be discerned and developed, or action may be taken to combat unfavorable aspects in the situation before they develop too far. Such awareness of the social and governmental milieu in which business operates is important for the preservation of free private enterprise in a democratic system.

Limitations and Problems of a Forecasting Program

Several problems are likely to be encountered in a forecasting program. One problem is that top management may expect a greater degree of accuracy from a forecast than is possible with the present knowledge of business and economic factors. Many top executives, especially in smaller concerns, feel that a forecast which is made once a year should be accurate enough to use as a basis for planning a year ahead with no further review or change. Such accuracy is seldom possible, however, since the numerous factors affecting business are changing constantly. Forecasting must be a continuous process.

Another problem is to obtain cooperation between various groups that participate in developing and using the forecast. At times sales departments are inclined to be overpessimistic when sales are bad. Other departments may argue for levels of production that are too high in order to make per unit costs look more favorable. This emphasizes the need for an independent forecasting group, not one under the direction of the sales or production planning departments.

Small businesses have a special problem in the forecasting area. Their forecasting problems may not keep one trained man occupied, and they cannot afford to pay a man of the required background and experience. They are also at a disadvantage in finding a good man since the number of men qualified in this area is small. A possible solution is to have forecasting services set up locally, serving clients in a manner similar to law offices or tax consulting services.

The Need for Forecasting in the Government

The many activities of the federal government and its widespread obligations in the economic sphere cannot be carried on without an analysis of current economic activity and a forecast of future economic activity. This has to be done to carry out governmental responsibilities under the Full Employment Act, and the Council of Economic Advisers has been established for this purpose. The level of economic activity must also be forecast to develop the annual budget of the federal government. In order to estimate receipts of the federal government, which come to a large degree from personal and corporate income taxes, it is necessary to forecast personal income and corporate profits. This, of course, cannot be done without forecasting the level of total economic activity and the level of prices.

The Department of Agriculture must forecast the prospective supply of farm products and the level of farm prices in general and the supply and prices of particular commodities in order to plan its crop control and price support programs. The Board of Governors of the Federal Reserve System must forecast the demand for money and the basic supply and demand factors at work in the economy to develop and carry out its monetary policies.

The various housing agencies must forecast supply and demand in developing their programs. In fact every agency that deals with economic matters must analyze the factors at work in the economy and forecast future economic conditions. Forecasting has become one of the important activities of government, and the skill and accuracy with which it is done are major factors in the success or failure of government programs in the economic sphere.

THE PLAN OF STUDY

This book is designed to give the student of economics and business administration an understanding of some of the major external factors which affect the economy and in turn decisions in business, labor, agriculture, and government. It is necessary to understand these factors in order to make intelligent decisions — decisions that will help shape the destinies of an organization and of the total economy rather than allow them to be buffeted around by forces which are not understood. For example, a decision on plant expansion including the size and timing of such expansion can only be made intelligently in the light of the trend of the economy and the industry and of seasonal and cyclical factors. It should also give the student an understanding of techniques that are available to measure and forecast levels of total economic activity and of the level of sales in an individual business. It provides an understanding of present programs for stabilizing economic activity, and a framework for classifying and analyzing such programs that may be proposed in the future.

Introduction

This first chapter has introduced the nature of economic fluctuations and their significance for individuals, the economy, and society. The nature of forecasting has also been considered in a preliminary way. The second chapter in this part will provide additional background on the basic characteristics of economic development and economic fluctuations in the United States.

Causal Factors in the Cyclical Process

Using the record of past trends and cycles as a background, an analysis is made in Part II of the causal factors at work in the business cycle. Consideration is given to individual factors, such as credit expansion and contraction, and the relationship between saving and investment; but major emphasis is placed upon a study of the interrelationship of all of the factors at work in the cycle.

A summary of the main strands in the history of business cycle thought is found in Chapters 4 and 5. The concluding three chapters of this part cover the basic elements of national income analysis as developed by John Maynard Keynes and post-Keynesian economists.

Measurement of Economic Fluctuations

In order to forecast future levels of activity, it is necessary to know the extent of changes in economic activity. Consideration is given in Part III to tools for measuring changes in aggregative economic activity and changes in production and prices. Statistical techniques for breaking down an economic time series into the trend, seasonal, cyclical, and irregular components are also considered, since such a breakdown of the data is a necessary preliminary to analysis and forecasting.

Statistical Record of Business Fluctuations

Before forecasting can be done effectively, it is necessary to summarize what is known about past fluctuations, especially the quantitative data available about such fluctuations. This summary in Part IV includes data on the cycle in general economic activity and in major sectors of the economy.

The pattern of events during the business cycle is also traced from the beginning of the revival in activity, through the upswing, the peak, the downswing and the trough at the end of the cycle. Chapter 13 in Part IV summarizes data on trends, seasonal factors, building cycles, agricultural cycles, and other fluctuations in economic activity.

Historical Record of Business Fluctuations

Part V covers the record of business fluctuations from 1918 to the present including major and minor cycles. This period is covered in some detail because the recent past is most significant in predicting what is most likely to happen in the future and also because events in this period still have a profound influence on the thinking of many men in business and in government today. Chapter 14 covers the period from 1918 to 1938, and Chapter 15 the period from 1938 to the present.

Forecasting Economic Activity

Scientific forecasting must be based on an understanding of the nature of fluctuations and of the causal factors which produce them. This understanding is developed in the preceding parts of this book. Procedures for analyzing economic conditions and forecasting them are considered in Part VI. Chapter 16 discusses methods used to project the trend of economic activity. Chapters 17 and 18 consider procedures for forecasting the level of general economic activity for the next year, Chapter 19 procedures for forecasting price changes, and Chapter 20 describes the services which are available to business from professional forecasting organizations.

Forecasting Sales

In many situations in government and in business a forecast of the trend of economic activity and of the level of general economic activity for the next year can serve as the basis for sound decisions. If business planning and budgeting is to be done effectively, however, it is necessary also to forecast the sales of a business. In Part VII methods of forecasting industry sales are described and discussed and also methods of doing so for an individual business.

Proposals for Achieving Economic Growth and Stability

The last part discusses proposals for stabilizing general economic activity. Chapter 23 in Part VIII discusses some of the major problems involved in establishing policies to promote economic stability and growth. A chapter is devoted to monetary policies and another to fiscal and other governmental policies. The role of business and labor in promoting greater stability and a rising trend of real income is also considered.

QUESTIONS

1. Review the nature of our economic development.
2. How do business variations affect individuals? society at large? governments?
3. What is the trend of economic activity?
4. Describe the nature of the trend in an industry.
5. Describe the business cycle. Comment on the use of the word "cycle" in describing this type of economic fluctuation.
6. Describe seasonal variations in business activity.
7. Give several examples of irregular fluctuations which may affect the level of economic activity.
8. How are economic analysis and forecasting related to determining business objectives?
9. Describe the role of forecasting in business planning.
10. What is the nature of forecasting as it is used in business planning?
11. Discuss the advantages and limitations of forecasting in business.
12. Discuss the role of forecasting in government activities.

See page 39 for Suggested Readings for Chapter 1.

CHAPTER 2 American Economic Development

The story of American economic development is one of dramatic growth in total output as a new continent was being populated and developed. It is also a story of increased output per capita and the development of many new goods and services to meet the needs and wants of consumers. This growth has not been continuous because it has been interrupted by many periods of decline in economic activity. Most of these have been short and mild, but several have been severe and protracted.

This chapter will briefly review this economic development of the United States. The first section will outline the major trends in the economy from 1783 to the present. The second section will discuss five major depressions during which economic activity declined for a protracted period of time.

Economic activity from the end of the War of Independence to the present can be divided into several periods in which the factors at work were somewhat different from what they were in the period taken as a whole. The first such period runs from 1783 to the beginning of the Civil War in 1861. The Civil War marked a distinct political turning point in our history and in many phases of activity also an economic turning point.

The second period starts at the outbreak of the Civil War and ends at the beginning of World War I in Europe. It was a period of rapid growth in which manufacturing replaced agriculture as the dominant American industry. The end of the period has been set at 1914 because World War I had a pronounced influence on the American economy, especially in its relationships to the rest of the world, and also because the passage of the Federal Reserve Act in 1913 materially changed the nature of banking and credit in the American economic system.

The third period begins with the outbreak of World War I in Europe in 1914 and runs to the present. The American economy was affected by this war from its beginning, even though this country did not go to war until fighting had gone on for several years. The

17

economy of the world was so profoundly affected by World War I that it did not return to many prewar relationships.

MAJOR TRENDS IN ECONOMIC ACTIVITY

In this section major trends affecting economic activity will be developed. Such factors as changes in population; agriculture, manufacturing, transportation, and trade; banking and the price level; and national income will be considered in each of the major periods into which the history of economic development has been divided.

From 1783 to 1861

The period from the end of the Revolutionary War in 1783 to the beginning of the Civil War in 1861 is one of rapid development on an extensive scale. The number of people in the country grew rapidly and this population pushed westward beyond the Eastern mountain ranges and on to the Mississippi River and beyond.

Population. When the first census of the United States was taken in 1790, the nation had a population of just under 4 million people. In each of the periods between the census dates from 1790 to 1860, population increased more than 30 percent.[1] Part of this population increase was due to the natural growth of numbers in a new country; part of it to an increased life span that, according to the best estimates, increased ten to fifteen years during this period; and part of it to an influx of immigrants.[2]

This rapidly growing population provided an expanding market for consumer goods and services. Demand was further increased because many young people entered this country and set up a home and reared a family a short time after their arrival.

The growth in population was not uniform in all sections of the country. During the period between 1790 and 1860, it was most rapid in the territory between the Alleghenies and the Mississippi River. The portion of this area north of the Ohio River had a rapid increase in population following the development of steamboat transportation on inland rivers and newly constructed canals in the period from 1825 to 1837. During the depression, which began in 1837, some of the unemployed moved farther west.

---

[1] U. S. Department of Commerce, Bureau of the Census, *Statistical Abstract of the United States* (Washington: U. S. Government Printing Office, 1949), p. 6.
[2] Harold F. Williamson (ed.), *The Growth of the American Economy* (New York: Prentice-Hall, Inc., 1947), p. 339.

Manufacturing, Agriculture, Transportation, and Trade. In the period to 1861 basic changes took place in the methods of producing goods. The factory system was begun in this period shortly after the turn of the century. Factories were first set up in the textile field to combine all phases of spinning and weaving under one roof. Within a short time, the preparation of meat for market began to be shifted to packing houses in such cities as St. Louis, Cincinnati, and Chicago. The flour milling industry and the leather industry made rapid strides, and there were beginnings of the canning industry and the liquor industry. Advancement also took place in the iron industry with the replacement of charcoal by coke as blast furnace fuel.

A revolution occurred in agricultural technology during this period. In 1790 the average farmer did his work with a clumsy axe, a plow with a wooden moldboard, a wooden-toothed harrow, a hoe, a scythe, a sickle, and a flail. By the time of the Civil War the typical farmer in the northern states had a seed drill, a reaper, a mower, a portable thresher, a grist mill, and modern plows, cultivator, and harrows. The economy of the South was affected profoundly by the invention of the cotton gin by Eli Whitney in 1792. The use of the gin made it possible to handle large quantities of cotton, which almost immediately became the leading southern crop.

Far-reaching changes in transportation occurred before 1860. Early in the period road building went on at a rapid rate, so that by 1820 all the major cities in the eastern and northern states were connected by a fairly good system of surfaced roads.

Between 1800 and 1840 there was also a large amount of canal building. After the invention of the steamboat in 1807, there was rapid development of transportation on rivers. According to one estimate over 1,000 steamboats were built from 1831 to 1840.[3] Railroad development did not take place to any large extent until after 1835; but from that year on development took place rapidly, especially between 1850 and 1860.

Foreign trade was an important factor in the economy of this period since large quantities of raw materials were exported and many manufactured goods were bought from abroad. Trade was affected by wars that began in Europe before the turn of the century and that continued with but brief periods of peace until the final defeat of Napoleon by the English in 1814. The volume of trade in war goods increased materially despite the interference with our

[3]*Ibid.*, p. 180.

commerce by the warring powers. After the depression following this war, trade again increased substantially and continued to do so for the remainder of the period.

The fields in which income was produced shifted materially between 1799 and 1859. Whereas agriculture accounted for about 40 percent of total income in 1799, it accounted for 30 percent in 1859. Manufacturing increased its contribution from 5 percent to 12 percent during the same period. There was also a significant increase in the percentage of income arising from trade, which was 5 percent at the beginning of the period and 12 percent at the end. The same thing was true to a lesser degree of service income, which increased from 10 percent to 14 percent of total income from production of goods and services.

Banking and the Price Level. At the beginning of this period there were only a few small banks in existence in the United States. As part of the program of the new government under the Constitution, the First Bank of the United States was set up in 1791 with a 20-year charter. The federal government did not own the bank directly but subscribed to one fifth of its stock. This bank had the privilege of issuing bank notes, which provided a sound currency. The bank and its branches also furnished needed credit for the development of business.

The bank's charter was not renewed in 1811 because the political party then in office felt that the bank had too much power for a private institution. State banks were chartered in large numbers, and their bank notes took the place of the notes of the First Bank of the United States. These state banks were not properly regulated and issued large amounts of currency during the War of 1812 without proper backing. This unregulated issuance of currency was largely responsible for the rapid rise of prices in this period.

As a result of this experience, the Second Bank of the United States was chartered in 1816, again with a 20-year charter. Its charter was allowed to lapse because of a change in the political situation, and state banks were chartered in large numbers. They again issued currency without proper backing. The inflation that followed was an important factor in the period just before the depression of 1837.

As a result of the failure of many banks in the depression of 1837, the various states revised their laws so as to provide for more effective regulation of banking practices, especially the issuance of notes. By the time of the Civil War, great strides had been made toward establishing a sound banking and currency system.

The long-term trend of prices during this period was downward except for a period of inflation during and after the War of 1812. On the average prices were about one third lower at the end of the period in 1860 than they were in 1800.[4]

National Income. At the time of the census in 1799, total realized income was $677 million according to estimates made for the National Industrial Conference Board by Robert F. Martin. By 1859 it had increased to $4.3 billion, an increase of 537 percent. If these income figures are adjusted by means of an index of the cost of living to put them in terms of 1926 purchasing power, the increase was 707 percent. On a per capita basis, however, income did not increase very much, since it was $131 per person in 1799 and $140 in 1859, an increase of only 7 percent. This increase is somewhat larger in dollars of constant purchasing power, since income in terms of the 1926 cost of living was $216 per person in 1799 and $296 in 1859, an increase of 37 percent.[5]

From 1861 to 1914

The period from 1861 to 1914 was one of continued rapid growth in population and in total economy activity. It was a period in which manufacturing and trade increased rapidly and surpassed agriculture in their contribution to the total production of goods and services in the economy.

Population. The rate of increase in population after 1860 was slower than it had been before that period, dropping to about 25 percent per decade until 1890 and 20 percent per decade between 1890 and 1910.[6] Population grew in all sections of the country in this period; but, as is to be expected, growth was more rapid in parts of the West than in the rest of the country. The westward movement of population was so rapid that by 1900 the frontier had all but disappeared. As a result, unemployment in the cities during depression periods became a more serious problem since, as long as free land had

---

[4]Jesse M. Cutts, "One Hundred and Thirty-Four Years of Wholesale Prices," *Monthly Labor Review* (July, 1935), p. 250.

[5]Robert F. Martin, *National Income in the United States, 1799 to 1938* (New York: National Industrial Conference Board, 1939), p. 6.

[6]U. S. Department of Commerce, Bureau of the Census, *Statistical Abstract of the United States* (Washington: U. S. Government Printing Office, 1949), p. 6.

existed, many of the unemployed had moved to the West to begin life anew.

Manufacturing, Agriculture, Transportation, and Trade. Manufacturing developed rapidly in the period between 1860 and 1914. In 1860 the most important manufacturing industries were the production of flour and meal products, cotton goods, lumber, and boots and shoes. By 1914 the slaughtering and meat-packing industry was at the head of the list, iron and steel production second, flour and mill production third, and foundry and machine shop production fourth.

Changes in agriculture that affected the whole economy took place during this period. In 1860 agriculture was based on the use of "cheap land," which could always be deserted for new land. By 1900 the frontier was gone and a period of intensive development of available land was begun. The development of machinery to harvest cereal crops, such as the combined harvester and thresher, made it possible to produce more food at a lower cost. It meant, however, that farming was becoming a business that required a high degree of managerial skill and sizable amounts of capital. Lowered costs and increased production also meant lower prices for farm products. Many farmers were unable to adjust to the new conditions and sought relief by supporting inflationary monetary policies. These policies affected the course of business in several of the major depressions in this period.

A major development in the field of transportation was the rapid growth of the railroad network. In 1860 there were 30,000 miles of railroad in the United States, and by 1916 the railroad network of the United States had increased to 260,000 miles of line.

The volume of foreign trade increased significantly from 1860 to 1914, and its composition also changed. In 1860 agricultural products accounted for 80 percent of total exports and finished manufactures for about 10 percent; by 1914 agricultural products constituted 40 percent of the total exports and finished manufactures 30 percent.[7]

The pattern of realized private production income from the various sectors of the economy shifted rather materially from 1859 to 1914. In 1859 agriculture accounted for 30 percent of the total; by 1914 it had declined to 20 percent. Manufacturing became more

---

[7]Ernest L. Bogart and Donald L. Kemmerer, *Economic History of the American People* (New York: Longmans, Green & Co., Inc., 1943), p. 635.

important, increasing from 12 percent of the total to 21.5 percent; and so did trade, which increased from 12 percent to 20 percent.

Banking and the Price Level. During the Civil War, Congress passed legislation authorizing the establishment of banks with a national charter. These banks were permitted to issue bank notes, using government bonds as collateral. A tax was placed on state bank notes that drove them out of circulation and left national bank notes as the most important form of money except for small change. Since the debt of the federal government was not increasing, the volume of national bank notes was restricted by the amount of available government bonds for collateral. This led to a shortage of money, especially in the fall of the year when crops were being marketed, and created problems in several depression periods.

There were some wide fluctuations in prices, but the level at the end of the period was not much higher than that at the beginning.

National Income. The level of national income showed a decided rise during this period. In 1859 realized national income was $4.3 billion; and by 1914 it had increased to $31 billion, an increase of 626 percent. Measured in terms of constant dollars based upon the 1926 cost of living, the increase was 508 percent. On a per capita basis, income increased from $140 in 1859 to $319 in 1914, an increase of 128 percent. On the basis of the cost of living as it was in 1926, the 1859 per capita income was worth $296 and that of 1914 was worth $565, an increase of 91 percent.[8]

From 1914 to the Present

The period from 1914 to the present was marked by wide variations in economic activity. The early years were boom years due to the demands for goods arising out of World War I. The decade of the 1920's was a period of boom and speculation, and that of the 1930's one of worldwide depression. This was followed by a new boom period during World War II and a period of prosperity during most of the 1940's, 1950's, and 1960's as international tensions and large-scale military expenditures continued.

Population. The rate of increase in population in this period was slower than in the preceding periods, especially in the years before World War II. Between 1910 and 1920 population increased 15 per-

---

[8]Martin, *op. cit.,* p. 6.

cent and between 1920 and 1930, 16 percent, but in the decade of
the 1930's only 7 percent.[9] In the 1940's population increased 15 percent and continued to increase in the 1950's at a somewhat faster
rate, increasing by 19 percent during this decade. The rate of increase slowed in the 1960's when the number of births started falling
in 1961 while the number of marriages increased. This pattern was
still in evidence in mid-1967.

These changing birth-rate patterns changed the composition of
the population by age groups. Before 1960 there were large increases
in the age groups under 20 and little change in the age groups of 20
to 40. Between 1960 and 1965, the 15-to-25-year age group increased
most rapidly; and between 1965 and 1970, it will be the 20-to-30-year
age group that shows the most significant rate of increase. The
number of persons over 65 years of age increased faster than the
total population during this whole period and especially after 1945.

The rapid increase in population after 1945 following the low
birth rates in the 1930's affected materially the economic situation
in the 1950's. The large number of children necessitated increased
productive facilities for children's products and increased housing.
Schools also had to be expanded to take care of the large number of
youngsters. At the same time the number of people entering the
labor force was relatively small because of the abnormally low birth
rates at the depth of the depression in the 1930's. This combination
of a strong demand because of increased population and a relatively
small addition to the labor force gave the economy underlying
strength to help prevent prolonged unemployment.

This situation changed somewhat during the 1960's. The number
of persons of working age increased sharply in the mid-1960's as
children born after the end of World War II reached age 18. An
increasing proportion of these young people went to college thus
greatly increasing the demands upon the nation's colleges and universities. The number of new workers to be integrated into the labor
force also increased materially in a period when the pool of executive
and management talent in the age group of 35 to 50 was not increasing materially. The employment of teenage workers became a
major economic challenge of the mid-1960's.

Manufacturing, Agriculture, Transportation, and Trade. The
trends in manufacturing in this period continued those of the pre-

---

[9]*Statistical Abstract of the United States,* 1949, *op. cit.,* p. 6.

vious period. The rate of output of manufacturing industries increased rapidly when measured either in terms of absolute output or on a per capita basis. The trend toward larger establishments also continued, and their efficiency increased because of scientific management and industrial research. The transfer of activities from the household to the factory also continued, especially in the baking and canning fields.

The period since the end of World War II has been marked by large-scale capital investment in almost all major industries. Automation has become a household word in our economy. In some fields, such as textiles and the production of automobile motors, factories have been established that use practically no direct labor in production. In those fields which have not gone so far as automation, there has also been a steady increase in the amount of work done by machines. From 1950 to 1965 output in manufacturing almost doubled, but employment increased by less than 15 percent. In mining, output also increased substantially and total employment decreased as more and more work was done by machinery.

The trend toward mechanization in agriculture progressed at a faster rate in this period. The most significant development in the early part of this period was that of the gasoline tractor, which replaced horses and mules to draw farm machinery. Power machinery was also developed for harvesting and threshing. This mechanization reduced the amount of labor needed to produce farm products and freed labor for jobs in industry. Use of tractors and self-propelled machines also materially reduced the number of horses and mules on farms, and this reduction freed millions of acres used to raise animal feed for other crops.

Agricultural productivity increased even more rapidly in the post-World War II period than it did earlier. This rapid increase in productivity was due to the use of more and better machinery, more and better fertilizers, chemical weed killers, improved seed, scientifically developed feeds for farm animals, and the like. Between 1914 and 1967 the output per man-hour of farm work more than tripled. About half of this increase in productivity occurred in the 10-year period from 1949 to 1958.[10]

A revolution in transportation also took place in the early part of this period with the development of the automobile. The automobile

---

[10]U. S. Department of Agriculture, *Agricultural Outlook Charts* (Washington: U. S. Government Printing Office, 1959), p. 65.

was a luxury for the few in 1914, but by 1929 over 5.6 million cars
were sold. The automobile was brought into the price range of the
middle-income group by the introduction of assembly line production, which cut costs drastically. The automobile made it possible
for people in agricultural areas to go to nearby towns of some size to
do their shopping and as a result trade moved from the general store
to larger shopping centers. The widespread use of automobiles
necessitated the development of a network of highways and of all of
the facilities related to automobile travel. As good roads were developed in the 1920's and the 1930's, motor carriers began to carry
sizable amounts of freight, especially on the shorter hauls.

The airplane was developed as a major form of transportation in
the late 1920's and early 1930's and continued to increase in importance throughout the remainder of the period, especially in the
1950's and 1960's with the development of jet planes.

No major new forms of transportation were introduced into the
economy after World War II, but significant shifts took place in the
relative importance of the various forms of transportation. Airlines
became the major factor in the passenger field and also developed a
substantial volume of freight business. Trucks and barges increased
their share of the freight business so that by 1967 railroads carried
less than one half of all freight.

The foreign trade of the United States increased rapidly and its
composition changed materially during this period. In 1914 exports
of goods and services were somewhat above $2 billion and they in-
creased to over $29 billion in 1966. The composition of exports
also changed during this period. In 1914 agricultural products were
more significant than manufactured goods, but by 1967 agricultural
products were but a minor proportion of the total of all goods exported.[11] The most significant change in the foreign trade picture in
the 1940's, 1950's, and 1960's was the changing role of the government. Large quantities of exports were financed during and after
World War II by means of government grants and loans.

Income from manufacturing increased significantly during this
period and income from agriculture declined materially. Income
from construction and the production of electric light, power, and
gas went up by a substantial percentage and that from mining and
quarrying and from transportation and communication went down.

---

[11]Bogart and Kemmerer, *op. cit.*, p. 803, and *Survey of Current Business* (September, 1967), p. 522.

Role of Government. The role of government in the economy was a minor one before this period except in the money and banking areas. During the depression that began in 1929 the role of government increased markedly. The Reconstruction Finance Corporation was set up to make loans to businesses that were in difficulty. Government programs were set up to aid business, labor, and agriculture. Large-scale public works programs were carried on, and the government incurred large deficits to put funds to work in the economy. Even though some of the programs enacted during the depression were later abandoned, the role of government in the economy continued as a major one.

The role of government, especially that of the federal government, increased spectacularly during and after World War II. Total expenditures by the federal government in the fiscal year 1940 were $10 billion and had increased in 1966 to over $150 billion. State and local government expenditures also increased steadily in the postwar period. Total personal taxes were just over 3 percent of personal income in 1940, but in 1966 had increased to 13 percent.[12]

Banking and the Price Level. The difficulties with the currency system led to the establishment of the Federal Reserve System at the beginning of this period. Provision was made for an elastic currency that would increase with the demands of industry and commerce. The total resources of the banking system increased materially during this period, but the number of banks decreased markedly.

One of the outstanding developments during this period was the growth in consumer credit, especially in installment financing of the sale of durable consumer goods. Such financing was begun before the turn of the century to finance the sale of sewing machines, pianos, books, and a few other types of goods, but it had not reached any sizable proportions by the time of World War I. It grew rapidly after the end of World War I as a method of financing the growing sales of automobiles and other consumer durables. Banks entered the field of consumer financing on a small scale in the 1920's and expanded such lending activities materially in the 1930's and especially in the post-World War II period. Other consumer financing agencies, such as sales finance companies, consumer finance companies, and credit unions, also materially expanded their volume of activity in this period. Savings and loan associations grew rapidly

<hr />

[12]*Federal Reserve Bulletin* (April, 1967), pp. 626, 655.

and played a significant role in financing the large-scale housing development in this period.

Wholesale prices experienced a rapid rise during World War I, a marked decline during the postwar depression that began in 1920, a period of stability during the 1920's, and another decline during the 1929 depression. Prices increased gradually in the 1930's after reaching a depression low point in 1932. They increased somewhat during World War II as price controls held them in check. When controls were lifted, prices went up rapidly and then stabilized in 1949. They increased again during the Korean War and continued to rise slowly through the remainder of the 1950's and 1960's. By 1967 consumer prices were somewhat more than double the level in 1939.

National Income and Gross National Product. National income increased materially during this period. In 1914 realized national income was at a rate of $31 billion per annum. It reached a high point in 1929 of $79.5 billion.[13] Comparable income data are not available for the period from 1914 to the present. National income data developed from more complete sources by the Department of Commerce show that national income was at a level of $86.8 billion in 1929. This was 9.2 percent higher than estimates of realized national income. The national income increased to $610.1 billion in 1966.

On a per capita basis, realized national income went up from $319 in 1914 to $654 in 1929. The comparable figure for 1929 based on national income figures is $713, and this increased to $3,100 in 1966. Adjusting the 1914 figure by adding 9.2 percent gives an adjusted per capita national income figure in 1914 of $348 compared with $3,100 in 1966. In dollars of constant purchasing power based on the BLS Consumer Price Index using 1957–59 as 100, per capita national income went up from an adjusted figure of $994 in 1914 to $1,188 in 1929 and $2,743 in 1966.[14]

Gross national product increased from $38.6 billion in 1914 to $739.6 billion in 1966. In constant dollars based on 1958 prices, GNP went up from $125.6 billion in 1914 to $647.8 billion in 1966. Per capita GNP in terms of 1958 prices went up from $1,267 to

---

[13]Martin, *op. cit.*, p. 7.

[14]*Long-Term Economic Growth 1860–1965* (Washington: U. S. Government Printing Office, 1966), pp. 218, 224, 225, 228; and *Survey of Current Business* (April, 1967), p. 7.

$3,292, an increase of over two and one-half times in this period of just over 50 years.[15]

CHARACTERISTICS OF FIVE MAJOR DEPRESSIONS

The business cycles that have interrupted economic growth have varied widely in length and in severity. The most frequent type of cycle is one that is about four years in length and results in changes in the level of economic activity that are no more severe than those experienced in the post-World War II economy. Several cycles, however, have been much more severe than all others and led to depressions which lasted for several years. Other cycles led to depressions which were less severe than these long, deep depressions, but were much more pronounced than the minor recessions in the post-World War II period. Five depression periods in our history stand out as being more severe than the others. These were the depressions following the Revolutionary War, and the War of 1812, and those which began in 1837, 1873, and 1929. Each of these will be considered in turn, the last only briefly since it is covered in more detail in Chapter 14.

Post-Revolutionary War Depression

The first major depression began at the end of the Revolutionary War in 1783. It arose out of the events of the preceding years in which America successfully waged a war for independence.

Background and Character of the Depression. In 1783 the American economy was in an unsettled political and economic condition. It was necessary to shift from a wartime status under the Second Continental Congress to a peacetime government for the new nation. This proved to be a difficult adjustment, and unsettled political conditions made it impossible for business to forge ahead. The economy suffered from the inflation of the currency during the Revolutionary War, which was due in a large measure to the issuance of paper money without backing of any kind. The use of depreciated paper money drove specie out of circulation and, as a result, trade had to be carried on in currency of doubtful value. The government of the United States was also heavily in debt to foreign countries and to citizens at home, and it found itself substantially in arrears

---

[15]*Long-Term Economic Growth 1860–1965, op. cit.,* pp. 166, 167, 169; and *Survey of Current Business* (April, 1967), p. 51.

in the payment of interest on the domestic debt. As a result, business activity declined substantially from wartime levels for a period of several years.

This depression lasted until 1787 when recovery began in various sectors of the economy. Business remained in an unsettled state until the early 1790's when the new government provided for in the constitution was firmly established and stabilized the financial situation. This first depression was different from all later depressions because of the almost complete collapse of former trade relationships and the breakdown of the financial system. In many ways it was a complete breakdown of the economy rather than a depression of the type experienced in later years.

Causes. The immediate cause of this depression was the ending of the Revolutionary War. The economy had been geared to the production of goods needed to carry on the war, and the demand for such goods suddenly ceased to exist. Conditions were much too unsettled to effect a smooth transition to the production of peacetime goods and, as a result, economic activity declined sharply.

Unsettled political conditions prevented normal economic development, but other serious problems existed, especially an imbalance in foreign trade. During the colonial period a large part of our trade — both exports and imports — was with England. These trade relations were interrupted during the war, and it was impossible to restore normal relations in the immediate postwar period. During 1784 and 1785 American merchants bought more goods from England than they were able to pay for. Before the war the colonists had exported large quantities of tobacco, bread, flour, dried fish, rice, and indigo to England. The war, however, practically destroyed the fishing industry, military operations in the Southern colonies destroyed a large part of the rice fields, and indigo could not be produced profitably without the British subsidies that had been paid previously.

This serious imbalance of trade led first of all to an export of specie on a large scale. The loss of specie would normally have resulted in a rapidly declining price level and did in fact have this tendency. Several of the states, however, issued paper money to take the place of the vanishing specie. Since such paper money had no backing, there was some question about its value, and prices in terms of it tended to increase.

Monetary problems were not the only ones in this period. New manufacturing industries, which had sprung up during the war, suffered serious losses because English merchants dumped excess goods into the United States at low prices in an attempt to win back American markets, which had been lost as a result of the war.

Depression Following the War of 1812

The second major depression was also related to the end of hostilities — this time the War of 1812. It likewise arose out of events in the preceding period of wartime boom.

Background and Character of the Depression. War in Europe affected the American economy during the first part of the nineteenth century. Business activity was at a high level as a result of sales of goods to England, France, and other warring powers, except during the period from 1807–09 when the Embargo Act made it illegal for American vessels to sail to the ports of any foreign power.

The period during and shortly after the war was one of inflation and boom. The War of 1812 was financed to a large extent by borrowing and by the issuance of treasury notes. The first of the treasury notes were regular interest-bearing debt obligations. In later issues, however, no definite provision was made for redemption and the denominations under $100 bore no interest, so that for all practical purposes they were issues of printing press money. The deficit of the government was large in each of the war years and in the first postwar year, 1815. The banking system also added to the flow of inflationary purchasing power. After the charter of the First Bank of the United States was allowed to lapse in 1811, many state banks were chartered and they issued paper money with little or no backing in specie. This period of inflation during the war was followed by a depression in 1815, when the inflationary pressure of war finance was removed. The depression following the War of 1812 was severe and protracted. Business declined from 1815 until 1822 and remained at fairly low levels for two more years. This depression was accompanied by a period of financial chaos in which the notes of various state banks circulated at different values, depending upon the safety of the issuing institution. Prices of commodities and of securities dropped drastically, and business failures were at a high level. This was in part due to the attempts of British merchants to flood the American market with cheap goods as they had done at the end of the Revolutionary War.

Causes. The immediate cause of the decline in business activity was the rapid decline in prices that occurred when wartime inflationary finance was halted. The economy, however, had more serious readjustments to make than the correction of imbalance due to inflation. Since the turn of the century, business had been geared to European wartime purchases. At the end of the war in 1814 peace was finally achieved in Europe, and the American economy had to readjust to a new pattern of production based on peacetime demands for goods. The war demands had lasted for over 15 years, and the economic system had become adjusted to such a pattern. The readjustment to a peacetime pattern in which different types of goods were demanded was slow.

Depression of 1837

The third major depression was not related to the cessation of wartime activities as were the first two. It occurred during a period of rapid development in the economy and interrupted such development for several years.

Background and Character of the Depression. The depression which began in 1837 was the result of activities in the economy during the period of the 1820's and the 1830's. Especially significant was the inflation of the money supply that took place because of President Andrew Jackson's action in regard to the Second Bank of the United States. Jackson vetoed the bill to renew the charter of this bank and made it an issue in the campaign of 1832. Since he was re-elected, he decided that the people had voted against the bank and began to remove the deposits of the United States government from it. As a result, the bank was forced to contract its loans and a panic developed in 1833. After the bank had readjusted itself to the loss of the government deposits and these federal funds were redeposited in other banks, the money shortage was relieved. The government placed its funds in state banks that were friendly to the administration, and this action gave them the basis for issuing additional paper money.

The increase in the number of banks and in bank note circulation helped cause the inflation of the period, but that inflation was also in part the result of speculative development in many parts of the economy as internal improvements were constructed at a rapid rate. Expenditures by the federal government on roads and canals were increased materially, especially after 1832. Among the states New York led in this development with the construction of the Erie Canal, which cost over $10 million, and a series of other canals, which cost almost as much. Massachusetts, Pennsylvania, and South Carolina were among the other states that spent large sums on internal improvements. The building of canals and turnpikes opened up new land for development, which in turn led to large-scale land speculation. Deposit of the receipts from the sale of public lands in banks in the western states provided the reserves for a further inflation of the money supply and thus reinforced the speculative boom.

The depression that began in 1837 was one of the most severe in our history. Unemployment was extensive and business failures were numerous. Prices dropped disastrously, and this added to the panic of the period. Cotton, for example, fell from 20 cents a pound to 10 cents, causing some of the largest financial institutions in New Orleans, as well as some large plantation owners, to fail. In all, over 600 banks failed during the 1837 depression.[16] With the resumption of specie payments by most banks in the latter half of 1838, business revived somewhat; but it collapsed completely with the failure of the Bank of the United States, which had been rechartered with a Pennsylvania charter.

Causes. The immediate factor that led to the end of the speculation in land and to the end of the boom was the issuance by President Jackson in July, 1836, of his now famous "specie circular," which required that all public land had to be paid for in specie rather than in the notes of state banks. The resulting demand for specie restricted the operations of the western banks and led to a good deal of opposition; but despite pressure on President Van Buren, who succeeded Jackson, the order was allowed to stand.

Another source of difficulty was the transfer of funds of the federal government from one section of the country to another occasioned when Congress voted to deposit with the several states part of the surplus that had developed from the sale of public land. The resultant scarcity of money in those sections of the country from which funds were withdrawn necessitated the suspension of specie payments by New York banks, and by banks in many other cities.

The situation was further aggravated because credit had been created in large amounts by privately owned banks chartered on a

---

[16]Bogart and Kemmerer, *op. cit.,* p. 369.

basis of political favoritism. The banks issued notes with little or no backing and, at least in the West, with little regard to the needs of business. The result was again a period of inflation followed by one of deflation.

The immediate cause of the depression of 1837 is to be found in the financial situation. The severe nature of this depression cannot be accounted for, however, by the financial situation. It was due in large measure to the nature of the economic development in the 1820's and 1830's. Canals were constructed at a rapid rate, and transportation was also developed on all important rivers. This was made possible by the development of the steamboat and the rapid building of such boats to haul freight and passengers. These changes made it possible to settle new areas rapidly and led to the large-scale development of western areas, which created a demand for new houses and also for new towns and cities with all of their facilities.

Additional production capacity was needed to build steamboats and the equipment needed to make them run. This created a demand for more iron and steel and more machine tools. Plants and equipment were also needed to meet the demands of the construction industry for materials to build houses and other buildings.

By 1837 this phase of economic activity had run its course. Canals had been built wherever it was feasible in the northern part of the country, and a few were also built in the South. Most of them did not turn out to be profitable ventures, and this slowed down new building. Some railroads had been built and had demonstrated their capacity sufficiently to help dampen the enthusiasm for more canal projects.

After this burst of development, the economy had to adjust itself to a less spectacular form of growth. Rapid population of new areas did not occur again until after the Civil War. The long depression was due to the readjustment from an economic pattern geared to the rapid development of the northern part of the country west to the Mississippi to one based on the more gradual growth of population and real income.

Depression of 1873

The fourth major depression was similar in some respects to the one which began in 1837. It too occurred during a period of rapid development in the economy and interrupted such development for almost six years.

Background and Character of the Depression. A financial crisis began in the fall of 1873, when several important financial institutions were forced to suspend operations. The first of these was the New York Warehouse and Security Company, which was organized to make advances on grain but which had been persuaded to tie up its funds in financing the Missouri, Kansas, and Texas Railroad. Several large brokerage firms failed in the next few days, and these failures led to a rapid calling in of loans by the banks. To meet these demands to repay loans, investment houses attempted to sell stocks to get cash to pay the banks and these sales broke the price of securities. On Saturday of the crisis week several of the large banks and trust companies were forced to suspend operations, and before the day was over stock prices were declining so rapidly that the stock exchange was closed.

The depression that followed this panic was long and severe. Business declined until the middle of 1879, a period of almost six years. This is the longest period of contraction in any cycle in American history. Business failures were not as spectacular during the downturn as they were during the panic, but they increased slowly year by year. Unemployment also increased and became a serious problem, especially in the industrial centers in the eastern part of the country. Prices declined steadily until they were at much lower levels than in 1873 and this led to distress in agricultural communities.

Causes. The financial crisis of 1873 was due in part to unsound commitments by the financial institutions and also in part to the operation of the money and banking system of that period. The banks had not engaged in any large-scale credit expansion before 1873 nor were their reserves unusually low. One of the factors leading to the financial crisis was the concentration of deposits of a large number of banks held in seven large New York banks. Under the National Banking Act, national banks were required to keep a set percentage of reserves against deposits and could keep part of them in other banks. Between 70 percent and 80 percent of these deposits were concentrated in seven large New York banks. There was normally a demand for funds late in the fall to meet the needs of the crop-moving period. As a result of this demand, these seven banks had a sizable deficiency in the required 25 percent reserve of legal tender notes and specie against their deposits by mid-

September of 1873. They were forced to call some of their loans to meet reserve requirements. This happened at the same time that several brokerage houses failed and banks called in loans in this field. This led to a financial panic and runs on the banks, and they were forced to suspend specie payments. Despite the financial panic and the suspension of specie payment, most of the national banks were sound since only a few of them failed during this period. Most of those that failed paid their depositors 50 percent or more.

The basic cause of the 1873 depression was the overexpansion of the preceding period, especially in railroads. The years from 1868 to 1872 witnessed extraordinarily rapid growth, especially in the upper Mississippi Valley.

The real cause for the decline was the completion of most of the railroad network that could be operated profitably at this time. The eastern part of the country had been given fairly adequate railroad coverage. There was still room for development, especially west of the Mississippi River; but railroads in this area found it difficult to operate profitably without being tied in with the eastern network of railroads. The lack of bridges across the Mississippi River made this impracticable. It was not until several years later that such bridges were successfully built and business increased sufficiently to resume profitable railroad development in the western part of the country.

Depression of 1929

The 1929 depression will be covered in some detail in Chapter 14. Its nature is similar in many respects to the earlier major depressions. Business declined from 1929 to 1933 and was below full employment levels throughout the 1930's. Industrial production dropped by 50 percent and employment by 25 percent. The basic causes of this depression are to be found both on the international and domestic scenes. Attempts during the 1920's to reestablish some of the pre-World War I economic relationships, especially in the monetary area, proved unsuccessful. Financial and trade problems arising out of the war were not solved successfully, and as a result international trade collapsed during the depression.

On the domestic scene a major shift in production patterns took place during the 1920's due to the rapid development of several new industries, the major of which was the mass production of automobiles. The general use of the automobile as a mode of transportation led to shifts in living and shopping habits. Other consumer durable goods were also developed during this period, especially electrical appliances, such as refrigerators and radios. The electric utility industry also experienced rapid growth in the 1920's. By 1929 the automobile had become a standard part of the living pattern of middle-income families, and the rapid developments accompanying its introduction slowed down. Most upper- and middle-income families in urban areas also owned an electric refrigerator, a radio, and other electrical appliances. The shift to a new pattern of development based on more intensive development of needs and resources rather than on the rapid expansion of major new industries was made slowly.

Summary of the Major Depressions

The study of the causal factors at work in major cycles shows that protracted depressions have occurred at the time of a basic shift in the nature of the capital investment in the economy. A long depression followed the end of the Revolutionary War when a shift had to be made not only from a wartime economy to a peacetime economy, but also from an economy of a colony dependent on England to one of an independent nation with no assured markets, or sources of raw materials not available at home. A long depression followed the War of 1812 as the economy of the United States and of the world shifted from a protracted period of war to one of relative peace. The depression that began in 1837 was severe and prolonged because a rapid period of development based on canals and the steamboat had been completed. In 1873 the railroad network had been largely completed in the portion of the country east of the Mississippi River, and it took some time to cross this natural barrier and resume railroad building. In 1929 a large part of the capital investment needed to make the automobile and some electrical appliances a part of the American way of life had been committed, and it took time to develop a new pattern of investment. Therefore, a study of the current investment pattern and of the trends in the major areas making it up is an integral part of any analysis of current business conditions and future prospects.

QUESTIONS

1. Describe the trend of population in the three major periods in the economic history of the United States.

2. Discuss the major changes in manufacturing, agriculture, transportation, and trade in the development of the American economy.

3. Discuss the trend of prices from 1783 to the present. Does this record of prices substantiate the proposition that prosperity can only take place when the price level is rising?

4. Describe the changes in the sources of production income by industries between 1800 and the present. How were changes in manufacturing, agriculture, transportation, banking, foreign trade, employment, and productivity related to such changes?

5. (a) Why was there a protracted depression after the end of the Revolutionary War? (b) How did this depression differ from all later depressions?

6. (a) What caused a long and severe depression after the end of the War of 1812? (b) How was it related to the development of the economy in the 15 years preceding the war?

7. (a) What was the immediate cause of a downturn in business in 1837? (b) What basic causal factors were at work?

8. Why was the depression following 1837 one of the most severe in our history?

9. In what respects were the depressions that began in 1815 and 1837 due to similar causal factors?

10. Describe the immediate and basic causal factors at work in the 1873 depression.

11. Why was the depression which began in 1929 a long and severe one?

SUGGESTED READINGS FOR CHAPTER 1

Economic Report of the President. Washington: U. S. Government Printing Office.

"Forecasting Sales," *Studies in Business Policy,* No. 106. New York: National Industrial Conference Board, 1963.

Maisel, Sherman J. *Fluctuations, Growth and Forecasting.* New York: John Wiley & Sons, Inc., 1957. Chapters 1 and 2.

McKinley, David H., Murray G. Lee, and Helene Duffy. *Forecasting Business Conditions.* New York: The American Bankers Association, 1965. Chapter 1.

SUGGESTED READINGS FOR CHAPTER 2

Bretzfelder, Robert B. "Variations in National Output," *Survey of Current Business* (November, 1960), pp. 14–20.

Cole, A. H. "Statistical Background of the Crisis of 1857," *Review of Economic Statistics.* XII (November, 1930), pp. 170–80.

Dewey, Davis Rich. *Financial History of the United States.* New York: Longmans, Green & Co., Inc., 1931. Chapters 12–21 inclusive.

Frickey, Edwin. *Production in the United States, 1860–1914.* Cambridge: Harvard University Press, 1947.

Hyndman, H. M. *Commercial Crises of the Nineteenth Century.* London: Swan Sonnenschein & Co., 1902.

Lauck, W. Jett. *The Causes of the Panic of 1893.* Boston: Houghton Mifflin Co., 1907.

McGrane, Reginald Charles. *The Panic of 1837.* Chicago: University of Chicago Press, 1924.

Mitchell, Wesley Clair. *A History of the Greenbacks.* Chicago: University of Chicago Press, 1903.

Rezneck, S. "Distress, Relief, and Discontent in the United States during the Depression of 1873–78," *Journal of Political Economy.* LVIII (December, 1950), pp. 494–512.

Schluter, W. C. *The Prewar Business Cycle, 1907 to 1914.* New York: Columbia University Press, 1923.

Smith, Walter Buckingham, and Arthur Harrison Cole. *Fluctuations in American Business, 1790–1860.* Cambridge: Harvard University Press, 1935.

Sprague, O. M. W. *History of Crises under the National Banking System.* Washington: U.S. Government Printing Office, 1910.

Stigler, George J. *Trends in Output and Employment.* New York: National Bureau of Economic Research, 1947.

PROBLEMS ON PART I

1. Calculate the average percentage increase per year in income per capita in the 1799–1859, 1859–1914, and 1914 to the present period in American economic history. Make a table for each of the three periods of economic development showing the major factors that may have led to an increase in economic activity, and the major factors that may have slowed it down. On the basis of your data, account for differences in the rate of growth.

2. A. Develop a chart showing similarities and differences in the factors at work in the depressions that began in 1815, 1837, and 1873.

   B. How might the pattern of business fluctuations in the 1790–1860 period have been affected if the steamboat had been perfected after a good system of roads had already covered the section of the country north of the Ohio River and east of the Mississippi River?

   C. Suppose that Henry Ford had begun assembly line production of automobiles in 1926 instead of before the United States entered World War I. Discuss the possible effects on economic fluctuations from 1920 to 1939.

PART II

CAUSAL FACTORS
IN THE CYCLICAL PROCESS

In the description in Chapter 2 of the major depressions that occurred in the economic development of the United States, some of the factors that were at work in these periods were pointed out. No attempt was made, however, to explain fully these causal factors. A discussion of the factors that cause the economy to grow in a cyclical fashion has been reserved for Part II.

Chapter 3 reviews some of the salient features of the American economy as it operates currently. This is done for two reasons. It provides a review of the background needed to understand what is happening in the economy during the cycle. These characteristics also help explain why the cycle develops as it does. If the economy were changed materially, the cycle would be changed or perhaps even eliminated in the form in which it has occurred.

Chapters 4 and 5 present various aspects of cycle theory, beginning with theories which explain the cycle by the cyclical behavior of some force outside the economy. There is no attempt to analyze all possible theories, nor are the theories presented in the chronological order of their formulation. The major types of theories are considered in order to emphasize the role in the cyclical process of the main points stressed by each group of theorists.

Chapters 6, 7, and 8 can be considered a unit on the basics of modern national income analysis. In Chapter 6 the familiar Keynesian model, including the multiplier, is developed. This model is

41

presented verbally, algebraically, geometrically, and in the arithmetic of period analysis. This analysis is extended in Chapters 7 and 8 incorporating the integration of the goods market and the money market, multiplier-accelerator systems, the role of government in national income determination, and the analysis of economic growth. Differences between the two main schools of thought, "Keynesians" and "classicists," are pointed out at various points.

CHAPTER 3

The American System of Finance Capitalism

The business cycles described in Part I were a phenomenon of capitalism that is organized on a pecuniary basis with a banking system having the ability to create credit. Changes in an economic system affect the characteristics of the cycles in that system. In order to understand economic fluctuations adequately, especially cyclical fluctuations, it is necessary to be familiar with the essential characteristics of our system of finance capitalism and also to have an understanding of changes in this system. Therefore, an outline of the major features of this system, especially those that are related to the monetary exchange of goods and services, will be presented as a background for the study of the causal factors at work in business fluctuations.

MONETARY AND CREDIT SYSTEM

The monetary system has a more significant effect on the nature of business fluctuations than any other facet of our capitalistic system. Therefore it is discussed at greater length than other institutional factors.

Monetary System

The *monetary system* of the United States is made up of the United States Treasury, the Federal Reserve System, and the system of commercial banks. All of these institutions have one feature in common that no other units of the economy have; that is, they are capable of creating and destroying money. They are peculiar in that they have money as a liability. The bulk of our money supply is in the form of demand deposits, which are liabilities of commercial banks. Our hand-to-hand money is made up of coins, a liability of the Treasury, and currency, which is a liability of either the Treasury or the Federal Reserve Banks.

The stock of money at any time depends primarily upon the actions of the members of the monetary system, the constraints

43

placed upon them by the law and its administration, and upon the actions of parties not included in the monetary system, such as households, business units, and the rest of the world. In much of our later analysis we shall have occasion to discuss the significance of variation in the money supply. At this point, however, our purpose is to demonstrate the means by which the variation comes about. In the analysis of business conditions, it is the total money supply that is important, not just the currency supply. If the money supply were, for instance, $100 billion, it would make very little difference whether it were $100 billion of currency or $100 billion of demand deposits. It is simply a matter of convenience for the nonmonetary system (the public) to have both kinds of money for different types of trans- actions. The monetary system accommodates the public by dividing the total money supply into the desired proportions. In restricting our attention to the stock of money, defined in the narrow sense of demand deposits plus currency and coin, we are not denying the importance of near monies, such as savings and time deposits, gov- ernment bonds, and savings and loan shares. These items are im- portant, but their effects should be considered separately from the effect of money itself.

A *commercial bank* is defined as a firm that has the power to accept accounts which are subject to immediate withdrawal by check. Commercial banks are either members of the Federal Reserve System, or they are nonmember banks. All National Banks, banks that received their charters from the Comptroller of the Currency of the Department of the United States Treasury, must be member banks. State banks, banks that received their charters from their state governments, may become member banks if they meet certain standards on capital and agree to abide by the laws and regulations of the Federal Reserve System.

Member banks are required to keep a legally prescribed minimum amount of *legal reserves*, at present defined as deposits with the district Federal Reserve Bank or as currency and coin (vault cash). Nonmember banks are required by the state banking authorities to maintain legal reserves, which typically are defined as balances held with other commercial banks and vault cash. The definition of legal reserves has changed from time to time, and this is a source of varia- tion in the stock of money. Likewise, the reserve requirements are changed occasionally, and this is another source of the variability of money.

Prior to July 28, 1962, there were three classes of member banks: Central Reserve City banks (downtown Chicago and New York banks), Reserve City banks (banks located in some 60 large cities), and Country banks (banks designated as neither Central Reserve City nor Reserve City banks). The banks of New York and Chicago are now classified as Reserve City banks. Thus there remain just the two categories of member banks. The Board of Governors of the Federal Reserve System has the authority to vary reserve requirements on demand deposits subject to the requirement between 10 and 22 percent in the case of Reserve City banks, and between 7 and 14 percent in the case of Country banks. The Board can vary the reserve requirement on time deposits of all member banks between 3 and 10 percent. The requirements in January of 1968 on demand deposits were 17 percent for Reserve City banks; 12 percent for small Country banks and 12½ percent for Country banks with deposits in excess of $5 million; and 3 percent on time deposits under $5 million, and 6 percent on those in excess of $5 million.

Credit Expansion

The term "credit expansion" is used somewhat loosely to refer to the process by which banks increase the money supply. One should distinguish between credit expansion and money supply expansion. The term "money supply expansion" points at the liability side of the balance sheets of the members of the monetary system. The former points at the asset side of bank balance sheets, and emphasizes the fact that bank credit normally increases as demand deposits grow. The purpose of this section is to review credit and money expansion as it takes place through the activities of commercial banks.[1]

If a bank receives a deposit, the customer brings either currency and coin or a check. The full amount is included as legal reserves immediately if currency and coin have been deposited, since vault cash is counted as legal reserves. If a check drawn against another bank is deposited, the check will be sent for collection and the collection will take the form of an increase in the bank's deposit account

---

[1]Throughout, we tend to speak of expansion, but the reader should realize that the contractionary process is equally important in business cycle analysis. The steps involved in the contraction are just the reverse of those cited for the expansion.

with the Federal Reserve Bank of its district. It may take a day or two for the collection to take place; but when it does, the full amount is added to the bank's legal reserves. If the deposited check is drawn on the receiving bank itself, neither its total deposits nor its legal reserves are affected.

The bank receiving the deposit now has 100 percent of its new deposit backed by legal reserves. If its reserve requirement were 15 percent, it could allow its legal reserves to fall by 85 percent and continue to operate within the legal minimum. It could expect that if it made a loan or purchased securities in the amount of the 85 percent, the borrower or seller of the security would write checks on his created balance and thus withdraw his deposit and legal reserves from this bank. The bank then would have the original deposit as its liability and, as assets, the 15 percent remaining in legal reserves and 85 percent in earning assets: loans or investments. But now the bank on whom the original deposited check was written has lost reserves and deposits in the amount of the check. Its required reserves went down by 15 percent of the amount of the withdrawal; so it will have to take steps to acquire 85 percent of the check amount of reserves. It will allow loans to expire or sell other earning assets in this amount so that the expansionary action by the one bank is exactly offset by the contractionary action of the other bank.

The key to most of the analysis of credit and money expansion or contraction comes exactly at this point — is there or is there not an offsetting action elsewhere in the system? If, for example, currency that had been in circulation for some time was returned to the banking system, there would be an increase in reserves of the bank receiving the deposit without a corresponding loss by another bank. Similarly, if the Federal Reserve bought securities, or if the Treasury paid off some of its debts or spent some money out of its account at the Federal Reserve, some banks would receive new reserves while no other commercial banks would lose reserves.

Now, suppose one of these things has happened. Let us assume that the Federal Reserve buys $100 million worth of Treasury bills on the open market. The sellers will receive checks drawn against the Federal Reserve Banks, which they will deposit in commercial banks, which will have new reserves as soon as the checks are sent to the Federal Reserve Banks. Since no commercial bank loses reserves in this transaction, there is a net increase of reserves in the banking system and in deposits of the sellers of the bills of $100 million. Now the affected banks have excess reserves of $85 million (assuming a 15 percent reserve requirement). Each bank could lend or purchase other earning assets by the amount of its excess reserves unless it wished to hold additional excess reserves. If, for example, banks on the average had a demand for excess reserves equal to 5 percent of their demand deposits, they would expand earning assets by $80 million rather than the $85 million that could legally be added. Borrowers or the sellers of the assets would spend the proceeds by writing checks, and those who received these checks would deposit them in their own commercial banks. In this process we might expect a currency drain to take place, since as the money supply is expanding it is likely that the public will demand more of both kinds of money, that is, currency and coin as well as demand deposits.

To the extent that currency and coin are drawn into circulation, the banks are losing reserves. If we assume that the currency drain is 10 percent of deposit expansion, the public will withdraw $10 million since demand deposits have increased by $100 million. This means that of the $80 million of earning asset expansion by banks, $70 million will be deposited to become new reserves for the depositors' banks. These banks, in turn, will have $56 million available for loans and investments (deposits and reserves increased by $70 million; required reserves went up by $70 million × .15 = $10.5 million; desired excess reserves increased by $70 million × .05 = $3.5 million). This process of banks making loans, losing reserves and deposits to other banks and to currency in circulation, will continue until all of the original $100 million is absorbed into required reserves, desired excess reserves, and currency in circulation. The interesting question in monetary theory is: By how much will the money supply increase?

In order to answer this question, it is necessary to discover the size of the monetary expansion multiplier. This multiplier is the number by which the monetary base must be multiplied to equal the size of the money stock; that is, $M = KB$ where

M = the amount of money in the economy,
K = the multiplier,
B = the monetary base.

The Simple Multiplier

If we were to introduce all, or even most, of the complications in the real world, the model would become extremely complex. In view of this, we will present first the simplest possible multiplier, and then develop one that is adequate for the analysis we shall need in this book.[2]

1. $M = KB$

2. $B = R$ Where R is the amount of legal reserves held by the Commercial Banking System (CBS).

3. $R = rD$ Where r is the reserve requirement and D is the amount of demand deposits held by the banking system.

4. $M = D$ Which states that in this model the only kind of money is demand deposits.

$$K = \frac{M}{B} \text{ from (1)}$$

$$K = \frac{D}{R} \text{ from (2) and (4)}$$

$$K = \frac{D}{rD} \text{ from (3)}$$

$$K = 1/r$$

Thus the simple multiplier is the reciprocal of the reserve requirement. If the reserve requirement is .20 (or 20%), the value of K, the multiplier is 5. This means that if legal reserves are $20 billion, the money supply will be 5 × $20 billion or $100 billion; and if R were increased by $100 million, the money stock would increase by $500 million.

A More Complete Multiplier

To use the simple model as a forecasting tool would obviously be absurd; other things would have to remain constant, and we can be quite certain that some very important things would not remain constant. We would expect, for instance, that, if the reserve base were increased and the amount of demand deposits were increasing, the public would increase their demands for currency and for time deposits, and the banks might want more excess reserves. Our next problem is to incorporate these factors into a model and add the

---

[2]The methodology of this section relies very heavily on the excellent work of Karl Brunner, *A Case Study of U. S. Monetary Policy; Reserve Requirements and Inflationary Gold Flows in the Middle 30's*, Reprint No. 20 (Los Angeles, California: Bureau of Business and Economic Research, University of California, 1959).

caveat that there are still a number of important variables which have not been included.

1. $M = KB$

2. $B = R + C_b + C_c$
   Where R is deposits of member banks in Federal Reserve Banks, C_b is vault cash, C_c is currency in circulation.

3. $R + C_b = rD = eD = r'T$
   Where e is the desired excess reserve ratio, r' is the reserve requirement on time deposits, T is time deposits.

4. $C_c = aD$
   Where a is C_c/D, the ratio of currency to demand deposits that the public wishes to hold.

5. $T = tD$
   Where t is T/D, or the ratio of time deposits to demand deposits the public wishes to hold.

6. $M = D + C_c$
   The money supply is made up of demand deposits and currency in circulation.

Solving for K:

$$K = \frac{M}{B} = \frac{D + C_c}{R + C_b + C_c} \quad \text{from (6) and (2)}$$

$$K = \frac{D + aD}{rD + eD + r'T + aD} \quad \text{from (4) and (3)}$$

$$K = \frac{D(1 + a)}{rD + eD + r'tD + aD} \quad \text{from (5)}$$

$$K = \frac{D(1 + a)}{D(r + e + r't + a)}$$

$$K = \frac{1 + a}{r + e + r't + a}$$

$$M = \frac{1 + a}{r + e + r't + a} \quad (B)$$

To demonstrate the value of this type of model, let us assume some values to the parameters and observe the resulting consolidated balance sheet of the commercial banking system:

$$a = .20$$
$$r = .15$$
$$e = .02$$
$$r' = .05$$
$$t = .60$$
$$B = 40 \text{ (in billions of dollars)}$$

Now we can insert these values into the equation for K:

$$K = \frac{1 + a}{r + e + r't + a} = \frac{1 + .20}{.15 + .02 + .05\,(.60) + .20} = \frac{1.2}{.40} = 3$$

Thus, the money supply multiplier, K, is 3, and since $M = KB$, $M = 3 \times \$40 = \$120$ billion. Now that the money supply is known, its division into currency in circulation and demand deposits can be determined. Since $M = D + C_c$ and $C_c = aD$, $M = D + aD$ or

$$M = D\,(1 + a) \quad \text{or} \quad D = \frac{M}{1 + a} = \frac{\$120}{1 + .20} = \$100. \quad \text{Currency in}$$

circulation is the difference between the money supply and demand deposits; that is $C_c = M - D$, or $C_c = \$120 - \$100 = \$20$. To check on that result, compare with Equation 4, which is $C_c = aD$. Thus $C_c = .20 \times \$100 = \$20$.

Commercial Banking System

$R + C_b$ = $ 20		$D = \$100$
Earning Assets = 140		$T = $ 60
Total Assets = $160	Total Liabilities	= $160

Legal reserves of deposits with the Federal Reserve plus vault cash were found by multiplying the reserve requirement r of .15 times D of $100, and the desired excess reserve ratio e of .02 times D, and r', the time deposit reserve requirement (.05) times T. T was found from Equation (5): $T = tD = .60\,(100) = \$60$. Earning assets are the difference between total liabilities and nonearning assets (cash).

If $1 billion is added to the base (B) through open-market purchases by the Federal Reserve, the changes in the consolidated balance sheet of the commercial banking system would be as follows:

Commercial Banking System

$R + C_b$	$= + \$ .5$	D	$= + \$2.5$
Earning Assets	$= + \ 3.5$	T	$= + \ 1.5$
Change in Total Assets	$= + \$4.0$	Change in Total Liabilities	$= + \$4.0$

The new balance sheet of the banking system now looks like this:

Commercial Banking System

$R + C_b$	$= \$ 20.5$	D	$= \$102.5$
Earning Assets $=$	143.5	T	$= \ 61.5$
Total Assets	$= \$164.0$	Total Liabilities $= \$164.0$	

The money supply increased by the multiplier ($K = 3$) times the change in the reserve base ($\Delta B = \$1$) or \$3 billion, \$.5 billion of currency in circulation, and \$2.5 billion of new demand deposits. While the money supply increased by \$3, credit expansion was \$3.5 (change in earning assets), and liquid assets of the public ($D + T$) increased by \$4, which is partly offset by the fact that the public's liabilities to the banks increased and/or their holdings of other assets such as government securities were reduced.

Money and Business Fluctuations

In this section we shall try to demonstrate the way the type of model that has just been presented can be of help in the analysis of the role of money in business fluctuations and in evaluating monetary policy. Later chapters develop these topics in more detail.

A quite dramatic example can be seen in the behavior of a, the currency/demand deposit ratio, which was approximately .16 in June of both 1928 and 1929 and rose to about .33 in the same month of 1933. If we insert these figures into our model, holding all other values constant, the money supply would decline by some 22 percent! In fact, of course, the other factors also changed. The ratio of time deposits to demand deposits (t) decreased from 1.28 in June, 1928, to 1.00 in June, 1933, which by itself would have increased the money supply by about 3 percent. The excess reserve ratio (e) increased over this same period from .002 to .026, sufficient to cause a 6 percent decrease in the money supply. It was after 1933 that the great increase in bank demand for excess reserves took place to put great contractionary pressure on the stock of money. The excess reserve ratio of member banks rose to .136 in 1936 and continued to rise to .214 in June of 1940.

Monetary policy, too, can be evaluated by means of our model. It probably is reflected in all of the variables, but the most direct relationship is in the reserve requirement parameters and in the monetary base.

Reserve Requirements

As was pointed out earlier, the Federal Reserve Board of Governors has the authority to vary the reserve requirements of member banks; so r (which should be a properly weighted average of the requirements of the different member bank classes) and r' are directly under the control of the Federal Reserve System. The size of the multiplier, the money stock, and bank credit rise when r or r' is decreased, and fall when r or r' is increased.

Member bank reserve requirements were unchanged from 1917 until 1936 when they were increased by approximately 50 percent. They were raised again in 1937 and on May 1, 1937, they were increased to their legal maximum, remaining at that level. Since this was a period of depressed economic conditions and large-scale unemployment, one might wonder why reserve requirements were kept so high. After all, we have just seen that an increase in r is contractionary to the money and credit supply! Some very eminent economists have also questioned this action. Defenders of Federal Reserve policy argue that it was desirable to lower the value of the multiplier because of the growth in the monetary base that was taking place during these years. There was a great fear in the System of what would happen if e were suddenly to decrease, that is, if banks were to decide to expand their earning assets significantly. The money supply could explode. Detractors of Federal Reserve policy respond that if the money supply were to expand at too rapid a rate, open-market operations could be used to dampen the rate of growth.

Open-Market Operations

The impact of open-market operations is directly on B, the monetary base. Whatever is happening within the multiplier, the effect can be offset by changes in B. Thus, if one of the components of the multiplier is changing in such a way as to cause an increase in the money supply and the Open-Market Committee finds this undesirable, the open-market agent can be told to sell enough securities to counteract the expansion. On the other hand, if additional expansion is deemed to be warranted, the orders will be to purchase securities.

There is no possibility of open-market operations failing to affect B. If the Open-Market Committee buys or sells, someone must sell to them or buy from them. Since all of the firms who deal directly with the Open-Market Committee are large dealers in government securities, the checks received in payment or the checks they pay for the securities immediately result in an increase or a decrease in some member banks' reserves held at the Federal Reserve Banks. These new reserves, of course, spread out pervasively throughout the system of banks.

Discount Rate

Another policy tool of the Federal Reserve that affects the money base is the *discount rate*, which is the rate of interest at which member banks may borrow from the Federal Reserve Bank of the district. When a bank borrows from the Federal Reserve Bank, it takes payment in the form of deposits at the Reserve Bank. Since no other commercial bank has lost reserves by this act, total reserves and B have increased by the amount of the loan. The borrowing is at the initiative of the individual commercial bank, but at the discretion of the Federal Reserve Bank, and is, therefore, not under the precise control of the monetary authority. The Federal Reserve can encourage borrowing by lowering the discount rate and discourage borrowing by raising the rate.

Many writers and practitioners of central banking have concentrated their attention on what is called the "announcement effect" of discount rate changes, arguing that an increased rate is taken as a signal that the Board of Governors views the current situation as one where contractionary action is in order, and that banks ought to be more cautious in their lending policies. In terms of our model, the expectation (or hope) is that e, the excess reserve ratio, will rise somewhat, causing a slight decrease in the size of the multiplier as well as decreasing B by decreasing member bank indebtedness to the Federal Reserve.

Other Factors Affecting the Base of the Monetary System

Federal Reserve policy is not the only determinant of B. There are other important sources of variation, but it should be kept in mind that if these other sources cause undesired changes, the Federal Reserve's policy can neutralize them, although it has not always done so.

One continuously perplexing feature of the United States monetary system is that both the Federal Reserve System and the United States Treasury have powerful ability to affect the money base. Although this is consistent with the political philosophy of checks and balances, it makes for divided responsibility and inconsistent policy actions, and sometimes a stalemate. Both the Treasury and the Federal Reserve System are capable of completely offsetting the effects of the policy action of the other.

The Treasury causes member bank reserves to vary inversely as its own deposit balances at the Federal Reserve Banks vary. A decrease in the Treasury's balance means that it has paid out money for the purchase of goods and services, transfer payments, or the retirement of its debt, the recipients have cashed the checks, and member banks have received new reserves. Reserves decrease when the Treasury's balance at the Federal Reserve increases because the balance falls when the Treasury directly transfers funds from its deposits at commercial banks, and when tax collections or the proceeds of government security sales are placed in its balance at the Federal Reserve Banks. The Treasury also adds to the base by its issuance of currency and coin.

Another important source of variation in the monetary base arises out of the flow of monetary gold. Purchase of gold bullion by the Treasury results in the receipt by the seller of the gold of a check drawn against the Treasury's balance at the Federal Reserve. The Treasury's balance may then be replenished by the issuance of gold certificates. In this way, the reserves of commercial banks are increased without a decrease in the Treasury's Federal Reserve Bank balance.

A table is published each month in the *Federal Reserve Bulletin* entitled "Member Bank Reserves, Federal Reserve Bank Credit, and Related Items." By means of this table one can see the various factors that have caused changes in the monetary base. To go from this table to the scheme we have presented, it is simply necessary to observe that member bank reserves plus currency in circulation are equal to the "factors supplying reserve funds" minus "factors absorbing reserve funds," not including member bank reserves and currency in circulation themselves.

Table 3-1

MEMBER BANK RESERVES, FEDERAL RESERVE BANK CREDIT, AND RELATED ITEMS

(In millions of dollars)

Column groups: Factors supplying reserve funds — F.R. Bank credit outstanding [U.S. Govt. securities[1]: Total, Bought outright, Repurchase agreements; Discounts and advances; Float[3]; Total[3]], Gold stock, Treasury currency outstanding. Factors absorbing reserve funds — Currency in circulation, Treasury cash holdings, Deposits other than member bank reserves with F.R. Banks [Treasury, Foreign, Other[2]], Other F.R. accounts, Member bank reserves [With F.R. Banks, Currency and coin[4], Total].

Period or date	Govt. sec. Total	Bought outright	Repurch. agree.	Disc. and adv.	Float[3]	Total[3]	Gold stock	Treas. curr. outst.	Curr. in circ.	Treas. cash hold.	Dep. Treasury	Foreign	Other[2]	Other F.R. acc.	MBR With F.R. Banks	Curr. and coin[4]	MBR Total
Averages of daily figures																	
1929 — June	179	179		978	61	1,317	4,024	2,018	4,400	210	30		30	376	2,314		2,314
1933 — June	1,933	1,933		250	12	2,208	4,030	2,295	5,455	272	81		164	350	2,211		2,211
1939 — Dec.	2,510	2,510		8	83	2,612	17,518	2,956	7,609	2,402	616		739	248	11,473		11,473
1941 — Dec.	2,219	2,219		5	170	2,404	22,759	3,239	10,985	2,189	592		1,531	292	12,812		12,812
1945 — Dec.	23,708	23,708		381	652	24,744	20,047	4,322	28,452	2,269	625		1,247	493	16,027		16,027
1950 — Dec.	20,345	20,336	9	142	1,117	21,606	22,879	4,629	27,806	1,290	615	920	353	739	17,391		17,391
1956 — Dec.	24,765	24,498	267	706	1,633	27,156	21,942	5,064	31,775	772	463	372	247	998	19,535		19,535
1957 — Dec.	23,982	23,615	367	716	1,443	26,186	22,769	5,144	31,932	768	385	345	186	1,063	19,420		19,420
1958 — Dec.	26,312	26,216	96	564	1,496	28,412	20,563	5,230	32,371	691	470	262	337	1,174	18,899		18,899
1959 — Dec.	27,036	26,993	43	911	1,426	29,435	19,482	5,311	32,775	396	524	361	348	1,195	18,628	304	18,932
1960 — Dec.	27,248	27,170	78	94	1,665	29,060	17,954	5,396	33,019	408	522	250	495	1,029	16,688	2,595	19,283
1961 — Dec.	29,098	29,061	37	152	1,921	31,217	16,929	5,587	33,954	422	514	229	244	1,112	17,259	2,859	20,118
1962 — Dec.	30,546	30,474	72	305	2,298	33,218	15,978	5,561	35,281	398	587	222	290	1,048	16,932	3,108	20,040
1963 — Dec.	33,729	33,626	103	360	2,434	36,610	15,562	5,583	37,603	389	879	160	206	1,215	17,303	3,443	20,746
1964 — Dec.	37,126	36,895	231	266	2,423	39,873	15,388	5,401	39,698	595	944	181	181	1,093	17,964	3,645	21,609
1965 — Dec.	40,885	40,772	113	490	2,349	43,853	13,799	5,565	42,206	808	683	154	231	389	18,747	3,972	22,719
1966 — Dec.	43,760	43,274	486	570	2,383	46,864	13,158	6,284	44,579	1,191	291	164	429	83	19,568	4,262	23,830
1967 — Jan.	44,066	43,847	219	389	2,215	46,802	13,158	6,350	43,957	1,225	566	153	442	203	19,765	c4,310	c24,075
Feb.	44,215	43,915	300	362	1,875	46,587	13,144	6,409	43,525	1,252	609	136	448	496	19,675	4,034	23,709
Mar.	44,620	44,351	269	200	1,606	46,524	13,108	6,473	43,673	1,297	505	136	443	647	19,404	4,001	23,405
Apr.	45,082	44,942	140	155	1,540	46,902	13,108	6,530	43,812	1,356	860	125	463	559	19,365	3,997	23,362
May	45,699	45,481	218	126	1,374	47,323	13,108	6,576	44,083	1,392	990	137	450	692	19,263	4,021	23,284
June	45,844	45,801	43	147	1,459	47,547	13,109	6,602	44,567	1,385	715	128	464	373	19,388	4,130	23,518
July	46,807	46,784	23	91	1,584	48,590	13,053	6,615	44,997	1,480	1,123	128	482	212	19,730	4,177	23,907
Aug.	46,612	46,558	54	89	1,423	48,210	13,007	6,665	45,011	1,488	1,036	128	453	65	19,600	4,191	23,791
Sept.	46,398	46,377	21	90	1,571	48,147	13,003	6,737	45,189	1,491	566	127	472	-80	19,980	4,220	24,200
Oct.	47,367	47,203	164	126	1,408	48,993	13,003	6,737	45,396	1,483	974	125	476	-211	20,402	4,206	24,608
Nov.	48,010	47,885	125	133	1,555	49,752	12,907	6,781	45,969	1,462	1,167	146	449	-204	20,458	4,282	24,740
Dec.	48,891	48,810	81	238	2,030	51,268	12,436	p6,777	p46,998	p1,430	902	150	451		p20,753	p4,503	p25,256

Source: *Federal Reserve Bulletin* (January, 1968), p. A-4.

A recent example is shown here as Table 3-1. All of the items shown on the left side of this table increase the monetary base when they increase, and the items on the right-hand side, other than currency in circulation and member bank reserves, decrease the base when they increase. Notice that from 1933 to 1939 the increase in the monetary base was due primarily to the great increase in the gold stock, whereas during the 1941–1945 period the increase was due to the great expansion of United States Government securities held by the Federal Reserve Banks.

PERSONAL INVESTMENT PATTERNS

According to national income determination theory, saving that is not matched by concurrent investment expenditures brings about a reduction in aggregate economic activity. Financial institutions have evolved over the years to aid in the process of accepting funds from those who are willing to give up their ability to command goods currently (savers), and make the funds (and, therefore, the ability to command resources) available to investors. In this sense financial institutions are intermediaries between savers and investors. They are also intermediaries between savers and dissavers, and to some extent between disinvestors and investors. In order to serve this important function, they must tailor their liabilities to the manifold needs and personalities of savers, and, on the other hand, the nature of the credit granted must be such as to fit the needs of those who wish to use the funds. As economic conditions change, financial institutions and financial instruments must also change if serious problems are to be avoided.

A very familiar class of financial institution or financial intermediary is the life insurance company. Life insurance as it is generally sold in America represents a combination of protection and investment. The growth of life insurance has resulted in a large volume of assets in the hands of life insurance companies. In late 1967 life insurance companies had about $173 billion in assets.[3] Since the major concern of a purchaser of insurance and of the insurance company is protection rather than maximum investment return, life insurance funds are invested on a conservative basis. Legal requirements have in most cases restricted insurance company investments to mortgages, real estate, high-grade bonds, a few well-

---

[3]*Federal Reserve Bulletin* (October, 1967), p. 1782.

protected issues of preferred stock, and a small proportion of high-grade common stocks.

Large sums are also deposited in savings banks and put into trust accounts in trust departments of banks and in trust companies. There are also legal restrictions on the use which such institutions may make of funds.

Such institutional investment makes large sums of money available for debt financing. This creates no problem so long as sufficient demand for debt capital exists. It may, however, make it more difficult to raise equity capital that is also needed if business is to maintain a sound capital structure.

A problem may also arise in periods of recession in keeping all funds invested. Especially in life insurance purchases savings go on year by year, in good years and bad, since the major aim is protection. This means that savings are available in large quantities when the demand has fallen off due to the lower level of business. Economic activity would hold up better if less were saved and more spent on consumption, but institutional arrangements prevent this.

There has also been a phenomenal growth in the postwar period in savings accounts in savings and loan associations. The total in such savings accounts was about $7.5 billion in 1945 and had increased to over $120 billion in late 1967.[4] Many savers put money into these institutions because the rate of return is somewhat more favorable than in alternative uses offering the same degree of liquidity and safety. This restricts a large volume of savings for use in financing residential real estate. It may also create problems because a large volume of liquid assets has been built up while the proceeds have been invested in permanent assets. Even though it is legally possible to require a time period for withdrawing savings, in practice they are paid on demand. This makes it possible for savers to withdraw funds for consumption purposes almost at will and without penalty. The funds may come from new savers in which case funds intended for saving are switched to consumption purposes. Or they may come from loans from the Home Loan Banks. Since they get most of their funds from the sale of debentures, the result is the same.

A large amount of personal investment is also in government bonds especially savings bonds. The volume of savings bonds outstanding in late 1967 was $51 billion,[5] and a substantial amount of

[4]*Ibid.*
[5]*Ibid.*, p. 1786.

marketable government securities was also held by individuals. These huge amounts of liquid assets may also affect the economy if large amounts are converted into cash at one time and used for consumption expenditures. The funds may come from credit creation, from funds previously held idle, or from funds intended for investment.

Thus the trends in personal investment patterns create additional problems of economic balance. On the one hand, savings are made available to limited sectors of the economy which may not be the sectors of greatest need. On the other hand, savers have a large degree of liquidity which makes it possible to shift funds to consumption expenditures with little or no delay and with little or no penalty.

CONSUMER FREEDOM OF CHOICE

Consumer sovereignty is a fundamental principle of democratic capitalism. By and large, freedom of the individual to make economic choices is characteristic of the economy of the United States, and in varying degrees this is true of other countries. The consumer is free to spend his income as he sees fit. He may choose among various types of goods and services, and he may choose the time at which he makes his purchases; or he may decide not to spend on goods or services, in which case he may decide to hold money; buy bonds, insurance, or equities; or repay debt. While this kind of freedom is priceless, it is also one of the factors that gives the economic system some of its unstable characteristics.

When consumers are free to decide the amount of consumption spending they will do, businessmen are free to decide the amount of investment spending, peoples of other countries are free to buy the amounts they choose from us, and governments are free to determine their purchases, it sometimes happens that the total spending is inadequate to bring into employment all of the resources that are willing and available to be used, or that the total spending is more than the value of the goods that can be produced. Consumers are also vital in determining the rate of economic growth of the system since capital expansion, which is the essence of growth, is limited by the amount of saving.

Classical economists admitted some temporary difficulties as consumer preferences shifted from certain goods to other goods, but flexible prices and mobility of the factors of production would eliminate them. It was inconceivable, however, to Ricardo and later classicists that a shift by consumers to less total spending could result in any excess of labor or other resources. Their way of phrasing this proposition was that a general glut was impossible. The reasoning was that the interest rate would fall, causing investors to increase their demand for resources and, at the same time, lead households to revise their spending plans upward so that total resources would be employed but with a lower percent of them devoted to present or consumption goods. This line of analysis, known as Say's Law, has played such an important role in the development of the understanding of how economic systems work that we shall come back to it again and again.

PROFIT MOTIVE

In our system, most production is done for the market. Most businessmen cannot wait until the orders come in and then produce precisely that amount. Instead, they try to estimate what the demand will be, when the goods will be ready for the market, and what the costs will be when they are actually incurred in the production process. Thus, the possibility of errors is quite great. Revenue forecasts as well as cost forecasts can be wrong so that either undesired inventory accumulation or attrition or serious price changes may easily arise. Unexpected outcomes provoke new responses by businessmen, causing further changes in the important variables of the economy. The problems are caused by the fact that production takes time. If output could be created instantaneously, no inventories would be maintained, and no possibility of errors of expectations would exist.

Sometimes government officials and other observers admonish businessmen to make decisions "for the good of the nation" rather than on the self-interest principle of the profit motive. During depressions business is asked to expand; and when inflation appears to be the problem, restraint is called for. In general, if there is a conflict between the two criteria, businessmen are well advised to ignore, and, in fact, do ignore such admonition. By relying on the profit motive, we get into difficulties, but it is in no wise clear that any alternative criteria would be superior, or, indeed, as good.

The decisions of businessmen concerning such items as price, production, and investment may be made upon the basis of careful, rational appraisals of all factors in the business situation. They may also be influenced by psychological factors, such as waves of optimism or pessimism; the desire to follow in the footsteps of competitors; or the fear of the future outlook because of international uncertainties, governmental policies, and the like.

The bases on which the decisions of businessmen are made have changed somewhat as the economy has developed so that the role of business decisions in the cycle is not necessarily the same today as it was a generation ago. More and more businessmen are taking a longer-range point of view, realizing that it is better to maximize long-run profits than short-run profits. This often means that in the short-run prices are set at a lower level than the market will bear in order to maximize long-run profits. This tends to narrow the range of price fluctuations over the cycle in those fields where such a policy is followed and thus to change the characteristics of the cycle to this extent.

In many cases modern management decides inventory policies, working capital policies, and the timing and the amount of investment in new plants and equipment on the basis of careful studies of the long-range demand for its product. As such action reaches sizable proportions, it eliminates excessive accumulation of inventory and the building of unnecessary plants and equipment and thus, by reducing activity somewhat during the boom, changes some of the characteristics of the cycle.

THE INDUSTRIAL STRUCTURE

Elements of great importance in the analysis of business fluctuations are the degree of price flexibility and output responsiveness to changing conditions. According to the traditional theory of the firm, both purely competitive firms and unfettered monopolies respond immediately to changes in supply or demand by altering price and output. Only casual observation is needed, however, to observe that the prices of some goods and services seem to be quite stable even though cost conditions and demand change markedly.

Competitive prices become rigid when governments impose controls over them, as under price control or agricultural price supports, and when government is the sole or major buyer as is the case with gold, and in other cases where it is deemed in the public interest, as with milk. Monopoly prices are rigid when set by government or when they must be approved by a governmental agency, which, of course, describes public utilities. Monopolies might also maintain constant prices to avoid more direct and pervasive involvement by government. Most firms in the real world are somewhere between the poles of pure competition and pure monopoly, and here our micro theory is less helpful.

There are a number of explanations for the price stability that is fairly characteristic of these oligopolistic markets. One is that collusion, tacit or overt, exists; and in this situation any change in price or other policy could precipitate a falling out among the members. This is a way the firms can live together without damaging price wars or extreme price fluctuations. Another explanation involves the kinked demand curve which is established if each firm believes that if it raises its price other firms in the industry will not raise their prices, and if the firm lowers its price the others will follow suit. Under these circumstances, variations in costs will not change price or output unless the cost changes are extreme. In some activities the cost of changing prices is considerable, and consequently will not be done unless circumstances have definitely changed and are expected to be relatively permanent. Sometimes price stability has as its source the organizational structure of the firm, and internal political considerations may lead to the no-change decision. If the firms are large, as they frequently are in the oligopoly case, fear of government involvement, in one way or another, may induce the firms to leave well enough alone, that is, keep prices where they are.

In general, where prices are relatively inflexible, the response to changes in demand or cost conditions is a more pronounced change in output than where prices are flexible. In unrestricted agricultural markets, for example, price varies considerably as demand changes and output variations are less pronounced. In contrast, automobile sales and output vary directly as demand varies, and price changes are more moderate. This relationship between price and output variability in particular industries and the differences in this respect among industries have a great deal to do with the character of business fluctuations, and so we shall come back to this question later.

LABOR UNION POLICIES

Still another factor that is important in shaping the cycle in present-day capitalism in America is the position of labor unions. When workers were largely unorganized, wages were cut rapidly in a period of declining business to bring costs into line with declining prices. This is what one would expect to happen under any perfectly competitive system in which workers compete with each other for the available jobs. With the advent of powerful labor unions, however, the wage is fixed by collective bargaining between the union and representatives of management. The wage rate is usually set for a specified period, though in some contracts it is tied to the cost-of-living index. Where wage rates are fixed through union contracts, or by minimum wage laws, a reduction in the demand for a product will result in a greater reduction of employment in that industry than would otherwise occur.

In business cycle analysis, it is important to distinguish between real wages and money wages. Constant money wages over a period of rising consumer goods prices result in falling real wages. Real wages rise if the consumer price index falls at a faster rate than money wages; and if money wages and prices rise or fall at the same rate, real wages remain constant. We raise the question, to be taken up later: Are business decisions, and the decisions of workers, based on the real wage or on the money wage?

THE ROLE OF GOVERNMENT IN THE ECONOMY

The role of government in the economy is a very large subject, and we cannot do justice to the topic here. The consensus of what the proper role of government is has changed considerably over the history of our nation. It always has been, and no doubt always will be, the subject of widespread debate; but the range of disagreement is narrowed by the understanding of how the economic system operates. But whether we agree or disagree with the actions taken by government, we must know what they are and take account of them in our analysis.

When our country was first established, the basic attitude was "that government is best which governs least." Interferences with the smooth functioning of the economy arose primarily out of war financing, or out of government changes in banking rules and regulations, such as those that occurred in the period of "wildcat" banking during the administration of Andrew Jackson prior to the crash of 1837. As time went on, government assumed a larger and larger role in the economic system. Beginning with the passage of the Interstate Commerce Act in 1887, which regulated railroad rates, government regulation spread to many sectors of the economy, and the government has engaged in business on a large scale in such projects as the production of electrical energy and atomic energy.

The role of the government in the pricing of agricultural products also has decided effects on the course of the cycle in business. Before the advent of the New Deal, agricultural production was left almost entirely to the decisions of the individual farmers, although some attempts were made to stimulate production during World War I and to take surpluses off the market during the Hoover administration. Since 1933, however, various aspects of agricultural production and pricing have been controlled by the government.

The prices of many of the nonperishable commodities are regulated by means of marketing agreements, as in the case of milk. The prices of basic commodities have a floor set by the prices at which the Commodity Credit Corporation will make loans to farmers on these commodities as collateral. These loans are in effect purchases by the CCC if the price does not rise above the loan value, since there is no legal recourse against the farmer if he does not repay the loan. Such loans, therefore, set a lower limit to farm prices.

In past cycles agricultural prices and food prices in general usually dropped rapidly and gave the cycles some of the characteristics which they had. With government control of some agricultural prices, this characteristic of the cycle has changed and past price-quantity interrelations have been altered.

We could continue to enumerate the points at which governments impinge upon the operations of the different segments of the economy. This kind of government policy might be termed *structural economic policy*, since it alters the relationships among the basic units of the system. Increasingly, especially in the past few years, the viewpoint has been growing that the government should not restrict its influence to structural policy, but it should take as its responsibility the assurance that the level of economic activity behaves in a desirable manner. We might refer to this kind of policy as *aggregative economic policy*. In this connection, the role of the government includes full employment policy, anti-inflationary policy, economic growth policy, and a balance of payments policy. The tools used are monetary and fiscal policy. Part VIII, Proposals for Achieving Economic Growth and Stability, is devoted to the study of these aggregative tools.

THE COBWEB THEOREM

The business cycle is a phenomenon that occurs over a span of time. Economic activity usually cannot take place instantaneously. A development may inspire a change in some action, but usually only with a lag in time.

Perhaps the clearest example of the way time lags are responsible for fluctuating economic behavior is to be seen in the "cobweb theorem." It is demonstrated here on a micro level of analysis, although it also has applications in macroeconomic theory.

In the usual price theory, quantities supplied and demanded of a particular commodity are said to be determined by the current price of that commodity and certain other factors. The analysis is termed "static" because it is essentially timeless. Implicitly, all activity takes place instantaneously. In dynamic analysis, the fact that some activity takes time is taken into account, and the results are sometimes considerably different from that flowing from static theory.

In the case of the cobweb theorem, it is assumed that quantity demanded of a good depends upon the price existing at the time the decision to purchase is made. The notation is $Q_{Dt} = f\ (P_t)$. (In words: quantity demanded in time period t is a function of price in period t). This isn't always the best assumption, but for many, perhaps most, commodities it is accurate. It is on the supply side where the most obvious time lag would seem to exist — the production lag. In the cobweb theorem, the assumption is made that the decision of the producers to sell different amounts of the good depends on the price of that good at some critical time in advance of the time of sale. A farmer, for example, must decide early in the spring how many acres of land he will devote to the production of a certain crop that will be harvested in the fall. He must also determine the amount of fertilizer and water and other care to be applied. In any event, these decisions which determine the quantity that will be produced must be made in some time period before the sale can take place. In other words, $Q_{St} = f\ (P_{t-1})$. (Quantity supplied in period t is a function of the price of the product in period $t - 1$).

Chart 3-1 has been drawn with the supply function slightly steeper than the demand function (ignoring the signs). We can suppose that the example is potatoes, and the current price (P_o) is above the equilibrium price (P_e) because of a severe drought last year. Potato farmers and potential potato growers, observing this

Chart 3-1

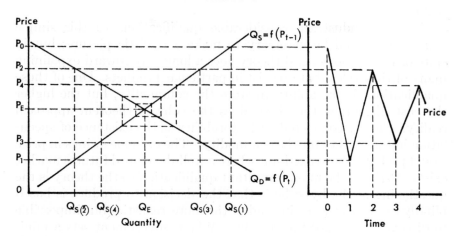

relatively attractive price, decide to produce relatively large quantities of potatoes, $Qs_{(1)}$. When this size crop comes on the market, however, buyers of potatoes will be willing to purchase the entire crop only if the price falls considerably, namely to P_1. P_1, being a price at which little or no profit can be expected, will induce farmers to plan on smaller crops next spring. Many will shift to more promising crops. Thus, the output in time period 2 will be expected to be just $Qs_{(2)}$, a very small output which, when it is grown and harvested, will bring the higher price (P_2). That high price will induce a larger output ($Qs_{(3)}$), which, in turn, can be sold only at the lower price, (P_3), and so on. A cycle is in operation, represented on the conventional time diagram. If we were to plot the output figures, they would be inverse to the price figures; that is, when price is high, output is low and vice versa.

The cyclical process just described is a convergent cycle, so-called because the variables converge toward equilibrium. If the reader will experiment a bit with different shapes of the demand and supply schedules, he will discover that if the demand curve is steeper than the supply curve, the result will be an explosive cycle, that is, one in which price and quantity move farther away from equilibrium each time period. If the two curves are drawn with the same slope, the cycle will be one of constant amplitude. When both functions are relatively steep, price will fluctuate widely and the output cycle will be within a more narrow range; whereas if both curves are relatively flat, the greatest fluctuation will be in output, and the price variation will be mild.

In most industries, considerable qualifications to this simple framework would be necessary to make a realistic picture; but in spite of these, the general theory goes a long way toward explaining many of the cycles that do exist in particular products. One of those qualifications is the ability to store the commodity, but the higher the cost of storage the closer does the cobweb theorem approach reality. Closely connected with storability is the existence of specu- lation in the market for the commodity. The extreme swings in price would probably be evened out where a well-developed futures market exists. Perhaps the most important qualification to the theory is the questioning of the hypothesis that the decision to produce is based blindly on present price instead of the more realistic (but impossible to discover) expected future price. Where government sets a mini- mum or maximum price or where noncompetitive conditions hold, further qualifications are necessary.

QUESTIONS

1. The text does not define "the financial system." What do you think should be the important elements in such a definition? Explain how "the monetary system" differs from your definition of "the financial system."

2. Using the model on pages 48–51, show the final balance sheets of the commercial banking system and the money supply in each of the following events:
   (a) Reserve requirements on demand deposits (r) increase to 35 percent.
   (b) Reserve requirements on time deposits are eliminated al- together.
   (c) Currency in circulation increases significantly so that the value of a becomes .50.
   (d) The monetary base decreases by $2 billion.

3. Discuss the events that will increase or decrease the monetary base. Organize your answer according to the agency responsible for the change, that is, the Treasury, the Federal Reserve, and "other."

4. Compare the basic economic problems of societies where con- sumption choice is left up to the individuals of the society with one in which governmental bureaus decide what shall be consumed.

5. Draw three charts depicting the cobweb cycle as (a) convergent, (b) explosive, and (c) one of constant amplitude.

6. How has the development of institutional investment affected economic stability?

7. Can managerial policies change the nature of business fluctuations?

8. How has the business cycle been affected by the increased role of government?

SUGGESTED READINGS

Adams, Walter. *The Structure of American Industry.* New York: The Macmillan Co., 1950. Chapters 14 and 15.

Brunner, Karl. *A Case Study of U.S. Monetary Policy: Reserve Requirements and Inflationary Gold Flows in the Middle 30's,* Reprint No. 20. Los Angeles, California: Bureau of Business and Economic Research, University of California, 1959.

Ezekiel, Mordecai, "The Cobweb Theorem," *Quarterly Journal of Economics.* Vol. LII, No. 1 (February, 1938).

Klise, Eugene S. *Money and Banking,* 4th ed. Cincinnati: South-Western Publishing Company, 1968. Chapters 7, 9, 11, 12.

Colm, G. *Essays in Public Finance and Fiscal Policy.* New York: Oxford University Press, Inc., 1955. Chapters 5 and 13.

The Federal Reserve System — Its Purposes and Functions. Washington: Board of Governors of the Federal Reserve System, 1964.

Hailstones, Thomas J. and J. Harvey Dodd. *Economics: An Analysis of Principles and Policies,* 5th ed. Cincinnati: South-Western Publishing Company, 1965.

Mitchell, Wesley C. *What Happens during Business Cycles: A Progress Report.* National Bureau of Economic Research, Studies in Business Cycles 5, 1951. See the Introduction by Arthur F. Burns.

Samuelson, Paul A. *Economics,* 5th ed. New York: McGraw-Hill Book Company, 1961. Chapters 1–10.

CHAPTER **4** *An Introduction to Business Cycle Theories*

In the next several chapters we deal with theories of the business cycle. Before embarking on this project, it might be well to ask why we take the time to study different and even conflicting theories rather than devoting all of our effort to the presentation of "the" theory of the business cycle. Fluctuations in economic activity are far too complex to be incorporated into a single universal theory applicable to every historical period. There is a great deal to be learned from each theory that is relevant to today's student even though the theory might have been developed many years ago. Each theory stresses certain forces or aspects of the economy, and necessarily slights others. A complete theory would have to incorporate all of these important causal factors in a systematic way. Even what may be considered errors of earlier writers are valuable to us, since they teach us not to make the same mistakes or which alleys are blind.

Virtually all of economic theory has been developed with the concept of equilibrium at its core. Movement or changes in any variables are viewed as returns to equilibrium (either to a new one or to an old one) following some exogenous or outside change. It is very difficult to break out of this method of comparative statics to the kind of theory needed to explain the continuity of successive rises and falls in economic activity resulting in cyclical behavior. This has been one of the stumbling blocks to the development of a satisfactory theory of economic fluctuations.

SAY'S LAW

Another and even more important reason that business cycle theory took so long to achieve a measure of respectability and success was the straight jacket of Say's Law as it was understood. The usual statement used to explain Say's Law is that "supply creates its own demand." This sounds like a slogan. But what does it mean? If it means that the total value of goods produced during a period of time (supply) is an amount sufficient to purchase (demand) all that was produced during the period, it is an important truism. Our national income accounting is based on it, although in that connection we usually state the fact in a slightly different way; namely, the total income earned in a period by the factors of production is equal to the total value of all the goods and services produced by those factors of production. Thus when we speak of Say's Law as a truism, or identity, supply and demand are equal by definition.

There is a much more exciting question that can be asked by Say's Law; that is, does the amount of goods and services that producers wish to produce and sell equal the amount of goods and services buyers want to buy? Since this statement involves intentions of people, it certainly is possible that supply and demand in this sense are not necessarily equal. In fact, their equality is a condition of equilibrium. Classical economists, with their basically Hedonistic view of the nature of man's motivations, believed that departures from equilibrium would be of only short duration. Their argument was that saving was unpleasant or onerous; that since present goods were valued more highly than future goods, a reward or premium would have to be paid to induce the public to save, which is to say abstain from present consumption. This reward is the interest paid to those who save, and the higher the interest rate, the more people would be willing to save. While high interest rates encourage saving (thrift) and low interest rates discourage saving, just the opposite is true of investment. A high interest rate makes it more costly to borrow or to use one's own funds for investment purposes, whereas a low rate of interest lowers the cost and is a stimulus to more investment. Briefly, then, the savings function which is the supply of resources available for investment is positively sloped with respect to interest, and the investment demand for savings is negatively sloped with respect to interest. Interest rate adjustments assure the equality of savings and investment and, hence, equilibrium in the aggregate demand and supply.

To understand the classicist's view of things, consider the implications of disequilibrium in Chart 4-1. At the interest rate r_a, which stands for any interest rate above the equilibrium rate, saving of S_a is greater than investment of I_a. Since investors are

willing to invest (or pay r_a to use saved resources) in just the amount
I_a, some savers would be unable to lend their surplus funds at all
and, therefore, their reward for saving is zero. Rather than accept
this state of affairs, the disappointed savers would offer to lend at
lower interest rates, but the lower interest rates would encourage
investors to invest more and induce some savers to save less. In this
way saving and investment come into equality and the interest rate
falls toward r_e.[1]

Chart 4-1

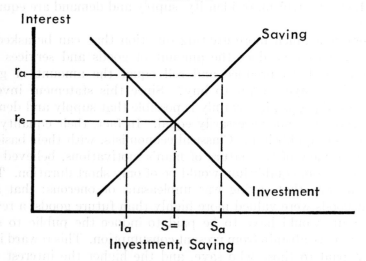

If you were to question this analysis, as later economists did,
by noting that people might be willing to forego the interest income
from saving by holding money instead of making it available to
investors, the classicist would have made two counter arguments.
First, he would probably assert that there is no advantage in holding
money; therefore, no one would be willing to pay to do it. Second,
even if there were such a thing as a demand for money to hold in
idle balances, the only result would be lower commodity prices and
a redistribution of goods and services from the foolish money holders
to the more reasonable members of the society who want money
only because it can be used to purchase things.

It was David Ricardo who represented the strongest adherent of
Say's Law, and the power of his logic was so great that few econo-

---

[1]We resist the temptation to explain the forces at work if the interest rate is
below equilibrium so that the reader can test his understanding by doing it himself.

mists were bold enough to challenge it. One who did was his contemporary and friend, the Reverend T. R. Malthus. Ricardo was interested in demonstrating the nature of the forces included in Adam Smith's "invisible hand," the forces that insured equilibrium in all economic activity. The fascination of this study caused him to be impatient with observations that the real world did not always coincide with his description of it. His interest was in the long run, not in the temporary aberrations. Malthus, on the other hand, lived in the short run. He saw what he thought was unemployment and overproduction and wanted to explain them, even though according to Ricardo's theory, they couldn't exist.

Malthus was not convinced that all of the resources which were being saved were automatically flowing into investment demand. In fact, he thought oversaving was a chronic problem in an economy where the demand for capital building was limited by the decisions of private entrepreneurs. The excessive saving was due to the unequal distribution of income in favor of the landlords and other wealthy individuals. His solution to the problem was to advise this group to spend more on nonproductive or intangible output, such as the services of armies, clergy, teachers, and other retainers whose output is not storeable.

It cannot be said that Malthus' position was accepted by any considerable number of economists, but it was one respected voice questioning the unquestioned acceptance of Say's Law, and it opened the way for others to make some attempt to explain fluctuations in economic activity.

We proceed now to a summary statement of a number of theories that have been advanced to explain the phenomenon of business cycles. The classification of theories will be that devised by Gottfried von Haberler in his definitive study, *Prosperity and Depression*.[2]

OUTSIDE FORCE THEORIES

Theories in which the cyclical nature of business activity is explained by the cyclical behavior of some outside force are known as outside force theories or exogenous theories of the business cycle. What is an exogenous or outside variable is sometimes difficult to say. We might all agree that the economic system has no influence on sunspot activity, but what of war, or the discovery of gold, or

[2]Gottfried von Haberler, *Prosperity and Depression* (3d ed.; Geneva: League of Nations, 1941).

innovations? A Marxist would probably consider wars to be endogenous (or internal) to the economy, something to be explained by the economist. Cassel argued that gold discovery was an endogenous variable in that lower prices and costs would encourage the prospecting for and mining of gold, the value of which would be higher when other prices were low. Schumpeter's theory depends heavily upon the argument that the volume of innovations was strictly dependent upon the stage of the business cycle.[3]

Thus, there is no rule that tells us which factors are really exogenous or endogenous. It depends completely on the theory or the theorist. In general, the procedure is to agree that there is no way for us to know which variables are really exogenous, so we adopt the convention that if the value of a variable is to be explained by the theory, it is endogenous; and if we are not concerned with explaining the behavior of the variable, we call that variable an exogenous one. A variable may actually be both exogenous and endogenous in the same theory. For example, spending by government might be increased for political reasons, in which case the economist will consider that as an exogenous change; whereas, if the increased spending were caused by an increase in national income, it would be counted as endogenous.

The appeal of exogenous explanations of the business cycle is easy to understand. We observe fluctuations in business activity. Business activity responds to outside forces. If an outside force behaves cyclically, cycles in business are explained by the cycle in the outside force. Even today, many people are involved in the search for statistical series which are so highly correlated to business conditions that they can be used as forecasting guides. If the movement in the series is not explained by theory, this amounts to an exogenous theory of the business cycle. In an earlier day, when the economy was dominated by agriculture, and variations in the yields of agricultural crops were dominated by weather conditions, it was natural to look for cycles in weather to account for cycles of good and bad trade.

Changes in Agricultural Yields

Some students of cycles claim to have found a high degree of relationship between cycles in agricultural yields and business

---

[3]Joseph Schumpeter, *Theory of Economic Development* (Cambridge, Massachusetts: Harvard University Press, 1934).

cycles. In particular, W. S. Jevons[4] and Henry L. Moore[5] searched for periodicity in meteorological phenomenon consistent with the periodicity in business fluctuations. Jevons found it in sunspot activity, and Moore in the peculiarities of the orbit of the planet Venus. Both went on to explain the connection between weather and agricultural activities, and between agricultural activity and general business conditions.

Other scholars, however, have come to exactly opposite conclusions, and in several cases shortcomings were found in the statistical techniques used to establish the relationship between agricultural and business cycles.

This is not intended to imply that changes in agricultural production have no effect on business conditions. When crops are bountiful, prices of agricultural commodities drop and costs in the industrial fields using them as raw materials are reduced. If prices are not reduced in the same proportion, profits increase and higher profits tend to stimulate further capital investment. If prices are reduced and the demand for the product is elastic, consumers buy larger quantities of such goods and thus industrial activity in that field expands. Higher agricultural prices resulting from small crops have just the opposite effect.

Changes in agricultural yields may also affect the income of agricultural areas. The income of agriculture is not changed at the same rate as the change in agricultural yields because prices of most farm products increase sharply when crops are small and drop markedly when crops are large. In those cases in which the demand for a product is quite elastic, however, farmers may get a larger total income in periods of large crops than they do when crops are small. This is especially true when crops are large in a year in which consumer income in general is increasing. More money is also paid to operators of farm services, such as combine crews for harvesting wheat when crops are large, and railroads and trucking companies get more revenue for hauling the products to market.

If exports are increased materially when crops are large, there is also a tendency for business activity to increase. Exports will reduce, in part, the price decline that would occur if all of the crop

---

[4]W. S. Jevons, *Investigations in Currency and Finance* (London: Macmillan and Co., Ltd., 1884).

[5]Henry L. Moore, *Generating Economic Cycles* (New York: The Macmillan Company, 1923). See also his earlier *Economic Cycles: Their Law and Cause* (New York: The Macmillan Company, 1914).

had to be marketed at home, and so the total income in the domestic economy is increased. As foreign funds flow into the country to pay for the larger exports, there is also a tendency for money supplies to increase and for interest rates to decline. This lowering of interest rates has a stimulating effect on business activity. Just the opposite effect takes place when crops are small and exports are reduced.

It is not clear, however, from the records of agricultural production and business fluctuations that such relationships exist between total agricultural yields and general business activity. This situation can be accounted for in several ways. In the first place, agricultural production does not move up and down as a unit. In the same year there may be a good cotton crop and a poor corn crop. The effects on business in general of a large crop of one commodity may thus be offset by the effects of a small crop of another commodity.

There have also been some farmers, especially those who operate on a large scale, who have held their crops in storage in years of low prices and sold them later when prices have been more favorable. This has helped to mitigate the effects of changes in crop yields. Since the early 1930's this storage of crops has been done on a large scale by the government.

As our industrial economy has expanded, agriculture has accounted for a smaller and smaller proportion of total income so that its influence on business has become less and less. Therefore, its role in initiating changes in economic activity has also become less important. Changes in agricultural yield cannot alone explain the cycle since such changes do not correspond to the regularly recurring cycles of recession and recovery in business.

Sunspots

One of the earliest of the outside force theories of the cycle, and in fact one of the earliest explanations offered for business cycles, was the sunspot cycle theory proposed in 1875 by an English economist of note, W. Stanley Jevons. From the available data on major English business cycles and from fragmentary data on sunspot cycles, he was led to believe that there was a correspondence between the two sets of cycles. He reasoned that sunspot cycles must cause changes in agricultural yields and these in turn cause business cycles. This thesis was refuted when research showed that the sunspot cycles were somewhat longer than Jevons thought they were, and that changes in agricultural yields did not correspond to business cycles.

The sunspot idea, however, continues to find support from time to time. Different measurements have been made of solar activity, especially of the total area of "bright spots" on the sun, and claims of high correlation between such measurements and business activity have been made in recent years. An explanation of the relationship suggested in a recent book is that sunspot changes cause changes in the quantity of ultra-violet rays reaching the earth and that this affects the emotional responses and general health of human beings.

A quite sophisticated chain of analysis was forged by Henry L. Moore relating the conjunctures of the sun, Venus, and earth to the weather conditions on earth, particularly in the amount of rainfall. The cycle of favorable and unfavorable weather conditions results in a cycle of high and low crop yields, which, in turn, generates a cycle in the prices of basic raw materials, which then produces a cycle in industrial production and general economic activity.

War Cycles in Population

Some students of cycles, especially in Germany, have reasoned that major cycles can be traced to changes due to major wars, especially population changes. The heavy casualties suffered during a war, especially in the wars preceding World War II, were primarily among young men and so reduced the size of the labor force. The birth rate was also reduced while the men were on the fighting fronts, but it increased sharply when the war was over. Such changes in the number of births affect the birth rate a generation later because many young people marry at about the same time, have some effect two generations later, and gradually disappear.

Some geopolitical theorists have carried the analysis further by arguing that this growth in population exerts such pressure on the limited national territories of some countries that the governments seek relief in attempting to claim the territory of other nations, which precipitates new wars. Thus, war itself is a periodic phenomenon, and produces cyclical economic responses.

The effect of wars on population seems well established, and the high birth rates in the years after World War II will affect the American economy for some time to come. The time intervals involved, however, are too long to account for business cycles in general, and certainly this factor cannot account for American cycles in the past.

UNDERCONSUMPTION THEORIES

Underconsumption theories of the cycle are about as old as the science of economics itself. These theories have appeared in various forms and have frequently been expounded by writers who lacked training in the field of economics. They lend themselves well to the justification for such political schemes as the Townsend Plan of large pensions for old people. The views of many underconsumptionists really do not constitute a complete theory of the cycle since most of them have attempted only to explain the downturn of the cycle and the depression period. A complete analysis of the cycle cannot be based upon such underconsumption theories.

Another difficulty in describing these theories is that the term "underconsumption" is not used in the same sense by all of them. Some of them use underconsumption to mean that the economic system does not pay out sufficient funds to purchase all of the goods that are produced. This point of view should be distinguished from a periodic hoarding of money or a slowing down of the velocity of money, which are integral parts of a monetary theory of the cycle. Others use underconsumption to describe a situation in which too large a proportion of income is saved in relationship to that which is spent on consumption.

Insufficiency of Purchasing Power

Major C. H. Douglas, of England, has received considerable publicity for an underconsumption explanation of the cycle based on the deficiency of payments. He tries to make this point by means of his *A plus B theorem*.[6] *A payments* are payments made to individuals, such as wages, salaries, or dividends; while *B payments* are payments made to other organizations, such as those for machinery, raw materials, and the payment of interest on bank loans. *A* payments, of course, automatically and directly become purchasing power for consumers. The difficulty arises with *B* payments, which do not go to consumers directly. These payments are made sometime before they are spent by the organizations that receive them. They are thus not available for spending on the present output of goods. In other words, the gap between the value of current output and income that is distributed currently constitutes a deficiency of purchasing power.

---

[6]C. H. Douglas, *Social Credit* (New York: W. W. Norton & Co., Inc., 1933).

Since both A and B payments are costs and enter into the price, there is a deficiency of purchasing power equal to B payments that must be made up. This deficiency can be overcome for a period of time through bank credit. Difficulty soon arises because, as businesses receive the B payments, they must be used to pay off earlier bank loans and are not returned to the income stream. If new loans were continuously made as old ones were extinguished, there would be no problem; but Douglas holds that this will not be the case under modern banking practice. This is partly true because interest is charged on each round and also because there are limits to bank credit expansion.

There is no evidence from the record of past cycles that the amount of bank credit continuously falls short of the needs of society. In fact, the opposite appears to have been the case more frequently since the Federal Reserve System was set up.

The underconsumption thesis is at times based on the failure of the money supply to keep up with the increased demands placed upon it. Improvements in technology and increases in population lead to an increase in the supply of goods that is not accompanied by an increase in the quantity of money, and this in turn leads to a deficiency of purchasing power for consumption. Such an explanation by itself cannot explain the cyclical process since it is based on a long-run unbalance between production and the money supply. There can be a cycle due to monetary factors only if the supply of money moves in a cyclical fashion; and this is, of course, the essence of the purely monetary explanation of the cycle.

Underconsumption as Oversaving

If we were tracing the chronological history of underconsumptionist thought, we would probably start with Malthus (recognizing his roots in Adam Smith's *Wealth of Nations*) and end with the theory of John Maynard Keynes. We could go further and include a later Keynesian such as Professor Alvin Hansen of Harvard. Probably the most important stop between Malthus and Keynes would be at John A. Hobson, the British economist who presented a persuasive case not only for underconsumption as the cause of the depression but also a theory of cyclical instability based on underconsumptionist principles.

Hobson challenged Say's Law directly, asking why, in a world in which human wants are said to be insatiable, large amounts of unsold commodities appear at the beginning of a business downswing. His answer is that a kind of cultural lag exists. Productivity, in modern societies, increases at a relatively rapid rate. There are no important deterrents in instituting new methods of production or other innovations that will increase the rate of output. Indeed, competition as we know it in capitalistic systems forces producers to introduce more productive methods as quickly as possible.

Consumption, on the other hand, is, according to Hobson, a very conservative art. Tradition, custom, and habit dominate. Most consumption is done in private, and, Veblen[7] to the contrary notwithstanding, the pressures to increase consumption when income increases are relatively mild. Society is faced with a problem of rapidly increasing powers of production with lagging willingness or ability to consume the increasing output.

In this view of things, if production and income are increasing faster than is consumption, savings are growing. This would seem to present no problem if there is sufficient investment demand to absorb this additional output. But if all of the additional savings go into new productive capacity by way of investment, the problem becomes still more acute when this new capital begins to add more goods and services to the aggregate supply. Unless one can conceive of a world in which capital goods are continuously being produced in order to produce more capital goods, a crisis must be pending. The additional productive capacity must either result in inventories of goods unsalable at current prices, or in drastic price reductions. In either case, the demand for investment will decline sharply and total production will be reduced to a level that can be sustained by consumer demand. This means idle workers and plants — a recession.

We can see in Hobson the beginnings of a dynamic theory of growth. The rate of savings must be just the amount needed to add to the capital stock the productive power to produce increased goods and services at the rate of increase consumers will demand. As we have just seen, if the rate of savings is greater than this a recession will inevitably ensue. When will the downward movement stop? The answer is when excess capacity has been eliminated by depreciation or capital consumption, and when consumers have learned to consume a larger portion of their income, which will happen as incomes fall.

---

[7]Thorstein B. Veblen, *The Theory of the Leisure Class* (New York: The Modern Library, 1934).

Typically, underconsumption theorists argue that the problem can only be eliminated by a redistribution of wealth and income. Hobson pointed out that most economists believe that the average level of saving is high for high income groups and low for low income groups. This means that a redistribution of income away from the high saving, high income recipients in favor of low saving, lower income workers would result in a lower ratio of savings to spending or income. Therefore, there must be some distribution that would produce a rate of savings compatible with the rate of increase in productivity. He recognized that if the redistribution were carried too far in the direction of equality, the rate of savings could be so low that economic progress would be impeded. On the other hand, he pointed out that progress was also slowed down by the intermittent periods of depressed business conditions under the present income distribution.

It must be conceded that the underconsumption theory, as presented by its most capable adherents, is highly convincing. It is not something out of the dead past. It is present doctrine for many, and aspects of it are accepted by virtually all economists. New Deal policies as well as many current government policies imply the acceptance of the basic hypothesis. Anyone who thinks that our economy would be in serious difficulty if the defense budget were slashed is an underconsumptionist.

It would be a mistake for the reader to decide at this stage that he ought to accept the underconsumptionist position. What is intuitively so plausible may not be true. Actually, the relationship of consumption and saving to income is not as simple and straightforward as it may seem at this point.

OUTLINE OF THE UNDERCONSUMPTION CYCLE

The expansion phase of the business cycle is characterized by underconsumptionists as a period when as income rises wages tend to lag behind the growth in other incomes, especially the profit component. Since it is contended that wage earners spend a larger proportion of their income on consumer goods than do the higher income profit recipients, saving grows at an increasing rate during the upswing of the business cycle. The rate of growth in savings must reach a point where it is in excess of the amount of investment that can feasibly be justified on the basis of the current amount of consumption. This brings about the crisis, or upper turning point.

During the resulting contraction phase incomes fall, but now profit incomes fall more rapidly than do the incomes of wage earners. Since profit earners have high saving to income ratios relative to wage earners, saving declines more rapidly than do consumption and income. In the early stages of the downswing, the supply of capital is large relative to the need for it as expressed by the demand for consumption. For this reason investment will fall off very sharply and will remain depressed until the forces of depreciation reduce the stock of capital to a level consistent with the current rate of consumer goods output. The downswing is supposed to stop when consumption stabilizes, and consumption will stop falling as income is transferred from the low consumption group of profit recipients to the high consumption group of laborers. The stage is then set for a reversal of direction of economic activity, which will happen when investment increases.

PSYCHOLOGICAL THEORY OF THE BUSINESS CYCLE

We shall consider the theories of economists who consider psychological factors as the dominant forces causing oscillations in economic activity. One should not get the impression from this that other economists ignore the psychology of decision makers in their theories. Since any economic decision has its psychological aspects, every economist is concerned with them to some degree. Those who are not included as psychological theorists, however, generally take the state of mind of the economic unit as given. Their usual reaction is that changes in psychology are very important, but that they have no ability to predict the cause of these changes beyond what is already incorporated in their theory. When prices have been rising for some time, for example, some people will expect them to continue to rise; others will feel that since they have gone up so long they are bound to fall soon. It is relatively easy, after the fact, to say that expectations were such and such. It is very difficult, if not impossible, to say what they are or what they will be.

In the study of economics, most of the important decisions that are analyzed involve forecasts of the future. If the period of time is relatively long, the outcome depends on many possible events that simply cannot be accurately forecast at the moment the decision is made. The businessman, or the householder, or the government official is forced to fall back on his judgment as to whether important innovations will occur, whether war or peace will be the environment, whether depression or prosperity will characterize the period, or whether more or less government intervention will take place. Pessimism and optimism will bias his judgment when he has few objective bases on which to forecast.

The economist who is best known for his stress upon emotional responses in business decisions is the great Cambridge economist, Arthur C. Pigou, and it is his theory we shall summarize.[8] Wesley Clair Mitchell, the outstanding American student of business cycles, quoted Pigou approvingly in this regard, and is, himself, considered an adherent of the psychological theory. The key features of Lord Keynes' explanation of business fluctuations are psychological in origin, as we shall see when we look in depth into his contributions. Though these economists subscribe to the general thesis that the psychological reactions of businessmen are important causal factors in the cyclical process, they do not ignore other important objective events. They hold, however, that even though changes in the supply of and demand for the factors of production can bring about fluctuations in economic activity, they are not sufficient to bring about business cycles in the absence of psychological factors.

They believe that the causal factors in the cyclical process are to be found in the ways in which changes in real underlying factors cause changes in the attitudes of businessmen. Pigou, for example, recognizes five real causes of business change: (1) changes in agricultural yield, (2) changes in the rate of investment, (3) discovery of new mineral resources, (4) industrial disputes, and (5) changes in consumer tastes. Changes in the first three of these have similar effects since they lead to an increase or a decrease in supply with no change in labor input, or at least to a change in the supply per unit of labor expended. The impact of any of these three factors on the economy may be illustrated by considering the effect of a change in agricultural yield. Changes in agricultural yield are believed to stimulate or to retard business activity since an increase in yield promotes business expansion, while a decrease in yield discourages expansion or may even lead to a contraction. If there is an increase in the yield of an agricultural commodity and if the demand for that product is such that the total amount spent on it is larger than before, total demand for all goods will tend to be increased. Farmers

---

[8]A. C. Pigou, *Industrial Fluctuations* (London: Macmillan and Co., Ltd., 1927) and *The Theory of Unemployment* (London: Macmillan and Co., Ltd., 1933).

will have more money to spend, and this fact will lead to increased
sales and production of goods demanded by them. A decrease in
agricultural yield will have the opposite effect. Such changes lead
to fluctuations in business activity, but not to a business cycle. The
same is true of increased production due to the discovery of new
resources or to inventions that reduce costs.

The last two of the real causes, namely, industrial disputes and
net changes in consumer tastes, are not considered important factors
causing business fluctuations. Industrial disputes in basic industries,
if prolonged, could lead to a downturn in the economy; but this does
not happen very often, if at all, and net shifts in consumer tastes
are not likely to be important enough in the short run to affect the
economy seriously.

Errors of Businessmen

When any of these real changes occurs, there will be a dual effect.
There will be the direct effect of the change that has taken place
and also an indirect effect caused by the reactions of businessmen to
the change. These reactions of businessmen will not always be consistent with the facts because they may be based on errors in
evaluating the situation. The scope or range of the errors of businessmen will be primarily determined by two basic factors, the capacity
of business forecasters and the accessibility of information.

In a capitalistic system with its roundabout processes of production, forecasting is a difficult procedure. The economic response
of businessmen to real changes will depend in part upon the skill
developed in forecasting the effects of these changes. Some error,
however, will always be involved in such forecasts.

Probably more important as a source of error is the lack of
information about all of the factors that will be affected by the
change. Under a competitive system, individual producers have no
real way of knowing what the demand for their product or the
supply of productive factors will be in the future. Each producer
endeavors to supply a part of the market without knowing the
portion of the increased demand that other producers are preparing
to meet. The result is that producers tend to overestimate the
quantity they can sell and the price at which they can sell their output during an expansion period and to underestimate these same
items during a period of declining business. They likewise underestimate the costs of production during the upswing and overestimate

them during the contraction. This is also true in regard to the cost of capital, that is, the interest rate.

A second reason for the lack of adequate knowledge on the part of businessmen is the tendency to order more goods than are really wanted during periods of rising prices in order to insure the receipt of at least those quantities that are needed. Such duplication of orders makes it impossible to know what the true state of demand is and causes producers to turn out goods in excess of the demand for them.

A third reason for the lack of knowledge of all pertinent factors is the large geographical area of the market. Raw materials are frequently purchased from various parts of the nation and from foreign countries. Production is also carried on for regional, national, and international markets. Under such conditions it is difficult to appraise properly future supply and demand conditions.

The basic reason for the lack of satisfactory knowledge of the market is the length of time required to produce a commodity, especially a capital good.

Pigou puts great stress on what he calls the *period of gestation*. This is the length of time required for the new output to come on the market after the decision to increase production has been made. Different commodities have different gestation periods. Very long gestation periods would characterize commodities that are produced with large amounts of complex capital goods. If capital goods are produced without the expansion of bank credit, nothing happens normally that should give rise to any serious errors. If, as actually happens, an expansion of bank credit takes place during the period of gestation, however, there is an overall increase in purchasing power without a corresponding increase in the volume of consumer goods. This excess purchasing power leads to higher prices until the capital goods are completed and the output of consumer goods increased. As a result, businessmen are misled about the real demand for their products. As the period of gestation ends and the new consumer goods begin to flow onto the market, the errors come to light. The length and severity of the expansion phase of the cycle is dependent upon the length of the gestation period.

Mutual Generation of Errors

These errors made by businessmen can only lead to a cyclical process if they are predominantly in the same direction. If they are made on a more or less random basis, they will tend to neutralize each other as errors of optimism are canceled out by errors of pessimism. The latter situation does not occur because of an existence among businessmen of a tendency toward common action.

Several factors cause errors of either optimism or pessimism to become general throughout the business world. One of these is the tendency for businessmen to influence each other's thinking. The continuous contact during the course of business and in the meetings of business organizations spreads feelings of optimism and pessimism widely. Furthermore, errors in forecasts of business conditions tend to create their own justification. An error on the optimistic side by one producer results in an increased demand for goods and services, thus brightening the prospects of other businessmen. Thus the errors of some producers lead other producers to commit errors in the same direction.

The debtor-creditor relationship also disperses errors through the various parts of the business system. If one optimistic businessman makes credit more easily available to his customers or relaxes his terms of credit, this in turn stimulates other businessmen to do likewise so as not to be at a competitive disadvantage.

The cycle occurs because errors on the optimistic side inevitably lead to errors of pessimism, and these in turn to errors of optimism, and so on in a continuous cycle. In a period of expansion errors of optimism do not become apparent during the period of gestation because the creation of credit and the length of time required to produce various goods prevent businessmen from recognizing that part of the demand is fictitious and that the shortage of consumer goods is only temporary. When the errors of optimism are revealed at the end of the period of gestation, the expansion comes to a halt and a recession begins. Optimism then gives way to pessimism since businessmen realize that their forecasts of the situation were wrong and, as business turns downward, errors of pessimism spread. As expenditures are curtailed, there is an oversupply of consumer goods and, as a result, producers underestimate the real demand for their products. As capital goods again need replacement, the errors of pessimism come to light and the stage is set for revival. This process by which errors of optimism lead to errors of pessimism and errors of pessimism to those of optimism is referred to as the *mutual generation of errors*.

Evaluation

Even though the psychological theorists have stressed psychological factors, their explanation of the cycle includes many factors that relate to investment and bank credit creation. They have made a valuable contribution to business cycle theory by showing how waves of optimism can lead to waves of pessimism and these in turn to waves of optimism. Since these are based upon real changes that have taken place in the economy, however, it can hardly be maintained that the cycle is due entirely to psychological factors. These factors help explain the cumulative nature of expansion and contraction, but are of little or no help in explaining turning points. Psychological factors should be considered in a complete explanation of the cycle, but they should not be given the only position of importance.

SERIES OF OUTSIDE FACTORS

Some economists contend that the cycle is caused by the many outside forces which are continually affecting the economy. These not only include weather changes, cycles in farm yields, wars, and war-induced changes in population, but also new inventions and discoveries. Since these occur in a more or less random fashion, they lead to cycles of different time intervals. Sometimes several factors occur at about the same time and thus lead to more severe cycles. Even though such outside influences do affect business activity, they alone cannot account for the cycle because they cannot explain the cumulative nature of the expansion and contraction. These explanations must be sought in the operation of the economic system itself. More recent work in this field involves the creation of formal economic models which incorporate the behavior relations of the economic system. When random disturbances or "shocks" are introduced into such a system, the response of the economy is to generate cyclical movement. We shall consider this variety of business cycle theory in a later chapter. The theories of Wesley Clair Mitchell, which will be considered next, attempt to explain the cumulative nature of expansion and contraction.

MITCHELL'S THEORY OF THE CYCLE

In his classic volume on business cycles published in 1913, Mitchell presented a synthesis of cycle theory based on the evidence available to him at that time.[9] Mitchell planned to revise his theory, if necessary, after the complete study of cycle data was made under his direction by the National Bureau. The work which he projected, however, was of such a magnitude that his career ended before the study was completed. In his latest book, published after his death, however, he indicated that in a general way the theory presented in his first book was still valid even though some details would have to be changed to bring it in line with the facts of the business cycle. Therefore, Mitchell might not have agreed at that time with all aspects of the theory here presented in his name, but the changes would hardly have been basic.

Upswing

A revival in business activity begins, according to Mitchell, with a legacy from the depression period. Prices during a depression are low in comparison with prices during prosperity. Business costs have been drastically reduced, profit margins are narrow, bank reserves are liberal, the policy in regard to the extension of credit is conservative, stocks of goods are moderate, and buying is cautious. The upturn is slow at first, but the process is cumulative. It has often been speeded up by some propitious event, such as unusually profitable harvests, large government purchases of goods, or a large increase in exports.

The revival begins at first in just a small sector of the economy but soon spreads to all fields. This is true because those concerns experiencing an increase in business buy materials from other enterprises, these latter from still others, and so on. As incomes increase, expansion increases in a cumulative fashion. Price increases and the expectation of future price increases lead to an increase in orders to beat the price rise, and this accelerates the upward spiral.

This would be of little interest if all prices rose in the same proportion. For instance, if the price of the product a firm sells were to increase by 10 percent, and the prices of all the services and materials that go into the product were also to increase by 10 percent, the profit rate would be as it was before the price rise. Mitchell's statistics indicated, however, that finished goods prices rise more rapidly during the business expansion than do the prices of those items entering into costs of production, particularly wage

---

[9]Wesley Clair Mitchell, *Business Cycles* (Berkeley: University of California Press, 1913).

rates, rents under leases, and interest on bonds. Thus, profits increase, and investment expenditures are encouraged which leads to further expansion of the physical volume of production and puts further pressure on prices.

Downturn

This cumulative process also sets in motion stresses which undermine prosperity. The lag in supplementary costs ceases when the limit to the business that can be handled with the present equipment of a firm is reached. A rise begins when the expiration of contracts forces renewals at higher rates of interest, rent, and salaries. At the same time other costs rise rapidly because less efficient equipment is brought into use, more overtime is paid, and prices of raw materials rise faster than selling prices on the average. Waste and inefficiency occur and increase the cost of doing business.

Stresses also develop in the investment and money markets as the supply of funds available fails to keep pace with the rapidly swelling demand. Tensions in the money markets are unfavorable to the continuance of prosperity. This is true because high rates of interest reduce prospective margins of profit and thus reduce the demand for additional capital goods for further expansion. As new orders fall off and as old contracts are completed, there is a serious reduction in the volume of production of capital goods and workers are laid off in this field.

Increases in prices at different rates also lead to unbalance in the system. Some prices cannot be raised sufficiently to prevent a reduction in profits because they are set by public commissions, by long-term contracts, or by custom. Consumer demand does not remain the same in all fields as money income increases and, as a result, prices rise faster in some fields than in other. In some cases prices do not rise as fast as costs, and profit margins are reduced. As profits decrease, cautious creditors fear for the safety of their loans, and stop making new loans and refuse to renew old ones as they come due. Thus prosperity ultimately brings about a liquidation of the huge credits piled up during expansion.

The process of contraction is cumulative, just as expansion was. The same factors that work to increase business on the upswing are also at work during the downswing. Depression spreads over the whole field of business and grows more severe as it spreads.

The rapid decline in business, however, sets into motion the very factors from which a revival will emerge. Prices fall, but again not uniformly in all fields. Wholesale prices drop faster than retail, the prices of producer goods faster than those of consumer goods, and the prices of raw materials faster than those of manufactured goods. Not only are the day-to-day costs of doing business reduced, but supplementary costs are also reduced by the reduction in rents, the refunding of loans, the charging off of bad debts, and the writing down of depreciable properties. Accumulated stocks left over from prosperity are gradually exhausted, and then current consumption requires current production. Consumer and producer durable goods wear out and must be replaced and, as population continues to grow, more food, clothing, and shelter are needed. The environment for investment also becomes more favorable as pessimism gives way to cautious optimism. New methods of production are developed, and these call for additional capital investment. As a result, revival begins and the cumulative cyclical process is once more under way.

This synthesis by Mitchell is still a reasonable explanation of the cyclical process. It does not give sufficient stress, however, to the factors at work in the investment process. In the next chapter we consider the theories which put prime emphasis on the role of investment in the business cycle. This prepares the way for the later study of the contributions of Keynes and his followers.

QUESTIONS

1. Using a chart similar to Chart 4-1, page 70, explain why the interest rate would rise if it were temporarily below equilibrium.
2. What is the basic difference between an exogenous and an endogenous theory of the business cycle?
3. Explain the conflict between the acceptance of Say's Law and the development of business cycle theory.
4. The distinction between Say's Law as an identity and as a condition of equilibrium is highly important. Discuss.
5. According to the underconsumption theory, what makes the collapse of an economic expansion inevitable?
6. Explain why a business cycle expansion would be of long duration if the gestation period for key commodities is long.
7. What do you see as the principal difficulty in constructing a theory of the business cycle based on waves of optimism and pessimism?

See page 120 for Suggested Readings for Chapter 4.

5 *Monetary and Investment Theories of the Cycle*

The structure of the monetary and credit system of the economy has an important influence on the nature of business fluctuations. In fact, since Say's Law would be true in a barter economy, business cycles as we know them could not exist. The important role of monetary factors led early business cycle theorists to give major emphasis to them in their analysis of the causal factors at work in the cycle. One group of monetary theorists held that changes which occur in this system are sufficient in themselves to produce cycles, another that the interaction of the monetary system with changes in investment activity leads to cyclical fluctuations. Since most of the writers who held these theories were, along with the majority of all economists of their day, quantity theorists, we start the chapter with a review of the quantity theory of money.

In this chapter consideration will be given also to those theorists who hold that the basic cause of the cycle is found in the process of investment rather than in the operation of the monetary system. One group of investment theorists has stressed a shortage of capital as the basic cause of the cycle; another, fluctuations in the investment process that are produced by innovations; and a third, changes in consumption that lead to magnified changes in the demand for producer goods and so lead to unbalance.

THE QUANTITY THEORY OF MONEY

The quantity theory is the oldest and perhaps the newest monetary theory. Of course, it has evolved with greater sophistication over a period of time. Its earliest statement was based on the simple observation that when currency in a country increased, the prices of commodities also increased, and when currency flowed out of the country, prices would fall. Later versions introduced refinements that involved the rapidity with which the money was spent and the volume of production.

The equation that is the starting point of any discussion of the quantity theory is called the *equation of exchange:*

$$MV = Py$$

In the equation, M stands for the money supply, V stands for the velocity of circulation of that money, P stands for the general price level, and y is a measure of the production of goods and services.

There is never any debate over whether the equation is true or not. If the components are carefully defined, it is a tautology, a truism, or identity. Looking at the left side, we multiply the number of units of money by the average number of times each unit was spent to buy the things included in y during a specified period of time. MV, then, is the total spending of that money for those things which took place in that period. If y is the total number of units of goods and services sold and P is their average price, then Py is the total value of those goods and services. No one questions that total spending for a particular group of commodities is equal to the total money received from the sale of those same commodities. In itself, this is a good disciplinary device. We must be careful not to say anything that contradicts a true statement. We can choose any set of goods, such as those which are included in gross national product, or all goods and services, or peanuts to define y. But once y has been defined, in order for the equation to be true, P and V must have reference to the same set.

An alternative statement, called the Cambridge equation, which involves the same variables is

$$M = k\,Py$$

The only new symbol introduced here is k, and the only one not included is V. The relationship between V and k is very simple. From $MV = Py$, it can be seen that $V = \dfrac{Py}{M}$. From $M = k\,Py$, obviously $k = \dfrac{M}{Py}$. Thus, $V = \dfrac{1}{k}$, and $k = \dfrac{1}{V}$. For example, if $V = 4$, it means that, on the average, each piece of money is spent four times per period (assume it to be one year). In that event $k = \dfrac{1}{4}$ which means that, on the average, each piece of money is not spent on y for one fourth of the year, or three months. Another way of looking at k is to observe that k is that portion ($\frac{1}{4}$) of annual spending (Py) that is held in cash balances (M).

Looked at in this last way, $M = k\,Py$ can be viewed as a demand for money function. But if it is that, it is no longer a truism; and if it is no longer a truism, we need a new definition of k. Now, instead of k being the portion of total spending held in the form of money, it is the portion of total spending economic units wish to hold in the form of money. In order to see the difference let us take an example in which the monetary system determines the money supply originally at $100 billion; the money value of national income is in equilibrium at $400 billion. Since equilibrium exists, k of the identity (call it k') is the same as k of the equation (call it simply k). Both have a value of $\frac{1}{4}$: $100 = \frac{1}{4}\,(400)$.

Now, suppose the operations of the monetary system act to double the money supply to $200 billion. The truism reads: $200 = \frac{1}{2}\,(400)$. k' has doubled from $\frac{1}{4}$ to $\frac{1}{2}$ because people are holding one half of total spending in the form of money. Since the money exists, someone must hold it, but our demand for money equation says that people wish to hold only $100 billion when income is 400, so $200 \neq \frac{1}{4}\,(400)$ — a disequilibrium condition. Economic units are holding twice as much money as they wish to hold, and we would expect them to take steps to reduce their money balances until they hold the desired amount. But by our assumption that only the monetary system can control the money supply, any individual can reduce his balance only by inducing someone else to increase his balance. This can be accomplished by buying more things at the old prices, or paying a higher price for the same number of things. In other words, either y or P will increase. If everyone holds rigidly to their original judgment on the portion of their income they should hold in money balances, and if no change in income distribution occurs, Py will continue to rise until it reaches 800. Only then will equilibrium exist where both k and k' are $\frac{1}{4}$: $200 = \frac{1}{4}\,(800)$. Notice that if real output remained constant so that all of the expansion were accounted for by the increase in the price level, then the real value of money holdings did not change even though more money was held.

The example we have just covered is, of course, too extreme. No contemporary quantity theorist believes that k is quite as rigid as the one in our example. There is the opposite extreme view that is characteristic of those we might call antiquantity theorists who believe that in certain circumstances, notably in a severe depression, k will change proportionately with any change in the money supply so that money supply changes have no effect on national income. Going back to our example, where the original equilibrium situation was $100 = \frac{1}{4} (400)$, a doubling of the money supply would cause both k and k' to become one half, $200 = \frac{1}{2} (400)$. This says that people are willing to hold any additional amounts of money the monetary system creates and that they will not increase their rate of spending because of it.

These two examples should make it clear that the usefulness of the quantity theory depends upon the degree of stability of k or its reciprocal, V, and even more importantly upon their independence of M. This is not as simple to determine as might at first appear since k itself cannot be measured directly. Statistically, we can measure only k', and even in the example above, where k was rigidly fixed, k' did vary. Quantity theorists, especially Irving Fisher, believed that the size of cash balances was determined mainly mechanically by institutional arrangements for payments in the system. Thus, the frequency of receipts and disbursements and the degree of correspondence between them would be important, as would the efficiency of the transportation and communication systems, the degree of specialization and integration of industry, population changes, habits of thrift and hoarding, and the use of trade credit. These are all factors that would change only slowly over time, and furthermore would seem to be not related in any systematic way to the money supply. A modern critic might point out that several important influences have been neglected, such as expectations of future price level and interest rate changes, and the relative attractiveness of substitutes for money, such as savings accounts and bonds and potential borrowing sources.

If k is assumed to be a constant for the moment, then an increase in the money supply must increase Py proportionally; but the question remains, will P increase, or will it be y, or might both increase? To the rigid classicist the answer has to be that P alone will increase since y is always at its practicable maximum through the efficiency of the free market system. Real income, of course, would be expected to rise secularly as the state of the arts, capital, and population grow; but in the short run, these could be assumed to be fixed. For this reason, the quantity theory was, above all, the explanation of the absolute level of prices, and was a supplement to the explanation of relative prices through micro supply and demand analysis. To some business cycle theorists, however, the quantity theory was used to explain variations in both output and prices. In contemporary analysis the point is usually made that the closer the economy is to full employment, the less y can change so that increases in M result in significant changes in P; but when large-scale unemployment exists, the increase in M can increase y with negligible effects on P.

THE PURELY MONETARY THEORY

Considering the pervasive role of money in modern economic systems, it would be strange indeed if it were not included in an important way in the explanation of business fluctuations. In fact, the only disagreement lies in the particular way and the degree of importance attached to money in generating business cycles. Even those theories that are called nonmonetary implicitly require the necessary response of the money supply to bring about the cycles described. These theorists argue that the initiating or causal force is something other than monetary, whereas the monetary theories place the monetary system in this critical position. The purely monetary theory takes the polar position that variations in money are the necessary and sufficient conditions for variations in economic activity. This is essentially the position taken by Ralph G. Hawtrey, a British economist whose name is virtually synonomous with the purely monetary theory.[1]

Without question the kind of cycles that have occurred in the economies of industrial nations could not exist in an economy with an inelastic monetary system. An increase in business activity could not develop in a cumulative fashion for any period of time under such a monetary arrangement. As the demand for goods increased in some sectors of the economy, more money would be used to make sales in these fields. With inelastic money and credit, this would leave fewer funds for other fields of business activity and prices would fall in these areas. Velocity could increase to some extent, but a cumulative expansion of sales in many fields at the same time would be impossible.

Such a cumulative expansion of sales, however, is one of the major characteristics of the cycle in the United States and other

---

[1]Ralph G. Hawtrey has written many books and articles detailing his view of the cycle. Two representative books are: *Trade and Credit* (London: Longmans, Green & Co. Ltd., 1928) and *Capital and Employment* (London: Longmans, Green & Co. Ltd., 1937).

industrial countries. Both the volume of goods sold and the prices of goods expand during prosperity. On the upswing the quantities of goods sold expand somewhat faster than do the prices at which they are sold. During the downswing both the prices of goods sold and the quantities sold contract. Prices decrease faster, however, than do the quantities of goods sold.

The usual situation in the case of individual products or services is for the quantities sold to increase as prices are lowered and to decrease as prices are raised. Prices of goods and quantities sold can only move together in the upswing and downswing of a cycle because the total supply of purchasing media is expanding and contracting as business goes up and down. This change in the supply of purchasing media is primarily due to a change in the volume of demand deposits that are expanded and contracted as borrowing from the banking system increases and decreases during the cycle.

The Upswing

It is proper in cycle analysis to have the turning points brought about by the conditions created in the phase just preceding them. Hawtrey's theory is a good example of this. The period of downswing develops a situation of the banking system accumulating excess reserves and growing desires on the part of bankers to make loans. On this account interest rates fall, and other credit terms and standards for borrowing are eased. The depression has also gone on long enough to eliminate any excess inventories that might have existed early in the downswing, weaker firms may also have been eliminated so that even though general business conditions are depressed, conditions for the remaining business units are at least stabilized. Lower interest rates obviously make borrowing more attractive, but the firm must expect the borrowed funds to add to its earning power enough to more than cover the costs of the borrowing.

Who will borrow during the depths of a depression? Certainly, the businessman who overcomes the pessimism of the times and anticipates an imminent period of good times. Most economists would expect borrowing to increase at some point during the downswing if innovations create expectations of significant improvements in sales or of lowering costs. The general opinion has been that lower interest rates will have the greatest effect on borrowers whose use for funds is very long term, such as public utilities and housing.

Hawtrey, however, concentrates his attention on the merchants or middlemen who have the carrying of inventories as a major expense of doing business. Since a major portion of the variable cost of maintaining inventories is the interest expense, any lowering of interest rates reduces these costs. If there are advantages to larger inventories, we would expect their lower costs to induce merchants to add to their holdings. The profitability of larger stocks of inventories comes because of such things as greater range of selections by customers, quicker service, and delivery of large orders. In other words, even if aggregate sales are low, any individual seller can gain some competitive advantage by increasing his inventory.

So, in Hawtrey's version of the monetary theory of the trade cycle, as he, being a British economist, calls it, the upswing begins when excess reserves build up sufficiently for interest rates to fall enough to bring about borrowing by middlemen to increase their inventories. In order for the new orders to be additions to total demand, the purchasing power must come from a source that would not decrease demand elsewhere. New or idle money is such a source. The new demand produces added income for the producers, and the upswing is in progress.

After the process of expansion has been started, it is cumulative for a period of time. As more goods are ordered, more are produced, more income flows into the hands of consumers, and consumer expenditures are increased. Traders finding their stock of goods decreased increase their orders for merchandise, which in turn increases production, consumer income, and consumer outlay in a cumulative process. As this process develops, there is a rise in the general level of prices because output in certain areas cannot be increased readily due to a scarcity of plant capacity or labor or both. The rise in prices adds further impetus to the expansion that is underway since it increases the profits of entrepreneurs and therefore makes them willing to increase the amount of credit used in their business. This credit expansion accelerates the expansion process and in turn adds to the pressure on prices and thus reinforces the upward movement.

According to Hawtrey, the expansion is reinforced by the expectation of rising prices that causes people to reduce the size of their cash balances relative to the amount of their transactions — that is to say that k falls (or, alternatively, velocity increases) during the expansion if rising prices are expected.

The Contraction

Prosperity comes to an end when the banks restrict the expansion of credit. Banks take such action because their excess reserves are being depleted by the increase in loans and deposits and by the withdrawal of cash for hand-to-hand circulation. The central banks could continue to supply additional credit, but they have usually felt that it was their function to prevent excessive expansion and therefore have refused to do so.

Some monetary theorists believe that, if the restriction of credit did not occur, the expansion phase of the cycle could be continued indefinitely although that would mean an indefinite rise in prices. The continuous increase in prices leads to an increasing demand for cash for hand-to-hand circulation, for till cash and petty cash funds by business concerns, for working cash balances by financial institutions, and for cash needed in day-by-day operations of banks. These increased demands for cash, being a drain on reserves, not only cause banks to stop expanding credit but also to contract the amount outstanding.

The upper turning point is brought about, according to Hawtrey, because of a lag between the growth in bank deposits and the outflow of currency into circulation. While Hawtrey was referring to a gold standard in which gold served both in the capacity of reserves for the banking system and as circulating currency, the general ideas are applicable to our present system. At the time the expansion begins, the skeleton balance sheet of the banking system might look something like this:

Commercial Banking System

Gold (reserves)	$ 20	Demand deposits $150
Earning assets	$130	

British banks did not have legal reserve requirements, but tradition did dictate a minimum reserve ratio. For purposes of our example, let us assume this to be 10 percent, so that in our initial situation the amount of excess reserves is $5 billion. At this stage the banks are lowering their interest charges, and merchants begin to borrow for the purpose of adding to their stock of inventory. Earning assets increase, and at the same time demand deposits are increasing *parri passus*. While this is happening, the incomes of workers who are producing the goods bought are growing, although with a lag. In Hawtrey's time workers kept their cash balances in the form of currency rather than demand deposits. Thus gold specie will be accumulating in the hands of the workers, leaving the banks; so the balance sheet of the banking system might approach a position like this:

Commercial Banking System

Gold (reserves)	$ 18	Demand deposits $180
Earning assets	$160	

At the 10 percent reserve ratio limit, the banks are loaned up at this point; but gold will continue to flow into circulation, which throws the banks into a deficient reserve position. This, of course, will force the contraction of earning assets. Interest rates will rise to encourage borrowers to get out of debt to the banks. Some forced liquidation of inventories will be imposed. Merchants will find the interest costs high enough to induce them to decrease the size of their inventories. Now the contraction is in process.

When bank credit is contracted, businessmen must reduce their stocks of goods to retire bank loans and thus they place orders for a smaller amount of goods than they are selling currently. This starts business on a downward movement, which is cumulative just as the upward movement was. As prices begin to fall, merchants expect them to fall further and therefore try to reduce their stocks. As producers receive smaller orders, they cut down production, consumer income is cut and so are consumer expenditures, so the reduction in stocks will be less than intended. The same lags that were observed in the expansion are at work in the contraction phase. Income reductions of workers lag behind the reduction in loans and demand deposits, and the inflow of currency into the banks which becomes bank reserves lags behind the decline in incomes. If people expect the continuance of the price declines, the velocity of money will fall and cash balances will increase accentuating the downswing.

Periodicity

According to the monetary theory, there are pronounced business cycles rather than minor oscillations around a point of equilibrium because of the cumulative, self-sustaining nature of the processes of expansion and contraction. These processes go on for a period of time because the expansion of bank credit and the use of the increased cash balances of the community are not instantaneous. It takes time for economic activity to expand to the point where increased cash balances are needed and for this loss of cash by the banks, along with increased borrowing, to put pressure on reserves. Likewise, during contraction, it takes time for these cash balances to return to the banking system and to increase bank reserves above normal levels.

When most of the commercial nations of the world were operating on the gold standard, this process took place with some regularity since the central banks acted to maintain the gold reserves. Since the abandonment of the automatic gold standard during World War I, however, the regular periodicity is no longer apparent because the intricate mechanism that produced regular periods of expansion and contraction has been altered materially.

Evaluation

Monetary factors are certainly active factors in the cyclical process. It is difficult, however, to agree that the cyclical phenomenon is entirely a monetary one. Changes in economic activity may be due to changes in demand, to new inventions, to changes in the cost structure, to changes in the methods of doing business, and so forth, which are not monetary factors but they do, of course, affect monetary factors. The monetary theorists have well described the cumulative processes of expansion and contraction that such factors set into motion. Their explanation of the turning points is, however, not a completely satisfactory one.

It is highly doubtful that businessmen generally are as sensitive to small changes in interest rates as the monetary theorists maintain they are. The most important factors affecting investment decisions generally are present and prospective levels of sales, and price, cost, and profit expectations rather than minor variations in interest rates. It is true that under any given state of expectations some individual businessmen may gain by increasing inventories and are encouraged to do so by lower interest costs, but this is not likely to be quantitatively important in bringing about an expansion unless expectations are favorable for increased business activity. A complete explanation, then, must account for changed expectations, not lower interest rates alone. The explanation of the upper turning point is likewise not fully satisfactory. Turning points have occurred when bank credit was easily available, and prosperity has continued when credit was severely restricted.

THE NONMONETARY OVERINVESTMENT THEORY

One group of investment theorists stresses overinvestment as a basic cause of the cycle and assigns only a subordinate role to monetary factors. Therefore, their theory has been referred to as the nonmonetary overinvestment theory.

It is a fact that investment spending fluctuates more severely than do the other major components of total spending in the economy over the course of the business cycle. This can be explained either as the response of investment to other forces at work in the system, as it was in the purely monetary and the psychological theories; or investment spending can be viewed as the causal factor that provokes the other elements to behave in a cyclical fashion. The nonmonetary overinvestment theory focuses upon investment as the factor that has an inherent tendency to fluctuate and causes the whole economy to react in a cyclical manner. These economists describe the monetary system as a passive agent in the cycle, expanding during the upswing and contracting during the downswing. In other words, the money supply is not an originating force but a response variable. Changes in the money supply are a necessary but not a sufficient condition for cycles.

The earliest writer of this group we have called the nonmonetary overinvestment theorists was Michel Tugan-Baranowsky.[2] In his version, the most important feature of the cycle was the conversion of free capital into fixed or real capital during the expansion and the opposite movement of fixed into free capital during the contraction. Free capital, which today we would call loanable funds, is converted into fixed capital, or capital goods, by the act of investment. Fixed capital is converted into free capital by way of the capital producing the receipt of funds, which are not used to replace the machine but are available for future spending. Free capital also builds up during the downswing because of people on fixed incomes whose savings cumulate without acceptable outlets for the use of these funds. Of course, investment in plant and equipment absorbs these funds during the expansion phase. A downswing comes to a halt, and the

---

[2]Tugan-Baranowsky, *Les Crises Industrielles en Angleterre*, 1913.

direction of the economy is reversed when free capital has accumulated in large enough amounts that great pressure to employ these
funds is felt, and the fixed capital, which was too large at the beginning of the downswing, has been reduced by way of depreciation in
use over this time. The low interest rate in effect at this time is further encouragement to the initiation of investment activity. The
upper turning point is explained by the absorption of all of the available free capital by real capital. Investment must stop because there
are no longer funds to pay for the new equipment and buildings.

Professor Arthur Spiethoff[3] improved upon Tugan-Baranowsky's
explanation of the overinvestment theory, especially of the turning
points. Spiethoff agreed with Tugan-Baranowsky that the lower
turning point would be initiated by the push of free capital, but he
was of the opinion that the pull of real capital might be a more
powerful force. This demand for capital goods would arise from
innovations that would open up new profit possibilities. Spiethoff's
addendum to the theory of the upper turning point is to observe that
the expansion will stop if the society runs out of loanable funds, as
Tugan suggested; but it will also come to an end if the investment
possibilities inherent in the innovations are exhausted. Thus,
Spiethoff has added the force of the pull of investment demand or
real capital at both the upper and lower turning points to the reliance that Tugan-Baranowsky had made of the push of free capital.

It remained for Professor Joseph A. Schumpeter[4] to explain why
innovations would occur with sufficient regularity to explain the
periodicity of the business cycle. The Schumpeter schema will be
considered immediately after we have summarized the events of the
cycle according to the nonmonetary overinvestment school.

The Upswing

This group describes the upswing and the cumulative process of
expansion in much the same way as the monetary overinvestment
group. After a period of depression, there are again profit possibilities
and an increase in investment activity. This revival of investment
generates income and purchasing power. This leads to an increase

---

[3]Arthur Spiethoff, *Business Cycles*, International Economic Papers, No. 3
(New York: The Macmillan Company, 1953).

[4]Joseph A. Schumpeter, *Business Cycles*, Vol. 1 (New York: McGraw-Hill
Book Company, 1939); also his *Theory of Economic Development* (Cambridge, Massachusetts: Harvard University Press, 1934).

in demand for capital goods and also for consumer goods. The increased demand for consumer goods stimulates further investment, and the increase in profits arising out of larger volumes of business and a rising price level provide a psychological stimulus for further expansion. Thus prosperity arises out of this cumulative process of expansion.

To describe the maladjustment, which develops in this expansion period, theorists in this group divide goods into four categories: nondurable consumer goods, durable and semidurable consumer goods, durable capital goods, and materials used to produce durable goods. Disequilibrium arises between these categories of goods during the upswing of the cycle. What actually occurs is a shortage and abundance at the same time, since there is too much of one type of goods and too little of another. Because of the development of new types of durable capital goods that can be used to reduce costs of production, a larger proportion of the factors of production are allocated to the making of durable capital goods and the materials used to produce such goods. As a result, insufficient resources are available for the consumer goods industries that are counted on to use the new capital goods.

Also contributing to the unbalance is the long interval between the construction of a plant or factory and the time when it begins to turn out products. This situation makes a correct forecast of demand very difficult. Additional income is being paid to workers and to capital in the field of producer goods, and this increased income leads to more demand for consumer goods. The increased demand cannot be satisfied until the new producer goods go into production and, as a result, prices rise. This rise in prices is temporary to the degree that supply of new producer goods will increase to an extent large enough to meet demand. It is difficult for individual producers to determine the industry's increase in capacity and also the price that will exist after production is in full swing. The higher prices may also lead to some expansion projects based on profit expectations at these prices, which will turn out to be unsound when supply is increased and prices return to lower levels.

The development of new durable consumer goods may also attract the factors of production to this field and away from the production of nondurable and semidurable consumer goods. The unbalance between the various types of production cannot be corrected because to do so would require additional labor and additional consumer goods to satisfy the demand of such labor. Since all resources are in use, the additional labor and consumer goods are not available.

The Downturn

The expansion continues until either a shortage of loanable funds develops, which forces investment to decrease, or because of the virtual completion of profitable investment projects. The capital goods industry becomes depressed and the downswing is under way. After a long period of high activity and high incomes the people who receive their incomes from this industry find their incomes, and hence their ability to purchase consumer goods, reduced at about the same time that the new plants and machinery are ready to turn out larger volumes of consumer goods. Now it can be seen that overinvestment has taken place. Projects, which would have been profitable had they been available when incomes were rising and resources were being devoted to capital building rather than consumer goods, are now excessive when large amounts of resources are available for the production of consumer goods and incomes are insufficient to buy them. Prices of consumer goods fall and a cumulative contraction is under way.

During the downswing, conditions are being created that make the lower turning point possible. The capital wears out over time and is not replaced so the stock of capital is reduced. The costs of building capital equipment are lowered, wages are reduced, prices of raw materials are cut, and interest rates are lowered as loanable funds accumulate in the system. The contraction will continue until investment is again stimulated by these conditions and/or the occurrence of an innovation requiring the expenditure on capital.

Evaluation

This form of the overinvestment theory is hardly satisfactory as a complete explanation of the business cycle. It has made a contribution, however, by pointing out that unbalance can occur between different categories of consumer goods as well as between producer and consumer goods. There is no completely satisfactory explanation given of the reasons for the unbalance between the different categories of goods. The minor emphasis on monetary factors cannot be fully accepted since changes in the monetary system have played an active role in many past cycles. The explanation of the factors that initiate an upswing after a business has declined during a recession period is inadequate in that it does not sufficiently explain why innovations occur at just the right time to produce the regularity of the business cycle. For this we turn to the work of Professor Schumpeter.

INNOVATIONS

The most thorough analysis of the role of innovations and the process by which they generate economic fluctuations was developed by Joseph A. Schumpeter. Changes in economic activity may be initiated by external factors, such as war, changes in tariffs, damage due to earthquakes, and changes in agricultural yield. Such external influences disturb economic equilibrium, but they do not of themselves lead to cyclical fluctuations of business activity. Fluctuations may also be due to internal changes in the economic system, such as changes in tastes of consumers, changes in the quantity or quality of the factors of production, and innovations in the methods of producing commodities.

The movement is cyclical because of the cumulative process that takes place. Conditions in a period of prosperity are unbalanced and therefore lead inevitably to depression; and in turn conditions in the depression become favorable to a revival of investment; and thus the cycle goes on in a regular fashion. After there has been an initial boom in capital construction, replacements tend to assume a cyclical character since much of the equipment must be replaced at about the same time in the future.

Crucial to the understanding of the Schumpeterian analysis is the distinction between inventions or discoveries, and innovations. The invention of new techniques, processes of production of new capital goods, of new consumer products, the discovery of new markets, or new sources of raw materials are the major categories. These would seem to happen any time, perhaps in a random fashion over time. The presumption is that individuals and organizations engaged in research to discover or invent do so at a fairly continuous rate but that there is no regular pattern to the actual occurrences. Innovations are the economic exploitation of these inventions or discoveries, that is, the introduction of them into the economy so that they are effective in causing the system to respond as it does in the business cycle. Innovations are introduced because a few business leaders see possibilities that are not generally seen by the rank and file. At first, they must strive hard to overcome inertia and introduce the innovation. After a time, others see the prospects for profits and they too get into the new field.

Schumpeter uses the construct of the "stationary state" or "static flow," an idealized situation of equilibrium — as complete an equilibrium as can be imagined. In it there is no uncertainty because there are no changes, and no changes because there are no innovations. There is no reason to invest except to replace worn-out equipment so there is no saving. All output and all spending are on consumption. The lack of uncertainty assures that no profit will exist. Management, having no risk to take, simply repeats what was done in the past and so receives only its wages. There would be no borrowing and lending between households and business because capital would earn no net return. Everything else is constant, including the money supply, the velocity of money, prices, output, and full employment.

Into this euphoric environment rides the dynamic entrepreneur, Schumpeter's hero. He is the risk taker, the innovator, the creator of change and uncertainty. Inventions or discoveries that may have been developed in the past are introduced by this entrepreneur.

Since this analysis starts with an economy that is in a state of equilibrium and has no unemployed factors of production, any new production must be financed by bank credit. This introduction of bank credit causes prices to rise, and it also causes an increase in money income and in the rate of interest.

If most of the great obstacles to change are conquered and the innovation is successful, profit will arise and hosts of imitators will be attracted into the new field and into peripheral areas. This expansion of investment will be paralleled by credit and monetary expansion, and savings will be forced to increase to equal the investment.[5] Since the expansion started from a condition of full employment there can be no net increase in total output. As a result, when more labor and capital are devoted to the production of additional capital goods, output of consumer goods must fall. At the same time, the demand for consumer goods will increase as the additional money arising through bank credit is paid out in wages, thus putting additional pressure on prices.

---

[5]The process of "forced saving" is detailed in the section on the monetary overinvestment theory.

This situation is changed as soon as the capital goods have been produced and the new consumer goods arising from putting them into production flow into the market. Since the innovations are more efficient than the processes they replaced, the volume of consumer goods will be greater than it was before the process began. Old plants will be modernized to keep up with competition from the efficient plants or will be forced out of business. The turning point in this process will come when entrepreneurial activity in introducing innovations ceases. This slowing down in the activity of the entrepreneurs will cause uncertainty in business, and for a time new projects will not be planned. This process, however, is not cyclical in the sense in which business cycles have occurred in our economy. It describes the disturbance from equilibrium and the expansion, and then the return to equilibrium. The return to equilibrium is a period of the adjustment of industry to the new innovations. Some old firms will go out of business as they are unable to compete with the new. Others will curtail the scale of their activity or in other ways readjust their output or ways of production. Some of the old firms whose products are complementary to the new innovation will adapt by expansion or other adjustments.

Secondary Wave of Speculation

The cycles that we have experienced in the past are described as due to a secondary wave of speculation. When business is in the process of readjustment because innovations are being introduced, many feel that the boom which is being produced, especially in the capital goods industries, will be permanent. As a result, the already established firms borrow money to increase their operations, and consumers also go into debt to buy additional goods. General expansion of inventories also takes place due to expected price increases. The excessive indebtedness that is built up during this speculative wave causes trouble.

When the additional goods and services that are made possible by the new capital equipment enter the markets, prices gradually drop. This leads to difficulties for businessmen and consumers who have gone into debt because they contracted their obligations under the impression that the boom would be permanent. When prices fall, many of these people cannot meet their obligations and a depression results. During the expansion, overoptimism and over-extension of debt took place. During the downswing, overpessimism takes over and forced liquidation of inventories and indebtedness go on. This situation can easily lead to a panic.

Evaluation

Beyond question, innovations are an important factor in the cyclical process. This was especially apparent with the introduction of such important new modes of transportation as the canal and the steamboat, the railroad, and the automobile. This analysis has shown how innovations can lead to a business cycle. They are not, however, the only factors leading to cyclical movements, but only a very important part of the total cycle picture.

THE MONETARY OVERINVESTMENT THEORY

One group of theorists stresses deviations in the structure of production that are caused by an expansion in economic activity which is initiated by monetary factors. During a boom a basic maladjustment occurs in the structure of the economy, not only a shortage of bank credit. The production of capital goods is increased faster and to a larger extent than is justified by the demand for consumer goods.[6]

The structure of production that exists at any period of time is not an accidental or an arbitrary one. It has been built up by businessmen who have invested in plant and equipment for the purpose of producing those goods that consumers demand. The amount and types of machinery used depend in part upon the stage of technology in the economy. Also of primary significance is the amount of savings that is available for investment in business plant and equipment and the rate of interest that must be paid to get the holders of savings to invest them. The relative costs of capital and labor are also significant because businessmen combine these factors of production so as to achieve the best possible combination from a cost standpoint.

To keep the economy in equilibrium, it is necessary that the factors of production be utilized so as to produce a pattern of production which corresponds to the pattern of consumption. The pattern of consumption is, in a general way, determined by the decisions of the population to spend or save its income and by the decisions concerning the distribution of expenditures between various

---

[6]For an excellent presentation of this point of view see F. A. Hayek, *Monetary Theory and the Trade Cycle* (New York: Harcourt, Brace & World, 1933), and *Prices and Production* (London: George Routledge & Sons, Ltd., 1935).

types of goods. If, as production increases, the division between the making of new producer goods and of new consumer goods does not correspond to the division of income between saving and spending on consumption, a vertical maladjustment occurs. If the pattern of production of consumer goods of various types does not correspond to the pattern of consumer expenditures for such goods, there is a horizontal maladjustment.

The terms "vertical maladjustments" and "horizontal maladjustments" are used because of the nature of the relationships of the industries to each other. Consumer goods industries are considered as being on one plane, and producer goods industries are thought of as being on a higher plane than consumer goods industries. There are also stages in the producer goods field since some plants produce consumer goods directly, some produce machinery for such plants, some produce machine tools needed to make production machinery, some the basic metals for the tools, and so on. The stages closest to the consumer have been referred to by the monetary overinvestment theorists as the "lower stages of production"; those further removed, the "higher stages of production."

Also basic in the monetary overinvestment theory of the cycle is the concept of the *natural rate of interest*. This is the rate at which the demand for loan capital is just equal to the supply of savings. It should be distinguished from the *money* or *market rate*, which is the actual going rate of interest at any time. If banks lower the market rate below the natural rate, the demand for credit will rise and exceed the available supply of savings. The supply of credit is supplemented by the creation of bank credit, which leads to inflation. If the market rate is above the natural level, the demand for credit will fall and, as a result, part of the supply of savings will not be used and deflation will occur.

The Upswing

The monetary overinvestment theorists have stressed an important economic phenomenon called "forced saving." Hayek, in particular, has made great use of the concept, and feels that this is the essence of the expansion process in the business cycle. In order to explain how forced saving occurs we shall first show how investment can increase *without* forced savings, that is, when savings are increased voluntarily. Chart 5-1, page 108, shows this case.

Chart 5-1

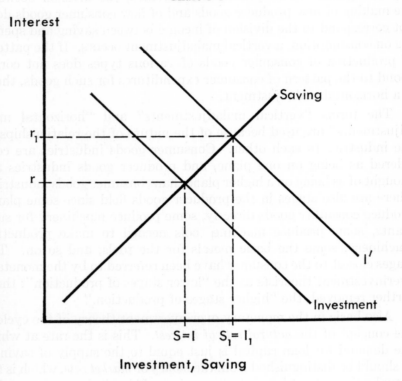

Investment, Saving

The original equilibrium condition is represented by the intersection of the savings and investment functions, where $S = I$ at the interest rate r. Now, we assume an increase in the demand for resources to produce capital goods because of, for example, an important innovation. This increased demand means that business units wish to increase investment spending and are willing to pay higher interest costs to do so. In this case investors *persuade* savers to increase saving (that is, reduce their consumption spending) by offering a higher reward for saving in the form of interest. In fact, households voluntarily relinquish their right to use resources for consumption in exactly the amount needed to satisfy the investors' demands. Saving increased (consumption decreased) from S to S_1, and investment increased from I to I_1. The rise in the rate of interest from r to r_1 induced the higher rate of saving and caused investors to invest less than they would have invested had the interest rate remained at r. There is nothing disruptive in this process.

Total income and output in the economy will not change since neither M nor V of the equation of exchange has changed. Only the composition of output has been altered — more capital goods produced, and in equal amount, less consumer goods produced. Austrian economists describe this alteration in output as a lengthening of the stages of production. When it happens in the manner just presented, no business cycle expansion occurs.

To demonstrate the contrast between the situation involved in Chart 5-1 and what happens in a business cycle, the monetary overinvestment theorists utilize the Wicksellian analysis involving the notions of the market rate of interest versus the natural rate of interest.[7] The natural rate is the rate that equates savings and investment and maintains equilibrium of the price level. In Chart 5-1, the market rate, the rate actually in existence is the same as the natural rate. Divergence between the two occurs if an increase or decrease in hoarding, that is, a decrease or increase in velocity, V, or an increase or decrease in the money supply takes place. An increase in the money supply or the release of funds from "hoards" can make resources available to buyers of capital goods just as surely as if the resources were derived from saving.

Chart 5-2 includes on the supply side savings plus changes in the money supply. For simplicity we have not incorporated increases in velocity, but the analysis would be basically the same. To start the analysis, we can take $S_e = I_e$ at interest rate r_n (natural rate) as the original equilibrium position, and some event causes the banking system to find itself in a position of having excess reserves that bankers want to lend. In order to get all the available funds borrowed, the interest rate will fall to r_m, the market rate of interest. Now, the market rate is below the natural rate. Investors can now command resources valued at I_1 amount. Of this total S_1 is supplied by savers and $I_1 - S_1$ is supplied by the expansion of the money supply. Notice the difference between this case and the case depicted on Chart 5-1. When investment increased on Chart 5-1 saving increased, that is, the use of resources for consumption purposes decreased. In Chart 5-2 when investment increased, planned saving actually decreased, which is to say that consumption demand increased at the same time that the quantity of investment demanded increased.

---

[7] Knut Wicksell, *Interest and Prices* (London: Macmillan & Co., Ltd., 1936)

Chart 5-2

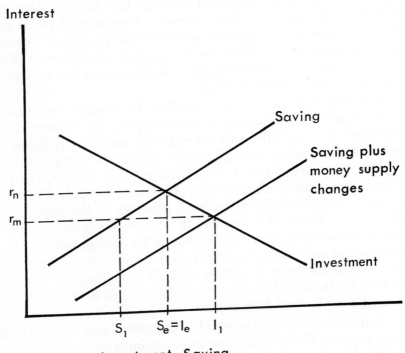

At this stage we must point out that Hayek assumes that we started from a position of full employment so that the total supply of output cannot increase. This being the case, if investors are successful in increasing the output of capital goods, they must lure resources away from their current employment in the production of consumer goods. This can be done only by raising factor prices and, therefore, also the prices of final goods. In other words, consumers are forced to decrease their real consumption by way of price inflation. This is what is meant by the term *forced saving*. Actual saving is equal to I_1, even though desired or intended saving is just S_1.[8]

The market rate of interest will continue to be below the natural rate as long as the money supply continues to expand (or dishoarding

---

[8]This description should be qualified to observe that the new investment demand would be expected to drive up the prices of resources used in both the consumption and the capital goods industries so that some forced reduction of investment will take place as well as some reduction in consumption. The amount of the reduction in each industry will depend largely on the length of the lag in receipts of wages and other income payments behind the expansion of the money supply.

continues); and as long as the rates differ in this way, the upswing of the business cycle will persist. But what happens when the source of expansion of the money supply dries up? Then, again, the supply of loanable funds will be limited to the desired amount of current saving and the market rate of interest will rise to become equal to the natural rate. At this point, in the Austrian terminology, a shortage of capital exists. Investment projects, which were expected to be profitable when evaluated in terms of the lower market rate of interest, cannot be justified at the higher rate. It is now the households whose desires are fulfilled. They will save the amount they wish to save, and investors will be able to invest just that amount. Investment must decline to I_e and savers will plan to increase their saving to S_e. Now there is a decrease in aggregate demand, since both investment and consumption demands have decreased and national income will fall.

The Downturn

According to the overinvestment theory, the process of monetary expansion and heavy investment must always end in a collapse. Here let us review very briefly the sequence of events of the expansion leading to this collapse. The artificial lowering of the interest rate causes businessmen to invest in capital equipment at a rate that cannot be maintained because it is out of balance with consumer demand. The effective demand for consumer goods is reduced by forced savings at the same time that additional capital is invested to produce consumer goods. In other words, the structure of production has become top-heavy since it is now out of balance with too many facilities in the higher stages of production in the capital goods field.

Forces that tend to reverse this pattern are then set in motion. As money is paid out to laborers, who are producing capital goods, the demand for consumer goods rises and the consumer goods industries become more profitable. This, in turn, entices the factors of production away from the higher stages of production back to the production of consumer goods. This demand for the factors of production in all fields causes an increased demand for bank credit and further inflation.

The immediate cause of the breakdown of the boom is almost always the inability or unwillingness of the banking system to continue the process of credit expansion. This is due to monetary reasons, that is, either the pressure on the reserve requirements of individual banks or to central bank policy.

When pressure develops on bank reserves and bank credit is restricted, the producers of capital goods can no longer obtain the funds to pay the higher prices and wages needed to bid raw materials and labor away from the consumer goods field. At the same time increased costs force these producers to charge higher prices for their products. These higher prices of capital goods lower the return to be received from investment in capital equipment at the same time that interest rates are rising because banks have used up most of their excess reserves and are no longer anxious to increase their loan volume. This combination of factors leads to reduced activity in the capital goods field. As workers are laid off, total income is reduced and the downward spiral sets in. The real cause of the collapse, however, is the shortage of real capital. It is not merely a shortage of investable funds but a real shortage of capital in the lower stages of production, which is needed to achieve a new balanced pattern of production in line with the additional investment in the higher stages.

During the depression the structure of production is again brought into balance. This is a lengthy and painful process of readjustment during which workers are thrown out of work in the higher stages of production and gradually reabsorbed in the lower stages as a new pattern of equilibrium is developed. The depression is intensified by the general deflation that accompanies the decrease in the velocity of circulation brought about by hoarding on the part of businessmen and consumers. Now, the market rate of interest will rise above the natural rate because of the increase in hoarding and the possible decrease in the money supply. If total output did not decrease, something like "forced consumption" would take place because the price level would decrease, and since investment has decreased consumption would have to increase. While this is apparently the assumption that Hayek makes, a more realistic position would be that unemployment does occur and total output falls such that both investment and consumption decline during the contraction phase of the cycle. The depression comes to an end when the money supply ceases to decline and when the pessimism that caused the hoarding dissipates. At this point, the natural rate and the market rate would again come into equality, and the stage would be set for another expansion phase that would take place whenever the banking system again finds it profitable to create more money.

Evaluation

There are several shortcomings to this theory as the sole explanation of the cycle. The thesis that credit, which is created when the market rate of interest differs from the natural rate, goes to the higher stages of production and leads to an unbalance between consumption and investment would be generally true under conditions of continuous full employment. However, the upswing of the cycle starts at a time when the economy has unused resources, and the production of both producer goods and consumer goods can be expanded before full employment of resources is reached. At full employment, if credit continues to be expanded to meet the demands of producers, forced saving and unbalance result. But unbalance also results if credit is created to meet the demands of consumers or of government.

The stress upon changes in interest rates as a determinant in the investment process may also obscure other factors that are at work. Investment decisions are based upon the interaction of the demand for funds with the supply of and cost of funds. The demand for funds at various stages in the cyclical process is affected materially by changes in prospects of sales and profits. An analysis of the reasons for the changes in these prospects is an integral part of an understanding of the cyclical process.

Answers to this question supplied by a group of theorists stressing changes in investment activity will be considered in the next section. The monetary overinvestment theorists have stressed an important factor in their analysis of unbalance during the cycle between producer and consumer goods and between different types of producer goods.

THE ACCELERATION PRINCIPLE

Both the monetary and the nonmonetary overinvestment theories, as well as the innovation theory, hold that the initiating force in the cyclical process comes from the investment sector of the economy. There is, however, a point of view, which has been used in explaining the cyclical process, which holds that the initiating impulses come from changes in consumer demand. According to this point of view, changes in consumption expenditures can lead to a cycle because slight changes in the demand for consumer goods can produce much more violent fluctuations in the demand for investment goods. This principle, known as the *acceleration principle,* has been used by many theorists as part of their explanation of the cycle, notably by the French economist Albert Aftalion, the American economist J. M. Clark, and the British economist R. F. Harrod.[9]

In its broadest aspect the principle of acceleration states that changes in the absolute rate of change in the demand for and production of finished goods and services tend to give rise to much more pronounced changes in the demand for and production of the producer goods that are needed for their production. This principle applies not only to finished consumer goods but to all intermediate goods with respect to their preceding stages of production. It also applies to changes in demand resulting from other factors than changes in final demand, such as changes in technology calling for the use of more machinery to produce a given level of output. It also holds true in a measure in the production of durable and semidurable consumer goods.

Producer Goods

The relationship in the case of producer durable goods may best be illustrated by means of a hypothetical example. Let us suppose that in a given economy 1,000 units of consumer goods are produced in a year and that it takes 100 units of producer durable equipment to turn out the consumer goods. If the producer equipment lasts 10 years, there is an average demand for 10 units of equipment each year to replace those that are wearing out so as to keep the stock of equipment intact.

Let us suppose, further, that there is an increase of 10 percent in the demand for this particular consumer good so that 1,100 units are now desired by consumers. In order to produce these additional 100 units, it will be necessary to have 10 more units of equipment. Even though this equipment will be useful for a period of 10 years, it is needed immediately. As a result, there is now a demand for 20 units of equipment, the 10 needed for replacement and the 10 additional units needed to take care of the increased consumer demand. Thus an increase of 10 percent in the demand for consumer goods has been magnified into an increased demand of 100 percent in the producer goods field.

---

[9] Mr. Harrod makes use of the acceleration principle in his analysis of the business cycle, but following his own terminology calls it "the relation."

The degree of this acceleration in the derived demand for capital goods depends upon the life of the capital equipment. If the machines in our example lasted only 5 years, there would be a normal demand for replacement of 20 per year. In this case a 10 percent increase in the demand for consumer goods would result in a 50 percent increase in the demand for producer goods since 10 additional machines would be needed and 20 are being produced regularly. On the other hand, if the machines lasted 20 years, the normal replacement demand would be only 5 per year and the 10 percent increase in the demand for consumer goods would lead to a 200 percent increase in the demand for producer equipment.

At the one extreme, if a machine was capable of producing an unlimited number of commodities, that is, would last indefinitely, there would be no activity in the replacement business and so any

Table 5-1

Changes in the Demand for Producer Goods
Resulting from Changes in Consumer Goods Demand*

PERIOD	COMMODITY DEMAND	EQUIPMENT STOCK (BEGINNING OF PERIOD)	DEMAND FOR EQUIPMENT FOR RE- PLACEMENT	DEMAND FOR NEW EQUIPMENT (NET IN- VESTMENT)	TOTAL DEMAND FOR EQUIPMENT (GROSS IN- VESTMENT)
1	1,000	100	10	0	10
2	1,100	100	10	10	20
3	1,150	110	11	5	16
4	1,150	115	11.5	0	11.5
5	1,000	115	11.5	−15	−3.5

*Assumptions:
  (1) Commodity demand figures arbitrarily selected.
  (2) One piece of equipment produces at the rate of 10 units of the commodity per period.
  (3) The equipment has a life of 10 periods, that is, its depreciation rate is 10 percent per year. In reality, the assumption is that in its lifetime the equipment is capable of producing 100 units of the commodity.
  (4) No depreciation occurs in the year in which equipment is added.

increase in primary demand would result in an increase in the demand for new equipment only. In that case, the total demand for equipment would be represented by our column headed "Demand for New Equipment." This is the most volatile case. At the other extreme, suppose the durability of the machines were just one period, that is, capable of producing just 10 units of commodity output. In that case, the replacement industry would be producing the existing stock of capital each period, and any increase in primary demand would result in exactly a proportional increase in total demand for equipment.

It is possible for the demand for new equipment to slow down while the demand for consumer goods is still increasing. If the demand for the consumer goods increases from 1,000 to 1,100 units, the demand for equipment increases by 10 or 100 percent. However, while the demand for the consumer goods continues to increase to 1,150 units, the total demand for equipment has already been cut to 16 units, a reduction of 20 percent. If in the next period the demand for the commodity remains constant, the only equipment demand is for replacement and, as a result, demand falls still further. This can be clearly seen from the example in Table 5-1.

Thus it can be seen that increases in the absolute rate of change in demand for consumer goods when an industry is at or near capacity will lead to an accelerated derived demand for producer goods, but this demand will be sharply curtailed as the rate of increase slows down.

Durable and Semidurable Consumer Goods

The second case of the principle of acceleration is similar to the first except that it pertains to durable and semidurable consumer goods. Identically the same example can be used with modifications in terms. Instead of the production of a consumer good, it is necessary to substitute the service received from it (as, for example, the service received from a house) and to substitute the supply of houses for the equipment used to produce consumer goods. An increase in the demand for housing accommodations leads to a greatly magnified demand for new houses because houses last for a long period of time.

The same situation is true in the automobile field where the basic demand is for transportation service. Since cars last for several years, there is a basic demand for automobiles for replacement; and an increase in the demand for transportation service leads to an accelerated increase in the demand for new cars. This relationship will be elaborated on more fully in a discussion of the methods of forecasting the demand for consumer durable goods in Part VII.

Inventories

The third case of the acceleration due to derived demand occurs in the case of inventories. Let us suppose that it is the practice of a dealer in men's suits to adjust his inventory to sales in such a way that he usually has a stock on hand about equal to the sales during two months, and that his sales are normally 100 suits a month. Because of an increase in demand, his sales rise to 110 suits a month. As a result, he will find that it is necessary to increase his orders for suits by more than the increase in sales if he is to maintain his regular relationship of inventory to sales. If the increased demand for suits is permanent, it will necessitate the addition of 20 extra suits to his stock of suits to maintain past inventory relationships.

This principle works on the downturn as well as on the upswing. It is, however, subject to some very definite qualifications. It is by no means clear that a relatively fixed relationship will be maintained at all times between sales and stocks, especially in the short run. In addition, the volume of stocks is subject to speculative changes that may easily overshadow any changes due to the acceleration principle.

Evaluation

The acceleration principle has been used as part of the explanation of the cycle by various theorists. It is another factor that explains the accelerated increase in demand in the upswing of the cycle. It is especially significant in a highly developed economy in which large amounts of capital equipment are in use, much of the equipment having a long period of usefulness. As has already been demonstrated, the longer the life of the equipment, the greater the acceleration due to derived demand. Since some of the new capital equipment is financed out of credit expansion, the additional credit intensifies the upswing. The acceleration in demand for durable goods and in demand for inventories also offers a further explanation of the factors leading to the cumulative nature of the expansion.

The acceleration principle also adds a new possibility for an explanation of the downturn. Instead of being due to a shortage of money or of equipment, the downturn may occur because the rate of increase in the demand for consumer goods has slowed down, thus reducing the demand for new equipment and leading to unemployment in the producer goods field. This further reduces the demand for consumer goods which still further reduces the demand for producer goods. As this cumulative process of contraction takes place, the boom must come to an end.

Attempts to verify the acceleration principle statistically have not always met with success. This is to be expected since it is only a greatly simplified statement of a principle, not an explanation of a phenomenon which happens in just that way in the real world. In the case of producers' durable equipment, for example, it is very unlikely in an economy which experiences marked fluctuations in demand that there will be any regularity in the replacement of equipment. Most replacement is likely to occur in prosperity periods when the demands for new equipment must also be met. Furthermore, when an expansion of business begins, there is usually unused capacity in an industry so that the first effect of an increased demand for consumer goods is a fuller utilization of existing capacity. As demand expands further, it is also possible in many plants to utilize existing equipment more fully by adding additional shifts of workers. Beyond that point it becomes necessary to place orders for new equipment, which will show the accelerated effect of derived demand.

As the economy approaches full employment of men and resources, however, it is no longer possible to increase production in all fields. The major result will be a bidding up of prices, especially those of basic raw materials utilized in both the producer and consumer goods fields. Thus, the acceleration principle cannot hold completely as full employment of men and resources is achieved. This explanation is in harmony with the record of business fluctuations as developed by the National Bureau of Economic Research. The most rapid rate of increase in the production of capital goods occurs early in the cycle, but the most rapid rate of increase in price does not occur until the last segment of expansion. This relationship is much too complex a one to be measured effectively in all of its ramifications; and, therefore, it is not surprising that the evidence on this point is at variance. It is, however, an integral part of the explanation of the cyclical process, especially the more pronounced fluctuations in demand for durable goods of all kinds than for nondurable goods.

Here, we have discussed the acceleration principle as it applies on the micro level, or the level of the industry. The principle has also been integrated into the general theory of national income analysis, and we shall take up this very important contribution in a later chapter.

QUESTIONS

1. Some writers state the Cambridge form of the equation of exchange as $\frac{M}{P} = k\,y$. Review the meaning of the terms, and interpret this equation.

2. Using the tautology $MV = Py$, what arguments would be necessary to defend such a statement as: labor unions (or monopolies) are the cause of inflation?

3. Show the balance sheet changes of the commercial banking system over a complete business cycle as implied in Hawtrey's analysis. Use successive T-accounts. The only items needed are reserves, earning assets, and demand deposits. Assume a 10 percent customary or required reserve ratio.

4. Trace the development of a full business cycle according to the purely monetary theory within the framework of the equation of exchange, either $MV = Py$, or $M = kPy$.

5. What weakness in Tugan-Baranowsky's theory did Spiethoff correct? What was Schumpeter's contribution to this same problem?

6. Would the nonmonetary theory of the cycle be an acceptable theory if the money supply were held completely constant? Defend your answer.

7. In the overinvestment theories, the upper turning point is associated with a decrease in investment. Why, then, are the theories called "overinvestment"?

8. Explain how inflation of the general price level operates to produce the phenomenon called "forced saving."

9. Explain why the acceleration principle is more pronounced the more durable the capital equipment is.

SUGGESTED READINGS FOR CHAPTERS 4 AND 5

American Economic Association. *Readings in Business Cycle Theory*, Vol. III. Homewood, Illinois: Richard D. Irwin, Inc., 1944.

Clark, John J., and Morris Cohen (eds.). *Business Fluctuations, Growth and Economic Stabilization*, A Reader. New York: Random House, 1963.

Estey, J. A. *Business Cycles, Their Nature, Cause, and Control.* Berkeley, California: University of California Press, 1941.

Hansen, Alvin H. *Business Cycles and National Income.* New York: W. W. Norton & Company, Inc., 1951.

——————————, and R. V. Clemence. *Readings in Business Cycles and National Income.* New York: W. W. Norton & Company, Inc., 1953.

Hawtrey, Ralph G. *Trade and Credit.* London: Longmans, Green & Co., Ltd., 1928.

Hayek, Friedrich. *Profits, Interest, and Investment.* London: Routledge & Kegan Paul, Ltd., 1939.

Hobson, J. A. *The Economics of Unemployment.* London: G. Allen & Unwin, Ltd., 1922.

Mitchell, W. C. *Business Cycles and Their Causes.* Berkeley, California: University of California Press, 1941.

Pigou, A. C. *The Theory of Unemployment.* London: Macmillan & Co., Ltd., 1933.

von Haberler, Gottfried. *Prosperity and Depression.* Cambridge, Massachusetts: Harvard University Press, 1958, Chapters 4–8.

Keynes and the Basic Framework of National Income Analysis

The next three chapters develop the modern theory of national income analysis. Chapter 6 begins with some comments on the contributions of Lord Keynes who was mainly responsible for initiating interest in this form of analysis. This chapter continues by presenting the basic framework of the theory. Chapter 7 extends the analysis by integrating the market for goods and services and the money market, and also includes a presentation of a multiplier-accelerator model that shows how business cycles can occur because of the form of the investment demand function. Chapter 8 incorporates further developments in national income theory and concludes with its application to the theory of economic growth.

THE KEYNESIAN CONTRIBUTION

This separate chapter is devoted to the theories of John Maynard Keynes on the nature of the business cycle for several reasons. One of these is the outstanding influence of the man as an economist and as an adviser on public policy. Few, if any, economists, at least since the days of Adam Smith, have had as pronounced an effect on economic theory as did Lord Keynes. In his *General Theory of Employment, Interest, and Money* he analyzed what he considered to be the weaknesses of classical economics and presented a new set of tools for economic analysis and a new formulation of the factors that determine the level of employment of men and resources. As is the case with any new approach to a problem, his work generated a great deal of discussion and controversy, some of which continues to this day. Those who refused to accept his general approach to economic analysis were forced to reexamine their concepts and to define them more accurately and more clearly. His followers were given the tools which led them to develop a greatly increased understanding of our economy, especially the factors that determine the level of consumption, saving, investment, and interest rates.

Keynes not only attained a standing as an economist held by few men, but he achieved a place as an adviser on public policy in the economic area that has seldom, if ever, been equaled. In his early twenties he was an adviser to the government of India on financial matters; in his early fifties governments in all parts of the world sought his advice on matters of economic policy. His position of preeminence as an economic adviser continued until his death. In his last years, he was one of the leading advisers responsible for the agreements that led to the establishment of the International Monetary Fund.

Another reason for devoting so much space to the work of J. M. Keynes is that he analyzed the factors determining the level of investment and consumption and developed the relationships between them in a fuller and in a different way from that of earlier cycle theorists. Since Keynes's analysis of these factors has become the wellspring of modern aggregative economic analysis, we use this chapter as the introduction to the basic elements of national income determination theory. A mastery of the material in this chapter will permit comprehension of the later developments in macroeconomic theory and contemporary business cycle thought discussed in later chapters.

Basic Concepts of the Keynesian Framework of Analysis

In order to understand the nature of the cycle as Keynes saw it, it is necessary to understand some of the basic concepts on which his system is based. These include the concepts of income, consumption, saving, and investment; the propensity to consume; the marginal efficiency of capital; liquidity preference; equilibrium; and the multiplier concept. Each of these will be developed and analyzed in some detail.

It is worth considerable effort to understand the meaning of these terms, since a great deal of confusion and disagreement have, at their source, different understandings of what a particular term involves. It would be very easy to give a half dozen different concepts embodied in such words as capital, consumption, saving, profit, and many other words that belong in the popular domain and are used by economists. Since each of these concepts represents a significant feature of economic behavior, they need to be incorporated in our analysis. We should use qualifying adjectives or explain which notion we have in mind, but frequently we simply hope that the concept intended is clear from its context.

One of the serious stumbling blocks in the understanding of economic relationships is the confusion between flow variables and stock variables. In popular discourse this distinction is often glossed over, but in the study of economics it should not be. For instance, the word "investment" to an economist is strictly a flow, and the associated stock is called wealth or capital. A flow variable can be measured only over a period of time, while a stock variable can be measured only at a point in time. Similarly, saving is an act that can be performed only over a period of time. The associated stock that results from saving is popularly called savings. A better practice would be to refer to the accumulated stock simply as assets.

In national income analysis, as in most of economics, there is usually a difference between the definition of a term designed to permit its measurement, and the definition designed for purely analytical purposes. For example, the idea of consumption has been the "using up" of goods and services, or the destruction of utility or value. Since this notion is measurable only in the aggregate, we usually find it expedient to define consumption as purchases by households for current use. Sometimes the two definitions are very close, but under other conditions they diverge so much that if one's analysis is based upon the one idea and his empirical evidence is based upon the other idea, he may be seriously misled.

Another source of difficulty is that economics deals with transactions and every transaction is two-sided — the buyers' and the sellers'. Sometimes our terms put the emphasis on the one side, and it is forgotten that forces are also operative on the other side. For this reason newspapers frequently report waves of selling on the stock exchange and ignore the "wave" of buying that is necessarily taking place simultaneously.

A long debate over the equality of saving and investment culminated in the warning of the necessity of distinguishing between planned or intended magnitudes on the one hand and actual or measured magnitudes on the other. It is always necessary to be clear in discussion and analysis whether one is referring to planned magnitudes, which are usually of most interest but difficult, if not impossible, to measure, and actual magnitudes, which are usually of less interest, but are measurable.

Concepts of Production, Income, Consumption, Saving, and Investment

In this section we will look first at the most fundamental meaning of these terms. *Production* is the creation of value. Thus any activity that results in someone being willing to pay more for a good or service than the value of the materials used has produced something. Defined in this way, production is the same thing as income, since all the value created must be allocated or distributed to someone. Under capitalistic principles, the rule is that the income will be distributed to the factors of production responsible for the production. In a complex process this is difficult to achieve, but we have a large body of thought, called income distribution theory, which attempts to explain this allocative process. It is customary to use the income categories of wages, rent, interest, and profit, even though a rigorous theoretical division of them is not possible. From the point of view of the business sector, wages, rent, and interest are elements of cost, and profit is a pure residual between total revenues from the sale of goods and services and contractual costs. From the factor-owner side, wages are the payment for human services; and rent, interest, and profit are derived from the provision of the services of property.

In the aggregate, *income* is the amount of goods and services that could be consumed during a period of time, leaving the stock of wealth of the society at the end of the period the same as it was at the beginning.[1] From this it follows that income is equal to consumption plus capital accumulation, where *consumption* is defined as the destruction of value; and *investment*, or capital accumulation, is the act of adding to the stock of capital or wealth. *Saving* is the process of not consuming all that was produced during the time period.

Now, if we let Y stand for national income, which we have said is equal to aggregate production, and let C stand for consumption, or destruction of value, the difference between them is what was produced and not destroyed. The result of destroying less than the amount produced is an increase in the stock of physical goods. This is what we defined to be investment, which we label I. But, by definition this is also saving, S, since it is the amount by which income exceeds consumption. Therefore: $Y \equiv C + I$ and $Y \equiv C + S$, or $I \equiv Y - C$, and $S \equiv Y - C$, and $I \equiv S$.

---

[1] This notion of income is discussed in J. R. Hicks, *Value and Capital*. (2nd ed.; London: Oxford University Press, 1946), Ch. XIV.

We should keep in mind that these fundamental notions are what we are really interested in, since questions of economic welfare, growth possibilities, and so on must be evaluated in these real terms. There are some analytical and statistical reasons for using approximations to these concepts, however. Consumption, for example, cannot be accurately measured so we use, as a close estimate of it, expenditures on consumer goods. The difficulty here is to define *consumer goods,* and we do this by including all goods purchased by households that are normally destroyed during the period in which we are interested. Likewise, we can't tell what part of the expenditures of government add to the society's wealth and what part are currently consumed for present utility. In this case, we devote our attention simply to government expenditures *in toto.* Expenditures by business units on capital account becomes our measure of investment.

AGGREGATE DEMAND

Aggregate demand is the summation of decision-making units' intentions to buy final goods and services. The usual procedure is to group the decision-making units into the various sectors of the economy. In general, it has been found helpful to use the categories of households, business, government, and the rest of the world. There are three reasons for this particular breakdown: (1) The decision-making process is somewhat different for each of the categories, or at least is handled differently in the theory explaining their behavior. (2) The impact of the expenditures of the various sectors on the future may be different. (3) Value judgments about the welfare effects of the expenditures of the several sectors may differ.

Households

Households include all of the human beings in the domestic economy. The *raison d'etre* of the economy is to improve the welfare, in some sense, of this sector. Consumption takes place to satisfy the desires of households, so that in the fundamental meaning of the term only households consume. A large and well-developed theory of household behavior exists in the literature where each consuming unit is viewed as an expected utility maximizer. A household is in equilibrium when the marginal utilities of all commodities relative to their prices are equal; that is: $\dfrac{MU_A}{P_A} = \dfrac{MU_B}{P_B} = \ldots = \dfrac{MU_N}{P_N}.$

Macroeconomic theory does not concern itself in any important way with the allocation of income among commodities, but it does concern itself with the allocation of income between present goods as a group and future goods as a group. In other words, in aggregative economic theory, the decision of households to spend on present consumption a part of current income implies a decision to save the remainder. On partial equilibrium grounds, then, the household is in equilibrium when the marginal utilities of all present goods relative to their prices are equal to the marginal utilities of all future goods relative to their current prices.[2] An increase in a consumer's income would be expected to increase his demands for both present and future goods. The precise manner in which a change in income will influence this decision is the subject of considerable controversy as will be seen in our review of consumption function studies. To the extent that households opt for more saving, they have, at once, increased the demand for future goods, and they have made resources available for future use.

All income from production accrues to the household sector in the sense that all factors of production are owned by members of that sector, either through personal, direct ownership, or indirectly through the intermediary of a corporation or government. In national income accounting, reference is made to business saving and government saving, but even in these instances where retained corporate earnings or government surpluses exist, saving will occur only to the extent that consumers acquiesce in the decision.

It stretches credulity too much to declare that consumption and household spending are identical. What should be included in consumption spending is the spending on goods and services that are normally destroyed in value during the period under analysis. The purchase of a new home or new automobile, for example, should be excluded since the largest part of the expenditure is not for current consumption but for future use. Thus spending for these items should be included in investment demand. But they should also be included in the category of investment because the decision to purchase is based on the same elements as the process of decision making by business firms. Since investment is the act of adding to the stock of

---

[2]The future price of commodities is, of course, unknown. If the price level were expected to remain constant, then the interest rate could be used in calculating the current price ratios of present and future goods. Similarly, the marginal utility of future goods in the future is unknown; our reference must be to the present utility of future goods, which, too, involves a forecast.

capital, it is clear that the purchase of a home or auto is an act of investment which increases the supply of future income.

The Business Sector

In the circular flow analysis, all productive activity takes place at the level of the business sector. Business firms employ the services of the factors of production owned by the households. Microeconomic theory asserts that business units utilize resources in such proportions as to maximize expected profits. The equilibrium of a firm occurs when an additional dollar spent on any given resource is expected to yield a return equal to that of that dollar spent on any other resource. In the manner of price theory textbooks: $\frac{MP_A}{P_A} = \frac{MP_B}{P_B} = \ldots = \frac{MP_N}{P_N} = 1$ where MP is the marginal product of the factors of production $A, B \ldots N$ and P is the per unit price of factors $A, B, \ldots N$. This means that the employment of any resource will increase if its productivity increases or if its cost decreases.

From the side of aggregate demand, the most important decision of the business firm is the amount of investment to be undertaken. The investment decision is based on the expected returns to the dollars invested compared to the expected cost of engaging in the investment.

If investment takes place, the stock of productive resources increases and the ability of the economic system to produce goods and services in the future has increased. In the case of investment in inventory the physical supply of goods available for future consumption has increased directly. It makes a great deal of difference to future employment and to future price prospects what kind of investment takes place. If the investment is primarily in increases in inventories of finished consumer goods, or in finished producers goods, or in raw materials stocks, or in the many types of plant or equipment, the implications for the future are clearly different. It is easy to conceive of cases in which the investment expenditures would be of the type that would put pressure on wages to move in one direction and prices of finished goods to move in the other direction. On the other hand, the investment might be of a kind that created an unemployment problem, or it might create an imbalance between agricultural versus industrial production. Such problems are discussed in greater detail at later stages of our study.

The Government Sector

The theory of government behavior has not been as well developed nor as generally accepted as has the body of theory on the private sector. On the one hand, we have the welfare oriented theory which states, in general terms, that marginal social benefits should be equal to marginal social costs. The problem of determining what these benefits and costs are to a society made up of individuals with different preference patterns is, of course, controversial. Theoretical analysis of actual government behavior runs the gamut from the extremely naive to the extremely cynical. One approach, which has attracted a number of adherents, runs in terms of votes gained from a particular action weighed against the number of votes lost by the action. It is at least conceivable that the two approaches lead to the same action, although at this stage in the development of the analysis, it cannot be proved nor disproved.

The place of the government sector in the circular flow picturization of the economy is to absorb purchasing power from the household sector by taxation, and to direct this purchasing power to the business sector (including government employees, therein) as governments purchase goods and services.[3] Some of the expenditures by government will result in current satisfactions of the public (thus being consumption type expenditures), and some increase the wealth of the society (thus being investment type expenditures). Classification of particular government spending into either category would involve us in serious philosophical debate, so we restrain ourselves, but it should be pointed out that the question which needs to be answered is whether the expenditures have the effect of increasing the stock of wealth of the society, or not.

For purposes of short-run analysis of national income behavior, it is insignificant whether government spending is classified as consumption or investment. All such spending acts as an injection of demand for the output of the economy, and becomes income for the owners of the factors of production responsible for the production of the goods and services.

The main reason for handling the government sector apart from the others is that its behavior is subject to political control, and its

---

[3]Government also distributes funds to some households without requiring any current goods and services in exchange. This is what is meant by "transfer payments," and we include transfer payments as negative taxes since the amount of taxes offset by transfer payments constitute no net outflow from the household sector.

taxing and spending can be adjusted to bring about what are believed to be desirable goals. The most important reason, ultimately, that the federal government differs from the other sectors is that it has the sovereign power, which makes its receipts from taxes different from the receipts of units that must sell a product or service; and its borrowing power is unlimited, as long, of course, as the general public has confidence in the monetary system.[4]

The Rest of the World Sector

Exports of goods and services result in an injection of demand by other economies for output and an increase in the incomes of the factors that produced the commodities. Imports into this economy can be looked upon as an outflow or withdrawal from the income stream, since these expenditures do not return purchasing power to our business sector. The international transactions are almost always handled as a net figure called *net foreign* investment or net exports of goods and services, which is the difference between what our nationals sell to foreigners and the amount foreign nationals sell to citizens of this country.

Selling goods or services to peoples of other countries is akin to other investment activities since the ability of our nationals to consume in the future is greater, while purchasing goods from the rest of the world decreases our ability to consume in the future. Another important reason for dealing with the net amount by which exports exceed imports is that it is impossible for us to measure directly the amount of foreign produced and domestically produced goods and services bought by our households, government, and our business sector. Many goods said to be "made in America" may actually contain raw materials from foreign countries, or perhaps foreign machines were used to produce the raw materials produced in this country.

The demand to import goods and services is primarily dependent upon national income and prices of foreign goods as represented by the exchange rates among currencies. The demand for exports depends on the incomes in other countries and the exchange rates. In addition to these factors, exports and imports are heavily influenced

---

[4]This statement may sound shocking, but it must be remembered that issuing money is the prerogative of all national governments, and money is a noninterest-bearing form of debt. We are not yet ready to discuss whether, or under what conditions, government ought to borrow at interest or at no interest.

by various government policies, such as quotas, tariffs, taxes, subsidies, and many others usually designed to encourage exports and
discourage imports of the country.

THE CIRCULAR FLOW

The process by which income is generated through production
and sales, and sales are made possible by income, is called the *circular
flow*. Business firms receive receipts from the sale of goods and services to all of the four sectors we have just described: households,
governments, the rest of the world, and what is not sold to these
three is purchased by business firms themselves. It is important to
understand that what business units buy may be voluntary purchases
by one firm from another, or the producing firm may not sell to other
buyers so that its inventory of its own product will increase. This
increase in inventories may be intentional or unintentional. Such
unintentional investment is of critical importance in the study of
national income because when it occurs, the business units can be
expected to attempt to reduce the unplanned accumulation by decreasing production, and therefore also incomes, or by maintaining
the old level of sales by lowering prices and thus also reducing
incomes. Unintended real investment also can take place when a firm
uses up less of its capital equipment than it had planned because
output was less than intended, while planned investment remains
the same.

The receipts of business units accrue as income to household
owners of the factors of production. Households allocate their incomes among the following uses: purchasing goods and services
directly from business units (consumption); paying taxes to governments; purchasing goods from other countries (imports); or if the
households do none of these, we say they have saved (personal
saving). This saving is a definitional residual, and whatever else
might be done with the money does not alter the fact that saving
took place.

Like investment, saving can be viewed as taking place either
voluntarily or involuntarily. Involuntary saving might occur because earners of income during a period do not receive it until some
future period. The payment lag is quite short for wage earners, but
for property income recipients, it might be considerable. Professor
Modigliani has pointed out that the strictly Keynesian analytical

framework implicitly assumes that consumers have their way so that intended saving is always the same as actual saving and that unintended saving never occurs. This assumption has the logical corollary that the impact of a disequilibrium income is always on the business sector. It always appears as a condition where unintended investment or disinvestment exists. These statements will be made more clear when we demonstrate the income equilibrating mechanism.

Symbolically, the circular flow can be described in the following identity:

$$Y \equiv C + G + I_B + (X - M) \equiv C + T + S_P$$

Where:

Y = income
C = consumption
G = government spending
I_B = business investment
X = exports
M = imports
T = taxes
S_P = personal saving

As a first approximation, it is convenient to reduce $G + I_B + (X - M)$ to I = injections; and $T + S_P$ to S = savings in the inclusive sense. In this way a simpler model can be constructed, where the supply side or value of goods and services produced is equal to $C + S = Y$, and the demand side is $C + I$.

The condition of equilibrium is that supply equals demand, that is, $Y = C + I$. It is necessary to see why equilibrium exists only if aggregate supply and demand are equal. First, suppose the total value of goods and services produced is greater than the demand for them. In that event, unintended inventories accumulate and business will attempt to reduce them by laying off workers and buying fewer materials and services from other firms. In other words, if income is greater than the equilibrium level, income will fall. If, instead of reducing production, firms with excess inventory lower the prices of the unsold goods, the profits of the sellers (which are their incomes) will fall. In later production the incomes of the other factors of production will also fall.

In the preceding paragraph, the case of aggregate supply exceeding aggregate demand was discussed. Now consider the case where demand is greater than supply: $C + I > Y$, or $C + I > C + S$.

Since $C = C$ it follows that $I > S$. It is also true that since purchases of goods and services $(C + I)$ are greater than the value of goods and services produced $(C + S)$, some of the goods sold must have been produced in prior time periods. In other words, the stock of capital, most importantly inventories, must have been drawn down. This is described as involuntary disinvestment or negative investment. In this situation, where business is in fact investing less than it intended to invest, we can expect the firms to try to build back their inventories to the desired level. This will necessitate the employment of additional workers and other resources, or an increase in the prices of goods and services as well as factor prices. Thus, when income is less than the equilibrium level $(C + I > C + S$, and $I > S)$, income will rise.

Parenthetically, it is worth noting that even in the disequilibrium situations where $S > I$ or where $I > S$ it is still the case that actual saving and actual investment are exactly equal in amount. In this framework it is usually assumed that savers do save the amount they intend to save. If this is so, then when $S > I$, involuntary investment in the amount $S - I$ must take place; and conversely, when $I > S$, involuntary disinvestment in the amount $I - S$ must take place.

The Simple Algebraic Model

What has just been verbalized can also be put in the form of a formal model. Certain propositions can be more easily demonstrated with such a model; but more importantly, more complete models or models closer to reality simply cannot be handled, or cannot be handled efficiently, verbally.

The first model to consider is the simplest that can be constructed. It is composed of the following three equations containing three unknowns:

$$(1) \quad Y = C + I$$
$$(2) \quad C = a + bY$$
$$(3) \quad I = I_o$$

The first equation is the condition of equilibrium. Our goal is to "solve" for Y, that is, to find the equilibrium value of Y in terms of the "knowns," (a, b, I_o).[5] The second equation is the "consumption function." It is a behavior equation, which is to say that it describes

---

[5]The meaning and significance of these terms are detailed later.

the expected behavior of households that consume specific amounts at specific levels of income. The third equation asserts that the amount of investment is exogenously determined. For purposes of this model, investment is not to be explained. We get the value of I_o from some other theory, or we simply ask all businessmen their intentions. For our present purpose, it is most important to observe that intended investment does not depend on the level of current income.

Now, solve for Y by substituting into equation (1). First, the unknown C can be replaced by $a + bY$ and the unknown I can be eliminated by using the known I_o.

Thus: $Y = a + bY + I_o$

Subtract bY from both sides of the equation: $Y - bY = a + I_o$

Factor out Y from the left side: $Y(1 - b) = a + I_o$

Divide both sides by $(1 - b)$: $Y = \dfrac{a + I_o}{1 - b}$

We now have one equation and one unknown (Y). Now, if we know the values of the knowns (the parameters), we can determine the value of the unknowns. Thus if:

$$a = \$20 \text{ billion}$$
$$b = 8/10$$
$$I_o = \$30 \text{ billion}$$

Then $Y = \dfrac{\$20 + \$30}{1 - 8/10} = \dfrac{\$50}{2/10} = \$250$ billion.

Since $C = a + bY$, $C = \$20 + 8/10 \,(\$250) = \$20 + \$200 = \$220$ billion.

No equation for S was given, but since we know that $S = Y - C$ we can derive the equation for S by substituting $a + bY$ for C.

Thus: $S = Y - a - bY$,

and factoring: $S = -a + (1 - b)\,Y$,

and $S = -\$20 + \left(1 - \dfrac{8}{10}\right) \$250 = -\$20 + \$50 = \$30$.

Since $I = I_o = \$30$, $S = I$.

The Geometry of the Simple Model

This model can now be demonstrated graphically. In general, the geometric approach is not as powerful as the equations approach since the charts get cluttered up quite quickly when many refinements are added. It is, however, a very handy method for attacking certain problems. The system just developed is shown in Chart 6-1.

Chart 6-1

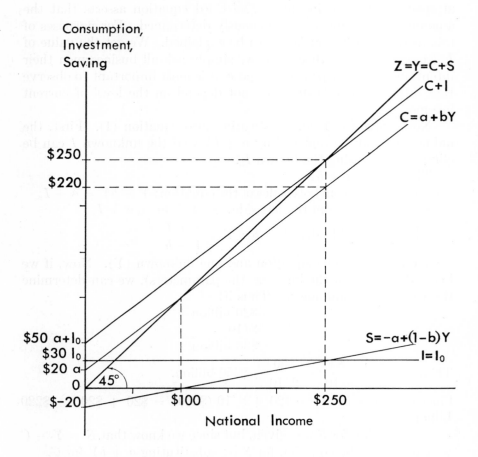

Each line on the graph is now to be explained. First consider the
Z line (Chart 6-2). It is drawn at a 45° angle from the origin, so that
triangles such as OYX and OXZ are identical right triangles. This is
significant in that it assures that $OY = OZ$. In this way, distances
measured along the horizontal axis can be compared to distances
measured along the vertical axis, since the equation for any straight
line is a constant, which measures the intersection of the line with the
vertical axis (call it α [alpha]), plus another constant which is the
slope of the line (call it β [beta]), times the value on the horizontal
axis. For the Z line we have drawn, its equation is: $Z = \alpha + \beta Y$
but $\alpha = 0$, and $\beta = 1$, so $Z = Y$. We know that $\beta = 1$ because the

slope can be measured by any triangle such as RWX. It is $\dfrac{XW}{RW}$, but $XW = RW$ (by right triangles, again) so $\dfrac{XW}{RW} = 1$, so the equation for the Z line collapses to $Z = Y$.

Chart 6-2

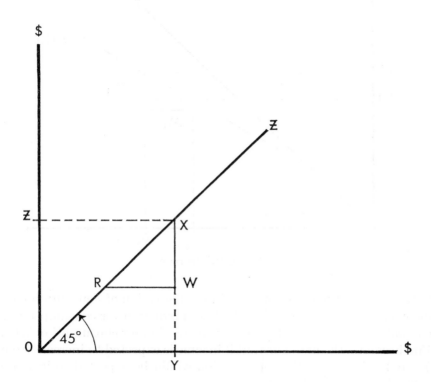

The Consumption Function

The C-line (Chart 6-3, page 136) has the equation $C = a + bY$, which makes it a straight line. The consumption function is the heart of the Keynesian system, and books have been written about it. It has been thought by some to be Keynes's most important contribution to the methodology of aggregate economic theory.

The C-line is drawn on the basis of the past behavior of consumption and income. It is the line which represents the best single estimator of what consumption was at various levels of income. Sta-

Chart 6-3

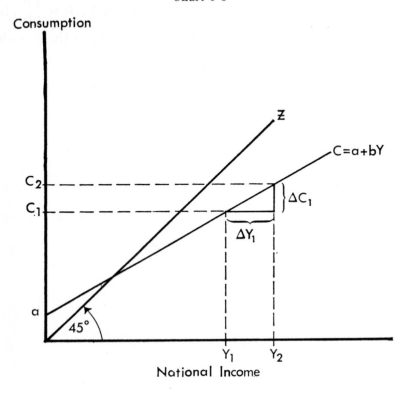

tistically, it is the least squares simple regression of consumption on income. When income is Y_1, the best prediction for consumption is C_1, and when income is Y_2, the best prediction for consumption is C_2. Furthermore, the line says that if income is expected to increase from Y_1 to Y_2 (i.e., by ΔY_1) consumption would be expected to increase from C_1 to C_2 (i.e., by ΔC_1).

The ratio of $\dfrac{\Delta C}{\Delta Y}$ is a very important element in the analysis. It is the *marginal propensity to consume*, the slope of the consumption function, b of our equation. In a straight line the slope is a constant, that is, it is the same wherever it is measured. Keynes reasoned that the marginal propensity to consume would get smaller as income gets larger; that is to say, he thought a curved line would be a closer approximation to the real world consumption function. More will be said about the realism of the function in the next chapter.

Less important than the marginal propensity to consume is the *average propensity to consume*, defined as $\dfrac{C}{Y}$. On a linear consumption function, the marginal propensity to consume (MPC) is constant, but the average propensity to consume (APC) declines as income gets larger. For this to be true, the intercept, a, must be positive. This is easy to see. Since $APC = \dfrac{C}{Y}$, and $C = a + bY$, $APC = \dfrac{a + bY}{Y}$.

If a were equal to zero the APC would be equal to $\dfrac{bY}{Y} = b$, and b is a constant. At very small incomes (Y) the APC would be dominated by a; in fact, if $Y = O$, then $APC = \dfrac{a}{O}$ which is customarily known as infinity. At that level of income at which $C = Y$, of course the $APC = 1$. At all smaller incomes $C > Y$ so $APC > 1$, and at all incomes larger than this, $Y > C$ so $APC < 1$ and falling. As a minimum, the APC approaches the MPC. This can readily be seen since in the expression $\dfrac{a + bY}{Y}$, as Y gets extremely large, the significance of a diminishes to nothing and for all practical purposes the APC becomes $\dfrac{bY}{Y}$ which reduces to b, the MPC.

It should be clear how important the consumption-income relation is to the entire analysis. In all economies, consumption is by far the largest component of national income, and this fact by itself means that if income is to be accurately forecast, consumption must also be predictable. The analysis being developed collapses if the consumption function is not relatively stable or at least if the shifts in it are not systematically predictable.

A word of warning. Students are frequently tempted to argue that a represents somehow the minimum standard of living for the economy. It does not! We have no idea how much consumption would be if income were, in fact, equal to zero. We have had no experience with such low levels of income. a should be thought of simply as the factor that establishes the height of the consumption function on the chart. Changes in the value of a can occur because of government restrictions on consumption, or because of changes in the social security system, or because of taxes and a number of other things; but this says nothing about what consumption would really be if income were zero.

The Saving Function

The saving function is derived from the definition of saving as the difference between national income and consumption. Since the 45 degree line labeled Z is equal to Y we can subtract the C-line from the Z line (Chart 6-4).

Chart 6-4

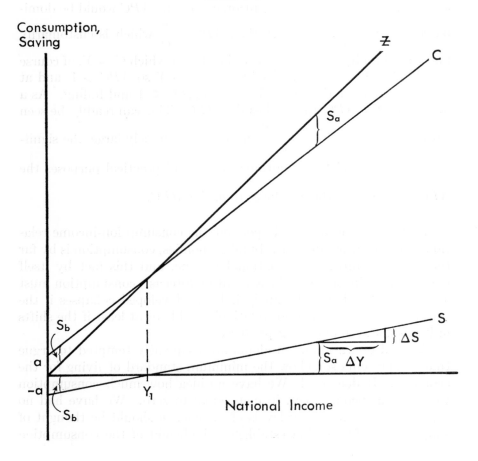

At $Y = 0$: $S = Y - C = Y - (a + bY)$, but if $Y = 0$, $S = -a$. At $Y = Y_1$: $Y = C$ so $S = Y - C = 0$. At incomes to the left of Y_1, $C > Y$ so $S < 0$ by the vertical distance between C and Z. At incomes greater than Y_1, $Y > C$ so $S > 0$ by the amount of the vertical distance between Z and C. Thus on the graph $S_a = S_a$; and $S_b = S_b$, etc.

It has already been shown that the equation for S is $S = -a + (1 - b) Y$. Thus the intercept is $-a$, and the slope of the S function is $1 - b$. Therefore, if b, the MPC, is $8/10$ the slope of the saving function is $1 - 8/10 = 2/10$.

In this example, if income were to increase by 20, consumption would increase by 16 and saving would increase by 4. Analogously to the consumption function, the slope of the saving function $(1 - b)$ is the marginal propensity to save (MPS) and is defined as $\dfrac{\Delta S}{\Delta Y}$.

Another way to demonstrate this is to start with the definition of $S = Y - C$, and observe that it is also true that $\Delta S = \Delta Y - \Delta C$. Now, dividing through by ΔY gives $\dfrac{\Delta S}{\Delta Y} = \dfrac{\Delta Y}{\Delta Y} - \dfrac{\Delta C}{\Delta Y}$; so, $\dfrac{\Delta S}{\Delta Y} = 1 - \dfrac{\Delta C}{\Delta Y}$, which says that the $MPS = 1 - MPC$.

The Investment Function

The investment function used in our present model is $I = I_o$, which appears graphically as a straight line parallel to the horizontal axis. Its intercept is I_o, a constant amount of investment. It has a slope of zero, which means that investment does not change as income changes. There are two reasons for adopting this form of the function: (1) Logically, current income should be irrelevant in the decision to invest. A decision to purchase investment goods for future production should be based on expected future income, which may be only influenced by present income. A theory of investment behavior using this proposition will be developed in the next chapter. (2) A statistical problem of discovering the investment-income relationship exists. If a regression of the actual amounts of investment and income were computed, the resulting function would be the same as our saving function because measured saving and investment are identical amounts. The justification for claiming that the regression is in fact the saving function, and not the investment function, lies in the belief that intended saving is relatively less volatile than intended investment, that investment is the active agent for change and saving is relatively passive.

The Multiplier

The concept of the multiplier, the notion that a given increase in investment or government spending would result in a multiplied effect on national income, was one of the most startling conclusions drawn from the Keynesian revolution. It is hoped that the section that follows will dispel any notions that any magic is involved, and that what happens to bring about this result is quite ordinary behavior by quite ordinary people. Money expansion multipliers were developed in Chapter 3, so the general idea is familiar. The procedure will be to demonstrate the multiplier algebraically, graphically, and in tabular form.

The Algebra of the Multiplier

We begin by defining multipliers in general as the change in a dependent variable per unit change in an independent variable. In aggregative economic analysis, the principal dependent variable of interest is national income, so we shall derive income multipliers. In the simple model we are using in this chapter, income would change if I changed, if a changed, or if b changed. What is usually referred to as "the" multiplier, or sometimes the "investment multiplier," is the amount by which income changes when investment changes, i.e., $\dfrac{\Delta Y}{\Delta I_o}$.

Recall the model presented earlier:

$$Y = C + I$$
$$C = a + bY$$
$$I = I_o$$

and the solution, or reduced form: $Y = \dfrac{a + I_o}{1 - b}$.

Now, if this same economy experiences an increase in the rate of investment of ΔI_o, the model appears as follows:

$$Y' = C' + I'$$
$$C' = a + bY'$$
$$I' = I_o + \Delta I_o$$

and the solution to this system is: $Y' = \dfrac{a + I_o + \Delta I_o}{1 - b}$.

We want to know the change in income (ΔY) which resulted from the change in investment (ΔI_o)

$$\Delta Y = Y' - Y = \frac{a + I_o + \Delta I_o}{1 - b} - \frac{a + I_o}{1 - b}$$

Subtracting: $\Delta Y = \dfrac{\Delta I_o}{1 - b}$.

If we now divide both sides of this statement by ΔI_o, we have discovered the multiplier: $\dfrac{\Delta Y}{\Delta I_o} = \dfrac{1}{1 - b}$.

Remembering that $1 - b = MPS$, we can say that this multiplier is the reciprocal of the marginal propensity to save.

Using the same numerical values of the parameters as before: $a = \$20$, $b = 8/10$, $I_o = \$30$, and adding $\Delta I_o = \$10$ we get the following results:

$$Y = \frac{a + I_o}{1 - b} = \frac{\$20 + \$30}{1 - 8/10} = \$250 \text{ billion}$$

$$Y' = \frac{a + I_o + \Delta I_o}{1 - b} = \frac{\$20 + \$30 + \$10}{1 - 8/10} = \$300 \text{ billion}$$

$$\Delta Y = Y' - Y = \$50 \text{ billion}$$

$$\frac{\Delta Y}{\Delta I_o} = \frac{50}{10} = 5 = \frac{1}{1 - b} = \frac{1}{1 - 8/10} = 5$$

The change in income of $50 billion is composed of the $10 billion of added new investment and $40 billion of added consumption. Our consumption function, $C = a + bY$, tells us that the original amount of consumption was $20 + 8/10 (\$250) = \$220$ and at the new equilibrium is $20 + 8/10 (\$300) = \$260$. Since the MPC is $8/10$, we can determine immediately that a change in income of $50 billion would induce 8/10's of $50 billion of additional consumption or $40 billion. The change in saving, we know, must be

2/10 of $50 billion or $10 billion, which is the amount necessary for saving to equal investment.

The Graphics of the Multiplier

Now we show the same events graphically. The graph is the same as the one shown previously, but with the new larger investment function.

Chart 6-5

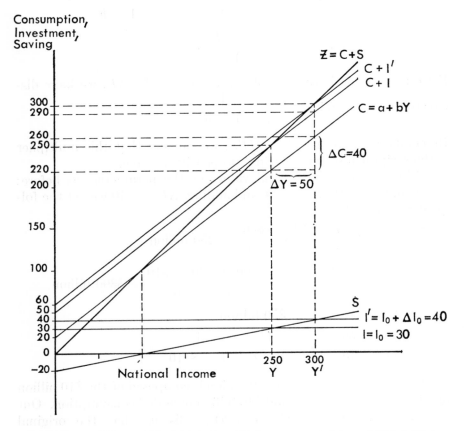

The original position of equilibrium income is at $250 billion, with consumption of $220 billion and saving and investment equal at $30 billion. Now the demand by business for investment increases by $10 billion per period. This means that aggregate demand is $260, still $220 billion of consumer demand plus the $40 billion of investment demand, whereas the current production of goods and services total just \$250 billion. Y is no longer an equilibrium income. The increased demand for investment creates new income, the recipients of which will increase their demand for consumption. In turn, this new demand for consumption generates new income which again stimulates further consumption. This process continues as long as aggregate demand $(C + I')$ exceeds aggregate supply $(C + S)$. It will stop when aggregate demand and aggregate supply are equal at Y' which is where the Z line intersects with the $C + I'$ line and where $S = I'$.

That the multiplier is the reciprocal of the slope of the saving function can be seen directly on Chart 6-5. Remembering the definition of the multiplier as $\dfrac{\Delta Y}{\Delta I_o}$, ΔY is the distance between the new and the old levels of equilibrium income $(Y' - Y)$, and ΔI_o is equal to ΔS, i.e. $(I' - I)$. The MPS is $\dfrac{\Delta S}{\Delta Y}$ which is the upside down, or reciprocal of $\dfrac{\Delta Y}{\Delta S}$, but this is equal to $\dfrac{\Delta Y}{\Delta I_o}$.

If the S-line is drawn very flat, that is, a very low MPS and hence a very large MPC, the change in income would be very large. Conversely, a steep S-function generates only a small change in Y.

The Movement to a New Level of Income

All of the preceding can be shown by means of a simple table, but it is now necessary to introduce explicit statements about the timing of the events. For this we attach time subscripts to the variables in the following way:

$$Y_t = C_t + I_t$$
$$C_t = a + bY_{t-1}$$
$$I_t = I_{ot} \text{ and } I'_t = I_{ot} + \Delta I_{ot}$$

Paul Samuelson has taught us the wisdom of checking up on our model in this way to be sure that the movement of the system is, in fact, toward the equilibrium position.[6] It would be a good exercise

---

[6] This involves what Samuelson calls the correspondence principle. See Paul F. Samuelson, *Foundations of Economic Analysis* (Cambridge, Massachusetts: Harvard University Press).

for the reader to test his understanding of this analysis by graphing a model in which the investment function has a steeper slope than the saving function. Now shift the investment function upward and find the new equilibrium. The next part of the exercise would be to construct a table similar to Table 6-1.

Table 6-1

PERIOD	Y	C	I	S	ACTUAL INVESTMENT	ACTUAL SAVING
0	250	220	30	30	30	30
1	260	220	40	30	40	40
2	268	228	40	32	40	40
3	274.4	234.4	40	33.6	40	40
4	279.5	239.5	40	34.9	40	40
.	.	.	,,	.	,,	,,
.	.	.	,,	.	,,	,,
.	.	.	,,	.	,,	,,
.	.	.	,,	.	,,	,,
n	300	260	40	40	40	40

Source: Hypothetical Data (see text).

The adjustment from the original equilibrium in Period 0 to the new equilibrium at Period n is a process of consumption increasing by continuously decreasing increments. Each increase in consumption is 8/10 (the MPC) of the preceding change in income. But each change in income (except the first one) is just the change in consumption, so each change in income is 8/10 of the change in income of the period before.[7]

Saving increases in every period also, but it increases by 2/10 of the preceding change in income. Intended saving is the same as actual saving only in the two rows representing equilibrium income. In the interim periods, intended saving is less than actual saving, and, of course, less than intended investment.

Notice that in this presentation, it is the household sector that makes all of the adjustment — not the business sector — in its inven-

---

[7]Another way to see the multiplier process is to observe that the summation of the changes in income are made up of the following series: $10 + 8/10\,(10) + (8/10)^2\,(10) + (8/10)^3\,(10) + (8/10)^4\,(10) + \ldots + (8/10)^n\,10 = \dfrac{10}{1-8/10} = 50$ which is the same as $10 \times \dfrac{1}{1-8/10}$, or the change in investment times the multiplier.

tories. Consumers are saving more than they intend to save because of our assumption that consumption spending lags behind the earning of income ($C_t = a + bY_{t-1}$). This can be justified by the observation that in this economy, income earned in a period is received at the end of the period, and hence is available for spending only in the next period.[8]

QUESTIONS

1. Give four definitions of "consumption" that incorporate the following words:
   (a) utility   c) production
   (b) destruction   d) spending
2. Do you think that a meaningful distinction between "capital goods" and "consumers goods" can be made?
3. Explain why income will move toward the equilibrium level when aggregate demand exceeds aggregate supply, and when aggregate demand is less than aggregate supply.
4. Consider the following model:

$$
\begin{aligned}
C &= a + bY & a &= \$30 \text{ billion} \\
I &= I_o & b &= 9/10 \\
Y &= C + I & I_o &= 25
\end{aligned}
$$

   (a) What are the equilibrium values of Y, C, S, and I?
   (b) What is the numerical value of the investment multiplier?
   (c) What would be the equilibrium values of Y, C, and S, if I_o became $30 billion?
   (d) What would be the equilibrium values of Y, C, S, and I, if a became $35 billion? (Assume $I_o = \$25$ billion.)
5. Draw Question 4 on graph paper.
6. Complete the following table for Question 4.

PERIOD		Y	C	I	S	ACTUAL SAVING
Equilibrium	(0)			25		
	1			30		
	2			30		
	3			30		
	4			30		
	5			30		
	.	.	.	.	.	.
	.	.	.	.	.	.
	.	.	.	.	.	.
Equilibrium	(n)			30		

See page 175 for Suggested Readings for Chapter 6.

---

[8]This is the technique contributed by Professor D. H. Robertson.

7 *Further Development of National Income Analysis*

The basic framework of the modern approach to national income determination was presented in Chapter 6. In this chapter some extensions and refinements are offered. We first develop the Hicksian analysis of equilibrium in the markets for goods and services called the *I-S* function, then the analysis of equilibrium in the money market, called the *L-M* function. This is followed by a comparison of some of the important elements in the theory as viewed by classical economists and by economists called Keynesians. The chapter is concluded with a discussion of the accelerator principle and the interaction of the multiplier principle and the accelerator.

THE GOODS MARKET

Three classes of markets can be distinguished in a modern economy — the market for goods and services of all kinds, the market for money, and the market for financial claims or securities. The three markets are interdependent. There can be an increase in the demand for goods and securities only if there is a decrease in the demand for money or an increase in the supply of money. Demand for money can be thought of as the supply of goods or of securities. Supply of goods and services can be thought of as the demand for money or for securities.

What is called the "goods market" is the market in which goods are exchanged for money, but money is merely the vehicle by which the exchange is effected. What is really involved is the exchange of goods and services for other goods and services. Productive goods and services are purchased by producing units and converted into final goods and services, which, in turn, are sold to those whose incomes were derived from the sale of the productive services.

The goods market is divided into the categories of goods that already have been described, namely, consumption, investment, government, and net foreign investment. All of these are incorporated in the *I-S* function that is developed in this chapter. Before the *I-S* curve is explained, however, a theory of investment must be considered.

Consumption theory is not explicitly covered in this section, but, since consumption is the difference between income and saving, everything that could be said about consumption is incorporated in the saving function. Likewise, government and net foreign investment are not explicitly covered. The reason for this is simply to keep the analysis from getting too complicated. The two demands, by government and by foreigners, can be added to the investment function.

The Marginal Efficiency of Capital and the Theory of Investment

It is now appropriate to ask the question: What will cause the investment function to shift upwards or downwards? Such a question can be answered only if one has a theory of investment behavior. The purpose of this section is to develop such a theory.

Decisions to invest are made by individual business units, not by business as a whole. Thus, the theory explaining investment expenditures must be based on the microtheory of the business firm. The firm's decision to invest in a physical asset will be affirmative if that asset is expected to yield a return greater than the return on alternative uses of funds. Presumably, businessmen would be able to rank the opportunities available to them at any moment according to their expected yields.

In this comparison, it is necessary to evaluate assets of differing durabilities. How, for example, would one choose between an asset expected to return $100 per year for 5 years with an asset expected to yield $20 per year for 30 years if they both cost the same amount of money? This brings up the more basic question of how one values any asset, the returns of which are to be received in the future. The answer depends upon what future returns are worth at the time the decision is made — in general, today. What, for example, is the value at this moment of $100 that is to be received one year from now, or of $100 to be received 50 years from today? In a society in which borrowing and lending take place, and in which positive interest rates exist, everyone adjusts to that rate. The value of $100 one

year from today is $\dfrac{\$100}{1+r}$, where r is the interest rate, and the value of

$100 fifty years from today is $\dfrac{\$100}{(1 + r)^{50}}$. This says that the present

value of a sum of money in the future is the amount needed today to
produce that sum in the future, if the interest rate remains at r.

We can look upon any physical asset as the present embodiment
of returns that will accrue in the future. Its worth in the present,
then, is the discounted value of all of its expected future returns.
The usual formula for the determination of present value is:

$$V = \frac{a_1}{1 + r} + \frac{a_2}{(1 + r)^2} + \frac{a_3}{(1 + r)^3} + \ldots + \frac{a_n + S}{(1 + r)^n}$$

Where V is the present value of any durable asset,
   a is the expected annual returns in dollars,
   r is the interest rate used to discount those returns, and
   S is the expected value of the asset at some date in the future,
   usually what is thought of as the "lifetime" of the asset, that is,
   the salvage value.

A very significant portion of the fields of accountancy and managerial economics is involved in the calculation of the a's. For most
physical assets, $a_1, a_2 \ldots a_n$ are different, i.e., $a_1 \neq a_2 \neq a_3 \neq \ldots \neq a_n$.
Each a is calculated as the expected net return from owning the asset
over not owning the asset. This means that the additional revenue
and the additional costs must all be estimated in all future periods.
These, necessarily, will all be forecasts since they involve the future
in an uncertain world. The most important cost to be included, from
the point of view of our development of the theory, is the cost of
uncertainty. This can be handled as a premium similar to an insurance premium, but it is the essence of business profit that certain
risks cannot be insured against, so the firm must absorb them in its
calculation of cost. This cost must include a subjective estimate on
the part of the firm's major decision makers, but, in part, it can be
scientifically computed.[1]

There is sometimes a question about which rate of interest to use
as the discounting factor. We hope we have avoided this problem by
including all the risk and other costs in the numerators of the equation so that the interest rate should be the pure rate, the rate reflect-

---

[1]There is a number of ways risk can be handled in these calculations, but it
would take us too far afield to properly develop any of them.

ing only time preference. In the real world, the closest we can get to this, probably, is the rate on short-term Treasury bills.

We have just seen how the value of any asset can be calculated. The firm will find it profitable to invest in any asset, the value of which to it is greater than its price to the firm. It is now to be demonstrated that where the value is greater than the cost the marginal efficiency of capital is greater than the rate of interest.

The *marginal efficiency of capital* (*MEC*) is to be defined with reference to the following equation:

$$C = \frac{a_1}{1 + m} + \frac{a_2}{(1 + m)^2} + \frac{a_3}{(1 + m)^3} + \ldots + \frac{a_n + S}{(1 + m)^n}$$

Where m is the *MEC*, the a's and S are defined exactly as before, and C is the price to the firm of the asset being considered — what Keynes called the supply price of capital. It should be obvious that since the a's are the same for a given asset, if V is greater than C, then m is greater than r. This leads to the assertion that firms will invest as long as the *MEC* is greater than the rate of interest.

As output in the capital goods producing industry expands, the price of capital goods will increase because the marginal cost of producing them is a rising function. It is clear from the equation of the preceding paragraph that as C rises, m falls. This argument is sufficient to establish the negative slope of the *MEC* in the aggregate economy. In other words, the statement that the marginal efficiency of capital declines as investment increases is tantamount to the assertion that the supply price of capital increases as investment increases.

It is now our purpose to derive the demand schedule for capital goods. The individual business unit ranks all of its conceivable investment outlets according to the *MEC* as in Chart 7-1, page 150. This particular firm could spend $10,000 on machines or other equipment, which would be expected to yield at least 10 percent. If it were to spend $20,000, it would have to buy lower yielding items; according to Chart 7-1, the last dollar spent would yield just 7 percent. This would happen for two reasons. First, less productive types of capital might be used; and second, even if homogeneous capital is involved, according to the law of variable proportions the marginal product of capital would be expected to decline as more capital is employed.

Chart 7-1

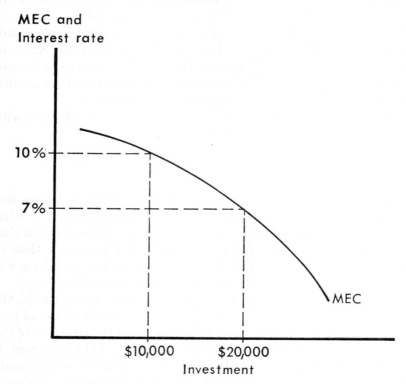

This firm would be expected to demand exactly $10,000 of investment, if the interest rate were 10 percent, because each of the dollars spent up to $10,000 has an *MEC* greater than the rate of interest; and, therefore, the value or worth to this firm of the asset purchased is greater than its price. Similarly, if the rate of interest were 7 percent, this firm would be expected to spend $20,000 on physical assets. Notice that it is immaterial whether the firm has its own funds to invest. For example, if it does have $50,000 of retained earnings and the interest rate is 7 percent, it would invest $20,000 in its own business and lend the rest at 7 percent. If it has no money of its own, it would be profitable to borrow at 7 percent in order to invest in all of the opportunities expected to yield more than 7 percent. Of course, the real world is not quite this neat and simple but the principle still holds.

Any *demand curve* is defined as a schedule of the quantities of the commodity buyers wish to buy at all conceivable prices. In this case, the price is the interest rate. The *MEC* schedule is a graph of the quantities of investment the firm would wish to make at all conceivable interest rates. Since the *MEC* curve for a single firm incorporates prices of capital goods, a decrease in the prices of such goods (*ceteris paribus*) would shift the whole schedule to the right. Now if we aggregate all of the individual *MEC* curves, we have the *MEC* curve for the whole economy as the demand for investment as a function of the rate of interest.

Knowledge of the kinds of events which will cause the *MEC* schedule to shift upwards or downwards is indispensable to the business conditions analyst. The subject is far too large for an exhaustive discussion here, but we can mention certain classes of events which would effect the *MEC*. The most important category in this connection is innovation in the broad Schumpeterian sense. The innovations may increase the physical productivity of capital by lowering the cost of production, or may affect the value of the output by increasing the demand for it. Outside events, such as changes in tax provisions, or other governmental policies or any number of other changes in the environment of business, will have an effect in one direction or the other. The class of events that projects uncertainty more or less into future forecasts of profits has been so often emphasized, particularly by Keynes and his followers. Greater uncertainty leads to a higher risk premium being included in costs and so a shift downward in the *MEC*. Pure optimism or pessimism, even if the cause for it cannot be found, will shift the function. All evidence leads to the conclusion that the *MEC* schedule is one of the most volatile functions with which economists have to deal.

The *I-S* Function

If the interest rate is known, the rate of investment is determined, and given a stable savings function the level of equilibrium income is established. Different rates of interest induce different rates of investment and, therefore, different levels of equilibrium rates of income. The *I-S* function is a set or locus of points with each point representing an interest rate and the corresponding compatible income. On this line intended saving equals intended investment, and the marginal efficiency of capital is equal to the rate of interest. Chart 7-2, page 152, demonstrates the graphic derivation.

Chart 7-2

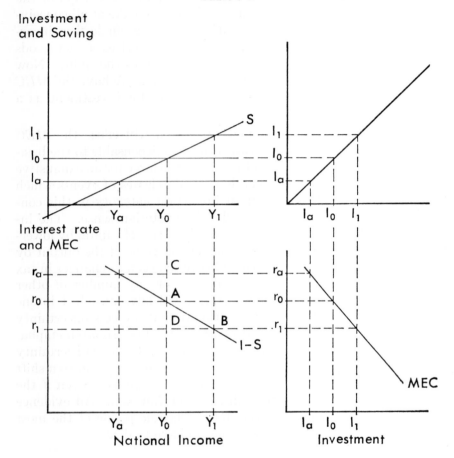

Investment
and Saving

Interest rate
and MEC

National Income

Investment

Chart 7-2 shows the derivation of two points on the I-S function. Starting at the lower right-hand chart, if the interest rate is r_o, the rate of investment will be I_o. The upper right-hand chart contains only the 45° line, which assures that I_o measured on the horizontal axis is equal to I_o measured on the vertical axis. Where the saving function of the upper left-hand chart intersects the investment function is the equilibrium income consistent with interest rate r_o. This then gives us one point on the I-S function, point A. Point B is found by the same technique as are all other points on the I-S curve.

What would happen if the economy had an interest rate of r_a, and income were at Y_o, that is, at point C to the right of the I-S curve?

Since r_a is a very high rate of interest, investment would be curtailed back to a level of I_a. At income Y_o, saving is greater than I_a, so either actual saving is less than intended saving, or actual investment is greater than intended investment. In either case, we know that income must fall. In this case, it would fall to Y_a, which is a point on I-S. Conversely, of course, at a point to the left of the I-S curve such as D, intended investment would exceed intended saving and income would rise.

THE MONEY MARKET

The determination of equilibrium national income in the goods market depends upon particular interest rates being given. For the model to be complete, the interest rate must be determined; that is, the reason that the interest rate is what it is and the kind of forces that will cause it to change must be explained. It is to the money market that we look for the theory of interest.

The Theory of Interest

The interest theory to be discussed now is called the liquidity preference theory. It was the theory Keynes advanced, although what is to be presented here draws from the work of later contributors as well. According to this theory, interest is determined by the supply of and the demand for money. We touched upon the supply of money theory in Chapter 3, and we will make no additions to it here. Remember that we defined money to include demand deposits and currency.

Every dollar of the supply of money must be held by someone, so there is no question of how much money people and business do hold. The question asked by demand-for-money theory is how much do they wish to hold.

The demand for money is divided into two basic categories. The first we shall refer to as working balance demand or active balances, and the second category will be referred to variously as pure liquidity preference, or as the speculative demand for money, or sometimes as the asset demand for money, or again as inactive balances.

Demand for Money for Working Balances

The demand for money for working balance purposes is a function of the money value of national income, in equation form: $M_W^D = f(Y)$.

According to classical economists, this was the only reason for holding money, that is, for transactions purposes. Every economic unit needs some cash to bridge the time span between receipts of money, during which time outflows of funds take place. Everyone is familiar to some extent with this reason for holding cash. To operate effectively as a going concern or as a household, one simply needs some money. How much one needs depends upon the nature of his receipts and expenditures. Different types of businesses need differing amounts of money, but it is probably a correct generalization to say that any household or business unit would need more money the larger its level of economic activity. This would seem to be true whether the increased activity is in increased physical output or in higher prices of the same output.

Chart 7-3

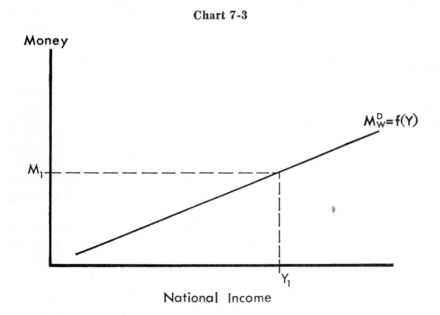

Chart 7-3 demonstrates the positive relation between the amount of money demanded for working balances and the level of national income. In it, income is the independent variable and the demand for money is the dependent variable; that is, when income is Y_1, money demanded for working balances will be M_1.

In the theory, it is assumed that the amount of money people wish to hold for this purpose is the amount they actually do hold.

Pure Liquidity Preference

The term liquidity preference is meant to indicate that money held for the speculative motive is held in preference to other assets. This is also why some economists refer to these balances as asset balances. In some respects money is superior to other assets, and in some respects other assets are superior to money. The price of money is constant in terms of the unit of account, and is, therefore, perfectly liquid. Its value, however, is variable in terms of the things it will command.

Debt instruments, which shall be referred to generally as bonds, are similar to money in that the legal obligation is stated in terms of the unit of account, so bonds and money share the quality of variable value in terms of the goods and services they will buy. This means that if inflation is expected, money and bonds would both be expected to lose value; and if deflation were expected, bonds and money would both gain in real value. On this consideration alone, bonds would be preferred to money in that an interest income is attached to the bonds.

There is a risk involved in holding bonds rather than money. The risk is that interest rates will rise because a rise in interest rates is equivalent to a decrease in the price of outstanding bonds. One would hold money if the expected loss in the capital value of the bond is greater than the interest income the bond yields over the relevant period of time. If the current interest rate is very high, two factors should be noted. One, the interest income to offset any losses in bond prices is high. Two, any given interest rate change (increase) will have a relatively small effect on the price of bonds. This leads to the conclusion that when interest rates are high, the demand for money in the expectation of rising interest rates will be smaller than when the interest rate is low.

A low current rate of interest induces more holding of money because the cost of holding it (the foregone interest income) is low. A given change in the interest rate has a relatively large capital value effect, and the earnings to offset such capital losses are small. Keynes and others have argued further that when interest rates are high, expectations are likely to be that they will fall so less money would be demanded. Whereas when interest rates are low, the bulk of anticipation will be that the rate will rise, and so induce more demand for money for the speculative motive.

All of this leads to the conclusion that the demand for money to hold as an asset is a negative function of the current rate of interest. Its general shape seems to be that shown in Chart 7-4. An interest rate of r_2 would induce M_2 amount of money to be held for pure liquidity preference purposes.

Chart 7-4

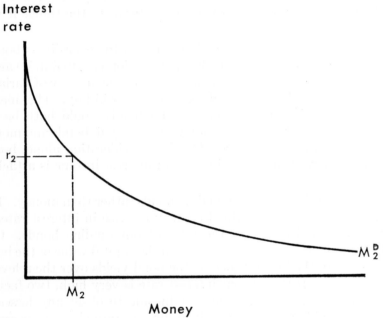

The *L-M* Function

Now we can combine the two types of demand for money and the supply of money to form a new function, the *L-M* curve.

In the derivation of the *L-M* function, it is convenient to start at the lower right-hand chart. Choose any income, such as Y_o, which indicates that the amount of money people wish to hold, and, in fact, do hold for working balance purposes is M_1. The total money supply is shown on the lower left-hand chart. There, a 45° line is drawn from the total money supply measured on the horizontal axis to the same amount measured on the vertical axis. Observe that OM_1 is equal to $\overline{OM}^S - OX_2$ (by right triangles) so that OX_2 is the amount of the money supply not being used for working balances. This is the

Chart 7-5

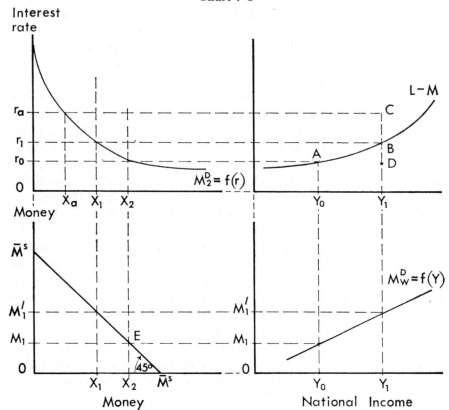

amount that is available for holding for other purposes, namely, as speculative balances.[2]   The interesting thing is that this money, because it exists, must be held whether people want to hold it or not. What makes them willing to hold it is a particular rate of interest. The graph in the upper left hand of the chart shows that the public is willing to hold exactly OX_2 only if the rate of interest is r_o.

Point A on the upper right-hand chart is a point of equilibrium of interest rate r_o, given an income of Y_o. Likewise, point B is a point

---

[2] Thus, $\overline{OM}_1 = X_2E$. $X_2\overline{M}^SE$ is a right triangle since $\angle X_2 = 90°$ and $\angle E$ and $\angle \overline{M}^S = 45°$. EX_2 is therefore equal to $X_2\overline{M}^S = O\overline{M}_1$. $X_2\overline{M}^S = O\overline{M}^S - OX_2$. Looking at the situation the other way, note that if $O\overline{M}_1$ is used for transactions balances, the rest of the money supply $(O\overline{M}^S - OM_1)$ is available for speculative balances. $O\overline{M} - OM_1 = M_1E$ because triangle $M_1E\overline{M}^S$ is a right triangle. Therefore, $OX_2 = M_1E$ is the part available for speculative holdings that is transferred to the chart above.

showing that income Y_1 is compatible with interest rate r_1, and so on for all other points on L-M. Any point on L-M represents a possible condition of equilibrium in the money market where supply of money and the demand for it are equal. As with the I-S function, any shift of the functions making up the L-M function will cause a shift in the L-M curve.

Suppose the system is not in equilibrium. What is the nature of the forces at work in the economy to drive interest rates and/or income to the position we have called equilibrium? Take a point such as C, a point to the left of the L-M curve. Income is Y_1, so the amount of money demanded for working or transactions purposes is OM_1', which means that OX_1 is available for speculative holdings. Point C interest rate is r_a, but if the interest rate is r_a, the amount of money the public wishes to hold is just OX_a, which is less than the amount they must hold. Now if more money is held than the holders wish to hold, we would expect them to try to get out of money and into bonds. The offers to buy bonds would drive the price of bonds up — thus driving current yields on the bonds, and hence current interest rates, down. Therefore, if interest rates are above equilibrium, competitive pressures in the bond markets will push the interest rates downwards towards equilibrium.

To cement his comprehension of this analysis, the reader is invited to prove that if the interest rate and income were at the point labeled D, that is, any point to the right of L-M, the forces operative in the system would move interest rates upward towards L-M.

Both the L-M and the I-S curves represent possible points of equilibrium of income and interest rates. But there is an infinity of points on both curves so equilibrium can exist only at that point which is common to both curves, that is, at their intersection. Chart 7-6 shows this situation.

A good exercise to see why income would really be Y_e and why the interest rate would really be at r_e is to ask the question: What would the economic environment be like if a different combination of income and interest existed? To do this select a point such as A on Chart 7-6, which is neither on the L-M nor on the I-S curve. Take the analysis in steps. First, since A is to the left of the L-M curve, by the reasoning we used above, the interest rate would have to fall to point B. Point B, however, is to the right of the I-S, and by our earlier argument (pages 152–153), income would fall to the level represented by point C. C is to the left of the L-M function so the interest rate would fall to the point represented by D, but since D is to the left of the I-S curve, income would rise to point E.

Chart 7-6

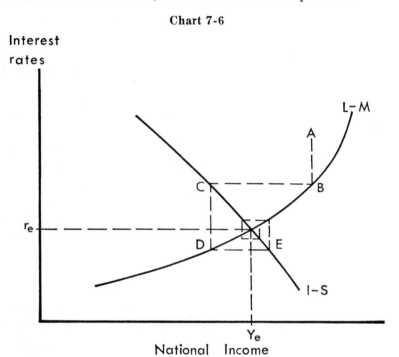

If this mechanism is continued, clearly, interest and income would oscillate in the direction of the equilibrium levels. Our approach here has been very mechanistic. The real world does not operate exactly in this step fashion, which we adopted for pedagogical reasons. The exact path by which the forces at work operate to move income and interest towards equilibrium is dependent upon several time lags. To be candid about the matter, we still have a great deal to learn about these lags. Professor Hicks, who first advanced the cobweb theorem in this context, proposed some rather complicated lags in both the money and the goods markets. It takes time for consumption spending (or saving) to react to changes in income, for investment spending to change when interest rates change, and for money balances to change as income and interest rates change.[3]

---

[3]J. R. Hicks, *A Contribution to the Theory of the Trade Cycle* (Oxford: Oxford University Press, 1950), Chapter XI.

KEYNES AND THE CLASSICS

If the analysis that has just been developed is to be of significant value, we should know something about the probable shapes of the various functions and about the events or circumstances that will cause the functions to shift. Such understanding cannot be achieved within the confines of this book, but some of the major questions can be considered.

Lord Keynes' *The General Theory of Employment, Interest, and Money* was written during the depressed period of the early 1930's and was inevitably influenced by the prevailing economic conditions. He made a number of observations about the nature of the relationships we have been discussing which have become associated with the term Keynesian since in several cases they were in sharp conflict with the prevailing view of economists. In large part, *The General Theory* was an attempt to refute what Keynes called the classical school though basically the direct target was his eminent colleague, Arthur C. Pigou.

Consumption and Saving

In previous chapters on the history of business cycle thought, we had occasion to observe that earlier economists stressed the interest rate as the major determinant of the division between saving and consumption and, therefore, given the level of income, saving is a function of the rate of interest. Keynes rejected this functional relationship completely, arguing that no one received interest for saving. To get interest one has to give up the holding of money and make it available to someone else. Such an argument has no validity in denying the interest-saving relation, but it does support the search for an alternative approach. The unusual features of Keynes' approach to interest theory, which we refer to as the liquidity preference theory, will be discussed below.

The Keynesian approach to saving was, as we saw earlier, to postulate that the major factor determining the volume of saving is the level of income. Classical economists would not necessarily disagree with that contention, but, according to their theory, it wouldn't be very pertinent since real income was determined primarily by the quality and quantity of the society's employed resources, and the money value of national income was determined by money and its velocity.

The particular form of the consumption or saving function suggested by Keynes was that the marginal propensity to consume declined as income increased, which implies that the marginal propensity to save increases as income gets large. Chart 7-7 shows such consumption and saving functions.

Chart 7-7

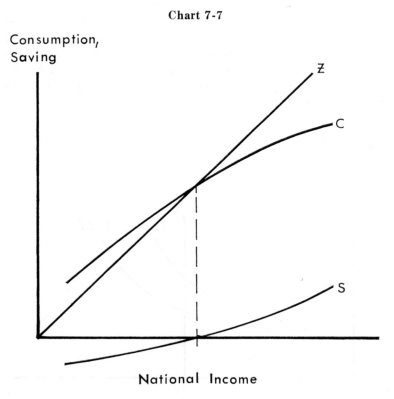

Consumption, Saving

National Income

These shapes seem so plausible by introspection that many economists accepted them without further evidence. Others have tested them empirically and posed new hypotheses about saving and consumption behavior. Some of the conclusions of these studies will be covered later. Also, we will consider the implications of such functions for economic policy.

Investment

The most significant Keynesian hypothesis regarding the marginal efficiency of capital refers to its elasticity. Classical economists believe that whenever the interest rate falls, the rate of investment increases; that is, the *MEC* curve is interest elastic. Keynes felt that, at least during depressed times and when interest rates are already low, a decrease in the rate of interest would have no effect in stimulating investment expenditures; that is, Keynes' *MEC* curve is interest inelastic.

This feature of the Keynesian system is one of the reasons for the extreme difference between the classics and the Keynesians on economic policy. Classical economists expect monetary policy to be effective in increasing national income, whereas Keynesians do not. The reasoning is easily seen with reference to the *I-S, L-M* framework as shown on Chart 7-8.

Chart 7-8

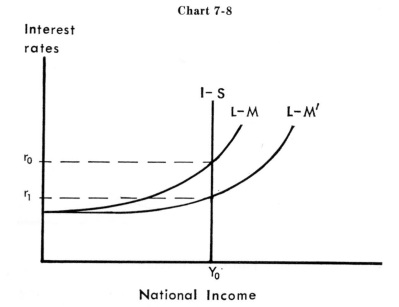

National Income

An inelastic *MEC* schedule means that the *I-S* function is also inelastic, so that an increase in the money supply which shifts the *L-M* function to the right has no effect on national income.

Liquidity Preference and the Rate of Interest

Another feature of the rigid Keynesian structure which makes monetary policy ineffective is the so-called "liquidity trap." This liquidity trap occurs when the liquidity preference function is infinitely elastic as in Chart 7-9.

Chart 7-9

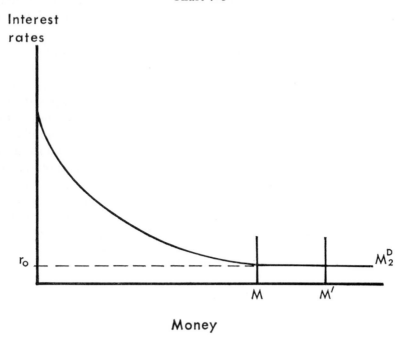

Money

In the range to the right end of the curve, an increase in the money supply available for speculative holdings of cash will have no effect on the rate of interest. Having no effect on the rate of interest, there will also be no influence on investment, and hence no change in income. This can be shown on the *I-S*, *L-M* graph. See Chart 7-10, page 164.

Increases in the money supply shift the *L-M* curve in the manner of *L-M'* and *L-M''*, and this will have the effect of decreasing interest and increasing income as long as the *L-M* function is less than completely elastic. Where the function is infinitely elastic, however, money supply changes are completely ineffective. Subjecting the liquidity preference theory to statistical evidence leads to the general conclusion that the shape is roughly consistent with those we have drawn.[4] It is not entirely clear, however, that a liquidity trap would ever exist, but even if it does not, the function may be so elastic at

---

[4] See W. L. Smith and R. L. Teigen, *Readings in Money, National Income and Stabilization Policy* (Homewood, Illinois: Richard D. Irwin, Inc., 1965). Ronald Teigen has summarized the empirical studies in the article, "The Demand for and Supply of Money," pp. 44–76. See particularly pp. 49–60.

times that a large increase in the money supply might be needed to effect a relatively small fall in interest rates. In this situation, fiscal policy might be the preferred policy tool.

The classical position is quite the reverse of the liquidity trap hypothesis. Based on the quantity theory of money,[5] the rigid classical conclusion is that any increase in the money supply would become a part of active (or transactions) balances, as opposed to the liquidity trap situation where all of the increased money would simply increase the holdings of inactive balances. In the classical case, income would increase enough to increase the demand for active balances in amount sufficient to absorb all of the new money. The rigid Keynesian case argues that income would remain constant so there would be no need for additional active balances. Most contemporary economists believe that the real world situation has to be described as being somewhere between these two polar positions.

Chart 7-10

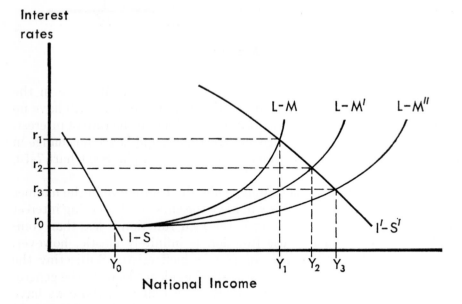

The Real System

Up to this point, the analysis has been cast in money value terms, but our primary interest is in the real system — the actual goods and

_____
[5]See Chapter 3.

services produced, consumed, and so on. If the price level is constant throughout the time of the events included in the analysis, this would constitute no problem. If, for instance, national income in value terms increased by 10 percent, real national income would also increase by 10 percent. At very large levels of unemployment and great excess capacity of productive facilities, this situation is likely to be closely approximated. At the other extreme, that is, full employment and near capacity utilization of capital, any change in the money level of national income is likely to be almost completely a change in the price level, since real output is near its maximum.

Classical economic theory concluded that full employment was the equilibrium to which the system would always adjust. Therefore, classical economists concentrated their attention on price level behavior, and their interest in saving and investment was directed at the impact on future production, not as a determinant of current income.

The Keynesian conclusion that the economy might be in equilibrium at less than full employment was a direct denial of the whole structure of classical thought. In order to bring out the issues of the controversy, we will present the classical reasoning, the Keynesian challenge, and the classical rebuttal.

If the economy exhibits unemployment, it signifies that the total demand for output is less than the potential output. A classical economist would contend that unemployed workers and the owners of other unused factors would lower the prices of their services making it economical for more of them to be reemployed.

Most classical theorists made the mistake of handling this question with the tools of partial equilibrium theory. They reasoned that the lower wages resulting from the pressure of unemployment would shift the firm's marginal cost curve downward, leading to increased output and lower product price. The increased output would absorb the unemployed resources, and the pressure for falling wages would continue until full employment was reached.

The great Swedish economist, Knut Wicksell, was probably the most adamant critic of this approach. He pointed out that in the total economy, the income earned by laborers and other resource owners was what they used to demand the output. Thus the demand curve for the product of a firm could be held constant while the marginal cost curve shifted due to lower wages paid by that firm, but it is completely erroneous to do so for the entire economy.

Keynes, too, adopted this position. He believed that wages, in particular, and prices, generally, were not flexible. While the upward movement of wages would take place quite easily, Keynes said that workers would vigorously resist the lowering of their wages. Furthermore, he argued, lower wages would be effective in stimulating increased output only if the real wage, that is, the money wage divided by the price level, were lowered and workers and their unions could have an influence only on the money wage rate.

Another way to see the issues involved is to observe that if labor agrees to lower the money wage rate such that the marginal cost curves of all firms decrease, the demand curve for the output of the firms will also decrease. According to Keynesians, there is no reason to believe that the marginal cost curve would shift more than the demand curve. The result of lowering money wages is shown in Chart 7-11.

Chart 7-11

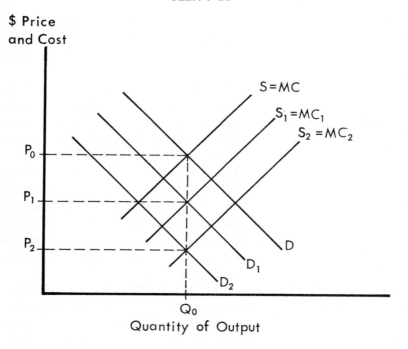

The situation depicted is what Keynes referred to as "doomsday," with wages and prices falling continuously while employment and production continue at a depressed level.

The Pigou Effect

The classical response to this argument was offered by A. C. Pigou; in fact, it has been titled "the Pigou effect." It is also called "the real balance effect," since it involves the real value of money balances.

Pigou says that as prices are falling in the manner just described there is an important reason for believing that the demand curve for the firm's output will not fall as much as does the supply curve when wages fall. That reason is that holders of money become wealthier in real terms without anyone else becoming less wealthy. With debt instruments other than money, the creditors become wealthier and so would be expected to increase their real demand for goods and services, but that increase in demand would be approximately offset by the decrease in demand of debtors who become less wealthy as prices fall, and the real burden of their debt becomes more severe. The government and the banks are the debtors in the case of money outstanding, and neither would be expected to react to an increase in the real value of their debt as would other debtors. However, the important characteristics of money as debt are that there is no interest paid by the debtor, and money is a perpetual debt so the principal need never be repaid.

Another way to look at the significance of the Pigou effect is to consider the Keynesian national income analysis in real rather than money value terms. According to this theory, national income is determined at the intersection of the saving and investment functions, and Keynes said that this intersection could occur at a level insufficient to provide full employment. Adding the real balance effect, however, amounts to saying that saving and consumption depend not only on current income but also on wealth. Falling prices have no effect on the real value of goods nor on the aggregate real value of financial instruments, except money. The real value of money would increase, causing real consumption to increase and, therefore, causing real saving to decrease.

The Pigou effect can be included in the theory by using as the saving function: $S = f\left(Y, \dfrac{M}{P}\right)$, where $\dfrac{M}{P}$ is the money supply divided by the price level and hence is a measure of the real value of money holdings. If P falls while M is constant, or if M rises when P is constant, real balances increase and S falls. On our familiar saving and investment chart, the classical system includes the proposition that the saving function will shift downward as long as unemployment exists.

Consider the situation of Chart 7-12. Income is at the Keynesian equilibrium of Y_1 where S and I are equal. The inclusion of the Pigou effect is to cause S to shift in the direction of S_f at which point the economy would be in equilibrium at Y_f, full employment national income.

Chart 7-12

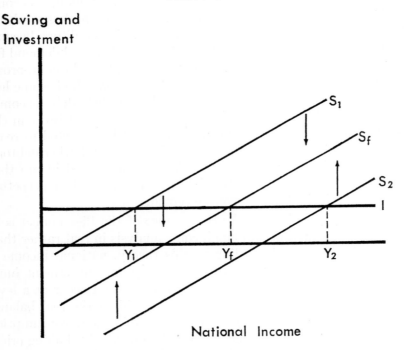

The analysis would presumably apply in the case of rising wages and prices as well. If, for example, the saving curve were to the right of (below) the S_f curve so that national income were greater than the full employment level, inflation would be in process. Rising wages and prices would reduce the real value of money balances $\left(\dfrac{M}{P}\right)$ so that economic units would attempt to increase their holdings of money by increasing their rate of saving. In other words, the saving function would shift from S_2 in the direction of S_f to return national income from Y_2 to Y_f.

MULTIPLIER–ACCELERATOR INTERACTION

In Chapter 5 the acceleration principle was seen to produce cyclical behavior in certain industries. The same sort of forces are operative on the macrolevel of analysis. The theory that is outlined here as the multiplier-accelerator interaction theory has become an important contemporary explanation of business cycles.

The multiplier process is capable of explaining why income and expenditures rise in a cumulative fashion once an expansive act occurs, or why economic activity declines cumulatively in response to some contractive action. The theory itself does not explain the turning points of business cycles. Other theories must be introduced for that purpose, such as Keynes' psychologically caused shifts in the marginal efficiency of capital.

The essential feature of introducing the acceleration principle into the theory is that cycles are generated as a part of the response mechanism of the economy. The basic difference between a "multiplier type" model and a model that incorporates the accelerator lies in the nature of the investment function.

A multiplier type investment function makes investment depend on the level of national income. A large national income is associated with a large level of investment. There is an aspect of this which is rather strange. It implies that if income were constant at some high level, investment would also be constant at a high rate. In a business firm, one would expect that if the level of production were constant, the firm would have no need for new equipment except to replace that which wears out or becomes obsolete, neither of which expenditures are a part of net investment. A firm would purchase additional capital only to meet expected increases in its rate of production.

An accelerator type investment function takes this reasoning into account, making investment depend on the change in national income and not on the level of income.[6] This implies that if national income is constant, no matter at what level, investment expenditures would be zero. The accelerator, then, is a dynamic theory where time plays an important role.

The easiest way to see why the accelerator generates cycles and why multiplier type investment relations do not is through the use of an example. First, compare the investment functions themselves:

[6]Frequently, writers relate investment to change in consumption, rather than in income, which sometimes leaves the impression that this is the distinctive feature of the accelerator. It is not! Making changes in consumption or income the independent variable has no effect upon the cycle generating capability of the model.

(1) $I = \bar{I} + iY$ (multiplier type investment function)

(1') $I' = \bar{I}' + A \, \Delta Y$ (accelerator type investment function)

In these two equations, $\bar{I}$ and $\bar{I}'$ are autonomous investment parameters, the portion of investment which does not vary as income varies. In the discussion we will ignore that portion and use the equations:

$$I = iY \text{ in place of (1) and}$$

$$I' = A \, \Delta Y \text{ in place of (1').}$$

A study of Tables 7-1 and 7-2 should bring out the distinction being made between a multiplier model and a model that incorpor-

Table 7-1

PERIOD	Y	C	$\bar{I}$	I_i	I
0	800.00	670.00	50.00	80.00	130.00
1	810.00	670.00	60.00	80.00	140.00
2	819.00	678.00	60.00	81.00	141.00
3	827.10	685.20	60.00	81.90	141.90
4	834.39	691.68	60.00	82.71	142.71
5	840.95	697.51	60.00	83.44	143.44
6	846.86	702.76	60.00	84.10	144.10
7	852.18	707.49	60.00	84.69	144.69
8	856.97	711.75	60.00	85.22	145.22
9	861.28	715.58	60.00	85.70	145.70
10	865.46	719.33	60.00	86.13	146.13
⋮	⋮	⋮	⋮	⋮	⋮
n	900.00	750.00	60.00	90.00	150.00

ates both the multiplier and the accelerator. Table 7-1 is the multiplier model constructed from the following equations and parameter values:

(1) $Y_t = C_t + I_t$

(2) $C_t = a + bY_{t-1}$

(3) $I_t = \bar{I}_t + iY_{t-1}$

$a = 30, b = 8/10, \bar{I}_o = 50, \bar{I}_1 = 60, i = 1/10$

The first row is found by solving for equilibrium income in period O, as follows:

$$Y_o = \frac{a + \bar{I}}{1 - b - i} = \frac{30 + 50}{1 - 8/10 - 1/10} = 800$$

$$C_o = a + bY_o = 30 + 8/10\ (800) = 670$$

$$I_o = \bar{I}_o + iY_o = 50 + 1/10\ (800) = 50 + 80 = 130$$

The latter rows are completed by first finding consumption as a function of income in the preceding period, then finding induced investment (I_i) also as a function of the preceding income, and adding $C + I$ to find Y.

In this table, Y will always increase because once the rate of autonomous investment has increased, consumption and investment must both increase. Increases in consumption and investment are an increase in income which, in turn, means that consumption and investment in the following period must increase. Each of the increases is smaller than the one which went before it, and all variables will approach new equilibria as shown in period n.

Table 7-2

	PERIOD	Y	C	$\bar{I}$	I_A	I
	0	800	700	100	0	100
	1	810	700	110	0	110
	2	828	708	110	10	120
	3	850.4	722.4	110	18	128
	4	872.72	740.32	110	22.4	132.4
	5	890.50	758.18	110	22.32	132.32
P	6	900.18	772.40	110	17.78	127.78
	7	899.82	780.14	110	9.68	119.68
	8	889.49	779.85	110	−.36	109.64
	9	871.26	771.59	110	−10.33	99.67
	10	848.78	757.01	110	−18.23	91.77
	11	826.55	739.03	110	−22.48	87.52
	12	809.02	721.25	110	−22.23	87.77
T	13	799.70	707.23	110	−17.53	92.47
	14	800.45	699.77	110	−9.32	100.68
	15	811.12	700.37	110	.75	110.75

Table 7-2 shows the accelerator in action and was constructed from the following (continued next page):

$$Y_t = C_t + I_t$$

$$C_t = a + b\,Y_{t-1}$$

$$I_t = \bar{I}_t + A\ (Y_t - Y_{t-1})$$
$$a = 60,\ b = 8/10,\ \bar{I}_o = 100,\ \bar{I}_1 = 110,\ A = 1$$

Equilibrium income is found from $Y_o = \dfrac{a + \bar{I}_o}{1 - b}$ at which income $C_t = a + b\,Y_{t-1} = 60 + 8/10\ (800) = 700$. Investment is 100, which is the autonomous portion $(\bar{I})$ only. Induced investment (I_A) is zero because income is at equilibrium, therefore constant, so $Y_e - Y_{o-1} = 0$.

Table 7-2 has been carried out to 15 periods to show that with these particular values of the MPC $(b = 8/10)$ and "the relation" $(A = 1)$ a cycle is indeed operating with a peak or upper turning point in period 6 and a trough or lower turning point at period 13. Other values of b and A would produce different behavior. This particular set creates a slightly explosive or divergent cycle; another set (both A and b) would lead to damped or convergent cycles; in other cases, the multiplier effect would swamp the accelerator so that income would move only in one direction.[7]

The acceleration principle is a good example for warning about too mechanistic an approach to determining cause and effect. On the basis of the statistics alone, one might conclude that, since investment declined earliest (period 5), this was the "cause" of the ensuing depression. But why did I fall? Because the increase in income from period 4 to 5 was less than the increase from period 3 to 4. Why was this true? We already know that the reason for the cycle is the relative sizes of the response mechanism and the structure of the economy. In this case, at least, the search for direct cause and effect would be fruitless.

The accelerator relation (A) can be related to the productivity of capital by observing that $A = \dfrac{I - \bar{I}}{Y_t - Y_{t-1}}$, or if we ignore the exogenous portion: $A = \dfrac{I}{Y_t - Y_{t-1}}$. Recalling that investment is the change in the stock of capital goods, and $Y_t - Y_{t-1}$ is the change in output, or income, A is almost the reciprocal of the national

---

[7]For more precision see the much quoted article by Paul A. Samuelson, "Interaction between the Multiplier Analysis and the Principle of Acceleration," *Review of Economic Statistics* (May, 1939). Reprinted in *Readings in Business Cycle Theory* (Philadelphia: The Blakiston Co., 1944).

average of the marginal product of capital. The marginal product of capital is defined as the change in total output per unit change in the stock of capital, with all other factors held constant. The important difference between the two ideas is that in the accelerator concept, the change in income is the independent variable and the change in wealth (I) is dependent, whereas in the marginal product concept income (or output) change is dependent upon the change in the stock of capital.

The marginal product of capital is a technological relation between capital input and the product output. In the theory of the firm, after some refinements, the marginal product schedule becomes the demand curve for the factor of production. In the case of capital, interest is the relevant price or wage. The accelerator, too, should be considered as an element of the demand for capital; here the quantity demanded varies as income varies. Higher or lower interest rates would be assumed to alter the size of the accelerator coefficient.

The speed with which business managers react to an increase in the demand for their product and the length of time required to construct new capital are also important elements in the determination of the size of A. The time lag involved in the model (such as that of Table 7-2) must be determined by the consumption lag, that is, the length of time for consumers to adjust their spending to their new income. Suppose the consumption lag to be one month so that $Y_t - Y_{t-1}$ is the change in the rate of income within one month. If all businessmen immediately ordered new equipment and producers of this equipment were able to produce it in less than a month, the accelerator would be very large. This is not very realistic for most industries. It would seem more likely that many investors would hesitate to evaluate the permanence of the increased demand, and take time to arrange financing. Furthermore, the cost of production of capital often dictates that a long period of time will be taken to produce it. The response will also depend in part upon the current degree of utilization of existing capital. If much excess capacity exists, firms need not increase their capital stock significantly when demand increases so A would be relatively small. On the other hand, if the capital goods producing industry is at, or near full capacity, it may take a relatively long time to supply new equipment to the users of the equipment — again a low value of A would exist.

On technological grounds, underdeveloped economies are likely to exhibit lower A values than are the well-developed, industrialized societies because the marginal product of capital relative to that of labor and land is quite high. This, in part, can be used to explain the observed phenomena that the business cycle is a greater problem in the well-developed systems than it is in the less industrialized.

This discussion would seem to indicate that the acceleration coefficient is complex. The lag is probably distributed over several periods. The numerical value of the relation fluctuates over a period of time, especially over the business cycle, and is different in different industries or geographical areas. Although we can find many qualifications to the simple theoretical system, it is nevertheless an important contribution to business cycle analysis.

QUESTIONS

1. Explain why the Pigou effect would not be expected to operate on corporate bonds, whereas it would be operative on Federal Reserve notes.

2. Without a numerical example, explain why a multiplier type investment relation can produce only single-direction movements of national income while the accelerator relation generates cyclical response to the same shock.

3. Would you expect the accelerator to operate differently in periods when the capital stock is being used only partially and when capital utilization is near capacity?

4. Continue Table 7-1 through the 15th period. Will there be a turning point?

5. Continue Table 7-2 through the 21st period. Have you reached another turning point?

6. Derive graphically the shift in the I-S function caused by (a) a shift to the right of the MEC schedule, (b) an upward shift of the saving function.

7. Refer to Chart 7-6 on page 159. Explain why a point to the left of the I-S function would not be an equilibrium point. What are the forces that would cause movement of the interest rate and income in the direction of the I-S curve?

8. Refer to Chart 7-6 on page 159. Explain why a point to the right of the L-M function (such as point D) would not be an equilibrium point. What are the forces which would cause movement of the interest rate and income in the direction of the L-M curve?

9. Derive graphically the shift in the L-M function caused by (a) an increase in the money supply, (b) a downward shift in the M_W^D function, (c) a shift to the right of the liquidity preference function.

10. Given the following condition, when would it be advisable to hold bonds? (Assume that the bonds available are all perpetuities, and can be exchanged only on one date each year.)
    (a) The current interest rate is 1 percent, and you forecast that the rate next year will be 2 percent.
    (b) The current interest rate is 2 percent, and you forecast that the rate next year will be 1 percent.
    (c) The current interest rate is 30 percent, and you forecast that the rate next year will be 31 percent.
    (d) The current interest rate is 10 percent, and you forecast that the rate next year will be 11 percent.
    (e) The current interest rate is 10 percent, and you forecast that the rate next year will be 12 percent.
11. How would you qualify your conclusions in Question 10 if the forecast of future interest rate behavior was clouded with a great deal of uncertainty?

SUGGESTED READINGS FOR CHAPTERS 6 AND 7

Dillard, Dudley. *The Economics of John Maynard Keynes.* Englewood Cliffs, New Jersey: Prentice-Hall, Inc., 1948.

Hansen, Alvin H. *Business Cycles and National Income.* New York: W. W. Norton & Company, Inc., 1951.

Hicks, J. R. *A Contribution to the Theory of the Trade Cycle.* Oxford: Clarendon Press, 1950.

——————————. "Mr. Keynes and the 'Classics': A Suggested Interpretation," *Econometrica.* Vol. 5 (April, 1937).

Keynes, John Maynard. *The General Theory of Employment, Interest, and Money.* New York: Harcourt, Brace & World, 1936.

Klein, Lawrence R. *The Keynesian Revolution.* New York: The Macmillan Company, 1947.

Modigliani, F. "Liquidity Preference and the Theory of Interest and Money," *Econometrica* (January, 1944).

Patinkin, D. "Price Flexibility and Full Employment," *The American Economic Review.* Vol. XXXVII (September, 1948).

Pigou, A. C. "Economic Progress in a Stable Environment," *Econometrica,* New Series. Vol. XIV (August, 1947).

Ritter, L. S. "The Role of Money in Keynesian Theory," in Deane Carson (ed.) *Banking and Monetary Studies,* sponsored by the U.S. Comptroller of the Currency. Homewood, Illinois: Richard D. Irwin, Inc., 1963.

Samuelson, Paul A. "The Simple Mathematics of Income Determination," *Income, Employment and Public Policy,* Essays in Honor of Alvin Hansen. New York: W. W. Norton & Company, Inc., 1948.

——————————. "Interactions between the Multiplier Analysis and the Principle of Acceleration," *Review of Economic Statistics.* Vol. XXI, No. 2 (May, 1939).

8 *Topics in*

National Income Analysis

In this chapter, the theoretical structure of national income determination is concluded. In the first part the role of government from both the spending side and the taxation side is discussed. The following segment deals with problems associated with the establishment of a useful consumption function, and some modern treatments of the topic. The last section of the chapter introduces the subject of long-run economic growth and some of the approaches to its study.

GOVERNMENT AND THE NATIONAL INCOME

In this section, government expenditures and taxation will be introduced into the theory of national income determination. Part VIII of this text deals with national policies to promote full employment, price stability, economic growth, and other goals; so at this juncture our concern is with the analytical framework rather than with the evaluation of such policies.

Government Expenditures

Purchases of goods and services by government are a portion of the total demand for the national output. They may be on capital account or on current account. They may be by state and local units or by the federal government. From the point of view of their impact on the level of national income, these distinctions can be submerged; but in using the theory as a framework for forecasting, they are quite important.

State and local units of government do not have the spending flexibility of the federal government. Borrowing is often restricted by provision of their constitutions or charters and is otherwise more difficult to accomplish. The federal government has and the smaller units do not have the power to create money. Thus, the state and local levels of government are necessarily more closely tied in their decisions to spend to their ability to tax.

The ability to tax is also restricted more for state and local units than it is for the federal government. The smaller the taxing jurisdiction the easier it is for the public to avoid the taxes by moving to another jurisdiction. The type of taxation available to the smaller levels of government is also usually quite limited. As a rule they are forced to depend more on taxes based upon property than on income.

The many difficulties involved in acquiring funds by the smaller units of government force their spending patterns to be dictated by their receipts rather than by considerations of their counter cyclical effect. It would probably be correct to make state and local spending a positive function of national income.

Spending by the federal government is such a large portion of aggregate demand that changes in its volume have an important impact on the national income. The national government must be concerned with the effect of its expenditures upon the economy, and we are concerned, here, with what that effect will be. Since it is a matter of policy, government expenditures are usually handled as an exogenous factor. The G-function is, therefore, autonomous, or not a function of income.

In Chart 8-1 government expenditures on goods and services have been added to business investment (I_B) to become the injections function ($I_B + G$). A new higher rate of spending by the government is indicated by adding ΔG to create a new total amount of injections. The multiplier is operative on the new spending demand in exactly the same way as it was for new investment demand. The government expenditures multiplier is defined as $\dfrac{\Delta Y}{\Delta G}$, and it would be derived exactly as the investment multiplier was on page 140. Graphically, it can be seen that income would increase from Y_0 to Y_1 when government spending was increased by ΔG, so $\dfrac{\Delta Y}{\Delta G} = \dfrac{1}{\dfrac{\Delta S}{\Delta Y}} = \dfrac{1}{1 - \dfrac{\Delta C}{\Delta Y}}$.

In other words, in the mechanics of income determination government spending can be handled in exactly the same manner as is investment. Since no new principles are involved in introducing government expenditures into the model we shall delay its incorporation into an algebraic model until we have also brought in the taxation component.

Chart 8-1

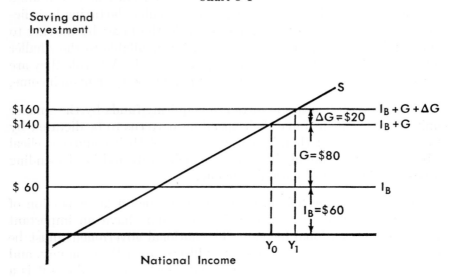

Taxation

Receipts by government are looked upon as a withdrawal from the income stream. Government has the ability to absorb purchasing power from the rest of the economy by its legal power to tax. The usual procedure is for the taxing authority to set the rate of the tax and the other conditions, and a forecast needs to be made of the amount of collections.

Taxes, being withdrawals, are not a part of aggregate demand. They are a part of aggregate supply but influence aggregate demand. Some taxes or rules for computing taxes will have their impact on the marginal efficiency of capital. Others will affect the net foreign investment figure. The most important classes of taxes, however, are those that reduce the disposable income of households, and thus influence the consumption function. It is these that will be introduced into our national income model at this stage.

The new consumption function that is to be utilized here is $C = \alpha + \beta Y_D$. We have switched from English to Greek letters for the parameters simply to indicate that this function is the after-tax consumption function. Y_D is disposable income, equal to national income (Y) minus taxes (T_x).

For the example we employ a linear tax function: $T_x = \overline{T}_x + tY$. This relationship is similar to a proportional tax in that a change in income results in a proportional change in the tax payments, i.e., $\frac{\Delta T_x}{\Delta Y}$ is constant. However, $\frac{T_x}{Y}$ is not constant. It is declining, so in that sense it is a regressive tax. A strictly proportional tax function would have both $\frac{\Delta T_x}{\Delta Y}$ and $\frac{T_x}{Y}$ constant, which could be accomplished by setting $\overline{T}_x$ equal to zero. This tax function relates to national income, not to personal or individual incomes; so we can say very little about the tax rate structure that applies to individuals. As national income changes, so may its distribution.

Formally, our model now looks like this:

$$1. \quad Y = C + I_B + G$$
$$2. \quad C = \alpha + \beta Y_D$$
$$3. \quad Y_D = Y - T_x$$
$$4. \quad T_x = \overline{T}_x + tY$$
$$5. \quad I_B = \overline{I}_B$$
$$6. \quad G = \overline{G}$$

And its solution can be shown in the following way:

$$Y = C + I_B + G$$
$$Y = \alpha + \beta Y_D + \overline{I}_B + \overline{G}$$
$$Y = \alpha + \beta (Y - T_x) + \overline{I}_B + \overline{G}$$
$$Y = \alpha + \beta Y - \beta T_x + \overline{I}_B + \overline{G}$$
$$Y = \alpha + \beta Y - \beta \overline{T}_x - \beta tY + \overline{I}_B + \overline{G}$$
$$Y - \beta Y + \beta tY = \alpha + \overline{I}_B + \overline{G} - \beta \overline{T}_x$$
$$Y (1 - \beta + \beta t) = \alpha + \overline{I}_B + \overline{G} - \beta \overline{T}_x$$
$$Y = \frac{\alpha + \overline{I}_B + \overline{G} - \beta \overline{T}_x}{1 - \beta + \beta t}$$

A tax multiplier can be constructed, if it is defined as $\frac{\Delta Y}{\Delta \overline{T}_x}$. The meaning of $\Delta \overline{T}_x$ here is that whatever the level of national income the amount of the tax will be $\Delta \overline{T}_x$ larger than before. Notice that it does not say that the tax will be $\Delta \overline{T}_x$ larger than before the additional tax was imposed. Since the change in the tax will change the national income, the tax will also change because income changes. The derivation of this multiplier can be accomplished by comparing the equilibrium income of the latest model with the income found to be equilibrium when the tax function includes $\Delta \overline{T}_x$. Thus, in place of Equation 4 use Equation 4': $T_x = \overline{T}_x + tY + \Delta \overline{T}_x$.

The new equilibrium income Y' can be found to be:

$$Y' = \frac{\alpha + \overline{I}_B + \overline{G} - \beta \overline{T}_x - \beta \Delta \overline{T}_x}{1 - \beta + \beta t}.$$

Our goal is to find $\dfrac{\Delta Y}{\Delta \overline{T}_x}$. ΔY is $Y' - Y$. Subtracting the equation for Y on page 179 from the equation just found for Y' gives:

$$Y' - Y = \Delta Y = \frac{-\beta \Delta \overline{T}_x}{1 - \beta + \beta t}.$$

Then, dividing both sides of this equation by $\Delta \overline{T}_x$ we get:

$$\frac{\Delta Y}{\Delta \overline{T}_x} = \frac{-\beta}{1 - \beta + \beta t}$$ which is the tax multiplier.

The tax multiplier is negative. Since $\Delta \overline{T}_x$ is positive ΔY must be negative; that is, an increase in taxes results in a decrease in national income.

Chart 8-2 shows how to develop a consumption function when taxes are imposed in the form described by the tax function: $T_x = \overline{T}_x + tY$.

Y_2 is disposable income (i.e., $Y - T_x$) when national income is Y_1 $(T_1 = Y_1 - Y_2)$. We make the assumption that households will spend on consumption the same amount if national income is Y_2 and no taxes are paid, or if national income is Y_1 and taxes of T_1 make disposable income Y_2. This is like saying that a man with an income of $150 and taxes of $50 would consume the same amount as he would were his income $100 with no taxes to pay. He acts on the basis of his take-home pay rather than his gross pay.

By this assumption we are able to draw an after-tax consumption function, $C' = a + bY$. At a given level of income, it is below the pretax function $(C = \alpha + \beta Y_D)$ by β times the amount of the tax at that income. The individual's disposable income has been reduced by the amount of the tax so we expect him to reduce his consumption by the marginal propensity to consume times the reduction in income. b is the marginal propensity to consume national income given this particular tax function. It will be a little smaller than β, the MPC disposable income. A little analysis will show that $b = \beta - \beta t$. With the given tax function, C' is the relevant consumption function. The C-function is needed to derive C' so it is kept in the diagram.

Chart 8-2

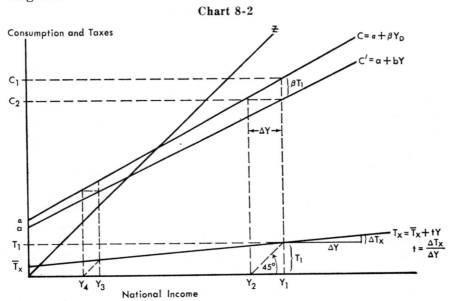

Now that taxes have been incorporated, aggregate leakages or withdrawals (S) include both personal saving and taxes: $S = Sp + T_x$. $S = Y - C'$, so $Sp + T_x = Y - C'$. Therefore, $Sp = Y - C' - T_x$. The aggregate saving curve can be derived by simply subtracting the C' line from the Z line. Then the Sp line can be found by $Sp = S - T_x$. Alternatively, the Sp line can be constructed by the same reasoning by which the C' curve was derived in Chart 8-2. Then Sp and T_x sum to S.

As before, equilibrium income occurs at that level at which aggregate saving ($Sp + T_x$) is equal to aggregate investment ($I_B + G$). An increase in government spending of ΔG will cause income to increase by that amount (ΔG) times the reciprocal of the slope of the S function $\left(\dfrac{1}{1 - \beta + \beta t} \right)$.

A decrease in taxes by a given amount will result in an increase in income, but the increase will be somewhat less than that resulting from the same increase in government spending. Likewise, if government expenditures and taxes were both increased by the same amount, national income would not be constant — it would increase. The reason for this asymmetry of taxes and spending is that while government purchases of goods and services become a part of national income, a decrease in taxation reduces consumption by less than the full amount of the tax. The change in taxes of $\Delta \overline{T}_x$ shifts the consumption function by $\beta \, \Delta \overline{T}_x$ and the aggregate saving function by the same amount but in the opposite direction. The shift of the saving curve can be viewed as a composite of the shift in the personal saving function and the shift in the tax function. For example, suppose the increase in the tax is $10 billion ($\Delta \overline{T}_x = \$10$ billion) and the MPS disposable income is 2/10. Then the tax function shifts upward by $10 billion, and the Sp function shifts downward by $2 billion — a net increase in the S function of $8 billion.

Chart 8-3 shows a balanced budget situation where taxes and government spending were both increased by an amount equal to $\Delta \overline{G}$. If only government expenditures had been increased, income would have risen to the rate Y_1. If only taxes had been raised, income would have fallen to Y_2. Since both were raised, the net effect is for income to rise to Y_3.

Chart 8-4 compares the effect of an increase in G and a decrease in T_x of equal amounts. Clearly, the increase in G has a larger impact on national income than does the decrease in T_x.

RECENT CONTRIBUTIONS TO THE THEORY OF CONSUMPTION

The statistical correlation between annual real personal consumption expenditures and annual real disposable personal income is extremely high. With the exception of the war years 1941–1945, virtually all the points from 1929 to the present fall on the regression line that has a slope of about .90, seeming to confirm the empirical relevance of the kinds of consumption functions we have been using.

Our confidence in the function is shaken considerably, however, if we go through the same procedure using quarterly or monthly data. Here the correlation is not nearly so impressive, the points appear to be scattered almost haphazardly. Some significant errors in forecasting consumption on the basis of income have inspired many economists to probe more deeply into the nature of consumer behavior. This can be done by study of individuals or groups of individuals with different characteristics such as age, urban vs. rural, wealth, and education, or it can be done by a more sophisticated theoretical attack on the aggregative level. Both of these approaches are being followed continuously. The final answers are not yet in.

Chart 8-3

Saving, Investment, Taxes, and Government Spending

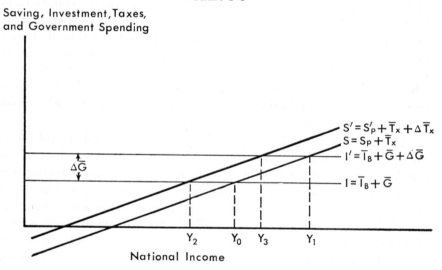

National Income

Chart 8-4

Saving, Investment, Taxes, and Government Spending

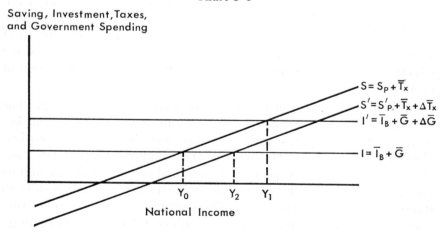

National Income

The significant errors in the short-run empirical consumption function suggest that factors other than disposable income contribute importantly to the consumption decision. Some of them will be discussed here. Some empirical evidence on them will be taken up in the chapters on forecasting.

Expectations of Changes in Income, Employment, and Prices

Households in any given income bracket would be expected to increase their current consumption if they anticipated a considerable increase in income in the near future. Such expansion of spending out of a given income is usually possible through the reduction of saving, or through spending out of assets accumulated during the past, or through borrowing against future income. If a person fears the possibility of becoming unemployed, he would be likely to become more conservative in his spending behavior. If the feeling is widespread, the consumption function might shift downward.

We would expect that uncertainty in and of itself would be an important reason for saving, so anything creating uncertainty in the minds of the family decision makers would shift the consumption function downward. Closely connected to this idea, but independent of it, is the reasoning that volatility of income would alter consumption behavior. Imagine two families whose incomes over a long period of time would be the same, but one of them had a constant income from an annuity and the other had an income that fluctuated greatly from month to month or quarter to quarter. The short-run consumption function for the two might be quite different, even though the longer run functions might be identical. The aggregate consumption function would probably be higher as uncertainty and volatility of income were diminished. This is one of the hoped for effects of the expansion of social security and other governmental economic policies.

The Survey Research Center of the University of Michigan has engaged in extensive research into consumer expectations and behavior, stressing particularly the psychological and sociological elements of the study. In general, their findings support the view that pessimism with respect to income and employment, as well as the vague feeling that "things are going to get worse," results in diminished consumer spending. The converse also seems to be true; that is, a general attitude of optimism about future income, employment, and the general economic and political climate acts as a stimulus to consumption expenditures.[1]

One would certainly anticipate that consumers who expect prices to rise would increase current spending in order to take advantage of the lower prices currently prevailing, and when expectations of lower prices are held that consumers would curtail present consumption as much as possible. Apparently, consumer psychology is more complex than this. It seems that when prices are rising and expected to rise further, they are already higher than they were, so there is reluctance to increase consumer purchases at what are thought of as "high" prices.

Expectations on the future price level will affect the demand for some goods more than others. For example, if prices are expected to fall in the near future, families will get along with their present automobile or household appliances, whereas their consumption of less durable items may remain about the same.

Prices

Rational consumer behavior implies that if all prices (and hence incomes) increased proportionally, consumption valued in current prices should also increase by the same proportion so that real consumption would remain constant. Frequently, households suffer from a type of myopia economists call the "money illusion." This means that the consumer might stress the rise in his income without realizing that the prices of the things he buys have also increased. Others might be so conscious of the higher prices of goods and services that they seemingly are insensitive to the fact that their incomes have also increased. Economists are not in general agreement as to whether a money illusion exists in dependable enough form to include the hypothesis in their analysis.

We saw earlier that the major effect of price level changes on consumer behavior came through the Pigou effect where increases in the general level of prices reduced the real value of money balances and so inspired consumers to attempt to add to their money holdings by reducing their consumption. The Pigou effect assumes that

---

[1]Most of the Center's publications are pertinent to this discussion. See, in particular, G. Katona and E. Mueller, *Consumer Expectations, 1953–56* (Ann Arbor, Mich.: Survey Research Center, 1957). Also, see G. Katona, *The Powerful Consumer* (New York: McGraw-Hill Book Company, 1960)

the money illusion is not operative. In fact, it assumes a high degree of awareness of the "real" effects of price level changes, unclouded by any veil of money.

Inflations and deflations as they have been experienced are not characterized by proportional price changes. Rather, some prices change very readily while others are termed "sticky." We saw earlier that this fact alone can be quite important in generating business fluctuations as described by W. C. Mitchell. We are not prepared to make empirically meaningful generalizations about the effect of nonproportional price variability on consumption spending. We can, however, observe that if it were true that price volatility was characteristic of goods whose income elasticity of demand was high and if price rigidity was true of goods with low income elasticity, then a general price level rise would reduce consumption. Of course, such statements are of very little value until a great deal more research on the problem is complete.

There are other considerations of this sort that can be observed. For example, a general increase in prices, even if proportional, will result in a shift of real income from the private sector to government where a progressive income tax is in effect. Assume all prices to increase by 10 percent so that all money incomes also increase by 10 percent. Since the income tax is progressive, the increase in tax payments will be more than 10 percent, the real disposable income will have declined. In this instance we should expect real consumption to be reduced.

Another possible source of change in consumption could come through a systematic redistribution of income by price level changes from those with a high marginal propensity to consume to those with a low marginal propensity to consume, or vice versa. In order to make significant statements about this, we would have to know that inflation does have this redistributional effect on particular classes of consumers, and that classes so affected do, in fact, have different marginal propensities to consume. Inflation could also cause a shift from the consumption of domestically produced goods to foreign produced goods as their relative prices changed.

Interest

In a number of connections, it has been pointed out that classical economists relied on the interest rate to explain the division of income into its consumption and saving components. In the logic of utility maximization, an increase in interest rates should cause households to save more and consume less out of any given level of income. A saver whose goal is to accumulate a particular sum of wealth at a particular date in the future, however, would save less when interest rates rise, since the same sum could be accumulated by that date with smaller periodic additions. In some instances, this may describe some households' behavior, but it is inconsistent with utility maximization and therefore somewhat suspect as a part of the theory.

Income Distribution

Many schemes to promote economic expansion are based on the belief that the marginal propensities to consume of low income groups are higher than those of high income groups. Consumption and income would increase if income were taken away from low MPC families and given to high MPC households. The hypothesis seems to be so intuitively appealing that many have accepted the policy proposal based on it. There are several fallacies incorporated into this position, quite aside from the most fundamental one which is that because an act has one desirable outcome it should be done.

The simple error of confusing the marginal propensity to consume with the average propensity to consume is often discovered. It is quite well established that the APC of high income families is significantly lower than that of low income families. The evidence on the MPC by income class is an entirely different matter. It is a very difficult thing to measure, and most attempts seem to indicate that the differences in the marginal propensities to consume of the various income classes are not significant. One reason for this surprising conclusion is that low income families might have debts to pay, cash balances to build up, insurance to buy, and so on. There are many nonconsumption uses for added income.

Even if it were discovered that low income households had high marginal propensities to consume, it would be advisable to determine whether some other factor might be the fundamental reason rather than the level of income. For example, it seems to be the case that young families have a high MPC and they are more likely to be lower on the income scale. Certainly, there are groups in the low income category who have low marginal propensities to consume, such as farmers and certain immigrant groups. The source of income seems to have some influence on consumption behavior. Profit recipients behave differently than do wage earners and interest and rent receivers. These considerations ought to give us pause before we recommend income redistribution as the preferred solution to a slumping economy. This is not to say that income redistribution may not be defended by some as a worthwhile goal, but its defense must rest on other grounds.

Wealth

The relationship of wealth to consumption behavior is difficult to ascertain. For one thing, wealth and income are themselves so highly correlated it is difficult to determine their individual effect upon consumption. Another difficulty is that the very fact of wealth ownership may indicate that the owners saved large portions of income in the past and thus are motivated differently than are those whose wealth is small. Again, considering any given level of income, wealth holding is likely to be concentrated in the older age group whose spending patterns are different from those of younger people.

Wealth of different kinds may have different effects on consumers' spending. Some consumer wealth requires additional spending if its value is to be maintained and services received. Automobiles and household appliances are in this category. On the other hand, the services of some kinds of consumer wealth substitute for new consumer goods and services. Thus, to some extent, a television set may reduce spending on other forms of entertainment, and ownership of an automobile reduces spending on other forms of transportation.

The influence of financial wealth on consumers' spending habits is the more serious question. It has been suggested that the unexpectedly high levels of consumption following World War II can be partially explained by the rapid accumulation of financial assets in the hands of consumers during the war years. It does seem plausible that of two families with the same income, the one with the larger holdings of financial assets would spend more on current consumption. Undoubtedly, the most important consideration is the level of wealth relative to the family's aspiration level. Unfortunately, this is not directly measurable.

Consumer Credit Terms

Consumption can be accomplished without regard to current income either by allowing the stock of assets to vary over a period of time, or by varying the amount of indebtedness over a period of time. The terms on which consumers can borrow are altered from time to time. The interest rate is of some consequence in these terms, but other conditions may be of equal or even more importance. Among these are the down payment requirement, the length of the repayment period, and the credit standards imposed by the lenders. Easing of these terms stimulates consumer borrowing and spending, and the tightening of the terms discourages new borrowing and spending. The major impact, of course, is on durable consumer goods, but revolving type charges involving the purchase of "soft goods" are also affected.

Short-Run versus Long-Run Consumption Functions

The statistical evidence on the consumption-income relation suggests that the consumption function over short periods of time has a positive intercept and a relatively small slope. The long-run function derived from empirical evidence is approximately proportional; that is, it is linear and its intercept is at the origin.[2] These seemingly contradictory findings demand an explanation. In fact, any explanation of consumer behavior must be consistent with these observations.   Chart 8-5 is drawn to serve as the basis for discussing the problem.

The consumption function labeled C_L represents the long-run consumption-income relationship.   Kuznets found remarkable stability in the average propensity to consume when he used decade figures from 1869 to the beginning of the great depression in 1929. During the 1930's the APC increased significantly when disposable income fell well below what it had been. During the years of World War II, the APC was very low as incomes again grew very rapidly. After the war the APC again returned to figures comparable to the long-run historical norms.

The short-run consumption functions of Chart 8-5 have the subscript s. They represent the consumption behavior in response to incomes in relatively short periods of time. The argument is that the short-run consumption function has been shifting upward because of some basic changes taking place in the economy such as the developments of new consumer goods, the accumulation of wealth,

---

[2]The study on which these statements are based is Simon Kuznets, *National Income: A Summary of Findings* (Princeton, New Jersey: National Bureau of Economic Research, Princeton University Press, 1946).

Chart 8-5

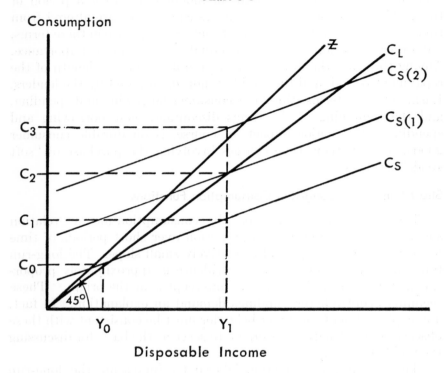

education to new desires, and the growth of urban populations and so on.

Start with income Y_o, at which level of income consumption is C_o. Now, if income increases to Y_1 within a year, consumption would increase to C_1; but if the changes we spoke of took place such that the consumption function shifted to $C_{s(1)}$, consumption would increase to C_2. Many years later, Y_1 might be a severe depression level of income, but since the consumption function had shifted upward considerably, consumption would then be at C_3. Arthur Smithies showed that the statistical evidence was consistent with this explanation of consumer behavior,[3] but, as we shall see, a number of other explanations are also consistent with the evidence.

One of these explanations is the "relative income hypothesis" of James Duesenberry. Where Smithies felt that the basic consumption

---

[3] Arthur Smithies, "Forecasting Postwar Demand," *Econometrica*, Vol. 13 (January, 1945).

relation was the short-run function and the long-run proportional function showed up as shifts in the short-run functions, Duesenberry believes that it is the proportional function that is the fundamental one.[4] In other words, if income were to continuously increase, consumption would increase proportionally, but since income fluctuates, consumer response is nonproportional.

This argument is based on the view that consumption is determined not simply by one's current income but, to an important extent, on one's position in his society which, in turn, depends partly upon his own past income and the income of his neighbors. Thorstein Veblen,[5] in his penetrating discussion of consumption, emphasized the degree to which people consume to impress others, "conspicuous consumption," and how socially approved consumption patterns were set by the higher ranking or higher income groups, "pecuniary emulation." Persons whose income is low relative to their neighbors will spend a larger proportion of their income, whereas those with relatively large income can consume smaller proportions of their income. Thus the least wealthy of the "jet set" may have a higher APC than the wealthiest persons living in a very poor neighborhood.

Duesenberry's description of consumption behavior is based on the dynamics of fluctuations and growth in income. Chart 8-6 can be used to explain the hypothesis. Consumption would be equal to C_1 if income were Y_1 and, if income grew steadily, consumption would follow the C_L line, so that as income increased to Y_2 consumption would increase to C_2. But when income hits a peak of Y_2 and declines, consumption would follow the $C_{s(1)}$ line down, so that if income fell all the way back to Y_1, consumption would be C_3 rather than C_1. The reason given for making the short-run (nonproportional) function the relevant one when income falls is that households having once reached a high standard of living (as represented by C_2) will give it up only very reluctantly. They will allow their savings to decline rather than give up the level of consumption attained during the boom. However, as income reaches its trough, say, at Y_1 and begins to rise again, consumption will increase again, but again along the $C_{s(1)}$ line. Now the argument is that, having become accustomed to the lower standard of living represented by

---

[4] J. S. Duesenberry, *Income, Saving, and the Theory of Consumer Behavior* (Cambridge, Massachusetts: Harvard University Press, 1952).

[5] Thorstein B. Veblen, *The Theory of the Leisure Class* (New York: The Modern Library, 1934).

Chart 8-6

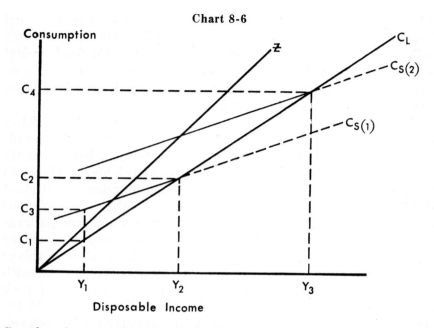

C_3, when income rises the desire to save seems more urgent. But when income again reaches Y_2 and continues to increase, consumption will again increase according to C_L until income reaches a new peak at, say, Y_3, at which point as income falls consumption behavior would follow a new short-run function $C_{s(2)}$.

Professor Friedman has approached the problem of the consumption-income relation in a novel way.[6] The underlying motivation and attitudes of consumers are similar to those described by Duesenberry, but Friedman makes consumption depend explicitly on what he calls "permanent income." The term, "permanent," should not be taken too literally. It is measured as a weighted average of incomes of the recent past. Actual income differs from permanent income by an amount called "transitory income." Friedman believes, and his statistical evidence supports his belief, that consumers will not respond to an increase in income by a proportional increase in consumption, but if that income continues for several years they will consume virtually all of it.

The rigid statement is that the marginal propensity to consume out of permanent income is one, and that the marginal propensity

---

[6]Milton Friedman, *A Theory of the Consumption Function* (Princeton, New Jersey: Princeton University Press, 1957).

to consume transitory income is zero. Transitory income is in the nature of a windfall gain or loss, and is, therefore, not incorporated into the consuming units' budget. Instead, people tend to use transitory income to pay off debts or accumulate assets for future use when income might fall or when heavy expenses might arise. The permanent income hypothesis is probably more meaningfully understood if viewed as an approximation to or proxy for expected future income.

Clearly the explanation of consumption behavior is not a simple thing. Many economists, besides those mentioned, have made important contributions to the study, and the research continues.

STAGNATION THESIS

The prolonged depression of the 1930's and some of the ideas developed by John Maynard Keynes led some economists to develop the stagnation thesis. Two factors are prominent in this point of view. The first is that investment opportunities become less attractive as an economy develops and, therefore, the long-run marginal efficiency of capital declines. The second is that consumers do not spend so large a proportion of their income as incomes go up since they already have satisfied a large proportion of their wants. In other words, the long-run average propensity to consume is a declining one.

Even if the average propensity to consume does not decline, a problem may develop because of the long-run decline in the marginal efficiency of capital. As more and more capital is put into place year after year, income must also increase if unemployment is to be avoided. As income increases, savings will also increase, and this means that still more investment opportunities must be found. This is no problem in a rapidly developing economy; but it can become a problem in a mature economy especially if innovations are not being developed, since the marginal efficiency of presently used types of capital decreases as more and more of it is built.

During the days of rapid economic development the real problem was to get sufficient savings to meet the demands for capital investment. This demand was due to several factors, one of the foremost being the necessity to provide for the needs of a rapidly growing population. More food, clothing, shelter, services, and the like, were required by more people, and large-scale capital investment was required to provide these.

There was also a large demand for capital because of the development of new territories in the United States and in South America, Australia, and Africa. Means of transportation had to be developed to penetrate into the new territory. New houses had to be built, new shopping centers had to be developed, wholesale centers had to be established. Gradually manufacturing also developed, and the new territory became integrated into the total economy. At this stage the demand for new capital decreased because it now depended on replacement of plant and equipment and the increased demand due to gradual increases in population, changes in technology, and the like. The rapid development of new industries also led to a large-scale demand for capital. This was especially true of the durable consumer goods fields, such as automobiles, radios, and refrigerators. These industries also made use of highly developed assembly lines to manufacture their products, and these required a larger proportion of capital in relationship to output than was the case in industry in general.

Those who have argued for the stagnation thesis hold that these factors making for large-scale investment have largely disappeared as economies have become more mature. Population growth slowed down, especially in the 1930's. The physical frontier is gone, in the United States at least. Especially during the 1930's new industries were not being developed as fast as in earlier periods. Moreover, in the face of reduced investment opportunities, there was a tendency for savings to increase. A larger percentage of people were receiving an income high enough to save a significant proportion of it. Saving was also taking place to an increasing degree through insurance and annuity programs. The advocates of the stagnation thesis hold that this combination of factors results in a chronic tendency for planned saving to outrun investment opportunities except for short boom periods due to wars and speculation. The result is chronic unemployment of a part of the labor force.

The stagnation thesis has not been so popular in recent years as it was in the 1930's. Population is again growing rapidly, and new industries are being developed on a large scale as the electronic and atomic age is coming into being. Automatic factories have been developed in some fields, such as textiles, and are being considered in other fields. Machines are again being developed to replace labor, and the amount of investment in capital required to produce many

products is going up.   Some still hold that these are temporary
phenomena and that stagnation will return in a few years at the
most.

During the period of the late 1950's in which unemployment was
somewhat higher than in earlier postwar years, the stagnation thesis
was again used by some to justify expanded government investment
programs to stimulate the rate of growth of the economy.   It is, of
course, possible for an economy to become stagnant in the sense
used in this thesis. There is, however, little evidence to indicate that
the needs for capital investment are being saturated.   In fact, the
supply of capital goods may well be growing too slowly to meet all
of the demands put on our economy.   This is especially true now
because of the role of America as the leader of the free world in the
"cold-war" struggle with the communists.

There is also no proof of any long-run tendency for the propensity to consume to decline. Demands of consumers for new goods
and services have kept pace with increases in income.   In fact, in
many postwar years the problem was not one of insufficient consumption expenditures, but of insufficient saving to meet the needs of
the economy without credit expansion and inflation.

Economic Growth and Fluctuations

The stagnation thesis discussion leads us into the study of long-
run economic problems.   We can visualize the situation by means
of Chart 8-7.   First, we observe that the equilibrium levels of income
where $S = I$ are only short-run equilibria because, if investment is
a positive amount, it means that the stock of capital is increasing
each period during which this situation holds.   For short periods of
time, this may not be very significant because the amount of investment may be a relatively small fraction of the total stock of capital.
But if this short-run equilibrium exists for many periods, the stock
of capital grows by I amount each period and must become a significant proportion of the total.

The growth of the capital stock must have some impact because
capital is productive.   At this point it is necessary to be clear on
whether we are speaking of real or money valued national income.
If Y_o is real national income, then factors of production other than
capital must be unemployed as investment takes place since the
given level of output can be produced with the larger amount
of capital goods and a smaller amount of labor.   The severity of the

Chart 8-7

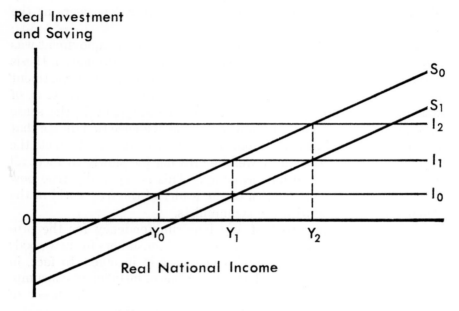

Real Investment
and Saving

Real National Income

unemployment of labor depends upon the nature of the new capital, how productive it is in terms of the displacement of labor.

Under these conditions, presumably prices and wages would continuously fall and, if the Pigou effect is operative, the saving function would decline causing real income to increase to absorb the unemployed. In this context the question is: Would the saving function shift downward at a rate fast enough to exactly compensate for the increased productivity of capital caused by its increase in the amount I?

To be more explicit, refer to Chart 8-7. If study would indicate that when I_o amount of investment took place, income would have to increase to Y_1 in order for employment of labor to remain constant, would the saving function shift to precisely the position represented by S_1? The answer depends most importantly on the degree of flexibility of prices and wages, and on the responsiveness of the public to these price changes in their saving behavior via the Pigou effect.

The stagnationists did not consider the Pigou effect. They reasoned that if income had to increase to Y_1, investment would have to shift upward to I_1, but $I_1 > I_o$ so in the following period income would have to increase by more than the difference between Y_o and Y_1. Income would have to increase to some level of income such as Y_2 to maintain employment. The problem of economic growth then would seem to be that saving and investment must increase at exactly the right speed, an increasing rate of increase.

Two considerations led the stagnation theorists to conclude that government spending was the solution to the problem. First, as pointed out above, these economists were pessimistic about the ability of the economic system to find profitable investment opportunities in ever-growing amounts sufficient to keep up the necessary growth rate. Second, to the extent that government spending is included in I and does not replace labor, the problem is avoided.

Since a downward shifting saving function also is a cure for the problem, government policy directed at achieving this end is also frequently suggested. While it can be accomplished in a number of indirect ways, the direct method would be by either lowering income taxes or by increasing transfer payments.

Domar's Growth Theory

In the preceding section it was pointed out that a positive amount of investment would lead to unemployment of labor unless income continuously increased. Excess capacity of capital might also occur that would discourage any further investment. In that event, national income would decline. We are forced to the conclusion that Schumpeter was correct in saying that the only complete static equilibrium is one in which saving and investment are both zero.

Growth theorists search for another kind of equilibrium, a dynamic equilibrium where savings and investment will be equal at growing levels of income. The first growth theory to be presented is that of Professor Evsey Domar.[7]

Central to the Domar model is the concept of the increase in productive capacity of the economy caused by an increase in its capital stock. He uses the symbol σ (lower case sigma) to stand for the ratio of the change in the amount of output that can be produced in the system (ΔY^*) divided by the increase in the stock of capital which brought about the increase in potential output. The

---

[7]Evsey D. Domar, *Essays in the Theory of Economic Growth* (New York: Oxford University Press, 1957). Essay IV is a straightforward nonmathematical treatment. The same model with the mathematical derivations is found in Essay III.

letter K is used to stand for the total amount of capital goods in the system, so ΔK (the change in that stock) is by definition the amount of investment (I). Thus $\sigma = \dfrac{\Delta Y^*}{I}$. If $\sigma = .25$, the ability of the system to produce goods and services will increase by $25 per time period for every $100 of new investment (in constant dollars.)[8]

To demonstrate the principle involved, Domar uses a very simple national income model. It is the same as the first model we presented in Chapter 6, except that he assumes that the long-run consumption function, and, therefore, also the saving function are proportional. The model is:

(1) $Y = C + I$

(2) $C = bY$ which implies that $S = (1 - b)Y$ or $S = \alpha Y$

(3) $I = \overline{I}$

If $b = .88$, $1 - b = \alpha = .12$, and $\overline{I} = \$18$, $Y = \dfrac{\overline{I}}{\alpha} = \dfrac{\$18}{.12} = \$150$.

Since $\sigma = .25$, the addition to the stock of capital of $18 means that in the next period potential output will be $.25 \times \$18 = \$4.5$ ($= \Delta Y^*$) larger than it had been. If "full employment" of capital is to continue, national income or aggregate demand must also increase by $4.5. Since the multiplier in this model is $\dfrac{1}{\alpha} = \dfrac{1}{.12} = 8.33$, investment must increase by $.54 (i.e., $\Delta Y = \dfrac{1}{\alpha} \times \Delta I = 4.5 = 8.33 \times .54$). If investment increases by $.54, saving will also increase by $.54 because $\alpha = \dfrac{\Delta S}{\Delta Y} = \dfrac{12}{100} = \dfrac{.54}{4.5}$.

The increase in investment of $.54 means that investment (and saving) in the second period will be 18.54, which implies that productive capacity (ΔY^*) and aggregate demand (ΔY) must both increase (by an equal amount) in the following period. To maintain full employment $\Delta Y^* = \Delta Y$.

---

[8]The value of σ incorporates the fact that some of the old capital may be retired early by virtue of the introduction of the new. In other words, the new investment might be capable of producing $30 of new output per period, but since some old capital was retired, the net increase in output per $100 of investment might be $25.

Since $\Delta Y^* = \sigma I$ and

$$\Delta Y = \Delta I \frac{1}{\alpha}$$

$$\sigma I = \Delta I \frac{1}{\alpha}$$

multiply both sides of the equation by α : $\alpha \sigma I = \Delta I$, and divide both sides by I: $\alpha \sigma = \dfrac{\Delta I}{I}$.

The right-hand side is the rate of change of investment necessary to keep the change in potential output equal to the actual change in output or income, that is, $\Delta Y^* = \Delta Y$. The left-hand side tells us what this rate of growth must be. In our example $\alpha = .12$, and $\sigma = .25$ so the rate of growth in investment per period needed to maintain the full use of capital is $.12 \times .25 = .03$ or 3 percent.

In this example, income must also increase by 3 percent.[9] Our original income was 150 and increased by 4.5 $\left(\dfrac{4.5}{150} = 3\% \right)$. This can be seen directly by observing that the rate of change of income can be expressed as $\dfrac{\Delta Y}{Y}$, and $\Delta Y = \dfrac{\Delta I}{\alpha}$, and $Y = \dfrac{I}{\alpha}$ so:

$$\frac{\Delta Y}{Y} = \frac{\dfrac{\Delta I}{\alpha}}{\dfrac{I}{\alpha}} = \frac{\Delta I}{I} = \alpha \sigma = .12 \times .25 = 3\%.$$

One shouldn't take all of this too literally. Our economy is much too complex to be represented by this model, but it does indicate that both the productivity of capital, as expressed in σ, and the habits of the population with respect to saving (and consumption), as expressed in α, influence the degree to which income must grow in order to avoid falling into a recession.

There is another side to the problem. That is that if aggregate demand increases at too rapid a rate relative to the growth of productive capacity, inflation will result. Thus, according to this theory, economic growth must proceed at a particular rate in order to maintain full employment and stable prices. A faster rate results in inflation. A slower rate results in unemployment. This problem has

---

[9]This result depends upon the assumption used here that the marginal propensity to save and the average propensity to save are the same.

been described as the "tightrope" or "knife-edge" problem. We look
more closely at this aspect in Harrod's growth model.

Harrod's Growth Theory[10]

In the Domar model, investment or the change in investment
was treated as exogenously determined. His problem was to show
the required change in investment to achieve an equilibrium rate
of growth in national income. Sir Roy Harrod, on the other hand,
uses a version of the accelerator as the equation explaining investment: $I = A \Delta Y$. In order to switch to Harrod's symbols, we note
that what we have called A, Harrod calls C_r — in other words, the
"capital requirement."

In our discussion of the acceleration principle we pointed out
that the equation could be looked upon both as a behavior relation
and as a technical production relation. Harrod uses both meanings.
As a behavior relation, $I = C_r \Delta Y$ is the demand by business for new
capital. If income increased in the last period, investment would be
positive in the current period; but if income fell, investment would be
negative as businessmen failed to replace worn-out capital. As a
behavior relation, the equation expresses the intentions to invest,
and may, therefore, be different from the actual amount of investment, and in the Harrod model the burden of adjustment in a disequilibrium situation is entirely on investors since he assumes that
savers actually save the amount they intend to save.

The rationale behind Harrod's acceleration type investment
demand function is that the change in income from the last period
to the present serves as a forecast of income (aggregate demand) in
the next period. In order to produce goods and services sufficient to
supply the amount demanded, new plant and equipment will be
needed. Hence, new investment will be proportional to the change
in income, the proportion being determined by the productivity of
capital; that is, $I = C_r \Delta Y$.

Like Domar, Harrod uses a proportional long-run saving function
without a time lag: $S_t = sY_t$. The concept of the warranted rate of
growth is central to his analysis. It is the rate of growth in national
income which keeps saving and investment equal and is labeled G_w.
Since (1) $I_t = C_r (Y_t - Y_{t-1})$ and (2) $S_t = sY_t$, the equilibrium

---

[10]Sir Roy Harrod, *Towards a Dynamic Economics* (London: Macmillan & Co.,
Ltd., 1949).

condition $I_t = S_t$ implies $C_r (Y_t - Y_{t-1}) = sY_t$. Dividing both sides by s gives (3) $Y_t = \dfrac{C_r}{s} (Y_t - Y_{t-1})$. $Y_t - Y_{t-1}$ is the change in income from one period to the next (call it ΔY). The rate of change in income is $\dfrac{\Delta Y}{Y}$. From Equation (3) we find that $\dfrac{\Delta Y}{Y} = \dfrac{s}{C_r}$. This is the warranted rate of growth (G_w).

If income grows at precisely this warranted rate, the amount of goods and services demanded will be exactly enough to employ all of the new capital as well as the previously existing stock of capital. Entrepreneurs who planned the investment expenditures made the right decisions, and will continue to plan to increase their investments in accordance with the forecasting procedure used before.

While income is growing at the warranted rate, income increases by just enough to generate the amount of saving needed to supply the resources for investment. In summary of the growth process described by the warranted rate of growth, output measured by consumption plus saving exactly balances with the demand for the output by consumers and investors.

Harrod finds no reason to believe that the economy would actually grow at the rate prescribed by the warranted rate, and herein lies the difficulty. If the actual growth rate (G) is greater than G_w, income will grow at a still faster rate, diverging farther and farther from G_w. For instance, suppose the propensity to save should suddenly decline to a figure less than equilibrium requires, which, of course, means that consumption demand would increase. This would mean that the output forecast on which investment expenditures were based was too small. Inventories would decline (unintentionally). Capital equipment would wear out faster than expected. Intended investment, in other words, would be greater than actual investment, so in the next planning period businessmen would increase their demands for investment, but this would aggravate the problem still more leading to a greater rate of growth of actual income.

If income expands faster than it should to maintain G_w, output has not increased as much as has aggregate demand. The reverse case, that is, where output increases faster than aggregate demand, will occur when $G < G_w$. A higher rate of saving or a lower demand for investment would bring about this result. An increase in saving (a decrease in consumption) or a decrease in investment demand would mean that output exceeds sales and inventories would build up (unintentionally) and capital would not be fully utilized. Actual investment, in this case, would be greater than intended investment which would, in turn, reduce demand for capital still further and income would decline. In this case, too, the actual growth rate would get continuously farther away from the warranted rate.

Harrod's warranted rate of growth is the rate that will assure the full utilization of the capital stock of the economy, and thereby assures the condition of equality of saving and investment. But Harrod also points out that if population and the labor force are also growing, there must be some rate of growth that will absorb into employment all of the additions to the labor force. The rate of growth needed to maintain exactly full employment — neither unemployment nor over full employment — he terms the natural rate of growth. The situation is complicated in that not only does the labor force grow but also the productivity of labor increases through the growth of capital and its quality and by the improvement of the labor force itself through education and training.

Harrod finds no systematic reason for believing that the rate of growth appropriate to both the growth of capital and to labor will be the same. Indeed, he finds it highly unlikely that they would be close enough to avoid the difficulties. What does happen when the natural rate and the warranted rate differ?

The actual rate of growth in output is restricted by the growth of the labor force and its productivity. Thus, if the natural rate is less than the warranted rate, actual income will grow too slowly and chronic stagnation will result. As we have just seen, under these conditions where $G_w > G$, actual investment including unintended investment in capital and inventory will exceed planned or intended investment.

The opposite case occurs when the labor force is growing fast enough to cause the natural rate of growth to be higher than that warranted rate by the need to keep capital utilized. In such a situation, $G_n > G_w$ and $G > G_w$, and we saw that this condition would lead to output continuously expanding as actual investment would be below intended investment.

QUESTIONS

1. List the attributes of families or individuals you would expect to produce a high level of consumption relative to income.

2. Do the same for those that produce a low propensity to consume.

3. Show that a high *APC* could be consistent with a low *MPC* and vice versa.

4. Consider how various types of consumer wealth might increase and/or decrease consumption out of current income.

5. Develop the thesis that the true consumption function is based on expected lifetime income rather than on current income. Remember that borrowing and lending and repayment are always possible, and that expected future income and expenses can be discounted to the present to give a present value estimate.

6. Using the Domar growth model, at what rate would income have to grow to maintain full employment of capital if the marginal (and average) propensity to consume were 8/10ths and if the ratio $\dfrac{\Delta Y^*}{I}$ were .20?

7. Explain the following of Harrod's terms:
   (a) Warranted rate of growth.   (c) Actual rate of growth.
   (b) Natural rate of growth.

SUGGESTED READINGS

Ackley, Gardner. *Macroeconomic Theory.* New York: The Macmillan Company, 1961.

Domar, Evsey D. *Essays in the Theory of Economic Growth.* New York: Oxford University Press, 1957.

Duesenberry, James S. *Income, Saving, and the Theory of Consumer Behavior.* Cambridge, Massachusetts: Harvard University Press, 1952.

Ferber, R. A. *A Study of Aggregate Consumption Functions.* New York: National Bureau of Economic Research, 1953.

Friedman, Milton. *A Theory of the Consumption Function.* Princeton, New Jersey: Princeton University Press, 1957.

Harrod, Sir Roy. *Towards a Dynamic Economics.* London: Macmillan & Co., Ltd., 1949.

Katona, G. *The Powerful Consumer.* New York: McGraw-Hill Book Company, 1960.

——————————————, and E. Mueller. *Consumer Expectations,* 1953–1956. Ann Arbor, Michigan: Survey Research Center, 1957.

Kuznets, Simon. *National Income: A Summary of Findings.* Princeton, New Jersey: Princeton University Press, 1946.

PROBLEMS ON PART II

1. Construct a table from data in the *Federal Reserve Bulletin* showing the following for the years 1955 to the present:
   (a) Gross National Product
   (b) Wholesale Commodity Price Index
   (c) Money supply (i.e., currency in circulation plus demand deposits)
   (d) Velocity of money (i.e., (a) divided by (b))
   (e) Index of Industrial Production

   Relate the behavior of these series to the equation of exchange and the quantity theory of money.

2. A. Assume that the economy is in a state of equilibrium in which the market rate of interest is equal to the natural rate. Analyze the changes, if any, that would be likely to occur if the following happened:
   (a) The Federal Reserve bought $3 billion of bonds in the open market.
   (b) A large new gold deposit was discovered and $2 billion added to the monetary gold stocks in a year.
   (c) There was a rapid development of automatic factories requiring large amounts of new capital.
   (d) A law was passed requiring steel mills to use more machinery around furnaces to eliminate hazardous jobs. Total costs of producing steel remain about the same.
   (e) Banks changed their credit standards so as to make it easier to get term loans for 15 years to build new plants.

   B. Business has been going up for several years. Bank credit has been increasing in volume, and prices have moved upward. Analyze the possible effects that could result from the following actions:
   (a) The Federal Reserve raises reserve requirements 2 points, and a month later the rediscount rate is increased 1 percent.
   (b) The federal government has been operating at a deficit during the upswing in business. A new administration cuts expenses drastically, but maintains tax rates so as to have a surplus for debt retirement.
   (c) The Federal Reserve supplies the banking system with $5 billion of added reserves.
   (d) The rate of consumer saving increases from 7 percent of disposable income to 9 percent.

   C. There is reasonable balance between the production of nondurable consumer goods, semidurable and durable consumer goods, durable capital goods, and materials used to produce durable goods. Analyze the possible effects of the following:

(a) A small, safe helicopter that can be sold for the price of a small car is developed. Consumer demand for this new means of transportation is strong.

(b) New machines are developed at a reasonable price to replace most men on assembly lines for durable goods. Industrial demand for such machines is far in excess of supply.

3. Using the *Federal Reserve Bulletin* Table, "Member Bank Reserves, Federal Reserve Bank Credit, and Related Items," account for the changes in the monetary base to the latest monthly figures from the same month one year earlier. Over this same span of time, what was the change in the money supply? The actual money expansion multiplier is M/B. What was it for your time period? Evaluate the behavior of the parameters in the money supply model on page 50 to determine whether any of them had a significant effect on the money supply.

4. In a textile factory 1 unit of machinery and equipment is required to produce 20 lots of cloth a day. The average life of the machinery and equipment is 10 years. Develop a table similar to Table 5-1, on page 108, showing the demand for equipment for replacement, the demand for equipment resulting from increased consumer demand, and the total demand for equipment when the output of textiles varies as follows:

Year	Average Production per Day
1	2,000 lots
2	2,200 lots
3	2,360 lots
4	2,360 lots
5	1,700 lots

5. A. Assume that business is operating at a level of full employment except for a normal amount of frictional unemployment. Several of the independent appliance companies are combined into an integrated company. Their forecast of demand for their appliances turns out to be decidedly overoptimistic, even though many businessmen thought it might be correct. How will business in general adjust to such an error in forecast according to the psychological theorists?

B. The economy is fairly well adjusted at full employment levels. Consumers are spending 92 percent of disposable income and saving 8 percent. As a result of bank and savings and loan thrift campaigns, savings increase to 12 percent of disposable income. Discuss the possible effects on the economy in the short run and long run of such a shift.

C. The economy is in equilibrium according to the Keynesian concept of equilibrium. The rate of savings is increased from 5 percent of disposable income to 8 percent. Few opportunities exist for capital investment of the deepening type. Explain how saving and investment are brought into balance (a) by the day analysis and (b) by the *ex ante* and *ex post* analysis.

6. Given the following model:

$$Y = C + I + G \qquad\qquad a = \$40 \text{ billion}$$
$$C = a + bY \qquad\qquad b = 8/10$$
$$I = I_o + iY \qquad\qquad I_o = \$30 \text{ billion}$$
$$G = G_o \qquad\qquad i = 1/10$$
$$G_o = \$50 \text{ billion}$$

(a) Calculate the equilibrium values of Y, C, I, S.

(b) Assume that autonomous investment (I_o) changes from \$30 to \$40 billion, and calculate the new values of Y, C, I, S. What is the value of the investment multiplier?

(c) Draw an accurate graph reflecting the original model and the change introduced in (b).

(d) Construct a period table showing the above events over time.

PART III

MEASUREMENT OF
ECONOMIC FLUCTUATIONS

In order to analyze business fluctuations, it is necessary to have measurements of the changes that have taken place in the past and of current changes. These measurements include data on total business activity and on activity in an industry or an individual business. Total business activity can be measured in two ways: by recording the total dollar figure for sales, or by developing a figure that expresses changes in the physical volume of activity on a percentage basis because it is impossible to add tons of steel, crates of oranges, sacks of wheat, and the like, and get a meaningful total. Methods have been developed for measuring total sales in the economy. In fact, a whole field of record keeping called *national income accounting* has been developed. The basic elements of this system will be described in the first part of Chapter 9. This will be followed by a description of a Federal Reserve series showing the flow of funds through the economy. Attention will then be directed to the most inclusive figure showing percent changes in industrial production, the Federal Reserve Board Index of Industrial Production. The last part of Chapter 9 will be devoted to index numbers that measure changes in prices.

In Chapter 10 consideration will be given to methods of measuring the various types of fluctuations in business and relationships among them. Attention will first be directed to methods of measuring seasonal fluctuations, and then the various methods of estimating the trend will be discussed. Two methods of arriving at the cycle will be presented next. The first is the residual method in which the trend and the seasonal are removed. The second is the National Bureau method, which measures the cycle more directly. The last section of this chapter discusses correlation analysis and develops the graphic approach to such analysis.

9 Measuring Changes in National Income, Production, and Prices

In order to understand fully the nature and the extent of the changes that have taken place and are taking place in aggregative economic activity, it is necessary to have a system of accounting. Such a system, which was developed under the sponsorship of the National Bureau of Economic Research, has been taken over by the National Income Division of the United States Department of Commerce, Office of Business Economics. Data on national income and related items are published regularly in the *Survey of Current Business*. These data, which give a complete and reliable record of what is taking place in the American economy, are available for historical study from 1929 on.

NATIONAL INCOME ACCOUNTING

This section on national income accounting begins with a discussion of the purpose and nature of such accounting. Then national income accounting will be contrasted with accounting for a private business, and lastly the structure of national income accounts and procedures for developing these accounts will be described.

Purpose and Nature of National Income Accounting

The major purpose of national income accounting is to measure total economic activity during a period of time, such as a year or a quarter. Since such activity is of many different types, a common denominator must be used. In national income accounts this denominator is the dollar value of activity. An additional purpose of national income accounting is to show the pattern of economic activity in various sectors of the economy, such as the consumer sector, the business sector, and the governmental sector.

Total economic activity can be measured from the point of view of each of the three patterns used to describe the aggregate circular flow of economic activity. It can be measured by the total value of goods and services produced in the pattern of production; it can also be measured by the total volume of income or, more broadly, of money flow receipts generated in the process of producing total output; or it can be measured by the total volume of expenditures used to purchase such output. It matters little whether total output is measured as total production, total income, or total expenditures. All three measures are used in national income accounts.

Since these patterns are part of the circular flow of economic activity in which production precedes the payment of income and such payment, in turn, precedes expenditures, they are not necessarily equal in any given period of time. In national income accounting, however, they are defined as conceptually equal in a given time period so that any of the measures will produce the same total figure for economic activity. The controlling factor is production of goods and services in a given time period. The income measure is based on the income generated by the output of goods produced during a time period. The expenditure measure also is adjusted to become an alternative measure of goods produced in a time period by making adjustments for such factors as a change in inventories.

The measure of aggregate output is based on the market value of goods and services and is restricted to those items having a market value. Therefore, the value of the services of housewives, in their own homes, for example, is not included in output. A value is imputed for the rental value of owner-occupied houses, however. This is done for consistency in the measure of housing services produced. The value used is estimated from current rental values for similar houses. A similar treatment is used for food consumed by farm families that has been produced on their farm.

In order to avoid double counting, only the value added at each stage of production is counted in measuring production. The expenditure pattern used is that for goods by end users, such as consumers in the case of food and clothing, and businessmen in the case of new lathes or assembly lines. This measure of expenditures is consistent with the production measure since the value of a product is equal to the value added at each stage in the process of producing and selling it.

National Income Accounting versus Business Accounting

The basic principles on which national income accounting is based are similar to those used in accounting for an individual business. At the present time the only data that are available regularly on a national basis are income data, since no detailed balance sheet for the total economy is regularly prepared. Furthermore, since information on many phases of economic activity is not available in income statement form, national income figures are developed by estimating some of the items used.

The form in which national income data are presented is different, however, from that used in reporting business income. The usual income statement of a firm begins with a statement of gross sales from which expenses of various types are subtracted to arrive at the net profit or loss. Such a statement is illustrated in Table 9-1. This form of the income statement can be revised somewhat to show the identity between current receipts from sales on one side and the uses or allocations of these receipts on the other side. An income statement so revised is shown in Table 9-2.

Table 9-1

Income Statement of the ABC Corporation for 1968

Sales...		$35,000
Less Cost of Goods Sold.........................		15,000
Gross Profit..................................		$20,000
Wages and Salaries..............................	$9,000	
Social Security Taxes............................	500	
Taxes, Other than Income........................	1,000	
Depreciation....................................	1.000	
Interest..	500	
		12,000
Net Income before Taxes........................		$8,000
Income Taxes...................................		2,400
Net Income after Taxes.........................		$5,600
Dividends Paid.................................		2,000
Added to Retained Earnings.....................		$3,600

Table 9-2

Income Statement for the ABC Corporation for 1968

ALLOCATIONS OF SALES RECEIPTS		RECEIPTS FROM SALES	
Goods and materials purchased from other firms....	$15,000	Sales to Co. A.........	$ 5,000
Wages and salaries.........	9,000	Sales to Co. B.........	10,000
Social security taxes........	500	Sales to Co. C.........	15,000
Taxes, other than income....	1,000	Sales to other companies	5,000
Depreciation..............	1,000		
Interest..................	500		
Corporate profit taxes.......	2,400		
Dividends................	2,000		
Undistributed profits.......	3,600		
	$35,000		$35,000

Such a revised income statement forms the basis for developing national income accounts. There is, however, a significant difference from general business accounting. It is standard accounting practice to recognize income when a sale is made, and to subtract the costs incurred in producing and selling the goods from the revenue received from their sale to arrive at the profit on the sale. The income statement for the year is a record of sales made, of all costs that are matched against those sales, and of the resulting profit or loss. Sales for the year usually are not the same as production since inventories have either been increased or decreased during the year.

In analyzing business operations cost accountants at times develop a production statement, which is a record of goods produced during the year and of all costs relating to such production. This is the type of statement needed to measure total output in the economy. If the total economy were considered as one large business unit, a production statement for the economy could be developed by consolidating production statements for each individual economic unit. In consolidating a series of financial statements, it is necessary to avoid double counting by eliminating intercompany transactions. In a consolidated production statement for the total economy, this can be done by eliminating the cost of raw materials, parts, and other goods purchased from other firms. The same result is achieved in national income accounting since only the value added to the product by each concern is used in arriving at the value of the total production of the economy.

National Income and Product Accounting

In developing a production statement for the total economy, the first step is to find the total sales to all groups. Sales made by all productive units in the economy can be divided into four major groups, that is, sales to individual consumers, sales to business firms, sales to the government, and sales to foreign countries. Goods and materials purchased from other concerns to be used in current production must be subtracted so as to include only the value added to the product by each concern. It is further necessary to make an adjustment for the net change in inventories to put the statement on a production basis. The sources of funds side of the statement, which corresponds to the receipts from sales side of a business statement, can then be shown as follows:

Sources of Funds

Sales to consumers
Sales to business firms
Sales to the government
Sales to foreign countries
Net change in inventories

Minus: Goods and materials purchased for
use in current production

This statement can be simplified by eliminating offsetting items. Sales to business firms include goods and materials intended for use in current production as well as for capital improvements. Some goods purchased from foreign countries are also used in current production, and some of them offset purchases by foreigners in this country. After subtracting these items the statement can be recast into the following form:

Sources of Funds

Sales to consumers
Sales to the government
Net sales to foreign countries
Sales to producers on capital account
Net change in inventories

This is essentially the form utilized in the national income and product account. However, in order to emphasize the highly volatile character of private investment expenditures, they are combined into one account called "gross private domestic investment." This account includes all sales to producers on capital accounts and the net change in inventories, and also expenditures on residential and other building by individual consumers and nonprofit institutions. Gross private domestic investment thus includes all expenditures on private construction and on producers' durable equipment, and the net change in business inventories.

Sales to consumers of durable goods, nondurable goods, and services are shown as personal consumption expenditures. Sales to the government of goods and services, including new public construction, are listed as government purchases of goods and services. Net sales to foreign countries are referred to as net exports of goods and services. The total of personal consumption expenditures, gross private domestic investment, net exports of goods and services, and government purchases of goods and services is called *gross national product.*

Sources of GNP — Definitions

Since forecasts of aggregative economic activity are frequently made by estimating gross national product from the sales or sources side of the statement, it is desirable to define each of these terms somewhat more precisely. *Personal consumption expenditures,* as the term is used in national income accounting, consist of the purchases of goods and services at market value by individuals and nonprofit institutions and also the value of food, clothing, housing, and financial services received as income in kind. They do not include the purchase of dwelling units, which are classified as capital goods, but do include an estimate of the rental value of owner-occupied houses.

Gross private domestic investment includes capital goods that are newly produced by private business and nonprofit institutions; all private new dwellings including those acquired by owner occupants; commissions arising in the sale and purchase of new and existing fixed assets, principally real estate; and the value of the change in the volume of inventories held by business.

Net exports of goods and services are the net differences between exports and imports of goods and services that have taken place in international transactions, excluding transfers under military grants. They measure the excess of exports of goods and services over imports of goods and services, net transfer payments from the United States government to foreigners, and net personal transfer payments to foreigners.

Government purchases of goods and services consist of the net purchases of goods and services by governmental bodies, except the acquisition of land and the current outlays of government enterprises.[1] Thus, this item consists of general governmental expenditures for the compensation of employees, purchases from business (net of sales by government of consumption goods and materials), net government purchases from abroad, and the gross investment of government enterprises. It excludes transfer payments for such items as relief, and veterans aid and bonuses. It also excludes government interest, subsidies to business, and loans and other financial transfers. These items are excluded because they do not represent payments to the factors of production for current production. Government interest payments are put into this category because most government debt has arisen out of war expenditures that are not, in the usual meaning of the word, productive. Private interest payments are included in the selling price of goods because they are one of the costs involved, representing a payment to capital used in production, and, therefore, they are included in the total of government purchases of goods and services.

Charges against GNP — Definitions

So far gross national product has been built up by adding all sales of goods and services to consumers, and the government, and net sales to businesses and foreigners. Also included was the change in inventories, which adjusts the sales figures to a production basis. In producing these goods and services, payments were made to the factors of production in the form of wages, rent, interest, and profit distributions. Some profits were retained by various business units. Taxes were also paid including income taxes and indirect business taxes and license fees. Some money was kept in the various firms as an allowance for depreciation. Some funds were also donated to various philanthropic organizations. Table 9-3 on page 216 shows the national income and product account for 1966. The breakdown of these various items into the pattern of money flow receipts is shown in the top portion of the table.

---

[1]The purchase of land is excluded since it is a national resource on which productive resources were not expended. The current outlays of government enterprises are excluded since these do not involve purchases of goods but payments to the factors of production to produce goods and services sold to consumers. The value of these goods and services is included at the time of sale.

Table 9-3

National Income and Product Account, 1966
(Billions of Dollars)

ITEM

1	Compensation of employees	435.7
2	Wages and salaries	394.6
3	Disbursements	394.6
4	Excess of accruals over disbursements	0
5	Supplements	41.1
6	Employer contributions for social insurance	20.3
7	Other labor income	20.8
8	Proprietor's income	59.3
9	Rental income of persons	19.4
10	Corporate profits and inventory valuation adjustment	82.2
11	Profits before tax	83.8
12	Tax liability	34.5
13	Profits after tax	49.3
14	Dividends	21.5
15	Undistributed	27.8
16	Inventory valuation adjustment	−1.6
17	Net interest	20.2
18	**NATIONAL INCOME**	**616.7**
19	Business transfer payments	2.7
20	Indirect business tax and nontax liability	65.1
21	Current surplus of government enterprises less subsidies	2.2
22	Capital consumption allowances	63.5
23	Statistical discrepancy	−2.6
	GROSS NATIONAL PRODUCT	**743.3**
24	Personal consumption expenditures	465.9
25	Gross private domestic investment	118.0
26	Net exports of goods and services	5.1
27	Exports	43.0
28	Imports	37.9
29	Government purchases of goods and services	154.3
	GROSS NATIONAL PRODUCT	**743.3**

Source: *Survey of Current Business* (September, 1967).

A more precise definition of some terms is again needed. *Wages and salaries* consist of the monetary payments to employees, including executives, whether in the form of regular wages, commissions, tips, or bonuses. It also includes the money value of wage payments made in goods or services.

As the term is used in national income accounting, *supplements to wages and salaries* include such items as employer contributions for social insurance, contributions to private pension and welfare funds, compensation for injuries, doctors' fees, pay for the military reserve, and a few other minor items.

Proprietor's income in unincorporated businesses is shown as one sum, since it is not ordinarily broken down on the books of such enterprises into wages of management, rent, interest, and profit. An inventory valuation adjustment is made in arriving at the income figure for this sector of the business community. Such an adjustment is necessary because, under most accounting systems, profits are taken inclusive of inventory profits or losses because of price changes, whereas only the value of the change in the physical quantity of inventories is considered in national income accounting.

The *rental income of persons* consists of the monetary earnings from the rental of real property, the imputed net rentals to owner occupants of nonfarm dwellings, and the royalties received from patents, copyrights, and rights to natural resources.

Corporate profits are measured without a deduction for depletion charges and exclusive of capital gains and losses, neither of which is related to the production of goods and services. Intercorporate profits are eliminated and the net receipts of dividends and profits from branches abroad are added. An inventory valuation adjustment is also made for corporations. It includes the profits of stock life insurance companies and of mutual financial institutions.

Net interest includes all interest accruing to the nation's residents except interest payments from the government and interest paid by consumers. Such payments are not included in the concept of national income because they do not add to the value of goods and services, since most government debt has arisen out of military expenditures. An item of imputed interest is added, which consists of the value of financial services received by individuals from banks and other financial institutions that render financial services free of charge rather than pay interest on balances on deposit and make specific charges for services rendered. Also included is imputed interest on reserves held for individuals by life insurance companies and similar financial intermediaries.

The total of these factor payments of wages, profits, interest, and rent is the *national income* of the economy. Various other factors must still be included to arrive at gross national product since it is the total market value of all goods and services produced in a period of time. It includes items such as indirect business taxes that are part of the total cost of production but are not payments to the factors of production, which are the only items included in national income. Gross national product also includes capital consumption allowances, which are an expense for the capital used in production, but likewise are not payments to the factors of production.

The first step is to add indirect business taxes and nontax payments, such as licenses and fees, and business transfer payments, such as contributions to charitable institutions and bad debts that have been written off. An adjustment must also be made by subtracting the amount of subsidies paid to business by the United States government, since they are not included in gross national product but represent a transfer of government funds to business. The current surplus of government business enterprise must also be added, since it is part of gross national product but is not included in national income under profits that are exclusively those of private enterprise. National income plus the adjustments for these factors equals *net national product*. Net national product plus capital consumption allowances, which include depreciation charges, accidental damage to fixed capital, and capital outlays charged to current expense, equal *gross national product*.

PERSONAL INCOME

For some purposes the most significant aggregative economic variable is neither gross national product, net national product, nor national income, but personal income, that is, all income actually paid to individuals in a given time period. All of the income to the factors of production is not paid out to individuals, and there are such items as transfer payments that are paid to individuals but are not included in national income. The items to be subtracted, because they were counted in national income but were not paid out to individuals, include undistributed corporate profits, corporate profits tax liability, corporate inventory valuation adjustment, contributions for social insurance, and the excess of wage accruals over disbursements (an adjustment for the accounting technique of charging as an expense the wages accrued to the end of the fiscal year rather than wages actually paid out). Items that should be included because they are paid to individuals but not included in national income are net interest paid by the government, interest paid by consumers, government transfer payments, and business transfer payments. After these adjustments are made, the resultant figure is personal income. The most important of these adjustments is shown graphically in Chart 9-1 on page 221.

When personal tax and nontax payments are subtracted from personal income, the remainder is *disposable personal income*. This is a very significant item for studying changes in consumer spending, since it is the amount of money consumers have available for the purchase of goods and services. The relationship between national income, personal income, disposable personal income, and consumption expenditures for each year from 1953 through 1966 is shown in Table 9-4 on page 220.

NATIONAL INCOME IN CONSTANT DOLLARS

Additional information about economic activity may be obtained from a study of national income figures in terms of constant dollars. In interpreting the current economic scene and especially in making production forecasts, it is imperative to know whether changes in strategic economic variables are due to changes in prices or in the quantity of goods produced. To meet this need, the Department of Commerce has deflated figures for GNP and its major components so as to put them in terms of constant dollars. Data for the period 1954–1966 in current and in constant dollars are presented in Chart 9-2 on page 222 and for 1945–1966 in Table 9-5 on page 223.

FLOW-OF-FUNDS ACCOUNTS

Data on the value of gross national product, national income, disposable personal income, production, and expenditures of all types are significant for determining the current and prospective future state of the economy. Economic units, such as businesses and households, however, make their decisions in the light of their whole pattern of receipts and cash outlays, including borrowing and lending and saving and investing. Changes in the availability of credit, liquidity positions, and the like affect spending decisions and output. On the other hand, changes in income, expenditures, output, and prices influence saving and investment decisions. Therefore, in order to have complete data on the operation of the economy and on its future prospects, it is necessary to have data on financial activity and on saving and investment.

Table 9-4

Relation of Gross National Product, Net National Product, National Income, Personal Income, Disposable Personal Income, and Personal Consumption Expenditures, 1953–1966

(Millions of Dollars)

	1953	1954	1955	1956	1957	1958	1959	1960	1961	1962	1963	1964	1965	1966
Gross national product	**365,385**	**363,112**	**397,469**	**419,180**	**442,769**	**444,224**	**482,056**	**502.6**	**518.2**	**554.9**	**589.2**	**628.7**	**676.3**	**743.3**
Less: Capital consumption allowances	26,526	28,809	31,986	34,412	37,443	38,139	40,491	43.0	44.3	49.4	52.8	55.7	58.7	63.5
Equals: Net national product	**338,859**	**334,303**	**365,483**	**384,768**	**405,326**	**406,085**	**441,565**	**459.6**	**473.8**	**505.5**	**536.5**	**573.0**	**617.5**	**679.8**
Less: Indirect business tax and nontax liability	30,203	30,151	32,865	35,692	38,186	39,350	42,571	46.4	49.1	53.0	54.6	58.0	62.0	65.1
Business transfer payments	1,369	1,262	1,457	1,616	1,790	1,845	1,801	2.2	2.3	2.3	2.2	2.3	2.3	2.7
Statistical discrepancy	1,283	853	988	−2,428	−601	−1,661	−1,826	−3.0	−1.9	−1.8	−.7	−.5	−.2	−2.6
Plus: Subsidies less current surplus of government enterprises	−431	−243	33	948	992	1,135	629	.5	1.7	1.7	.7	1.2	1.2	2.2
Equals: National income	**305,573**	**301,794**	**330,206**	**350,836**	**366,943**	**367,686**	**399,648**	**414.5**	**426.1**	**453.7**	**481.1**	**514.4**	**554.7**	**616.7**
Less: Corporate profits and inventory valuation adjustment	37,314	33,743	43,126	41,990	41,669	37,448	46,556	44.5	43.8	47.0	58.1	64.5	73.1	82.2
Contributions for social insurance	8,728	9,695	10,995	12,586	14,522	14,827	17,303	20.6	21.4	23.9	26.8	27.8	29.5	38.2
Excess of wage accruals over disbursements	−76	0	0	0	0	0	0	.0	.0	.0	.0	.0	.0	.0
Plus: Government transfer payments to persons	12,887	14,961	16,050	17,190	20,089	24,517	25,243	27.3	31.3	32.5	33.0	34.2	36.8	41.2
Net interest paid by government	5,171	5,407	5,389	5,745	6,204	6,175	7,091	7.8	7.7	8.0	17.5	19.1	20.6	22.3
Dividends	9,225	9,839	11,215	12,132	12,588	12,364	13,363	14.5	15.3	16.6	15.8	17.2	18.9	21.5
Business transfer payments	1,369	1,262	1,457	1,616	1,790	1,845	1,801	2.2	2.3	2.3	2.2	2.3	2.3	2.7
Equals: Personal income	**288,259**	**289,825**	**310,196**	**332,943**	**351,423**	**360,312**	**383,287**	**401.3**	**417.4**	**442.1**	**464.8**	**495.0**	**530.7**	**584.0**
Less: Personal tax and nontax payments	35,785	32,940	35,748	40,001	42,632	42,440	46,021	51.4	52.9	57.7	60.9	59.2	65.4	75.2
Federal	32,359	29,155	31,521	35,180	37,342	36,740	39,842	44.0	45.1	49.0	51.2	48.6	53.6	61.7
State and local	3,426	3,785	4,227	4,821	5,290	5,700	6,179	7.3	7.8	8.7	9.7	10.6	11.8	13.5
Equals: Disposable personal income	**252,474**	**256,885**	**274,448**	**292,942**	**308,791**	**317,872**	**337,266**	**349.9**	**364.4**	**384.4**	**403.8**	**435.8**	**465.3**	**508.8**
Less: Personal consumption expenditures	232,649	238,025	256,940	269,917	285,164	293,495	313,835	328.2	336.8	355.4	383.4	409.5	441.5	479.0
Equals: Personal saving	**19,825**	**18,860**	**17,508**	**23,025**	**23,627**	**24,377**	**23,431**	**21.7**	**27.6**	**29.1**	**20.4**	**26.3**	**24.9**	**29.8**
Addendum: Disposable personal income in constant (1958) dollars	275.4	278.3	296.7	309.3	315.8	318.8	333.0	340.2	350.7	367.3	381.3	406.5	430.8	456.3

Source: *Survey of Current Business* (July, 1960), pp. 8, 10; (Aug., 1963), pp. 5–6; (May, 1966), pp. 4–5.

Chart 9-1

Relationship of Gross National Product, National Income,
and Personal Income

The VALUE of the

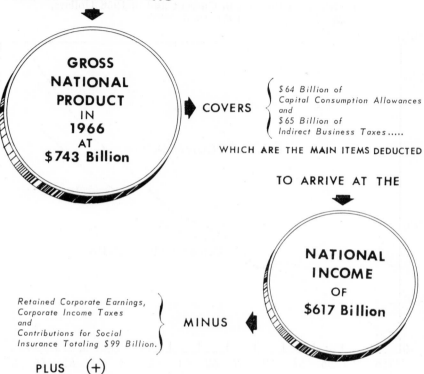

GROSS
NATIONAL
PRODUCT
IN
1966
AT
$743 Billion

COVERS

$64 Billion of
Capital Consumption Allowances
and
$65 Billion of
Indirect Business Taxes.....

WHICH ARE THE MAIN ITEMS DEDUCTED

TO ARRIVE AT THE

NATIONAL
INCOME
OF
$617 Billion

Retained Corporate Earnings,
Corporate Income Taxes
and
Contributions for Social
Insurance Totaling $99 Billion.

MINUS

PLUS (+)

Transfer Payments and Government
Interest of $66 Billion.....

EQUALS THE

PERSONAL
INCOME
OF
$584 Billion

Source: *National Income — 1951 Edition*, A Supplement to the *Survey of
Current Business* (Washington: U. S. Department of Commerce,
1951), p. 22. Figures for 1966 from the *Survey of Current Business*
(September, 1967).

Chart 9-2
Gross National Product in Current and in 1958 Dollars,
1954–1966

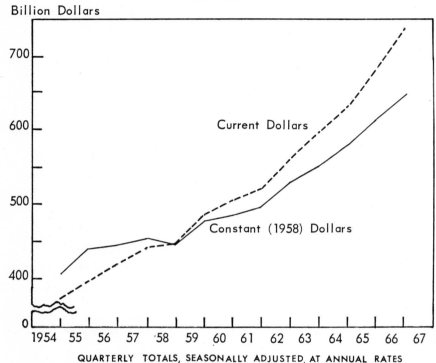

QUARTERLY TOTALS, SEASONALLY ADJUSTED, AT ANNUAL RATES

Source: *The National Income and Product Accounts of the United States,*
1929–1965, Statistical Tables, A Supplement to the *Survey of Current
Business.* Figures for 1966 from the *Survey of Current Business*
(August, 1966).

Such data on financial flows and on saving and investment have
been developed by the Board of Governors of the Federal Reserve
System. They are available on a quarterly basis in the *Federal
Reserve Bulletin,* with about a four-month lag. The quarterly data
are shown in general without seasonal adjustment. Quarterly data
are available for the period from 1952 to the present, and annual
estimates are available from 1946.

Sector Statements of Sources and Uses of Funds

The basic form of the flow-of-funds statements is a set of sources
and uses of funds statements of major sectors of the economy. These
statements of sources and uses of funds include current income of all
types, current expenditures, capital expenditures, borrowing and

Table 9-5

Gross National Product in Current and in Constant Dollars, 1945–1966
(Billions of Dollars)

YEAR	CURRENT DOLLARS	CONSTANT (1958) DOLLARS
1945	211.9	355.2
1946	208.5	312.6
1947	231.3	309.9
1948	257.6	323.7
1949	256.5	324.1
1950	284.8	355.3
1951	328.4	383.4
1952	345.5	395.1
1953	346.6	412.8
1954	364.8	407.0
1955	398.0	438.0
1956	419.2	446.1
1957	441.1	452.5
1958	447.3	447.3
1959	483.7	475.9
1960	503.7	487.7
1961	520.1	497.2
1962	560.3	529.8
1963	590.5	551.0
1964	631.7	580.0
1965	681.2	614.4
1966	739.6	647.8

Source: *The National Income and Product Accounts of the United States,
1929–1965*, Statistical Tables, A Supplement to the *Survey of Current
Business.* Figures for 1966 from the *Survey of Current Business*
(August, 1966).

lending, and other acquisitions of financial assets such as transfers
and gifts.[2] These statements are similar to statements of sources and
uses of funds in general accounting for a business. They cover many
of the same transactions as the national income and product accounts, since most income in the United States is received in money,
and most products are purchased for money. The two systems of
accounting do not have the same purpose any more than do the income statement of a corporation and a sources and uses of funds
statement of that corporation. One shows the sales and the related
expenditures and income arising from such sales during a period of

[2]Description of the current series can be found in the *Federal Reserve Bulletin*
(August, 1959), pp. 828–859. Further revisions are described in the *Federal Reserve
Bulletin* (November, 1965), pp. 1533–1538.

time; the other shows all of the funds made available during a period of time, not only from sales but also from borrowing, sale of assets, gifts, and the like, and the uses of such funds.

Statements of sources and uses of funds are available for the following major sectors of the economy:

Households { 1. Consumers and nonprofit organizations

Business {
2. Farm business
3. Nonfarm noncorporate business
4. Corporate business

Government {
5. Federal government
6. State and local government

Financial {
7. Commercial banking and monetary authorities
8. Savings institutions (mutual savings banks, savings and loan associations, credit unions)
9. Insurance companies and private pension plans
10. Finance not elsewhere classified (security brokers and dealers, open-end investment companies, sales finance companies, etc.)

International { 11. Rest of the world

The statement for each sector of the economy records all of the transactions of that sector, divided into current transactions and capital transactions. The transactions in the current account differ in the statements of the various sectors. This is true in the amount of detail shown and in the degree to which transactions are shown on a net basis. For example, in the government sector, tax receipts are shown net of tax refunds. The most detail is shown in the consumer and government sector accounts.

Transactions are also divided into nonfinancial flows and financial flows. Nonfinancial flows deal with such items as purchases of consumer goods, purchases of plant and equipment, and net change in inventories; financial flows deal with such items as changes in the volume of demand deposits, time deposits, and credit instruments.

The financial flows for each sector are generally recorded on a net basis for each type of transaction. This means that for each category of assets the funds obtained by disposing of such assets are subtracted from the funds used to acquire these assets in order to arrive at a net figure. Similarly with liabilities, the funds used for repayment are subtracted from the funds raised by borrowing. There are several cases, however, in which transactions are not recorded on a net basis. This is true when transactions involve similar asset and liability categories of transactions. For example, consumer borrowing to purchase securities and consumer purchases of securities are shown as separate transactions rather than as a net figure for investment in securities by consumers. This is also true of some assets and liabilities in the same category of transactions. For instance, consumer assets in the form of mortgages held and consumer mortgage debts are shown separately, not on a net basis.

Table 9-6 shows a sources and uses of funds statement for the consumer and nonprofit organizations sector annually from 1960 through 1966, and by quarters for 1955 and 1966. It shows that personal income minus personal taxes and nontaxes and personal outlays equals personal saving. Adding to personal saving, credits from government insurance and other minor adjustments, the net addition to the stock of durable consumers goods equals net saving by the household sector. Gross saving by this sector is net saving plus capital consumption of consumer durables, owner-occupied homes, and the plant and equipment of nonprofit organizations.

In the capital account there are two major sections, capital expenditures and net financial investment. Capital expenditures are divided into residential construction, consumer durable goods, and nonprofit plant and equipment. Net financial investment is divided into the following major subheads:

> Net acquisition of financial assets
>> Demand deposits and currency
>> Savings accounts
>> Life insurance reserves
>> Pension fund reserves
>> Credit and equity market instruments
>> Net investment in noncorporate business
> Net increase in liabilities

Partial balance sheets are also available for each sector of the economy. They show estimates of financial assets and of liabilities outstanding. Table 9-7 shows such a statement for the household sector of the economy, annually from 1953 through 1966.

Table 9-6

Sources and Uses of Funds in the Consumer and
Nonprofit Organization Sector, 1962–1966

(In Billions of Dollars)

Category	1962	1963	1964	1965	1966	1964 IV	1965 I	1965 II	1965 III	1965 IV	1966 I	1966 II	1966 III	1966 IV	
									(A) Households¹						
1 Personal income	442.6	465.5	496.0	535.1	580.4	507.5	518.1	527.6	541.9	552.8	564.6	573.6	585.2	598.2	1
2 Less: Personal taxes & nontaxes	57.4	60.9	59.4	66.0	75.1	60.9	64.9	66.6	65.7	66.7	69.5	73.7	77.4	79.8	2
3 Personal outlays	363.7	384.6	412.1	443.4	478.3	420.0	430.3	438.6	447.1	457.6	468.4	473.3	483.3	488.0	3
4 Equals: Personal saving	21.6	19.9	24.5	25.7	27.0	26.6	22.8	22.4	29.0	28.5	26.7	26.6	24.5	30.4	4
5 Plus: Credits from Govt. Insur.²	3.5	4.0	4.4	4.1	4.0	4.2	4.1	4.4	4.1	1.8	3.8	4.5	3.9	3.9	5
6 Other adjustments³	.5	.5	.6	.9	1.3	.7	.7	.6	.7	1.8	1.8	.6	.8	2.1	6
7 Net durables in consumption	6.7	8.9	11.3	14.6	14.3	9.5	14.9	13.4	14.8	15.2	16.6	12.6	14.8	13.3	7
8 Purchases	49.5	53.9	59.4	66.1	69.3	58.8	65.1	64.4	66.7	68.0	70.3	67.1	70.2	69.6	8
9 Less: Cap. consumption	42.9	45.0	48.0	51.5	55.0	49.3	50.2	51.0	51.9	52.8	53.7	54.5	55.4	56.3	9
10 Equals: Net saving	32.3	33.3	40.8	45.3	46.7	41.0	42.5	40.8	48.6	49.1	48.8	44.2	44.0	49.7	10
11 Plus: Capital consumption⁴	49.8	52.4	56.0	59.9	63.9	57.4	58.4	59.4	60.4	61.4	62.4	63.4	64.4	65.4	11
12 Equals: Gross saving	82.0	85.8	96.8	105.1	110.6	98.5	100.9	100.1	109.0	110.5	111.2	107.6	108.4	115.2	12
13 Gross investment (14 + 18)	83.5	87.2	99.3	107.8	112.8	107.5	99.7	106.3	112.4	112.8	111.0	109.1	111.5	119.4	13
14 Capital expend. (net of sales)	71.5	76.3	82.6	89.7	93.2	82.1	88.1	87.6	90.3	93.0	95.0	91.5	94.4	91.9	14
15 Residential construction	18.7	19.0	19.6	19.5	19.4	19.5	18.8	19.0	19.6	20.7	19.9	19.9	19.8	17.8	15
16 Consumer durable goods	49.5	53.9	59.4	66.1	69.3	58.8	65.1	64.4	66.7	68.0	70.3	67.1	70.2	69.6	16
17 Plant and equip. (nonprofit)	3.2	3.4	3.7	4.2	4.5	3.8	4.1	4.2	4.0	4.3	4.7	4.5	4.3	4.5	17
18 Net finan. investment (19 − 37)	12.1	10.9	16.7	18.1	19.6	25.4	11.6	18.7	22.1	19.9	16.0	17.7	17.1	27.5	18
19 *Net acquis. of finan. assets⁵*	*32.6*	*37.2*	*43.9*	*47.8*	*43.0*	*52.5*	*39.9*	*47.9*	*51.1*	*52.3*	*41.9*	*43.9*	*39.7*	*46.8*	19
20 Demand deposits and currency	2.7	4.3	6.7	7.2	2.1	13.9	6.3	.9	6.1	15.4	-3.4	2.6	.5	8.9	20
21 Savings accounts	23.4	23.0	23.9	26.4	18.9	26.4	26.8	22.1	29.1	27.6	21.0	19.8	17.9	16.7	21
22 At commercial banks	10.3	7.9	8.2	13.3	11.6	11.2	13.5	9.8	15.8	13.9	11.3	15.0	12.6	7.4	22
23 At savings institutions	13.0	15.1	15.8	13.1	7.3	15.2	13.3	12.3	13.2	13.6	9.7	4.8	5.3	9.4	23

24 Life insurance reserves	3.7	4.2	4.3	4.8	4.7	4.2	4.6	4.8	4.9	4.8	4.7	4.7	4.8	4.7	24
25 Pension fund reserves	8.8	9.9	11.2	10.9	12.1	12.0	10.4	11.6	11.2	10.6	11.9	11.0	12.6	12.7	25
26 Cr. market instr.	-1.7	.4	3.4	2.7	11.1	1.2	-3.0	11.7	3.8	-1.9	12.2	10.4	15.1	6.5	26
27 U.S. Govt. securities	*	3.5	1.7	2.6	7.8	2.2	.5	9.9	1.3	-1.3	9.8	9.9	5.3	6.3	27
28 Savings bonds	.4	1.2	.9	.6	.6	1.0	.8	.4	.5	.8	.3	.7	.3	.9	28
29 Short-term mkt.	.4	2.8	-1.8	-3.0	2.1	-.5	5.5	5.2	2.0	-.4	.4	6.4	-6.2	7.7	29
30 Other direct	-1.1	-.9	1.7	-1.2	1.1	1.3	-3.6	1.0	-1.3	-.7	6.7	-7.3	6.8	-1.9	30
31 Nonguaranteed	.3	.4	.9	.1	4.1	.3	-2.1	3.4	.1	-1.0	2.4	10.1	4.3	-.5	31
32 State and local oblig.	.8	.7	2.5	2.2	3.5	1.6	.8	1.5	2.4	4.4	1.9	.7	4.0	7.3	32
33 Corporate and foreign bonds	-.7	-1.0	-.8	-.1	-.2	.3	-2.6	2.7	1.7	-2.1	1.8	-3.5	4.0	-3.2	33
34 Corporate stock	-1.8	-2.5	-1.5	-1.5	*	-3.0	-.8	-1.7	-.5	-2.9	1.2	3.0	.9	-5.0	34
35 Mortgages	*	-.3	-.1	-.6	*	*	-.9	-.6	-1.1	.1	-2.5	.3	1.0	1.1	35
36 Net invest. in noncorp. bus.	-4.9	-5.3	-6.6	-5.8	-7.1	-5.8	-6.1	-6.0	-5.7	-5.4	-7.4	-7.4	-7.1	-6.4	36
37 *Net increase in liabilities*	*20.5*	*26.3*	*27.2*	*29.7*	*23.4*	*27.1*	*28.3*	*29.1*	*28.9*	*32.4*	*25.9*	*26.3*	*22.6*	*18.8*	37
38 Credit mkt. instruments	20.4	24.1	27.1	28.5	23.2	27.3	28.0	28.2	28.5	29.4	24.9	24.8	24.3	18.9	38
39 1- to 4-family mortgages	12.9	14.8	16.0	15.8	13.5	15.3	15.5	15.2	15.9	16.7	15.0	14.1	13.4	11.4	39
40 Other mortgages	.9	.9	.9	1.1	1.3	1.0	1.1	1.1	1.1	1.2	1.2	1.2	1.3	1.3	40
41 Consumer credit	5.5	7.3	8.0	9.4	6.9	7.2	10.0	9.6	9.3	8.9	9.2	7.0	6.9	4.6	41
42 Bank loans n.e.c.	.5	.4	1.4	1.3	-.2	3.1	.6	1.4	1.3	1.9	-1.4	-.8	.3	-.4	42
43 Other loans	.7	.6	.8	.8	1.8	.7	.8	.9	.9	.7	1.0	1.6	2.5	2.0	43
44 Security credit	-.1	2.0	-.2	.8	-.1	-.5	-.1	.7	.1	2.8	.6	1.2	-2.0	-.3	44
45 Discrepancy (12 - 13)	-1.5	-1.5	-2.5	-2.7	-2.2	-9.1	1.2	-6.2	-3.5	-2.3	.2	-1.5	-3.1	-4.3	45

Notes to Table

(A) Households

[1] Includes nonprofit organizations serving individuals.

[2] Imputed saving associated with growth of government life insurance and retirement reserves.

[3] Capital gains dividends from open-end investment companies plus life insurance reserve revaluations.

[4] Line 9 plus capital consumption on owner-occupied houses and nonprofit plant and equipment.

[5] Includes net free balances with security brokers not shown separately.

[6] Policy loans, hypothecated deposits, and U.S. Government loans to nonprofit organizations.

Source: *Federal Reserve Bulletin* (May, 1967), p. 853.

Table 9-7

Statement of Financial Assets and Liabilities of the Household Sector, 1952–66

(A) Households

Category	1953	1954	1955	1956	1957	1958	1959	1960	1961	1962	1963	1964	1965	1966	
Total financial assets	512.9	604.9	683.7	728.1	714.2	848.9	911.0	931.0	1073.6	1047.4	1171.8	1300.1	1438.9	1414.1	1
Demand deposits and currency	61.8	63.2	63.7	64.7	63.5	65.2	66.7	65.9	66.6	69.4	73.5	79.5	86.7	88.6	2
Savings accounts	87.6	96.7	105.5	115.0	127.0	141.1	152.8	165.3	182.7	206.0	229.1	253.0	279.5	297.5	3
At commercial banks	38.9	41.4	43.1	45.3	50.5	55.8	59.4	62.2	68.4	78.7	86.6	94.8	108.0	118.7	4
At savings institutions	48.7	55.3	62.4	69.7	76.6	85.3	93.5	103.1	114.3	127.3	142.5	158.3	171.5	178.8	5
Life insurance reserves	63.7	66.3	69.3	72.7	75.5	78.5	82.0	85.2	88.6	92.4	96.6	101.1	105.9	110.8	6
Pension fund reserves	37.0	41.9	49.6	55.6	61.6	71.6	81.1	89.4	102.1	107.7	121.3	136.1	150.8	159.2	7
Credit market instruments	252.7	325.7	384.4	408.5	374.5	479.8	515.1	511.3	618.9	556.6	635.4	713.5	797.3	738.2	8
U.S. Government securities	65.7	64.3	66.8	67.9	68.0	65.3	70.3	69.8	69.1	69.1	72.8	74.7	77.7	85.7	9
Short-term marketable	7.3	5.0	5.4	6.9	9.1	6.9	10.4	7.8	7.4	7.8	10.8	9.0	12.3	14.1	10
Other direct	8.6	10.3	10.9	9.7	8.8	9.2	11.0	13.6	12.6	11.5	10.6	12.9	11.8	13.3	11
Nonguaranteed					1.9	1.5	3.0	2.7	2.6	2.9	3.3	3.8	4.0	8.1	12
Savings bonds	49.4	50.0	50.2	50.1	48.2	47.7	45.9	45.6	46.4	46.9	48.0	49.0	49.6	50.1	13
State and local obligations	13.5	15.2	18.6	21.6	23.6	23.8	25.7	28.7	31.6	34.2	33.8	36.6	38.4	40.6	14
Corporate and foreign bonds	3.7	3.7	4.8	5.5	6.2	6.9	6.7	6.7	6.5	5.8	4.8	4.4	4.6	5.7	15
Corporate stock, market value	160.9	233.3	284.9	303.6	266.0	372.3	400.8	394.3	500.0	435.9	512.6	586.4	666.3	596.3	16
Mortgages	8.8	9.1	9.3	9.9	10.8	11.5	11.6	11.8	11.6	11.6	11.4	11.2	10.3	9.9	17
Security credit	.7	1.0		.9		1.0	1.0	1.1	1.3	1.2	1.2	1.2	1.7	1.6	18
Miscellaneous	9.6	9.9	10.4	10.7	11.2	11.6	12.2	12.8	13.5	14.1	14.7	15.7	17.0	18.2	19
Total liabilities	106.9	119.2	139.9	156.3	169.2	181.9	203.8	221.9	238.7	259.2	285.6	312.7	342.5	363.6	20
Credit market instruments	101.5	112.5	132.2	148.3	161.2	172.6	194.2	212.2	227.4	247.9	272.0	299.0	327.6	348.5	21
1- to 4-family mortgages	58.9	67.5	79.7	90.9	99.8	109.1	121.9	133.2	144.4	157.3	172.1	188.0	204.0	216.3	22
Other mortgages	3.9	4.6	5.2	5.9	6.6	7.4	8.2	9.0	9.8	10.7	11.6	12.6	13.6	14.8	23
Consumer credit	31.4	32.5	38.8	42.3	45.0	45.1	51.5	56.0	57.7	63.2	70.5	78.4	87.9	94.8	24
Bank loans n.e.c.	3.7	4.1	4.4	4.8	5.0	5.7	6.7	7.2	8.1	8.6	9.1	10.5	11.8	11.6	25
Other loans	3.5	3.8	4.1	4.4	4.9	5.3	5.9	6.7	7.4	8.1	8.7	9.5	10.3	11.0	26
Security credit	3.0	4.1	4.8	4.8	4.4	5.5	5.5	5.4	6.7	6.6	8.6	8.4	9.2	9.0	27
Trade credit	1.2	1.3	1.4	1.6	1.7	1.8	1.9	2.0	2.1	2.1	2.2	2.3	2.4	2.5	28
Deferred and unpaid life insurance premiums	1.3	1.3	1.5	1.7	1.8	2.0	2.2	2.4	2.5	2.7	2.9	3.0	3.3	3.7	29

Source: *Federal Reserve Bulletin* (February, 1968), p. A-65.14.

Summary Statement for the Total Economy

For the latest quarter for which flow-of-fund estimates are available, a summary table is presented. It shows sources and uses of funds for each of the sectors of the economy and also for all sectors combined. The major transactions categories are:

Gross saving
Gross investment
Private capital expenditures (net)
Net financial investment
Financial uses, net
Financial sources

Supplementary tables show more detail of saving and investment and of the principal financial flows for the total economy. Table 9-8 shows the summary statement by sectors and major transactions categories for the first quarter of 1967.

Concepts of Saving and Investment

Various definitions of saving and investment are used both in the description of cycles and in cycle theory. In this series of accounts *saving* is defined as the excess of current receipts over current expenditures. *Investment,* which is defined from the point of view of capital transactions, is the sum of the net purchases of tangible capital assets and net acquisitions of financial assets less net increases in liabilities. Saving and investment are equal because all current funds not used for current expenditures are classed as investment. In the accounts there is some statistical discrepancy, since these categories are estimated separately from different data.

Defining saving and investment in this way does not determine which items are included. All transactions are classified either as current or capital, but judgment is involved in deciding on the category into which to place many items.

One area of decision involves government investment expenditures in capital goods. These have all been listed under current transactions, and only financial transactions are shown under government investment. Also expenditures on research and development and on education and training are classed as current transactions in all sectors. Expenditures on consumer durable goods and on housing

Table 9-8

Summary of Flow-of-Funds Accounts for First Quarter, 1967 — Seasonally Adjusted Annual Rates

(In Billions of Dollars)

Transaction category (Sector)	Private domestic nonfinancial sectors								U.S. Govt		Financial sectors								Rest of the world		All sectors		Discrepancy	Natl. saving and investment
	Households		Business		State and local govts.		Total				Total		Monetary auth.		Coml. banks		Nonbank finance							
	U	S	U	S	U	S	U	S	U	S	U	S	U	S	U	S	U	S	U	S	U	S	U	
1 Gross saving	122.2		75.1			−1.7		195.6		−12.6		3.3		*		1.7		1.6		−2.5		183.9		186.3
2 Capital consumption	67.0		55.5					122.4				1.1				.5		.6				123.5		123.5
3 Net saving (1 − 2)	55.2		19.7			−1.7		73.2		−12.6		2.2		*		1.2		1.0		−2.5		60.3		62.8
4 Gross investment (5+10)	119.0		74.0		−2.2		190.8		−9.9		3.0		*		1.6		1.4		−1.4		182.6		−2.8	181.2
5 Private cap. expend., net	88.3		90.5				178.8				1.0				.5		.5				179.8			179.8
6 Consumer durables	69.4						69.4														69.4			69.4
7 Residential constr.	14.3		7.1				21.4														21.4			21.4
8 Plant and equipment	4.7		76.3				80.9				1.0				.5		.5				81.9			81.9
9 Inventory change			7.1				7.1														7.1			7.1
10 Net financial invest. (11 − 12)	30.7		−16.4		−2.2		12.0		−9.9		2.1		*		1.1		.9		−1.4		2.8		−2.8	1.4
11 Financial uses, net	50.2		10.4		10.7		71.3		4.3		80.7		3.7		37.0		40.0		1.9		158.2			3.3
12 Financial sources		19.5		26.9		12.9		59.3		14.1		78.6		3.6		35.9		39.1		3.3		155.4		1.9
13 Gold & off. U.S. fgn. exch.									−1.0		−3.1		−3.1						.2	−3.9	−3.9	−3.9		
14 Treasury currency										.9	.7		.7								.7	.9	.2	
15 Dem. dep. and currency											.9	6.2		5.0		1.3		.9		4.3	4.3	6.2		
16 Private domestic	9.2		−4.1		1.8		7.0					10.6		3.3		7.4				7.9	7.9	10.6	2.7	
17 U.S. Govt												−2.4		1.8		−4.2				−1.6	−1.6	−2.4	−.9	
18 Foreign												−2.0		−.1		−1.9				−2.0		−2.0		

Line																	Line
19	Time and svgs. accts..	34.6	17.9	10.0		50.3		.2	51.8		1.5	−1.3	.2	1.2	51.8		19
20	At coml. banks....	18.1				33.9			35.1				.2		35.1		20
21	At svgs. instit....	16.4				16.4		.2	16.7			35.1	.2	16.7	16.7		21
22	Life insr. reserves....	6.4				6.4			6.3				6.3		6.4		22
23	Pension fund reserves.	11.8			2.7	11.8	2.7		8.4	1.5			8.4		11.8		23
24	Consol. bank items¹..							.2	.2	1.5 −1.3	1.5	.8			.2 76.4		24
25	Credit mkt. instr....	−9.5 17.9	−.4 31.5	3.0 10.1	5.0	−6.8 59.5	10.8	74.9 .6	4.5	−1.3	37.4 .8	32.9 −.2	3.4 5.5	76.5 76.4		25
26	U.S. Govt. securities	−5.5	−6.2	−3.5	10.8	−15.2		23.2	4.8		18.7	−.3	2.7			26
27	State and local oblig.	−1.2	.7	−.4 9.8		−.9 9.8		10.7			8.7	2.0		10.8		27
28	Corp. and fgn. bonds	.6		6.6		7.2 13.1		8.4 2.3		.8		8.4 1.5	.6	9.8		28
29	Corp. stocks....	−3.1	13.1			13.1		3.1				3.1		16.2		29
30	1- to 4-family mtgs..	−.3 9.7	.9	.4	1.6	−3.1		7.5		.8		7.5	.6	4.2		30
31	Other mortgages....	1.3	.1		.9	.1 9.8		8.7 .6		*	1.1	7.6	−.2	10.4		31
32	Consumer credit....	4.3	5.2			6.5		5.7			1.0	4.7		6.5		32
33	Bank loans n.e.c....	1.4	2.1		1.6	4.3		2.2	*		1.4	.9		4.3		33
34	Other loans....	1.3	6.5		.9	7.9		1.4 −5.6	−.9		1.3	−5.6	.3 5.5	12.9 12.7	−.1	34
35	Open mkt. paper....	*	3.0 5.6	.2	2.5	3.0 7.1	2.5	7.1 .1	−.3		5.2	2.3 2.9	.3	12.7 8.3		35
36	Federal loans....		3.0 4.7	.3	2.5	3.0 4.7	2.5	5.1 2.9	−.3		5.2	.2 −2.8	4.7	8.3 2.5		36
37	Security credit....	3.5 1.4			1.4	3.5 1.4		3.4 5.5	5.5		2.1	1.3 5.5		6.9		37
38	To brkrs. and dealers	3.5				3.5		2.0 5.5	5.5		2.6	−.6 5.5	*	5.5		38
39	To others....	1.4			1.4	1.4		1.4			−.4	1.8	*	1.4		39
40	Taxes payable....			.1	1.1	.1			.2		.1			2.0	−1.6	40
41	Trade credit....	*	2.1 1.3	.1	1.9 2.0	2.1 1.4	−.7	.2				.2		4.3	−3.5	41
42	Equity in noncorp. business....	−6.8	−6.8		−6.8	−6.8 −6.8		3.3	−.5		−1.2 −3.0	4.4 2.4	−1.0 1.7	4.0 −6.8	.4	42
43	Misc. financial trans..	.9 .2	2.8 .8	.4	3.8 1.0	3.8 1.0	2.3	−.5	*					4.4		43
44	Sector discrepancies (1 − 4)....	3.1	1.1	.5	−2.7	4.7		.3		.1		.2	−1.0	1.3	1.3 5.1	44

¹Claims between commercial banks and monetary authorities: member bank reserves, vault cash, F.R. loans to banks, F.R. float, and stock at F.R. banks.

Source: *Federal Reserve Bulletin* (August, 1967), p. 1428.

are classed as investment. Transactions in existing assets have also been excluded from investment, except for business purchases of used plants from the government and the sale of plants to insurance companies, which are then leased from the companies.

Some problems also arise in defining financial investment. For example, the saving element in life insurance may be estimated in various ways. It has been treated as the difference between total life insurance company assets and claims against these assets in the form of policy reserves and dividend accumulations. Private pension plans and government employee and railroad retirement plans are treated as financial investment. Old-age and survivors insurance and unemployment compensation programs are treated as current transactions. Net retained earnings of unincorporated businesses are treated as if all were paid to the owners and are shown as consumer saving rather than business saving. Commodity Credit Corporation Loans under crop-support programs are treated as purchases of commodities with the seller having an option to repurchase, not as an investment.

There are many minor differences in the way saving and investment are handled in these accounts and in national income accounts. Gross national investment in the flow-of-funds accounts is larger than in national income accounts because consumer purchases of durable goods and business purchases of used plant and equipment from the government are included. Personal or consumer saving is larger because of several items. This includes the treating of the purchase of consumer durables as an investment expenditure, and the inclusion of saving through government life insurance and through government employee and railroad retirement funds. On the other hand, the national income saving series includes internal saving of life insurance companies and mutual financial institutions under personal saving, whereas they are excluded in the flow-of-funds accounts.

MEASURING CHANGES IN PRODUCTION AND PRICES

National income figures when deflated for price changes give an indication of the changes in the quantity of goods and services produced. At times it is desirable to have a more direct measure of these changes, especially those which occur in such fields as manufacturing and mining. In order to obtain such a measure, it is necessary to utilize an index number that shows composite levels of production as percentages of a base year or period, since such quantities as tons of steel and bushels of wheat produced cannot be added together directly. Index numbers are also useful in showing changes in prices that have occurred over a period of time. In fact, they can be used to explain changes in any economic variable when no other common denominator exists.

Use of Index Numbers

In developing index numbers for production or prices several problems require solution. One is to determine the items that are to be included in the index, since it is usually impossible to include more than a fraction of the universe being studied. A decision must also be made concerning the sources from which the data are to be collected and the methods of collection to insure accuracy and uniformity over a period of time. It is also necessary to determine the relative importance of the various items that have been selected for inclusion in the index and then to assign proper weights to those items. Furthermore, a decision must be made concerning the base year or period for the index. A fairly recent year or period that is reasonably representative of the years covered by the index should be chosen.

It is also necessary to select the method of computing the index number. Two basic methods are available — the aggregative and the average of relatives. A simple example will be used to illustrate the basic principles involved in calculating indexes. A fruit merchant sells 20 bushels of apples and 500 pounds of bananas each year. Prices change in the following fashion over the next three years:

	AVERAGE PRICE	
YEAR	BUSHEL OF APPLES	POUND OF BANANAS
1	$1.50	$0.04
2	1.20	0.12
3	.75	0.16

In order to obtain a weighted aggregative type of index, the average price of each fruit each year is multiplied by the quantity sold. These products are then added. The values for the second and third years are expressed as percentages of the first or base year, taken as 100. These figures then become the index numbers.

YEAR	APPLES	BANANAS	TOTAL	INDEX NUMBER
1	$30	$20	$50	100
2	24	60	84	168
3	15	80	95	190

The same result may be achieved by an alternative method known as the average of relatives type of index number. The first step is to reduce the price for each year to a percentage of the price in the base year as follows:

PRICE RELATIVES

YEAR	APPLES	BANANAS
1	100	100
2	80	300
3	50	400

These relatives are then weighted by multiplying them by the total value of each commodity in the base year, that is, $30 for 20 bushels of apples at $1.50 and $20 for 500 pounds of bananas at 4 cents. The value for the base year is again taken as 100 and the values for subsequent years expressed as a percentage of the base year.

YEAR	APPLES PRICE RELATIVES × 30	BANANAS PRICE RELATIVES × 20	TOTAL	INDEX
1	3,000	2,000	5,000	100
2	2,400	6,000	8,400	168
3	1,500	8,000	9,500	190

In this simple form these two methods of calculating index numbers give identical results. However, the methods may be modified in calculating more complicated indexes and then the results obtained will differ somewhat.

Federal Reserve Board Index of Industrial Production

The Federal Reserve Board of Governors has developed an index of industrial production including manufacturing, mining, and utilities. It is available on this basis from 1947 to the present, and for manufacturing and mining only from 1919 to 1947. The index is available on two base periods: 1947–1949 and 1957–1959.

The items in the index are grouped in two different ways, that is, by industry and by market. The first industry grouping is by manu-

Table 9-9

Major Groupings in the Federal Reserve Board Index of Industrial Production and Their Relative Importance

Industry Grouping	1957–1959 proportion	Market Grouping	1957–1959 proportion
Total index........................	100.00	Total index........................	100.00
Manufacturing, total.................	86.45	*Final products, total*...................	47.35
Durable.............................	48.07	Consumer goods...................	32.31
Nondurable.........................	38.38	Equipment, including defense........	15.04
Mining..............................	8.23	Materials..........................	52.65
Utilities............................	5.32		
Durable manufactures		**Consumer goods**	
Primary and fabricated metals.........	12.32	*Automotive products*....................	3.21
Primary metals.....................	6.95	Autos.............................	1.82
Iron and steel...................	5.45	Auto parts and allied products........	1.39
Nonferrous metals and products.....	1.50		
Fabricated metal products...........	5.37	*Home goods and apparel*...............	10.00
Structural metal parts..............	2.86	Home goods........................	4.59
Machinery and related products........	27.98	Appliances, TV, and radios..........	1.81
Machinery..........................	14.80	Appliances......................	1.33
Nonelectrical machinery............	8.43	TV and home radios..............	.47
Electrical machinery................	6.37	Furniture and rugs................	1.26
Transportation equipment............	10.19	Miscellaneous home goods..........	1.52
Motor vehicles and parts...........	4.68	Apparel, knit goods, and shoes.......	5.41
Aircraft and other equipment.......	5.26		
Instruments and related products.....	1.71	*Consumer staples*.....................	19.10
Ordnance and accessories.............	1.28	Processed foods....................	8.43
		Beverages and tobacco.............	2.43
Clay, glass, and lumber...............	4.72	Drugs, soap, and toiletries.........	2.97
Clay, glass, and stone products......	2.99	Newspapers, magazines, and books.....	1.47
Lumber and products................	1.73	Consumer fuel and lighting.........	3.67
		Fuel oil and gasoline.............	1.20
Furniture and miscellaneous...........	3.05	Residential utilities..............	2.46
Furniture and fixtures..............	1.54	Electricity....................	1.72
Miscellaneous manufactures...........	1.51	Gas...........................	.74
Nondurable manufactures		**Equipment**	
Textiles, apparel, and leather..........	7.60		
Textile mill products.................	2.90	*Business equipment*....................	11.63
Apparel products....................	3.59	Industrial equipment...............	6.85
Leather and products...............	1.11	Commercial equipment.............	2.42
		Freight and passenger equipment.....	1.76
Paper and printing...................	8.17	Farm equipment....................	.61
Paper and products.................	3.43		
Printing and publishing.............	4.74	*Defense equipment*....................	3.41
Newspapers......................	1.53		
		Materials	
Chemicals, petroleum, and rubber........	11.54		
Chemicals and products..............	7.58	*Durable goods materials*...............	26.73
Industrial chemicals................	3.84	Consumer durable..................	3.43
Petroleum products.................	1.97	Equipment........................	7.84
Rubber and plastics products........	1.99	Construction......................	9.17
		Metal materials n.e.c...............	6.29
Foods, beverages, and tobacco..........	11.07		
Foods and beverages.................	10.25	*Nondurable materials*..................	25.92
Food manufactures.................	8.64	Business supplies..................	9.11
Beverages.......................	1.61	Containers.....................	3.03
Tobacco products...................	.82	General business supplies..........	6.07
		Nondurable materials n.e.c.........	7.40
Mining			
Coal, oil, and gas....................	6.80	Business fuel and power.............	9.41
Coal................................	1.16	Mineral fuels..................	6.07
Crude oil and natural gas.............	5.64	Nonresidential utilities.............	2.86
Oil and gas extraction.............	4.91	Electricity....................	2.32
Crude oil.......................	4.25	General industrial.............	1.03
Gas and gas liquids..............	.66	Commercial and other..........	1.21
Oil and gas drilling...............	.73	Gas...........................	.54
Metal, stone, and earth minerals........	1.43		
Metal mining.......................	.61	**Supplementary groups of consumer goods**	
Stone and earth minerals.............	.82		
Utilities			
Electric.............................	4.04	Automotive and home goods..........	7.80
Gas................................	1.28	Apparel and staples.................	24.51

NOTE — Published groupings include some series and subtotals not shown separately.

Source: *Federal Reserve Bulletin* (August, 1966), pp. 1228–1229.

Table 9-10

Federal Reserve Board Index of Industrial Production by Industry Groupings, 1962–1966

1957–59 = 100

(Seasonally adjusted)

Annual Average

Grouping	1962 average	1963 average	1964 average	1965 average	1966 average	1967 Jan.	Feb.	Mar.	Apr.	May	June	July
Total index	118.3	124.3	132.3	149.3	156.3	158.1	156.4	156.4	156.3	155.6	155.5	156.7
Manufacturing, total	118.7	124.9	133.1	144.9	158.7	160.1	158.5	158.1	158.2	157.2	156.9	157.9
Durable	117.9	124.5	133.5	148.4	165.1	165.5	163.2	162.9	162.8	162.5	161.7	162.7
Nondurable	119.8	125.3	132.6	140.7	150.7	153.3	152.4	152.0	152.4	150.7	150.9	151.7
Mining	105.0	107.9	111.3	114.4	120.3	123.0	122.4	121.6	122.1	120.2	123.5	127.7
Utilities	131.3	140.0	151.3	161.0	173.4	179.6	178.2	180.6	179.2	182.5	183.6	183.0
Durable manufactures												
Primary and fabricated metals	110.0	117.7	130.7	142.0	151.5	147.0	146.3	143.9	142.7	142.8	142.5	142.8
Primary metals	104.6	113.3	129.1	137.5	142.7	131.9	131.9	129.2	129.1	128.9	129.3	128.9
Iron and steel	100.6	109.6	126.5	133.6	136.2	124.9	124.8	123.7	122.7	122.9	120.5	122.2
Nonferrous metals and products	119.1	126.7	138.3	152.1	166.5	163.2	167.2	162.1	161.4	154.4	156.0	153.0
Fabricated metal products	117.1	123.4	132.7	147.8	162.8	166.6	165.0	162.9	160.2	160.8	160.8	160.7
Structural metal parts	113.2	120.2	130.3	145.4	158.8	160.7	160.9	160.1	158.1	156.4	156.9	156.1
Machinery and related products	122.1	128.7	136.4	154.3	176.5	179.6	176.2	177.0	177.1	177.0	176.1	178.3
Machinery	123.5	129.2	141.4	160.4	183.8	189.2	186.4	183.8	181.8	180.5	177.5	180.5
Nonelectrical machinery	119.7	126.9	142.1	160.3	181.9	190.7	187.3	185.2	183.4	181.7	181.3	182.6
Electrical machinery	128.5	132.3	140.6	160.6	186.5	187.2	185.3	182.0	179.7	178.9	172.5	177.8
Transportation equipment	118.3	127.0	130.7	149.2	168.3	164.6	159.4	164.5	167.7	169.0	170.8	172.2
Motor vehicles and parts	134.1	146.1	150.1	175.2	171.3	151.5	140.6	148.0	153.8	155.2	157.7	160.0
Aircraft and other equipment	103.9	109.5	112.4	125.3	165.2	176.0	175.6	178.8	179.8	181.4	181.8	182.6
Instruments and related products	123.0	130.2	136.4	151.4	176.5	186.2	183.4	185.8	185.2	185.3	184.1	183.2
Ordnance and accessories	.....	.....	.....	.....	.....	.....	.....	.....	.....	.....	.....	.....
Clay, glass, and lumber	109.3	114.4	121.1	127.6	132.9	129.3	129.6	129.5	130.7	127.8	126.7	126.8
Clay, glass, and stone products	111.1	117.5	126.0	133.5	140.7	137.2	136.9	134.9	136.0	134.8	133.5	133.7
Lumber and products	106.1	108.9	112.6	117.4	119.3	115.7	116.0	120.2	121.5	115.6	114.9	.....
Furniture and miscellaneous	124.5	129.1	138.4	151.7	165.0	166.3	163.9	162.4	162.9	162.3	161.5	159.5
Furniture and fixtures	126.8	133.1	143.4	157.4	171.9	172.1	170.6	166.5	166.5	166.5	166.3	163.9
Miscellaneous manufactures	122.2	125.0	133.4	146.0	157.9	160.3	157.1	158.2	159.2	158.1	156.7	155.1

Nondurable manufactures

Textiles, apparel, and leather	115.1	118.5	125.2	135.7	141.6	139.8	136.4	134.5	134.2	134.0	133.3	133.6
Textile mill products	115.2	116.9	122.9	134.8	142.3	139.3	136.7	134.6	135.1	135.2	135.3	135.3
Apparel products	118.9	125.6	134.1	145.0	150.3	150.2	146.4	143.6	141.9	141.2	141.5	.....
Leather and products	102.3	99.8	102.6	107.8	111.9	107.7	103.7	100.5	107.1	105.0	101.9	.....
Paper and Printing	116.7	120.1	127.5	135.3	146.3	149.0	148.7	149.1	149.3	149.1	148.9	148.6
Paper and products	119.7	125.1	133.4	142.3	152.1	154.0	152.4	152.7	150.7	151.4	150.3	148.6
Printing and publishing	114.6	116.4	123.3	130.3	142.2	145.5	146.1	146.8	148.3	147.4	147.8	148.5
Newspapers	108.5	108.0	117.0	124.2	134.2	133.7	134.8	130.9	133.8	133.1	134.3	136.1
Chemicals, petroleum, and rubber	131.2	141.8	152.5	161.6	181.7	186.7	187.3	186.1	185.8	181.7	182.8	186.4
Chemical and products	136.1	148.6	159.6	173.3	193.0	198.6	200.5	199.3	199.2	199.2	199.2	200.1
Industrial chemicals	147.5	162.7	178.4	196.1	220.1	228.5	230.8	227.9	227.7	228.8	226.6	.....
Petroleum products	112.9	117.1	121.0	123.4	128.4	128.7	127.4	130.1	133.1	132.1	132.8	131.5
Rubber and plastics products	130.6	140.0	156.3	172.2	191.9	198.8	196.3	191.5	186.9	164.0	169.7	.....
Foods, beverages, and tobacco	113.4	116.8	120.8	123.1	127.7	130.9	130.5	130.5	132.4	130.9	131.3	131.1
Foods and beverages	113.5	116.9	120.8	123.3	128.4	131.9	131.3	131.7	132.7	132.0	131.9	131.7
Food manufactures	113.8	116.8	120.1	124.8	126.6	130.4	129.5	129.7	130.2	130.3	129.9	129.7
Beverages	111.5	117.8	124.4	128.4	137.8	140.2	141.1	142.3	146.3	141.2	142.9	.....
Tobacco products	112.0	115.2	120.8	120.5	119.8	118.5	120.2	116.2	128.8	117.4	123.9	.....

Mining

Coal, oil, and gas	103.8	107.0	109.8	112.2	117.6	119.6	118.9	117.7	118.7	118.0	121.3	127.5
Coal	95.3	102.5	107.1	111.8	115.2	120.7	115.7	115.1	125.5	120.1	122.5	122.6
Crude oil and natural gas	105.5	107.9	110.4	112.3	118.0	119.3	119.6	118.3	117.5	117.5	121.1	128.5
Oil and gas extraction	107.2	110.9	113.4	116.0	123.8	125.7	125.4	125.3	125.5	125.3	129.0	137.3
Crude oil	105.1	108.1	109.9	111.8	119.4	121.0	120.0	120.1	119.6	119.6	123.5	133.2
Gas and gas liquids	120.4	128.7	136.1	142.8	151.7	155.7	.....	.....	.....	.....	.....	.....
Oil and gas drilling	94.2	87.4	90.1	87.1	79.2	76.3	80.5	71.0	61.8	65.5	67.7	69.0
Metal, stone, and earth minerals	110.9	112.2	118.1	124.8	133.2	139.4	138.9	140.0	138.7	130.8	133.6	123.8
Metal mining	112.6	113.3	117.4	122.6	132.7	140.3	142.1	143.7	149.5	132.9	133.9	121.9
Stone and earth minerals	109.7	112.1	118.7	126.5	133.5	138.7	136.6	137.2	130.6	129.2	133.3	133.9

Utilities

Electric	133.1	142.6	153.9	165.5	179.7	185.7	183.7	186.7	185.2	189.6	190.8	.....
Gas	125.9	131.9	143.4	147.0	156.1							.....

Source: *Federal Reserve Bulletin* (December, 1963), p.1707; (December, 1964), p.1587; (December, 1965), p.1775; (October, 1966), p.1795; (September, 1967), p.1633.

facturing, mining, and utilities; and manufacturing is divided into two major subgroups, durable and nondurable manufactures. Each group is further subdivided as shown in Table 9-9 on page 235. Index numbers are available monthly for each subgroup, both seasonally adjusted and without such adjustment.

The first market grouping is by final products and materials. Final products are divided into two groups, consumer goods and equipment including defense equipment. Consumer goods are further divided into automotive products, home goods and apparel, and consumer staples. Materials are divided into three basic groups, that is, durable goods materials, nondurable materials, and business fuel and power. Each of the subgroups is further divided as shown in Table 9-9 on page 235. Monthly indexes are available for each of these groups and subgroups, both with and without seasonal adjustment.

Figures for the Index of Industrial Production by industry groupings in 1962 through 1966, with the first seven months in 1967, are shown in Table 9-10 on pages 236–237.

Whenever possible physical production units are utilized as the basis for measuring changes in production. In about half of the industries included in the index, however, changes are measured by the use of series on man-hours worked in each field. In order that these series may measure changes in production, it is necessary to adjust them for changes in the output per man-hour. The use of man-hours series makes it possible to get a better measure of changes in such fields as machinery, furniture, chemicals, baking, canning, and shipbuilding, where quantity figures are not too meaningful because the product is not homogeneous and there is no convenient unit in which output can be expressed directly.

In weighting the various factors to be included in the index, the importance of the individual series is measured by the value added by manufacture as shown in the Census of Manufactures and Minerals and by annual census surveys and other benchmark data. The most recent census years are 1963, 1958, and 1954.

In order to present an accurate index, allowances must be made for the number of nonworking days in a year. This has been done by a study in each field of the regular weekly closing days, if any. Seasonal factors, including holidays, have also been studied in each field so as to develop a seasonally adjusted index for each component as well as for the total index. These seasonal factors are studied continuously and changed as the seasonal changes in any field are made.

Bureau of Labor Statistics Wholesale Price Index

Several indexes are available for measuring changes in prices. One of the most comprehensive is the Wholesale Price Index of the Bureau of Labor Statistics. This index is based on the prices of nearly 2,000 commodities and is classified into 15 major groups and 88 subgroups. The index for all commodities and for each of the major groups for the years 1958 through 1966, and monthly from July, 1966–July, 1967, are shown in Table 9-11 on page 240.

The wholesale price index measures price changes in primary markets, that is, at the level of the first commercial transaction for each commodity. Most of the prices are those quoted by producers rather than by wholesalers in the strict sense. The term "wholesale" in the index refers to sales in sizable quantities, not to prices at which goods are either sold to wholesalers or by wholesalers.

For almost all of the items in the monthly index three or more price quotations are averaged. Detailed specifications are drawn up for each item on which prices are collected. Some of the wholesale prices are obtained by mail from individual reporters, others are obtained from trade journals, a few from boards of trade or commodity markets, and several from federal and state agencies.

Each price used in the index applies to only one day each week, but the day varies for different commodities. The monthly price is the average of the four or five one-day a week prices that fall within the month.

Indexes for the subgroups are first computed and then the total index developed from these indexes. When necessary, adjustments are made because of major changes in the specifications of commodities, shifts in the relative importance of sales to different types of purchasers or by different types of sellers, and alterations in the distribution pattern of the industry.

In using this index several limitations should be borne in mind. It is not a measure of the general price level or of the purchasing power of the dollar, since it does not include changes in the price of real estate, securities, services, etc. Furthermore, it does not cover

Table 9-11

Wholesale Prices by Groups of Commodities, 1958–1967

(Index Numbers of the Bureau of Labor Statistics, 1957–59 = 100)

Period	All commodities	Farm products	Processed foods and feeds	Industrial commodities													
				Total	Textiles, etc.	Hides, etc.	Fuel, etc.	Chemicals, etc.	Rubber, etc.	Lumber, etc.	Paper, etc.	Metals, etc.	Machinery and equipment	Furniture, etc.	Nonmetallic minerals	Transportation equipment	Miscellaneous
1958	100.4	103.6	102.5	99.5	98.9	96.0	98.7	100.4	100.1	97.4	100.1	99.1	100.0	100.2	99.9	n.a.	100.6
1959	100.6	97.2	99.9	101.3	100.4	109.1	98.7	100.0	99.7	104.1	101.0	101.2	102.1	100.4	101.2	n.a.	100.8
1960	100.7	96.9	100.0	101.3	101.5	105.2	99.6	100.2	99.9	100.4	101.8	101.3	102.9	100.1	101.4	n.a.	101.7
1961	100.3	96.0	101.6	100.8	99.7	106.2	100.7	99.1	96.1	95.9	98.8	100.7	102.9	99.5	101.8	n.a.	102.0
1962	100.6	97.7	102.7	100.8	100.6	107.4	100.2	97.5	93.3	96.5	100.0	100.0	102.9	98.8	101.8	n.a.	102.4
1963	100.3	95.7	103.3	100.7	100.5	104.2	99.8	96.3	93.8	98.6	99.2	100.1	103.1	98.1	101.3	n.a.	103.3
1964	100.5	94.3	103.1	101.2	101.2	104.6	97.1	96.7	92.5	100.6	99.0	102.8	103.8	98.5	101.5	n.a.	104.1
1965	102.5	98.4	106.7	102.5	101.8	109.2	98.9	97.4	92.9	101.1	99.9	105.7	105.0	98.0	101.7	n.a.	104.8
1966	105.9	105.6	113.0	104.7	102.1	119.7	101.3	97.8	94.8	105.6	102.6	108.3	108.2	99.1	102.6	n.a.	106.8
1966—July	106.4	107.8	113.8	105.2	102.4	122.7	101.4	97.9	95.1	106.6	103.2	108.8	108.3	99.0	102.7	n.a.	107.1
Aug.	106.8	108.1	115.7	105.2	102.4	121.2	102.0	97.9	95.1	106.2	103.2	108.5	108.5	99.1	102.7	n.a.	107.1
Sept.	106.8	108.7	115.5	105.2	102.2	119.9	102.2	98.0	94.7	105.9	103.1	108.4	108.9	99.2	103.0	n.a.	107.1
Oct.	106.2	104.4	113.9	105.3	102.2	118.7	102.6	97.9	94.6	104.8	103.1	108.6	109.4	99.7	103.2	n.a.	107.2
Nov.	105.9	102.5	112.6	105.5	102.1	117.5	102.7	98.0	95.0	103.0	103.0	109.0	110.2	100.3	103.3	n.a.	107.4
Dec.	105.9	101.8	112.8	105.5	101.8	117.3	102.0	98.2	95.0	102.5	103.0	109.0	110.7	100.4	103.3	n.a.	107.5
1967—Jan.	106.2	102.6	112.8	105.8	102.0	117.9	102.6	98.4	95.6	102.6	103.1	109.4	111.1	100.4	103.6	n.a.	107.9
Feb.	106.0	101.0	111.7	106.0	102.0	118.0	103.4	98.5	95.8	103.6	103.3	109.6	111.2	100.4	103.7	n.a.	108.0
Mar.	105.7	99.6	110.6	106.0	101.8	117.0	103.7	98.8	95.9	103.6	103.6	109.4	111.5	100.6	103.8	n.a.	107.7
Apr.	105.3	97.6	110.0	106.0	101.8	115.7	103.3	98.8	95.9	104.1	103.9	109.1	111.6	100.6	103.9	n.a.	108.0
May.	105.8	100.7	110.7	106.0	101.6	115.2	104.4	98.8	95.8	104.2	103.9	108.9	111.6	100.8	103.8	n.a.	108.0
June.	106.3	102.4	112.6	106.0	101.6	115.6	104.0	98.5	95.8	104.7	103.9	108.9	111.6	100.8	103.9	n.a.	109.6
July.	106.5	102.8	113.1	106.0	101.5	115.2	103.9	98.3	95.8	105.3	104.1	109.0	111.6	100.9	104.2	n.a.	109.7

Source: *Federal Reserve Bulletin* (September, 1967), p. 1640.

transactions at all levels of marketing but only at the wholesale level. In addition prices used in computing the index are those prevailing in national markets and are therefore not effective in any specific locality.

A weekly series of the index that includes a much smaller number of commodities than the monthly index is also published. It is designed as a counterpart of the monthly index and in a general way indicates weekly changes in the same field covered by the monthly index. This index is published each Friday for the week ending the previous Tuesday.

Bureau of Labor Statistics Consumer Price Index

In addition to measuring changes in a comprehensive series of prices, such as is done in the Wholesale Price Index, it is desirable to have special price indexes for more restricted segments of the economy. One such index that measures changes in the purchasing power of consumers was initiated during World War I by the Bureau of Labor Statistics and is currently available as the Consumer Price Index. It measures changes in prices that are paid for goods and services usually bought by moderate income families in large urban centers of the United States. In addition to the composite index, figures are also available for the following groups of commodities:

Food

Housing — Total and rent, home ownership, fuel oil and coal, gas and electricity, furnishings, and operation

Apparel and upkeep

Transportation

Health and recreation — Total and medical care, personal care, reading and recreation, other goods and services

This index is based on the average of 1957 to 1959 as 100. Weights are based on surveys of family expenditures determined by an extensive study of family consumption. Prices are gathered by part-time and full-time employees by means of shopping trips and personal interviews. A few prices, such as those for fuel, are obtained directly from dealers, and electric power rates are obtained from the Federal Power Commission.

It is again necessary to note some of the limitations in the use of this index. It does not show changes in the amounts that urban families spend for living, since to develop such a measure it would be necessary to have information reflecting changes in income and in the manner of living. It also does not show changes for any group other than typical moderate income families. It does show changes in the prices of a representative aggregate (or market basket) of goods and services bought by city wage-earner and clerical-worker families.

Implicit Price Indexes

What index does one use if he is interested in the general price level or the value of the dollar? Most of the readily available price indexes are more or less specific; that is, they measure the price behavior of a particular class of commodities or services such as farm products, transportation, lumber, or consumer goods. While it is probably usually the case that when general inflation is taking place these indexes will also be rising, it is not necessarily so. We need an index that reflects price movements in all segments of the economy.

The best index for overall price movements is constructed by the Department of Commerce and is called the implicit GNP deflator. The deflator itself is found very simply by dividing the actual GNP (GNP in current dollars) by real GNP (GNP in constant dollars) and multiplying by 100. For example, in Table 9-5 on page 223, we have shown GNP in current and in constant (1958) dollars for the years from 1945 through 1966. GNP in 1966 was 739.6, and in 1958 dollars was 647.8 which means that the implicit price deflator was $\frac{739.6}{647.8}$ (100) or 114.2. In other words, the general price level rose about 14 percent from 1958 to 1966.

The important thing to understand is the method the Department of Commerce uses to construct the series of GNP in constant dollars. This series is extremely important in its own right, being our best estimate of what we are interested in, namely, the total output of goods and services corrected for price level changes.

The GNP is broken down into the smallest groupings for which specific price indexes are available. The total output of the particular commodity or group of commodities is then corrected to reflect the price changes in those specific commodities. This yields a figure of output in constant dollars, or in base year prices. If this is done for all of the components of GNP, all categories corrected for price changes can be summed to the corrected GNP, or GNP in terms of prices in the base year. Incidentally, the deflators used for the various subgroups are also available in the *Survey of Current Business.*

There are still some shortcomings in this price index. Some gaps remain in that more refined subgroup indexes could be used. Estimates in the government sector, the service sectors, and in the construction industries are thought to be particularly subject to error. Furthermore, its method of construction leads to a chronic bias toward the overstatement of inflation. The index is available only quarterly and with a lag so it is not usable for month to month or other short-run purposes. In spite of these weaknesses, the implicit price index is still clearly superior to any other available index to measure general price movements.

QUESTIONS

1. How does the form in which national income data are presented differ from the income reporting form for private business?
2. How does a production statement differ from an income statement?
3. Why is the value added by each firm considered in national income accounting?
4. Define each of the following from the point of view of national income accounting:
   (a) Personal consumption expenditures.
   (b) Gross private domestic investment.
   (c) Government purchases of goods and services.
   (d) Net exports of goods and services.
5. Which items are included in national income?
6. How does national income differ from gross national product?
7. How is disposable personal income found?
8. Explain how each of the following are related to personal income:
   (a) Personal income taxes.
   (b) Personal and real property taxes.
   (c) Personal saving.
   (d) Contributions for social insurance.
   (e) Net interest paid by the government.
   (f) Government payments to veterans.
   (g) Corporate contributions to the American Red Cross.
   (h) Dividend payments.
   (i) Corporate income taxes.
9. Describe the nature of the flow-of-funds accounts.
10. How are flow-of-funds accounts related to national income and product accounts? How do they differ?

11. What significant information for analyzing business conditions is available in the flow-of-funds accounts?
12. How can changes in production or prices be measured?
13. Which factors must be considered in developing an index number?
14. Briefly describe the following indexes:
    (a) Federal Reserve Board Index of Industrial Production.
    (b) Bureau of Labor Statistics Wholesale Price Index.
    (c) Bureau of Labor Statistics Consumer Price Index.
    (d) GNP implicit price index.

SUGGESTED READINGS

"A Description of the Revised Wholesale Price Index," *Monthly Labor Review* (February, 1952), pp. 180–187.

Mudgett, Bruce D. *Index Numbers.* New York: John Wiley & Sons, Inc., 1951. Especially Chapters 1–4 and 10.

The National Income and Product Accounts of the United States, 1929–65 Statistical Tables, A Supplement to the *Survey of Current Business.*

"Revised Industrial Production Index," *Federal Reserve Bulletin* (December, 1959), pp. 1451–1474.

Ruggles and Ruggles. *National Income Accounts and Income Analysis.* New York: McGraw-Hill Book Company, Inc., 1949.

U.S. Department of Labor, Bureau of Labor Statistics, *The Consumer Price Index — A Short Description of the Index as Revised, 1953.* Washington: U.S. Government Printing Office, 1953.

U.S. Income and Output, A Supplement to the *Survey of Current Business.* Washington: U.S. Government Printing Office, 1958.

Also see the chapters in any standard statistics text on index numbers.

CHAPTER 10

Analysis of Time Series

In analyzing any series of economic data over a period of time, it is helpful to segregate the major types of factors that have influenced it. It may contain seasonal variations, it may have a long-term trend of growth or decline, there may be cyclical fluctuations, and it may also include irregular movements caused by strikes, droughts, floods, etc. In order to understand the influences that affected a particular series, it is necessary to isolate each of these factors.

MEASUREMENT OF SEASONAL VARIATIONS

Seasonal variations are the results of changes from one season of the year to the next that may be due to changes in the weather, in customs related to the seasons of the year or to holidays, or to the unequal number of days in the month in our calendar. A *seasonal variation* exists in any economic series when there is a regular pattern of variation in the series over a specific period of time, usually a year, but sometimes less than a year. This may be a regularly recurring pattern from year to year; or it may be a changing pattern in which changes are taking place on a regular basis as, for example, an increased proportion year by year of December sales of a commodity as more and more of it is used in Christmas giving.

There are several reasons for calculating a measure of seasonal variation. The best form for data for measuring cyclical changes and for forecasting them is that in which an adjustment has been made to eliminate the effects of seasonal variations. This eliminates the effect of a regular factor and puts the major stress on the variable factors at work.

A measure of seasonal variation is also needed in developing a sales forecast for an industry, and especially for an individual business. The basic forecast is made without regard to the seasonal. A measure of seasonal variation is then used to put the data in the annual forecast of sales on a month-by-month basis throughout the year.

Before calculating a measure of seasonal variation, the analyst should be sure that regular variations of this type exist. This means that the factors causing them should be studied to make certain that any observed variation is due to them. Random factors may at times produce variations for a period of time that appear to be regular. If a measure of seasonal variation is calculated from them, it is not only useless for analysis and prediction but also adds a source of error that may make such analysis and prediction impossible.

The most widely used measure of the seasonal variation is found by the ratio-to-moving-average method. A 12-month moving average is calculated from monthly data of sales or production for a period of several years. Since such a moving average always includes each of the 12 months of the year, it averages out the seasonal fluctuations in the data. This means that the moving average contains the trend, the cycle, and any irregular factors that may have affected the data. By dividing the original monthly data by the 12-month moving average, which includes everything but the seasonal, it is possible to obtain a measure of the seasonal variation.

The basis for this procedure may be shown in equation form, using the following symbols: T for the trend, S for the seasonal factor, C for the cyclical factor, and I for irregular factors.

The original data may then be expressed in terms of the above symbols as $T \times S \times C \times I$. The 12-month moving average averages out the seasonal factor and, therefore, contains the trend, and cyclical and irregular factors. It may be expressed as $T \times C \times I$.

Dividing the original data containing trend, seasonal, cyclical and irregular factors by the 12-month moving average containing the trend, cyclical, and irregular factors gives a measure of the seasonal factor. This may be seen from the following equation:

$$\frac{T \times S \times C \times I}{T \times C \times I} = S$$

The following hypothetical example of the calculation of the seasonal index of the sales of the Super Ice Cream Company illustrates the method. For simplicity a period of only four years has been used, but in actual practice it is best to use a period of ten or twelve years. Sales for each month from 1965 through 1968 are presented in Table 10-1.

Table 10-1

Monthly Sales of the Super Ice Cream Company, 1965-68
(In Thousands of Dollars)

	1965	1966	1967	1968
January...............	50	52	55	58
February..............	60	62	65	68
March................	77	79	83	86
April.................	96	99	102	106
May..................	137	140	144	149
June.................	158	163	165	170
July.................	167	174	175	180
August...............	159	165	166	171
September............	108	114	116	120
October..............	75	78	81	85
November............	61	62	64	67
December............	54	56	58	61

Source: Hypothetical data.

The first step is to find a 12-month moving average of the sales data. To do this, it is necessary to find a 12-month moving total and then to divide it by 12 to get the moving average. These calculations are shown in Table 10-2 on page 248.

The original data is divided by the 12-month moving average and the result expressed as a percent to determine the year-by-year seasonal factors. For example, the sales figure of $52,000 for January of 1966 is divided by the 12-month moving average for that month of 101.58 to get a seasonal factor of 51.2 percent. The results of these calculations are shown in Table 10-3 on page 249.

Since unusual factors may affect the seasonal pattern in any one year, the seasonal factors for several years are averaged to obtain a typical figure for each month. If necessary, these typical seasonal factors are then adjusted up or down proportionately to make them total 1200 percent or an average of 100 percent a month. These steps are shown in Table 10-4 on page 250.

When a longer period of years is utilized, it is often desirable to use some average other than the arithmetic mean in arriving at a

Table 10-2

Calculation of a 12-Month Moving Average of the Monthly Sales of the Super Ice Cream Company, 1965–1968

	12-MONTH MOVING TOTAL CENTERED AT THE 7TH MONTH[1]				12-MONTH MOVING AVERAGE CENTERED AT THE 7TH MONTH			
	1965	1966	1967	1968	1965	1966	1967	1968
January......		1219	1263	1297		101.58	105.25	108.08
February.....		1226	1264	1302		102.17	105.33	108.50
March........		1232	1265	1307		102.67	105.42	108.92
April.........		1238	1267	1311		103.17	105.58	109.25
May..........		1241	1270	1315		103.42	105.83	109.58
June.........		1242	1272	1318		103.50	106.00	109.83
July.........	1202	1244	1274	1321	100.17	103.67	106.17	110.08
August......	1204	1247	1277		100.33	103.92	106.42	
September....	1206	1250	1280		100.50	104.17	106.67	
October......	1208	1254	1283		100.67	104.50	106.92	
November....	1211	1257	1287		100.92	104.75	107.25	
December....	1214	1261	1292		101.17	105.08	107.67	

Source: Table 10-1.

[1] Actually the average for the first set of data from January through December, 1965, is the average for the middle of the year, that is, between June and July. For greater refinement, the July figure can be calculated by taking this figure and the figure between July and August found by averaging the data from February, 1965, through January, 1966, and averaging these two figures.

Table 10-3

Original Monthly Sales Data of the Super Ice Cream Company
for 1965–1968 Divided by the 12-Month Moving Average

	1965	1966	1967	1968
January..........		51.2	52.3	53.7
February.........		60.7	61.7	62.7
March...........		76.9	78.7	79.0
April............		96.0	96.6	97.0
May.............		135.4	136.1	136.0
June............		157.5	155.7	154.8
July............	166.7	167.9	164.8	163.5
August..........	158.5	158.8	156.0	
September........	107.5	109.4	108.7	
October..........	74.5	74.6	75.8	
November........	60.4	59.2	59.7	
December........	53.4	53.3	53.9	

Source: Tables 10-1 and 10-2.

typical seasonal pattern. This may be done by placing the items in an array, that is, arranging them from low to high and then taking the middle item or median, or by taking an average of the middle three or five items. It is also possible to use a modified arithmetic mean, that is, to eliminate any unusually low or high items and then take an arithmetic average of the rest.

If the seasonal variation in any field is changing over the course of time, it is necessary to alter the procedure in finding typical seasonal factors. Instead of calculating an average January figure, for example, the proper procedure is to plot the January crude seasonal figures for the period being studied and then to draw a trend line showing the change that is taking place. It is usually best to draw this trend line freehand, especially if it is being done by someone who has a thorough knowledge of the changes taking place. The trend may also be fitted by means of a formula either for a straight line or for a curve. The use of such formulas is considered more fully in the next section of this chapter on the measurement of the secular trend. The same thing is done for each of the 12 months. The current seasonal factors are then found by projecting the trend line for each of the 12 months one year ahead and then adjusting these figures on a proportionate basis to add to 1,200.

Table 10-4

Calculation of the Refined Seasonal Factors from the Crude Seasonals
of the Super Ice Cream Company

	JAN.	FEB.	MAR.	APR.	MAY	JUNE	JULY	AUG.	SEPT.	OCT.	NOV.	DEC.
1965............							166.7	158.5	107.5	74.5	60.4	53.4
1966............	51.2	60.7	76.9	96.0	135.4	157.5	167.9	158.8	109.4	74.6	59.2	53.3
1967............	52.3	61.7	78.7	96.6	136.1	155.7	164.8	156.0	108.7	75.8	59.7	53.9
1968............	53.7	62.7	79.0	97.0	136.0	154.8	163.5					
Average Seasonal........	52.4	61.7	78.2	96.5	135.8	156.0	165.7	157.8	108.5	75.0	59.8	53.5
Seasonal Index........	52.4	61.6	78.1	96.4	135.7	155.9	165.6	157.7	108.4	74.9	59.8	53.5

Source: Table 10-3.

A seasonal index such as that calculated from the sales of the Super Ice Cream Company shows the percentage which sales of each month are in relationship to average monthly sales as 100. For example, January sales are 52.4 percent of the average, July sales 165.7 percent, and so on. It is helpful at times to express the seasonal factor for each month as the average percent of the business for the year done in that month. January sales in this case are $\frac{52.4}{1200}$ of the year's business or 4.4 percent. Figures for each month as a typical percentage of the year's business are shown in Table 10-5.

Table 10-5

Typical Seasonal Factors for the Super Ice Cream Company
Expressed as a Percentage of the Year's Business

January	4.4	May	11.3	September	9.0
February	5.1	June	13.0	October	6.2
March	6.5	July	13.8	November	5.0
April	8.0	August	13.2	December	4.5

Source: Table 10-1.

MEASUREMENT OF THE SECULAR TREND

After the seasonal has been calculated and then eliminated from a series of data, it is possible to calculate the long-term or secular trend. This trend is the persistent underlying movement that has taken place in a series of data over a period of time long enough to cover several business cycles. It is the basic growth or decline that would be there if there were no cycle.

In the absence of the cycle the growth of any economic series, such as the production of a new product like nylon, would probably approximate a curve like an elongated S. Any new industry will probably grow slowly at first, will then experience a period of rapid growth while it is becoming integrated into the economy, and will then grow more slowly in relationship to increases in total economic activity.

The long-term trend in total economic activity in the United States has been a gradually rising one at a more or less constant rate. This is true in part because of increases in population that are continuing although at a reduced rate of increase. Increases in productivity and in the proportion of the population in the labor force have in all probability more than offset the decreasing rate of population growth. The quantity of capital in use has been increasing, and from all available evidence it appears that its effectiveness has also increased. American industry has likewise developed methods of economizing on materials and labor by improving design, by using by-products, by developing more efficient planning of work, and by introducing labor-saving techniques. In some fields natural resources of the highest quality are being depleted, but this factor leading to a slowing down in the rate of growth has been more than offset by the development of substitute materials and synthetic products. The system of distribution is also becoming more efficient through the introduction of self-service facilities and the development of larger, more economical units. The net result of all of these factors has been a more or less constant rate of increase in total economic activity.

There are several reasons for calculating a measure of the trend of an economic series. It can be used to project the most likely level of that series over a long period as, for example, ten years or twenty years in the future. Such a projection is only valid if the factors that led to its growth in the past continue. It is possible to calculate a measure of the trend from any series showing a significant change in magnitude over a period of time even when year-by-year changes are largely random, but projections made from such measures are useless. A measure of the trend is also useful as a means of analyzing the changes due to the business cycle in the past. In forecasting for a calendar quarter or a year ahead, the cycle may easily overshadow the trend so that a measure of the trend is of limited usefulness in short-run forecasting.

Since most economic series are in that stage in which they are growing in relationship to changes in population and national income, their current growth can be effectively measured by a straight line trend, even though an S-shaped curve would be needed to describe their total growth. The straight line that most closely approximates the growth in the total economy or in an industry which is growing in relation to increases in population and national income is the line of least squares. It is a line from which the sum of the squared vertical deviations is at a minimum. This line was not developed as a logical explanation of the growth in these series but was adapted from the physical sciences because it produces a good fit.

The following example shows the calculation of this line for the sales from 1964 through 1968 of the Super Ice Cream Company. This is much too short a period for calculating a trend, which should cover several cycles, but it is used to illustrate the method of getting the least-squares line. The formula for any straight line is $Y = a + bx$ in which Y is the trend value for each year expressed in terms of the original data. The symbol a is the average of the original data and establishes the height of the trend line in the middle year of the series. The slope of the line is determined by the value of b, which measures the annual deviation from the average value of the trend at the midpoint of the series. The following example shows its calculation.

Sales of Ice Cream for Each Year
(Thousands of Dollars)

1964	—	$1,080
1965	—	1,202
1966	—	1,244
1967	—	1,274
1968	—	1,321

YEAR	PRODUCTION	YEARS FROM MIDPOINT	xY	x^2
	Y	x		
1	1080	−2	−2160	4
2	1202	−1	−1202	1
3	1244	0	0	0
4	1274	1	1274	1
5	1321	2	2642	4
	6121		554	10

The value of a is found by dividing the sum of the original data (Y) by the number of years or N. $a = \dfrac{\Sigma Y}{N} = \dfrac{6121}{5} = 1224.2$. The value of b is found from the following formula: $b = \dfrac{\Sigma xY}{\Sigma x^2}$. In this case it is $\dfrac{554}{10}$ or 55.4. The straight line formula is then $Y = 1224.2 + 55.4x$. The values of Y for each year are found by adding and subtracting 55.4 for each year from the midyear, as follows:

(Thousands of Dollars)

1964	1113.4	(1224.2 minus 2 × 55.4)
1965	1168.8	(1224.2 minus 1 × 55.4)
1966	1224.2	(average value)
1967	1279.6	(1224.2 plus 1 × 55.4)
1968	1335.0	(1224.2 plus 2 × 55.4)

At times it may be desirable to express the long-term trend by means of a curved line rather than a straight line. This should be done, however, only if the analyst is convinced that such a curve actually represents the basic growth of the economic series at hand. Formulas are available for many types of curves such as the second degree parabola, the compound interest curve, and several different forms of S-shaped curves.[1] In most cases it is probably better to draw a trend line freehand rather than use a formula that may not accurately express the rate of growth.

MEASUREMENT OF CYCLICAL FLUCTUATIONS

One of the most complete definitions of the business cycle has been developed by the National Bureau of Economic Research. The working concept used in its research is as follows:[2]

> Business cycles are a type of fluctuation found in the aggregate economic activity of nations that organize their work mainly in business enterprises: a cycle consists of expansions occurring at about the same time in many economic activities, followed by similarly general recessions, contractions, and revivals which merge into the expansion phase of the next cycle; this sequence of changes is recurrent but not periodic; in duration business cycles vary from more than one year to ten or twelve years; they are not divisible into shorter cycles of similar character with amplitudes approximating their own.

Several important factors are included in this definition. They are as follows:

---

[1] For a discussion of the methods of deriving such curves the reader is referred to a comprehensive text in statistics such as John R. Stockton, *Introduction to Business and Economic Statistics* (3d ed.; Cincinnati: South-Western Publishing Company, 1966); and Werner Z. Hirsch, *Introduction to Modern Statistics* (New York: The Macmillan Company, 1959). The latter book also discusses a method of testing the significance of a measure of the trend. This test is designed to differentiate a measure based on random data from one based on a true trend. Such tests are also described for measures of seasonal and cyclical variations.

[2] Wesley C. Mitchell, *What Happens during Business Cycles* (New York: National Bureau of Economic Research, Inc., 1951), p. 6.

(1) The business cycle refers to fluctuations in aggregate economic activity rather than in a particular industry or sector of the economy.

(2) It is a phenomenon of an economy that has developed sufficiently to organize its activity in business units.

(3) Expansions and contractions occur at about the same time in many phases of economic activity.

(4) This sequence is recurrent but not periodic; that is, one cycle follows another in a continuous process but the cycles are not of equal length.

(5) These cycles cannot be further subdivided into shorter cycles that have similar characteristics or the same amplitude of fluctuation from the low point of activity to the high point, and from the high point to the next low point.

The cycle in any particular economic series is one that corresponds, in a general way, in its timing to the general business cycle; that is, it has troughs and peaks that occur at about the same time as such troughs and peaks occur in the general economy.

A measure of the cycle is valuable for historical analysis of past cyclical movements. It cannot be used for mechanical projection into the future since cycles do not develop in a regular pattern. Some of the factors in the cycle do develop in somewhat similar ways, and there is some consistency in cycle patterns. This makes a measure of past cycles of some value as an aid in analyzing the present situation. Such elements of similarity in the cyclical pattern will be described in Part IV.

Several methods have been developed for measuring the business cycle. The most widely used is the residual method in which the cycle is found by eliminating the other factors in the data. In recent years the National Bureau of Economic Research has developed a method of determining the cycle directly. It has become significant since more and more of the data from the intensive business cycle research of the National Bureau are being published in this form. These two methods will be considered in this section. The diffusion index which is useful for determining turning points in aggregate economic activity will also be described.

Residual Method

The residual method of calculating the cycle is based on the elimination of the trend and seasonal factors. The first step is to find a normal factor by multiplying the trend by the seasonal. The original data are then divided by the normal factor to obtain the cyclical and irregular factors. For example, the trend value of sales of the Super Ice Cream Company for 1964 was $1,113,400.[3] Since the trend of sales was increasing at a rate of $55,400 a year or $4,600 a month, the trend figure at an annual rate for January, 1964 is, $1,088,000 ($1,113,400 minus 5½ × $4,600); for February, 1964, it is $1,092,700, and so on. The seasonal pattern shows that business in January is normally 4.4 percent of the business for the year. In this case normal sales in January are 4.4 percent of $1,088,000 or $47,900, normal sales in February 5.1 percent of $1,092,700 or $55,700, and so on.

Deviations from such normal sales based on the trend and the cycle are due to cyclical and irregular factors. In the above examples actual sales for January, 1964, were $40,000 so they were $7,900 below normal due to cyclical and irregular factors.

Actual figures may also be expressed as a percentage of normal sales. Sales of $40,000 in January, 1964, for example, were 83.5 percent of normal sales of $47,900. Deviations due to cyclical and irregular factors for each month of 1964 are shown in Table 10-6.

The irregular factors cannot be eliminated from the data but can be smoothed out by means of one or a series of moving averages. The most frequent procedure is to use a three-month moving average, since most irregular factors affect a series for only a few months.

This residual method leaves a cyclical pattern that is correct only if the trend and seasonal have been correctly measured. It shows the cycle completely divorced from the trend and may thus give somewhat of a false impression, since the trend which has occurred during the period of the cycle is an integral part of the fluctuations that are taking place.

National Bureau Method

The National Bureau has developed a method for isolating and analyzing cyclical and irregular fluctuations directly, rather than by first calculating a normal figure and expressing these factors as deviations from normal.

Since business fluctuations go on in a continuous process, it is necessary to agree on a consistent method of isolating individual

---

[3]The trend value for 1964 is 1,113.4 expressed in thousands of dollars, or $1,113,400.

Table 10-6

Calculation of the Cyclical and Irregular Factors in the
Sales of the Super Ice Cream Company for Each Month of 1964

(Thousands of Dollars)

MONTH	TREND (Monthly Figures at an Annual Rate)	NORMAL (Trend and Seasonal)	ACTUAL SALES	CYCLICAL AND IRREGULAR FACTORS	
				DEVIATIONS FROM NORMAL	PERCENTAGE OF NORMAL
January....	1,088.1	47.9	40	−7.9	83.5
February...	1,092.7	55.7	47	−8.7	84.4
March.....	1,097.3	71.3	64	−7.3	89.8
April......	1,101.9	88.2	81	−7.2	91.8
May.......	1,106.5	125.0	122	−3.0	97.6
June.......	1,111.1	144.4	143	−1.4	99.0
July.......	1,115.7	154.0	154	0.0	100.0
August.....	1,120.3	147.9	149	+1.1	100.7
September..	1,124.9	101.2	102	+0.8	100.8
October....	1,129.5	70.0	71	+1.0	101.4
November..	1,134.1	56.7	58	+1.3	102.3
December..	1,138.8	51.2	49	−2.2	95.7

cycles. A cycle could be considered as the interval from one peak of business activity to the next, from one trough or low point to the next, or perhaps in other ways. The National Bureau measures the cycle from trough to trough. Thus a cycle begins at the initial trough at point A in the simplified pattern in Chart 10-1, develops to the peak at point C, and ends at the terminal trough at point E.

It is also necessary to establish the dates of the initial trough and terminal trough to isolate a cycle and, for some purposes, to establish the peak. This may be done for a series by noting the low point in the cycle, the high point, and the following low point. These points should, of course, correspond in a general way to the time period of the cycle in total economic activity. Since there is no comprehensive series available that covers all economic activity, it is necessary to get at the dates of the cycle in total activity in a different way. The National Bureau has analyzed many areas of economic activity and on the basis of this study has developed reference dates showing the time of the initial trough, peak, and terminal trough of the cycles in total economic activity. For example, March, 1933, is the initial

Chart 10-1

Simplified Cycle Pattern

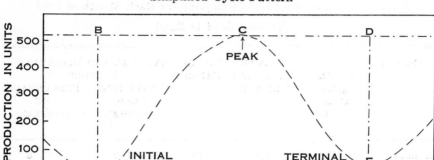

trough of the cycle in the 1930's; May, 1937, is the peak; and June, 1938, is the terminal trough.

In order to analyze the data for any series on economic activity the first step is to eliminate the variations due to seasonal factors. The seasonally adjusted data are then studied to find the specific cycles in the data by looking for troughs and peaks, which correspond in a general way to the reference dates for troughs and peaks. The specific cycles are measured from the initial trough through the peak to the terminal trough in those series that fluctuate in a similar manner to total economic activity. In those series that move in an inverse fashion from general economic activity, as for example commercial failures, the cycle is measured from the initial peak through the trough to the terminal peak.

In order to get a pattern of the cycle in any series, such as coke production, the seasonally adjusted data for each month of the specific cycle are averaged to find the cycle base. The seasonally adjusted figure for each month of the specific cycle is then expressed as a percent of the cycle average or base. These percent figures are referred to as specific cycle relatives.

The data on coke production are also analyzed in the same way during the period of the reference cycle. The data for each month during the reference cycle are averaged to find the cycle base, and then each month is expressed as a percent of this average. These percents are referred to as reference cycle relatives.

From such data it is possible to derive significant information about the cycle in any series. It is possible to calculate the timing of the cycle in any series by obtaining the number of months' lead or lag of the specific cycle troughs and peaks from the reference cycle troughs and peaks. For example, the peak of the reference cycle was in June, 1929, but the peak of the specific cycle in coke production was in July, 1929, a lag of one month. The trough of the reference cycle was in March, 1933, but the trough of the coke production series came in August, 1932, a lead of 7 months.

The duration of the cycle may be calculated by finding the number of months in the specific cycle and also the time periods covered by expansion and contraction. For example, the average period of the cycle in coke production for the 5 specific cycles from 1914 through 1932 was 42.6 months. The average for expansion was 24.0 months and for contraction 18.6 months.

It is also possible to compare the length of the specific cycle with the length of the reference cycle, and to do the same for the expansion and contraction phases, to see if any regular pattern exists. The specific cycle in coke production was 1.2 months shorter on the average between 1914 and 1932 than the reference cycle. The period of contraction was 1.6 months shorter and that of expansion .4 months longer on the average than the periods of expansion and contraction of the reference cycle. Data on the timing and duration of the cycles in coke production from 1914–1932 are shown in Table 10-7.

The amplitude of the specific cycle can be measured by the difference between the relatives at the initial trough and the peak, and between those at the peak and the terminal trough. In order to reduce the influence of random factors, three-month averages centered on the troughs and peaks are used in making such calculations. For example, such an average specific cycle relative of coke production at the initial trough in November, 1927, was 105.5. The average relative at the peak in July, 1929, was 141.6 and at the terminal trough in August, 1932, was 41.7. The amplitude of the rise was then 141.6 minus 105.5, or 36.1, the amplitude of the fall, 141.6 − 41.7, or 99.9; and the combined amplitude of the rise and fall, 136.0. The amplitude may also be expressed on a per month basis. Table 10-8 on page 262 gives an example as calculated by Burns and Mitchell for pig iron production showing the total amplitude of the rises and falls in this series as well as the per month amplitudes.

Table 10-7

Sample of Table S1: Timing and Duration of Specific Cycles
Coke Production, United States, 1914–1932

DATES OF SPECIFIC CYCLES TROUGH-PEAK-TROUGH (1)	TIMING AT REFERENCE PEAK		TIMING AT REFERENCE TROUGH		DURATION OF CYCLICAL MOVEMENTS (MO.)						PERCENT OF DURATION OF SPECIFIC CYCLES	
					SPECIFIC CYCLES			EXCESS OVER REFERENCE CYCLE				
	NO. OF MONTHS LEAD(−) OR LAG(+) (2)	DATE OF REFERENCE PEAK (3)	NO. OF MONTHS LEAD(−) OR LAG(+) (4)	DATE OF REFERENCE TROUGH (5)	EXPANSION (6)	CONTRACTION (7)	FULL CYCLE (8)	EXPANSION (9)	CONTRACTION (10)	FULL CYCLE (11)	EXPANSION (12)	CONTRACTION (13)
Nov. 14..........			−1	12/14								
Nov. 14–July 18– May 19..........	−1	8/18	+1	4/19	44	10	54	0	+2	+2	81	19
May 19–Aug. 20– July 21..........	+7	1/20	−2	9/21	15	11	26	+6	−9	−3	58	42
July 21–May 23– July 24..........	0	5/23	0	7/24	22	14	36	+2	0	+2	61	39
July 24–Feb. 26– Nov. 27..........	−8	10/26	−1	12/27	19	21	40	−8	+7	−1	48	52
Nov. 27–July 29– Aug., 32..........	+1	6/29	−7	3/33	20	37	57	+2	−8	−6	35	65
Average..........	−0.2		−1.7		24.0	18.6	42.6	+0.4	−1.6	−1.2	57	43
Average deviation..........	3.4		1.9		8.0	8.3	10.3	3.5	5.5	2.6	12	12

Source: Arthur F. Burns and Wesley C. Mitchell, *Measuring Business Cycles* (New York: National Bureau of Economic Research, 1947), p. 26, Table 5.

In a similar fashion the amplitude of the reference cycle may be calculated. For the rise, it is the difference between the reference cycle relatives at the dates of the initial trough and the peak of the reference cycle; and for the fall, the difference between the reference cycle relatives at the dates of the peak and the terminal trough of the reference cycle.

Cycle Pattern

In order to obtain a fairly smooth cycle pattern that is not affected materially by irregular factors, the full cycle is divided into nine stages. Stage I includes the three months centered at the initial trough; Stage V, the three months centered at the peak; and Stage IX, the three months centered at the terminal trough. Stages II to IV cover successive thirds of the expansion phase, and Stages VI to VIII successive thirds of contraction. The reference cycle relatives for Stage I are averaged to find the standing at Stage I, those for Stage II are averaged to find the standing at Stage II, and so on. The simplified example below illustrates this procedure. The standings at each stage are plotted at the midpoint of the stage and the points connected to form a cycle pattern. Such patterns may be developed for each specific cycle and also for each reference cycle for any economic series.

Reference Cycle Dates[4]

Initial trough — March, 1980
Peak — April, 1982
Terminal trough — November, 1983

Stages of the Cycle

Stage I   March, 1980
II   April through November, 1980 (8 months)
III   December, 1980, through July, 1981 (8 months)
IV   August, 1981, through March, 1982 (8 months)
V   April, 1982
VI   May, 1982, through October, 1982 (6 months)
VII   November, 1982, through April, 1983 (6 months)
VIII   May, 1983, through October, 1983 (6 months)
IX   November, 1983

[4]Hypothetical dates. Such dates are based on an analysis of overall economic activity rather than on any specific series or groups of series.

Table 10-8

Sample of Table S2: Amplitude of Specific Cycles
Pig Iron Production, United States, 1914-1932

DATES OF SPECIFIC CYCLES	3-MONTH AVERAGE IN SPECIFIC CYCLE RELATIVES CENTERED ON			AMPLITUDE			PER MONTH AMPLITUDE OF		
TROUGH-PEAK-TROUGH	INITIAL TROUGH	PEAK	TERMINAL TROUGH	RISE	FALL	RISE & FALL	RISE	FALL	RISE & FALL
(1)	(2)	(3)	(4)	(5)	(6)	(7)	(8)	(9)	(10)
Nov. 14-July 18-May 19....	55.5	119.6	74.5	64.1	45.1	109.2	1.5	4.5	2.0
May 19-Aug. 20-July 21....	88.7	125.9	45.0	37.2	80.9	118.1	2.5	7.4	4.5
July 21-May 23-July 24....	44.3	144.0	82.6	99.7	61.4	161.1	4.5	4.4	4.5
July 24-Feb. 26-Nov. 27....	69.4	118.2	92.1	48.8	26.1	74.9	2.6	1.2	1.9
Nov. 27-July 29-Aug., 32...	105.5	141.6	41.7	36.1	99.9	136.0	1.8	2.7	2.4
Average..........	72.7	129.9	67.2	57.2	62.7	119.9	2.6	4.0	3.1
Average deviation.........	19.5	10.4	19.1	19.8	22.2	23.0	0.8	1.7	1.2

Source: Arthur F. Burns and Wesley C. Mitchell, *op. cit*, p. 27, Table 6.

Production of Toy Autos 1980–1983
(Adjusted for Seasonal Variations)
(In Thousands)

	1980	1981	1982	1983
January................	13	18	33	21
February...............	11	19	34	21
March..................	10	20	34	20
April..................	11	20	35	18
May....................	11	21	33	17
June...................	12	22	31	16
July...................	12	23	30	16
August.................	13	24	28	15
September..............	14	27	26	15
October................	14	29	24	14
November...............	16	31	24	13
December...............	18	32	22	14

Average monthly production over the cycle (in thousands) — 21.27 units

Average monthly production in Stage I—February, March, and April, 1980—
10.67 units

Standing at Stage I —

$$\frac{10.67}{21.27} \times 100 = 50.2 \text{ percent}$$

Average monthly production in Stage II—April through November, 1980—
12.88 units

Standing at Stage II —

$$\frac{12.88}{21.27} \times 100 = 60.6 \text{ percent}$$

The patterns for successive cycles may be plotted on the same chart to determine if there is a typical cycle pattern. If there is, the cycle may be drawn in freehand or may be determined by averaging the cycles that have occurred during the period studied.

The conformity of the specific cycle to the general business cycle may be studied by plotting the typical specific cycle pattern and the typical reference cycle pattern when such patterns exist. Chart 10-2 shows such a pattern for the average of the five specific cycles and the five reference cycles in coke production from 1914 to 1932.

This National Bureau method of measuring cyclical fluctuations gives a visual picture of the average cycle in any series and of its relationship to the reference cycle. Such a picture is useful only if a typical cycle exists. It is easy to develop such a pattern from the

Chart 10-2

Sample Chart of Cyclical Patterns in Coke Production, 1914-1932

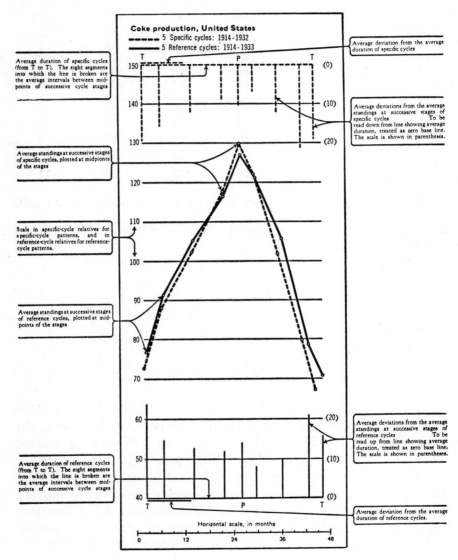

Source: Arthur F. Burns and Wesley C. Mitchell, *op. cit.*, p. 35.

relatives of several cycles by averaging the data for the nine stages of the cycle. Caution must be used in interpreting such a pattern, however, since it obscures the variation between cycles, which is often greater than the uniformity.

This cycle pattern also includes the influence of the trend during the period of the cycle. The trend between cycles is eliminated by expressing each monthly relative as a percent of the average relative for the cycle, but this procedure preserves the intra-cycle trend. Fluctuations during the course of the cycle include both of them, therefore it is worthwhile to study them together. If the trend is changing, however, it is necessary to have an estimate of such change. In this case the residual method may be the better one to use. The two methods can well be used to complement each other, especially if any question of a changing trend exists.

To follow the process of expansion and contraction, the cycle is also divided into eight segments. Segment 1 begins at the initial trough and runs to the midpoint of Stage II, Segment 2 runs from the midpoint of Stage II to the midpoint of Stage III, and so on. These procedures for dividing the cycle into segments are illustrated in Chart 10-3.

Chart 10-3

Cycle Stages and Segments

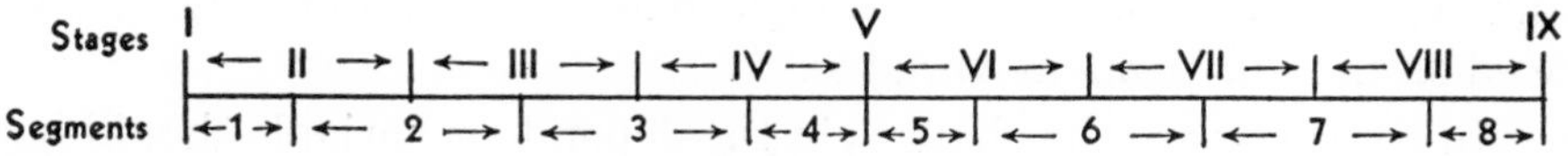

```
Stages     I                         V                              IX
           |← II →|← III →|← IV →|← VI →|← VII →|← VIII →|
Segments  |←1→|←  2  →|←  3  →|←4→|←5→|←  6  →|←  7  →|←8→|
```

Additional information about the cycle can be obtained from a study of the monthly rate of change in cycle standings in each of the segments of the cycle. In the example on page 263 production of toy autos had a standing of 50.2 at Stage I and 60.6 at the mid-point of Stage II, the period of Segment 1. Segment 1 is four months long. The average rate of change per month in reference cycle standings during this segment, therefore, is 2.6 points.

Diffusion Index

The turning points of the reference cycle must be determined from an analysis of many series on economic activity, since all areas of the economy do not move up and down at the same time. As one indication of turning points, the National Bureau has made use of a measure called a *diffusion index* to determine when the greatest proportion of economic series is turning. The diffusion index is the percentage of the series in any group being studied that is expanding in any period of time, such as a month or a quarter. For example, if out of a group of 50 series 30, or 60 percent, are expanding in a month, the diffusion index is 60; if 35, or 70 percent, are expanding the next month, it is 70; and so on. Turning points are indicated when after an upturn the diffusion index ceases to expand and starts to contract, and when after a downturn the diffusion index ceases to contract and starts to expand. Judgment is still required since series that cover different phases of economic activity have somewhat different turning points. When only a small number of series is used, the diffusion index becomes erratic and may turn for a short period when total economic activity has not reversed itself.

MEASURING CORRELATION BETWEEN SERIES

One of the basic methods of obtaining information when analyzing any economic variable, such as a time series, is to investigate its relationship to other variables. When two series move together consistently, the variations in one may be used to predict the variations in another. The pattern of relationship is developed by correlation analysis. Correlation is similar in some respects to trend analysis; but instead of using time as one variable, another series is used as the independent variable.

In a strict sense the changes in the dependent variable should be caused by changes in the independent variable. However, such strict causal relationship seldom, if ever, holds in economic analysis. Usually a whole series of forces are at work even though one or two may be dominant. However, unless a relationship exists that has remained fairly stable over time and is likely to do so, the use of measures of correlation can lead to serious errors in prediction. The only situation in which a measure of correlation can be reliably used in forecasting is when it is known that the changes in the variables are related.

The period used to develop a correlation relationship should cover more than one complete cycle. This is desirable to establish the validity of the relationship. Generally the effects of price changes should also be removed by putting value series in real terms. This is essential when correlating a value series with a physical volume or other nonprice series.

In developing correlation relationships between time series, it is often desirable to correlate year-by-year changes in the series rather than the original data. The trend of many time series is so strongly upward that a high degree of relationship exists because of this factor alone. If a significant relationship exists in the year-by-year changes in each series, it is frequently more useful for prediction than the relationship between the series themselves.

The development of a measure of correlation is similar to the determination of the trend in that it is a curve-fitting operation. The line of relationship is usually developed in one of two ways. The line of least squares may be used just as for the trend. The straight line relationship is expressed by the formula $y = a + bx$ just as for the trend, only x is the independent variable instead of time. When used to develop the relationship among variables rather than the relationship of one variable over time, the method of least squares is called *regression analysis*.

The second method is the graphic method in which the data are plotted and the line of relationship is drawn in by inspection of the data. Such a line is illustrated in Chart 10-4 on page 268 which shows the relationship between the sale of women's shoes and disposable personal income. Both shoe sales and disposable personal income are expressed as index numbers based on 1935–1939 as 100 to put the major stress on changes in each series since both increased materially in the period being analyzed. The first five years of the data on which this relationship is based are shown in Table 10-9 on page 269. The first step is to plot the data on the chart. In 1935 the index number of women's shoes sales was 87 and that of disposable personal income was 90. This is plotted at 87 on the sales axis and at 90 on the disposable personal income axis. Each set of figures is plotted in this way.

After the figures are all plotted, a line must be drawn that expresses the relationship shown by the dots on the chart. The line in Chart 10-4 passes through or near all dots except in the World War II period when shoes were in short supply and were rationed.

Even when mathematical methods are used to express the relationship, it is usually worthwhile to first use the graphic method to see the general nature of the relationship. In this example the formula based on the line of least squares is as follows:

$$Y = 24.3 + .704 \, X$$

This means that for each 10 percent increase in disposable personal income, there was just over a 7 percent increase in women's shoe sales.

Chart 10-4

Sales of Women's Shoes v. Disposable Personal Income

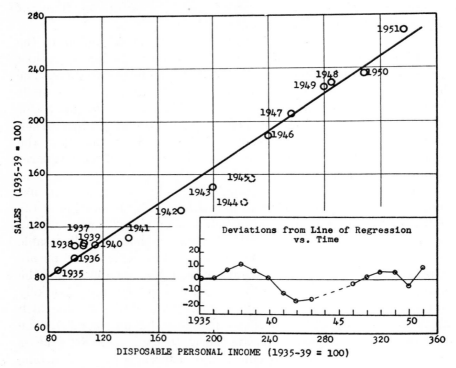

DISPOSABLE PERSONAL INCOME (1935-39 = 100)

Source: Calculations developed from data in the *Boot and Shoe Recorder*, the *Survey of Current Business*, and the files of the Bureau of Labor Statistics by Jurgis Bendikas as part of a graduate research project.

Frequently a relationship exists between a series and two or more other series. Such a multiple correlation relationship may be developed mathematically, but it is generally done graphically at least as a first step. A regression line is developed between the dependent variable and the most important independent variable. Deviations from this line are plotted against a second independent variable, and a regression line developed from these relationships.

Table 10-9

Index Numbers of the Sales of Women's Shoes and of
Disposable Personal Income, 1935–1939
(1935–1939 = 100)

YEAR	INDEX OF SHOES SALES	INDEX OF DISPOSABLE PERSONAL INCOME
1935	87	90
1936	96	99
1937	107	107
1938	105	98
1939	105	105

Source: Developed from data in the *Boot and Shoe Recorder*, the *Survey of Current Business*, and the files of the Bureau of Labor Statistics by Jurgis Bendikas as part of a graduate research project.

An example of the technique of doing this is presented in Chart 10-5 on page 271. It presents the relationship between food consumption per capita and real income per capita and real food prices. It is based on data shown in Table 10-10 on page 270.

The first part of the chart shows the relationship of an index number of food consumption and an index of disposable income. The related figures for each year are plotted in a similar fashion to the data in Chart 10-4 on page 268. Then a line of relationship is drawn in freehand. In this case the line passes through most of the dots in the prewar period, but it is above those in the postwar period. This is to be expected since the relative price of food increased in the postwar period over the prewar period. This line of regression shows an average change of one percentage point in food consumption for each change of three percentage points in disposable income.

The next step is to measure the deviation of each dot for each year from the line of regression. These deviations are then plotted in Part B of the chart against an index number of the price of food which has been deflated by the consumer price index. For example, in 1932 the vertical deviation from the line of regression was plus 2 index number points and in this year the relative food price index was 73.3. The dot is plotted at plus 2 on the deviation scale and at 73.3 on the price scale. After all points are plotted in this way, a line is drawn expressing the relationship, if any. In this case a good fit is obtained by a line which shows a change of two percentage points in food consumption per capita for each ten percentage points of change in the real price of food.

Table 10-10

Index Numbers of Food Consumption, Disposable Income, and
Retail Food Prices in the United States, 1922–1941 and 1948–1956

(1947–1949 = 100)

YEAR	PER CAPITA		PRICE OF FOOD[1]	YEAR	PER CAPITA		PRICE OF FOOD[1]
	CONSUMPTION OF FOOD	DISPOSABLE INCOME[1]			CONSUMPTION OF FOOD	DISPOSABLE INCOME[1]	
1922	89.0	61.0	83.0	1937	90.4	72.5	84.9
1923	90.9	68.3	84.2	1938	90.6	67.8	80.3
1924	91.5	67.4	83.2	1939	93.8	73.2	79.3
1925	90.9	68.5	87.7	1940	95.5	77.6	79.8
1926	92.1	69.6	89.9	1941	97.5	89.5	83.0
1927	90.9	70.2	88.3				
1928	90.9	71.9	88.4	1948	99.1	100.6	101.3
1929	91.1	75.2	89.5	1949	98.9	100.1	98.2
1930	90.7	68.3	87.4	1950	99.9	106.8	98.4
1931	90.0	64.0	79.1	1951	98.1	106.6	101.4
1932	87.8	53.9	73.3	1952	100.4	107.6	101.0
1933	88.0	53.2	75.2	1953	101.5	110.8	98.6
1934	89.1	58.0	81.1	1954	101.4	110.3	98.1
1935	87.3	63.2	84.7	1955	102.8	115.5	96.9
1936	90.5	70.5	84.5	1956	104.0	118.4	95.9

[1]Deflated by dividing by the Bureau of Labor Statistics Consumer Price Index.

Source: Frederick V. Waugh, *Graphic Analysis in Agricultural Economics* (Washington: United States Department of Agriculture, 1957), p. 35.

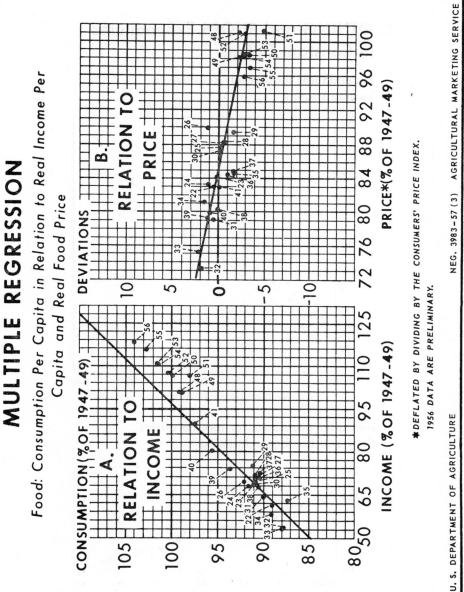

Chart 10-5

MULTIPLE REGRESSION

Food: Consumption Per Capita in Relation to Real Income Per Capita and Real Food Price

U. S. DEPARTMENT OF AGRICULTURE   NEG. 3983–57 (3)   AGRICULTURAL MARKETING SERVICE

Source: Frederick V. Waugh, *Graphic Analysis in Agricultural Economics* (Washington: United States Department of Agriculture, 1957), p. 35.

Chart 10-6

CLOTHING and SHOES Expenditures in Constant Dollars

Expenditures moderately sensitive to income change . . .

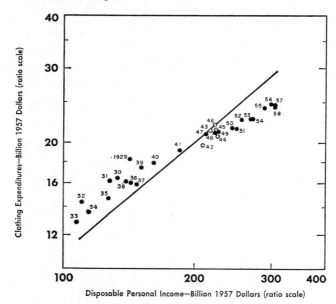

and after allowance for income effects the trend has been declining

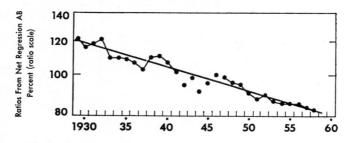

Source: *Survey of Current Business* (March, 1959) p. 27.

One of the forms of multiple correlation is that in which time is one of the variables that is used in developing the relationship. If technological or other factors have affected the relationship so as to introduce a time trend, the deviations from the first line of regression may be plotted year by year on a second chart to see if a consistent pattern appears. This is true in the case of consumer expenditures on clothing and shoes in constant dollars that show a relationship to disposable personal income, but one that has been decreasing gradually for some years. This relationship is expressed graphically in Chart 10-6. In this case the line of relationship to disposable income has a strong upward slope. When plotted on an arithmetic scale, it is a curvilinear relationship. It has been plotted here on a ratio scale in which equal spaces represent equal rates of change. This has the same effect as if logarithms of the numbers were plotted. On this scale the relationship becomes a straight line.

QUESTIONS

1. Describe the ratio-to-moving-average method of calculating the seasonal.

2. How is a changing seasonal calculated?

3. Describe the method of calculating a trend line by the least-squares method.

4. Describe the residual method of isolating the cycle.

5. What can be done to remove the effect of irregular factors?

6. How does the National Bureau use the term reference cycle? specific cycle?

7. How are reference cycle relatives calculated? specific cycle relatives?

8. How can the amplitude of the cycle be determined from specific cycle relatives?

9. How is a cycle pattern determined?

10. How can a cycle pattern be used to judge the conformity of a specific series to the reference cycle?

11. Describe the segments into which the cycle is divided.

12. How is the rate of change during a segment of the cycle determined?

13. How do the residual method and the National Bureau method differ in handling the trend?

14. How may a diffusion index be used in the analysis of cyclical turning points?

15. Discuss the nature of correlation.

16. Which factors should be considered in deciding on the series to correlate and the time period to use?

SUGGESTED READINGS

Burns, Arthur F., and Wesley C. Mitchell. *Measuring Business Cycles*. New York: National Bureau of Economic Research, 1947.

Gordon, Robert A. *Business Fluctuations*, 2nd ed. New York: Harper & Brothers, 1961.

Kuznets, Simon. *Seasonal Variations in Industry and Trade*. New York: National Bureau of Economic Research, 1933.

Spencer, Milton, Colin G. Clark, and Peter W. Hoguet. *Business and Economic Forecasting: An Econometric Approach*. Homewood, Illinois: Richard D. Irwin, Inc., 1961.

Stockton, John R. *Business Statistics*. Cincinnati: South-Western Publishing Company, 1958. Parts IV and V.

PROBLEMS ON PART III

1. A. From tables and charts in *Economic Indicators* and the *Survey of Current Business* prepare a table showing quarterly changes during the last complete cycle and for the current cycle in each of the following categories of GNP:

> Personal Consumption Expenditures
>> Durable goods
>> Nondurable goods
>> Services
> Government Purchases of Goods and Services
>> Federal
>>> National defense
>>> Other
>> State and local
> Net Exports of Goods and Services
> Gross Private Domestic Investment
>> Residential construction
>> Other private construction
>> Producers' durable equipment
>> Change in business inventories

   B. Calculate the percentage increase in the last cycle from the low quarter to the high quarter for each category. Calculate the percentage decrease during the downturn.

2. Calculate an index number of the price of fruit sold by a fruit merchant from the following data:

Month	Average Price			Average Quantities Sold per Month
	Bushel of Apples	Box of Pears	Pound of Bananas	
1	$3.00	$4.00	$0.18	Apples — 30 bushels
2	3.25	4.50	0.16	Pears — 20 boxes
3	3.50	5.25	0.14	Bananas — 400 pounds
4	3.40	5.00	0.10	

3. Plot gross national product figures in constant dollars for the period from 1949 to the present. On the same chart using the right-hand side for a scale for this series plot the figures for the Federal Reserve Board Index of Industrial Production for the same time period. Discuss the similarities and differences in the fluctuations in these two series and insofar as possible account for them.

4. The following data are available on the cycle of an industry producing kitchen gadgets:

Initial trough of the cycle................September, 1927
Peak of the cycle........................March, 1929
Terminal trough of the cycle.............January, 1933

Average specific cycle relatives for the nine stages of the cycle are
as follows:

Stage I	85	Stage VI	111
Stage II	95	Stage VII	100
Stage III	102	Stage VIII	90
Stage IV	111	Stage IX	85
Stage V	120		

(a) Plot the cycle pattern.
(b) Calculate the timing and duration of this cycle.
(c) Calculate the amplitude for the rise and for the fall. Also the
amplitude per month for the rise and for the fall.

5. Select a company for which you can get monthly sales data for
January, 1954, to the present. (This data will be used in this project
and for the forecast project in Part VII.) Using this data calculate:

(a) The trend of sales since 1954 (use annual sales data).
(b) The seasonal pattern.
(c) The cycle pattern (National Bureau Method). Plot this pattern.
(d) Timing and duration of the cycle.
(e) Cyclical amplitude.

PART IV

STATISTICAL RECORD OF
BUSINESS FLUCTUATIONS

To forecast the level of economic activity it is generally helpful to consider the trend, the seasonal pattern, the cycle, and any other factors that may be at work.

When forecasting business six months to a year ahead, the trend is of relatively minor significance, since it does not cause material changes in so short a period of time. Seasonal variations are very significant in some sectors of the economy, such as department stores, but relatively unimportant in others. The seasonal pattern can usually be predicted fairly accurately from a study of past seasonal variations.

The most difficult factor to forecast is the cycle, since it is the result of the interaction of all of the factors at work in the economy and, in turn, affects all of them. In order to analyze the cyclical forces at work, it is necessary to study the empirical evidence on the behavior of the cycle in some detail. Such a study should determine which factors, if any, are typical, and the extent of deviations from a typical pattern.

The first chapter in this part (Chapter 11) will be devoted to a study of the statistical record of the cycle in general economic activity and in various sectors of the economy. The following chapter (Chapter 12) will present the general cycle pattern as it develops during the expansion and contraction phases. The last chapter (Chapter 13) will deal with the empirical evidence on other types of business fluctuations, such as those in construction and in agriculture.

Behavior of the Cycle

This study of the statistical record of the behavior of the cycle will begin with an analysis of the most common length of the cycle and of its expansion and contraction phases, and of the extent of the deviations from these patterns. Attention will next be directed to the international conformity of business cycles, especially in the major industrial countries. The extent to which the cycle has affected all phases of American business will then be considered, followed by a study of the timing of various phases of economic activity in relationship to the turning points in the reference cycle. Special attention will be given to important series that lead and lag in the cyclical process. The varying amplitudes of different economic series in past cycles will be described and analyzed. Consideration will also be directed to the differences in the characteristics of the cycle in different regions of the United States. Lastly the nature of the cycle in inventories will be described and analyzed.

LENGTH OF THE CYCLE

In forecasting changes in the level of economic activity it is helpful to know what pattern, if any, has existed in the length of the cycle and in the expansion and contraction phases of the cycle. These factors will be considered in turn in this section.

Length of the Cycle in Years

Using the definition of the National Bureau of Economic Research, American business cycles from 1854 to the present have varied in length between 1 and 8 years. The average length of the cycle has been 4 years, and the most common length 3 years. Over two thirds of the cycles have been between 3 and 5 years in length. Table 11-1 on the next page shows the length of American business cycles from 1854 to 1961.

Table 11-1

Length of American Business Cycles
1854 to 1961

LENGTH IN YEARS	NUMBER OF CYCLES
1	0
2	2
3	10
4	7
5	3
6	2
7	1 (June, 1938–October, 1945)
8	1 (December, 1870–March, 1879)

Sources: Adapted from Willard Thorp, *Business Annals*; and Burns and Mitchell, *Measuring Business Cycles*; and carried forward to date.

Length of the Cycle in Months

For those cycles between 1854 and 1961 for which the National Bureau has established monthly reference dates, the full cycle varied from 28 months to 99 months, with an average of 49 months. The expansion periods varied from 10 months to 80 months, with an average of 30 months; and the contraction periods from 7 months to 65 months, with an average of 19 months. Thus it can be seen that there is no uniform length of the cycle, and there is also no uniform period of expansion or contraction.

There is no uniform relationship between the length of the expansion phase in an individual cycle and the length of the contraction phase in that cycle. In some cases the expansion period is much longer than the contraction period, as was the case in the cycle that reached its peak in May, 1937. In others, the two periods are of about equal length; and in still others the contraction phase is decidedly longer than the expansion period, as was the case in the cycle that reached its trough in March, 1879.

In the post-World War II period expansions have been about 20 percent longer than the average and contractions have been only about half as long as the average. The four postwar contractions have been 11, 13, 9, and 9 months long. Since 1920, 8 of the 10 contractions have lasted 14 months or less. The contraction in the post-World War I depression, however, lasted 18 months and in the depression, which began in 1929, 43 months.

The duration of expansion and contraction periods, and of the full cycle for reference cycles from December, 1854, through February, 1961, is presented in Table 11-2 on page 282.

CONFORMITY IN BUSINESS CYCLE PATTERNS

This section will review the degree to which the business cycle pervades all areas of economic activity. Consideration will be given, first, to the international pattern of cycles and, then, to the domestic pattern of activity during cycles.

International Pattern

Business cycles affect all countries that have their economies organized on a free enterprise-pecuniary basis. The most highly organized countries show the most pronounced cyclical patterns. Major cycles have occurred at about the same time in industrial countries, such as England, France, Germany, Austria, and the United States. This was true in the cycles that reached their peaks in 1815, 1837, 1847, 1857, 1890, 1907, 1920, and 1929.

Minor cycles have not occurred at the same time, nor has each country had the same number of cycles. The United States has had more cycles than England, France, the Netherlands, Sweden, and Germany. Furthermore, some countries may be in a recovery or in a prosperity stage while others are still in a recession stage.

This lack of conformity in international cycle patterns has continued in the post-World War II period. The 1949, 1953, and 1960 downturns were not experienced by most countries. The recession that began in 1957 in the United States was more severe than earlier postwar recessions, but it was still a relatively mild recession. It affected most industrial countries of the world to some degree, however. Canada and Japan had a recession at about the same time as the United States, and economic activity leveled off in most other industrial nations. The 1960-1961 recession was not experienced by most other countries, but there was some decline in economic activity in Canada and Japan.

Domestic Pattern

The cycle in the United States is also by no means an all-pervasive phenomenon, which carries every economic activity with

Table 11-2

Duration of Business Cycle Expansions and Contractions in the
United States, 1854–1961

Business Cycle			Duration (in Months) of —		
Trough	Peak	Trough	Expansion	Contraction	Full Cycle
Dec., 1854	June, 1857	Dec., 1858	30	18	48
Dec., 1858	Oct., 1860	June, 1861	22	8	30
June, 1861	Apr., 1865	Dec., 1867	46	32	78
Dec., 1867	June, 1869	Dec., 1870	18	18	36
Dec., 1870	Oct., 1873	Mar., 1879	34	65	99
Mar., 1879	Mar., 1882	May, 1885	36	38	74
May, 1885	Mar., 1887	Apr., 1888	22	13	35
Apr., 1888	July, 1890	May, 1891	27	10	37
May, 1891	Jan., 1893	June, 1894	20	17	37
June, 1894	Dec., 1895	June, 1897	18	18	36
June, 1897	June, 1899	Dec., 1900	24	18	42
Dec., 1900	Sept., 1902	Aug., 1904	21	23	44
Aug., 1904	May, 1907	June, 1908	33	13	46
June, 1908	Jan., 1910	Jan., 1912	19	24	43
Jan., 1912	Jan., 1913	Dec., 1914	12	23	35
Dec., 1914	Aug., 1918	Mar., 1919	44	7	51
Mar., 1919	Jan., 1920	July, 1921	10	18	28
July, 1921	May, 1923	July, 1924	22	14	36
July, 1924	Oct., 1926	Nov., 1927	27	13	40
Nov., 1927	Aug., 1929	Mar., 1933	21	43	64
Mar., 1933	May, 1937	June, 1938	50	13	63
June, 1938	Feb., 1945	Oct., 1945	80	8	88
Oct., 1945	Nov., 1948	Oct., 1949	37	11	48
Oct., 1949	July, 1953	Aug., 1954	45	13	58
Aug., 1954	July, 1957	Apr., 1958	35	9	44
Apr., 1958	May, 1960	Feb., 1961	25	9	34
Average, all cycles:					
26 cycles, 1854–1961			30	19	49
10 cycles, 1919–1961			35	15	50
4 cycles, 1945–1961			36	10	46
Average, peacetime cycles:					
22 cycles, 1854–1961			26	20	46
8 cycles, 1919–1961			28	16	44
3 cycles, 1945–1961			32	10	42

Source: *Business Cycle Developments* (January, 1965), p. 56. Based on National
Bureau of Economic Research data.

it. In a sample of economic time series studied by the National Bureau of Economic Research, which includes all of the series studied by the Bureau except a few that do not have regular cyclical movements, it was found that some series were reaching their peak in almost every month.[1] Many series do not move in complete conformity with the general business cycle but are undergoing expansion and contraction at different times. During a prosperity period many, but by no means all, of the series are expanding; and during a recession not all series are contracting.

A study of the profits of American industrial corporations reveals a similar diversity in the profit record of individual companies. In every stage of the business cycle the results of the operation of some companies run counter to the main stream of profits or losses. Even in the quarter in the 1929 to 1937 depression that had the fewest rises in profits, 26 percent of the corporations in one group which was analyzed by the National Bureau had rising profits. In other words, the depression did not cause business to decline rapidly enough to reduce profit levels in all fields. When minor fluctuations are disregarded, the exceptions are fewer but they are still there.[2]

CYCLICAL TIMING OF ECONOMIC SERIES

Most types of economic activity expand and contract in phase with overall economic activity. Some series are inverted; that is, they are moving in opposition to the direction of business in general.

Inverted timing occurs to a large extent because of the form in which economic data are reported. If the employment series being studied is the number of men at work, it will move with the business cycle, showing positive timing. If, instead, the employment situation is viewed from the number of men unemployed, the series will show inverted timing. Since in most cases the form in which economic data are expressed is not arbitrary but is designed for ease of use and compilation, the National Bureau has kept all of the time series it has studied in their original form. This explains the inverted position of such series as commercial failures and idle freight cars, in addition to unemployment.

---

[1] Arthur F. Burns, *New Facts on Business Cycles* (New York: National Bureau of Economic Research, 1950), p. 6.

[2] Thor Hultgren, *Cyclical Diversities in the Fortunes of Industrial Corporations* (New York: National Bureau of Economic Research, 1950), p. 11.

In several groups of inverted series, however, the inversion is not due to the form in which the data are expressed. In some of them it is due to the choices made by consumers in periods of shifting incomes. For example, the series on sheep and hog slaughter are often inverted since most people who can afford beef prefer it, and shift to pork and mutton only when incomes are cut during depression periods. In other cases a series is inverted because the supply of a product is not reduced during a recession to as great an extent as is the decline in demand. For example, when the demand for cotton expands, a larger fraction of the output is used domestically and therefore exports are less; but during contraction less is used at home and more exported. Thus the exports of cotton show inverted timing in many cycles. Some series on inventories are also inverted in short cycles, since it is difficult to keep stocks adjusted to sales without a lag; and, as a result, in short cycles they may decrease as business expands and increase as business contracts.

Even though most economic series expand and contract with general business, they do not move in perfect unison with the cycle in overall activity. Many of them typically have leads and lags at reference cycle peaks and troughs. Such leads and lags can be measured from the reference cycle turning point dates as developed by the National Bureau. These are the dates presented as the troughs and peaks of cycles since 1854 in Table 11-2.

General Economic Activity

As is to be expected, indexes that reflect aggregate economic activity correspond fairly closely with reference cycle dates. Gross national product for the period for which the figures are available moved closely in harmony with reference cycle dates.[3] The Federal Reserve Board Index of Industrial Production reaches its peaks at about the same time as the reference peaks, and on the average has a short lead at reference troughs.

Construction

Indexes for the construction industry almost always lead reference cycle peaks and troughs. The index of the F. W. Dodge Com-

---

[3]The data on leads and lags in this section are taken from Geoffrey H. Moore, *Statistical Indicators of Cyclical Revivals and Recessions* (New York: National Bureau of Economic Research, 1950), and Geoffrey H. Moore, *Business Cycle Indicators*, Vol. I (New York: National Bureau of Economic Research, 1961).

pany for the amount of floor space represented in residential contracts leads at reference peaks and at reference troughs, as does the number of housing starts. The same is true of the index of commercial and industrial building contracts. There are also leads at peaks and troughs in indexes of total construction contracts awarded on a value basis, of total contracts adjusted for changes in cost, of total building permits, of total residential construction on a value basis, and of the number of commercial building projects. There is also a tendency for related series, such as the production of southern pine lumber, oak flooring, and plumbing fixtures, to move in about the same fashion.

Since contracts lead construction, a lead would be expected in this series even if construction moved in complete conformity with the cycle. The lead of construction itself at many upper turning points is due to several factors that are inherent in the nature of the cyclical process. The accelerator can cause construction to turn down while demand is still increasing, but at a lower rate. Innovations lead to building early in the cycle, but this slows down when plant and equipment have been built to produce the new product. The slowdown in construction before the economy turns down may also be due to overbuilding in some fields, which has often been one of the factors producing unbalance. The lead at the lower turning point is due to some of the factors at work in the economy that produce an upturn, such as an innovation, a need for more capacity in some fields as population expands, the lowering of interest rates that makes some projects profitable, the building of new plants to cut costs, and the like.

Industrial Durable Goods

New orders for industrial durable goods lead at both peaks and troughs. New orders for locomotives, freight cars, and railroad passenger cars also show a tendency to lead at reference peaks and troughs. The reasons for such leads are similar to those for construction.

The movements in pig iron production and in steel ingot production are fairly coincidental with the cycle but show some lead at the troughs and some lags at the peaks. The lead at the trough is based on leads in construction and industrial durable goods. The lag at the peak is probably due to the time required to fill orders at the mill, which were placed before the downturn became apparent.

Employment and Hours of Work

Indexes of employment correspond to cyclical peaks and troughs fairly closely. Employment in nonagricultural establishments is practically coincidental with the reference cycle turns at the peak, but has at times had a short lead at the troughs due to the lead in construction and in industrial durable goods. The index of unemployment of the Department of Commerce, as is to be expected, moves in a fashion similar to nonagricultural employment. The tendency for indexes of employment to be roughly coincidental at peaks and troughs is also shown in series on employment in the durable goods field and in such industries as cement, clay, glass, iron and steel, and machinery. The Bureau of Labor Statistics index of average hours worked per week, however, shows a tendency to lead at reference peaks and at reference troughs.[4] In other words, one of the first reactions of businessmen to a change in economic conditions is a change in the average hours worked per week rather than in the number of men employed.

Wholesale Prices

The Dun & Bradstreet Wholesale Price Index of Basic Commodities shows a tendency to lead the business cycle.[5] The wholesale price index of the Bureau of Labor Statistics, excluding farm products and foods, behaves in a similar fashion. This is probably due in part to changes in demand arising out of industries that lead. It is also due to the action of traders in commodity markets who try to determine future conditions of demand and supply in setting prices at which they are willing to trade.

Consumer Income and Spending

In the prewar period there was some tendency for consumer income and spending to lag somewhat in the cyclical process. This lag has disappeared in the postwar period in part because of governmental programs to maintain purchasing power and also because of the mild nature of postwar recessions. Personal income has in recent years moved about in harmony with turning points in the cycle and the same is true of retail sales.

---

[4]For the period from 1932–1958 based on the Bureau of Labor Statistics figures on Average Hours Worked per Week in Manufacturing.

[5]War cycle observations omitted.

Profits

An index of quarterly corporation profits developed by the National Bureau moved in fairly close harmony with the general cyclical process. A study of the profits of industrial corporations made for the National Bureau of Economic Research found that there was no constant lead or constant lag in aggregate profits. It did find, however, that some companies were experiencing increasing profits while others were experiencing decreasing profits.[6] This is to be expected since profits are a residual after all expenses are met, and expenses are affected as soon as business turns. Since all of business does not turn at the same time, profits can be expected to follow business and also show a spread.

In the postwar period profits have shown a short lead. The Department of Commerce quarterly series on Corporate Profits after Taxes had a median lead of two months for the period from 1939 to 1961. Since profits are a residual after all expenses have been met, they fluctuate much more widely than sales. They are already declining in some industries before business has reached a peak and increasing before business has reached a trough. In the postwar period the magnitude of changes in profits in such industries was large enough to give profits in total a short lead.

Common Stock Prices

Common stock prices as measured by the Dow-Jones Industrial Index show a tendency to lead at peaks and troughs. Stock traders base their purchases on the future prospects of the economy and of a particular company whose stock they are buying and have generally succeeded in determining changes before they have occurred.

Business Failures

Business failures have a long lead at reference peaks and at reference troughs. When the upturn begins, costs lag and profits increase. As costs catch up and as an increasing volume of goods is available from new plants constructed in the upturn, it is more difficult to operate profitably. Some weak concerns fail at this stage, and the number increases as prosperity develops. In the recession period there is also a lead because most weak concerns have failed after the

---

[6]Thor Hultgren, *op. cit.*, p. 12.

full effects of lower business levels have had their impact. The concerns still in business are by and large the stronger ones that have weathered the storm.

Interest Rates

Interest rates have a tendency to lag in the cyclical process. A quarterly index of bank rates on business loans of the Federal Reserve Board shows a lag at reference peaks and at reference troughs. This same tendency for interest rates to lag is also shown in bond yields. This is, in part, due to the contractual nature of interest payments. Loan contracts are usually signed for a minimum of 90 days, and in many cases run for years. The lag is also due to the "sticky" nature of interest rates in many situations. They are changed infrequently and only when there are clear indications that the underlying demand and supply factors have changed.

Summary

Table 11-3 presents some of the most important series that typically lead at reference cycle peaks and troughs, those which move at about the same time as the reference cycle, and those which typically lag. This table appears on the opposite page.

CYCLICAL AMPLITUDE

This section will consider the amplitude over the cycle of various phases of economic activity. First some observations will be made on the general pattern of cyclical amplitude and then the pattern in gross national product and in industrial production will be described.

General Pattern

Various phases of economic activity have different amplitudes during the cycle. In the prewar cycles for which data are available in National Bureau studies, some general patterns are evident. Prices had a lower average amplitude than production in manufacturing inasmuch as producers adjusted to changed demand primarily by reducing output. The amplitude in employment was substantially less than that in production because many workers were put on part-time employment rather than laid off. Payrolls fluctuated somewhat more than production due to changes in the work week and to overtime pay in prosperity. Profits had a much larger am-

Table 11-3

Timing at Peaks and Troughs of Important Economic Series

Leads

Average hours worked per week
Layoff rate — manufacturing
Business failures — liabilities
Common stock prices
Corporate profits after taxes
Housing starts
New orders — machinery and equipment industries
Construction contracts awarded for commercial and industrial buildings
Newly approved capital appropriations
Change in manufacturers' unfilled orders — durable goods industries
Change in book value of manufacturing and trade inventories

Roughly Coincident

Bank debits outside New York
Corporate profits
Employment — nonagricultural
Gross national product
Industrial production
Personal income
Retail sales
Unemployment rate
Wholesale prices excluding farm products and foods

Lags

Bank rates on short-term business loans
Consumer installment debt
Manufacturers' inventories in current prices
Plant and equipment expenditures
Index of labor cost per unit of output — total manufacturing

Source: Based on data in Geoffrey H. Moore's *Statistical Indicators of Cyclical Revivals and Recessions* (New York: National Bureau of Economic Research, 1950), and Geoffrey H. Moore, *Business Cycle Indicators*, Vol. 1 (New York: National Bureau of Economic Research. 1961).

plitude than production or payrolls. This is to be expected since it is a residual after all expenses are paid and fixed costs represent a large part of total business costs.[7]

---

[7]Wesley C. Mitchell, *What Happens during Business Cycles* (New York: National Bureau of Economic Research, 1951), p. 173.

The relationships have generally held true in the postwar period. Prices have had such an upward bias that they have declined little or not at all in recession periods. An example of such postwar relationships may be seen from Table 11-4, which shows changes in major economic variables in the 1954–1958 cycle. Changes in the earlier postwar cycles show the same general pattern, but the amplitude was smaller in the 1958–1961 cycle, especially in the contraction phase.

Several other significant relationships exist. The amplitude of production of durable goods is much greater than that of nondurable goods. This would be expected from the operation of the accelerator principle and other causal factors at work in the cycle, especially those affecting the marginal efficiency of capital and interest rates. Consumer durables show a more pronounced variation than durable manufacturing in total. This was not generally true in the prewar period. This is probably due to several factors. More consumers have significant amounts of discretionary income and so can buy durables in prosperity periods. They seem to have been motivated more by the changing economic outlook than by prospects for long-run changes in income. Business has done more investing than it did during the prewar period on a long-run basis instead of on a short-run profit basis, and so has reduced the amplitude in the producer durable field. This has been true in part because of a desire to cut costs by introducing more modern machinery and equipment.

One of the significant factors is the very small change in personal income in the downturn, much smaller than prewar. This is due to a series of factors, such as unemployment compensation, compensatory fiscal policy, agricultural price-support programs, more stable dividend policies, and the like. These are discussed in some detail in Part VIII.

Gross National Product

Gross national product has increased significantly in each of the cycles in the postwar period. In the first postwar cycle it increased 34 percent over the 37-month expansion 'period, or .92 percentage points a month; and in the second cycle 44 percent over the 45-month expansion period, or .98 percentage points a month. The rate of advance in the third and fourth postwar cycles was somewhat

Table 11-4

Changes in a Selected Group of Economic Series
in the 1954–1958 Business Cycle[a]

SERIES	PERCENTAGE INCREASE FROM INITIAL TROUGH TO PEAK	PERCENTAGE DECREASE FROM PEAK TO TERMINAL TROUGH
GNP — Current Dollars	25	4
GNP — 1954 Dollars	14	5
Production — FRB Index	18	13
Nondurable Goods	16	6
Durable Goods	22	20
Consumer Durables	38	37
Nonagricultural Employment	10	6
Manufacturing-Payrolls	24	15
Personal Income	25	1
Wholesale Prices	7	(1)[b]
Profits — Mfg. Corporations	173	39

[a]The initial trough of this cycle is August, 1954; the peak is July, 1957; and the terminal trough is April, 1958.
[b]Increase.

Source: Based on data in the *Survey of Current Business*.

slower. In the third cycle GNP increased 25 percent in an expansion period of 35 months, or .71 percentage points a month; and in the fourth cycle 15 percent in a period of 25 months, or .60 percentage points a month. The fifth postwar expansion was still in progress in mid-1966 and was being influenced to a significant degree in 1966 by the Vietnam War. During the 70-month period to the end of 1966, GNP increased by 50 percent, or .71 percentage points a month.

The decline in GNP has been modest in each of the postwar cycles. In the first two cycles it decreased by 3 percent, in the third cycle by 4 percent, and in the fourth cycle by only .03 percent. The percentage point decreases per month are .27, .23, .33, and .003 respectively for the four cycles.

Chart 11-1 on page 292 shows the cyclical pattern of GNP in the four postwar cycles since the fourth quarter in 1949 both in current dollars and in 1958 dollars. Price changes were especially significant in the first period of expansion, but the increases in prices were smaller in the 1954–1958 cycle and modest in the 1958–1961 cycle and in the cycle which began in the first quarter of 1961.

Chart 11-1

GNP in Postwar Cycles from 1949 to 1966

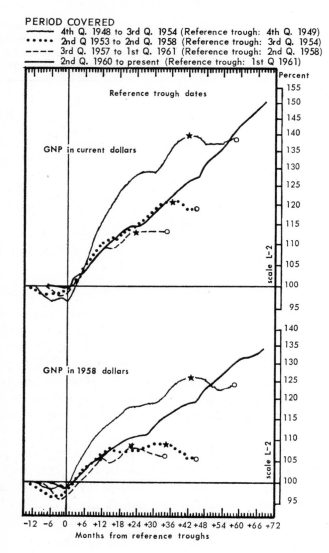

PERIOD COVERED
——— 4th Q. 1948 to 3rd Q. 1954 (Reference trough: 4th Q. 1949)
• • • • 2nd Q 1953 to 2nd Q. 1958 (Reference trough: 3rd Q. 1954)
– – – – 3rd Q. 1957 to 1st Q. 1961 (Reference trough: 2nd Q. 1958)
——— 2nd Q. 1960 to present (Reference trough: 1st Q 1961)

Reference trough dates

GNP in current dollars

Percent
155
150
145
140
135
130
125
120
115
110
105
100
95

scale L-2

140
135
130
125
120
115
110
105
100
95

GNP in 1958 dollars

scale L-2

-12 -6   0 +6 +12 +18 +24 +30 +36 +42 +48 +54 +60 +66 +72
Months from reference troughs

Data expressed as a percentage of the level at the previous peak.

Scale L-2 is a logarithmic scale with 2 cycles in that distance.

★ Point at which this expansion reached a new reference peak.

O Point at which a new reference trough was reached.

Source: Adapted from *Business Cycle Developments* (March, 1967), p. 60.

Industrial Production

The changes in industrial production are more pronounced than changes in GNP in real terms, especially in the downturn. In the postwar cycles the decline in industrial production was less severe than it was on the average in the prewar period, and the expansion was somewhat less vigorous than in minor cycles in the prewar period. The average per month percentage point changes during

Chart 11-2

Industrial Production in Postwar Cycles
from 1949 to 1966

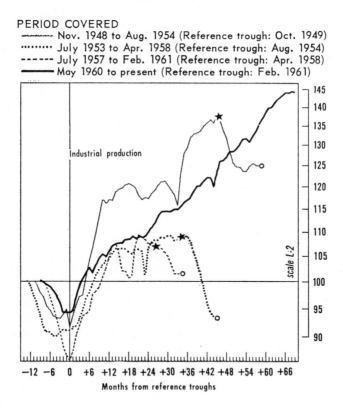

PERIOD COVERED
———— Nov. 1948 to Aug. 1954 (Reference trough: Oct. 1949)
••••••••• July 1953 to Apr. 1958 (Reference trough: Aug. 1954)
------ July 1957 to Feb. 1961 (Reference trough: Apr. 1958)
———— May 1960 to present (Reference trough: Feb. 1961)

Months from reference troughs

Data expressed as a percentage of the level at the previous peak.

Scale L-2 is a logarithmic scale with 2 cycles in that distance.

★Point at which this expansion reached a new reference peak.

O Point at which a new reference trough was reached.

Source: Adapted from *Business Cycle Developments* (March, 1967), p. 59.

the contraction phase of specific cycles in industrial production since July, 1948, were as follows:

July, 1948 – October, 1949	−0.48
July, 1953 – April, 1954	−1.01
February, 1957 – April, 1958	−0.98
January, 1960 – September, 1961	−0.45

The monthly increases in industrial production during expansion periods were not much different from those in contraction periods, but expansion periods were almost four times as long as contraction periods. The average per month percentage point changes during the expansion phase of specific cycles in industrial production since October, 1940, were as follows:

October, 1949 – July, 1953	+0.85
April, 1954 – February, 1957	+0.55
April, 1958 – January, 1960	+1.05
February, 1961 – December, 1966	+0.77

Chart 11-2 on page 293 shows the cyclical pattern of industrial production in the four postwar cycles since October, 1949.

REGIONAL ASPECTS OF BUSINESS CYCLES

Some additional knowledge of the business cycle process can be gained from a study of the course of cycles in different regions of the country. If the timing, duration, and amplitude of cycles are different in some sections of the country than in others, this is important information both from the standpoint of national policy and of individual business planning. If there were regular leads and lags between business conditions in various sections of the country, the experiences of areas with leads would provide an excellent means of forecasting for those areas with lags.

The most detailed information available on regional aspects of business cycles has been developed by Philip Neff and Annette Weifenbach. This study covers business cycles from 1919 through 1945 in six industrial areas — Los Angeles, San Francisco, Chicago, Detroit, Cleveland, and Pittsburgh. At the time of the 1940 census, about 45 percent of the population of the United States lived in 33 industrial areas and about one fourth of these lived in the 6 areas

covered in this study.[8] These areas vary widely in their economic
pattern. All of them have substantial manufacturing industries.
Durable goods production is the major industry in Detroit, Pittsburgh, and Cleveland and is also very important in Chicago.

There was a clear tendency for Detroit to lead the general
economy at peaks and troughs. This is due to the heavy concentration of durable manufacturing, especially durable consumer goods
manufacturing. The data of the timing and duration of cycles clearly
show that there is no definite pattern for cycles to move from East to
West or in any other regular geographic pattern. The data also indicate rather clearly that there is no standard cycle pattern for the
country as a whole. The economy of each area is affected differently
by the factors that are at work in each cycle. The consistent lead of
Detroit in employment, however, substantiates the lead of automobile production shown by aggregate data.

There is no uniformity in the amplitude of change in economic
activity during the cycle in these regions. Cycles in national economic activity affect all of the areas substantially, with Detroit
showing a cycle of greater amplitude than the others. The amplitude,
however, does not seem to be directly related to the industrial pattern of the area except for Detroit. Pittsburgh with its concentration
in producers' durable goods does not have abnormally severe swings,
nor does Los Angeles or Chicago with large consumer and nondurable
goods industries have milder swings.

A more recent study has analyzed regional cycles in manufacturing employment in the United States for the period 1914–1953.[9] This
study found that there are lasting differences in the amplitude of
cyclical fluctuations in manufacturing employment in different
states. Those are due in part at least to the differences among the
states in the types of industries operating within their borders.
These differences in the severity of the cycle in different states have
tended to diminish as industry has become more diversified within
the states.

---

[8]The material in this section is based on a study by Philip Neff and Annette
Weifenbach, *Business Cycles in Selected Industrial Areas* (Berkeley and Los Angeles:
University of California Press, 1949).

[9]*The Study of Economic Growth*, Thirty-ninth Annual Report, National Bureau
of Economic Research, Inc. (New York: National Bureau of Economic Research,
1959), pp. 49–51.

In major contractions in economic activity states with important industries that have high cyclical fluctuations have had severe cycles in their total economy including industries which normally are less severely affected by the cycle. This effect on industry in general was not apparent in minor recessions, but only in the case of major recessions in economic activity.

There was also some tendency for states with high rates of long-run growth to have larger cyclical variations than states which were growing more slowly. This is due in part to the fact that rapidly growing states have industries which experience wide cyclical amplitude. Some states, however, have grown rapidly and still have had moderate cycles, especially Texas, North Carolina, and Iowa; whereas, such states as Connecticut, Pennsylvania, and Mississippi have grown slowly but have had severe cycles. States that experience a slowing down in the rate of growth frequently show larger cyclical fluctuations than states which have no retardation in growth. This is true even when allowance is made for the effect that different industry patterns in a state have on cyclical fluctuations within the state. The patterns are so widely varying that an analysis of each region is necessary to forecast the effect of the cycle on that region.

FLUCTUATIONS IN INVENTORIES

Inventories are an important factor in the cyclical process. In the five cycles between World War I and World War II, the average increase from trough to peak in gross national product, that is, the total value of all goods and services produced, was about $12 billion in terms of 1929 prices. The average increase in the investment in inventories during these cycles was almost $3 billion, or about 25 percent of the average expansion. Therefore, inventories constituted one of the most important elements of change in the cycle and reinforced other movements that were in process.

In the post-World War II period, changes in inventories continued to play a major role in changes in total economic activity even though inventories were maintained at a lower level in relation to sales than in the prewar period. This influence was more pronounced in downturns than in expansion periods.[10] During the first

[10]Moses Abramovitz, *The Role of Inventories in Business Cycles* (New York: National Bureau of Economic Research, 1948) and Manufacturers' Inventories in *The Study of Economic Growth*, Thirty-ninth Annual Report (New York: National Bureau of Economic Research, 1959), pp. 43, 44.

postwar recession the change in the rate of inventory purchases was somewhat larger than the decline in GNP. In the second recession inventory adjustment was equal to about 55 percent of the change in GNP and in the third recession to almost 60 percent. In the fourth postwar recession in 1960–1961 the change in inventory investment was more than twice as great as the decline in GNP.[11]

This significance of the role of inventories in the cycle is to be expected because of the causal factors at work. The accelerator principle leads to a more than proportionate change in the rate of inventory accumulation on the upswing and in the rate of liquidation in the downturn. Speculative activity also leads to inventory accumulation in a recovery period and liquidation in a recession.

A detailed study of several series on manufacturer's inventories was made for the National Bureau by Moses Abramovitz. He found that fluctuations in the volume of inventories conformed well with those of the reference cycle. There was, however, somewhat of a lag in inventory movements behind those of general business. Inventory series in terms of current prices showed a lag of somewhere between 3 and 6 months, while deflated series showed a longer lag that was somewhere between 6 and 12 months.[12] This lag has continued in the postwar recessions, but it has been somewhat shorter.

This lag in inventory adjustment is also present in the total inventories of all types of manufacturing and trade, that is, all nonfarm inventories. This can be seen in Chart 11-3, which shows the ratio of nonfarm stocks to total GNP in 1958 dollars for the period from 1947 to 1965. This ratio has a lag in the postwar downturns beginning in 1948, 1953, 1957, and 1960 and also in the upturns beginning in 1950, 1954, and 1958. A striking feature of this chart is the relative stability of the ratio of nonfarm inventories to GNP in constant prices in the 1961 to 1965 period.

Factors Determining the Level of Inventories

In order to understand the reasons for the fluctuations in inventories during the course of the cycle, it is necessary to analyze the factors involved in holding inventories. The most common reasons cited by businessmen for holding inventories are to gain the savings from buying materials and supplies in larger quantities, to achieve

---

[11]Based on data in the *Survey of Current Business*.

[12]Moses Abramovitz, *op. cit.*, pp. 87, 97.

Chart 11-3

Ratios of Nonfarm Stocks to Total GNP in 1958 Dollars
1947–1965

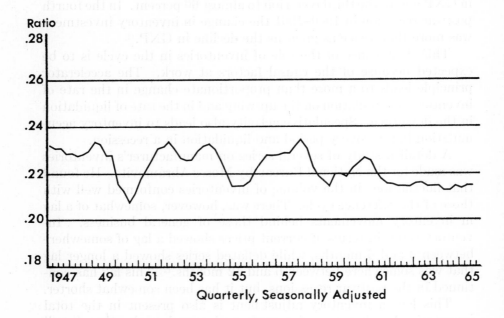

Quarterly, Seasonally Adjusted

Source: Adapted from *Survey of Current Business* (November, 1965), p. 4.

the cost savings resulting from smoothing production over a period
of time, and to provide a buffer stock against unforeseen contin-
gencies. These benefits from holding inventories are offset in part
by the costs incurred in carrying inventories. The level of inventories
that a business will normally desire to hold will depend, therefore,
on a balance between costs of holding inventories and the benefits
from doing so.

In determining the optimum level of inventories, the costs
associated with holding different levels of inventories are first
calculated on the basis that the various costs will remain constant
over short periods of time and vary only with different levels of
inventories. The major costs involved are such factors as interest,
insurance, taxes, spoilage, obsolescence, storage, and possible price
changes. A change in any of these costs will change the costs of

holding different levels of inventories and, therefore, also the optimum level of inventories based upon an analysis of costs and benefits.

Two of the major costs of holding inventories have a significant cyclical fluctuation, that is, interest charges and price changes and expectations of such changes. An increase in the rate of interest will increase the cost of holding inventories and so lead to a reduction in optimum levels, and a reduction will do just the reverse. An expected rise in prices will lead to a reduction in the cost of holding inventories and so lead to an increase in optimum inventory levels, and an expected decline will have the opposite effect. Since reductions in costs of holding inventories due to price rises and expected price rises are generally greater in the early stages of expansion in business activity than increases in costs due to higher interest rates, the net effect from the cost side is to lead to an increase in inventories as expansion gets under way. The opposite is generally true as business contracts, especially in the early stages.

Changes in some of the factors that lead to cost savings from holding inventories also have a cyclical pattern. Consideration will be given in turn to savings from buying in larger quantities, savings from smoothing production, and benefits from holding buffer stocks. In most industries cost savings are usually realized by buying goods in larger quantities. These savings include quantity discounts both in the purchase price and in transportation costs and also savings from placing and processing fewer orders.

In order to consider the effect of these factors independently of other factors, let us assume that savings result only from buying in larger quantities and that conditions in the industries supplying the goods have not changed. Under these conditions a change in the rate of sales would not ordinarily lead to a change in the level of inventories since savings have been calculated on the basis of savings associated with quantity discounts and less frequent ordering. As the rate of sales increased, a firm would ordinarily consider one of two alternatives, either order more frequently or order in larger quantities. The effect on the level of inventories in either case would be minimal. The increases in the rate of sales associated with an upswing in business activity do not, therefore, lead to a significant increase in inventory due to cost savings arising from purchasing in larger quantities.

Inventories are also held to achieve the benefits resulting from smoothing production. Savings result from producing goods at a more or less constant rate rather than adjusting to seasonal shifts in demand. When production is geared to sales, added costs are incurred to hire and lay off workers, to pay overtime or add extra shifts in periods of peak demand, to pay for raw materials that are likely to be in short supply in periods of peak demand and therefore cost more, and the like. If attempts are made to spread sales more evenly and so to smooth production levels, there are added selling costs. The optimum policy balances the costs of holding inventory against the savings from smoothing production. If production is completely smoothed, or almost so, and average inventory holdings are large enough to meet seasonal needs, an increase in sales will have some effect on average inventories, but it will ordinarily not be as great as a percentage of peak stocks. This is not true, however, if production is only partially smoothed.

When sales go up cyclically in an industry, costs associated with peak periods of production will go up more than normally because of greater delays in getting raw materials, more overtime and shift work, and the like. In this situation there is a significant saving to be realized from adding to stocks early in an upswing in business. When few firms in an industry smooth production fully, there are significant savings to be gained from increasing stocks early in an expansion period. This is another factor in explaining increases in inventory investment early in the upswing of a cycle.

A third major reason for holding inventories is to provide a buffer stock to serve as a safety factor if there is a delay in delivery of raw materials or parts and to be prepared for an unexpected surge in sales. This is true because there are significant costs associated with being out of materials and parts and having to slow down production and also costs associated with lost sales. The relevant cost factor is the actual cost of being out of stock, multiplied by the probability that this will occur. Cyclical factors will affect the amount of inventory to be held as a buffer. An increase in the rate of sales will increase the probability of running out of finished goods and so lead to an increase in inventories. However, in industries in which stocks are relatively large in relationship to sales, the effect will not be large since the chances are good that production can be increased to meet the added demand before the inventory is depleted.

If sales go up when the supply of raw materials or other goods needed in production is tight or is expected to be, the chances of running out of stock are greatly increased and this leads to an attempt to increase inventories early in an expansion. The effect is again greater in an industry in which stocks are relatively low in relationship to production than when they are high.

In summary, the result of optimal inventory policy will be an increase in stocks in an upswing in business that is proportionately greater than the increase in sales and a similar reduction in a downturn. These effects will be greatest when significant price rises are expected and when conditions are such that raw materials and parts are expected to be tight. This is generally the situation in the early stages of an upturn. Some analysts have attributed the slow rise in inventories in the expansion period after 1961 to the increased use of scientific inventory management. This is probably true in part, but as our analysis has shown inventories will go up significantly if prices rise and supplies get tight or if they are expected to do so. The major explanation for the relatively slow growth of inventories from 1961 to mid-1965 is probably the relative price stability and ease of supply of goods. When prices started to rise in the second half of 1965 and shortages again became a possibility, inventories began to rise more rapidly in relationship to sales.

Goods in Process and Purchased Materials

Little information is available on the stocks of goods in process, but fortunately it is possible to figure out logically what their relationship must be to activity in manufacturing. There may be a small lead in goods in process over output, but in a general way there must be a direct and proportional variation. It is true that when production is divided into several distinct stages, manufacturers could allow partly completed goods to remain in one of these stages; but this does not appear to happen very often. Most manufacturers do not like to have semifabricated goods on hand for any great length of time, so that in all probability most goods in process move proportionately with the cycle.

There is one exception to this generalization, that is, stocks of goods in process in industries in which production is divided into several distinct stages. This is especially true in the manufacture of durable goods in which metals and various component parts are produced in separate stages from the assembly of the final product.

These stocks have become much more important as a proportion of the total in the postwar period than they were in the prewar period. These stocks are built up more than proportionately as business expands and reduced more than proportionately as business contracts. They are rather sensitive to changes in business activity and cause stocks of goods in process to expand and contract more than they did in the prewar period. These stocks turn at about the same time as general economic activity.

The behavior of stocks of raw materials and other purchased materials, especially in the durable goods field, is similar to that of stocks of goods in process between stages of manufacture. Such stocks show a high degree of cyclical sensitivity both because they are affected by demand for finished durable goods and because they are in a large measure easily obtained.

Investment in these stocks has led the upturn in the cycle and has provided for a stimulus to economic activity in the expansion phase of the cycle. Investment in such stocks has dropped off before the economy, in general, reached a peak, and this decline in activity has been one of the causal factors in the downturn.

These shifts in inventory investment of raw materials and purchased materials can be explained by practices in these industries and the factors that govern the level of inventories. Durable goods industries produce primarily to order, and backlogs of orders vary over the cycle. When expansion begins, the backlog of orders increases and inventories are increased to take advantage of expected price rises and to guard against shortages. When demand and supply come into better balance late in expansion, the reasons for increasing stocks no longer hold; in fact, optimum policy may call for a lower level of inventories. It is easy to curtail inventory investment since orders for goods can easily be postponed or even canceled. Availability of goods is easy in a downturn and prices weaken, thus calling for lower stocks. In a short recession the planned reduction in stocks may not have been completed when the recession ends, and this may lead to a short lag in adjustment at the lower turning point of the cycle.

Finished Goods

Stocks of finished goods must be divided into two groups for analysis: those that are made to order, and those made for stock. It should be kept in mind that the finished goods of manufacturers are not all ready for the ultimate consumer, since some are going to other manufacturers for further fabrication and some to wholesalers for distribution. It is obvious that goods made to order rise and fall with production or shipments. They are in inventory only during that brief period between their completion and shipment. Probably 20 percent of all finished goods are in this category.

Stocks of finished staples made from nonagricultural commodities had a fairly long lag in prewar cycles. In short cycles they had a tendency to move inversely to the general business cycle, decreasing as business increased and increasing as business approached the trough of a cycle. This lag has been materially reduced in the postwar period. There is now a short lag of several months, which is somewhat longer for durable goods than for nondurable goods. Such inventories reach their peak in the early stages of a recession and their trough in the early stages of expansion.

Finished goods inventories are more sensitive than other inventories to changes in economic activity. If there are sizable unexpected changes in shipments of goods or if changes turn out to be much greater than expected, immediate changes are made in the planned levels of stocks. However, increases or decreases in the level of activity may take place gradually and manufacturers may want to maintain rates of production to keep costs at a minimum level. In such cases, inventory investment may not be adjusted except with a lag and, therefore, inventory investment will lag turning points in the rate of change in economic activity.

Lags can also occur especially in a recession period when stocks are allowed to grow to prevent layoffs and the possible loss of valuable workers. This may also happen in expansion if stocks are temporarily depleted to avoid paying overtime, but this is much less likely since other factors such as increased prices of materials and threatened shortages provide the justification for increasing stocks. If inventory management is done successfully, however, leads can occur. If rates of change in activity are anticipated and inventory investment is adjusted accordingly, the turn in inventory building will lead the turning points to economic activity. This has happened increasingly in the post-World War II period.

Although there is no empirical evidence to substantiate the conclusion, stocks of perishable commodities or those affected by rapid changes in style probably do not show this cyclical pattern. Stocks of finished staples produced from agricultural raw materials behave irregularly over the course of the business cycle. A rise in the production of the raw material leads to a rise in manufacturing with only a short lag, and stocks soon outrun consumption. Since agricultural cycles in production do not move consistently with business cycles, such stocks vary in a random fashion over the business cycle.

QUESTIONS

1. What has been the average length of the cycle? the most common length?
2. How do the lengths of the periods of expansion and contraction compare?
3. Describe the international pattern of business cycles.
4. Discuss the extent to which various phases of economic activity in the United States move with the cyclical tide.
5. Study the list in Table 11-3 of series which typically lead, move with the cycle, and lag. Account for the timing of (a) common stock prices, (b) new orders for industrial durable goods, (c) bank debits outside New York City, (d) retail sales.
6. Describe and account for the general pattern of amplitude in various phases of economic activity.
7. Describe the fluctuations in GNP in cycles in the postwar period.
8. Describe the fluctuations in industrial production during postwar cycles.
9. Discuss the pattern of the cycle in various regions of the country.
10. How important are fluctuations in inventories over the cycle?
11. Discuss the factors that affect the level of inventories and the effect that cyclical factors have on them.
12. Describe the cyclical fluctuations of goods-in-process inventories.
13. Account for the adjustment of inventories of raw materials to cyclical fluctuations.
14. How do finished goods inventories change with the cycle in business?

SUGGESTED READINGS

Abramovitz, Moses. *The Role of Inventories in Business Cycles.* New York: National Bureau of Economic Research, 1948.

Business Cycle Developments, Bureau of the Census, U. S. Department of Commerce. U. S. Government Printing Office, January, 1965, and current issues.

Mitchell, Wesley C. *What Happens during Business Cycles.* New York: National Bureau of Economic Research, 1951. Part II.

Monhollon, Jimmie R. *Manufacturers' Inventory Investment and Monetary Policy.* Washington: Board of Governors of the Federal Reserve System, 1965.

Moore, Geoffrey H., (ed.), *Business Cycle Indicators*, Vols. I and II. Princeton, New Jersey: Princeton University Press, 1961.

Neff, Philip, and Annette Weifenbach. *Business Cycles in Selected Industrial Areas.* Berkeley, California: University of California Press, 1949.

CHAPTER ■12■ *The General Cycle Pattern*

From the records of the behavior of the many economic series studied by the National Bureau of Economic Research, it is possible to develop some of the features that have been typical of an American business cycle, especially for the period since the end of World War I. A complete picture must await further study, since many of the National Bureau series have not been fully analyzed, since their series do not include some important sectors of the economy, and since much of the data has not been analyzed fully for the post-World War II period. Such evidence as is available indicates that many of the features of the cycle have continued to operate in a fashion similar to the prewar period. Some factors, such as those associated with the rapid rise in prices in the early postwar years after the period of wartime price controls and the effects of the Korean and Vietnam Wars, are not likely to be typical of future cycles.

The differences that existed prewar and postwar in the general cycle pattern are due in part, at least, to differences in the kind of cycles that occurred. The postwar cycles were mild, the prewar depression beginning in 1929 was the most severe in our history, and the 1937 downturn was also more severe than any postwar downturn. Postwar cycles were also marked by inflationary pressures that were not present at all or were mild in prewar cycles. This resulted in a policy of monetary restraint by the Federal Reserve, which affected the financial situation. Postwar recessions were also mild because many governmental programs helped sustain purchasing power, and this had an effect on the contraction.

SERIES USED TO DESCRIBE THE GENERAL CYCLE PATTERN

Several groups of data are available to give a preliminary picture of the typical general cycle pattern. One group is a series on buyers' outlays, which were analyzed for price and quantity variations during the various stages of the cycle. Buyers' outlays are the total sums spent on a commodity by all purchasers: individuals, institutions, businesses, and government. They may also be considered as the total revenues from sales of all sellers of the commodity. Another group is made up of comprehensive series, that is, series which themselves reflect a cross section of economic activity, such as the Federal Reserve Index of Industrial Production. There is also a series developed by the National Bureau of Economic Research for the post-World War II period on costs, prices and profits, and another one on the behavior of interest rates.

Buyers' Outlays

Frederick C. Mills made a study for the National Bureau of Economic Research on the relative roles of price and quantity in changes in buyers' outlays during the business cycle in the pre-World War II period. This study was based upon 64 commodities for which comparable price and quantity data are available on a monthly basis. The number of separate commodities included in the list is only 56, however, since two different sets of quantity records are used for 8 of the products. For example, petroleum products are in the list twice, once for total petroleum production and again for production in the Appalachian region, since data for these two different series are available. The periods covered in the data are not uniform, but range from 14 to 80 years. The 64 series covered constitute about one third of the aggregate value of manufactured goods, raw materials, and agricultural commodities sold in the United States.[1]

Comprehensive Series

Buyers' outlays are but one factor in the economic process. Additional areas can be studied in the pre-World War II period from the data on 34 comprehensive series analyzed by the National Bureau. These series include those on production, transportation, prices, trade, employment, income payments, investments, dealings in securities, business profits, business failures, and bank debits, and also several indexes of general business activity. They are not inclusive enough, however, to cover all important sectors of economic activity. Omitted are such important factors as inventories, orders for goods, real estate transactions, wage rates, hours of work per

---

[1]Frederick C. Mills, *Price-Quantity Interactions in Business Cycles* (New York: National Bureau of Economic Research, 1946), p. 25.

week, output per man-hour, interest rates, the volume and velocity of money, taxes, and savings. Series in some of these areas are available and will be analyzed, but others are not available for a long enough period of time. Another defect is the diversity of time periods covered by the various series. Enough data are available, however, to present a preliminary picture of the typical cycle.[2]

Such a typical pattern of general economic activity can be obtained from the cycle patterns of indexes of total business activity. Chart 12-1 shows typical cycle patterns plotted for each of the eight segments of the cycle for three such indexes of business activity. They are unadjusted for the long-term trend, the form in which the National Bureau generally presents cyclical data.

Chart 12-1

Typical Cycle Patterns of Indexes of Business Activity

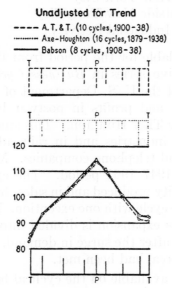

Unadjusted for Trend

---- A. T. & T. (10 cycles, 1900 – 38)
·········· Axe-Houghton (16 cycles, 1879–1938)
——— Babson (8 cycles, 1908 – 38)

Source: Wesley C. Mitchell, *What Happens during Business Cycles* (New York: National Bureau of Economic Research, 1951), p. 267.

Data on the complete group of comprehensive series are not available for postwar cycles. Information is available, however, on

---

[2]Wesley C. Mitchell, *What Happens during Business Cycles* (New York: National Bureau of Economic Research, 1951).

the behavior of a representative group of eleven comprehensive series for the postwar period from 1945–1958 covering three complete cycles.[3] These series are:

Federal Reserve Board Index of Industrial Production
Bureau of Labor Statistics Wholesale Price Index
Federal Reserve Board Index of Department Store Sales
Bureau of Labor Statistics Production Worker Employment in Manufacturing Industries
F. W. Dodge Corporation Value of Construction Contracts Awarded
Number of Shares of Stock Sold on the New York Stock Exchange
Par Value of Bonds Sold on the New York Stock Exchange
Dun & Bradstreet Number of Business Failures
Bank Clearings in New York City
Bank Clearings Outside New York City
A T & T Index of Industrial Activity

Data are also available for the period from 1948 to the present on many comprehensive series in *Business Cycle Developments,* a monthly publication of the U. S. Department of Commerce. Some data on costs, prices, and profits in postwar business cycles are available in a study by Thor Hultgren.[4] This study covers cycles in fifteen manufacturing industries and in railroads, public utilities, construction, trade, and telephone companies. Most of the data is for the cycles in the 1947–1961 period. The cycles used are the specific cycles in quantity produced and in sales, but they correspond closely to the reference cycle with one exception. In many industries the 1949–1953 business expansion is divided into two periods since demand fell for a time after the surge in demand, resulting from the outbreak of war in Korea, had been met.

Some data are also available on the cyclical behavior of interest rates in the period from 1945–1961 in a study by Reuben A. Kessel.[5] This study analyzed the cyclical behavior of short-term and long-

---

[3]From an unpublished research project at Washington University by Robert L. Virgil, Jr., *Comparative Patterns of Behavior by Economic Time Series during Prewar and Postwar American Business Cycles.*

[4]Thor Hultgren, *Cost, Prices, and Profits: Their Cyclical Relations* (New York: National Bureau of Economic Research, 1965).

[5]Reuben A. Kessel, *The Cyclical Behavior of the Term Structure of Interest Rates* (New York: National Bureau of Economic Research, 1965).

term interest rates including commercial paper rates, the yield on Treasury bills, and on Moody's Aaa corporate bonds.

Total economic activity as measured by the A T & T Business Index shows less fluctuation in the postwar period than it and similar business indexes did in the prewar period. The amplitude[6] during expansion is about one-third smaller and during contraction about one-half smaller. Some of the series have a smaller amplitude during the cycle than indexes of business activity. Included in this group are agricultural marketings, bond prices, wholesale prices of all commodities, and department store sales. The amplitude is much greater for industrial production, construction contracts, factory payrolls, liabilities in failures, and net corporate profits. Table 12-1 on page 310 presents the reference cycle amplitude for each of the comprehensive series in the prewar period, Table 12-2 on page 311 in the postwar period.

TYPICAL CHANGES DURING SEGMENTS OF THE CYCLE

Since the cycle is a dynamic process, a full understanding of its nature may be obtained by studying what happens in each of the eight segments of the cycle. For this purpose, data on the comprehensive series will be used in the main, but they will be supplemented by data on buyers' outlays for the prewar period, and on costs and profits, and the behavior of interest rates in the postwar period.

The Expansion Phase of the Cycle

This record of the general cycle pattern will begin at the initial trough of the cycle. The expansion phase will be divided into the four segments used by the National Bureau in describing the cycle.

Segment 1 — Prewar. In Segment 1 the 32 comprehensive series that have regular cyclical patterns all show that the level of business is increasing. The two series on business failures are falling, as is to be expected, and the other 30 series are rising.

The series on buyers' outlays also show that most of the economy is moving with the cyclical tide. In fact, 84 percent of the series is moving with the tide, which is a larger percentage than at any other time in the cycle, except Segment 3.

---

[6]Based on the National Bureau method of calculating the amplitude of the cycle as described in Chapter 10.

Table 12-1

Average Reference Cycle Amplitudes of Comprehensive Series in the
Prewar Period

SERIES	AVERAGE AMPLITUDE		
	EXPAN-SION	CONTRAC-TION	FULL CYCLE
Agricultural marketings.............	+1.4	−0.8	+2.2
Bond prices......................	−3.5	+6.4	−9.9
Exports........................	+15	−1	+16
Prices, wholesale.................	+9	−9	+18
Department store sales.............	+16	−10	+26
Deposits activity.................	+14	−17	+31
Business index, Ayres.............	+17	−19	+36
Wholesale trade sales.............	+18	−19	+37
Bank clearings outside N. Y. City....	+26	−11	+37
Incorporations...................	+27	−10	+37
Production of fuels................	+26	−15	+40
Income payments.................	+23	−18	+40
Imports........................	+26	−19	+45
Factory employment..............	+22	−23	+45
Business index, Persons...........	+22	−23	+45
Common stock prices.............	+27	−20	+47
Failures, number.................	−22	+26	−48
Business index, A T & T, adj........	+23	−25	+48
Bond sales......................	−15	+35	−50
Business index, Axe-Houghton.......	+29	−21	+50
R. R. freight ton miles.............	+28	−23	+51
Bank clearings, total..............	+30	−21	+51
Business index, Babson...........	+29	−23	+52
Business index, A T & T...........	+32	−23	+55
Bank clearings, N. Y. City.........	+32	−28	+60
Industrial production..............	+35	−32	+68
Construction contracts.............	+43	−30	+74
Factory payrolls..................	+36	−40	+76
Shares traded...................	+41	−36	+77
Security issues...................	+47	−46	+93
Cash from issues on N. Y. Stock Ex-change......................	+58	−39	+97
Pig iron production................	+54	−45	+99
Failures, liabilities...............	−67	+59	−125
Net corporate profits..............	+169	−175	+343

Source: Wesley C. Mitchell, *What Happens during Business Cycles* (New
York: National Bureau of Economic Research, 1951), p. 286.

Table 12-2

Average Reference Cycle Amplitudes of Eleven Comprehensive Series
in the Postwar Period

SERIES	AVERAGE AMPLITUDE		
	EXPAN-SION	CONTRAC-TION	FULL CYCLE
Federal Reserve Board Index of Industrial Production...............	18.9	−9.5	28.4
Bureau of Labor Statistics Wholesale Price Index......................	19.1	−2.0	21.1
Federal Reserve Board Index of Department Store Sales..............	22.1	−3.9	26.0
Bureau of Labor Statistics Production Worker Employment in Manufacturing Industries.................	14.3	−10.1	24.4
F. W. Dodge Corporation Value of Construction Contracts Awarded...	42.1	33.0	9.1
Number of Shares of Stock Sold on the New York Stock Exchange........	−20.3	34.5	−54.8
Par Value of Bonds Sold on the New Stock Exchange..................	−21.5	15.1	−36.6
Dun & Bradstreet Number of Business Failures..........................	42.4	42.9	−.5
Bank Clearings in New York City....	17.4	11.0	6.4
Bank Clearings Outside New York City	36.3	−1.7	38.0
A T & T Index of Industrial Activity.	21.0	−13.7	34.7

Source: From an unpublished research project at Washington University by Robert L. Virgil, Jr., *Comparative Patterns of Behavior by Economic Times Series during Prewar and Postwar American Business Cycles.*

Even though all of the comprehensive series are moving with the cycle, there is a wide variation in the rates of change. The data on the monthly rates of change are expressed according to the regular National Bureau method,[7] which is based on the average monthly rate of change in reference cycle standings during a segment of the cycle. Prices of all commodities are going up only 0.5 points per month in Segment 1, and agricultural marketings are increasing at the same rate. Department store sales are also increasing slowly at 0.7 points per month. Production is increasing 2.0 points per month, construction 3.7 points, shares sold on the New York Stock Exchange 6.6 points, and corporate net profit 11.8 points.

---

[7]See Chapter 10 for a discussion of the procedures involved in calculating the monthly rate of change in a series.

The series on buyers' outlays show that the maximum monthly rates of increase in outlays occur in Segment 1 in 13 of the 16 groups, that is, for all groups but foods, consumer goods, and nonmetallic minerals. The most rapid rate of increase in quantity comes in this segment for 11 of the groups. The rate of increase in a twelfth group, farm products, is as rapid in Segment 3 as it is in Segment 1. Consumer goods, foods, domestic crop products, and nonmetallic minerals have their most rapid quantity increases in other segments.

The most rapid monthly rate of increase in price occurs in Segment 1 for 9 commodity groups. A tenth group, manufactured goods, has the same rate of increase in price in Segment 4 as in Segment 1. The most rapid rates of increase in prices of metals, capital equipment, durable goods, nonmetallic minerals, goods other than American farm products, and consumer goods do not come until the last segment of expansion.

Segment 1 — Postwar. In the postwar period all of the eleven comprehensive series were rising in this segment except the number of business failures. The most rapid rate of increase in industrial production occurred in this segment just as it did prewar. The same was true of department store sales and construction contracts awarded. It was also true of employment in manufacturing industries in the first three postwar cycles, but there was little increase in employment in the early months of the 1958–1961 cycle or the cycle which began in 1961. Wholesale prices showed the slowest rate of increase in this segment, whereas prewar they had increased most rapidly in Segments 1 and 4. In all but the 1958–1961 cycle this is the only segment in which business failures were decreasing, whereas prewar they were decreasing throughout the expansion period.

In the fifteen manufacturing industries in the Hultgren study, prices were rising in 41 percent of the observations, the smallest percentage for any of the segments of expansion, while costs per unit of output were rising in only 22 percent of the observations, which is also the smallest for any of the segments of expansion. In Segment 1 profit margins as a percentage of sales were rising in 83 percent of the observations and total profits in 89 percent, the highest figures for any of the segments of expansion.

Long-term and short-term interest rates were generally rising in Segment 1. The rates of increase in commercial paper rates is the slowest for any segment in the expansion period, and on Treasury bills it is slower than in any segment, except the last segment of expansion. The rate of increase in Moody's Aaa corporate bond yields is also the slowest of any segment in the expansion period.

Segment 2 — Prewar. The expansion of business continues in Segment 2. All of the series with a regular cycle pattern continue to move with the cyclical tide except the par value of bond sales and the number of shares of stock sold on the New York Stock Exchange, which begin to fall after rising rapidly in Segment 1. The other series with regular cyclical patterns, however, move more slowly than they did in Segment 1.

The rate of increase in industrial production is only half what it was in Segment 1. Total income payments increase almost as fast as in Segment 1, and so do factory employment and payrolls. Department store sales adjusted for price changes increase about as fast as in Segment 1, but wholesale trade increases only about a quarter as fast. Net profits still show the largest rate of increase of any series, but the rate is less than half that in Segment 1.

This same retardation in the rate of expansion is shown in buyers' outlays. Whereas in Segment 1, 84 percent of the commodities studied had increases in outlays, only 64 percent have increases in Segment 2. In none of the 16 subgroups do all of the commodities show an increase in outlays; but the percentage having an increase is still high in capital equipment, nonmetallic minerals, metals, and durable goods. It is below 50 percent for domestic animal products, American farm products, and domestic crop products. None of the 16 groups has the maximum rate of increase in outlays in Segment 2, or the maximum rate of increase in either price or quantity.

Segment 2 — Postwar. The pattern in the postwar period is similar in some ways to the prewar pattern. Only eight of the eleven series expanded in this segment; the value of construction contracts, common stock sales, and bond sales were falling. Common stock sales and bond sales were falling in prewar cycles, but construction contracts were still increasing. The number of business failures was also moving against the cyclical tide by increasing, whereas prewar it was decreasing in this segment. None of the series showed the greatest rate of increase in this segment. The rate of growth clearly slowed from that of the first segment as it did prewar. However, wholesale prices were going up more rapidly, whereas in prewar cycles they went up less rapidly than in Segment 1.

The Hultgren study of manufacturing industries shows price rising in 63 percent of the observations compared with only 41 percent in Segment 1. Costs per unit of output are rising in 39 percent of the observations compared with only 22 percent in Segment 1. Profit margins are still rising in 75 percent of all observations, which is somewhat less than in Segment 1, but total profits are still rising in 89 percent of all observations, the same rate as in Segment 1.

Yields on Treasury bills are rising at the most rapid rate of any segment of expansion and so are commercial paper rates. Rates on Moody's Aaa corporate bonds are rising more rapidly than in Segment 1, and at about the same rate as in Segment 3.

Segment 3 — Prewar. After the retardation in Segment 2, most of the series again rise at a faster rate as the pace of expansion quickens. Of the 32 series with regular cycle patterns, 28 rise and 4 fall. The two series on business failures are expected to fall as business increases and are thus moving with the tide. Moving against the tide are the value of bond sales at par and bond prices.

Most of the other series are increasing faster than in Segment 2, but this is by no means true of all of them. Those increasing faster include industrial production, fuel and electricity production, the series on transportation, all of the series on trade having a regular cyclical pattern, factory payrolls, income payments, the number of incorporations, shares sold on the New York Stock Exchange (this series was falling in Segment 2 but is now rising again), and net profits of business enterprises. Liabilities in business failures also show improvement by falling faster. The various business indexes are moving up at about the same rate as in Segment 2. The same is true of wholesale prices and of common stock prices.

The following series are increasing at a slower rate than in Segment 2:

Pig iron production (rate down only slightly)
Factory employment
Value of construction contracts
Value of security issues (down from 2.5 to 0.8)
Cash from security issues on the New York Stock Exchange (down from 1.8 to 0.1)

The number of business failures is decreasing more slowly than it was in Segment 2, but liabilities in failures are decreasing much more rapidly.

Buyers' outlays also show this increased tempo in the cyclical tide. In Segment 3 increased outlays are made for 89 percent of all commodities, the highest percentage for any segment of the cycle. All commodities in the durable goods, metals, and nonmetallic minerals group are moving with the tide; and even in the lowest group, domestic animal products, 80 percent of all commodities shows increases in outlays.

The monthly rates of increase of both price and quantity are faster than in Segment 2. Price is moving only slightly faster, 0.7 points per month compared with 0.6 in Segment 2; but quantity is moving more than twice as fast, that is, 0.9 points as compared with 0.4.

The fastest rate of increase in outlays on consumer goods comes in this period. No group has its maximum rate of increase in price in this segment; but domestic crop products show the greatest rate of increase in quantity in this period, and American farm products are increasing as fast in quantity in this segment as they are in the first one.

Segment 3 — Postwar. In the postwar period all of the eleven comprehensive series were rising in this segment, except the number of shares of stock sold on the New York Stock Exchange. This series was decreasing, but at a much slower rate than in Segment 2, whereas in prewar cycles it rose in Segment 3. The par value of bond sales was again increasing very slightly after having fallen off significantly in Segment 2, whereas in prewar cycles it fell more rapidly than in Segment 2. The value of construction contracts was again increasing in this segment as it was prewar after having fallen somewhat in Segment 2. Industrial production did not increase more rapidly as it did prewar, but at only half the average rate of Segment 2. Employment in manufacturing industries went up only one quarter as fast as in Segment 2, a more rapid slowdown in the rate of expansion than in the prewar period. The number of business failures was going up much faster than in Segment 2, whereas in the prewar period it was falling in this segment. In the early postwar cycles wholesale prices showed their greatest rate of increase in this segment, 2.6 points per month on the average compared with 0.9 points in

Segment 2 and 0.5 in Segment 1; whereas prewar they increased about as fast in Segment 3 as in Segment 2, but at a slower rate than in Segment 1. In the 1958–1961 cycle wholesale prices remained stable in Segment 3 and also during the first three years of the cycle that began in 1961.

In the manufacturing industry study, prices were rising in 74 percent of the observations in Segment 3, and unit costs were rising in 67 percent of the observations, up materially from 39 percent in Segment 2. As a result, profit margins were rising in only 59 percent of the observations compared with 75 percent in Segment 2, but because of increased volume total profits were still rising in 70 percent of all observations.

Yields on Treasury bills were still rising but at a somewhat slower rate than in Segment 2, and commercial paper rates were rising at a significantly slower rate than in the preceding segment. Yields on Moody's Aaa corporate bonds continued upward at about the same rate as in Segment 2.

Segment 4 — Prewar. Business continues to rise during Segment 4, but fewer series participate in the rise.

SERIES	RATE OF CHANGE IN POINTS PER MONTH	
	SEGMENT 3	SEGMENT 4
Industrial production	1.4	1.6
Fuel and electricity production	1.4	1.8
Pig iron production	1.5	2.3
Railroad freight ton-miles	1.2	1.3
Wholesale prices	0.3	0.5
Factory employment	0.6	0.7
Factory payrolls	1.3	2.2
Cash from security issues on the New York Stock Exchange	0.1	2.2
A T & T index of business activity	0.6	0.8
Axe-Houghton index of business activity	1.0	1.1
A T & T index of business activity (not adjusted for trend)	1.0	1.3

Still moving with the tide are 24 series, but 8 are already moving against it, as follows:

Liabilities of failures (moving against the tide by increasing)
Bond sales
Bond prices
Number of shares of stock sold on the New York Stock Exchange

Prices of common stock
Bank clearings in New York City
Snyder's index of deposit activity
Value of corporate security issues

Thus, most of the series on financial transactions are falling in this last segment of expansion.

Of the 24 series moving with the cyclical tide, 11 are moving faster than in Segment 3, as shown on the preceding page.

The Babson Index of Business Activity adjusted for the long-term trend is increasing at the same rate as in Segment 3.

The remaining 11 series are increasing at a slower pace.

SERIES	RATE OF CHANGE IN POINTS PER MONTH	
	SEGMENT 3	SEGMENT 4
Wholesale trade	1.4	0.4
Department store sales	0.6	0.4
Imports, value	1.1	1.0
Income payments	1.0	0.7
Construction contracts	1.6	0.8
Number of incorporations	1.1	0.4
Net profits	5.5	3.0
Bank clearings	1.3	0.2
Bank clearings outside New York City	1.2	0.6
Ayres index of business activity	0.5	0.3
Persons index of business activity	0.7	0.6

The number of failures is still moving with the tide by decreasing, but at a slower pace than in Segment 3.

The most rapid increase in production in Segment 4 is in pig iron production. Factory payrolls are still increasing rapidly. Cash from security issues on the New York Stock Exchange is increasing much faster than in Segment 3. This is not completely logical since cash from all security issues and the number of new security issues are falling, but the explanation may be that larger issues are being floated late in the cycle. The most pronounced retardation in the rate of increase occurs in wholesale trade, construction contracts awarded, new incorporations, and bank clearings.

Buyers' outlays are increasing for 80 percent of all commodities, compared with 89 percent in Segment 3. Outlays for capital equipment show increases for 90 percent of the series included in this group. The lowest group is consumer goods.

The rate of increase in price has slowed down a little from 0.7 to 0.6 points a month, whereas the rate of increase in quantity remains

0.9 points per month. The maximum rate of increase in outlays for nonmetallic minerals is in this segment. This group also has the greatest rate of increase in both price and quantity in this segment.

Manufactured goods increase as fast in price in this segment as in Segment 1. Metals, capital equipment, durable goods, goods other than products of American farms, and consumer goods have the most rapid rate of increase in price in this last segment.

Segment 4 — Postwar. In the postwar period eight of the eleven series were still expanding in Segment 4, that is, all but the value of construction contracts awarded, common stock sales, and bond sales. Contracts awarded dropped slowly after increasing materially in Segment 3, stock sales continued to drop at about the same rate as in Segment 3, and bond sales dropped materially after increasing slowly in Segment 3. Stock sales and bond sales were dropping in Segment 4 in the prewar period, but construction contracts awarded were still increasing but at a much slower rate than in Segment 3. Industrial production and employment continued upward at about the same rate as in Segment 3. Price rises were slowed as wholesale prices went up only 0.9 points per month compared with 2.6 points in Segment 3. In the 1958–1961 cycle wholesale prices remained stable in the last segment of expansion. Thus the more rapid increase in production, employment, and prices in Segment 4 compared with Segment 3 which took place in the prewar cycles did not occur in postwar cycles. Department store sales went up at a much slower rate than in Segment 3. This slowing down in the rate of advance also occurred prewar, but it was not as pronounced. The number of business failures continued to increase and did so at a more rapid rate than in Segment 3, whereas they were still falling in this segment in the prewar period.

Prices in manufacturing industries were rising in 80 percent of the observations and unit costs in 74 percent, the highest figures for any segment of expansion. Profit margins were rising in only 46 percent of all observations, the lowest figure for any segment of expansion. Because of increased volume total profits were still increasing in 70 percent of all observations.

Yields on Treasury bills went up very slowly at the slowest rate in any segment of expansion. Commercial paper rates went up at a much slower rate, and the yields of Moody's Aaa corporate bonds went up at a somewhat slower rate than in Segment 3.

The Contraction Phase of the Cycle

The contraction phase of the cycle will be described in a similar manner to the expansion phase. In each segment the prewar pattern will be given first, then the postwar pattern.

Segment 5 — Prewar. As business passes the peak, all of the regular series decline in line with the tide of contraction. The series that began to fall before the peak of the cycle all fall faster now except bond prices, which are decreasing at a somewhat slower rate. The rate of decrease in commodity prices is small, as is that in income payments. Rapid rates of decrease occur in the value of construction contracts, the value of new security issues, and the number of shares of stock sold on the New York Stock Exchange. The most rapid change for the worse occurs in corporate profits, and the liabilities in business failures are also going up very rapidly.

Buyers' outlays drop rapidly primarily because quantity is going down 1.6 points a month, but price is also decreasing 0.7 points. Only 23 percent of commodities show increases in outlays, compared with 80 percent in the last segment of expansion. The largest percentages of commodities showing increases are in foods and consumer goods. No metals show increases in outlays, and only 5 percent of the items in the capital goods and durable goods fields show increases.

Even though there is a rapid drop in outlays after the downturn, only a few commodity groups show the most rapid rate of decline in buyers' outlays in this segment. Those which do are domestic crop products, American farm products, and manufactured goods. Nondurable goods and food outlays fall at the same rate in this segment and in the second segment of contraction, and then fall more slowly. No group has the maximum rate of decline in price in this segment, since prices drop faster as the rate of business activity declines for a period of time. Most of the groups have the maximum rates of decline in quantity in this first period of contraction. The decline in quantity leads to the rapid decreases in price, and these in turn help slow down the rate of decrease in quantities. Two groups drop as fast in Segment 5 as in a later segment; namely, durable goods, which drop as fast in quantity as in Segment 7, and raw materials, which drop as fast as in Segment 6. Nonmetallic minerals experience their greatest rate of decline in quantity in Segment 7.

Segment 5 — Postwar. The postwar cycles did not show the same degree of downturn in Segment 5 as did prewar cycles. In the prewar cycles all eleven series moved with the tide, all decreasing except business failures which went up as business turned down. Postwar, in addition to failures, there were also increases in the value of construction contracts awarded, the number of shares of common stock sold, the par value of bond sales, and bank clearings in New York City.

Wholesale prices, department store sales, and bank clearings outside New York City had their most rapid rate of decrease in this segment, whereas prewar it was in Segment 6. Employment in manufacturing had its slowest rate of decrease just as it did prewar.

In manufacturing industries prices were still rising in 85 percent of all observations, the highest percentage for any segment of the cycle; and unit costs were up in 85 percent of all observations, a higher percentage than in any segment of expansion. Profit margins were rising in only 28 percent of all observations, and because of decreasing volume total profits were up in only 19 percent of the observations.

Yields on Treasury bills dropped at the sharpest rate in any segment of contraction, and commercial paper rates also started to drop significantly. Yields on Moody's Aaa corporate bonds likewise started to decline slowly.

Segment 6 — Prewar. There is no retardation in the rate of decline in the second segment of contraction as there was in the second segment of expansion. Instead the most rapid rates of decline are taking place in this segment in most sectors of the economy. The only sector of the economy moving counter to the tide is the bond market. Railroad bond prices have ceased falling and remain about stable, while the par value of all bonds sold on the New York Stock Exchange is increasing 0.9 points per month. This is due to the decrease in interest rates, which forces up the price of high-grade bonds carrying high coupon rates, and also to a search for safety on the part of investors, which increases the demand for bonds.

The rate of decline is faster in this segment for most, but not all, sectors of the economy. Department store sales are falling at about the same rate as in Segment 5, and so are two of the business indexes. The value of construction contracts is falling somewhat more slowly, as are bank debits in New York City. The value of corporate security issues is falling much more slowly, and the liabilities in business failures are increasing at a much slower rate.

Buyers' outlays are falling at the most rapid rate in the cycle. Prices are now the most important factor leading to a decline: they drop 1.6 points per month while quantity is dropping 1.1 points.

Outlays are increasing for only 16 percent of all commodities. Nonmetallic minerals, consumer goods, and food head the list; but even the highest group has only 30 percent of the commodities showing increases in outlays. Producers goods and metals have the smallest percentage of commodities with increases in outlays.

Most groups have the maximum rate of decline in this period. Included are the following groups:

Metals
Capital equipment
Durable goods
Goods other than products of American farms
Producer goods
Raw materials
Producer goods for human consumption
Human consumption goods
Domestic animal products

Nondurable goods and foods move at about the same rate in this segment as in Segment 5.

No group has its maximum rate of decrease in quantity in this segment, but raw materials decrease at the same rate in this segment as in Segment 5. Most groups have their maximum rates of decrease in price in this segment. This is true of all groups but the following, which have faster price decreases in the next period:

Goods other than products of American farms
Consumer goods
Manufactured goods
Nonmetallic minerals

Domestic animal product prices decrease at the same rate in Segment 6 as in Segment 7, but more slowly in both the first and the last periods of contraction.

Segment 6 — Postwar. The downturn in Segment 6 was not as pervasive in postwar cycles as it was prewar when only the par value of bond sales was moving counter to the tide. Stock and bond sales and bank clearings were still going up as they were in Segment 5. Department store sales also showed a slight upturn. Construction contracts awarded turned down in this segment in the early postwar cycles after rising in Segment 5. In the 1960–1961 contraction construction contracts awarded continued to move upward in this segment. Business failures moved with the tide by increasing in number.

The most rapid rate of decline in this segment occurred in industrial production, in employment, in manufacturing, and in the A T & T Index, just as it did prewar. In the 1960–1961 contraction the most rapid rate of decline in industrial production was in Segment 7. Construction contracts awarded also went down most rapidly in this segment in the early postwar cycles, whereas prewar the most rapid rate of decline was in Segment 5.

In manufacturing industries prices were still rising in 78 percent of all observations and unit costs in 90 percent. Profit margins were rising in only 26 percent of all observations and total profits in the same percentage of observations.

Yields on Treasury bills continued downward at a slower rate than in Segment 5, while commercial paper rates and yields on Moody's Aaa corporate bonds continued downward at about the same rate as in the previous segment.

Segment 7 — Prewar. The depression still worsens in Segment 7, but at a slower rate. Most series still fall, and the number of business failures increases. The liabilities in failures, however, are starting to decline. The par value of bonds sold on the New York Stock Exchange continues to rise at the same rate as in Segment 6, and so do bond prices.

Most series, however, fall at about the same or a slower rate than in Segment 6. The exceptions are fuel and electricity production, railroad freight ton-miles, department store sales, income payments, the value of corporate security issues, and shares sold on the New York Stock Exchange, all of which are falling faster.

Consumer outlays still decline, but not so rapidly as in Segment 6. Price decreases at a rate of 1.3 points per month, and quantity 0.9 points. Only 17 percent of all commodities show increases in outlays. The highest percentages of increase are in domestic crop products, consumer goods, and foods; and the lowest in producers goods, durable goods, and metals.

The maximum rate of decrease in outlays takes place in this segment for only two groups, nonmetallic minerals and consumer goods. The maximum rate of decrease in price occurs in this segment for consumer goods other than products of American farms, manufactured goods, and nonmetallic minerals. Domestic animal product prices drop equally fast in this segment and in Segment 6.

The most rapid rate of decrease in quantity occurs in only one group, nonmetallic minerals, but durable goods quantities drop just as fast as in Segment 5.

Segment 7 — Postwar. In Segment 7 postwar only five of the series were contracting, whereas all but bond sales and business failures went down prewar. Also expanding postwar were stock sales, construction contracts awarded except in the 1960–1961 contraction, and the two series on bank debits. No series were going down most rapidly in Segment 7 in the early postwar contractions, but industrial production was in the 1960–1961 contraction.

Prices in manufacturing industries are now rising in only 45 percent of all observations, down from 78 percent in the preceding segment, and unit costs were rising in 65 percent of all observations compared with 90 percent in the preceding segment. Profit margins and total profits are rising in only 26 percent of all observations, the same percentages as in Segment 6. Yields on Treasury bills drop somewhat faster than in Segment 6, while commercial paper rates and yields on Moody's Aaa corporate bonds drop at about the same rate.

Segment 8 — Prewar. The decline in economic activity is no longer as pervasive as it was in the previous segment, since 14 series with regular cyclical patterns are already rising. This group includes the series on the number of failures, which is still going up but at a slower rate than in Segment 7. The liabilities in failures, which were decreasing in Segment 7, continue to decrease at a slightly accelerated rate.

The series that are increasing include those shown at the top of page 324, in addition to the number of failures, which is still moving with the cycle.

These series are almost all related to financial and investment activity, which involves preparation for investments soon to be made. The increases show that the financial situation has become favorable and that plans are under way for a renewal of expansion.

Imports

Value of corporate security issues

Cash from security issues

Number of shares of stock sold on the New York Stock Exchange

Par value of bonds sold on the New York Stock Exchange

Common stock prices

Three series on bank clearings and the business index based on deposit activity

Value of construction contracts

Number of incorporations

Railroad bond prices

Of the series that are still declining, that is, those on production, transportation, prices, trade, employment, and incomes, all but two are decreasing more slowly. Wholesale trade is still going down at the same rate as in Segment 7, and department store sales are going down a little faster.

In the area of buyers' outlays 45 percent of all commodities now show an increase, contrasted with only 17 percent in the last period. Buyers' outlays in total have become almost stationary in this segment. Price is still going down slowly at a rate of 0.3 points per month, but quantity is increasing 0.1 points per month. No group has its greatest rate of decrease in outlay in this segment, nor the greatest rate of decrease in price or quantity.

The fastest rate of increase in outlay on food occurs in this last segment of contraction. The maximum rate of increase in quantity in consumer goods, as well as in foods, is in this last segment of contraction. These rates of increase are probably responsible, in part at least, for some of the increase in investment activity.

Segment 8 — Postwar. Prewar many series already moved upward in Segment 8 and the same was true postwar. All were expanding except industrial production, manufacturing employment, and the A T & T Index. Industrial production and the A T & T Index declined at the slowest rate during this last segment, just as they did prewar. Manufacturing employment declined at a more rapid rate than in Segment 7, but slower than in Segment 6, whereas prewar the rate in Segment 8 was much lower than in Segments 6 and 7. Wholesale prices were stable in Segment 8 postwar, whereas they declined somewhat prewar in the last segment of the downturn. Department store sales were already expanding, whereas prewar they had the most rapid rate of downturn in this segment. The ex-

Chart 12-2

Diffusion Indexes from 1948–1967, Roughly Coincident Series

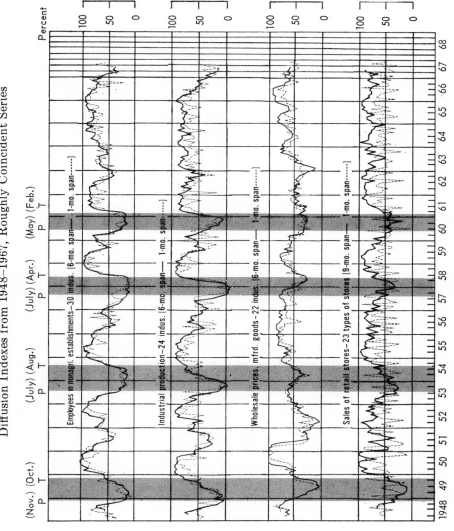

Source: Adapted from *Business Cycle Developments* (August, 1967), p. 48.

pansion of construction contracts awarded, which began in Segment 7, was going on more rapidly in Segment 8 whereas prewar they began an upturn in this segment. In the 1960–1961 downturn construction contracts continued to decline during this final segment of the contraction period.

Prices in manufacturing industries were rising in only 35 percent of the observations, the lowest rate in any segment of the cycle, and unit costs in 45 percent of the observations, the lowest rate in any segment of contraction. Profit margins were rising in only 19 percent of all observations and total profits in only 11 percent, the lowest percentages in any segment of the cycle.

Yields on Treasury bills continued downward, but at a very slow rate. Commercial paper rates continued downward at about the same rate as in previous segments of contraction, but yields on Moody's Aaa corporate bonds about stabilized.

CYCLE-TO-CYCLE VARIABILITY

This picture of typical movements in each of the eight segments of the cycle should not be allowed to obscure the differences that exist from cycle to cycle. There are wide differences in the length of cycles, in the amplitude of total economic activity and of various phases of economic activity from cycle to cycle, and in the standings of many series at reference cycle stages in different cycles.

These characteristics of cycles are clearly shown in Chart 12-2, which shows diffusion indexes for several series that are roughly coincident with movements in total economic activity. This chart shows the differences in the length of the expansion and contraction phases of the postwar cycles and in the development of each cycle, as well as the general similarity of pattern in several cycles. It also reveals that the cycle, which began in early 1961, has developed somewhat differently from earlier cycles, especially in employment, industrial production, and wholesale prices.

QUESTIONS

1. Briefly describe the series on buyers' outlays during the cycle.
2. Describe the comprehensive series used to describe the cycle.
3. Which areas of the economy are not covered by these series?
4. Describe what happens in each of the segments of the cycle during expansion. Contrast the prewar and postwar record.

5. Give some possible explanations for the retardation in the rate of expansion in Segment 2.
6. (a) Which series are increasing at a slower rate in Segment 3 than in Segment 2? (b) Are they related in any way? How does this differ postwar from prewar?
7. (a) Which series are moving against the cyclical tide in Segment 4? (b) What characteristics do they have in common?
8. Which series continue to increase at a faster rate in Segment 4?
9. Briefly describe the contraction phase of the cycle. Contrast the prewar and postwar record.
10. Discuss the changes that take place in Segment 8.
11. Discuss possible reasons for the differences between prewar and postwar cycle patterns.
12. Why is it necessary to study individual cycles in addition to the typical cycle?
13. Study the diffusion indexes in Chart 12-1. Discuss similarities and differences in the cycle patterns in the several cycles shown on the chart.

SUGGESTED READINGS

Business Cycle Developments. Washington: U. S. Department of Commerce. Current monthly issues.

Hultgren, Thor. *Cost, Prices, and Profits: Their Cyclical Relations.* New York: National Bureau of Economic Research, 1965.

Kessel, Reuben A. *The Cyclical Behavior of the Term Structure of Interest Rates.* New York: National Bureau of Economic Research, 1965.

Mills, Frederick C. *Price-Quantity Interactions in Business Cycles.* New York: National Bureau of Economic Research, 1946.

Mitchell, Wesley C. *What Happens during Business Cycles.* New York: National Bureau of Economic Research, 1951. Part IV.

CHAPTER 13

Other Fluctuations in Economic Activity

Business cycles are usually the most important fluctuations to analyze for the purpose of making forecasts. In some fields, however, seasonal fluctuations lead to wider swings in business activity than those due to the cycle, but they are more regular in their pattern and thus easier to predict. Several other types of fluctuations must be understood if a forecasting program is to be successfully carried out. These fluctuations will be analyzed in this chapter.

Consideration will be given first to cycles in building activity. These are treated separately from the business cycle since the movements do not always coincide, and some special factors affect the volume of building at times. Special cycles in agricultural production will be studied next.

Attention will then be directed to seasonal variations that occur in different sectors of the economy. The long-term trend will be considered next, and along with it the idea that long-run development may also move in waves. This chapter will be concluded with an analysis of long-run fluctuations in prices and their relationship to long-run movements in business.

CYCLES IN BUILDING ACTIVITY

The construction field is subject to regular cyclical movements that have not always coincided with fluctuations in general business and which have often been more severe. The cycle in building activity plays an important part in economic fluctuations since the building industry is of major importance. In 1966, for example, out of a total employment of 63.9 million in nonagricultural establishments, 3.3 million were employed in contract construction. This by no means indicates the total economic influence of the construction industry since many people are employed in the development of timber, the mining of metals, the manufacture of various building materials, and the furnishing of services related to the construction field. Expenditures on new construction in 1966 amounted to over $74 billion out of total expenditures of about $740 billion.[1]

Characteristics of the Building Industry

Some of the characteristics of the building industry are important in explaining fluctuations in the volume of building activity. It must be recognized first of all that the building industry is a combination of different types of concerns, some of which build small homes, some skyscrapers, others specialized industrial plants and equipment and so on. The industry is also made up of an unusually large number of small firms and of a much smaller number of large contractors engaged in developing large projects or specialized buildings. There are also local differences in the industry in the way of union organization; in the types of buildings permitted under building codes; in the availability of building materials such as stone, sand, and gravel; and in the seasons in which operations are possible.

One of the most important characteristics of the building industry is that it produces a product of unusual durability. Most buildings, especially of the residential type, last for forty years or more. In fact, obsolescence is often more important than actual physical depreciation. The immobility of buildings is also of economic importance since, as population shifts, new buildings must be constructed to take care of the people who change locations. Another important factor is the variation in different buildings, which is especially pronounced in industrial units. Buildings are not directly interchangeable so that, as the pattern of production and income shifts, there is a demand for some types of buildings that are currently not in existence and a slackening of demand for some types which exist.

Building Cycles

Various students of fluctuations in building activity have found that cycles exist in almost all types of building. Clarence D. Long, Jr., made a study of building cycles for the period from 1868 through 1936, starting with one city in 1868 and increasing the number of cities studied to 27 after 1911. He has found that there are cycles in total building, in residential building, in nonresidential

---

[1]*Federal Reserve Bulletin* (April, 1967), pp. 649, 650, 654.

Chart 13-1

The Timing of Long Cycles in Building Activity

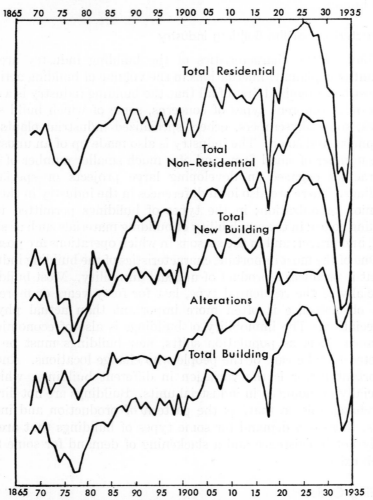

Source: Clarence D. Long, Jr., *Building Cycles and the Theory of Investment*
(Princeton: Princeton University Press, 1940), p. 131.

building, and in alterations.[2]   His index for total building and for the
major components on a 1920–1930 base is reproduced in Chart 13-1.

William H. Newman found similar cycles in building activity,
which he has divided into major cycles and minor cycles.   His work

---

[2]Clarence D. Long, Jr., *Building Cycles and the Theory of Investment* (Princeton:
Princeton University Press, 1940), pp. 226–227.

Table 13-1

Major Cycles in Building Activity

PHASE OF MAJOR CYCLE	CYCLE I	CYCLE II	CYCLE III
Turn from decline to rise..........	1876–1877*	1897–1899	1917–1918
Rise............................	1877–1892	1900–1908	1918–1924
Turn from rise to decline..........	1892–1893	1908–1912	1925–1926
Decline.........................	1894–1897	1912–1917	1926–1933

*While the Newman index extends back no further than 1875, 1876–1877 was considered a major low on the basis of building activity in Chicago and real estate activity in San Francisco, Los Angeles, and St. Louis during the preceding decade.

Source: William H. Newman, *The Building Industry and Business Cycles* (Chicago: University of Chicago Press, 1935), p. 10.

is based on Bradstreet's monthly index of building permits in 120 cities from 1911 to 1933, on Babson's permit data for 20 cities from 1903 to 1911, on Ayres' figures for 50 cities from 1900 to 1903, and on his own data for permits for from 3 to 13 cities from 1875 to 1900. He found three major cycles between the upturn in building activity in 1876 and the last low point of a building cycle in 1933. Data on these cycles, showing the starting point, the peak, and the period of decline, are presented in Table 13-1 above.

Some students of the construction industry have questioned the existence of long cycles in urban nonresidential building believing that the work of Long was based on too limited a survey of data. A very thorough study of construction data has been made under the sponsorship of the National Bureau of Economic Research by Moses Abramovitz and published in an occasional paper under the title *Evidences of Long Swings in Aggregate Construction Since the Civil War.* This study found that the weight of the evidence indicates that a series of long cycles or waves have occurred in aggregate construction activity and in construction work in all important sectors of the industry. In aggregate construction activity each wave was not followed by a distinct long-swing decline, but it was followed by a long period of retardation in growth. Waves similar to those in aggregate construction occurred in all major sectors of the construction field. Table 13-2 on page 332 shows the timing and duration of the long waves in aggregate construction activity.

These cycles are all between 15 and 20 years in length, except for the last complete cycle. This cycle was cut short in 1941 by

Table 13-2

Timing and Duration of Long Waves in Aggregate Construction
1861–Present

| Trough | Peak | Trough | Duration in Years | | |
			Upswing	Downswing	Cycle
1861	1871	1878	10	7	17
1878	1892	1898	14	6	20
1898	1912	1918	14	6	20
1918	1927	1933	9	6	15
1933	1941	1944	8	3	11
1944	1959		15		

Source: Adapted from Moses Abramovitz, *Evidences of Long Swings in Aggregate Construction Since the Civil War.* (New York: National Bureau of Economic Research, 1964), p. 90.

wartime restrictions on building. The contraction phase of the last cycle represents a slowing down in the rate of advance, rather than an absolute decline in building activity. A new trough was probably reached in late 1963 or 1964, after which activity started to increase again due to demands arising out of the Vietnam War.

Residential construction has shown somewhat more variation during the period since 1933 than construction in the aggregate. The number of nonfarm dwelling units constructed increased sharply from 1933 until 1942 when wartime restrictions greatly reduced the level of home building. At the end of the war residential construction increased rapidly until early 1950, after which there was somewhat of a contraction. A low point was reached in 1957, after which there was again some increase in home building. The 1950 level had not been reached, however, by 1967.

Nature of the Building Cycle

An analysis of the data on major cycles in building activity shows that they have an average length of about 18 years. Newman has found that the duration of major cycles varied between 15 and 21 years with an average length of almost 19 years.[3] C. F. Roos states

[3]William H. Newman, *The Building Industry and Business Cycles* (Chicago: University of Chicago Press, 1935), pp. 8–11.

that typical swings last from 10 to 20 years with an average of about 15 years.[4] John R. Riggleman has found a variation from 13 to 22 years with an average duration of 17 years.[5] Clarence Long agrees with John R. Riggleman that the average duration for the six cycles since 1830 is 17 years and for the last three cycles is just over 18 years.[6] The average duration of the cycles identified by Abramovitz is 17 years and if the cycle cut short by the outbreak of World War II is omitted, it is 18 years.

Clarence Long made a study of the turning points in the cycles of various classes of building, such as residential, nonresidential, and public. He found that the troughs in all of these series showed a high degree of coincidence, usually coinciding or varying only one or two years. The peaks varied a good deal. They rarely coincided and showed many deviations of as much as three or four years. There is a persistent tendency for public building to lag on the downturn of the cycle.[7]

Long also found that, when turning points in building were studied from city to city, the agreement was surprisingly high, especially at the lower turning points. This has been especially true in recent cycles, for in both 1918 and 1933–1934 the average deviation was only a fraction of a year and, even at the peak of the cycle in the middle 1920's, the deviation was not much more than a year.[8] This tendency for cycles to occur at the same time from city to city has continued in the postwar period.

There is no disagreement about the severity of the building cycle. Fluctuations in building cycles are usually two or three times as great as those in general business. It is to be expected that some individual industries would have fluctuations greater than those in total business activity, but building fluctuations are wider than those in almost any other component of business activity.

Long has found a tendency for each cycle since the 1878–1900 cycle to increase in intensity. The increase since 1933 has been more vigorous than earlier increases. The decrease in housing construc-

---

[4]Charles F. Roos, *Dynamic Economics* (Bloomington: The Principia Press, Inc., 1934), p. 69.

[5]John R. Riggleman, "Building Cycles in the United States, 1875–1932," *Journal of the American Statistical Association*, XXVIII (1933), pp. 174–183.

[6]Long, *op. cit.*, p. 159.

[7]*Ibid.*, p. 139.

[8]*Ibid.*, p. 145.

tion since the 1950 high point, however, has been much less severe than earlier declines.

The major movements in building and in general business appear to be associated in the absence of war, but the minor cycles are not parallel. Building reached a peak in the last years of the 1860's and in the early 1870's, and a major depression began in 1873. Building reached its next peak in the middle 1880's and turned downward in the early 1890's preceding the depression of 1893. The next cycle reached a peak in 1916 and declined in 1917 and 1918 because of America's entry into World War I; but indications are that, had it not been for the war, it would probably not have reached a peak until several years later. The cycle, which began at the end of World War I, was interrupted briefly during the sharp depression in 1920; but it then rose to a spectacular peak in 1925 and started to decline rapidly after 1928. It reached a trough in 1933 when general business reached a trough. The next peak of housing construction in 1950, was, however, not a peak in general economic activity that has gone on to new high ground since that time with but minor recessions. Thus it can be seen that major turning points in building have corresponded reasonably well with major turning points in business and have usually preceded them by one or more years.

Causal Factors

The causes of the differences in the building cycle from the general business cycle, especially the greater length and severity of the major building cycles, are inherent in the nature of the building industry. One of the major reasons for these long and severe fluctuations is the durability of buildings. The basic demand in the economy is for a certain stock of buildings, the vast majority of which are currently in existence since buildings last anywhere from 20 to 50 or more years. For example, let us suppose that a community with 10,000 people has 2,500 dwellings. Suppose further that, on the average, one new house is constructed for each increase of four persons in the population. As population increases, the need for housing in succeeding years varies as shown on Table 13-3.

The demand for houses in this example increases along with the increases in population, one house being required on the average for each four persons. As population increases by 1.6 percent in the second year, the demand for houses also increases by 1.6 percent, that is, from 2,500 to 2,540 houses. The 160 additional people create a demand for 40 new houses in the second year. In the third year, population continues to increase, but at a slower rate. The demand for houses increases at the same rate as the increase in population. The demand for new houses, however, is only half of what it was in the previous year, 20 in the third year compared with 40 in the second year. In the fifth year population and housing demand increase by 1.2 percent, but the demand for new houses doubles from that of the fourth year. Thus, while population increases by a small amount each year but not by the same amount each year, the demand for new houses shows wide fluctuations. This is another application of the accelerator principle discussed as one of the causal factors in the cycle.

Fluctuations in the demand for new buildings are not as extreme as the above example indicates, since a certain amount of building is required for the replacement of existing structures. If buildings

Table 13-3

Effect on Housing Demand of Changes in Population

YEAR	POPULA-TION	INCREASE IN POPULA-TION	PERCENT OF INCREASE IN POPULA-TION	NUMBER OF HOUSES REQUIRED	NUMBER OF ADDI-TIONAL HOUSES REQUIRED	PERCENT OF DIFFER-ENCE IN ADDI-TIONAL HOUSES NEEDED
1	10,000	——	——	2500	—	————
2	10,160	160	1.6%	2540	40	————
3	10,240	80	0.8%	2560	20	−50%
4	10,300	60	0.6%	2575	15	−25%
5	10,420	120	1.2%	2605	30	+100%

Source: Hypothetical data.

on the average lasted 50 years in this community, there would be a demand for about 50 houses a year for replacement. The demand for from 15 to 40 new houses a year due to increases in population, however, is between 30 and 80 percent of the demand for houses for replacement. In actual practice houses would not be replaced at a steady rate, and as a result fluctuations in building activity would be further magnified.

Thus it can be seen that minor shifts in population growth can lead to large shifts in the rate of demand for new housing. Cycles may easily develop even while population continues to increase but at different rates. Especially in small areas population does not grow at a smooth rate, and there have been fluctuations in the rate of population growth of the United States as large as or larger than those used in the above example. In individual communities local factors have led to varying rates of population growth, and shifts of population have taken place as some neighborhoods in a city have declined. In addition, changes in income have led to a demand for different types of housing, which has increased the demand for new buildings.

In order to test the relationship between population growth and building cycles, Newman made a study of annual population series for 17 major cities. He found a striking similarity between the population growth series and building permit series for the same cities. Both curves showed three major cycles for the period studied and had approximately the same turning points and the same degree of magnitude. He found a tendency for population growth to precede major changes in building activity by a year or two.[9]

Availability of Financing

Another factor of importance in determining the demand for buildings and hence the character of the building cycle is the availability of new financing. Most building is done on borrowed capital. It seems clear from the studies of Newman and Long that changes in interest rates will not explain major cycles in building activity. Even when interest rates move in the same direction as building, they show such minor variations that it is impossible to assign any important causal significance to them. Interest as a cost is overshadowed by such important factors as amortization, taxes, and insurance. The availability of credit, however, rather than the cost, is an important factor in the building cycle. Roos lists it, the growth in the number of families, and the net rental income as a percent of replacement cost as the three major factors affecting residential building. In fact, he holds that the supply of funds for investment in real estate is by far the most important factor affecting cycles in

---

[9] Newman, *op. cit.*, pp. 35, 36.

residential building.[10] Credit stringency was an important factor leading to the decline in home building in 1956, 1957, 1960, and again in 1966; and credit availability was a major factor leading to an upturn in 1958 and also in 1961.

Building Costs

Building costs, it would appear, are also one of the factors that should affect the demand for building and thus the building cycle, but studies by Newman indicate that no direct relationship exists. He found that costs usually moved independently of changes in building activity and that such relationship as did exist indicated that building activity caused changes in building costs rather than vice versa. The relationship between the income to be obtained from a building and the cost of the building, however, is an important factor in determining the level of construction. In a study of residential building in St. Louis from 1890 to 1933, Roos found that a 10 percent current net rental rate on current replacement cost usually led to a high level of construction activity, whereas 5 percent led to a low level.[11]

AGRICULTURAL CYCLES

Fluctuations in agriculture are directly related to cycles in general business since the purchasing power of farmers forms an important part of the pattern of expenditure for consumer goods. The income of nonfarm consumers also has a substantial effect upon the demand for and price of agricultural products; however, some cycles in this field have a pattern different from that of the business cycle.

Two-Year Cycles in Agriculture

There is a tendency toward a two-year cycle in the price and production of many crop products. If extremely favorable weather makes it apparent that there will be an unusually large crop of some commodity, such as soy beans, the price will drop to a relatively low level. This price will prevail during most of the crop season and will be the one in existence when new sowings are made. As a result of the low price, some farmers may not feel that it is profitable to raise soy beans and will cut the acreage for this crop.

---

[10]Roos, *op. cit.*, p. 70.

[11]*Ibid.*

As a consequence the price in the next crop year, barring other factors of major importance, will tend to be higher. As this higher price will prevail when another crop is sown, the tendency is to sow a larger acreage, which will lead to a larger crop and lower prices, in turn followed by a smaller crop and higher prices. Thus there is a tendency toward two-year zigzag cycles.

These cycles result from the way in which supply and prices interact. Supply reacts to the price of a commodity only after a lag because the production period of most agricultural commodities is more or less fixed. Thus an exogenous factor, such as the weather and the reaction of producers to prices and profit prospects, leads to cycles in production. The theory that describes such production-price cycles is called the *cobweb theorem* which was explained in Chapter 3.[12]

Hog and Cattle Cycles

In those fields in which the cycle of production is longer, this same tendency will lead to a longer cycle. One of the best examples is in the hog market, although cattle and other animal markets show the same general pattern. The production and slaughter of hogs has a tendency to move in a series of cycles that are three to four years in length and have been longer. These cycles did not exist during the World War II period, but have developed again in the postwar period. These cycles were due to a significant degree to variations in corn production and the relative price of corn and hogs before the period of government price support and storage programs that helped to stabilize corn prices. In recent years these cycles have been due primarily to the reaction of hog producers to prices received for hogs, but they have been longer than the two-year agricultural cycles because of the time required to produce hogs for market. The number of hogs slaughtered in any year is determined by the number of sows that were bred in the preceding year. The spring pig crop, which is marketed from September to March, was born six to nine months previously from sows bred ten to thirteen months previously. The same time relationships hold for the fall pig crop, which is marketed from April to August.

---

[12]For a discussion of the cobweb theorem see Mordecai Ezekiel, "The Cobweb Theorem," reprinted in American Economic Association, *Readings in Business Cycle Theory* (Homewood, Illinois: Richard D. Irwin, Inc., 1951), pp. 422–442.

This cycle can be explained as follows. Assume that in the first period under consideration hog slaughter is low, causing relatively high hog prices, and that the pig crop is about normal in size. Slaughter will tend to increase and prices to decrease to more normal levels in the second period as the normal pig crops come to market. The attractiveness of hog prices in period one, however, leads to an above normal pig crop in period two. In the third period this larger pig crop will produce a larger than normal rate of slaughter and prices will drop. The pig crop has, however, declined because of the normal prices in period two. As a result, slaughter and prices will return to normal levels in period four. However, the pig crop will be below normal because of the relatively low prices for hogs in period three, and forces are set in motion to start the cycle over again. These relationships may be summarized as follows:

Period	Slaughter	Prices	Pig Crop
1	Below normal	High	Normal
2	Normal	Normal	Above normal
3	Above normal	Low	Normal
4	Normal	Normal	Below normal
5	Below normal	High	Normal

Hog cycles are somewhat more complicated than the above example because hog production is governed to some degree by the relative price of corn and also of other feeds. The production of hogs and the production of corn are interrelated, since most of the corn crop is fed to hogs and corn makes up about two thirds of the feed used in pork production. Before government price support programs helped stabilize the price of corn, changes in the corn crop had a significant effect on hog production and the cycle was a corn-hog cycle to a large degree.

An unusually large corn crop, which resulted from large plantings or unusually good growing conditions, depressed the price of corn. This low price of corn made it cheaper to raise pigs and thus had a tendency to lead to larger pig crops. The most significant price was not the absolute price of corn, but the relative prices of corn and hogs, or the ratio of the price of hogs to the price of corn. When corn was cheap relative to the price of hogs, the pig crop was increased; and when corn was high, the pig crop was decreased. This led to cycles similar to those described above that are based on the price of hogs without regard to the relative price of corn and hogs. The situation was, however, somewhat more complex and less regular since weather conditions could change the expected yields from a given acreage of corn that was planted on the basis of past price relationships.

The cycle was also accentuated by variations in the length of time that hogs were kept on the farm instead of being sent to market. When the corn-hog ratio was such that it was more profitable to feed hogs and sell them than to sell corn, hogs were kept on the farm and fed longer than normally and supplies of pork become even smaller than expected on the basis of the pig crop and prices rose further. When the point was reached at which feeding was no longer profitable, slaughter increased and prices were reduced to more normal levels. There is still some tendency for this to happen at the present time, but it has been reduced materially by more stable corn prices and by relatively stable prices of feed supplements.

The hog cycle may be further complicated and increased somewhat in length by the number of sows that are available, which is, in part at least, determined by earlier price situations and price expectations. Data, which are available for the period from 1900 to the World War II period, indicates that in this period there was at least a rough approximation to a five-year cycle,[13] compared with a three-to-four-year cycle at present.

Since the production period in raising cattle is considerably longer than that in raising hogs, the cattle cycle is of longer duration. It is also less regular, since the longer the time involved, the greater is the possibility of outside factors affecting the cycle.

Coffee Cycle

One of the longest of the agricultural cycles occurs in the coffee market because it takes seven years from the time that a coffee tree is planted until it yields coffee beans. Therefore, a cycle of 15 or more years occurs in this field. This cycle is no longer as clearly

---

[13]Norman J. Silberling, *The Dynamics of Business* (New York: McGraw-Hill Book Company, 1945), pp. 48–51.

visible as it was some years ago because of the interference of the Brazilian and other governments in the coffee market. However, it has continued to affect coffee production and prices in the post-World War II period.

SEASONAL VARIATIONS

Seasonal fluctuations in the volume of business are important in many fields.

Causes of Seasonal Fluctuations

Various factors are responsible for these fluctuations in economic activity that take place during the course of the year. Some segments of the economy are affected by the yearly cycle in weather. Other segments are affected by the customs of society, especially those related to holidays. A third factor that causes data to have seasonal fluctuations is our present calendar.

Climate. Climatic conditions influence the periods of growth and the time of maturity of crops, and also to a lesser extent of livestock, and thus economic activity related to agriculture experiences pronounced seasonal fluctuations. The weather also determines the period of ice-free navigation on various bodies of water and thus influences economic activity. For example, iron ore cannot be transported on the Great Lakes during part of the winter. In some parts of the country the weather also influences operations in the lumber industry and in some types of open-pit mining. In many places climatic conditions necessitate different types of clothing during various seasons of the year, and the manufacture and sale of clothing show the influence of these variations. In addition, the weather determines which sports are carried on at different times and so leads to a seasonal variation in the sale of sporting goods.

Customs. Human institutions and customs also materially affect the volume of business during the course of a year. Holidays materially affect retail activity, and these influences extend into the manufacturing field. There is a demand for various types of merchandise for Christmas gifts, for new clothing at Easter, for fireworks on the Fourth of July, and so on.

The Calendar. The construction of our calendar gives monthly economic data the appearance of seasonal variations greater than the actual fluctuations in business. The months of the year vary from 28 to 31 days. February, for example, is usually almost 10 percent shorter than January, and April is about 3 percent shorter than March. In addition, February has several holidays which make the comparison of the volume of business in February with that in January or March less valid as an indication of the true course of economic activity. The number of Saturdays or Sundays in a month is another cause of spurious variations. A factor that affects sales differently in different years is the changing date of Easter.

Seasonal Patterns in Production

For purposes of analysis, industries with definite seasonal influences may be divided into four basic groups.

The first group consists of those industries in which the supply of raw materials is subject to large seasonal variations, while the demand for the finished product is fairly constant. Most food products belong in this classification.

The second group includes those industries in which the supply of raw materials and the demand for finished products are both subject to large seasonal fluctuations. Examples of this type of industry are the natural fibers, such as cotton and wool, in which there are definite seasonal fluctuations in the demand for the finished products as well as in their production.

The third category embraces industries that make use of raw materials with a fairly constant supply but have a final product that is subject to fairly large seasonal variation in demand. The automobile industry and industries related to it, such as the petroleum industry, are characterized by this type of fluctuation.

The fourth group includes primarily the construction industries, in which there is no necessary seasonal fluctuation in the manufacture of raw materials or in the demand for the final product.

The seasonal movements in some of the component activities of each of these four groups will be presented in general outline, and some comments will also be made on seasonal variations in phases of economic activity other than production.[14]

---

[14]For indexes of seasonal variation the reader is referred to the Board of Governors of the Federal Reserve System, *Federal Reserve Index of Industrial Production* (Washington: Federal Reserve System, 1943) and to Appendix D in a current issue of *Business Cycle Developments*.

The supply of most food products is subject to seasonal fluctuations while the demand is not, but the seasonal fluctuations work out differently in such fields as wheat and flour, dairy products, and fruits and vegetables.

Group 1 — Wheat and Flour. The harvesting of wheat is subject to pronounced seasonal fluctuations since it usually occurs between early June in the southern part of the wheat belt in Texas to late July in the northern wheat belt. Flour milling shows a peak in activity in October but not nearly to the same extent as that for the harvesting of wheat in the summer. There is some peak in flour consumption during the winter months, which is in turn much smaller than that in flour milling.

Stocks of wheat are held at various places — on the farms, in elevators, and at flour mills. The stocks of flour, on the other hand, are usually carried by wholesalers and large bakers.

Group 1 — Dairy Products. Seasonal fluctuations in dairy products differ somewhat from those in wheat because the industry is dealing with a perishable commodity. Since more milk is produced in summer than in winter and since the demand for it shows little seasonal variation, the surplus of summer milk is converted into evaporated milk, butter, and cheese, which are then stored until needed. The summer peak in the production of durable dairy products has a tendency to lower their price and thus produces a seasonal price fluctuation. This fact, in turn, affects the price and production of substitutes. Margarine, for example, is produced in larger quantities during the winter than during the summer.

Group 1 — Fruits and Vegetables. The demand for raw fruits and vegetables would probably remain fairly stable throughout the year in the absence of a seasonal cycle in production. However, their consumption is much heavier in summer, when the supply is large, than it is during other times of the year. The development of the frozen-food industry is tending to smooth out the seasonal fluctuation in consumption, but this industry also has a pronounced seasonal fluctuation since the freezing of food can be done only at the height of the season for each crop. This is also true of other forms of food processing, such as canning and drying; however, a large part of the seasonal adjustment in this field is made by consumers who adjust their purchases to fluctuations in production.

Group 2 — Cotton. In some ways the seasonal pattern in the movements of raw cotton and cotton textiles is similar to that in the field of wheat and flour milling. The consumption of raw cotton by textile mills does not have any major seasonal fluctuation even though the harvesting of cotton is concentrated in four months. As in the case of flour, the seasonal peak in mill activity occurs several months after the peak in the harvesting of the crop. This is the case because the farmer carries large and seasonally variable stocks of raw cotton. Cotton differs from wheat, however, since there is also a pronounced variation in manufacturing based upon the seasonality of the demand for cotton goods. This seasonal variation becomes greater in amplitude the closer one gets to the final consumer. In other words, the retailer has a larger seasonal fluctuation than the wholesaler, and the wholesaler a larger seasonal variation than the manufacturers in the various stages of production. Probably the major stocks of finished goods are held by retailers, and more are held by wholesalers than by manufacturers.

Group 3 — Automobile Field. There is some seasonal variation in the demand for automobiles. This variation is based in part upon the increased demand during the summer months for cars for vacation travel and also in part upon the dates of the introduction of new models. Increased summer demand is normally more pronounced in low-priced cars than in higher priced cars. Seasonal variation has a smaller amplitude in the field of trucks than in passenger cars.

These seasonal variations in automobile purchases lead to seasonal variations of almost the same magnitude in the manufacture of automobiles because it is not the policy of the industry to stock very many cars. These variations are carried over to a certain extent into the fields producing parts for automobiles, such as spark plugs and tires, and to a lesser degree to such industries as the manufacture of upholstery materials and sheet steel. The seasonal variation also carries over into the gasoline field, but here most variation takes place in stocks rather than in production since the technical characteristics of the industry make it difficult to vary production in response to demand.

Group 4 — Construction. In the construction field rain and low temperatures impede activity and thus lead to fluctuations in building activity. Many seasonal problems have been overcome in the construction of major buildings, such as industrial plants and office and apartment buildings, but in the construction of smaller buildings and in the laying of roads and highways some activity is still impossible in severe weather. Most contractors carry no stocks of raw materials, and consequently there are extreme fluctuations in the demand for materials as building speeds up in the summer months.

The seasonal peaks do not come at the same time but follow the progress of building since some materials are needed early in the process of construction and others somewhat later. Some stocks of these materials are kept by dealers; but a large part of the task of meeting fluctuations in demands falls upon manufacturers, especially in the case of heavy equipment, such as furnaces and radiators. Production of construction materials proceeds at a much more even rate than the shipment of these materials, except in the case of some types of brick and lumber, the production of which is itself subject to changes in the weather.

Seasonal Patterns in Other Fields

Seasonal variations characterize economic activities other than the production of goods. Fluctuations in employment and in payrolls are of the same types as those in production in the various fields, but their amplitude is not as great.

Prices usually fluctuate in an inverse fashion to the seasonal variations in production. In some cases retail prices are quite sensitive to seasonal fluctuations in production, as for example the prices of pork and dried fruits, especially prunes. Changes in prices are much less responsive to changes in production of potatoes, flour, and coal.

There is some seasonal variation in the volume of credit and currency. For example, total loans by reporting member banks of the Federal Reserve System show low levels during the first half of the year and high levels in the autumn and winter with a peak at the end of the year. The total money supply shows a similar variation. These fluctuations are based primarily upon seasonal variations in the distributive trades.

Quarterly dividend payments are more frequently made in January, April, July, and October than in any other months. Furthermore, payments during July are heavier than in April and October since many companies pay semiannual dividends. Payments

Chart 13-2

Trend of Output of Portland Cement since 1870

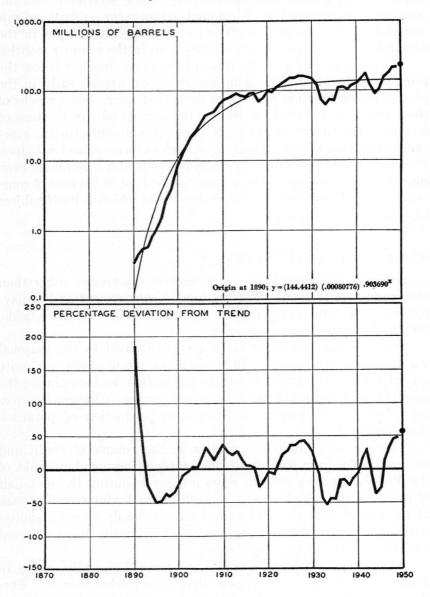

Origin at 1890; $y = (144.4412) (.00080776)^{.903690^x}$

Source: National Industrial Conference Board, *Growth Patterns in Industry*
(New York: National Industrial Conference Board, 1952), p. 34

in the last days of December and early January are heaviest of all since some companies pay dividends only once a year or pay extras at that time.

THE GROWTH TREND

The growth trends in individual industries vary, depending upon the age of the industry and its place in the economy. Most industries start slowly and then expand at a rapid rate as they become integrated with the rest of the economy. After that, they grow more slowly, increasing with increases in real income and in the population. This typical pattern can be seen in Chart 13-2 showing the trend of output of Portland Cement.

An old established industry that is still growing has a gradually increasing rate of output as population and real income increase. An example is the trend of cotton consumption shown in Chart 13-3.

At times the uses of a product may change, and this change may affect the trend. An example is the rubber industry, which was in the slow increase in output stage between 1870 and 1910 and then experienced a new wave of growth with the development of the automobile. This changing pattern is shown in Chart 13-4.

LONG WAVES IN ECONOMIC ACTIVITY

A theory of long waves in economic activity was developed by N. D. Kondratieff while he was director of the Conjuncture Institute of Moscow. He studied various series, such as indexes of wholesale prices in England, France, and the United States; bond prices in France and England; and series on wages, foreign trade, and the output of coal, pig iron, and lead.[15] After smoothing out all cycles with a duration of nine years or less from the late 1780's to 1920, he found two complete long waves and the beginning of a third. The first wave began in the late 1780's, rose until 1810–1817, and then declined until 1844–1851. The second wave began at this time, rose until 1870–1875, and then declined to around 1890–1896. The third wave began at that time with an expansion which continued to the period from 1914 to 1920 and then began to decline.

This theory of long waves has not been generally accepted by economists. Economic data expressed in money terms do show

---

[15]Kondratieff's articles have been translated and summarized in the following article: N. D. Kondratieff, "The Long Waves in Economic Life," *Review of Economic Statistics* (November, 1935).

Chart 13-3

Trend of Cotton Consumption since 1870

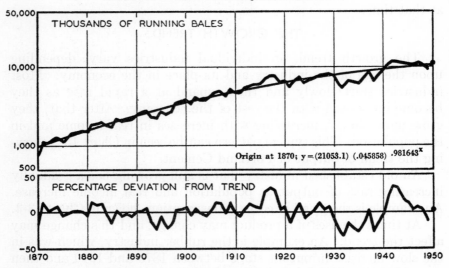

Origin at 1870; $y = (21053.1) (.045858)^{.981643^x}$

Source: National Industrial Conference Board, *Growth Patterns in Industry*
(New York: 1952), p. 50.

Chart 13-4

Trend of Rubber Imports since 1870

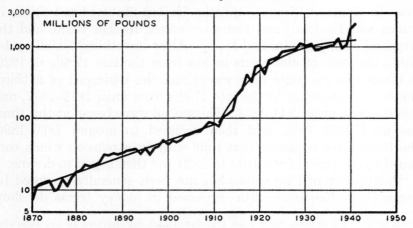

Source: National Industrial Conference Board, *Growth Patterns in Industry*
(New York: 1952), p. 19.

fluctuations that correspond in a general way to Kondratieff's long waves. This relationship is due to the inflation which occurs during major wars, but that does not mean that there were true waves in economic activity. There is no statistical evidence in production series in the United States of any long wave fluctuations of 50 or 60 years' duration.

Burns and Mitchell in their study of business cycles have sought to determine if there is any difference between business cycles occurring during the upswing of long waves in commodity prices and those occurring during the downswing. On the basis of a study of deflated bank clearings, pig iron production, railroad stock prices, the number of shares of stock traded, call money rates, railroad bond yields, and freight car orders, they decided that the cyclical patterns during the upswing and downswing in the long-period movements in commodity prices are broadly similar.[16]

They did find that business cycles in the United States, Great Britain, France, and Germany are somewhat longer on the average during a period of declining wholesale prices than they are when such prices are increasing. It is difficult, however, to draw any accurate conclusion from this relationship since longer business cycles may influence the direction of price movements rather than vice versa, or more complex factors may influence both the length of the cycle and the movement of prices.[17]

Joseph Schumpeter has adopted the idea of long cycles in describing economic fluctuations. According to his pattern of the cycle the Kondratieff cycle of 50 to 60 years' duration contains six Juglar cycles of 9 to 10 years' duration, and each Juglar cycle contains three Kitchin cycles of about 40 months' duration.[18] Schumpeter does not always find this regular pattern in actual practice; but whenever one of the cycles is omitted, he believes that some special factor is responsible. The statistical work of Burns and Mitchell, however, does not bear out this relationship between cycles. In the first place less than a third of the business cycles since 1854 have a length between 37 and 43 months.[19] Furthermore, attempts by

---

[16]Arthur F. Burns and Wesley C. Mitchell, *Measuring Business Cycles* (New York: National Bureau of Economic Research, 1946), p. 432.

[17]*Ibid.*

[18]Schumpeter named each of these cycles after the men who, in his opinion, did the first important work in describing each type.

[19]Burns and Mitchell, *op. cit.*, p. 462.

Burns and Mitchell to group monthly cycle data into patterns of three consecutive cycles produced no approximation to a Juglar cycle of 9 to 10 years.[20]

LONG SWINGS IN ECONOMIC GROWTH

Studies by the National Bureau of Economic Research have found that economic growth moves in recurrent waves of acceleration and retardation that last for between 15 and 20 years. Based on data for the United States since 1814, there is evidence that such successive swings have occurred at about the same time in such series as production, prices, population growth, and international movements of people and capital. There is still no complete agreement on the timing of such swings. This depends in part on the procedures used to smooth out the business cycle. Table 13-4 shows the peaks and troughs of long swings in the rate of growth of output according to one chronology developed by Moses Abramovitz as part of a National Bureau of Economic Research study.

These long swings in the rate of growth of output result from similar swings in the basic factors that determine the rate of growth. From available data it appears as if there are similar long swings

Table 13-4

A Chronology of Peaks and Troughs in Long Swings in the
Rate of Growth of Output in the United States

Long Swing Peaks	Long Swing Troughs
1814	1819
1834	1840
1846	1858
1864	1874
1881	1886
1890	1892
1899	1911
1914	1920
1923	1930
1938–9	

Source: "Long Swings in United States Economic Growth," *The Study of Economic Growth*, Thirty-ninth Annual Report, National Bureau of Economic Research (New York: National Bureau of Economic Research, 1959), p. 25.

---

[20]*Ibid.*

in the rate of growth of productivity, in the volume of additions to resources used to produce goods including both labor and capital, and in the intensity with which resources are used.

Each retardation in the rate of growth of output is marked by a depression of unusual severity. The evidence suggests that the swings consist of alternations between periods of relatively severe and long depressions and of relatively mild and short ones.

There is no complete analysis of the causal factors at work in these long swings. The evidence suggests, however, that they are related to the construction cycle. As long as construction grows fast enough so that total investment can absorb the growing volume of saving and so that total expenditures for all types of goods and services are equal to the growing level of output, total output follows a rising secular trend interrupted by only mild recessions. But when the rate of growth of construction slows down significantly and especially when the volume of construction turns down, a serious and long depression is likely to occur. This reduces the secular growth to its low point in the long swing of growth.

LONG-RUN FLUCTUATIONS IN PRICE

A study of prices for the last 160 years shows wide fluctuations, which have at times been described as price cycles. To the extent that such cycles exist, they are primarily related to fluctuations in prices that have occurred as the result of inflationary policies during major wars. If wars are considered as political factors impinging upon the economy, then these are not cycles in the same sense as other economic cycles. To those students of our economy, such as Karl Marx and N. C. Kondratieff, who believe that wars are an integral part of the capitalistic process, such cycles would, of course, be true economic cycles. These long-run price movements have also been influenced by major discoveries of gold as, for example, in the period after 1896. They may also have been influenced to some degree by increased demand resulting from major innovations, such as the railroads and automobile.

In the United States prices rose to high levels during the Revolutionary War and then declined after the end of the war. They fluctuated more or less in harmony with the business cycle until the War of 1812, when they again reached high levels due to wartime inflationary finance. There was a downward trend after the war, and then prices again moved more or less in harmony with business cycles until the Civil War period. During this war wholesale prices more than doubled under the impact of wartime fiscal policy.

After the Civil War, the downward movement of prices was again repeated so that by 1896 wholesale prices were not much over one third of the level of the Civil War peak. Prices then began a gradual upward movement that was greatly accentuated during World War I. From this point on, prices moved downward, reaching a level in 1932–1933 of about 40 percent of the World War I peak, and then they started up again and continued upward through World War II. There was only a slight falling off in prices after the end of World War II, and prices resumed their upward movement in the summer of 1950 after the outbreak of the Korean War.

From 1958 through 1964 prices remained about stable and then started to rise again due to the demands arising out of the intensification of the Vietnam War.

A cursory examination of the history of prices may give the impression that prices have moved in long waves. More careful examination of price data, however, will show that this is not the case. Prices have moved upward sharply during wartime periods and then have gradually declined. These sharp wartime peaks give price data the appearance of long waves, which is largely illusory.

QUESTIONS

1. What is the nature of the building cycle?
2. How are building cycles related to business cycles?
3. Account for the length and severity of the building cycle.
4. Describe the hog and cattle cycles. What accounts for them? How has the situation changed since the introduction of agricultural programs to stabilize corn prices?
5. Why is the coffee cycle one of the longest on record?
6. Briefly describe the factors that lead to seasonal fluctuations in business.
7. Identify the four basic types of seasonal variations in production industries.
8. What seasonal variations exist in fields other than production?
9. Describe the long-term trend of economic activity in the United States.
10. What is the nature of the trend of an established industry?
11. Account for abrupt changes in trend.
12. Briefly analyze the Kondratieff theory of long waves.
13. (a) Describe long swings in economic growth. (b) What explanation has been given for their existence?
14. Are there cycles in price movements?

SUGGESTED READINGS

Abramovitz, Moses. *Evidences of Long Swings in Aggregate Construction Since the Civil War.* New York: National Bureau of Economic Research, 1964.

American Economic Association, *Readings in Business Cycle Theory.* Homewood, Illinois: Richard D. Irwin, Inc., 1944. Chapter 2.

Burns, Arthur F. "Long Cycles in Residential Construction," *Economic Essays in Honor of Wesley Clair Mitchell.* New York: Columbia University Press, 1935.

————————. *Production Trends in the United States Since 1870.* New York: National Bureau of Economic Research, 1934.

Kondratieff, N. D. "The Long Waves in Economic Life," *Review of Economic Statistics* (November, 1935).

Kuznets, Simon. *Seasonal Variations in Industry and Trade.* New York: National Bureau of Economic Research, 1933.

Long, Clarence D., Jr. *Building Cycles and the Theory of Investment.* Princeton, New Jersey: Princeton University Press, 1940.

National Industrial Conference Board, *Growth Patterns in Industry.* New York: The National Industrial Conference Board, 1952.

Newman, William H. *The Building Industry and Business Cycles.* Chicago: University of Chicago Press, 1935

PROBLEMS ON PART IV

1. Study the record of economic activity in the 1960's from articles in the *Survey of Current Business* and the *Federal Reserve Bulletin*. Select monthly reference dates for peaks and troughs and bring Table 11-2 on page 282 up to date. How does the most recent cycle (or cycles) compare with earlier cycles in duration of expansion and contraction?

2. A. Using ratio paper, develop a chart for each of the following series showing sales and inventories for each month of the current cycle:
   Manufacturing — total
   Wholesale trade — total
   Retail trade — total
   Retail trade — durable goods
   Retail trade — nondurable goods

   B. Analyze the relationships between sales and inventories on each of the charts.

3. Make a list of the three or four most important factors in each of the eight segments of the cycle. On the basis of your reading and analysis on the current state of the economy, determine in which segment the economy is at present. Review your answer throughout the semester and revise it if you feel the economy has moved into the next segment.

4. A. Plot the number of nonfarm dwelling units started in each year since 1951 on ratio paper, using data from the *Construction Review*. On the same chart also plot the following:
   (a) Annual increase in population from the Bureau of the Census, *Current Population Reports* or *Statistical Abstract*.
   (b) Average interest rates on long-term government bonds from the *Federal Reserve Bulletin*.

   B. Discuss the relationships, if any, among these three series. Which additional factors are likely to have caused some of the fluctuations in residential construction?

5. Analyze the fluctuations during the current cycle in each of the following sectors of economic activity:
   (a) Industrial production
   (b) Gross national product
   Compare these fluctuations with those in these fields in past cycles. Describe similarities and differences, and insofar as possible account for them.

PART V

HISTORICAL RECORD OF
BUSINESS FLUCTUATIONS

In order to understand the present and to face the future with any degree of assurance, it is necessary to study the past. History repeats itself to some degree even though each period has new factors at work which lead to a somewhat different course of events than would have been predicted from a study of past events alone. Since this is also true of business fluctuations, it is desirable to study the past record of such fluctuations.

Some data on economic development was presented in Part I, and in Part IV the nature of past cyclical movements was described and analyzed in some detail. In this part the record of major and minor cycles since 1918 is discussed in chronological order. This most recent period is analyzed more fully than earlier periods because the changes that occurred in this period still affect the thinking of many people in government and in business. Another reason is that, since the economy is constantly changing, the situation in the present period resembles that of the most recent period more than it resembles the situation in any of the earlier periods.

Chapter 14 analyzes the record of business cycles from the end of World War I in 1918 to the beginning of World War II in Europe in 1939. This is a period of a postwar boom and collapse followed by a period of prosperity and then by one of severe depression. Chapter 15 covers the record of cycles from 1938 to the present. This is a period of all-out war, and a postwar period marked by the Korean and Vietnam Wars and the cold-war struggle with Russia.

CHAPTER **14** *Business Cycles from 1918 to 1938*

The economic and political changes arising out of World War I affected the American economy during the war period and also to some extent during much of the twenties and thirties. The level of economic activity in the United States increased materially when World War I broke out in Europe in 1914 and America supplied military equipment to some of the European countries engaged in the war. The level of activity grew even more when America entered the war in 1917.

The increased demand for goods and also the inflationary methods used to finance the war led to rapid increases in prices. The Treasury calculated the total cost of the war, including $10 billion advanced to our allies, at about $33 billion. Of this amount less than one third was raised by taxation. In the four Liberty Loan drives and in the Victory Loan drive the government sold over $21 billion in bonds. Prices increased sharply, wholesale prices moving from a level of 135 in 1914 on an 1890–1899 base to 280 in September, 1918. An index of ten sensitive commodity prices increased from 128 on the same base to 340 in November, 1918.[1]

At the end of the war in November, 1918, most economists and businessmen expected a severe slump in business activity; and after the Armistice there was some decline in the volume of business. For example, production of iron and steel declined to about 65 percent of capacity shortly after the end of the war.

By the summer of 1919 the American economy was again in a boom period, and prices moved up rapidly. The index of ten sensitive commodities had declined to 262 in April, 1919, but was at a level of 353 at the end of the year. It continued upward at a rapid rate in the early part of 1920, reaching 396 in June. Wholesale prices dropped to 265 in February, 1919, but increased through May,

---

[1]Warren M. Persons, *Forecasting Business Cycles* (New York: John Wiley & Sons, Inc., 1931), pp. 143–147.

Chart 14-1

Bureau of Labor Statistics Index of Wholesale Prices, 1913–1932
(1926 = 100)

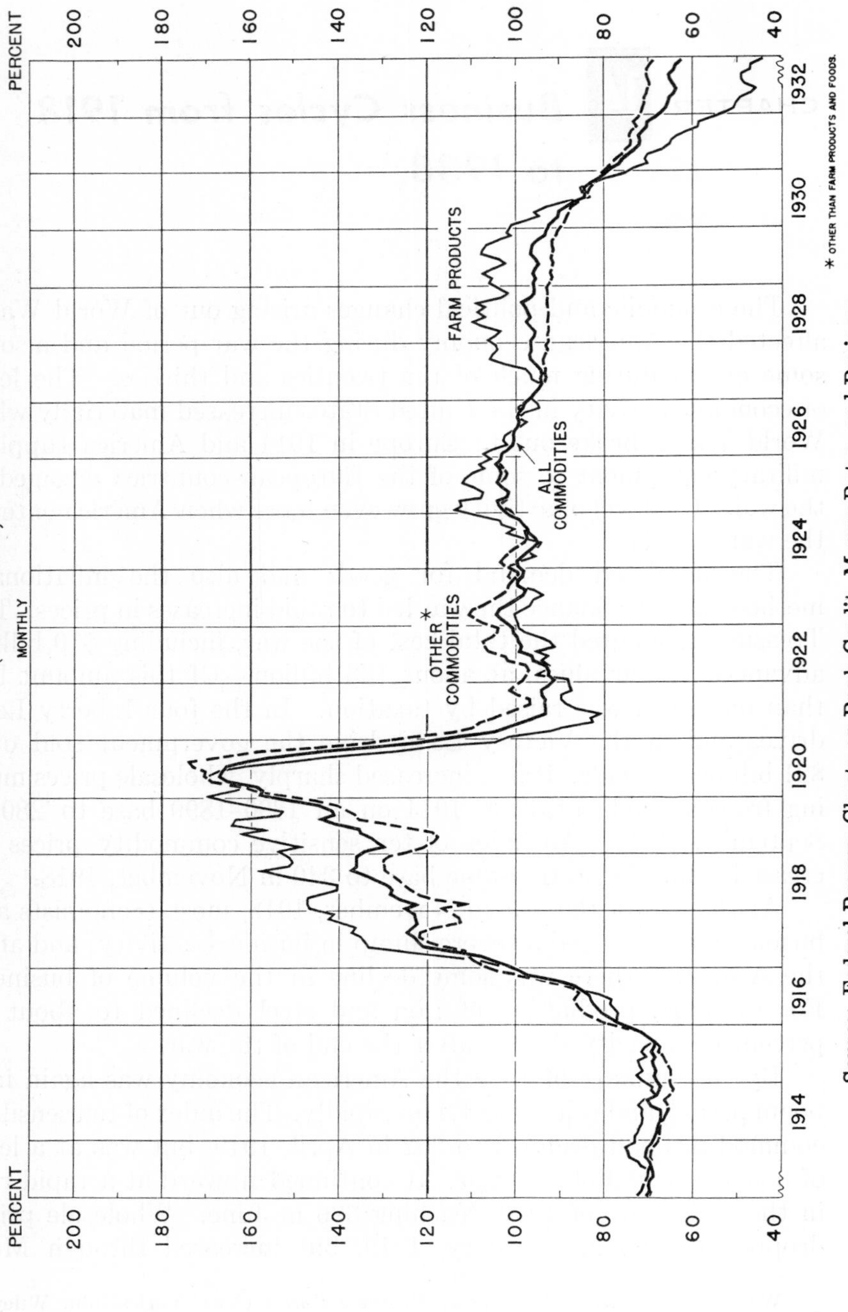

MONTHLY

PERCENT

PERCENT

200
180
160
140
120
100
80
60
40

1914 1916 1918 1920 1922 1924 1926 1928 1930 1932

FARM PRODUCTS

ALL COMMODITIES

OTHER * COMMODITIES

* OTHER THAN FARM PRODUCTS AND FOODS.

Source: Federal Reserve Charts on Bank Credit, Money Rates, and Business.

1920, to 342. There was a serious break in August, 1920, and a drastic drop in December that carried the index of sensitive prices down almost 170 points and the general wholesale price index down almost 100 points.[2] These price shifts are shown in Chart 14-1.

THE 1920 DEPRESSION

The break in commodity prices was followed by a depression in 1920 as business readjusted to lower price levels. The early postwar boom and the depression that followed arose out of the policies during the war and in the transition to a peacetime economy.

Character of the Depression

The slump in business activity that began in 1920 was rather severe, but it did not last very long. The Federal Reserve Index of Industrial Production on a 1935–1939 base was at a level of 75 in 1920, and then it dropped to a depression low of 58 in 1921. In 1922 it had recovered to about the 1920 level and was well above it in 1923. Factory employment dropped almost 25 percent from 1920 to 1921, but it had almost reached 1920 levels in 1923.

The wartime boom and inflation did not end shortly after the Armistice for several reasons. The demand for peacetime goods by European countries increased rapidly at the end of the war, and the favorable merchandise balance of trade for 1919 was in excess of $4 billion. Part of this demand arose because European currencies were pegged to the dollar at the prewar rates, and prices had gone up faster in those countries than in the United States. The federal government also continued to operate at a deficit until the late summer of 1919. Another factor was that the Federal Reserve System did not restrain the supply of money and credit until the beginning of 1920, since the banks were committed to take up a large part of the Victory Loan floated at the end of April and the beginning of May in 1919. Even after this bond issue was sold the Treasury continued short-term borrowing until the late summer of 1919, and the Federal Reserve System acted to keep credit freely available to aid government financing. This was done because the Federal Reserve had agreed to lend money to member banks for six months at rates equal to those borne by the Victory Bonds to facilitate the sale of these bonds.

---

[2] *Ibid.*

Immediate Causes

By late 1919 and early 1920 the monetary situation was completely reversed. In the third quarter of 1919 the federal government balanced its budget, and in the fourth quarter of 1919 and in 1920 it had a surplus. With the unpegging of foreign currencies they fell rapidly in value and, as a result, foreign trade was reduced early in 1920. The United States still had a favorable commodity balance of trade in 1920, but it was materially smaller than in the previous year. People generally felt that inflation would not continue and expected a recession to take place and, as a result, business began to adopt a more cautious policy toward expansion and the increasing of inventories. When the Federal Reserve System was free from its commitments in connection with government financing, it raised rediscount rates in an effort to discourage borrowing. The effect of this action at the late stage in the boom at which it occurred was probably mostly psychological since, as long as prices were going up rapidly, an increase of 1 or 2 percent on an annual basis in the cost of borrowing was of negligible significance. It did, however, clearly show that it was the intention of the monetary authorities to stop the inflationary boom.

Basic Causes

The 1920 depression was the result of the unbalanced situation created by inflation during the war. The rise in the price level was caused primarily by the inflationary methods used to finance the war. This inflationary finance continued into the postwar period for a time until the government balanced its budget. Added to this factor were the unusual demands for goods from Europe due to wartime shortages and improperly adjusted currency exchange rates. When these inflationary stimulants were removed, the price level dropped rapidly. During the period of rapid price declines, business was on a day-to-day basis. As soon as it was apparent that prices were stabilized, business picked up. There were no serious maladjustments to correct other than those caused by price unbalance and, as a result, the depression was short.

Recovery

Several factors were responsible for the rapid return to prosperity conditions in the early part of 1922. During 1920 the debts of federal, state, and local governments were decreased by $600 million, but in 1921 the debts of these governmental bodies increased by $545 million. In other words, the net effect of governmental fiscal policy was to add over $1 billion more to the income stream in 1921 than in the previous year.[3] Other funds were added to the income stream during the depression period by a reduction in the propensity to save. In 1920, 86.4 percent of national income was spent on consumers goods, and this percentage increased to 88.9 in 1921 and 89.8 in 1922. The total savings of business concerns and of various governmental units declined from $15.8 billion in 1920 to about $11 billion in 1921 and $9 billion in 1922.[4]

There was also a rapid increase in automobile production between 1920 and 1923, and that increase carried related industries, such as petroleum, with it. In addition the greatest building boom in our history began to get under way in 1921 and gathered momentum in 1922. The index of the value of total construction contracts awarded increased 50 percent from 1920 to 1923 and that of residential construction contracts 170 percent.[5]

THE 1922 TO 1929 PROSPERITY PERIOD

The depression of 1920 ended in 1922 and was followed by a period of record prosperity. Development was especially marked in the construction and automobile fields, and a boom of unprecedented proportions occurred in the stock market.

Character of the Period

The period from 1922 to 1929 marks one of the greatest periods of prosperity in the history of this country. There were slight recessions in 1924 and again in 1927, but they were so minor that many people have referred to this whole period as one of sustained prosperity. Industrial production rose rapidly from a depression low of 58 in 1921 (1935–1939 = 100) to 110 in 1929.

The increase in production was by no means uniform in all fields. For example, the Federal Reserve Index of Petroleum Production (1923–1925 = 100) increased from 86 in 1923 to 168 in 1929,

---

[3]Simon Kuznets, *National Income and Its Composition*, 1919–1938 (New York: National Industrial Conference Board, 1941), p. 814.

[4]Simon Kuznets, *National Income and Capital Formation, 1919–1935* (New York: National Bureau of Economic Research, 1937), pp. 24, 53.

[5]*Federal Reserve Bulletin* (June, 1950), p. 719.

that of rubber tire manufacture from 86 to 135, and that of motor vehicle production from 102 to 135. During this same period, however, production of manufactured food products declined from 99 to 97 and that of leather and leather products from 110 to 105.[6]

In addition to the boom in production, especially in the automobile and related fields, there was a tremendous boom in the construction industry. The index of the value of all construction contracts awarded increased from a level of 84 in 1923 to 135 in 1928 and then dropped to 117 in 1929. Residential construction increased from 81 in 1923 to 126 in 1928, and construction other than residential from 86 in 1923 to 142 in 1928.[7]

During these years the price level was experiencing some minor fluctuations, but on the whole it remained remarkably stable. The index of wholesale commodity prices, which was at a level of 98 in 1921, was at its highest point in 1925 at 104 and ended the period in 1929 at 95. The consumers price index exhibited the same stability. In 1922 it was at a level of 120, then rose to 126 in 1926, and declined slightly by 1929 (1935–1939 = 100).

Stock Market Boom

One of the most spectacular features of the 1922–1929 period was the rapid increase in the prices of common stocks. The index of common stock prices of the Standard and Poor's Corporation showed stocks at a level of 62 in January, 1922. They rose to 238 in September, 1929, an increase of 284 percent. From January, 1922, to September, 1929, industrial stock prices rose from 50 to 195, railroad stocks from 168 to 446, and utility stocks from 74 to 375. The boom had not lost any of its momentum in the summer of 1929; the index of common stock prices increased from 230 in August to 238 in September. The stocks that moved up most rapidly were public utility stocks, which in January, 1929, were at a level of 225; in May, 248; in June, 319; in August, 355; and in September, 375.[8]

The rapid rise in stock prices was in part based upon a similarly rapid increase in the amount of credit used in the stock market. According to Federal Reserve figures on March 31, 1927, loans to

[6]*Sixteenth Annual Report* (Washington: Board of Governors of the Federal Reserve System, 1929), p. 210.

[7]*Federal Reserve Bulletin* (June, 1950), p. 719.

[8]*Banking and Monetary Statistics* (Washington: Board of Governors of the Federal Reserve System, 1943), pp. 480–481.

brokers totaled $3,290 million. These loans had increased by March 31, 1928, to $4,640 million and by March 27, 1929, to $6,825 million. By June 29, 1929, the amount had gone up again to $7,070 million and by October 4 to $8,525 million. The majority of this money was not supplied by New York City banks or by outside banks but by individuals and businesses. On October 4, 1929, $1,095 million was loaned by New York City banks, $790 million by outside banks, and $6,640 million by others.[9]

This credit structure for stock purchases was especially vulnerable because stocks were purchased with small margins of the purchaser's funds, often only 10 percent. This down payment could be pyramided in a period of rising prices since, as prices went up, the potential capital gain was available for margin for additional purchases. For example, assume a man bought $10,000 worth of stock and had a margin of $1,000 and borrowed the remaining $9,000. If the stock went up to $12,000 in price, he now had a margin of $3,000 and could buy $30,000 of stock in total, and so on. This easy pyramiding of credit led to stock prices that were not based on the discounting by the market of future prospects for the economy, but on profits from rapidly increasing price rises in stocks based on an inflated demand for them. This credit structure was very vulnerable in a downturn since, if prices dropped about 10 percent, the banks would ask for additional margin to protect themselves, which the investors frequently did not have. The banks, therefore, sold the stocks thus adding greatly to supply in any downturn and giving added impetus to it.

THE DEPRESSION OF THE EARLY THIRTIES

The first generally recognized sign of real difficulty in the business situation began in the security markets. Several breaks in security prices in October, 1929, foreshadowed the difficulties that were to come. On October 29 the most severe break occurred, and selling was so fast that the combined volume of the New York Stock Exchange and the New York Curb Exchange was 23.5 million shares. Standard and Poor's index of common stock prices declined from 213 in October to 160 in November.[10] This rapid decline can be seen clearly from Chart 14-2 on page 364.

---

[9]*Ibid.*, p. 494.
[10]*Ibid.*, pp. 480–481.

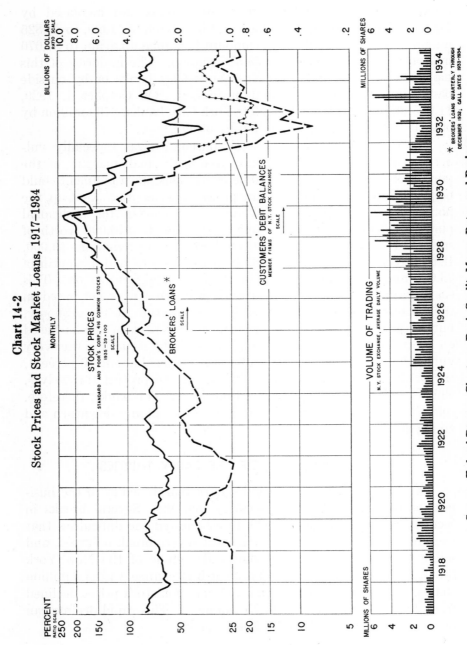

Chart 14-2

Stock Prices and Stock Market Loans, 1917–1934

Source: Federal Reserve Charts on Bank Credit, Money Rates, and Business.

The collapse in the stock market was a spectacular turning point in one phase of the total economic situation, but in retrospect it appears that the upper turning point in business was reached about the middle of the year. Indexes of industrial production rose through June, 1929, and then began a slow decline in July. Employment rose slowly through July, remained constant in August, and then began to fall in September.

In some countries this worldwide depression had begun earlier than 1929. In Australia and in the Dutch East Indies the depression began at the end of 1927. In 1928 business turned downward in Germany, Finland, and Brazil; and in 1929 Poland, Canada, and Argentina showed signs of depression before the United States. The depression, however, was not severe in any nation until after the decline began in the United States in the third quarter of 1929.[11]

Scope of the Depression

Industrial production decreased about 17 percent from 1929 to 1930, and dropped another 18 percent in 1931 and 23 percent in 1932 as the depression continued to deepen. By 1932 the level of production was just over 50 percent of prosperity levels. The decline in durable goods production was more pronounced than in nondurables. By 1932 the index of durable manufactures decreased to about 30 percent of 1929 levels.

General employment decreased about 25 percent by 1932, and factory employment by one third. Factory payrolls decreased still more rapidly because of the reduction in number of hours worked and in wage rates. By 1932 these payrolls were not much over 40 percent of the 1929 level.

The slump was especially severe in the construction industry, which had been one of the mainstays of the boom through 1928. By 1932 the value of construction contracts awarded dropped to about 20 percent of the 1928 level. Residential construction dropped even further, to about 10 percent of prosperity levels.

This decline in all phases of business activity led to a rapid decrease in wholesale prices. On a 1926 base, wholesale prices decreased from 95 in 1929 to 65 in 1932, and on a 1935–1939 base

---

[11]*The Recovery Problem in the United States* (Washington: The Brookings Institution, 1936), pp. 27, 28.

consumer prices declined from 122.5 to 98.[12]   The decline in the price of food products and raw materials was especially pronounced during this depression period. By June, 1931, the price of wheat had declined somewhat more than 60 percent from the average price during 1928, the price of corn 60 percent, of rice slightly over 50 percent, of bacon 50 percent, and of sugar 48 percent. The drop in the prices of basic raw materials was in many cases even more severe than that of foodstuffs. The price of rubber declined 72 percent by June, 1931, from the average price in 1928; that of wool, 68 percent; hides, 65 percent; cotton, 55 percent; petroleum, 43 percent; and copper, 42 percent.[13]

World trade also declined rapidly, and international investment was drastically curtailed during this period. The flow of foreign funds from such leading lending countries as the United States, the United Kingdom, and France was materially reduced during 1930 and disappeared completely in 1931. In fact, there was a flow of funds into France, rather than out, in 1930 and 1931 and also to Great Britain in the latter year. Funds flowed out of debtor countries, such as Germany, Poland, Australia, India, and Argentina, during 1931 because they were repaying existing debts and getting no new credits. In Germany a fear for the value of the mark caused a rapid flight of funds.[14]

International Situation

The international situation led to new complications in 1931, and these in turn led to a deepening of the depression during the remainder of that year and in 1932. The ability of debtor countries to meet their international obligations arising out of trade, investments, reparations, and war debts was seriously impaired by the deepening depression in the individual countries and by the contraction in world trade. In addition, political factors were superimposed on the already weakened debt structures, and this situation led to a financial and monetary collapse. Elections held in Germany in October, 1930, showed that the Nazi party was rapidly growing in strength. This development frightened foreign creditors, especially those in France, and led to a substantial withdrawal of short-term

---

[12]*Federal Reserve Bulletin* (June, 1950), p. 719.
[13]*The Recovery Problem in the United States, op. cit.,* p. 31.
[14]*Ibid.,* pp. 33–34.

funds invested in Germany. Many Germans also transferred their funds abroad. This led to a decrease of more than $100 million in the gold and foreign exchange holdings of the Reichsbank between December, 1930, and March, 1931.

In March, 1931, Germany and Austria announced an agreement for a customs union, which many believed was a violation of the Versailles Treaty. This announcement led to a renewed withdrawal of funds from Germany and Austria, and this, together with the difficulties occasioned by the depression, led to the failure of the largest bank in Austria, the Kredit Anstalt. The rapid withdrawal of short-term funds caused the abandonment of the gold standard in various countries and the suspension of payments on most international debts. President Hoover declared a moratorium on reparations and war-debt payments in June, 1931, for a period of one year, and the foreign creditors of Germany and Austria agreed to suspend their withdrawals of funds or reduce them to a minimum. Attempts were made to improve the situation by extending new short-term loans to Germany, Austria, and Hungary. The mad scramble for the return of short-term funds continued, however, and this placed a strain on Great Britain since her short-term obligations abroad exceeded her short-term claims against other countries and her long-term investments were not liquid.

Despite loans from the United States and France, Great Britain was forced to abandon the gold standard on September 21, 1931. This led to a flight of capital from other countries whose currency was tied to the pound sterling, since confidence in their ability to maintain currency stability was impaired. There was also a fear on the part of investors that funds would cease to be readily available. The pound sterling countries were forced off the gold standard shortly after England was forced off of it. These actions led to the withdrawal of short-term funds invested in the United States. Funds were withdrawn in part to provide a ready source of funds to offset sterling losses, but primarily because of a fear for the stability of the dollar. As a result of this flight of capital gold left this country in large volume.

Before the year was over, fifteen countries had followed the lead of Great Britain in abandoning the gold standard, including not only the Dominions but also such countries as Denmark, Finland, Japan, and Sweden. Because of uncertainties in international financial relationships, foreign trade declined at a more rapid rate, and this helped deepen the depression in the United States. Not only did it add to general uncertainty, but it also led to a more rapid decline in the prices of agricultural products and raw materials. The price of wheat, for example, dropped from 76 cents a bushel in May, 1931, to 46 cents in December, 1932, while cotton fell from 10.9 cents a pound in March, 1931, to 5.3 cents in June, 1932.[15]

Governmental Action

During this period of deepening depression from 1929 through 1932, the administration of President Hoover took various steps to stem the economic tide. The first reaction of the government to the collapse of stock prices was that an orgy of speculation had come to an end and that business was in excellent condition. The President conferred with industrial leaders and encouraged them to continue their capital expansion programs as planned and at first received a large amount of support from them. The President also encouraged businessmen to maintain wages in order to keep purchasing power at high levels. The general attitude was one of watchful waiting but, as the unemployment and financial situations grew worse, additional steps had to be taken.

Early in 1932 the Reconstruction Finance Corporation was established to lend money to railroads, insurance companies, banks, building and loan associations, various agricultural credit agencies, and business corporations that were in financial difficulties. In addition to its capital of $500 million advanced by the government, the RFC was allowed to borrow up to $1.5 billion in government guaranteed bonds. The bill authorizing the RFC was signed by the President on January 22, 1932, and operations began almost immediately. During the remainder of the year actual disbursements were about $1.5 billion. The largest amount of loans by the RFC was to banks and trust companies, but rather substantial sums were loaned to railroads, and smaller sums to building and loan associations, to mortgage loan companies, and to insurance companies. As the depression deepened, the RFC was empowered to borrow an additional $1.5 billion to provide loans to public and private agencies to construct self-liquidating works of a public character, such as

---

[15]*Ibid.*, p. 50.

toll bridges, and an additional $300 million for loans to states for unemployment relief.

Additional capital was also made available by the federal government to the Federal Land Bank System to increase long-term credit to agriculture, and the Federal Home Loan Bank System was set up with an initial capital of $125 million to discount first mortgages on residential real estate and thus provide additional credit in the housing field.[16]

Banking Crisis

Despite the financial assistance rendered to the banking system by the RFC, large numbers of bank failures continued. The banking system had not been without its weak spots during the 1920's, since almost 7,000 banks became insolvent between 1921 and 1930. In 1928 the number of bank failures was 491, in 1929 it rose to 642 and in 1930 to 1,345. Before the depression most of the banks that failed were in small towns in agricultural areas, especially in the cotton, corn, and wheat belts. During the depression, however, banks in larger cities joined the procession of failures. In 1931, 2,298 banks with total deposits of $1.7 billion suspended operations. In 1932, 1,456 banks with deposits of $716 million suspended.[17] As banks in various communities got into difficulties, the state governors declared holidays to enable them to adjust their affairs. In February, 1933, banks in Michigan were closed due to the acute problems of Detroit banks as a result of the low level of automobile production. Bank holidays were declared in Indiana on February 23, in Maryland on the 25th, in Arkansas on the 27th, and in Ohio on the 28th.

By March 3, seventeen more states had closed their banks. This led to a demand for funds from New York banks and a steady outflow of funds to other parts of the country. During the early hours of March 4, 1933, the day on which President Franklin D. Roosevelt was inaugurated, the New York banks were closed, and they were followed by banks in other parts of the country. The new President took office with all of the banks of the country closed. He called Congress into emergency session March 9, and on that day it passed

---

[16]Horace Taylor, *Contemporary Economic Problems and Trends* (New York: Harcourt, Brace & Co., 1938), p. 57.

[17]Broadus Mitchell, *Depression Decade* (New York: Rinehart & Company, Inc., 1947), pp. 127–128.

a hurriedly drawn emergency banking act that provided for additional funds for distressed banks and for the reopening of banks which were basically in a sound condition. This firm action by the President dispelled a great deal of fear and uncertainty, and money flowed back into the banks and confidence in the banking system returned.

New Deal Legislation

The emergency banking legislation also gave the President authority over gold during the continuance of the crisis. All gold was ordered turned in to the Federal Reserve System, and the Treasury began to raise the price of gold by buying at increasing prices all gold that was presented to it. The new government embarked upon a policy aimed at raising prices to predepression levels. The first Agricultural Adjustment Act, which was passed shortly after the banking legislation, provided for the restriction of agricultural production in exchange for payments to farmers. These payments were designed to increase the purchasing power of farm products in order to bring it back to a pre-World War I relationship with manufactured goods.

The National Recovery Act was likewise passed in the early days of the New Deal. It gave business groups the right to draw up codes of fair competition and to set minimum prices on their products or services provided they set maximum hours of work and minimum wages for labor. Large sums of money were appropriated for direct relief and for public works projects. An extensive social security program of unemployment insurance and old-age and other benefits was instituted. Various reform measures, such as those providing for the regulation of investment banking and security markets, were also enacted into law during the early years of the New Deal. These measures provided for full disclosure of all pertinent information in the sale of a new issue of securities and for the regulation of trading on the securities markets so as to eliminate manipulation of stock prices. The Securities and Exchange Commission was established to carry out these regulations.

Causal Factors

The immediate causes of the 1929 depression were the stock market collapse and the uncertainty of the international situation and its effect on financial markets. The basic causes went much deeper than these more spectacular events. During the 1920's significant changes took place in production patterns, in consumer expenditure patterns, and in capital goods development that led to basic maladjustments in the economy. These factors will be considered in some detail.

Shifts in Production. The treaty of peace at the end of World War I caused shifts in production, many of which could not be justified on an economic basis. When, as a result of the breakup of the Austro-Hungarian Empire, the Balkan countries were divided into a series of autonomous countries with boundaries based upon the political principle of the self-determination of peoples, each one tried to become self-sufficient insofar as possible, especially in food supplies. This was done by means of tariff barriers, embargoes, and quotas; and, as a result, production of goods in the Balkan area was shifted to less economic locations than before 1914.

These shifts in production, especially the increased production of raw materials, had their effect upon the position of the farmer in the American economy. In the prewar period the position of the farmer compared with workers in industry was improving. During the war period agricultural prices moved up faster than other prices, and the farmer experienced unusual prosperity. During the 1920–1922 depression the price of farm products fell rapidly so that, at the average prices in 1921, the purchasing power of raw farm products was 18 percent below the 1913 level.[18] Between 1921 and 1929 agricultural prices increased and the farmer made substantial gains. The 1929 depression, however, interrupted this improvement in the position of agriculture before the farmers had reached their prewar status of purchasing power. While this agricultural improvement was fairly general during the period from 1922 until 1929, the price of wheat reached a high point in 1925 and then began to decline as world production exceeded effective demand; and similar trends were apparent in the prices of cotton, wool, silk, sugar, coffee, and several other basic commodities.[19]

Changes in Consumption Expenditures. The flow of consumer purchasing power was also increased temporarily and its pattern

[18]Frederic C. Mills, *Economic Tendencies in the United States* (New York: National Bureau of Economic Research, 1932), p. 209.

[19]*The Recovery Problem in the United States, op. cit.,* p. 16.

shifted by the substantial profits that were being made in the security markets. It has been estimated from a study of income tax returns that between 1924 and 1929 there were realized capital gains of $10,087 million on stocks held for a period less than two years and an additional $7,550 million on stocks held for over two years.[20] Undoubtedly a large part of these realized profits went back again into the purchase of securities, but part of them was spent on consumer goods. Thus some money arising out of the savings of the purchaser or out of bank credit used to finance the purchase of the stock was used for consumption expenditures. This additional source of funds for consumption expenditures was only available so long as stock prices increased and made capital gains possible.

The volume of consumer expenditure was also changed by the rapid increase in sums spent for life insurance. The reserves of life insurance companies increased from $6,338 million to $14,948 million between 1920 and 1929. The number of policies in force almost doubled.[21] This meant that there was a rapid increase in savings on the part of the great mass of American people because of the development of the insurance business and, as a result, a smaller volume of funds was available for consumer goods and more for investment.

The amount of consumer income and the pattern of spending were also materially affected in an opposite fashion by the rapid increase in installment credit. In 1923 the amount of outstanding consumer credit was $4,350 million, and this increased to $8,180 million in 1929. This rapid increase not only added to consumer purchasing power but also helped change its pattern since a substantial portion of consumer credit was used for the purchase of consumer durable goods.[22]

The net result of these and other factors that affected the level and the pattern of consumer expenditures was a change in the rate of consumption from year to year. As can be seen from Table 14-1 the rate of increase in consumption decreased from 7.4 percent between 1927 and 1928 to 1.5 percent between 1928 and 1929. Since income was increasing in 1929, this change in the growth of

---

[20]James Alexander Ross, *Speculation, Stock Prices, and Industrial Fluctuations* (New York: The Ronald Press Company, 1938), pp. 345–346.

[21]*Life Insurance Fact Book 1949* (New York: Institute of Life Insurance, 1949), p. 44.

[22]Rolf Nugent, *Consumer Credit and Economic Stability* (New York: Russell Sage Foundation, 1939), p. 124.

Table 14-1

The Rate of Change of Consumption

1921–1922	+6.4	1925–1926	+7.9
1922–1923	+9.3	1926–1927	−1.0
1923–1924	+5.8	1927–1928	+7.4
1924–1925	−1.2	1928–1929	+1.5

Source: Thomas Wilson, *Fluctuations in Income and Employment* (New York: Pitman Publishing Corp., 1948), p. 118.

consumption was not due to a decline in income but to a change in the consumption function. A similar but more drastic change took place between 1924 and 1925, but 1925 was a year of prosperity nevertheless. The same situation was true between 1926 and 1927. In those two periods, however, the decrease in consumption was more than offset by the rapid increases in construction, primarily residential construction in the earlier period and public utility and governmental construction in the second period.

Capital Goods Developments. In 1929 there was no increase in construction or in other activity to offset the changing pattern of consumption and again carry business forward. There seems to be ample evidence that the building industry had reached its high point in 1928 and was declining in 1929. This decrease in activity was not the result of rising costs since indexes of building costs show practically constant levels from 1925 through 1929. There is also no evidence to indicate that there was any stringency in real estate credit during the period of the late 1920's. An index of rents would indicate that they were falling from 1925 on and were lower in 1929 than in 1928. It seems that the basic reason for a decline in construction was an exhaustion of the effective demand for new building.[23]

The supply of houses had not only been increased to such a level that the index of residential contracts awarded dropped from 76 in 1928 (1947–1949 = 100) to 52 in 1929, but the demand for non-residential construction had also reached a saturation point. The index of all other construction had increased only from 68 in 1927 to 70 in 1928 and remained at the same level in 1929, while it had increased from a level of 32 in 1921 to 67 in 1926.[24] The rapid increase

[23]Thomas Wilson, *Fluctuations in Income and Employment* (New York: Pitman Publishing Corp., 1948), p. 157.

[24]*Federal Reserve Bulletin* (July, 1959), p. 776.

in the level of nonresidential construction came to a halt because the rapid expansion in the automobile and related industries had slowed down as the demand for these new consumer goods reached a saturation point at current income levels.

From 1920 to 1929, while the production of all manufacturing industries increased 32 points (1920–1929 = 100), that of automobiles increased 77 points. By 1929 the automobile industry had passed its point of rapid growth and had become integrated with the rest of the economy. From that point on, its growth was in response to changes in population and in real income. During the period of rapid growth of the automobile industry large amounts of capital were invested in plants to produce automobiles and also in the materials used to make them, such as steel sheets, plate glass, upholstery, and rubber. Rapid development also took place in related fields, such as gasoline refining. Much capital was also invested in highway construction and in the development of business establishments along the highways. The coming of the automobile also led to a revolution in rural America. Shopping habits were changed as motor cars made it possible to go to larger towns for goods. New facilities were built to meet these changed habits. In short, the automobile and related developments led to large-scale capital investment in the period of rapid development prior to 1929.

When this investment was largely completed, men and materials were available for further expansion in other fields. The changes required in the pattern of production to adjust to this new situation led to the protracted period of depression in the 1930's.

The stock market collapse was not a basic cause of the depression, but it undoubtedly intensified the depression once it began. In the first place, the income received by consumers from realized capital gains all but disappeared. In addition, the reduction in the price of stocks created uncertainty in the minds of individuals, which undoubtedly caused some of them to cut their rate of expenditures from current income and caused businessmen to postpone purchases for inventory and expenditures for capital expansion and improvement.

Monetary and Fiscal Policies

Monetary policies must share some of the blame for the economic unbalance which led to the depression, beginning in 1929. This is particularly true since credit helped materially to finance the boom in real estate and in the security markets. In fact, the stock market boom led to actions that made bank credit more easily available. Because of high stock prices, many corporations raised funds beyond their immediate needs and put them into time deposits in banks. The volume of time deposits grew, and since banks were required to keep a smaller percentage of reserves against them than against demand deposits, they had additional reserves for credit expansion.

The Federal Reserve authorities took no action to curb the speculative boom until 1928. In 1924 and 1927 they followed a policy of monetary ease to curb the mild recessions that occurred in these years and also to help maintain monetary stability in Europe. Lower interest rates made investment of short-term funds in the United States less desirable and helped increase the supply of short-term funds invested in European markets.

In 1928 the Federal Reserve acted to restrain the boom in security markets by increasing the discount rate and by selling securities. This action was offset in part, however, by the purchase of acceptances arising out of the financing of foreign trade under a policy to stimulate the use of such acceptances. The banks sold acceptances to the Federal Reserve because this was the cheapest way to get credit, and thus they offset part of the action designed to restrict domestic credit expansion.

Stock market speculation continued unabated in 1929 but the Federal Reserve took no vigorous action to halt it. This was due to a controversy between the Board and the twelve Federal Reserve Banks on the proper policy to follow. The Federal Reserve Banks urged the use of quantitative measures, such as a higher discount rate and open-market operations, but the Federal Reserve Board urged direct pressure on banks making security loans. The major action taken in 1929 was the adoption of a policy that banks, which were large-scale lenders to the stock market, could not get credit from their Federal Reserve Bank. This conflict on the proper course to follow was, in large part, a conflict between policies that would help promote business activity and those that would restrain stock market speculation. The policies adopted in 1928 and 1929 were not restrictive enough to halt stock speculation but were too restrictive to help promote a vigorous business expansion. Any course of action taken during this period would have created some problems, but the middle course that was followed was not successful and, therefore, monetary policy must share a significant part of the blame for the excessive speculation in security markets.

There is also a serious question about the effectiveness of monetary policy after the decline in the stock market and in business activity had begun. The Federal Reserve added somewhat to bank reserves during the stock market collapse in late 1929, but did not pursue a vigorous policy of monetary ease during most of 1930. In fact, the increase in security holdings was smaller than the increase in the minor recession of 1924. And no vigorous action was taken to ease the money supply during the financially unsettled year of 1931. A large open-market operation was conducted in the spring of 1932, which helped banks meet the growing demand for currency and to reduce their indebtedness to the Federal Reserve. This action helped reduce pressure for further credit contraction.

One reason for not acting more vigorously to increase the money supply in 1930 and 1931 was the shortage of short-term commercial paper for backing for loans from the Federal Reserve Banks and for collateral for Federal Reserve notes. The Glass-Steagall Act of 1932 authorized the use of government securities as collateral for Federal Reserve notes, and thus removed any doubt about the ability of the Federal Reserve to increase the money supply. There was also a feeling that a larger money supply would not help stimulate the economy because most banks had excess reserves during this period and could not force the use of bank funds. One vigorous critic of monetary policy during this period, Professor Milton Friedman, feels that reserves were in excess only in a narrow legal sense because banks had found that the Federal Reserve would not lend them funds as a "lender of last resort" when they really needed them.[25] The debate over Federal Reserve policy in the great depression is not resolved, but it is clear that it failed to act vigorously enough in the early stages of the downturn to prevent a financial crisis.

Fiscal policy must also share some of the blame for the deteriorating financial situation. The federal government ran modest deficits in the depression years, but total government spending by all levels of government declined. The policy of the Hoover Admin-

---

[25]Milton Friedman and Anna Jacobson Schwartz, *A Monetary History of the United States, 1867–1960.* (Princeton, New Jersey: Princeton University Press, 1963), p. 348.

istration and during the first years of the Roosevelt Administration was to balance the budget if at all possible. In fact, tax rates were increased sharply in 1932 in an attempt to balance the budget. Thus fiscal policy contributed to the deepening depression instead of remaining neutral or offsetting other decreases in expenditures.

Recovery

Under the impetus of the government program, industrial production increased after 1933 and continued upward to 1937. The construction industry also increased its volume of activity; the index of construction contracts awarded increased about 2.4 times from 1933 to 1937, and residential construction almost quadrupled. Factory employment increased by one half, and factory payrolls more than doubled. Under the impetus of the inflationary policies of the government, wholesale prices increased almost 35 percent from 1932 to 1937 and consumer prices about 11 percent.[26]

Common stock prices, as measured by Standard and Poor's Index, had reached a low point of 36 in June, 1932, and increased to a level of 137 in February, 1937. The prices of industrial and railroad securities increased more rapidly than those of utility securities. Industrial production had recovered sufficiently by 1937 so that in May it passed the 1929 levels, and many railroads had overcome earlier difficulties in maintaining reasonable profits. The stocks of the public utility industry continued to be depressed, however, because of the uncertainty due to breakup of the public utility holding companies. This breakup was ordered under the Public Utility Holding Company Act of 1935.

By the early summer of 1937 business had reached the peak of a new cycle, but it had not grown during this recovery period at anything like the rate of the 1920's. Industrial production in 1937 was at a level of 113 (1935–1939 = 100), only 3 points higher than the 1929 top.[27] Employment was at about the same level as in 1929; but since the total labor force had grown materially between the two periods, approximately 8 million people were out of work in 1937.

The failure of the economy to continue its rapid growth during the 1930's was due to several factors. For one thing there were no innovations equal in their effect on production and national income

---

[26]*Federal Reserve Bulletin* (June, 1950), p. 719.

[27]*Ibid.*

to that of the automobile and related fields in the 1920's. Electric power production did increase much more rapidly from 1929 to 1937 than in the period from 1920 to 1929; but it did not create the same derived demand for the products of other industries as did the rapid development of the automobile, and it did not account for anything like the same amount of increased employment.

Another reason for the failure of the prosperity period that ended in 1937 to achieve 1929 proportions was the reduced rate of residential construction. The index of residential construction contracts awarded, which was at a level of 126 in 1929 (1923–1925 = 100), had increased to only 41 by 1937. This period of a low level of activity in the housing field was in part an aftermath of the vigorous housing boom of the 1920's in which housing construction was pushed beyond the point of effective demand. Since so many houses had been built during the 1920's, there was little need for replacement during the 1930's; and the low rate of economic activity did not create the demand for any large-scale new construction. Construction other than residential also failed to equal the 1929 boom since it reached a level in 1937 of only 74 compared with a 1929 high of 142.[28]

Foreign lending, which played an important part in the 1929 boom, was at a much lower level in this recovery period. Trade barriers were intensified during the depression, and world trade had not recovered to anything like predepression levels by 1937.

Some of the policies of the federal government, irrespective of any long-range merits, contributed to uncertainty in the business field and thus probably also delayed recovery. This was true of such legislation as the Security Act of 1933, the Securities Exchange Act of 1934, and the Public Utility Holding Company Act of 1935.

THE 1937 RECESSION

Recovery had not carried the economy back to full employment levels when another recession occurred in 1937. This recession was short, lasting only about a year, but it was quite severe.

Character of the Recession

The decline in business activity, which began in the latter half of 1937 and continued into the first half of 1938, was rapid. Industrial

---

[28]*Ibid.*

production dropped by over 25 percent in a short time, but it did not reach the low levels of 1932 or 1933 as can be seen from Chart 14-3 shown on page 380.

As is to be expected the greatest decline during this depression occurred again in the production of durable goods.   Residential construction, which had not recovered to anything like 1929 levels, showed no new decline but continued upward in 1937 and 1938. There was somewhat of a drop in the level of wholesale commodity prices late in 1937 and in 1938 and this continued into 1939.

Causal Factors

Several factors account for the downturn in business activity in 1937.   During the recovery period governmental deficits added to the income stream.   In 1933 the total expenditures of all governmental units in the United States exceeded receipts by almost $1.3 billion.   This sum was increased in 1934 to $2.4 billion, dropped somewhat in 1935 to $1.85 billion, and then increased substantially in 1936 to $2.9 billion.   In 1936 the deficit of the federal government was unusually large due to the cashing of the bonus certificates of veterans of World War I, which was authorized at this time.   In 1937 receipts of all governmental units exceeded expenditures by $685 million.[29]

In addition to the decrease in the deficit of the federal government, funds in the hands of consumers were further reduced when social security tax collections increased by over $1 billion in 1937 from the 1936 level and no provision was made for paying out any funds until a later period.   The net result of the operations of the federal government was a decrease in borrowing from $3.8 billion in the calendar year of 1936 to about $300 million in 1937.[30]   This rapid shift in government finances was a major factor leading to the downturn in 1937.

Another factor that influenced the business situation at this time was the June, 1936, Revenue Act, which contained an undistributed profits tax.   This tax caused the payment of a larger sum in dividends on 1936 corporate income than would otherwise have been the case,

---

[29]*National Income Supplement* to *Survey of Current Business* (July, 1947), pp. 21–23.

[30]Wilson, *op. cit.*, p. 177.

Chart 14-3

Industrial Production 1919–1942

MONTHLY, SEASONALLY ADJUSTED

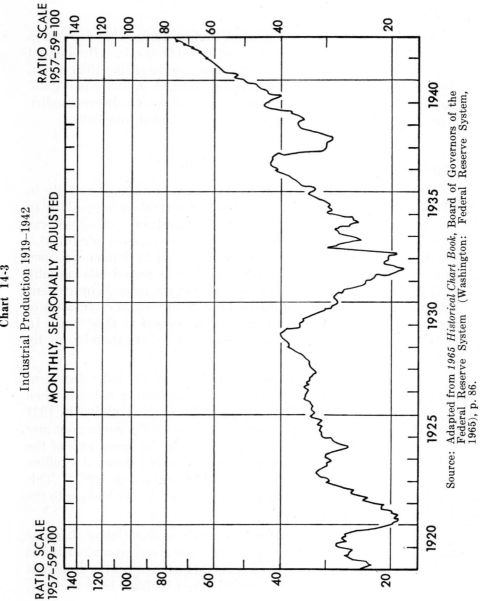

Source: Adapted from *1965 Historical Chart Book*, Board of Governors of the Federal Reserve System (Washington: Federal Reserve System, 1965), p. 86.

and this added to consumer income in the latter part of 1936 and the early part of 1937. Its long-range effect on business expansion, however, was repressive in that many businessmen were afraid of the implications of such a tax. It also made it difficult for small businesses to expand since they could not easily get new funds in the capital markets and had relied largely on the reinvestment of earnings.

Prices also played a part in the 1937 recession. Prices of agricultural commodities increased in 1936 because of the severe drought. Prices of some raw materials other than agricultural likewise increased late in 1936 and early in 1937 as European demand for them increased, in part because of an increase in industrial prosperity and in part because of armament expenditures. There was a decline in speculative activity in world commodity markets in April, 1937, and the prices of raw materials declined after that time and with them the speculative demand for goods.

These factors all contributed to the decline in business activity in 1937. By far the most important factor, however, was the rapid decrease in the contribution that various governmental units made to national income, when they shifted their operations from a deficit of almost $3 billion in 1936 to a surplus of almost $700 million in 1937.

Recovery

The reaction of the federal government to the decline in business in 1937 was to step up its public works program, which was financed by increasing its deficit. In 1938 the combined deficit of all governmental units was $1.5 billion, and in 1939 it increased to $1.9 billion. Orders for airplanes and other armaments were placed in this country in increasing quantities by European countries as the international situation deteriorated, and these orders helped increase the level of business activity. With the advent of war in 1939 these orders were stepped up materially and production in this country increased rapidly.

By 1939 production had almost expanded to the 1937 level, and by 1940 it was substantially above the level of the 1937 peak. Residential building continued upward through the recession and recovery.

QUESTIONS

1. Account for inflation during and immediately after World War I.
2. What were the basic causal factors at work in the 1920 depression?
3. Why was the 1920 depression sharp but short?
4. Discuss the outstanding features of the 1922–1929 prosperity period.
5. Briefly describe the scope and severity of the 1929 depression.
6. How did the international situation intensify the 1929 depression?
7. Discuss the Hoover program for reversing the economic decline.
8. What factors led to a banking crisis in March, 1933?
9. Briefly describe New Deal measures to increase prices and economic activity.
10. Discuss the basic factors that led to a deep and protracted depression after 1929.
11. Why did business turn down in 1937 before full employment was achieved?
12. In what respects was the 1929 depression similar to those of 1837 and 1873?
13. Discuss the reasons for short, sharp depressions in 1920 and 1937, and a deep, protracted depression after 1929. In developing your answer stress deviations from the typical cycle pattern, changing patterns of consumption, price developments, and the influence of governmental agencies.

SUGGESTED READINGS

Beard, Charles A., and George H. W. Smith. *The Future Comes, A Study of the New Deal.* New York: The Macmillan Company, 1933.

Dewey, Davis Rich. *Financial History of the United States.* New York: Longmans, Green & Co., Inc., 1931. Chapters 22–24, inclusive.

Hacker, Louis M. *Short History of the New Deal.* New York: F. S. Crofts & Co., 1934.

Mitchell, Broadus. *Depression Decade From New Era Through New Deal, 1929–1941.* New York: Rinehart & Company, Inc., 1947.

Payne, Wilson F. *Business Behavior 1919–1922.* Chicago: University of Chicago Press, 1942.

Roose, K. D. "The Recession of 1937–38," *Journal of Political Economy,* LVI (June, 1948), pp. 239–248.

Stigler, George J. *Trends in Output and Employment.* New York: National Bureau of Economic Research, 1947.

CHAPTER 15 *Business Cycles from 1939 to the Present*

The expansion in economic activity which began in the latter part of 1938 was accelerated in 1939 in part because of the increased demand for military equipment arising as a result of the deteriorating international situation. Almost all phases of economic activity in the United States increased rapidly after World War II began in the fall of 1939 and America became the Arsenal of Democracy in 1940 and 1941.

THE WORLD WAR II PERIOD

When America entered the war on December 7, 1941, the total effort of our nation was directed to winning the war as speedily as possible. This involved a mobilization of economic forces, as well as military forces, to a degree well beyond that in any past war.

Character of the Period

During 1941 the production of civilian goods was at a high level, but there was enough slack in the economy to turn out large quantities of military goods without any appreciable strain. When the United States entered the war in December, 1941, over five million people were still unemployed in this country. Within a short time, however, military demands became so large that it was impossible for the economy to produce enough of these goods without reduction of production in industries serving civilian needs and wants.

The task of getting sufficient production allocated to war needs was turned over to the newly created War Production Board early in 1942. This board stopped the production of various consumer durables and issued limitation orders on the nonwar use of metals to insure sufficient supplies for the production of war equipment. To make sure that the limited supply of scarce materials would be used to produce those goods most urgently needed, a system of priorities and allocations had already been set up in August, 1941. This system was taken over and expanded by the War Production Board. As war production increased rapidly at the end of 1942, the system of priorities proved inadequate and a controlled-materials plan was set up. Under this plan, production was controlled by basing schedules on the available quantities of three basic metals — carbon and alloy steel, copper, and aluminum.

The increased demand for goods for military operations, as well as increased purchasing power in the hands of a much larger labor force as the unemployed were absorbed in war production, led to price control and rationing in an attempt to prevent inflation. In April, 1941, the Office of Price Administration and Civilian Supply was set up, but in its early form it lacked real power to enforce its regulations. Under the Emergency Price Control Act signed by President Roosevelt on January 30, 1942, the Office of Price Administration was given the power it needed to enforce a price control and rationing program. The OPA rationed such items as tires, automobiles, typewriters, gasoline, bicycles, fuel oil, shoes, processed foods, and meats and fats. It also established maximum prices on various commodities, first at the wholesale level and then at the retail level, and it set ceilings on rent. The controls were tightened in April, 1943, when the President issued a hold-the-line order as increases in prices that were not included in the controls program threatened the whole price structure. The President ordered ceilings put on all commodities affecting the cost of living and the reduction of any prices judged "excessive."

The War Manpower Commission was established on April 18, 1942, by executive order in an attempt to assure a more efficient utilization of the nation's manpower in the war effort. It recruited men for private industry and government service, developed lists of individuals with particular skills so that they would be available when needed, set up training programs, and encouraged the utilization of women in the war effort.

Early in 1942 the President established a National War Labor Board to hear all controversies that might interrupt any work which contributed to the effective prosecution of the war. Nevertheless the number of strikes increased even though most of them were of short duration and were not sanctioned by the union leaders. As a result of strikes in the coal mines, Congress passed the Smith-Connally Act over the President's veto on June 25, 1943. This Act gave the President power to seize plants that were producing goods needed in the war effort in which a strike was in progress. The employees could appeal to the National War Labor Board for changes in wages or working conditions. Before any strikes could occur in the plant of a war contractor, the Secretary of Labor, the War Labor Board, and the National Labor Relations Board had to be notified; and the National Labor Relations Board was required to take a secret ballot after thirty days to determine whether the employees would strike.

The wage policy used by the War Labor Board in developing its stabilization program was referred to as the "Little Steel Formula." The War Labor Board decided in a dispute involving the workers of the Bethlehem, Youngstown, Inland, and Republic Steel companies that a top wage increase on June 16, 1942, of 15 percent above the straight-time rates which prevailed on January 1, 1941, would adequately compensate employees for the increased cost of living from January 1, 1941, through May, 1942. This was the date when the President sought to stop the ruinous price-wage race. This formula was used to determine wage increases needed to compensate for the increased cost of living, and above that no increases were allowed except to correct inequities.

Agricultural production increased rapidly during the war and the Department of Agriculture did all that it could to encourage such production. The War Food Administration and its successor, the Foreign Economic Administration, allocated foodstuffs to foreign countries. The number of workers on the farms decreased because of young men entering the army and farm hands getting higher pay in war plants, but nevertheless the production of agricultural commodities increased materially. The production of major crops in the four war years exceeded any previous four-year period.[1] The net income from farming increased from $6 billion in 1939 to $14.5 billion in 1944.

War Finance

Under the impact of war expenditures, the total budget of the federal government increased rapidly. In the fiscal year of 1941 the federal government spent $12.8 billion, of which approximately half

---

[1]Department of Agriculture, *Agricultural Statistics, 1945* (Washington: U. S. Government Printing Office).

Table 15-1

United States Budgetary Expenses, 1941–1945

(Fiscal Years July 1–June 30)

(Billions of Dollars)

YEAR	WAR		MAINLY RELATED TO WAR[1]		OTHER[2]		TOTAL	
	AMOUNT	PER-CENT	AMOUNT	PER-CENT	AMOUNT	PER-CENT	AMOUNT	PER-CENT
1941	$ 6.3	49.3	$1.8	13.8	$4.7	36.9	$12.8	100.0
1942	26.0	80.1	1.9	5.9	4.6	14.1	32.5	100.0
1943	72.1	92.2	2.5	3.2	3.6	4.6	78.2	100.0
1944	87.0	92.8	3.6	3.8	3.1	3.3	93.7	100.0
1945	90.0	89.7	7.4	7.4	3.0	3.0	100.4	100.0
Total	$281.5	88.6	$17.2	5.4	$18.9	6.0	$317.6	100.0

NOTE: Figures are rounded and will not necessarily add to totals.

[1]Interest on the public debt, veterans' pensions and benefits, and refunds of taxes and duties.

[2]Includes statutory debt retirements.

Source: John R. Craf, *A Survey of the American Economy, 1940–1946* (New York: North River Press, Inc., 1947), p. 120.

was directly related to the war. Total expenditures increased to a level of $100.4 billion in the fiscal year 1945, of which 90 percent was for war expenditures. The expenditures for war and nonwar purposes for each of the war years are shown in Table 15-1 above.

Part of the cost of the war was raised through increased taxation, but a substantial part was raised by government borrowing since in the seven War Loans and in the Victory Loan the United States Treasury sold almost $157 billion of securities. In the fiscal year 1941 the federal government had a deficit of $6.2 billion, and this was increased in 1942 to $21.5 billion. In 1943 it jumped to $57.4 billion, and was over $50 billion in 1944 and 1945, but dropped materially in 1946 to $20.7 billion.[2]

After the Second War Loan, commercial banks were not permitted to buy bonds during the war bond drives. However, they bought large quantities between the bond drives. As of December 31, 1939, all banks in the United States held over $19 billion of United States government obligations. This had increased to $25.5 billion at the end of 1941 and rose to $101 billion by the end of 1945. The

---

[2]*Tax and Expenditure Policy for 1950*, A Statement on National Policy by the Research and Policy Committee of the Committee for Economic Development (New York: 1950), p. 38.

Federal Reserve System facilitated the financing of the war by supplying reserves to the banking system through the purchase of over $20 billion of government securities.[3]

THE RECONVERSION PERIOD

The reconversion period was viewed with misgivings by many who felt that the economy would return to prewar depression levels. There was also some uncertainty because of the major problems in adjusting from a highly controlled economy to a more normal situation.

Character of the Period

In the fall of 1944 Congress ordered the establishment of the Office of War Mobilization and Reconversion to coordinate government planning for reconversion of men and resources to peacetime uses. As the economy shifted back to peacetime production at the end of 1945 and in 1946, the controls were lifted, one by one. Control over prices was modified shortly after the end of the war and was allowed to lapse on June 30, 1947, except for rent control in housing shortage areas.

Production decreased in 1946 and employment decreased somewhat. Most of the difference in production, however, was accounted for by the elimination of overtime work. In 1947 production and employment again increased, the year was one of virtually full employment of men and resources, and a strong seller's market continued. Prices continued upward during 1947 as supply and demand were seeking a new balance. During the second quarter of the year there was some tendency for domestic business to level off.

As the world agricultural situation became worse because of poor crops in 1947, the foreign demand for farm products caused new pressure on prices. During the second quarter of 1947 exports rose rapidly and, since imports remained about the same, net foreign investment rose to an annual rate of over $10 billion from a rate of about $5 billion in the last quarter of 1946.[4] This foreign demand reversed the easing tendencies that were beginning to appear in some lines of business. Foreign countries drew on their dollar

---

[3]*Federal Reserve Bulletin* (January, 1950), p. 61.

[4]"Progress of Postwar Transition," *Survey of Current Business* (February, 1948), p. 2.

resources so rapidly that they soon were all but exhausted. This led Secretary of State George C. Marshall to suggest a foreign aid program, and Congress passed an interim aid program late in 1947 and the European Recovery Program in the next year. These programs kept foreign demand at a high level, but not at the level of the second quarter of 1947.

Prices were held in check during the war and the immediate postwar period by the OPA. When the price control legislation was allowed to lapse on June 30, 1947, rapid increases in commodity prices occurred. The index of wholesale prices of all commodities, based on 1947–1949 as 100, was at 64 in 1942 when price controls were established. It increased to 67 in 1943 and then rose to only 69 in 1945. In 1946 it increased to 79 as price controls were relaxed and then, as controls were abandoned completely, to 96 in 1947.[5]

Factors Leading to Inflation

Several factors accounted for the postwar increases in prices after the period of wartime price control. There was a large demand for durable consumer goods, such as automobiles, refrigerators, washing machines, and radios, since the output of these goods had been drastically curtailed during the war. This unsatisfied demand built up during the war years was further augmented by the rapid increases in income that took place during the war. Wartime savings, larger than usual because of patriotic appeals and the shortage of goods, were available for postwar purchases.

The changed situation from a partially employed economy in the prewar period to a fully employed economy in the postwar period also made price increases likely. In 1941 the economy was geared to the production of goods for an economy in which income was lower than normal because millions of people had been out of work for years. As these people went to work during the war years and continued to work in the postwar period, they demanded a much larger amount of consumer goods of all kinds than the economy was producing before the war.

The most important reason for inflation in the postwar period was the method of wartime finance. As already pointed out, the government resorted to borrowing on a large scale and the banks of

---

[5]*Federal Reserve Bulletin* (November, 1952), p. 1225.

the country bought government bonds from private investors in large quantities. The total investment of all banks in government bonds was over $65 billion higher at the end of 1946 than it was in 1939. It had been even greater, but a large part of the Victory Loan was not used by the government and the funds were utilized to retire bank-held debt. Under the impact of inflationary war finance, the total deposits and currency outside banks increased rapidly. The total on December 31, 1939, was $63,253 million. By the end of 1947, it had risen to $170,008 million.[6] With this greatly increased money supply and the increased demand for goods, it was inevitable that prices should rise.

The economy continued to operate at close to capacity levels during 1948. Price rises were not as general, however, as in the two preceding years because the supply of goods in many fields had been increased sufficiently to meet the demand. During the latter part of the year there was a decline in agricultural prices and a general tendency for industrial prices to stabilize. Physical production in 1948 rose about 3 percent over 1947, and new construction increased between 10 and 15 percent in physical terms. There was a strong demand for all goods, especially for new producers' durable equipment. Wartime income tax rates were cut in the spring of 1948, and the extra income left in the hands of consumers had an expansionary effect on the economy.

The 1949 Readjustment

In 1948 the price level increased more slowly than in 1947, and consumption expenditures also began to level off. Businessmen did not adjust immediately to this change in the rate of increase in business activity and, as a result, found themselves with excessive inventories. Toward the end of 1948, businessmen adopted cautious buying policies and, during the first quarter of 1949, substantial inventory liquidation took place. During 1948 inventories were increased by some $5 billion, while in 1949 they were reduced by $2.5 billion.

As a result of the change in inventory policies, industrial production declined somewhat. It fell from 192 in 1948 on a 1935–1939 base to 176 in 1949, a drop of 8 percent. Durable goods production fell 10 percent, but nondurable production fell only 5 percent. Total employment declined but slightly, but manufacturing employment

---

[6]*Federal Reserve Bulletin* (January, 1950), p. 60.

fell off 9 percent. Construction continued upward through 1949, and expenditures on producers' durable equipment were down by only about 5 percent.

One reason that business did not decline further was that personal consumption expenditures held up and even increased slightly toward the end of 1949. This was due in part to the payment of unemployment compensation to most of the workers who were out of work and also to the effects of lower federal income taxes under the 1947 Revenue Act. Perhaps most important of all was the willingness of consumers to keep expenditures up even in the face of some falling off in business. Total economic activity as measured by gross national product was at about the 1948 level in 1949.

It became evident in the second half of 1949 that inventory liquidation had gone too far. Buying for stock was resumed in more normal proportions and business picked up early in 1950. A new boom began later in the year as the Korean War and large-scale rearmament led to an intensified demand for goods.

THE KOREAN WAR PERIOD

The Korean War started on a small scale as a United Nations police action, but it developed into a major conflict lasting several years. This war had a significant effect on our economy because the bulk of the UN forces were American and most of the war material was also supplied by this country.

Background

The demand for goods arising out of the Korean War led to renewed inflationary pressures. Government deficits were not the cause of price rises in the last half of 1950, since the Treasury had an excess of cash income over cash outgo in the last half of the year of almost a billion dollars. The explanation lies in private spending. Consumers, fearing the shortages of World War II, spent large sums on various types of durable and semidurable goods. Business also spent heavily for inventories and for capital investment. The annual rate of gross private domestic investment went up over $12 billion from the second to the fourth quarter of 1950. Loans of insured commercial banks rose nearly $7.5 billion from June to December.[7] Life

---

[7]Charles Cortez Abbott, *The Federal Debt* (New York: The Twentieth Century Fund, 1953), pp. 92, 93.

insurance companies also supplied long-term funds by selling government bonds and putting the funds in mortgages and corporate obligations.

Under these conditions Federal Reserve Bank credit increased materially. The Board of Governors of the Federal Reserve System wanted to act to restrict expansion, but could not so long as it felt obligated to support the bond market by buying all government securities at par or better. The Treasury wanted to follow a pattern of low rates as it did in World War II, and this, of course, required price-support operations since interest rates would have gone up in a free market as the demand for funds increased.

Monetary Problems and Policies

The controversy between the Treasury and the Federal Reserve System developed into an open conflict in the summer of 1950, especially after the Federal Reserve System had to engage in large-scale open-market operations to assure the success of some financing at a rate the market did not find attractive. When the Secretary of the Treasury stated in a speech in January, 1951, that the Treasury had not changed its position and was not willing to allow even fractional increases in interest rates, the controversy became acute. Not only Reserve officials but the press and members of Congress entered it. Such a situation could not last long, and President Truman appointed a committee to study ways and means to provide the necessary restraint on private credit expansion and at the same time to maintain stability in the market for government securities. Before this committee could report, however, an agreement between the Treasury and the Federal Reserve System was announced in March, 1951.

Before looking at this agreement, it is desirable to see the basis of the opposing viewpoints. Treasury officials wanted to keep interest rates on the debt at a low level. They favored low rates, not only to keep the cost of servicing the debt at a minimum but, also from a belief that low interest rates were necessary to keep investment in plant, equipment, housing, local public works, and the like at high levels. They felt that an emergency, such as that arising out of the Korean War, should be met by direct controls, such as materials allocation, rationing, and price controls.

Federal Reserve officials felt that in the absence of all-out war such controls were unnecessary if proper monetary and fiscal policies were followed. They believed that, if the government kept cash outgo and income reasonably in balance, monetary controls would be sufficient to prevent inflation. Such a course would also prevent the building up of idle funds by consumers as was done during World War II and led to inflationary pressures when controls were taken off.

The Federal Reserve was opposed to pegging interest rates because such a policy rendered their tools of credit control ineffective. They could not raise the discount rate because this would change the structure of interest rates. They could not raise reserve requirements significantly because to do so would decrease available free reserves and force interest rates up. Worst of all they had to buy government securities in sufficient volume to hold the price at par or above, thus increasing the money supply at the very time they wanted to act to restrict it.

The accord that was announced in March, 1951, was designed to check credit expansion without the use of direct controls. One result was the offer to exchange long-term 2½ percent bonds, which were being sold to the Federal Reserve in quantities, for a non-marketable 29-year issue at 2⅔ percent. These bonds were non-marketable but could be exchanged at the option of the holder into marketable 5-year, 1½ percent notes. At the same time, government bonds were no longer bought in the market by the Federal Reserve to any appreciable degree. Toward the end of the year the price of the longest term government bonds had dropped to below 97 in a free market.

The Federal Reserve did not stay out of the market completely but continued to buy and sell some securities so as to maintain an orderly market. As the private demand for funds increased because of a boom in residential building and in the capital markets, interest rates rose and long-term securities dropped somewhat further.

The Republican Administration that was elected in November, 1952, followed the same general line of policies reached in the accord in the spring of 1951. They decided to issue long-term government securities whenever funds were available in the market. Early in 1953 the Treasury issued 30-year bonds at 3¼ percent. As available funds were already at a low level, this helped to tighten the money markets and raise interest rates.

THE 1953 RECESSION

Business continued upward in the first half of 1953. By summer the rate of increase in business activity had slowed down, and there was some fear that a recession might occur. The Federal Reserve System eased credit in order to prevent a downturn or to make any downturn that might occur less serious. A downturn began in the third quarter of 1953 and continued through the third quarter of 1954. Industrial production dropped about 10 percent from July, 1953, to April, 1954, and unemployment increased to about 4 million workers. Gross national product decreased by only about 2 percent and personal income remained almost unchanged during the recession. Expenditures on construction leveled off in the second half of 1953 and the first quarter of 1954, and then increased rapidly during the remainder of the year.

The 1953–1954 downturn was largely a readjustment to a lower level of defense expenditures made possible by the end of the Korean War. Defense expenditures dropped from $49.3 billion in 1953 to $40.2 billion in 1954, and other federal government expenditures from $9.0 billion to $6.7 billion. Thus, total federal expenditures were cut by $10.5 billion from 1953 to 1954. The decreased demand for war goods also led to some decrease in business investment expenditures. Expenditures on machinery and equipment were reduced by some $2 billion and inventories were liquidated in late 1953 and 1954, whereas they were being increased before that time. Consumers also reduced expenditures on durable goods somewhat, especially on automobiles. This was due to the fact that most consumers had late-model cars because of large-scale purchases in the postwar period and also the uncertainty of the economic outlook as unemployment increased.

This readjustment to a lower level of government expenditures, especially on war goods, and the resulting decline in investment expenditures and reduction in inventories did not result in a protracted depression for several reasons. Personal income held up well during the recession due to several factors. This was true not only because most sectors of the economy were not affected but because personal taxes were cut by over $3 billion, and unemployment compensation of over $2 billion helped cushion the decline in income of the unemployed. Consumers increased expenditures on services by $4.5 billion from 1953 to 1954 and by over $1 billion on nondurable goods.

Construction also increased during the recession, especially residential construction which was $1.6 billion higher in 1954 than in 1953. The increase in residential construction was due in part at least to more favorable financing arrangements under government guaranteed loans. State and local governmental units also increased expenditures by about $3 billion from 1953 to 1954.

THE 1955–1957 PROSPERITY PERIOD

Economic activity increased rapidly in 1955. Gross national product increased almost $35 billion over 1954 levels and another $22 billion in 1956. Personal consumption expenditures increased rapidly in 1955, especially on durable goods. Automobile sales increased from about 5.5 million cars in 1954 to almost 8 million in 1955. This increase in automobile sales was financed to a significant degree by consumer credit and, as a result, total consumer installment credit outstanding increased $5.4 billion from 1954 to 1955.

Consumers spent over $1 billion less on durable goods in 1956 than in 1955. They spent more money, however, on nondurable goods and services so that total consumer expenditures increased by $12.5 billion between these two years.

Residential construction increased by over $3 billion from 1954 to 1955, and then declined somewhat in 1956 and 1957. This decline was due to several factors. One was the decreased rate of family formation as the smaller number of children born during the depression years reached marriageable age. Another was the increased cost of financing and reduced volume of funds available for housing resulting from restrictive credit policies of the Federal Reserve and the government.

One of the most rapid increases in investment expenditures was on business plant and equipment. Such expenditures increased from about $27 billion in 1954 to $35 billion in 1956 and about $37 billion in 1957.

Inflationary pressures began to develop during this prosperity period. The wholesale price index (1947–1949 = 100) increased from 110.7 in 1955 to 114.3 in 1956 and 117.6 in 1957. The consumer price index showed a similar rise. In order to prevent serious inflation, the Federal Reserve System followed a highly restrictive monetary policy. Reserve requirements were raised, and the rediscount rate was raised several times from the 1½ percent level in effect in April, 1954, to the 3½ percent level put into effect in August, 1957.

THE 1957–1958 RECESSION AND RECOVERY

In the late summer of 1957 the economy experienced the beginning of the third postwar recession. This recession was in some ways the most severe of the three readjustments. It was also unique in that the period of decline was the shortest of the three recessions. Industrial production dropped 13 percent from August, 1957, to the low point in April, 1958, compared with 10 percent in the two earlier recessions. In August, 1958, unemployment had increased to 7.7 percent of the civilian labor force. Gross national product declined from an annual rate of $446 billion in the third quarter of 1957 to $426 billion in the first quarter of 1958, a drop of 4.5 percent. Disposable personal income decreased only 1.2 percent during the same period. This was due to unemployment compensation, to rising farm income resulting largely from agricultural aid programs, and to increased governmental expenditures during the decline.

All sectors of the economy were not affected uniformly by the recession. One of the hardest hit was the capital goods industry since business expenditures on plant and equipment dropped by 16 percent. Consumer durable goods expenditures also declined, especially those on automobiles. Automobile sales dropped from over 6 million in 1957 to just over 4 million in 1958, a decline of about a third.

The decline in capital goods production and in consumer durable goods production had severe repercussions on the metals and minerals industries. The sales and price of nonferrous metals dropped rapidly, and steel production dropped to 54 percent of capacity in the first half of 1958 from 91.5 percent the year before.

Textile production in the first half of 1958 declined about 8 percent from the same period in 1957. Sales of food and drugs and service expenditures continued upward during the recession.

One of the major factors leading to the decline in production and in gross national product was the liquidation of inventories. In the third quarter of 1957 inventories were being built up at a rate in excess of $2 billion per year. During the first quarter of 1958 inventory liquidation was at an annual rate of $9.5 billion and $8 billion in the second quarter.

A number of causal factors were at work in the 1957–1958 recession. One was the slowing down of capital expenditures because plant and equipment had been expanded faster than the increase in demand for goods and services. Another was the shift in consumer expenditures. Less money was spent on durable goods and more on nondurables and services. This continuing shift is due to many factors. One is the increased demand for food, clothing, and services of the large group of children born in the postwar period. Another is represented by the increased prices for services that have been catching up with the increases in the general price level, but with a long lag.

Shifts in foreign trade also affected the economy in the 1957 downturn. Exports of goods and services increased in the early part of 1957 because of the crisis in Egypt and the Middle East which closed the Suez Canal and disrupted some pipelines carrying oil. The annual rate of exports dropped about $5 billion from early 1957 to the spring of 1958.

Another factor leading to the recession was the shift in expenditure patterns caused by the 5 percent increase in consumer goods prices in 1956 and 1957. Many individuals on social security, pensions, and other fixed incomes and many workers whose wages were not adjusted promptly to this price increase had to adjust their expenditure patterns to this reduction in real income. As a result, the demand for some types of goods dropped.

Business reached the low point of the recession in April, 1958, and then started upward. The boost did not come from any sharp reversals in the areas leading to the downturn, that is, investment in plant and equipment, auto sales, and exports. It came in part from the ending of inventory liquidation in the last quarter of 1958 and some increase of inventories in the first quarter of 1959. A major impetus for recovery came from the consumer section as consumers increased expenditures on nondurable goods and services. There was also an increase in residential construction as interest rates eased and mortgage funds were made more easily available under FHA and VA programs.

Increased government expenditures also helped increase business activity. Federal government expenditures increased by almost $3 billion from the third quarter of 1957 to the third quarter of 1958, and state and local government expenditures by almost $4 billion. By the spring of 1959 economic activity had passed the prerecession levels in most sectors of the economy. Unemployment remained a problem, however, since it was at 6 percent of the labor force and had been about 4 percent in the 1955–1957 prosperity period.

The Federal Reserve helped business recovery by supplying banks with excess reserves during the decline in business and in the early stages of recovery. By late summer of 1958 the Federal Reserve authorities began to reduce excess reserves and raised discount rates. They raised them again in mid-autumn and in the early spring of 1959. This was done in an effort to prevent further inflation and to try to stop the price increases that had continued throughout the recession.

The first half of 1959 was a year of strong economic recovery that showed some signs of turning into a boom. The economy suffered a severe setback, however, when the longest steel strike on record began shortly after midyear. The shortages resulting from the strike led to a drop of about 7 percent in industrial production between June and October.

When the steel strike ended in November, there was a new surge in economic activity. Inventories were rebuilt rapidly through the first quarter of 1960, and production and gross national product reached new highs by midyear.

THE 1960 – 1961 RECESSION

The fourth postwar recession began in the second half of 1960. Industrial production dropped during the second half of the year and into early 1961. Gross national product eased somewhat during the last quarter of 1960 and fell somewhat further in the first quarter of 1961. Unemployment, however, posed more of a problem than in earlier postwar recessions. It had been more severe in the 1957–1958 recession than in the earlier postwar downturns and continued to be a problem in the recovery period. During the 1960–1961 recession unemployment almost reached the 1958 peak even though the downturn in production was mild. One reason for the increased unemployment was the increasing size of the labor force due to an increasing birth rate after 1939. Another was the accelerated pace of automation resulting from new technological advances and rising labor costs.

The 1960–1961 recession was due to several factors. Inventories that had been depleted by the steel strike were rebuilt rapidly in the first quarter of 1960 and then more slowly in the second quarter. This build-up led to an increase in production which could not be sustained when inventory building ceased in the third quarter. Residential construction also slowed down since the huge backlog of deferred demand had been met and also because mortgage money for residential financing was more difficult to obtain and more costly than it had been during the period of credit ease in the 1957–1958 downturn and early recovery period. Consumer buying also weakened somewhat after midyear, especially the purchase of durable goods. Consumers had a good stock of automobiles and other durables so demand was no longer pressing. Rapid increases in the volume of consumer credit outstanding in 1959 and in the first half of 1960 also led consumers to slow down purchases so as to again increase their equity position.

Plant and equipment expenditures were cut during this recession, but the amount was so small that this was not a major factor in the downturn. The decrease took place because sales and profits were not up to expectations and because excess capacity developed in many fields.

A favorable factor during the downturn was the increased spending by foreigners for our goods and services. Increased spending by government at all levels also provided support for the economy.

The Federal Reserve System relaxed pressures on the money supply early in 1960, and in the second half of the year moved to a policy of monetary ease. This helped cushion the decline. It also led to a problem in our foreign exchange position and a large outflow of gold for a period of time during the latter part of 1960. Short-term interest rates dropped due to the Federal Reserve policy of monetary ease. At the same time interest rates were rising in many foreign countries as business continued upward and reached boom proportions. This disparity in interest rates led to an outflow of short-term funds for more profitable investment abroad. To counter this movement the Federal Reserve took measures to make money more readily available without depressing short-term rates further. Among other steps open-market operations were broadened to include longer-term certificates, notes, and bonds so as to supply funds to the economy without reducing short-term rates unduly.

THE PROSPERITY PERIOD OF THE SIXTIES

The prosperity period that followed the mild recession of 1960–1961 has been the longest in our history. Gross national product in current dollars increased year by year at a more or less constant rate from a level of about $500 billion in early 1961 to over $750 billion in late 1966.   There was some retardation in the rate of advance in economic activity in late 1962, which was more pronounced in industrial production than in gross national product. There was some intensification of economic activity in 1965 and especially 1966 as American participation in the Vietnam War was increased greatly.   Policies that were designed to slow inflation led to a slowing down in the forward movement of the economy in the first quarter of 1967, but the economy moved forward again in the second quarter.   Chart 15-1 on page 400 shows some characteristics of this cycle and other cycles in the period since 1948.

Several characteristics of the early years of this prosperity period before it was affected by the Vietnam War are somewhat unusual. Wholesale prices remained almost completely stable from 1961 through 1964 and then started to move upward slowly in 1965 and 1966, as demand accelerated. Labor cost per unit of output remained relatively stable throughout the period from 1961 through 1966. This was due to wage increases that were to a large extent held within average increases in productivity and to major expenditures by industry on more efficient production plant and equipment. Business expenditures on new plant and equipment increased moderately in 1961, 1962, and the first part of 1963, and then increased sharply through 1966.   Manufacturers' inventories increased very gradually through 1964 and then increased more rapidly in 1965 and 1966.   Bank rates on short-term business loans remained stable through the third quarter of 1965 and then rose sharply through 1966.

The money supply was also increased gradually during most of this period rather than being decreased during the prosperity period. There was a reduction in the money supply in the early part of 1962, but the supply was increased sharply in the second half of the year as retardation in the rate of advance took place.   The federal government had a cash deficit that did not vary significantly in amount during the first four years of this period.   The cash budget was almost in balance early in 1965 and then moved to a deficit position until mid-1966 due to the effects of tax cuts and large expenditures related to the Vietnam War. One of the major reasons for the unusual length of this prosperity period was that many of the things which lead to cyclical unbalance did not occur until 1965 and 1966.

Chart 15-1

Some Coincident Business Cycle Series from 1948 to 1966

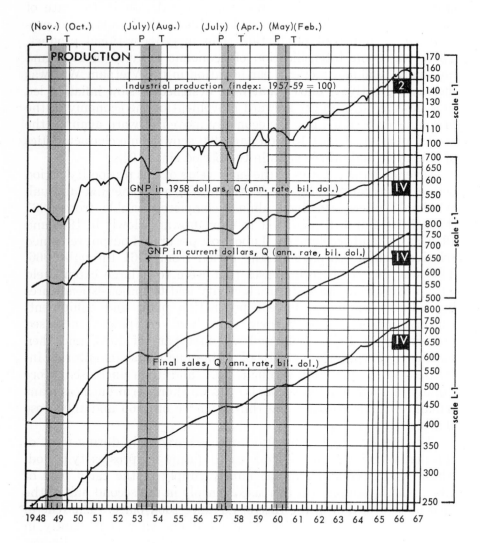

Notes: Arabic numbers in black blocks indicate the latest month for which data are plotted ("2" = February), and Roman numerals indicate the latest quarter ("IV" = fourth quarter). Scale L-1 is a logarithmic scale with one cycle in a given distance.

Source: Adapted from *Business Cycle Developments* (March, 1967), p. 16.

This does not mean that this prosperity period was without problems. The unemployment rate did not fall below 5 percent of the labor force until late 1964, and unemployment was especially severe among teenagers. The unemployment rate dropped gradually during 1964 as the economy expanded somewhat faster due to the effects of tax cuts, and dropped more rapidly during 1965 to 4 percent of the labor force as the Vietnam War led to additional demands for men, goods, and services. Even under the impetus of war demands, the rate did not drop much below 4 percent in 1966. Many of those who were still unemployed were for all practical purposes unemployable in a highly mechanized economy without an upgrading of their labor skills.

The problem of a deficit in the balance of payments also persisted during this period of prosperity. Campaigns to increase exports had some measure of success, and foreign investment was reduced by a Voluntary Foreign Credit Restraint program. Under this program the Board of Governors of the Federal Reserve System issued guidelines to banks and to other financial institutions for restricting lending and investing in foreign countries. This program changed an outflow of bank credit in 1965 to a small net inflow in 1966. These measures taken were not sufficient, however, to completely solve the problem of the balance of payments.

A new problem arose in 1966 when interest rates rose to the highest levels since the early twenties. The demand for funds from all sectors of the economy was high and increasing, especially the demand for bank loans from business. In order to prevent serious inflation arising out of the demands of the Vietnam War, the Federal Reserve raised the discount rate in December, 1965, and also acted generally to restrict the supply of money and credit. Such action did not reduce the money supply, but cut its rate of growth materially in the summer of 1966. Interest rates went up significantly on all types of loans and credit became tight, especially in residential mortgage markets. The result was a slowing down in residential construction during the summer of 1966. The stock market also reacted to higher interest rates and reduced profit prospects and by mid-1966 the average price of industrial common stocks had dropped by some 20 percent from high points reached in 1965. The rise in the wholesale price level was almost halted, but consumer goods prices continued to advance.

There were signs in late 1966 that the economy was slowing down and the Federal Reserve acted to stimulate the economy by increasing the money supply at the end of the year and into the first half of 1967.   Economic activity slowed down in the first quarter of 1967 when GNP in real terms did not increase over the fourth quarter of 1966. GNP in current dollars went up 0.66 percent as price pressures continued. Economic activity again moved forward in the second quarter of 1967, but not at the rate in 1966. The housing industry did not reach 1966 levels nor did commercial and industrial construction.   Industrial production also remained somewhat below the 1966 high.   The stock market was again at 1965 highs in the fall of 1967 and interest rates moved up again, and in some cases passed 1966 highs.   The Administration asked Congress for a temporary tax increase to help prevent renewed inflationary pressures.

QUESTIONS

1. Outline the steps which were taken to adjust the economy to the demands of World War II.
2. (a) How was World War II financed? (b) How did the methods used to finance this war differ from those used to finance earlier wars?
3. Why did prices drop sharply after 1920, but not after World War II?
4. Why did the price level increase rapidly in 1946 and 1947?
5. How would economic conditions probably have differed in 1946 and 1947 if almost all of the cost of the war had been raised by taxation?
6. What led to the 1949 readjustment?
7. Evaluate the arguments of the Treasury and the Federal Reserve System in the dispute that arose over the inflation control policy during the Korean War.
8. (a) Describe the nature of the 1953–1954 downturn. (b) Discuss the factors which led to this downturn.
9. Which factors were unusual in the 1955–1957 prosperity period?
10. (a) Describe the extent of the 1957 recession. (b) Which factors were responsible for this recession? (c) Why was the 1957 recession sharp, but short?
11. Discuss the nature of and causal factors at work in the 1960–1961 recession.
12. Describe the prosperity period of the 1960's. Why was it longer than earlier prosperity periods?

SUGGESTED READINGS

Baruch, B., and J. M. Hancock. *War and Postwar Adjustment Policy.* Washington: U. S. Government Printing Office, 1944.

Chandler, Lester V. *Inflation in the United States, 1940–1948.* New York: Harper & Row, Publishers, 1951.

Craf, John R. *A Survey of the American Economy 1940–1946.* New York: North River Press, Inc., 1947.

Economic Report of the President. Washington: U. S. Government Printing Office, 1947 to date.

Harris, Seymour E. *The Economics of Mobilization and Inflation.* New York: W. W. Norton & Company., 1951.

Murphy, Henry C. *The National Debt in War and Transition.* New York: McGraw-Hill Book Company, 1950.

Nadler, Marcus. *Recession and Recovery,* New York: Hanover House, 1958.

"Recent Expansion of Demand," *Federal Reserve Bulletin* (March, 1966), pp. 305–314.

PROBLEMS ON PART V

1. Analyze the current situation in the economy. Which past period does the current situation resemble most? Are there any changes on the horizon that could lead to major readjustments of the 1929 type?

2. Using data from the *Survey of Current Business*, the *Federal Reserve Bulletin* and *Economic Indicators*, make a table showing the following for the 1953–1954, 1957–1958, and 1960–1961 recessions:

   (a) Percentage change from the high quarter to the following low quarter in gross national product, personal consumption expenditures, government purchases of goods and services, residential construction, other construction, producers' durable equipment, and business inventories.

   (b) Decline in the hours worked per week from the high month to the low month.

   (c) Drop in personal income from the high month to the low month.

   (d) Drop in employment from the high month to the low month.

   (e) Changes in wholesale prices during the period from the high month in personal income to the low month.

   (f) Changes in retail sales during the period from the high month in personal income to the low month.

After studying the data in your table, discuss the similarities and differences in the periods of readjustment.

PART VI

FORECASTING
ECONOMIC ACTIVITY

One of the important reasons for studying the nature of business fluctuations and the causal factors that have produced them is to be able to determine the most probable future levels of economic activity. This is of significance in developing governmental policies in the monetary and fiscal areas, and it is also of primary importance to the businessman who must develop plans in the light of future prospects for the economy. This part will deal with techniques and procedures currently used to forecast future levels of economic activity.

The first chapter in this part considers various procedures for projecting the trend of activity in the economy for several years into the future and describes and analyzes various approaches to such forecasting. The next two chapters deal with short-run forecasting of economic activity for a year ahead and present procedures for building a model of gross national product for the next year. Chapter 19 discusses methods of predicting long-run price trends and of making short-run price forecasts. The last chapter, Chapter 20, describes services offered in the forecasting field by a representative group of professional forecasting services.

Forecasting is at the stage medicine was in its early days, but early medicine was a good deal better than were the witch doctors. Even today when the practice of medicine is an applied science based on the underlying biological sciences, there is an element of an art left in it. Forecasting is largely an art, but it is developing into an applied science with an element of an art as medicine has done.

The science of forecasting is based on an understanding of the causal factors at work in the economy. Future events can only be predicted when the causal factors at work are understood. Forecasting is also based on a knowledge of past reactions to a given set of causal factors. To provide such knowledge, the record of past cycles is analyzed. If the causal factors at work and the reactions to them are fully known, an analysis of the present situation should make prediction possible. In our present state of knowledge, much is still not known about the causal factors at work in the economy and about the reactions of the economy to such factors. Therefore, a full science of prediction is not possible, and a large area of judgment remains. As this stage of development forecasts will therefore be subject to some error and may at times be completely wrong. A forecast based on available techniques is, however, on the average far superior to intuition, chart reading, and the like.

CHAPTER 16 *Projecting the Trend of Economic Activity*

In any business important decisions must be made in the light of the long-term trend in sales of that business. If sales are likely to be growing over a period of time, plans must be made for the expanded facilities necessary to handle the increased volume of business and for the necessary financing for such facilities. This planning must be done on the basis of the long-term trend of the total economy, of the industry of which this business is a part, and of the business itself. Studies of these trends must take into consideration the varying rates of growth in different sections of the United States.

If the business is regional, the trend of economic activity in its region will affect its sales in the future. If the business is national, the trend of sales in different regions will affect the location of future plant additions so as to be most economically located in relationship to raw materials, labor, and future markets.

PROJECTING THE GROSS NATIONAL PRODUCT TREND

One of the best ways of making a long-range projection of total economic activity is to project the level of gross national product since this is the most comprehensive series on economic activity in general use. This is done by such organizations as the National Planning Association, the National Industrial Conference Board, and the Department of Commerce. These projections are not forecasts of the actual level of economic activity to be expected in the future but projections of long-run trends in the economy, made on the assumption of full employment in the forecast year and in terms of prices current at the time they are made. Such projections are useful as a guide to the building of plant and equipment on the basis of the long-run demand for a product, not on the basis of the cyclical fluctuations.

Since trends change slowly, such projections can be made with reasonable accuracy for several years into the future. As the period of time involved is lengthened, the projections become less reliable since unforeseen factors can have considerable influence on economic activity in the future and since trends may change materially over a period of time. Projections have been made for as many as fifty years ahead, but these are only rough general estimates of the potentialities of the economy. Fortunately for planning most types of capital expenditures, projections for five years are usually sufficient and these can be made with reasonable accuracy.

Various procedures with different degrees of refinement may be used for projecting gross national product. The simplest technique is to project the trend for the past few years either on a freehand basis or by using the line of least squares. Another possibility is to find the average annual rate of growth for a period of years in the past and then project this rate of growth to the forecast year. A more complex approach is based on a determination of the number of persons likely to be in the labor force and of the most likely output per employed worker in the forecast year. This approach can be refined by determining the most likely distribution of employees by fields and also the most likely output per worker in each field. Each of these procedures will be considered more fully.

Line of Least-Squares Trend

In projecting the trend, it is necessary to consider which time period in the past shall be used for such projection. GNP, for example, grew more rapidly from the depths of the depression in 1933 through the end of World War II than it has since that time or can be expected to grow in the future. The period since 1947 is one that is not affected by these abnormal developments. Prices rose rapidly in 1947 and 1948, but this effect is largely eliminated by using GNP in constant dollars as a basis of projection. This is done since increases in real output are to be projected, not price changes. Table 16-1 gives GNP figures from 1947 through 1965 in terms of 1958 dollars. The formula for the line of least squares applied to this data for the period 1947–1965 is:

$$Y = 443.7 + 15.2x \ (x \text{ is the forecast year minus 1956})$$

The value for 1975 for GNP in 1958 dollars is $732.5 billion. Adjusting this to 1965 prices by means of the 1965 GNP price deflator of 110.9 gives a GNP figure for 1975 in 1965 dollars of $812.3 billion.

Table 16-1

Gross National Product for 1947–1965
(In Billions of 1958 Dollars)

Year	GNP	Year	GNP
1947	309.9	1957	452.5
1948	323.7	1958	447.3
1949	324.1	1959	475.9
1950	355.3	1960	487.8
1951	383.4	1961	497.3
1952	395.1	1962	530.0
1953	412.8	1963	551.0
1954	407.0	1964	580.0
1955	438.0	1965	614.4
1956	446.1		

Source: *Survey of Current Business* (August, 1965), p. 27 and (September, 1966), p. 11.

Extending Average Rates of Growth

An alternative method of making a projection of GNP is to extend the average rate of growth in a past period into the future to the forecast year. It is necessary to select a period for calculating average rates of growth just as it is necessary to do so to determine and project the line of least squares.

The average rate of growth of GNP in real terms for the period from 1947 through 1965 was about 3.75 percent per year. Extending this rate of growth to 1975 from the 1965 level of GNP of $681 billion gives a value of GNP of $984 billion in 1975 in terms of 1965 prices. This may be calculated by the following formula:

$$681 \ (1.0375)^{10} = 681 \times 1.445 = 984.0$$

Estimating GNP from the Supply of Factors of Production

A more refined approach is to project GNP from the basis of the ability of the economy to supply goods and services. This is done by estimating the most likely level of the labor force and the GNP output per workers. The GNP output is total output of GNP arising from labor itself and also from the other factors of production.

This procedure also projects GNP in terms of current prices. Furthermore, it assumes full employment in the forecast year. This means that results will be somewhat higher than projections based on extending past growth from a period in which significant unemployment existed in some years. This will be true in the 1947–1965 period since there was unemployment of some magnitude above frictional unemployment in 1948–1949, 1953–1954, the second half of 1957 and 1958, and in 1961 and 1962.

Population and Labor Force. The first step in this procedure for projecting gross national product is to estimate the population at the future date selected for the forecast. This step requires a study of the trend of population and a projection of this trend into the future. Such estimates are made by the Bureau of the Census of the Department of Commerce, and individuals and private agencies. Table 16-2 on page 411 shows the increases in population since 1920. It also shows the total labor force, the labor participation rate, and the unemployment rate.

After the size of the population has been estimated, the number of individuals who will be in the labor force must be estimated. Such projections are based upon a study of the long-term trend of the labor force in relationship to the total population and the population of working age. From 1900 until about 1950 the labor force was growing when compared with total population. It has started a slow decline since then. The labor force is also declining when compared with the population of working age, that is, age 14 and over. It is also true that more married women have been seeking work. All of these factors must be considered in estimating the total labor force from an estimate of population. The Bureau of the Census makes estimates of individuals who will be in the labor force and calculates their probable distribution as to sex and age groups.

The number of persons 14 years of age and over in the labor force in 1965 was 78.4 million persons, or 40.3 percent of the population of 194.6 million.

The average of the range of population estimates for 1975, as developed by the Bureau of the Census, is about 225 million persons. The labor participation rate is likely to increase somewhat because the large number of children born after the end of World War II will enter the labor force. Assume a 41.5 percent participation rate in 1975. The total labor force estimate for 1975 is then 93 million.

Estimates of GNP are usually based on production of goods and services by the civilian labor force. Therefore, the number of men likely to be in the armed forces must be subtracted. This number

Table 16-2

Population and Employment, 1920–1965

YEAR	POPULATION*	TOTAL LABOR FORCE*	LABOR PARTICIPATION RATE†	UNEMPLOYMENT RATE‡
1920	106.5	42.8	39.9	4.0
1930	123.2	50.1	40.6	8.7
1940	132.6	56.2	42.4	14.6
1945	140.5	65.3	46.5	1.9
1946	141.9	61.0	43.0	3.9
1947	144.7	61.8	42.7	3.9
1948	147.2	62.9	42.7	3.8
1949	149.8	63.7	42.5	5.9
1950	152.3	64.7	42.5	5.3
1951	154.9	66.0	42.6	3.3
1952	157.6	66.6	42.3	3.1
1953	160.2	67.4	42.1	2.9
1954	163.0	67.8	41.6	5.6
1955	165.9	68.9	41.5	4.4
1956	168.9	70.4	41.7	4.2
1957	172.0	70.7	41.1	4.3
1958	174.9	71.3	40.8	6.8
1959	177.8	71.9	40.4	5.5
1960	180.7	73.1	40.5	5.6
1961	183.8	74.2	40.4	6.7
1962	186.7	74.7	40.0	5.6
1963	189.4	75.7	40.0	5.7
1964	192.1	77.0	40.1	5.2
1965	194.6	78.4	40.3	4.6

*In millions of persons

†Percentage of total population in the labor force, that is, persons who are able and willing to work.

‡Percentage of the civilian labor force which is unemployed.

Source: Bureau of Census data.

was about 2.6 million in early 1966 and had been going down gradually for several years before it increased again in the summer of 1966 due to the demands of the Vietnam War. Let us assume it is 2.5 million in 1975. Our estimate of the civilian labor force is then 90.5 million workers.

After the size of the civilian labor force in the forecast year has been projected, the amount of frictional unemployment must be estimated. *Frictional unemployment* includes unemployed workers who are entering the labor force for the first time, who are shifting from one seasonal job to another, who are shifting the concern for which they work, who are changing their line of work, and the like. Even in such years of high business activity as 1929, 1948, 1950, 1951, 1952, and 1966, unemployment did not drop below about 3 percent of the civilian labor force and was as high as 5 percent. Therefore, about 4 percent can be used as a good approximation of frictional unemployment. The above estimate of the civilian labor force for 1975 was 90.5 million workers. If about 4 percent or 3.5 million workers are unemployed, civilian employment in 1975 will be about 87 million workers.

Production. After the size of the employed civilian labor force in the forecast year has been determined, the volume of goods and services that will be produced must be estimated. This estimate depends upon the number of hours that will be worked and the rate of output per hour. The long-run trend of the number of hours worked has been going down; but it is unlikely, according to most observers, that it will drop much below 40 hours a week in most fields, at least not during periods of full employment that are assumed to exist as a basis for estimating the long-term trend. The average hours worked per week were about 39.5 in 1965. This was about the same as the level in the previous six years, but was more than one-half hour lower than the level 10 years before. The annual average is, however, likely to continue to drop somewhat because of a tendency toward more paid holidays and longer vacations. Let us assume for our projection of GNP that the average number of hours worked per week is 38 in 1975. This assumes a reduction in the work week, which is about three times as great as that in the previous decade, but the trend toward longer vacations is accelerating.

The next step is to estimate the amount of gross national product that is likely to be produced for each hour of civilian employment in the forecast year. The rate of increase in gross national product per man-hour since 1900 has been 2.3 percent per year. For the period since 1947, it has been 3.2 percent per year. From 1953 to 1960 it was materially below the postwar average. Let us assume that it will be 3 percent per year between 1965 and 1975. In 1965 GNP per hour of civilian employment was $4.71 (GNP of $681 billion ÷ 144.5 billion hours of work [39.5-hour average work week × 52 weeks × 72.2 million civilian employees]). At an average annual rate of increase of 3 percent per year GNP per civilian man-hour will be $6.31 in 1975. Gross national product in 1975 is then based on the following factors:

Civilian employment — 87 million workers
Average hours of work per week — 38
GNP per hour of civilian employment — $6.31

The average hours of work per year per worker are 1,976 (52 × 38), and the total number of hours of work in the year is 171.9 billion (1,976 × 87 million workers). Multiplying by an average projected rate of output of $6.31 gives a GNP figure of $1,085 billion.

More Refined Estimates of GNP

Estimates of GNP based on expected employment levels and expected output per worker may be refined by making separate estimates for major sectors of the economy and totaling these to arrive at an estimate of GNP. One such refinement is to estimate the civilian and governmental contribution to GNP separately. This is done for several reasons. One is that it is impossible to measure trends in productivity in government employment since government services are not sold in the market place. Another is that trends in wage rates in government and private employment have not always been the same.

The private contribution to GNP is found by determining private employment, hours to be worked per year, and output per hour. Such output can be projected on the basis of trends of productivity in general, or by figuring trends in productivity of labor and capital separately. The government contribution is developed from figures on the number of workers and the average pay per worker. The number of workers in government employment is determined from past trends in the number of government employees and a qualitative evaluation of the factors likely to affect it in the future as, for example, the large number of teachers required to educate the increasing number of children of school age because of increased birth rates in the postwar years. The average wage per government worker is likewise determined from trends of wages and from a consideration of qualitative factors. For example, the demand for teachers and

the increased emphasis on education due to the Russian challenge
are likely to lead to more than average increases in pay for teachers.

A further refinement calls for estimating output in major fields
of civilian employment separately. This is, at times, done only for
agricultural and nonagricultural production because of varying rates
of productivity and hours of work in these fields. At times nonagricultural employment is further subdivided. For example, the
National Planning Association has divided this sector of the economy into the following fields:[1]

Processed food	Eating and drinking places
Other manufacturing	Finance and insurance
Communication	Real estate and rental
Transportation	Mining
Trade	Utilities
Business, professional, and re-	Construction
pair service	Private households

ESTIMATING GNP FROM THE DEMAND
FOR THE FACTORS OF PRODUCTION

Gross national product can also be estimated from the demand
side by making an estimate of each of the major categories of GNP
in the forecast year. This is done by estimating personal consumption expenditures, gross private domestic investment, government purchases of goods and services, and net exports of goods
and services. These categories are estimated from past trends in
each of its major subdivisions, from an analysis of qualitative
factors, and from past relationships between them. The procedure
is similar to that described in Chapter 18 for making a short-run
forecast.

More refined estimates may be made by estimating receipts and
expenditures in each major sector of GNP and determining the
excess of receipts or expenditures in each sector. The total of these
must, of course, balance *ex post*, and estimates should be evaluated
and modified if need be. A lack of balance between total receipts and
disbursements may indicate that some of the estimates are not
accurate or that they have not been made consistently. It may also
indicate that the economy will tend to behave in this way, but that

---

[1]*National Economic Projections*, 1962–1965, 1970 (Washington: National
Planning Association, 1959).

forces will be put in motion to adjust the lack of *ex ante* balance between savings and investment. These factors are considered more fully in Chapter 18 which considers an expenditure model of GNP.

Estimates of GNP made from the supply side and from the demand side can also be compared and differences analyzed. If the figure from the supply side is above that from the demand side, it indicates that unemployment is likely to exist; if the demand figure is above the supply figure, it indicates that inflationary pressures will exist. In making a final forecast, it is necessary to consider the most likely actions by government, business, and labor if deflation or inflation is likely to be present and to estimate the effect these actions will have on GNP.

National Planning Association Projections

The National Planning Association has been making estimates of future levels of GNP for some time. These estimates have been made by using various approaches to projecting GNP and developing the most likely figures on the basis of the judgment of the economists making the estimates. The size of the labor force and the most likely output per hour of employment are used as one approach. Estimates are also made for the demand for GNP from purchases of goods and services by consumers, for domestic investment, by government, and from net international purchases. In developing the estimate for each sector, disposable receipts as well as purchases are estimated, and the projected excess or deficit of receipts is determined for each sector as well as the balance for the total economy. The National Planning Association has developed estimates that are in balance under each of the following sets of circumstances:

High Consumption Models   High Government Model
  Slow Growth   Slow Growth
  Fast Growth   Fast Growth
High Investment Models   Alternative Defense Models
  Slow Growth   Low Defense
  Fast Growth   High Defense

PROJECTION OF THE DISPOSABLE PERSONAL INCOME TREND

In many areas of economic decision making and especially in projecting consumer expenditures, it is necessary to have a forecast of disposable personal income as well as a forecast of gross national product. The amount of income individuals have to spend after taxes is one of the major factors determining the level of many consumer expenditures. The following adjustments must be made to GNP to get disposable personal income:

SUBTRACTIONS
Capital consumption allowances
Indirect business tax and nontax liability
Current surplus of government enterprises
Corporate profits taxes
Retained corporate earnings
Contributions for social insurance
Personal tax and nontax payments

ADDITIONS
Government transfer payments to persons
Government subsidies to business
Interest paid by government (net) and by consumers

Each of these items must be estimated in the forecast year to develop a forecast of disposable personal income. Minor items, such as the surplus of government enterprises and government subsidies to business, are usually ignored. An estimate of capital consumption allowances requires estimates of the year-by-year increases in plant and equipment, and of the depreciation on them. Also needed are estimates of losses of capital by destruction and of capital expenditures charged to income currently. These estimates are made on the basis of past relationships and the qualitative factors in the present situation.

Indirect business taxes, mainly sales and excise taxes, must also be estimated and subtracted, since they are not available for consumer expenditures. These taxes are usually estimated by applying present tax rates to estimates of future increases in business.

Corporate profits taxes and retained earnings are also not available for consumer expenditures. Except during the depression years, corporate profits after taxes have had a fairly stable relationship to gross national product. This past relationship can be used along with present and projected tax rates and qualitative factors to estimate corporate income taxes. Estimates of retained earnings can also be made from an analysis of past trends in the division of profits after taxes between dividends and retained earnings.

Deductions for estimates of social insurance contributions are also necessary. These can be estimated from past trends and any expected changes in social security tax rates, and from projected levels of employment and increases in the income of workers.

Personal taxes must be estimated and subtracted to determine disposable personal income. This is usually done by assuming that current tax rates will continue, but this assumption must be varied at times in keeping with expected changes in tax rates.

Several items must also be added to arrive at disposable personal income. One of these items is government transfer payments. These can be projected from past trends and also from a thorough study of present programs for veterans, for agricultural aid, and the like. The other important item to be added includes government interest payments. This involves a projection of interest rates and the levels of government and consumer debt. The level of the debt can be developed from a study of probable surpluses or deficits in government budgets and from trends and current developments in consumer borrowing. To estimate interest rates involves a study of supply and demand factors.

An alternative approach starts with a projection of national income. This is built up by projecting the trend of the various payments to the factors of production — essentially wages, interest, rent, and profits. Then the various items that must be added to and subtracted from national income in order to arrive at personal income must also be estimated. These items, as well as the various payments making up national income, were described in Chapter 9.

PROJECTING THE TREND OF CONSUMER EXPENDITURE

A study of past and prospective relationships to disposable personal income can be used to arrive at estimates of personal consumption expenditures. Chart 16-1 on page 418 shows such a relationship of consumer purchases to income in constant dollars for the period from 1920 to 1958.

Long-range estimates of retail sales in various fields can be developed from estimates of disposable personal income. These relationships have been studied by various analysts in the Department of Commerce. They have developed the relationship between changes in the disposable income of individuals and sales of various types of goods by calculating the correlation between disposable personal income and such sales. See Table 16-3 on page 419.

Chart 16-1

**Consumer Purchases Related to Income in Constant Dollars,
1920–1958**

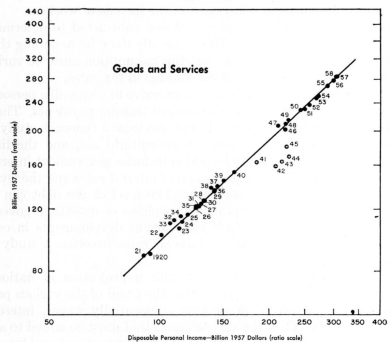

Source: *Survey of Current Business* (March, 1959), p. 22.

Real personal consumption expenditures on services based on constant 1957 dollars, for example, are expressed by the equation $C = (0.443 \times I)^{.956}$. C is real expenditures on services. For any projected value of I, or real disposable income, it is $0.443 \times I$ raised to the power of $.956$. For a real disposable personal income of $350 billion 1957 dollars the equation is:

$$C = (0.443 \times \$350 \text{ billion})^{.956} = \$155.1 \text{ billion}^{.956} = \$124.2 \text{ billion.}$$

Real expenditures on clothing and shoes have been declining in relationship to real disposable income so this equation has a time factor in it. It is $C = 0.192 \times 0.987^t \times I^{.887}$. C is real expenditures on clothing and shoes and t is the time trend factor with 0 at 1940. C is found by first multiplying 0.192×0.987 raised to the power by which the year in question is removed from 1940. Then this factor is multiplied by disposable personal income raised to the

Table 16-3

Equations for Consumption-Income Relationships

Major groups	Long-term (twenties and postwar)	Prewar (1929–40)
	Based on constant (1957) dollars*	
Goods and services.............	$C = 1.108\ I^{.969}$	$C = 2.920\ (1.002)^t\ I^{.777}$
Durable goods.................	$C = 0.0407\ I^{1.203}$	$C = 0.000391\ (0.984)^t\ I^{2.094}$
Nondurable goods..............	$C = 0.723\ I^{.919}$	$C = 2.197\ (1.012)^t\ I^{.716}$
Services†......................	$C = 0.443\ I^{.956}$	$C = 3.019\ (0.997)^t\ I^{.565}$
	Based on current dollars‡	
Goods and services.............	$C = 1.048\ I^{.979}$	$C = 1.628\ I^{.874}$
Durable goods.................	$C = 0.0702\ I^{1.113}$	$C = 0.00721\ I^{1.608}$
Nondurable goods.............	$C = 0.446\ I^{1.013}$	$C = 0.735\ (1.010)^t\ I^{.914}$
Services†......................	$C = 0.538\ I^{.913}$	$C = 1.146\ (0.991)^t\ I^{.729}$
Selected groups	Postwar	Prewar
	Based on constant (1957) dollars*	
Automobiles and parts..........	$C = 0.0317\ I^{1.096}$	$C = 0.00000384\ (0.980)^t\ I^{2.819}$
Furniture and household equipment.	$C = 0.0759\ I^{.951}$	$C = 0.00197\ (0.988)^t\ I^{1.639}$
Food (excluding alcoholic beverages)§	$C = 0.929\ I^{.743}$	....
Clothing and shoes§............	$C = 0.192\ (0.987)^t\ I^{.887}$	....
Gasoline and oil§..............	$C = 0.198\ (1.031)^t\ I^{.594}$	....
Housing and household operation‡..	$C = 0.0224\ I^{1.354}$	$C = 2.123\ (1.002)^t\ I^{.464}$
All other services‡ §............	$C = 0.626\ I^{.781}$	....

*C is real personal consumption expenditures; I is real disposable personal income, both in billions of 1957 dollars; and t is time with 0 at 1940.

†In the case of services, the average of current and previous years' income was used.

‡C is personal consumption expenditures; I is disposable personal income, both in billions of current dollars; and t is time with 0 at 1940.

§Both prewar and postwar years were used in this regression.

Source: *Survey of Current Business* (March, 1959), p. 28.

power of .887. For a real disposable personal income of $350 billion 1957 dollars in 1960, the equation is:

$$C = 0.192 \times 0.987^{20} \times \$350\ \text{billion}^{.887}$$

Estimates made from past relationships to disposable personal income can be checked by studying the long-term trend of an industry itself. In those cases in which an industry has reached maturity, retail sales should fluctuate pretty well in line with their relationships to disposable personal income, cash farm income for industries selling primarily to farmers, or other related variables.

Many industries, however, are either growing or declining relative to total economic activity so that it is necessary to study the trend of the particular industry. In the textile field, for example, cotton production has been growing at a rate somewhat slower than that of national income. Wool production was also growing at a slower rate until the middle of the 1930's, and then it started to grow at a rate faster than national income because of the development of improved lightweight woolen fabrics that were used in the manufacture of women's clothing and also because of the increased demands for woolen fabrics from the military. It has been declining again in recent years because of competition from synthetic fibers. The manufacture of synthetic yarns, on the other hand, has been growing much more rapidly than national income.

Growth rates for a group of products and services for the postwar period are given in Chart 16-2. Divergent rates of growth must be studied when forecasting trends in any industry or field.

The importance of factors which cannot be predicted when a long-term projection is made is well illustrated in the crude oil field. Crude oil was used at first primarily as a source of kerosene, and the trend of its production would undoubtedly have been downward but for the increased demand for gasoline because of the development of motor vehicles after the turn of the century. In more recent years in which motor vehicle production has been growing at a slower rate, crude oil production has continued sharply upward because of new uses in the manufacture of synthetic chemicals.

In projecting the long-term trend of an industry, the best procedure is to correlate sales with projected disposable personal income, cash farm income, or gross national product, whichever is most applicable, and also to study the growth of the industry in question considering all qualitative factors as well as its growth curve. On the basis of this information, a tentative estimate may be made of the long-term trend of the industry; but it must be kept in mind that this trend can be altered by changes in any of the factors that determine the trend. Continual study is necessary.

REGIONAL FACTORS

In developing the trend for a particular business, it is necessary to consider trends in the region and in the state or states in which the business is conducted. For national businesses such trends are also

Chart 16-2

Growth Rates of Some New and Established
Products in the Postwar Period

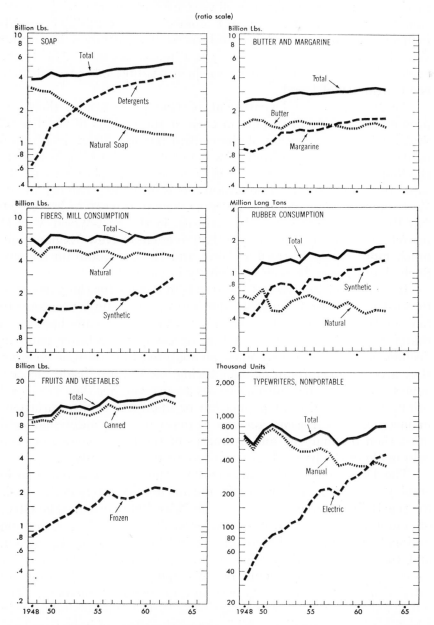

(ratio scale)

Source: Adapted from Frances L. Hirt, "Patterns of Output Growth," *Survey of Current Business* (September, 1964), pp. 21-28.

important in deciding on plant location in relationship to future
markets and labor supply, as well as sources of raw materials. From
time to time the Department of Commerce makes studies of trends
in income payments by regions and states. They compare income for
years in which economic activity was at about the same stage in the
cycle. They also divide longer periods into subperiods to see if there
is a continuity of trend.

According to the Department of Commerce study, there are
pronounced trends in income in each of the regions of the United
States with the exception of the central region. There has been a
relative shift in income from New England and the Middle East to
the South and West with the central region maintaining about the
same relative position. Population has grown more rapidly in the
West than in other sections. Average income per capita has grown
rapidly in the Southeast and Southwest in the post-World War II
period. It grew at a rate faster than average in New England and
much more slowly in the Far West and Rocky Mountain regions.
Such changes may be seen graphically in Chart 16-3.

In using such analyses of the trends in income for the purpose of
forecasting the trend of a particular business, it again is necessary to
look at the qualitative factors to see why these trends have been
taking place. This means that the sources of the relative gains or
declines in regional income must be analyzed to determine whether
they arose from shifts in manufacturing, agriculture, trade, service,
government, etc. It is also necessary to see whether they are based
primarily upon shifts in population or upon per capita variations
in income. The reasons for the changes in each individual field
must then be analyzed and estimates of the future course of each
field made in the light of future economic developments.

The Department of Commerce has studied growth patterns in
employment on a regional basis and on a county-by-county basis
for the 1940–1950 period and for the 1950–1960 period. The effect
on employment is shown in three ways — the effect based on
national growth, that based on the industrial mix of the region,
and that based on the region itself. The national growth effect
shows what the result would be on employment based on overall
rates of national economic growth in an expanding economy. The
industrial mix effect is the change due to the type of industry in
which a region specializes. This shows the effect of industries that
are growing faster or slower than total economic growth. For

Chart 16-3

Regional Trends in Population and Income, 1947–1957

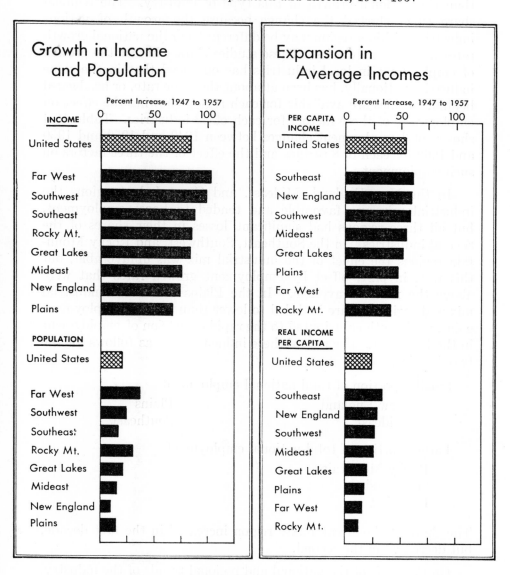

Source: U.S. Department of Commerce, *U.S. Income and Output, A Supplement to the Survey of Current Business* (Washington: U.S. Government Printing Office, 1958), pp. 27 and 28.

example, during 1950–1960 a region with a large electronics industry received a lift in employment because its growth rate was faster than the national growth in this type of industry. The regional share effect showed the change because the growth of various industries within a region may be different from the national growth rates for these industries. These studies show whether the growth of employment in local industries has outpaced that in the same industries nationally, has been at about the same rate, or has lagged behind. Tables are available for each region showing the effect on employment of these factors for each of 32 industries. Table 16-4 shows total employment changes between 1940 and 1950 and 1950 and 1960 for each of 8 regions and the effect of the three factors on such employment.

In the New England, Mideast, and Great Lakes regions the industrial mix was favorable and tended to boost employment, but all three regions had significant losses in their shares of the several industries. In the Southeast, Southwest, and Rocky Mountain regions the effect of the industrial mix was unfavorable; but this was, in part, offset by employment growth rates that were above the national average. In the Plains States the industrial mix and regional share both led to lower than average employment gains, while both contributed to the rapid expansion of employment in the Far West. The rest of these influences was as follows for the two decades:

Smaller portion of total national employment
　　　New England　　　　　　　　　Plains
　　　Mideast　　　　　　　　　　　　Southeast

Larger portion of total national employment
　　　Rocky Mountains
　　　Southwest
　　　Far West

The share of the Great Lakes region increased in the first decade, but decreased in the second.

On the basis of the national and regional trends of the industry, the future trend of sales in an individual business may be determined. The first step is to find the trend of sales of the business and to compare it with the industry trend. Since trends are different in

Table 16-4

Employment and Components of Employment Change, Regions, 1940–1950 and 1950–1960[1]
(Thousands of Employees)

	Employment			1940-50					1950-60				
				Changes related to[2]					Changes related to[2]				
	1940	1950	1960	National growth	Industrial mix	Regional share	Total change[3]	Net relative change[4]	National growth	Industrial mix	Regional share	Total change[3]	Net relative change[4]
	(A)	(B)	(C)	(D)	(E)	(F)	(G)	(H)	(I)	(J)	(K)	(L)	(M)
United States...	45,375.8	57,474.9	66,372.6	12,099.1	0.0	0.0	12,099.1	0.0	8,897.7	0.0	0.0	8,897.7	0.0
New England...	3,060.1	3,661.2	4,137.9	816.0	225.2	-440.1	601.0	-214.9	566.8	198.2	-288.2	476.8	-90.0
Mideast...	10,876.2	13,363.2	14,892.1	2,900.0	821.6	-1,234.6	2,487.0	-413.0	2,068.8	758.4	-1,298.3	1,528.9	-539.9
Great Lakes...	9,256.8	11,931.3	13,403.4	2,468.3	507.1	-300.8	2,674.5	206.3	1,847.1	277.1	-652.1	1,472.1	-375.0
Plains...	4,513.5	5,378.9	5,683.3	1,203.5	-316.6	-21.5	865.4	-338.1	832.7	-320.9	-207.4	304.4	-528.3
Southeast...	9,878.3	11,913.4	13,414.1	2,634.0	-1,299.7	700.8	2,035.1	-598.9	1,844.3	-1,062.4	718.8	1,500.7	-343.6
Southwest...	3,087.5	4,091.5	5,065.6	823.3	-220.7	401.4	1,003.9	180.7	633.4	-100.8	431.5	964.1	330.7
Rocky Mountain...	929.4	1,264.1	1,558.3	247.8	-33.1	120.0	334.7	86.9	195.7	-64.6	163.1	294.2	98.5
Far West...	3,773.9	5,871.3	8,227.9	1,006.3	316.2	774.9	2,097.4	1,091.1	908.9	315.0	1,132.6	2,356.6	1,447.6

[1]Derivation of each component is explained in the text. Detail will not add to totals because of rounding.
[2]Components are the result of summation across analytical results for each of 32 industrial categories. Data are from the U.S. Census of Population.
[3]Sum of Components D, E, and F for 1940–50 and J, K, and L for 1950–60.
[4]Sum of Columns E and F for 1940–50 and K and L for 1950–60.

Source: *Survey of Current Business* (February, 1966), p. 10.

different regions of the United States, the trend of sales of the business should be compared to industry sales on a region-by-region basis. The next step is to explain any differences in rates of company and industry growth. Little sales effort may have been put into some regions, or high transportation costs may have cut down sales. On the bases of industry trends, of past relationships to industry trends, and of future sales policies, it is possible to build up projected sales for the company in each region and in total.

QUESTIONS

1. On what assumption is a projection of the trend in economic activity based?
2. Outline the steps involved in projecting gross national product by (a) projecting the line of least squares, (b) extending past average rates of growth, (c) estimating the number of employed workers and the output per worker.
3. What problems are involved in projecting the size of the labor force?
4. How are trends in output per hour of employment determined?
5. Why is projection of GNP made by estimating the labor force and output per worker likely to give somewhat higher results than projecting the trend of GNP?
6. Outline several procedures for making more refined estimates of future levels of GNP.
7. Describe the National Planning Association procedure for projecting GNP.
8. Outline the procedure for developing estimates of disposable personal income from estimates of GNP.
9. Describe a procedure for estimating consumer expenditures in total and for major categories of expenditures from estimates of disposable personal income.
10. How do varying regional growth trends affect long-run business decisions?
11. How have population, total income, and per capita income by regions shifted since 1947?
12. Summarize regional changes in employment in the 1940–1950 and 1950–1960 decades. Account for such changes.
13. Outline a procedure for projecting sales on a regional basis.

See page 446 for Suggested Readings for Chapter 16.

CHAPTER 17 · Short-Run Forecasting of General Business Activity

Since forecasting is still much more of an art than a science, it is to be expected that economists will use varying approaches in making forecasts. This is especially true in making short-run forecasts of general economic activity. Most forecasters also use several approaches to forecasting since none of them is completely accurate at this stage of development. This approach is especially useful when economic activity is believed to be near an upper or lower turning point. The major approaches to short-run forecasting of overall economic activity will be considered in this chapter.

FAVORABLE AND UNFAVORABLE FACTORS

A simple, but valuable, approach to forecasting is to list all of the favorable and unfavorable factors in the current situation. Favorable factors are those whose effect is likely to keep the level of overall economic activity expanding, while unfavorable factors are those that have a tendency to cause a slowing down or decline in economic activity. This procedure is worthwhile only if the current situation is carefully analyzed. The analyst must also understand the factors that are likely to lead to further expansion or to contraction. For example, a list of favorable and unfavorable factors made in the summer of 1966 might have contained the following items:

FAVORABLE
1. Demand for goods arising out of the Vietnam War.
2. Plans for increased capital expenditures.
3. Inventories in reasonable balance with sales.
4. Low rate of unemployment.
5. Labor costs per unit of output remaining about stable.
6. Increasing consumer purchases.
7. Increasing state and local government purchases.
8. Moderate rise in family formation.
9. Short-run improvement in the balance of payments.

UNFAVORABLE
1. Restrictive monetary policy.
2. High interest rates.
3. Rising costs.
4. Rising prices and threat of further inflation.
5. Decline in home building.
6. Possible saturation of automobile demand.
7. Labor troubles.
8. Continuing balance of payments problem.
9. Stock market decline.

This method is valuable because it requires a thorough analysis of the current situation. When all factors are listed, judgment is used to decide what the impact of all of these factors in combination will be on the economy. This is especially difficult after economic activity has expanded for a time and unfavorable factors develop in greater number.

One of the important factors to consider in such analyses, especially in judging the severity of an impending recession, is the state of the building cycle. Recessions in business activity that have occurred when the building cycle was on the upswing have seldom led to deep or protracted depressions. When building is in a downward phase of the building cycle, however, depressions are usually of some severity.

Major depressions have usually occurred when major new industries, especially those related to the transportation field, have reached a point where their rate of growth has slowed down materially. This was true in 1929 when the automobile industry reached such a stage in its development. It was true for the railroad field in such major depressions as 1873 and 1893 and for the canal building field in 1837. It should be kept in mind that major developments in transportation have not only led to increased demand for capital goods in this field and in related fields, but have changed past living patterns and have thus stimulated investment to an even greater degree. Therefore, a study of the trend of major new industries should form a part of the process of forecasting cyclical change.

CONSENSUS OF OBSERVERS

In an area as important as forecasting is to many businesses and governmental units, and as subject as it is to error, it is natural to want to get the opinion of other analysts who have studied the economic outlook. Therefore, getting the consensus of qualified observers is part of the program of almost every forecaster. For some, it is the major approach to forecasting.

Several sources of such opinions are available. At the turn of the year financial papers and journals, as well as the financial sections of many daily newspapers, publish the opinions on the outlook of leaders in government, industry, and education. The National Industrial Conference Board has a discussion meeting on the outlook attended by prominent economists engaged in forecasting, and publishes the proceedings in a pamphlet called the *Business Outlook*. The First National Bank of Chicago publishes the opinion on the outlook for their industry by leaders in many fields every six months. Several such forecasts are described in Chapter 20, which covers the services offered by several organizations in the forecasting field.

As long as forecasting is subject to considerable error, it is possible for many experts to be wrong at the same time. Their reactions to the situation in their fields are, however, valuable background in developing a forecast by any method or combination of methods.

LEADING AND LAGGING SERIES

Economists have searched for years for a series that would give a signal of changes in economic activity by turning upward and downward before the overall economy turned. No single series has had such a relationship on a regular basis. Several series usually lead at turning points, however, and others usually lag. An analysis of a group of such series has been used to get an indication of the direction of economic activity.

The most complete studies of cyclical leads and lags have been made by the National Bureau of Economic Research. Geoffrey H. Moore and Julius Shiskin have chosen 88 indicators out of the large number of series studied by the National Bureau of Economic Research, 36 of which they have placed in a leading group, 25 in a roughly coincident group, 11 in the lagging group, and 16 in a group unclassified as to timing. These series cover a wide range of economic processes representing all sectors of the economy. Table 17-1 on page 430 shows the various economic processes represented by the economic indicators and the median lead or lag of the series in each process group.

Table 17-1

Economic Processes Represented in Leading, Coincident, and Lagging
Economic Indicators

Economic Process and Number of Series in Group	Median Lead (−) or Lag (+) in Months[a]
Leading Indicators	
Marginal employment adjustments (5)	−5
Formation of business enterprises (2)	−6
New investment commitments (8)	−6
Inventory investment and purchasing (7)	−6
Sensitive commodity price indexes (1)	−2
Stock price indexes (1)	−4
Profits and profit margins (4)	−5
Flows of money and credit (6)	−9
Credit difficulties (2)	−5
Roughly Coincident Indicators	
Job vacancies (2)	0
Comprehensive employment series (3)	−1
Comprehensive unemployment series (3)	0
Comprehensive production series (3)	0
Comprehensive income series (2)	0
Comprehensive consumption and trade series (3)	0
Backlog of investment commitments (2)	0
Comprehensive wholesale price indexes (2)	0
Money market interest rates (4)	0
Bank reserves (1)	−1
Lagging Indicators	
Long duration unemployment (1)	+2
Investment expenditures (2)	+2
Inventories (2)	+4
Unit labor costs (2)	+8
Outstanding debt (2)	+3
Interest rates on business loans and mortgages (2)	+4

a. Median for the group is the median of the medians for the individual
series.

Source: Adapted from Goeffrey H. Moore and Julius Shiskin, *Indicators of
Business Expansions and Contractions*, National Bureau of Economic
Research, Inc. (New York, 1967), pp. 44, 45.

Of the 88 indicators a series of 25 has been selected as a short list
of some of the most consistent indicators which involve little duplication of economic processes. This short list contains 12 leading, 7
coincident and 6 lagging series. The series included in this list and
this median lead or lag are presented in Table 17-2.

Table 17-2

Short List of Economic Indicators

Classification and Series Title	First Business Cycle Turn Covered	Median Lead (−) or Lag (+) in Months
Leading indicators (12 series)		
Average workweek, production workers, manufacturing	1921	−5
Nonagricultural placements, BES	1945	−3
Index of net business formation	1945	−7
New orders, durable goods industries	1920	−4
Contracts and orders, plant and equipment	1948	−6
New building permits, private housing units	1918	−6
Change in book value, manufacturing and trade inventories	1945	−8
Industrial materials prices	1919	−2
Stock prices, 500 common stocks	1873	−4
Corporate profits after taxes, Q*	1920	−2
Ratio, price to unit labor cost, mfg.	1919	−3
Change in consumer installment debt	1929	−10
Roughly coincident indicators (7 series)		
Employees in nonagricultural establishments	1929	0
Unemployment rate, total (inv.)†	1929	0
GNP in constant dollars, expenditure estimate, Q	1921	−2
Industrial production	1919	0
Personal income	1921	−1
Manufacturing and trade sales	1948	0
Sales of retail stores	1919	0
Lagging indicators (6 series)		
Unemployment rate, persons unemployed 15 + weeks (inv.)	1948	+2
Business expenditures, plant and equipment, Q	1918	+1
Book value, manufacturing and trade inventories	1945	+2
Labor cost per unit of output, mfg.	1919	+8
Commercial and industrial loans outstanding	1937	+2
Bank rates, short-term business loans, Q	1919	+5

*Quarterly series.
†Inverted.
Source: Adapted from Goeffrey H. Moore and Julius Shiskin, *Indicators of Business Expansions and Contractions*, National Bureau of Economic Research, Inc. (New York, 1967), p. 68.

This latest group of series was developed because earlier groups of series established a good record for forecasting changes in the direction of economic activity. Fourteen of the series in the short list were on the 1960 list, and six series on the new list are closely related to series on the earlier list. A still earlier group had 21 series of which 15 were still on the 1960 group.

It is interesting to examine the behavior of these series in the immediate postwar period. All of the series in the leading group were contracting by the middle of 1948. In the prewar peak in 1936–1937 the peaks in these leading series came within a short space of time, but in the postwar period they were scattered over several years as such series as business failures and stock prices began to decline early in 1946. The roughly coincident series rose during 1946 and 1947 and reached their peak in 1948 with the exception of freight carloadings, which reached a peak in December, 1947. The lagging group reached peaks in 1948–1949. The pattern, therefore, had been maintained.

Since the recession in business in 1948 was mild, took place in different fields at different times, and did not affect to any degree two major groups, namely residential building and automobile production, the series acted as would be expected in such a situation.

The leading series forecast the 1953 recession, although somewhat less clearly than the 1949 recession. Wholesale prices turned down and business failures up about two and one-half years before the recession began. New durable goods orders and commercial construction were higher in mid-1953 than in the fall of 1951, but were well below their peaks in early 1951. Residential construction declined in 1951, recovered in 1952, and then declined again in the first half of 1953. The average hours worked per week dropped sharply and stock prices fell somewhat before the downturn. New incorporations had only a slight drop, and this change did not come until the economy turned down. The picture of the leading series in the 1953 downturn was not as clear as it might have been because an adjustment took place in 1952 to lower levels of defense expenditures as the Korean War was stabilized and brought to a halt.

The upturn was also foretold by the leading series since, by the second quarter of 1954, four were expanding. The same was true of the 1957 downturn. By the end of 1956 five of the eight leading series had turned down. They also foreshadowed the upturn in 1958 and the downturn in 1960, and the upturn in 1961. They gave a false signal of a recession, however, in 1962 that turned out to be only a period of retardation in the forward advance of economic activity.

A series of diffusion indexes has also been developed for several leading and coincident series as follows:

LEADING INDICATORS

Average workweek, production workers, manufacturing
New orders, durable goods industries
Newly approved capital appropriations
Profits, First National City Bank of New York, percent reporting higher profits
Stock prices, 500 common stocks
Industrial materials prices
Initial claims, state unemployment insurance

COINCIDENT INDICATORS

Employees in nonagricultural establishments
Industrial production
Wholesale prices
Sales of retail stores

Their turning points tend to lead the turning points of the aggregate of the items in the series on which they are based. Widespread increases in the components of a series are often associated with a period of rapid growth and widespread declines with a sharp reduction in activity.

Diffusion indexes based on the National Bureau series behaved perfectly in postwar cycles. The diffusion index of leaders passed 50 percent on the way up before each peak and on the way down before each trough. The diffusion index of coincident series passed 50 at peaks and troughs and that of lagging series after the trough. They also, however, gave a false indication of a recession in 1962 just as the leading series themselves did.

The leading series and diffusion indexes have indicated every turn in general economic activity. They have also turned for a short period when no turn occurred, however, so they cannot be used alone as a forecasting device or without judgment. They also do not tell the exact timing of turning points or the intensity of changes in economic activity. They are, nevertheless, valuable as one tool in a forecaster's kit.

Data on all of these series and on many more are available currently in *Business Cycle Developments*, a monthly publication of the United States Department of Commerce. One of the major advantages of this publication is the speed with which the data are made available since publication is scheduled for around the twenty-second of the month following the month of the data.

RELATIONSHIP OF NEW ORDERS, INVENTORIES, SALES, AND PRODUCTION

Another method or group of methods for short-run forecasting involves a study of the relationships between sales and inventories and sales and new orders, and, in turn, the effect of changes in such relationships to changes in production. The ratio of inventory to sales for the manufacturing field as a whole and for major sectors of it, such as durable goods manufacturing, often gives an indication of turning points in production. During the upswing of a cycle, inventories are first reduced as sales go up faster than expected. They are then increased to bring them back into line with sales. Inventories have in the past been increased too much, and this has led to a downturn. As sales have declined, inventories have become even greater in relationship to sales until substantial inventory liquidation has occurred.

Such changes in the 1956–1958 period of the downturn and the recovery may be studied from Chart 17-1. Inventories of durables, for example, increased faster than sales in the first half of 1956 and especially in early 1957. This led to a decrease in production at midyear as the economy went into a recession, especially in durable goods production. During the second half of 1957 and the first quarter of 1958, inventory-sales ratios went up involuntarily as inventories were not reduced as rapidly as sales. This led to a decrease in production of a greater magnitude than the decrease in sales in real terms. As sales increased, inventory-sales ratios dropped rapidly during the second and third quarters of 1958 and more slowly into 1959. This led to increases in production to meet the increased sales, as well as demand for goods to rebuild inventory levels. The pattern in 1959 was obscured by the effects of the steel negotiation deadlock and steel strike. The normal pattern is one of relative stability for a short period and then a new increase of inventories in relationship to sales. Inventories went up again in relationship to sales before and during the 1960–1961 recession, especially inventories of durable goods. This ratio also went up in the 1967 slowdown, but not to the levels reached in 1960–1961 or 1957–1958.

Chart 17-1

Manufacturers' Inventories and Sales

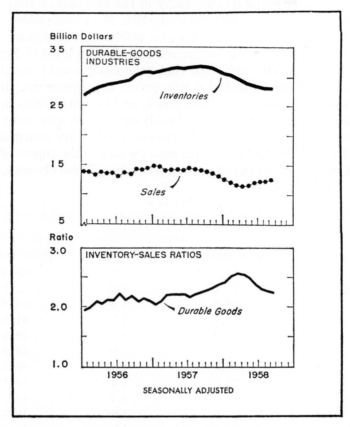

Source: *Survey of Current Business* (November, 1958), p. 4.

By studying such relationships of inventories to sales it is possible to predict turning points in production. Since the leads are not uniform and the ratios give some false signals judgment is still required to pinpoint changes.

An analysis of new orders and of new orders in relationship to sales and production can also be used as an indication of turning points. For example, the turning point in new orders during a recovery period is preceded by a period of a slowing down in the rate of decrease in new orders. When new orders turn up, the turning point in production is usually only several months away.

Such relationships may be observed in the 1958 recovery period. New orders in manufacturing declined slowly in January and February of 1958 after going down rapidly in the last half of 1957. Sales were decreasing more rapidly in early 1958 than new orders. While new orders went up, inventories and production continued to decrease. In March new orders increased over the level of February and of January. This indicated that production would shortly stop decreasing and start upward if new orders kept going up. In May production was somewhat above April, and in June it was substantially above May levels. After midyear, inventories were about stabilized, and as new orders increased, production continued upward. In 1959 the building of inventories due to the threat of labor difficulties in steel obscured normal patterns. These changes can be seen in Table 17-3.

Table 17-3
New Orders, Production, and Inventories in Manufacturing
January, 1958–June, 1959

1958	NEW ORDERS*	PRODUCTION†	INVENTORIES‡
January	24.4	135	52.9
February	24.1	131	52.4
March	24.8	129	52.0
April	24.5	128	51.5
May	25.0	130	50.9
June	25.8	134	50.2
July	26.5	136	49.8
August	26.1	138	49.4
September	27.0	139	49.3
October	27.9	140	49.3
November	27.8	143	49.3
December	28.4	144	49.2
1959			
January	28.5	145	49.5
February	29.7	148	49.9
March	30.2	150	50.5
April	31.2	153	51.0
May	30.5	156	51.6
June	31.4	158	52.1

*Department of Commerce Series, seasonally adjusted, in billions of dollars.
†Federal Reserve Index, seasonally adjusted, 1947–1949 = 100.
‡Department of Commerce Series, seasonally adjusted, in billions of dollars.
Source: *Survey of Current Business* and *Federal Reserve Bulletin.*

These series were also useful in predicting increased business in the second half of 1961 as the economy recovered from the 1960–1961 recession. By June new orders had advanced 9 percent from January levels, while production was up only about 7 percent. New orders for durable goods were up over 15 percent, whereas production was up less than 11 percent. Since inventories were at low levels, the new orders could not be filled out of stock and, as a result, production had to be increased further to meet demand.

Forecasting of production for one to two quarters in the future is done by some forecasters by studying patterns of new orders, unfilled orders, inventories, sales, and production in the major sectors of durable and nondurable goods production. From past relationships and typical time intervals between new orders, production, sales, and inventory levels, it is possible to forecast what production is likely to be in the future. This cannot be done purely mechanically because relationships change and factors, such as a threatened strike, alter business decisions on inventories and production.

SERIES ON EXPECTATIONS AND EXPENDITURE PLANS

Another approach to forecasting is to try to develop data on future expectations of business conditions by businessmen whose decisions determine the economic outlook. This approach has been expanded to include expectations and expenditure plans for most of the major spending sectors of the economy. Information on the expectations of major executives who make business decisions is published by *Dun's Review* in its quarterly survey of *Businessmen's Expectations*. It is based on interviews with a sample of over 1,500 businessmen regarding their expectations for their respective businesses. They are asked if they believe there will be an increase, a decrease, or no change in net sales, net profits, selling prices, the level of inventories, and the number of employees, compared with the same quarter a year ago. Data are presented for all concerns and also separately for manufacturers, wholesalers, and retailers.

The National Association of Purchasing Agents obtains the reaction of some of its members to business conditions through a monthly survey of a committee selected so as to reflect both regional and industrial diversification. These members are asked to indicate whether production, new orders, commodity prices, inventories of purchased raw materials and purchased finished materials, employment, and their level of buying were higher than a month ago, lower, or the same. The questionnaire also asks for specific commodity price changes and the reasons for them, for items that are in short supply, for business changes in the member's area, and for general business factors that may affect purchasing policies. A summary and an analysis of the answers of the purchasing agents in the Survey Committee are published in the Bulletin of the Association.

These surveys have been valuable gauges of changes in business conditions during the month since the results have been accurate and are available within two weeks or less after the questionnaires are filled out. In the period since 1947, during which the surveys were made on the present basis, they forecast the 1948, the 1953, the 1957, and 1960 downturns several months in advance, but were not always accurate on the magnitude of changes in business.

A major problem with this series and that of expectations of executives by *Dun's Review* is that they show changes in sentiment from time to time when general business conditions do not experience a turning point. They give signals of changes when overall activity changes, but they also give false signals and can, therefore, not be used alone to predict changes in the economy. They are, however, valuable as one in a series of methods used by the forecaster because they provide a check on forecasts obtained by other methods.

Another way to use data on expectations is to get information on expenditure plans by major spending sectors in the economy. These are available for many of the major categories of expenditures into which gross national product is divided. Surveys of consumer buying plans were begun in 1946 by the Survey Research Center of the University of Michigan. They interview a sample of about 2,000 families during January and February and conduct supplemental surveys at other times. They gather information on consumer intentions to buy durable goods including automobiles, furniture and appliances, and also new houses. The National Industrial Conference Board conducts a monthly survey and publishes it in the *Conference Board Record*. The Census Bureau conducts quarterly surveys on the percentage of families planning to buy new or used automobiles, new or existing houses, and new or used household equipment. In the fall of 1967 the Commercial Credit Company began publishing the results of these surveys and also its forecasts for the next six months of consumer demand in these fields in units and in dollars. These consumer surveys have been generally accurate in predicting changes in expenditures, that is, downturns and upturns. They have not, however, been accurate on a regular basis in predicting the magnitude of the changes in purchases of durable goods. There are no data on plans for expenditures on nondurable goods and services, but these do not change much in the short run.

Data on plans for spending by the federal government are available in the budget, which is presented by the President almost six months before the beginning of the new fiscal year. This is generally a good guide to the direction of change in expenditures, if any, but it cannot be used without analysis and revision as an estimate of the amount of change. To date no series exists on the expenditure plans of state and local governments. The same is true of exports and imports; but the net figure, which is all that is included in gross national product, is usually so small that it makes little difference in the general direction of economic activity.

Series on expenditure plans exist for most components of gross private domestic investment. The Department of Commerce and Securities and Exchange Commission jointly survey plans of businessmen for expenditures on plant and equipment. The McGraw-Hill Publishing Company also makes such surveys. They have been accurate in predicting turning points in expenditures. These series and their quantitative record are discussed in some detail in Chapter 18. Series on building permits can be used to show future changes in the volume of new building. Changes in plans for the level of inventories can be obtained from surveys by the National Association of Purchasing Agents and also the United States Department of Commerce.

Thus there are series on expenditure plans on every major sector of spending, except state and local government expenditures and consumer expenditures on nondurables and services, and these have not changed direction abruptly in the past. A study of all of these series can be used to judge the direction of business. When all these expenditures are moving in the same direction, as they are in the early stages of recovery, this procedure is relatively easy and effective. Later in prosperity, some expenditures may show increases and some a leveling off or decreases; and then it is difficult, if not impossible, to judge future business from changes in direction of spending alone. This requires estimates of the magnitude of changes that is done in model building. Chapter 18 presents a technique for building a model of GNP by the expenditure approach.

MONETARY FACTORS

After the Federal Reserve data on money flows are available for a period of time, it may be possible to develop a forecast of the level of business activity for several quarters in the future from an analysis of changes in money flows. If this can be done, it will add another approach to the forecaster's kit, which should prove valuable as a cross-check on forecasts made by other methods. At present, monetary factors can be used to give some indication of changes in business conditions.

Changes in the money supply have in the past led to changes in business activity. This is true whether the money supply is defined as demand deposits plus currency adjusted for seasonal variation, or in the broader concept to include time deposits. A six months' moving average of the money supply plotted in the sixth month has led all business declines since 1909 by an average of 19.9 months. Since the middle of the 1920's, the lead has varied from 20 to 29 months if the World War II period and the 1945 downturn due to the transition from war to peacetime activities are excluded. Recoveries have also been preceded by an increase in the money supply. The six months' moving average led general business consistently since 1909, the average lead being 8.6 months.[1] The lead in the 1949, 1953–1954, and 1960–1961 recessions was 8 months, but in the 1957–1958 recession it was only 3 months. This series helps give the forecaster an indication of turning points in economic activity, but analysis and judgment are still required to predict their timing and the magnitude of changes in economic activity.

Bank debits outside of New York City have been used at times as a measure of the total amount of trade spending in the United States, and bank debits in New York City as a measure of financial spending. Since these series are available a short time after the transactions have taken place, they are used by some people as a forecast because they show what is occurring in the economy before it has become general knowledge.

There is usually a high degree of correlation between bank debits of all commercial banks, excluding those in New York City, and

---

[1]Beryl W. Sprinkel, "Monetary Growth as a Cyclical Predictor," *Journal of Finance* (September, 1959), pp. 333–346.

gross national product. During periods of intense speculation, such as that occurring before 1929, financial transactions assume a larger than usual role in banks outside of New York City. As a result bank debits were higher than past relationships would indicate they should have been in 1928 and 1929. During World War II debits were lower because the large sales of goods to the government eliminated many intermediate transactions usually involved when goods are sold to private consumers. Since changes due to such factors cannot be measured currently, complete reliance cannot be placed on estimates of current levels of gross national product derived from bank debit figures. Thus the most that can be done at the present time by a study of monetary factors is to obtain an indication of the direction of change of business activity.

CYCLES AND TRENDS

Some attempt has been made to forecast economic activity by projecting the trend and cycle. If a regular cycle with uniform duration and amplitude existed, this would be the only procedure needed for accurate forecasting. Since such a cycle does not exist, however, this procedure cannot be used with any degree of assurance of success. Some analysts have at times tried to develop a cyclical pattern in GNP or industrial production by developing a multiple correlation relationship with a series of factors that they consider to be most significant in determining the course of the cycle, such as prices, interest rates, and unit labor costs. Such techniques must be viewed with scepticism since it is possible to recreate the movement of a series, such as GNP or industrial production, with formulas which relate the past behavior of the variable to the future behavior of that same variable. The correlation method is called *auto-correlation*, and the technique based on it is called *autoregressive forecasting*.

Some forecasters have used cycles and trends to develop a general picture of the pattern of economic development for five or ten years in the future. This may be done, for example, by using a future cycle pattern based on the average duration and amplitude of postwar cycles. Such a pattern is easy to develop and can serve a useful purpose in business planning and in assessing the possible effects of cycles on plans, but it cannot be used to make forecasts. The outstanding characteristic of cycles is their variability.

ECONOMETRIC MODELS

The development of economic models was discussed in Chapters 7, 8, and 9 as part of the theory of national income determination. Such models have been used with increasing success as a basis for forecasting gross national product and its major components. The Research Seminar on Quantitative Economics at the University of Michigan has been making forecasts for some time with the Klein-Goldberger model based on 32 equations. This model has been revised and improved on a regular basis since it was first used to make forecasts in 1953. The results have been good in most years so far as total GNP is concerned, but not as good on individual components. This model did forecast the 1954, 1957–1958 and 1960–1961 recessions.[2]

An analysis of the forecasts of econometric models for the postwar period made under the sponsorship of the National Bureau of Economic Research concluded that they have not been able to forecast the levels of aggregate economic activity as well as some forecasts based on more general methods. The errors have resulted primarily from the forecasts of price movements that have often been wide of the mark. The forecasts of changes in economic activity, which exclude price movements, have been about as accurate as the better forecasts made by other methods.[3]

The Department of Commerce has begun research and experimentation with a quarterly economic model of GNP that is based on a variant of the model developed by Professor Lawrence Klein. This model is based on 49 equations including identities. There are equations for each of the major components of GNP, and on factors such as prices, the labor force, income to the factors of production, monetary factors, new orders, and depreciation. This model has been developed for the period from 1953 on and used on an *ex post* basis to make forecasts for each year. In 9 of the 13 years the error in total GNP was $3 billion or less, and the average error was $2.9 billion. Errors in the components were larger than in GNP, as is generally true of all forecasts. In 5 out of 6 cases turning points were forecast within one quarter plus or minus the actual turning points. The equations developed from the 1953–1964

[2]Daniel B. Suits, *"Forecasting and Analysis with an Econometric Model,"* American Economic Review (March, 1962), pp. 104–132.

[3]*Forty-Fifth Annual Report* (New York: National Bureau of Economic Research, 1965), p. 60.

period were used to forecast GNP in 1965 and the error was less than 8 percent of the change in GNP from 1964, despite the increased activity resulting from the intensification of the Vietnam War. The result was not as good for GNP in 1958 dollars since this model also had difficulties in predicting price changes,[4] predicting greater increases in prices than actually occurred in 1965. A model cannot be evaluated on the basis of *ex post* forecasts, and one year is too short a period for any evaluation. The Department of Commerce plans to continue work on this model and report on its record from time to time.

A more limited approach also has proved of value. Equations are developed using demand and supply factors in various major spending sectors of the economy to explain variations in sales. Such equations are then used to develop estimates of future spending. The values of the factors in these equations must still be predicted. Total spending for the economy can then be developed by adding up spending in the various sectors. Some examples of the use of such series to forecast the demand for producers' durable equipment and consumer durable goods will be presented in the next chapter.

JUDGMENT MODELS

At this stage of knowledge of the economy it is impossible to use an econometric model to develop a completely accurate forecast. Therefore, models are also built that use the judgment of the forecaster to determine the most likely figure for each sector in the model. Such models have been developed primarily for gross national product and for industrial production. A gross national product model is generally developed by the expenditure approach. All available data are gathered on each major sector of GNP, including expenditure plans, analysis of supply and demand factors using formulas based on past experience, monetary factors, and leading series. A preliminary figure is developed for each spending sector based on the best judgment of the forecaster. These figures are then checked for consistency based on past relationships among them and revised if need be. A step-by-step approach to such model building to forecast GNP by the expenditure approach is presented in the next chapter.

---

[4]Maurice Liebenberg, Albert A. Hirsch, and Joel Popkin, "A Quarterly Econometric Model of the United States: A Progress Report," *Survey of Current Business* (May, 1966), pp. 13–41.

At times a judgment model of GNP is developed from the income or money flow receipts approach. This involves many more estimates and is a more complex procedure. It adds several valuable items of information, however. For one thing it provides forecasts of income payments for wages, interest, rent, and profits. These are needed by the Treasury Department when it forecasts budget receipts for the year since the major sources of revenue of the federal government are personal and corporate income taxes. A judgment model of GNP developed from this approach is also helpful as a cross-check on a model developed from the expenditure approach.

Models are also developed using the Federal Reserve Board Index of Industrial Production. The divisions of the index itself can be used to build up a model. They are at times reclassified into groups that have similar factors affecting them. One such classification uses the following groups:

Consumer perishable goods	Capital goods
Consumer semidurable goods	Fuels
Consumer durable goods	Materials and supplies
Construction materials	

A judgment figure is developed for each sector using techniques similar to those used to build up a model of GNP by the expenditure approach. When adequate productive capacity exists, the major emphasis is put on demand factors.

An alternative approach, which is often used at the same time as an analysis of changing demand factors, is a study of new orders and production in each sector of the economy into which the model is divided. Time lags that occur between changes in new orders and production are studied for a period covering several of the most recent cycles. In some cases it is easier to get data on new orders and on sales or expenditures rather than on production. Time lags between production and sales must then be determined in each sector of production into which the model is divided. Then changes in new orders can be used to predict changes in production based on past relationships. A study must continually be made of any tendency for past relationships to change.

Chart 17-2 shows such a relationship between capital expenditures and new orders in the machinery industry.

Chart 17-2
Capital Expenditures and Machinery Orders
1953–1959

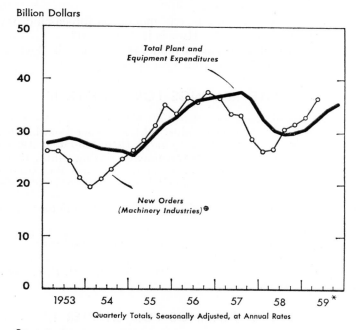

Billion Dollars

*Total Plant and
Equipment Expenditures*

*New Orders
(Machinery Industries)* ⊕

Quarterly Totals, Seasonally Adjusted, at Annual Rates

⊕ *Excludes farm, household, and electronics industries*
＊ *3rd und 4th quurters anticipated*

Source: *Survey of Current Business* (September, 1959), p. 6.

QUESTIONS

1. Describe and evaluate the use of a listing of favorable and unfavorable factors as a method of forecasting.
2. How may the concensus of qualified observors be used in forecasting?
3. Describe the use that can be made of leads and lags in forecasting.
4. Evaluate the record of the National Bureau's statistical indicators in the post-World War II period.
5. What is a diffusion index? How may it be used in forecasting?
6. How are new orders, inventory, production, and sales series used in forecasting?
7. How may expectations about future business conditions be used in forecasting?
8. Describe and evaluate the use of series on spending plans as a method of forecasting.

9. Discuss the use of monetary factors as a means of forecasting income.
10. Of what value is a projection of cycles and trends in forecasting and in business planning generally?
11. What is the record of econometric models as forecasting devices?
12. What is a judgment model? How is it developed?
13. Describe the use of a judgment model to forecast the Federal Reserve Board Index of Industrial Production.

SUGGESTED READINGS FOR CHAPTER 16

The Conference Board. *Economic Potentials of the United States in the Next Decade.* New York: National Industrial Conference Board, 1965.

Growth Patterns in Employment by County, 1940–1950 and 1950–1960. Vols. 1–8. Washington: U. S. Government Printing Office, 1966.

Long-Range Economic Projection, Studies in Income and Wealth, Volume 16. Princeton, New Jersey: National Bureau of Economic Research, 1954, Part I.

National Economic Projections 1962–1965, 1970. Washington: National Planning Association, 1959.

United States Department of Commerce. *Personal Income by States since 1929.* Washington: U. S. Government Printing Office, 1957.

United States Department of Commerce. Bureau of the Census. *Long-Term Economic Growth 1860–1965.* Washington: U. S. Government Printing Office, 1966.

SUGGESTED READINGS FOR CHAPTER 17

Business Cycle Developments, U. S. Department of Commerce, monthly.

Business Outlook, National Industrial Conference Board, annually.

Garvy, George. *Debits and Clearing Statistics, Their Background and Interpretation.* Washington: Board of Governors of the Federal Reserve System, 1959.

Liebenberg, Maurice, Albert A. Hirsch, and Joel Popkin. "A Quarterly Econometric Model of the United States: A Progress Report," *Survey of Current Business*, May, 1966, pp. 13–41.

Moore, Goeffrey H. and Julius Shiskin. *Indicators of Business Expansions and Contractions.* New York: National Bureau of Economic Research, 1950.

Platt, Henry M. *Economic Indicators*, Hanover: The Amos Tuck School of Business Administration, 1959.

"What Businessmen Expect," Quarterly in *Dun's Review*.

Also see the "Business Roundup" section of *Fortune* and the "Business Situation" section of the *Survey of Current Business* for current analyses of inventories, sales, and new orders.

Short-Run Forecasting of GNP by Building an Expenditure Model

This chapter will consider the procedures involved in forecasting gross national product by building up for the next year estimates of government purchases of goods and services, gross private domestic investment, net exports of goods and services, and personal consumption expenditures. The factors involved in building up estimates of each of these categories will be considered first, and then procedures for developing a consistent overall forecast from such sector expenditure forecasts will be described. A general overview of this method of model building was presented in Chapter 17.

In making forecasts of gross national product, it is necessary to keep in mind the major factors that cause shifts in economic activity. Money flows through the economy in a circular fashion since expenditures of one group are income for another. Changes in economic activity occur because individuals, businesses, private institutions, and governmental units change the amount of their spending or change the relationship of such spending to the amount of income received. Changes may also occur because the spending units decide to spend their income in a pattern different from that in which goods are being produced and, as a result, demand exceeds supply in some fields and is less than supply in others. Since labor and capital are not completely mobile, these changes lead to shifts in the level of economic activity.

The circular flow of economic activity may appear to create a problem in forecasting since there is no clear-cut starting or stopping point. However, since time elapses between various economic activities, such as an increase in production due to an increase in sales, the receipt by consumers of income from such production and the resultant further increase in sales, it is possible to break into the process at any point and to determine what is likely to happen during a future period of time. As long as the proper time relationships between the variables are considered, it makes little difference at what point in the economic cycle forecasting is begun.

The most commonly used procedure is to build up forecasts of gross national product for a year ahead by estimating expenditures by consumers, businesses, government, and foreigners. Such forecasts must include factors due to the trend and the business cycle. Seasonal variations do not affect the annual forecasts, and quarterly forecasts are usually made at seasonally adjusted annual rates. Therefore, the effect of the seasonal variations can be ignored in a GNP forecast.

The factors involved in estimating levels for the next year of government purchases of goods and services will be analyzed first because they are, in part at least, based on decisions that are not related to the circular flow of economic activity. The level of these items, nevertheless, affects general business activity materially. The factors involved in forecasting gross private domestic investment will be considered next. This is a highly fluctuating variable that plays a large part in determining the level of economic activity. Next attention will be directed to forecasting net exports of goods and services. Forecasts of consumer expenditures will be considered last since they are greatly influenced by the level of investment expenditures and government purchases of goods and services.

GOVERNMENT PURCHASES OF GOODS AND SERVICES

Government purchases of goods and services have fluctuated widely especially since 1929. However, since they are to a large extent not dependent upon the general level of business activity and since the democratic process requires a great deal of time, especially when money is being appropriated, it is possible to forecast government expenditures with a reasonable degree of accuracy for a year ahead. Attention will first be directed to federal expenditures and then to state and local government expenditures.

Federal Government Purchases of Goods and Services

The level of governmental purchases of goods and services can be forecast by analyzing the budget of the federal government and political and international factors in the current and future situation. The government of the United States uses a fiscal year that runs from July 1 to June 30. The fiscal year is designated by the number of the calendar year in which it ends; thus, fiscal 1968 ran from July 1, 1967, to June 30, 1968.

The President must submit a budget to Congress in January of each year. The budget as submitted is in great detail and involves a large amount of work by the Bureau of the Budget. The salient features of the budget are contained in a pamphlet called *Budget in Brief*, which is available as soon as the budget is transmitted to Congress. The economic implications of the budget are analyzed a few days later in the Economic Report of the President. After Congress has passed all tax and expenditure bills, the Bureau of the Budget puts out a *Budget Review*.

In dealing with the contribution of the federal government to overall economic activity, three sets of budget figures must be distinguished. These are the administrative budget, the consolidated cash budget, and the national income accounts budget which is used for arriving at government purchases of goods and services. They are all consolidated budgets in that transactions taking place wholly within the federal government, as each set of budget figures defines it, are excluded.

The *administrative budget*, or conventional budget, includes expenditures and receipts financed out of the general fund of the federal government, that is, the fund provided by receipts not legally set aside for a special use. Included are those agencies for which Congress makes regular appropriations. Activities of trust funds, such as social insurance and the highway fund; quasi-public agencies, such as the Federal Home Loan Banks; and self-financing agencies, such as the Post Office, are excluded. Expenditures and receipts in the administrative budget are generally recorded on a cash basis, but interest expense is recorded on an accrual basis.

The *consolidated cash budget* includes expenditures and receipts for the whole of the activities of the federal government, except the expenditures of government enterprises that are matched by receipts of such enterprises. The major items included in the consolidated cash budget, which are not in the administrative budget, are the operations of federal trust funds and government sponsored agencies. The major funds are those maintained under the Social Security System and for the federal highway program. This budget does not show the full magnitude of cash flows between the federal government and other sectors of the economy because activities of government business agencies, such as the Post Office, are recorded on a net basis.

Table 18-1

Reconciliation of Various Measures

	Fiscal Year		
	1965 Actual	1966 Estimate	1967 Estimate
RECEIPTS			
Administrative budget receipts............	**93.1**	**100.0**	**111.0**
Plus: Trust fund receipts...............	31.0	33.5	41.6
Less: Intragovernmental transactions....	4.3	4.5	5.5
Receipts from exercise of monetary authority	.1	.9	1.6
Equals: Federal receipts from the public....	**119.7**	**128.2**	**145.5**
Less: Cash transactions excluded from Federal receipts account (District of Columbia, financial transactions, etc.)....................	1.0	.6	.7
Plus: Items added to Federal sector account but not in cash receipts (netting differences, timing differences, etc.)..................	.9	1.2	−2.6
Equals: Federal receipts, national income accounts.....................	**119.6**	**128.8**	**142.2**
Plus: Adjustment for tax receipts because of deviation of economy from high employment..................	5.9	2.0	.5
Equals: High-employment receipts........	**125.5**	**130.8**	**142.7**

The *national income accounts budget* contains those items that reflect the direct impact of federal programs on the flow of current income and output. To get at the national income account budget, two major sets of adjustments are necessary in the cash budget. The first is capital transactions adjustments, which exclude expenditures on existing assets and loans and loan repayments. The second is timing adjustments. Expenditures are recorded when delivery is made to the government rather than at the time of payment, and tax receipts are recorded when the tax liability is incurred rather than when the tax is collected.

In determining the most probable level of government expenditures and the full economic impact of government spending, it is also necessary to consider "new obligational authority." Congress

Table 18-1 (continued)
of Federal Receipts and Expenditures (Billions of Dollars)

	Fiscal Year		
	1965 Actual	1966 Estimate	1967 Estimate
EXPENDITURES			
New obligational authority...............	106.6	126.0	121.9
Plus: Authorizations enacted in prior year but spent in current year........	—	—	30.7
Less: Expenditures to be made in future years.........................	—	—	39.8
Equals: Administrative budget expenditures	96.5	106.4	112.8
Plus: Trust fund expenditures..........	29.6	33.8	37.9
Less: Intragovernmental transactions....	4.3	4.5	5.5
Debt issuance in lieu of checks and other adjustments..............	− .6	.7	.2
Equals: Federal payments to the public.....	122.4	135.0	145.0
Less: Cash transactions excluded from Federal expenditures account (District of Columbia, financial transactions, etc.)	5.8	4.0	1.6
Plus: Items added to Federal sector account but not in cash payments (netting differences, timing differences, etc.).................	1.7	—	− .7
Equals: Federal expenditures, national income accounts.................	118.3	131.0	142.7
Plus: Adjustment for expenditures because of deviation of economy from high employment..........	− .2	− .2	.2
Equals: High-employment expenditures....	118.1	130.8	142.9
SURPLUS OR DEFICIT			
Administrative budget....................	−3.4	−6.4	−1.8
Cash budget............................	−2.7	−6.9	+ .5
National income accounts budget..........	+1.2	−2.2	− .5
High-employment budget.................	+7.4	0	− .2

Source: *The Budget of the United States Government for the Fiscal Year Ending June 30, 1967,* pp. 47, 377, and Federal Reserve Bank of St. Louis.

does not vote on expenditures as such, but provides new obligational authority. Expenditures may lag months behind new obligational authority for such items as military hardware. The budget shows the expenditures to be made in the current year from authorizations in prior years, as well as in the current year.

The full economic effect of government programs may be felt before the expenditure appears in the budget. When new military equipment is ordered, such as planes or missiles, the supplier makes expenditures for materials and labor after the contract is signed for their production, but the expenditure for the equipment does not show up in the budget until delivery is made to the government.

A final budget item of some importance is the high-employment budget. It is an estimate of what receipts and expenditures would be in the national income budget for a high level of employment. The figure generally used is for a 4 percent unemployment rate. Table 18-1, on pages 450 and 451, shows these various budget figures and new obligational authority for fiscal years 1965, 1966, and 1967.

To arrive at the figure for federal government purchases of goods and services, it is necessary to subtract the following items from the budget figure for expenditures on national income accounts:

		Estimates for 1967, in Billions of Dollars[1]
Transfer payments......................		$39.2
To persons....................	$37.0	
Foreigners (net).................	2.2	
Grants-in-aid to state and local governments.		14.7
Net interest paid.......................		9.7
Subsidies, less current surplus of government enterprises...................		4.7
Total........................		$68.3

Subtracting $68.3 billion from projected expenditures of $142.7 billion in the national income budget gives a projected figure of $74.4 billion for federal government purchases of goods and services.

The forecast of government purchases of goods and services should begin with an analysis of the budget for the remainder of the current fiscal year and for the next fiscal year. The budget review can be used to get the final figures for the current fiscal year. As early as the first part of December, the size of the budget to be proposed to Congress is usually reported in the press. When the budget is available, it cannot be taken as presented as a forecast of what will happen. This is true because Congress is unlikely to go

---

[1]Estimates made by the Department of Commerce as published in *Survey of Current Business* (February, 1966), p. 6.

along with all items and because of some bias in the budgetary process itself.   Expenses are usually overestimated somewhat, especially on new military programs.   Also revenues are usually underestimated, especially in a recovery period.   In the postwar period, final expenditures have in most years been within 10 percent or less of the President's budget.   But more accurate estimates are possible if they are based upon some analysis of the budget and the current situation.

One factor that needs consideration is an analysis of appropriations for new programs or agencies.   When a new agency is set up or appropriations are made for a new program, expenditures are often below the budget in the early stages.   This is due to such factors as overestimating the speed with which a new program can be set up, delays in getting the proper employees, delays in getting equipment, and the like.

It is also helpful to consider new and unused obligational authority for such programs as military equipment and public works. When obligational authority is increased significantly, budget expenditures are frequently below estimates because of various delays in producing and delivering the equipment.

Requests for changes in governmental programs should also be considered carefully in the light of the present and prospective political and international situation.   Adjustments should be made in the budgeted figures for items the analyst feels Congress will raise or cut.

The budget expenditure figure as presented should therefore be adjusted for three types of factors:

1. Bias in estimates of spending when new programs are introduced.
2. Effect of unused and new obligational authority on short-term expenditures.
3. Estimates of changes Congress will make in the President's budget.

State and Local Government Purchases of Goods and Services

If data and resources were available, it would be possible to forecast state and local government expenditures in the same way as federal government expenditures.   However, there are well over 100,000 such governmental units, and many do not publish budget figures and others have little classification of items in their budgets. Since 100 of the largest spending units account for about half of all spending at the state and local level, an analysis of their budgets can be made to get some idea of what is happening. This may be supplemented by analyzing a sample of the budgets of smaller spending units.

The most generally used approach in recent years has been to extend the trend of the last several years into the future for one year. This trend line may be modified if recent elections and political trends have shown a tendency to defeat tax increases, new bond issues, etc. This procedure is likely to be reasonably accurate for some years to come. Increased population in the past has increased the need for governmental services. This has also increased the need for capital expenditures that are likely to be spread out due to limits on the debt governments can incur, limits on taxes, and the like. Until some research organization develops figures on state and local government expenditure plans, the average analyst must rely on a projection of recent trends that are modified by an analysis of qualitative factors when necessary.

GROSS PRIVATE DOMESTIC INVESTMENT

The most volatile component of gross national product is gross private domestic investment, which includes new construction, producers' durable equipment, and the net change in business inventories. These categories are all difficult to forecast, but procedures have been developed that make it possible in most years to develop reasonably accurate forecasts of each of them.

Only the value of private construction is included in gross private domestic investment. Government construction is included under government purchases of goods and services. Forecasts of the level of construction can be made with some accuracy several quarters in the future because it takes at least that much time to finish most buildings. Since it is necessary to obtain permits to build, it is possible to use such data for forecasting changes in building activity.

Private building is usually divided into several categories for forecasting purposes. The major categories are the following:

Residential building, nonfarm
Nonresidential building, nonfarm
Farm construction
Public utility construction
   Railroads
   Telephone and telegraph

Other public utilities
    Local transit
    Petroleum pipelines
    Electric light and power
    Gas

All of these, except construction on farms and by public utilities, can be estimated from contracts awarded or from building permit data. The level of farm construction is estimated from past trends and relationships, and that of public utility construction from capital expenditure plans.

Residential Construction

The level of residential construction may be estimated in several different ways. One method is based upon data on building starts developed by the Bureau of the Census. Since 1959 building starts are being measured directly rather than estimated from building permits. This data covers all residential buildings both in areas requiring permits and in those that do not. It is subject to sampling error since it is based on sample data. The Bureau of the Census also develops data on the value of housing under construction. These figures are published monthly in the *Construction Review* by the Business and Defense Services Administration of the Department of Commerce.

The next step is to develop patterns of construction from the housing starts and value data. A study of past construction activity will show the average expenditures over the period of construction for various types of projects. For example, a project costing $25,000, which is begun in January, may typically involve expenditures of $2,500 in January, $5,000 in February, $10,000 in March, $5,000 in April, and $2,500 in May. In making such estimates, it is necessary to consider qualitative factors, such as the shortage of materials or of labor, that may lead to a stretching out or perhaps even some speeding up of activity. Similar procedures that are based on permit data developed by the F. W. Dodge Company may be followed.

The demand for residential construction may also be forecast from an analysis of the most likely number of housing starts and the average cost per house. The starting point in such a forecast is an estimate of net family formation and net household formation. Net family formation can be forecast with accuracy since the age at which persons marry and the percentage of persons of marriage-able age who marry change slowly. To develop estimates of net household formation, it is necessary to make allowances for changes in doubling up of families in one housing unit and for the net change in single-member families and nonfamily households. The Bureau of the Census publishes projections of the number of families and of households for periods up to twenty years into the future.

New houses may also be demanded for reasons other than new household formation. Houses may be demolished due to accidents, such as fires and tornadoes. Houses are torn down because of housing projects resulting in slum clearance, to make way for commercial centers, for highways, and the like. Additional houses are also needed because population is shifting, thus leading to vacant houses in some sections and the need for new houses in others. This demand has been largely due to a shift from rural to urban areas in the post-World War II period. A small housing demand also exists for second houses. These factors may be summarized as follows:

> Net family formation
> + or — Undoubling or doubling
> + or — Changes in single-member and nonfamily households
> =s Net household formation
> + Replacement demand
> + Net demand due to population shifts
> + Net demand due to an increase in two-house families
> =s Total housing units required

This unit forecast can be put on a dollar basis by a fairly simple procedure. The dollar value of housing for the past year can be divided by the number of houses built to get the average cost per house. This figure can be adjusted for expected changes in construction costs and in the size of houses, and an average unit cost and total cost figure arrived at for the forecast year.

Such a preliminary forecast of housing expenditures must be adjusted in the light of the following qualitative factors. Individuals buy houses somewhat more easily when income is rising than when it is falling. Housing demand increases significantly when credit terms on government underwritten mortgages are favorable and financing is easily available, and drops when credit is harder to get. Housing demand is increased when monthly payments are less than rentals for comparable units. Housing demand is slowed somewhat by rising costs of new houses. Some indication of the effects of changing rental rates and construction costs may be obtained by comparing rates of change in the rent index section of the consumer price index and a residential construction cost index. Housing demand will also be slowed when demand is close to, or somewhat ahead of, available supplies of building materials. This has a tendency to slow construction and so reduce the number of houses built in a year. The effect of these factors cannot be put into quantitative terms, but judgment must be used by the analyst to raise or lower his forecast in the light of his analysis of these factors.

A sum must be added to the forecast of expenditures for new houses for additions, alterations, and structures, such as new garages. This category is an increasing one on which complete data have only recently become available. It probably responds closely to changes in consumer income, to the cost of the work, and to the ease of getting it done. The Census Bureau in its survey of consumer buying plans asks about plans for major expansions or improvements, which are helpful in gauging trends.

A forecast prepared from an analysis of demand and one based on permit data can well be compared to see to what extent they are in harmony. Any significant differences call for a thorough analysis of all factors in the forecasts and such revisions as seem necessary to bring the forecasts into line. A forecast prepared in this manner is published in *Construction Review*, usually in the November issue.

Other Construction

Private nonfarm, nonresidential building is forecast in much the same way as housing from contract data of the F. W. Dodge Company. Several adjustments must be made of their data to use them as a basis for a forecast. Adjustments must be made in the data to take cancellations into consideration. The F. W. Dodge Company reports cancellations or corrections in the month in which they are ascertained. It is necessary to make such adjustments to the data for the month in which the contracts were reported. The F. W. Dodge Company data include permits for offices, warehouses, and other buildings constructed by public utilities that are usually estimated separately and must therefore be excluded.

The same pattern that was used for residential construction can be used to forecast nonresidential construction from a record of permits. A study of the progress of past projects of various types, such as the construction of schools, hospitals, and churches, is used to determine the rate at which building is likely to take place. Qualitative factors are again considered and these, along with the past patterns, are used to develop the final forecast.

Estimates of farm construction are developed from forecasts of farm income. There has been a high degree of relationship in the past between the trend of cash farm income and the amount of building done on farms. By using the past trend and studying qualitative factors, such as the relationship of building costs to farm prices, it is possible to forecast farm building.

Forecasts of the level of construction activity by railroads and public utilities are made somewhat differently. The Interstate Commerce Commission prepares monthly estimates of expenditures for all Class I railroads. These must be adjusted upward on the basis of past experience to make allowance for expenditures by smaller railroads. From developments in the past year or so and from a study of plans of the major railroad systems, it is possible to project construction levels for a year ahead with reasonable accuracy and a quarter ahead with a fairly high degree of accuracy.

Data for capital expenditures of electric light and power, gas, and petroleum pipeline companies are published quarterly by the Securities and Exchange Commission. Since such projects often take several years to complete, changes do not occur quickly. From a study of the figures for the past five or six quarters and from a study of expansion plans that are made several years ahead, it is possible to arrive at reasonable forecasts. The Securities and Exchange Commission makes surveys of plans for plant and new equipment expenditures for a year ahead and for the next quarter.

Local transit expenditures on construction have not been large in recent years and have followed the trend of expenditures by other utilities. Figures published annually in the *Transit Fact Book* are projected according to the changes expected in other utility construction expenditures.

The American Telephone & Telegraph Company publishes monthly estimates of telephone construction by its subsidiaries and by independent companies. Since the A.T.&T. system accounts for the bulk of the construction, its plans for the coming years form the basis for forecasting the level of activity. These must be raised on the basis of past experience to allow for construction by independent companies. Since A.T. & T. plans several years ahead, such forecasts for a year ahead are reasonably accurate. A similar procedure is followed in regard to Western Union Telegraph Company construction. *The Construction Review* in its forecast number contains forecasts of the most likely volume of construction in each of these areas.

Producers' Durable Equipment

Forecasts of private construction include only business plant, not expenditures on producers' durable equipment. The latter are treated as a separate subcategory of gross private domestic investment and must be projected independently.

A statistical method of forecasting the demand for domestic producers' durable equipment has been developed by the late C. F. Roos, of the Econometric Institute. He has done this by studying the factors that influence businessmen to invest in such equipment. There is an incentive to invest in equipment when the expected return from that equipment in relationship to its supply price is greater than the interest rate. Since it is impossible to determine accurately the future rate of return, Roos believes that most businessmen solve this problem by projecting the present rate of profit and he, therefore, uses current profits in his calculations. In order to determine a measure of the interest rate that is significant in business decisions, he worked with both AAA bond yields and a combination of AAA bond yields and short-term interest rates, since some capital equipment is financed by short-term borrowing. Since he found that adding short-term rates made little difference in the accuracy of forecasts, he used only AAA bond yields.

No index is available to show changes in the supply price of capital assets. The closest approximation to it is an index of machinery and machinery products prices. Unfortunately this index is not available for a long enough period to make an adequate study but, for the period for which it is available, it fluctuates in much the same way as the Bureau of Labor Statistics index of the price of metals and metal products. Therefore this index has been used by Roos as a proxy of changes in the supply price of capital assets.

He found, furthermore, that changes in real wage rates influence the demand for investment goods. This relationship may well be twofold since, as real wages go up, there is a greater demand for capital equipment to cut production costs. At the same time, increases in wages also lead to an increase in the demand for consumer goods and thus in the derived demand for capital equipment. Since there was no index available to measure changes in real wage rates, Roos used the Bureau of Labor Statistics index of nonfarm prices as the best approximation of such changes. The relative prices of consumer goods to producer goods also influence the level of demand for investment goods; a high level of consumer goods prices to producer goods prices encourages investment, whereas a low level discourages it. From this data he calculates capitalized profits based upon corporate profits and the supply price of capital assets, and adjusts them for changes in nonfarm prices. This capitalized relative profits factor is calculated as follows:

$$X = \frac{\text{Corporate profits}}{\text{AAA bond yields}} \times \frac{\text{Nonfarm prices}}{\text{Price of metals and metal products}}$$

This factor is then correlated with producers' durable equipment six months later. There was a high degree of correlation in the past as can be seen from Chart 18-1 on page 461.

The lag in the production of producers' durable equipment is to be expected, since some time must elapse between the decision to invest in new equipment and the fabrication of this equipment. The formula that expresses this relationship is as follows:

$$\text{Y (Producers' durable equipment 6 months in the future)} = .021X + 2{,}500 \text{ million}[2]$$

Thus from this formula it is possible to make a preliminary forecast six months ahead with some degree of accuracy. Forecasts for a year ahead can also be made fairly accurately, since it is necessary to forecast the four factors involved in capitalized relative profits for only six months in the future.

Roos has found that the demand for producers' durable equipment is greater than that which would be expected from past relationships when the economy is operating at or near capacity levels. At such times upward adjustments must be made in the figures to take the effects of this capacity "squeeze" into consideration. This has been done successfully according to the Econometric Institute. During the period of the Korean War beginning with 1951, an additional adjustment was made because of the provision of the

---

[2]Charles F. Roos, "The Demand for Investment Goods," *American Economic Review* (May, 1948), pp. 314–316.

Chart 18-1

Domestic Producers' Durable Equipment v.
Capitalized Corporate Profits and Relative Prices

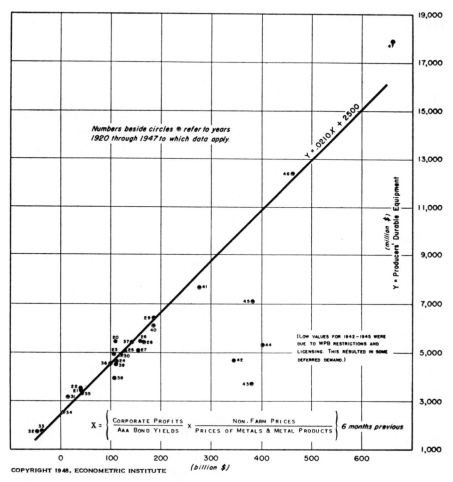

Numbers beside circles ⊛ refer to years 1920 through 1947 to which data apply.

$Y = .0210X + 2500$

Y = Producers' Durable Equipment (million $)

(Low values for 1942–1945 were due to WPB restrictions and licensing. This resulted in some deferred demand.)

$$X = \left\{ \frac{\text{Corporate Profits}}{\text{Aaa Bond Yields}} \times \frac{\text{Non-Farm Prices}}{\text{Prices of Metals & Metal Products}} \right\} \text{ 6 months previous}$$

COPYRIGHT 1948, ECONOMETRIC INSTITUTE   *(billion $)*

Source: Charles F. Roos, "The Demand for Investment Goods," *American Economic Review* (May, 1948), p. 314; and Econometric Institute.

income tax law permitting accelerated depreciation of assets vital to the defense program. This accelerated depreciation provided an additional source of corporate funds for new plant and equipment, and upward adjustments were made in the estimates to allow for it.

Some research organizations develop their forecasts of producers' durable equipment by following new orders, unfilled orders, inventories, and shipments. This is the method frequently used to forecast the Federal Reserve Index of Industrial Production, which was discussed in the previous chapter.

New Plant and Equipment

The value of new construction and producers' durable equipment is often broken down differently for forecasting purposes than it is in national income statistics. Businessmen do not as a rule differentiate clearly in their planning between new buildings and new equipment. Therefore, business expenditures on new plant and equipment are often projected as one unit. This reduces the number of classes of new construction that must be projected separately to the following:

Capital outlays by business charged to the current account
Residential construction
Nonresidential construction for nonbusiness purposes, such as institutions and private schools
Farm construction

Expenditures on farm machinery and equipment must also be projected separately since they are included in producers' durable equipment, but not in business expenditures on plant and equipment. The same is true of expenditures on professional equipment and that for private institutions.

The Department of Commerce and the Securities and Exchange Commission have in the post-World War II period surveyed businessmen's plans for expenditures on new plant and equipment. Data are gathered by the SEC on plans of all corporations registered with them under the Securities Acts, and the Department of Commerce uses a large sample to get data from nonregistered corporations.

McGraw-Hill also conducts a similar survey, which it publishes in *Business Week*. It is based on a smaller sample that is somewhat less representative, since it concentrates to some extent on larger concerns. The sequence of these surveys is as follows:

Fall (usually a November issue of *Business Week*)
Preliminary McGraw-Hill report for the coming year.

December
Commerce-SEC revised report for the current quarter and report for the first quarter of the coming year.

March
>Commerce-SEC revised report for the current quarter and
report for the second quarter.
Commerce-SEC report for the current year.

April
>McGraw-Hill revised report for the current year.

June and September
>Commerce-SEC revised report for the current quarter and
report for the next quarter.

Such a forecast is presented in Table 18-2.

Table 18-2

Plant and Equipment Expenditures
1964–1966

(Billions of Dollars)

	Actual 1964	Actual 1965	Antici- pated 1966	Percent Changes	
				1964 to 1965	1965 to 1966
All industries............	44.90	51.96	60.23	+16	+16
Manufacturing..........	18.58	22.45	26.75	+21	+19
Durable..............	9.43	11.40	13.50	+21	+18
Nondurable...........	9.16	11.05	13.25	+21	+20
Mining...............	1.19	1.30	1.51	+ 9	+16
Railroad...............	1.41	1.73	1.83	+23	+ 6
Transportation other than rail..................	2.38	2.81	3.15	+18	+12
Public utilities..........	6.22	6.94	8.04	+12	+16
Communications, com- mercial and other......	15.13	16.73	18.95	+11	+13

Source: Securities and Exchange Commission, *Statistical Series Release 2110,*
>p. 2.

These surveys have established a good record in anticipating the
change in investment expenditures. The Department of Commerce-
SEC annual surveys from 1947 through 1967 had a median deviation from actual expenditures of only 3 percent. In 13 of the 21
years for which the annual survey was conducted, anticipated
expenditures have been within 3 percent of actual expenditures.
In only two years, 1947 and 1950, were the deviations in excess

of 6 percent. The direction of change was predicted accurately in all years except 1950.

The 1947 figure was low because of the rapidly rising prices during that year as industry emerged from a period of price control. The larger volume of expenditures in 1950 was due largely to the impact of the Korean War on the economy, which could not have been foreseen at the beginning of the year. The survey would probably have been off, however, even if the Korean War had not occurred, since in the first two quarters outlays approached the 1949 levels and businessmen had scheduled a rise in output in the third quarter before the War began. The 1951 and 1952 figures were again somewhat low because of events related to the Korean War. Large increases in defense expenditures required more plant and equipment than businessmen anticipated. Prices of capital equipment also increased faster than they were able to foresee.[3] Under more normal conditions such errors should not occur. Since business plant and equipment programs must be planned some time in advance, it is reasonable to expect that fairly good estimates of such expenditures can be made.

In the fall of 1956 the National Industrial Conference Board introduced a new survey, which is published quarterly in the Conference Board *Business Record*. This is based on a survey of capital appropriations of the 1,000 largest manufacturing companies. The survey gives data on newly approved capital appropriations and on total outstanding capital appropriations. The difference between spending plans and new appropriations is essentially that between new appropriations and expenditures in the government budget. Thus, the Conference Board survey gives additional information that should prove useful in projecting capital spending more accurately several quarters ahead. This survey predicted the 1957 downturn and the following upturn and also the 1960 downturn, but it is still too new to fully assess its value as a quantitative forecasting tool.

The figures reported in the surveys of expenditures on plant and equipment should be analyzed in the light of conditions in the economy and revised if need be. It is impossible to check them quantitatively with building permit data, but an analysis of such data for several quarters will show if the surveys are in conformity

---

[3]Murray F. Foss and Vito Natrella, "Ten Years' Experience with Business Investment Anticipation," *Survey of Current Business* (January, 1957), pp. 16–24.

with future building as shown in permits. The same kind of check can be made with the Department of Commerce series on new orders and order backlogs in the durable goods manufacturing industries. If these series have been moving in the same direction as the expenditure surveys indicate that expenditures on plant and equipment will move, they help substantiate the survey figures. If not, they raise serious questions about the figures in the survey and may call for some revision of these figures in making the forecast for this sector of the economy.

The survey figures should also be checked in the light of their feasibility, both from a physical and a financial point of view. If the construction and equipment industry is operating at or near full capacity, additional spending plans cannot be fully met on time and the figures should be adjusted downward. This, for example, was the situation in 1956. If indications are that money will become extremely tight, some downward revision may also be necessary. Large concerns usually can get the funds to carry out plans for the current year, but some of the smaller firms may have to postpone some expenditures because of difficulties in financing. The effects of tight money are probably felt primarily in making plans for the next year, not in completing those for the present year.

Expenditure plans may also have to be changed because the analyst believes sales and profits will be substantially different from those which businessmen expected at the time of the survey. Minor changes in sales do not affect spending decisions significantly, but a sharp drop in sales and profits will. There is, however, a lag of three or four quarters before significant changes occur. The analyst has information on the sales picture expected because the Commerce-SEC report for the year asks businessmen about their expectations of sales for the year.

Other Capital Items

After expenditures on plant and equipment have been forecast from surveys of business plans, it is necessary to estimate the levels of the remaining items. Capital outlays charged to the current account fluctuate in about the same way as capital outlays in general. They are usually forecast by adjusting the figure for the past year by the same percentage by which the expenditure survey shows that spending on plant and equipment will change. Methods of forecasting residential construction, nonresidential construction for non-business purposes, and farm construction have already been considered.

Expenditures on farm machinery and equipment show a reasonable degree of correlation with cash farm income. They can therefore be forecast by adjusting levels in the past year by expected changes in cash farm income. Expenditures on professional equipment are not a large part of total investment expenditures and do not change rapidly. They can be estimated from expenditures during the past year and trends over the past five years or so.

Change in Business Inventories

The last item in the gross private domestic investment group to forecast is the net change in business inventories. This is the most volatile series of all and so, in many ways, the most important one to forecast accurately, especially in minor recessions. It is also one of the most difficult to forecast.

In analyzing inventory changes, it is well to keep in mind the adjustments businessmen are trying to make in inventory levels. In the retail and wholesale fields, and in major segments of the manufacturing field, goods are no longer made to order but are kept in stock and sold out of stock. The competent businessman has a pretty good idea of the relationship of inventory to sales that he would like to maintain to run his business effectively. Inventory acts as a cushion, however, since it is depleted as sales increase in an upturn and is increased when sales decrease in a downturn.

In such fields as the manufacture of major types of industrial equipment, goods are still made to order. In these industries, for example in machine tools, sales and production are almost the same. The cushion is in unfilled orders because new orders are above sales in an upswing and below sales in a downturn. In most manufacturing industries some goods are made to order, but enough are kept in stock so that inventories perform a major cushioning function.

The attempt of manufacturers to adjust inventories to sales has been reasonably successful, but with a lag. Sales, however, vary somewhat more than inventories, and the latter do not respond to fluctuations in sales occurring in short periods of time. There is, however, a lag of about two quarters of inventories behind sales. For example, after the turn in sales in 1929 inventories did not begin to drop until the second quarter of 1930. In 1937, manufacturers'

Chart 18-2

Manufacturers' Inventories: Actual and Calculated

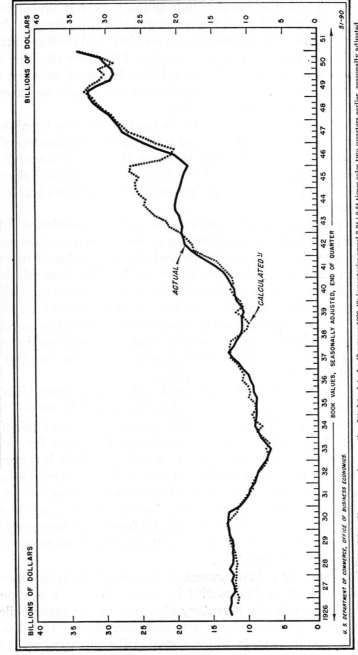

ACTUAL

CALCULATED ¹⧸

U. S. DEPARTMENT OF COMMERCE, OFFICE OF BUSINESS ECONOMICS.

BOOK VALUES, SEASONALLY ADJUSTED, END OF QUARTER

¹ Calculated values obtained from linear regression equation fitted to data for the years 1926-40; inventories equal 3.24+0.54 times sales two quarters earlier, seasonally adjusted.

Source: *Survey of Current Business* (April, 1951), p. 19.

sales ceased rising in the first half of the year, but inventories did not turn down until the final quarter. When business picked up toward the end of 1932, inventories continued to decline until after the middle of 1933. Chart 18-2 on page 467 shows the high degree of relationship, except for the World War II period, between manufacturers' inventories and calculated inventories based on the correlation with sales two quarters earlier.

Retail inventories likewise lag behind retail sales by about two quarters. There was a downward trend in the relationship of retail inventories to sales from 1920 to about the end of World War II. The relationship appears to have been about stabilized since 1947 or 1948. The lag in wholesale inventories behind sales is also about two quarters.

The relationship of inventories to sales has continued into the postwar period. A close relationship exists between average monthly sales in manufacturing and trade and the book value of inventory. This can be seen clearly from Chart 18-3. This close relationship also holds for retail trade inventories and for the volatile durable goods sector of manufacturing as well as for nondurable goods.

The first step in forecasting inventories is to develop an estimate of the level of inventories expected from past relationships and to compare them with current levels in order to see the size and direction of changes that are likely to occur.

Such changes should be compared with manufacturers' inventory and sales expectations as reported in the quarterly survey by the Department of Commerce. This survey shows manufacturers' expectations for changes in inventories and in sales for the next two quarters. It also gives their evaluation of their inventories as about right, too high, or too low, If the analyst is expecting a level of sales different from that expected by manufacturers, he can make the appropriate change in inventory figures. The data on the condition of inventories will also help adjust a forecast of inventory levels based on past relationships, since it will show any tendency to change inventory-sales relationships.

Before making a final forecast of the change in inventories, it is desirable to look at inventories in major fields. It is especially significant to study the inventory situation in the automobile field because significant changes often take place here. This has been especially true in years in which a steel strike threatens or in which sales have not been up to expectations.

Chart 18-3

The Relationship of Inventory to Average Monthly Sales in
Manufacturing and Trade, 1948–1966

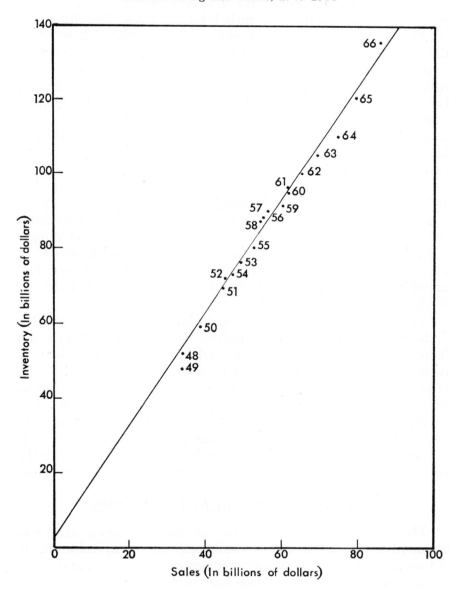

Source: United States Department of Commerce, *Business Statistics*, 1965
ed., p. 22, and *Survey of Current Business* (March, 1966), p. S-4.

NET EXPORT OF GOODS AND SERVICES

Net exports of goods and services do not constitute a large item. In recent years, it has not been much more than 1 percent of gross national product and has frequently been much less. Therefore, even sizable errors in this forecast would have had a negligible effect on the total forecast. In 1946 and 1947, however, the sums involved were about 2 percent and 4 percent respectively. This situation resulted from heavy foreign purchases in the United States, in part because of pent-up war demand and in part because exchange rates were so regulated as to make some American goods cheaper than domestic goods in many countries. In each year large amounts of long-term foreign investments were liquidated to help pay for the goods purchased here.

The volume of imports is related to domestic business activity. It is affected by the level of income in the United States and by the relative prices of domestic and imported goods. There is a reasonable correlation between gross national product in real terms and imports adjusted for the difference between domestic and foreign prices. In estimating the level of imports, qualitative factors, such as unbalanced inventories in some fields that may lead to price cuts and fewer foreign purchases, must also be considered.

The volume of exports is related to business conditions and the financial situations in foreign countries. A complete analysis would involve an analysis of the present and future levels of business in each foreign country, its prospects for selling goods abroad, its long-term borrowing from foreign countries, and its reserves of gold and foreign exchange. Such detailed analysis is impracticable and, as a result, exports are usually forecast in the aggregate. Changes in total volume in the past year or two are analyzed and, on the basis of such changes and a study of the major qualitative factors in the current situation, an estimate is made of exports for the coming year.

PERSONAL CONSUMPTION EXPENDITURES

The forecast of the major sectors of gross national product can be completed by forecasting personal consumption expenditures. It is possible to take each of the major subcategories in the durable goods field, the nondurable goods field, and the service field and to develop estimates of consumer expenditures in each of them by studying changes in the recent past and the effect that foreseeable changes in current conditions will have upon them. This can also be done for all of the individual categories that form the twelve major subdivisions of consumer expenditures used in national income accounting, but it becomes a formidable undertaking. A common procedure is to develop separate forecasts for expenditures on durable goods and nondurable goods.

The surveys of consumer buying intentions discussed in Chapter 17 are of some help in forecasting expenditures on durable goods, since they have gauged the changes in the direction of consumer expenditures accurately. Studies have been made to determine which factors cause consumer purchases to vary from intentions.

On the basis of such studies, the Commercial Credit Company began in the fall of 1967 to publish forecasts of expected expenditures six months in the future for automobiles and for major household durables. Until such forecasts have proved reliable, the forecasts must also rely on other techniques for a quantitative forecast of this sector of the economy, and will probably always want to use them as a cross-check.

Some analysts calculate a normal volume of automobile sales by figuring a total of expansion demand and replacement demand. Expansion demand can be calculated from the trend in the number of cars in use over the last several years. The trend must be modified to account for significant changes in the number of households such as are likely to occur in the middle 1960's. Replacement demand can be calculated from the trend in automobile scrappage for five or more years in the past.

This procedure, however, will not in itself give an accurate year-by-year picture of automobile demand, but it does give a fairly good picture of average demand over a period of years. Replacement in any one year is determined to a large extent by changes in income and psychological factors, however. When more new cars are purchased, more used cars are available, thus depressing their price. This drops the value of older used cars to the point where selling them as scrap is the most profitable course. Thus, years of good new car sales are also years of high scrappage.

In developing forecasts of new car sales, the sales picture of the last few years should be analyzed, especially in relationship to long-run demand. Then the effect of probable changes in income must be considered. The Department of Commerce has found that on the average an increase of 1 percent in real disposable income has been associated with a rise of 2.5 percent in automobile sales. Prices of automobile sales must also be considered, since a rise of 1 percent in auto prices in comparison with general consumer prices has led to a 1.3 percent decrease in car sales.[4]

Sales figures must also be adjusted for psychological factors. Major changes in new models have a stimulating effect on sales. The extent, of course, depends on consumer acceptance. The general attitude of optimism or pessimism on the part of consumers also has an effect, and in any model year car manufacturers can push sales and get dealers to move cars as they did in 1955. This may, of course, reduce sales below long-term levels the next year.

The sales of other durables depend, to a large degree, on the trend in the number of households and disposable income and on changes in disposable income. Thus, expected income changes are a major factor in forecasting changes in demand and sales. Years of major increases in home building are also likely to show more than normal increases in sales of home furnishings and appliances. In determining sales levels, increases in prices due to cost increases must also be considered.

In making a forecast of demand for all consumer durables, the financial position of consumers must be considered. Years in which consumer debt has increased markedly are followed by years of a smaller increase as consumers get into a more liquid position. The total of consumer expenditures on durables and personal saving that includes net repayments on consumer credit is more stable than either series alone. Thus, when consumers go into debt at an unusually rapid rate, a slowdown in new debt and also durable goods sales is to be expected as consumers plan their finances. This factor must be considered in making the forecasts of automobile and other durable consumer goods sales.

Forecasts of demand for nondurable goods and services are easiest to make. The volume of these purchases is little affected by small changes in income. Even in years of severe depression the effect is negligible until economic activity has been declining for a year or more. Such sales have increased in the postwar period in line with changes in real income, population, and the price level. These factors can be analyzed separately, or the trend of several years in the past

---

[4]The factors affecting automobile sales and sales of other durables are discussed in more detail in Chapter 21, Forecasting Sales for an Industry.

can be projected. When this is done, allowance must be made for expected price changes different from the average for the last few years. Some upward adjustment is also desirable because of an above average increase in expenditures on household operation in recent years. This is likely to continue so long as high levels of residential building are maintained.

DEVELOPING THE FINAL FORECAST OF GNP

After figures for each sector have been developed, the resulting product will not necessarily be the final forecast of GNP; in fact, it is very unlikely to be. The whole forecast should be cross-checked and revised as need be. The first step calls for a comparison of the total of GNP with the level of activity considered most likely when such sectors as residential construction and consumer durable goods purchases were forecast. If it appears that total economic activity will be greater or less than originally expected, these estimates should be revised.

Then the forecast can be cross-checked in several ways, using past relationships. One such check uses the relationship between real disposable income and real consumer expenditures on goods and services. It is first necessary to make a series of estimates to arrive at disposable income from estimates of GNP. The steps needed to make such estimates were described in Chapter 17. The estimate of disposable income should be adjusted for price changes that were assumed in building up GNP. The past relationship between real consumer expenditures and real disposable income as shown on Chart 16-1 on page 418 can be used to check estimates of current consumer expenditures in real terms. If the figures used in building up the forecast, after adjustment for price changes, are not in line with those expected from past relationships, adjustments must be made.

As a first approximation, consumer expenditures can be revised. Past relationship of real durable sales, nondurable sales, and service expenditures to real disposable income can be used to divide the adjustments among these categories. These relationships are considered more fully in Chapter 21.

A second approximation calls also for adjustment in other factors, such as capital goods expenditures, that are likely to be affected as consumer sales levels change. These changes affect GNP and, in turn, call for more revision of consumer expenditures. This process

Table 18-3

Total Output, Income, and Spending
The Nation's Income, Expenditure, and Saving

Current estimates indicate that gross national product rose by $9 billion (seasonally adjusted annual rate) in the second quarter.

(Billions of dollars; quarterly data at seasonally adjusted annual rates)

Period	Persons — Disposable personal income — Total[1]	Less: Interest paid and transfer payments to foreigners	Equals: Total excluding interest and transfers	Personal consumption expenditures	Personal saving or dissaving (−)	Government — Net receipts — Tax and nontax receipts or accruals	Less: Transfers, interest, and subsidies[2]	Equals: Net receipts	Government — Expenditures — Total expenditures	Less: Transfers, interest, and subsidies[2]	Equals: Purchases of goods and services	Surplus or deficit (−), income and product accounts
1959	337.3	7.1	330.3	311.2	19.1	128.9	34.0	95.0	131.0	34.0	97.0	−2.1
1960	350.0	7.8	342.3	325.2	17.0	139.8	36.5	103.3	136.1	36.5	99.6	3.7
1961	364.4	8.1	356.3	335.2	21.2	144.6	41.3	103.3	149.0	41.3	107.6	−4.3
1962	385.3	8.6	376.6	355.1	21.6	157.0	42.8	114.2	159.9	42.8	117.1	−2.9
1963	404.6	9.7	394.9	375.0	19.9	168.8	44.4	124.3	166.9	44.4	122.5	1.8
1964	438.1	10.7	427.4	401.2	26.2	174.1	46.7	127.3	175.4	46.7	128.7	−1.4
1965	472.2	11.9	460.3	433.1	27.2	188.8	49.7	139.1	186.1	49.7	136.4	2.7
1966	508.8	13.1	495.7	465.9	29.8	213.0	55.5	157.5	209.8	55.5	154.3	3.2
1965: III	479.4	12.2	467.2	436.4	30.9	188.3	51.9	136.4	190.0	51.9	138.1	−1.7
IV	489.4	12.4	477.0	447.8	29.3	193.2	50.4	142.8	192.6	50.4	142.3	.6
1966: I	497.5	12.6	484.9	458.2	26.6	204.3	53.4	150.9	199.8	53.4	146.5	4.6
II	503.3	13.0	490.3	461.6	28.7	210.6	53.1	157.5	204.4	53.1	151.2	6.1
III	512.4	13.1	499.3	470.1	29.2	216.3	56.1	160.2	213.7	56.1	157.7	2.6
IV	522.7	13.5	508.5	473.8	34.6	220.9	59.4	161.5	221.2	59.4	161.7	−.3
1967: I	532.7	13.8	518.9	480.2	38.8	222.8	63.1	159.7	233.6	63.1	170.4	−10.8
IIP	540.0	14.3	525.7	489.7	36.0	223.3	63.3	160.0	238.1	63.3	175.0	−14.9

Period	Business			Net transfers to foreigners by persons and government	International				Total income or receipts	Statistical discrepancy	Gross national product or expenditure
	Gross retained earnings[3]	Gross private domestic investment[4]	Excess of investment (−)		Net exports of goods and services			Excess of transfers or of net exports (−)[5]			
					Exports	Less: Imports	Equals: Net exports				
1959	56.8	75.3	−18.5	2.4	23.5	23.3	0.1	2.3	484.5	−0.8	483.7
1960	56.6	74.8	−18.0	2.4	27.2	23.2	4.0	−1.7	504.8	−1.0	503.7
1961	58.7	71.7	−13.0	2.6	28.6	23.0	5.6	−3.0	520.8	−.8	520.1
1962	66.3	83.0	−16.8	2.7	30.3	25.1	5.1	−2.5	559.8	−.5	560.3
1963	68.8	87.1	−18.4	2.8	32.3	26.4	5.9	−3.1	590.8	−.3	590.5
1964	76.2	94.0	−17.8	2.8	37.1	28.6	8.5	−5.7	633.7	−1.3	632.4
1965	83.7	107.4	−23.8	2.9	39.1	32.2	6.9	−4.1	685.8	−2.0	683.9
1966	89.7	118.0	−28.3	2.9	43.0	37.9	5.1	−2.2	745.9	−2.6	743.3
1965: III	84.2	108.2	−24.0	2.9	40.3	32.9	7.4	−4.5	690.7	−.6	690.0
1966: I	86.2	112.3	−26.1	2.6	40.5	34.4	6.1	−3.4	708.6	−.5	708.4
II	87.6	115.2	−27.6	3.4	42.0	36.0	6.1	−2.7	726.8	−.9	725.9
III	88.4	118.5	−30.1	2.8	42.5	37.1	5.4	−2.5	739.1	−2.2	736.7
IV	89.5	116.4	−26.9	2.8	43.7	39.0	4.6	−1.8	751.8	−3.2	748.8
1967: I	93.6	122.2	−28.6	2.5	44.0	39.7	4.3	−1.8	766.1	−3.8	762.1
IIp	88.9	110.4	−21.5	2.9	45.3	39.9	5.3	−2.5	770.4	−4.0	766.3
	89.3	105.1	−15.8	3.0	45.1	39.8	5.3	−2.3	778.0	−3.1	775.1

[1]Personal income less personal tax and nontax payments (fines, penalties, etc.)

[2]Government transfer payments to persons, foreign net transfers by government, net interest paid by government, and subsidies less current surplus of government enterprises.

[3]Undistributed corporate profits, corporate inventory valuation adjustment, capital consumption allowances, and wage accruals less disbursements. Does not include retained earnings of unincorporated business, which are included in disposable personal income.

[4]Private business investment, purchases of capital goods by private nonprofit institutions, and residential housing.

[5]Net foreign investment with sign changed.

NOTE.—Revised series beginning 1964. For details, see *Survey of Current Business* (July, 1967). Data for Alaska and Hawaii included beginning 1960.

Source: *Economic Indicators* (August, 1967), p. 1.

could go on indefinitely, but rather than do it mechanically the analyst should use his best judgment and make all revisions in one step.

A last check is worthwhile before the forecast is accepted as final. This involves an analysis of the excess of receipts or expenditures for each sector of the economy. The sum of these must, of course, in actual fact balance out to zero. A good form for doing this is that of the Council of Economic Advisers in its monthly publication *Economic Indicators*. This form is shown in Table 18-3.

At this stage the analyst has all of the necessary figures available for making such estimates, except for several in the government area that he can get from the budget. He needs estimates of tax and non-tax governmental receipts and also net transfers of funds to foreign countries.

Any significant lack of balance of the excess of receipts or disbursements calls for adjustments since the economy will set forces into motion that will balance them. No set rules can be given for doing this. The analyst must make needed adjustments based on his knowledge of the economy, past cycles, and the causal factors at work in the cycle.

Such cross-checking helps refine a forecast and make it internally consistent. At this stage of knowledge of the cycle, it cannot assure accuracy because the economy does not always react as it did in the past. Forecasting is still to a large degree an art even though the amount of guesswork is being reduced.

QUESTIONS

1. What is the relationship between the circular flow of economic activity and forecasting?

2. Explain the terminology used in federal government budgets.

3. Distinguish the administrative budget, consolidated cash budget, national income accounts budget, and high employment budget.

4. Describe the adjustments needed in federal budget figures to use them as a basis for developing a forecast.

5. Explain how a forecast of federal government purchases of goods and services may be developed from adjusted budget figures.

6. Explain a procedure for forecasting state and local government purchases of goods and services.

7. Outline a division of private building for forecasting purposes.

8. Describe, step-by-step, two alternative procedures for forecasting the volume of residential construction.

9. Explain how other construction may be forecast.

10. Explain a procedure for forecasting the volume of producers' durable equipment.

11. How is the Department of Commerce series on new plant and equipment related to the construction and producers' durable equipment series?

12. Explain a procedure for forecasting expenditures on new plant and equipment.

13. How are the remaining capital items forecast?

14. Explain a procedure for forecasting inventory investment.

15. Explain a procedure for forecasting net exports of goods and services.

16. How may durable goods sales be forecast?

17. Describe the process for forecasting nondurable goods and services expenditures.

18. Describe the process of checking a forecast for consistency and revising it in the light of such checks.

SUGGESTED READINGS

Bassie, V. Lewis. *Economic Forecasting.* New York: McGraw-Hill Book Company, 1958. Part Two.

"Business Investment and Sales Expectations," *Survey of Current Business* (annually in March issue).

Butler, William F., and Robert Kavesh (eds.). *How Business Economists Forecast.* Englewood Cliffs, New Jersey: Prentice-Hall, Inc., 1966.

Economic Indicators. Monthly publication of the Joint Economic Committee and the Council of Economic Advisers. Washington: U. S. Government Printing Office, Annual.

Lewis, John P., and Robert C. Turner. *Business Conditions Analysis.* 2nd ed. New York: McGraw-Hill Book Company, 1967. Part Four.

McKinley, David H., Murray G. Lee, and Helene Duffy. *Forecasting Business Conditions,* New York: American Bankers Association, 1965.

Short-Term Economic Forecasting, Studies in Income and Wealth, Volume 17. New York: National Bureau of Economic Research, 1955, Parts 1 and 2.

Wolfe, Harry Dean. *Business Forecasting Methods.* New York: Holt, Rinehart & Winston, Inc., 1966.

Wright, Wilson. *Forecasting for Profit.* New York: John Wiley & Sons, Inc., 1947. Chapters 4–11, 13.

CHAPTER 19

Forecasting Price Changes

A forecast of probable price changes is frequently necessary or desirable as part of a forecasting program. It may be necessary as a basis for converting a dollar forecast into a unit forecast. On the other hand, if the basic forecast is in units, a price forecast is needed to put it on a dollar basis.

The government needs price forecasts in planning monetary and fiscal policy. Such forecasts are needed to estimate both expenditures and income in governmental budgets, especially that of the federal government. Price forecasts are also needed in planning programs in the agricultural area. The purpose of federal price forecasts is often to provide a basis for action that will prevent the forecast of an unfavorable situation from actually taking place.

Prices and unit forecasts are usually also needed in business, the unit forecast to plan production and the dollar forecast to plan finances. Data on prospective price changes are also useful in other phases of business operations. Price forecasts are necessary if prices must be set months ahead for inclusion in a catalog. They are useful in planning a program of purchasing raw materials. A forecast of changes in the general price level may be helpful also in bargaining with labor on wages. Data on long-term price trends are helpful if long-range planning of capital expenditures is to be carried on effectively. Thus a price forecast is an integral part of any forecasting program.

Methods of determining price trends and forecasting price changes will be considered in this chapter. Consideration will first be directed to projecting the trend of prices, since short-run price forecasts are affected by the general direction in which prices are moving. Then the factors involved in forecasting short-run changes in the general price level will be considered. This discussion will be followed by an analysis of the factors involved in forecasting prices

478

of specific commodities. A final section will consider some of the schemes that purport to forecast common stock prices. Forecasting in this area is all but impossible because of the changing psychological reactions of a changing group of investors.

ANALYZING AND PROJECTING PRICE TRENDS

In projecting price trends, it is necessary to consider the basic factors that affect prices in the long run and the effect those factors have had on price levels over the years. Several factors seem to indicate that the long-run price level in the United States should have a downward bias. Prices should move downward gradually because increases in technology and in the skills of the labor force and of management are making it possible to produce increased quantities of goods and services per capita at a lower per unit cost. A study of long-run price movements, however, fails to show such a downward trend.

This is true primarily because prices have been inflated substantially during the major wars and have not in all cases dropped to prewar levels before new forces caused them to go up again. Since 1900, prices have increased materially, primarily as a result of the inflationary financing of World War I and of World War II. Even at the low point in the 1933 depression, they were well above prosperity levels in 1900. After the end of World War II there was not only no tendency for prices to decline materially, since the government continued to pursue inflationary policies for some years, but also new pressures pushed prices upward.

Factors Determining Long-Run Prices

As was pointed out in the description of the salient features of the American economy, there are several important sources of new purchasing media in the American monetary system. The stock of money is supplied by the Treasury, the Federal Reserve System, and the system of commercial banks; the bulk of it is in the form of demand deposits that are liabilities of commercial banks. Coins are provided by the Treasury and currency by both the Treasury and the Federal Reserve Banks. The size of the money supply depends on the action of these three supplier agencies and is determined in part by the constraints placed upon them by laws and by the procedures developed to administer the programs of these agencies. The money supply also depends upon the actions of governmental units, households, business units, and the rest of the world in demanding credit to meet their needs. The potential for monetary expansion depends on excess reserves that are available in the banking system and on the monetary expansion multiplier. This multiplier is based on reserve requirements but is reduced by such factors as increased demand for currency in circulation, increased demand for time deposits, and increased demand by banks for vault cash and other excess reserves when the money supply is increased. These factors were discussed in Chapter 3.

In the discussion of the quantity theory in Chapter 5, it was pointed out that changes in the money supply can lead to changes in the price level; but the cash balances which spending units desire to hold, or the level of goods and services that are produced, or both, may also change. The institutional arrangements on which cash balances depend to a large degree are not likely to change rapidly; but the desire to hold cash is also affected by such factors as expectations of price level changes, expectations of interest rate changes, the relative attractiveness of near money substitutes, such as savings accounts, and the ease of borrowing money. If the desire to hold cash balances or its reciprocal, the velocity of money, does not change, either the general price level or the output of goods and services must change. Output is likely to increase in part, at least so long as there are unused resources. But as full utilization of plant and equipment and full employment are approached, the major impact of an increase in the money supply will be on the price level.

This has happened during wartime when the money supply has been increased by the creation of credit for the government in the form of credits to the Treasury's checking accounts arising out of bank purchases of government bonds out of excess reserves or newly created reserves. When government deficits are financed in this way, the effect on the economy is potentially inflationary because the money supply is increased without increasing the supply of goods. This type of action was used in part to finance World War II expenditures. Prices were held in check by price control laws, but the basis was laid for an increase in the price level. The money supply was increased about threefold between 1939 and 1947, while physical output went up somewhat less than 50 percent. In other words, the supply of money went up somewhat over twice as fast as the supply of goods. Prices went up by only about 75 percent by 1947, since the velocity of money slowed down. When the velocity of money increased in 1948, 1949, and 1950, the full impact of the increased money supply was brought into play.

Projecting Price Trends

A projection of price trends involves a projection of the supply of purchasing media and the velocity of circulation of money and also a projection of the level of output of goods and services. The level of output can be projected several years ahead by the methods described in Chapter 16. The projection of the money supply involves an anaylsis of many factors, but most of them generally change slowly except in unusual periods such as wartime. The level of coins and currency in circulation can be projected from past trends, and this is also true to a large degree of the level of demand deposits held by businesses and consumers. However, such factors as the general state of the money markets and the level of interest rates must be considered since these affect the degree to which businesses and some individuals invest idle short-term funds in short-term obligations. Trends in demand deposits of governmental units can be projected from a study of past trends and present and prospective fiscal policies. Policies being followed by the Treasury and the Federal Reserve must also be analyzed, and the effect of likely changes must be projected. Changes in the velocity of circulation of money can also be projected from past trends. These must be modified by an analysis of the factors that may lead to a change in cash balances, such as the relative attractiveness of short-term obligations like commercial paper; the attractiveness of keeping liquid funds in other institutions, such as savings and loan associations; and the ease of obtaining credit in emergencies.

So many variables are involved that it is difficult to work with all of them at one time. Part of the difficulty may be overcome by working with rates of change in each of the basic series, that is, the output of goods and services, the money supply, and the velocity of circulation of money. Data on all of them are published in the *Federal Reserve Bulletin* and information on rates of change of many monetary and related series is available in a monthly release of the St. Louis Federal Reserve Bank called *Monetary Trends*. This method involves many broad estimates and cannot be expected to give completely accurate results. It can determine the level of prices in a general way by a comparison of the trend of output with the trend in the size of the supply of purchasing media.

Effect of Costs on Prices

A rise in the price level may also be caused by an increase in the costs of production. Increases in productivity have in the past reduced total costs, especially in manufacturing. In recent years, however, powerful labor unions have had sufficient bargaining power to win increases in wage rates in some industries at a faster rate than increases in overall productivity. This situation raises costs and in industries in which prices are not set in perfectly competitive markets, prices are raised to cover such increased costs. This type of inflation has been referred to as "cost-push inflation" or "administered-price inflation." Such price increases are possible only if the demand for the product is such as to maintain total sales and output, or at least to lead to equal or greater profits at the new level of sales than at the level based on the original price. It is also necessary for the money supply to be increased to support the new level of aggregate sales or for the velocity of money to increase to support such sales.

The aggregate demand for goods in recent years has been great enough to enable some producers to pass on higher costs associated with higher wage rates in the form of higher prices. This has been true because of rapidly increasing demands by state and local governments and, in some periods, by the federal government and by business for investment expenditures. The velocity of money has gone up in the postwar period, and the money supply has been increased slowly in prosperity and materially in every cyclical downturn, thus making higher prices possible, Inflation from the cost side must be considered in projecting price trends as long as wage increases are greater than increases in productivity.

SHORT-RUN PRICE FORECASTING

The direction of prices in the short run may be determined in a fashion similar to that for projecting long-run price developments. But in the long run it is usually sufficient to know the general direction of prices and to have some idea of the average rate at which they are moving, whereas in the short run it is often desirable to have more definite information about future prices.

Reasonably successful methods have been developed for forecasting the Bureau of Labor Statistics Wholesale Price Index and also the prices of many individual raw materials. In forecasting either an index of prices or individual prices, it is necessary to consider factors that affect supply and demand, and also autonomous monetary factors.

In forecasting the level of wholesale prices, general measures of supply and demand are called for. The supply of all goods is determined by the supply of the factors of production, that is, natural resources, real property, capital goods, and labor. The supply of natural resources and real property is not a significant variable, since for all practical purposes it remains constant in the short run. The capacity of capital equipment to turn out goods is, however, an important variable. It is almost impossible to arrive at a general measure of the productive capacity of all plants and other capital improvements used in producing goods and services. An index is available, however, of manufacturing capacity based on 1957-1959 as 100.[1]

The supply of labor is continually measured by the Bureau of the Census, and figures on the size of the labor force are regularly published by the Bureau of Labor Statistics. The measure of manufacturing capacity and figures on the size of the labor force thus provide a measure of the supply of the factors of production. Changes in these measures will show the degree to which pressure on prices is changing because of the rate of utilization of labor and capital.

It is impossible to find a true measure of the aggregative demand of the community. It is, however, possible to use GNP figures to show changes in demand that have taken place, since the demand for goods is translated into expenditures. Many analysts feel that it is better to use the Federal Reserve Board Index of Industrial Production as a measure of past changes in demand. Production in the manufacturing field is adjusted rather quickly to changes in demand; and, therefore, changes in the Index of Industrial Production provide a reasonable measure of current changes in demand. If goods are being produced for inventory rather than for sale, total

---

[1]For a description of this index see the *Federal Reserve Bulletin* (November, 1966), pp. 1605-1615.

demand is increased and this results in pressure on prices; but if stocks are being depleted, the situation is reversed. Therefore, the Index of Industrial Production provides a fairly good measure of changes in the aggregative demand for goods.

The third group of factors that must be considered are changes in the monetary factors which affect the general price level. These could be measured in detail, but such a procedure adds too many factors for practicable forecasting. Therefore, changes in the money supply and in the velocity of circulation have been utilized as a general measure of monetary influences on prices.

The first step in developing a forecast of prices from these supply, demand, and monetary factors is a study of past relationships of these factors. This may be done in several ways. One technique is to plot supply, demand, and monetary factors on ratio paper and analyze past relationships between them and wholesale prices as changes in the various series took place. Another possibility is to develop a multiple correlation relationship between wholesale prices and supply, demand, and monetary factors.

The next step is to forecast each of the major factors that affect prices. Methods of forecasting industrial production and the size of the money supply and the velocity of circulation have already been considered. The size of the labor force changes slowly and factors affecting it are continually studied by the Bureau of Labor Statistics. Forecasts of the size of the labor force are made regularly by the Bureau of the Census. The index of manufacturing capacity changes slowly, but not necessarily at a regular rate. Changes can be forecast from past trends and from data on plans for capital expenditures in manufacturing. A forecast of each of these factors for several quarters in the future and past relationships can be used to arrive at a preliminary forecast on wholesale prices.

Factors other than those considered in studying past relationships between supply, demand, and monetary factors also have an effect on prices, and the preliminary forecast must be adjusted in the light of them. This is especially true of such factors as foreign aid programs that stimulate exports and wartime price controls and materials allocation. It is also true of general increases in costs, such as increases in raw material prices due to import restrictions and increases in labor costs resulting from general wage increases that are greater than increases in productivity. It is, therefore, necessary to study all qualitative factors in the situation before making a final forecast of wholesale prices. Continual study of the relationship between the basic forecasting factors is also needed, since past relationships among so large a group of variables can change readily.

Leading series and series on expectations may also be used in short-run price forecasting either independently or in conjunction with forecasts based on supply, demand, and monetary factors. One of the leading series is the sensitive industrial materials index,[2] a subgroup of theWholesale Price Index. This index usuallyleads theWholesale Price Index, but the time period of the lead is not uniform. Price increases in sensitive industrial materials that are rapid or sustained tend to be followed by price increases in other industrial materials and these, in turn, by price increases in finished goods. The daily spot price index of 13 raw industrials may also be used as an indicator of present and future price developments. This index must be studied for basic underlying movements since it is subject to erratic movements on a day-by-day basis. This index like all leading series must be considered along with other factors in the situation since it often gives false signals.

Price diffusion indexes may also be used to help gauge future price developments. When a diffusion index moves above 50 percent, price increases are outnumbering price decreases and this is usually an indication that the aggregate price index will rise. Diffusion indexes can be used to gauge the direction of price changes, but they cannot be used to determine the timing or magnitude of such changes. One such index is based on the National Association of Purchasing Agents monthly survey of price developments. The index shows the percentage of purchasing agents reporting higher prices from the previous month, plus one half the percentage reporting unchanged prices. When this index has fallen below 50 percent, the industrial section of the Wholesale Price Index has declined or shown weakness; when it has passed 50 percent, prices have firmed or risen. This index had a sharp increase from 55 percent in June, 1964, to 76 percent in January, 1965, which forecast the increases in the price level that began in late 1964 and continued into 1965 and 1966.[3] Another diffusion index, which is published monthly in *Business Cycle Developments*, is that of industrial materials prices

---

[2]This index includes iron and steel scrap, nonferrous metals, lumber, plywood, wastepaper, rubber, hides, leather, textile fibres and intermediate products, and residual fuel oil.

[3]Federal Reserve Bank of Cleveland, *Economic Review* (April, 1966), p. 10.

based on the Index of Industrial Materials Prices of the Bureau of
Labor Statistics.   This index has also foreshadowed major price
movements, but it must be used with care since it can give false
signals.

Another approach to price forecasting is the use of series on
price expectations. Dun and Bradstreet in its quarterly survey asks
1,600 businessmen what they expect will happen to prices in the next
quarter in relationship to the same quarter a year ago.[4]   The net
percentage of businessmen expecting price increases, that is, the
percentage expecting price increases minus the percentage expecting
price decreases, gives some indication of future price developments.
Businessmen are more often right than wrong about future price
changes. But this series must be used with care since businessmen's
expectations at times lag behind price developments, especially in
periods when prices are declining.

FORECASTING THE PRICE OF AN INDIVIDUAL COMMODITY

In forecasting the demand for an individual commodity, such as
a farm product, it is necessary to consider the same three groups of
factors, that is, supply factors, demand factors, and monetary
factors.   The specific items used are different from those for the
general price level because only one commodity is involved.

As far as the supply is concerned, the most important factor is the
volume of production. If the commodity is purely a domestic one,
United States production is all that need be studied; but if it has a
world market, foreign production must be studied also. Inventories
also have an effect when they are unusually large or small, especially
in the case of agricultural raw materials.

Disposable income is one of the basic demand factors. For some
commodities it may be desirable to use lower bracket disposable
income, which is composed principally of wages and salaries, since
changes in this income are one of the best guides to changes in the
demand for basic commodities.   Other demand factors are consumption in the United States and, for a product having a world
market, consumption outside the United States.

Monetary factors can be measured, as was done in the forecasting of wholesale prices, by determining the degree of credit

---

[4]*Ibid.*, p. 12.

creation. For individual commodities, however, it is usually satisfactory to use disposable personal income as a measure of such changes, since such changes reflect the monetary factors that have been at work. Thus it can be seen that disposable income should be a significant factor in forecasting the prices of many individual commodities because it is related to demand factors and monetary factors at the same time.

Agricultural Prices

The first step in forecasting annual price changes of agricultural commodities is to decide upon the dating of the year to be used. For such a commodity as butter, which is produced continually throughout the year, the calendar year may be used for convenience. For crops such as wheat, which are produced only once a year, it is best to use the crop year, beginning with the month in which the new crop is harvested. For livestock there is a fairly distinct marketing year that should be used.

Selection of Factors for Study. The next step is the selection of the supply, demand, and monetary factors to be analyzed. As has already been indicated, consumer disposable income is one of the most important of these factors. Next in importance is the annual variation in supply. This variation may be analyzed as one factor, that is, production plus carry-over, or the two may be treated separately. If the amount of carry-over has a significant influence upon price, it should be considered as a separate factor. Consumption may also be considered as one of the factors in the analysis. If most of the product is consumed in the United States, domestic consumption may be utilized. If not, a separate measure of consumption outside the United States may be needed.

In order to determine which factors to use in correlation analysis, it is usually best to plot several of the most significant factors on a line graph, plotting past price variations of the commodity at the top of the graph and the related factors underneath. The two or three factors which fluctuate most nearly like that of the price in question should be selected for correlation. In forecasting individual prices, it is seldom practicable to use more than three related factors and two are often enough.

Past Relationships of Selected Factors. The past relationship
between these factors may be determined by multiple correlation
analysis. However, graphic correlation analysis can also be used
quite effectively with about the same degree of accuracy and it has
the added advantage of visual presentation. The period selected for
correlation analysis should be long enough to cover several business
cycles so that almost any conceivable combination of factors which
may affect prices is included. If graphic correlation is to be employed, the factor fluctuating most nearly like that of the price
being forecast should be used first and deviations from it then
plotted against the factor having the next closest variation. In this
way it is usually possible to explain past variations by two or three
variables, usually disposable personal income or lower bracket income and some measure of production or consumption or both.
In those cases in which stocks are extremely important in determining price, it may be advantageous to use disposable personal
income, production, and inventories or stocks as the three variables
to be correlated.

The factors affecting the price of cotton may be used to illustrate
this method. The price of cotton is affected materially by lower
bracket income, United States consumption, and United States
production. It is also affected by foreign consumption and by stocks
in the United States and in foreign countries. Chart 19-1 on page 489
shows cotton prices plotted along with lower bracket income, United
States consumption, and United States production. Past relationships between cotton prices and these factors were used to develop
the calculated price line shown in the chart. It is close enough in
most years so that other factors can be considered as qualitative.

Forecast Procedure. After past relationships have been established, it is necessary to forecast the related factors in order to
obtain the price forecast. Methods of arriving at disposable personal
income have already been considered. For basic agricultural raw
materials, the Department of Agriculture and private organizations
make continuous crop forecasts. Changes in consumption may be
estimated from past changes in relationship to disposable personal
income, and future stocks of goods may be estimated from the
differences between estimated production and consumption. Qualitative factors in the situation, such as government controls and
changes in them, unusual demands due to war, and shifts in con-

Chart 19-1

COTTON PRICE AND RELATED FACTORS

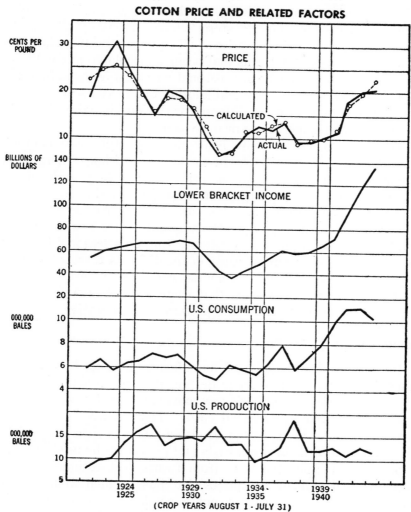

Source: Charles F. Roos, *Charting the Course of Your Business* (New York: Funk & Wagnalls Co., 1948), p. 30.

sumer tastes should also be continually studied and forecasts modified in the light of these studies.

After annual prices have been forecast, it is necessary to superimpose a forecast of seasonal movements on them to describe prospective price changes during the year. Seasonal variations in raw material prices may be determined by the method described in

Chapter 10, watching carefully for changes in seasonal patterns. This is important because changes such as the gradual introduction of improved methods of cold storage have materially affected the seasonal variations of some prices. Of more significance, however, are different seasonal patterns that occur under different conditions. For example, there may be one seasonal variation in years following a small crop of a commodity and another one in years after a large crop.   There may also be different variations in years in which national income is increasing or decreasing.

The relationship in some fields may be still more complex. Since the price of corn is related to the price of hogs, there is one seasonal pattern when the major price trend of hogs is downward in the years following a large corn crop, and another in the years following a small corn crop. There are different patterns following large and small corn crops when the major hog price trend is upward. Some of the most accurate price forecasting on a seasonal basis has been done by a very careful study of the different seasonal patterns under different conditions. Of course, care must be exercised so as not to use so many seasonals that there are not enough past examples of each type to make the patterns representative.

Manufactured Goods Prices

In forecasting the price of manufactured goods in which administered prices hold to some degree, it is necessary to forecast not only the price of the basic raw materials used but also changes in labor costs and in overhead costs. This involves estimates of wage increases to be granted and also a study of internal business costs. Past patterns between costs and prices can be used to arrive at preliminary price forecasts from future cost estimates.   This procedure will indicate the prices that businessmen would like to charge. Whether they can or not depends upon the prospective demand for their product. A forecast of demand and a study of past relationships between the level of demand and prices in relationship to costs can be used to make any needed adjustments in the price forecast.

FORECASTING COMMON STOCK PRICES

Probably no phase of economic activity has received as much study as the fluctuations in the security markets. Spurred on by a desire to make profits in the stock market, a large number of individuals and institutions have attempted to forecast the future course of stock prices.   Many of the forecasting services have proved to be of little value, and some individuals have sold forecasts that were not even based on a study of stock market behavior.   For example, in 1947 an individual who had a large number of clients for his forecasting service was arrested in New York. The authorities became suspicious because he claimed to have inside information. Upon checking they found that he claimed that he obtained his information through his sister who insisted that she had contacted the spirits of some of the great speculators of the past and that they had given her the secret of the security market. According to this source of information, the market was rigged every day, and clues to the security market could be found in the Maggie and Jiggs cartoon. The amazing thing about this situation was that many of the clients of this forecasting service maintained that it had an unusual degree of accuracy.

It should be recognized that a forecaster could be right a number of times purely on a chance basis. For example, if 100 people are forecasting the direction of the market, 50 could be right the first time purely by chance. Of those 50, 25 could be right the second time, 12 the third time, 6 the fourth time, 3 the fifth time, and at least 1 the sixth time, purely by chance. About 11 of the forecasters would be expected to be correct at least 5 times out of the 6 chances even if they were all to flip coins to make their choices. There can, therefore, be no acceptance of a system for forecasting the market or its record of calling four or five turns correctly without a study of the scientific basis underlying it.

Numerous attempts have been made to forecast the security market by finding a number of economic series which, when combined over a past period, have moved in conformity to an average of stock prices. For example, one such service was inaugurated in 1948 on the basis of a study of the market from 1919 through 1947. By combining several series, a line was developed which gave buy and sell signals that had been correct in practically every case over the past test period. The hypothetical results if money had been invested beginning in 1919 and held through 1947 were phenomenal, since a fund would have increased by over six hundred times. In the first year in which the line was used to make actual forecasts, however, it gave a major sell signal at a point below the last buy signal and several false indications in between.

This has happened frequently because by combining several series and weighting them properly it is possible to pass through or near almost any series of points. In fact, it can be shown mathematically that a combination of three curves properly weighted can be made to pass through or near ten points chosen almost at random. Therefore, little faith should be placed in any forecasting service in which the series chosen and the weights used in combining them are not based upon a logical study of the movements of the market but only upon the excellence of past fit.

Other approaches to forecasting the level of stock prices are based on the technical approach that assumes that a relationship exists between prices in one period and prices in another period. This assumption has been questioned and some have suggested that stock price movements are more like a *random walk*, that is, that past price behavior is no indicator of future price behavior. A major statistical study to test this hypothesis has been carried on at the Center for Research in Security Prices at the University of Chicago. This Center has made use of computer analysis to study various aspects of the stock market.

One study was designed to test two of the major theories of market behavior. The chartist approach holds that past market behavior gives information on future behavior because price patterns develop and such patterns tend to recur. If this is true and the patterns can be identified, it should be possible to develop a forecasting technique based on past developments. The random walk approach holds that no regular pattern exists and that the future of prices is no more predictable than the path of a series of random numbers which have been cumulated. In other words, successive price changes are independent, random variables with no identifiable pattern. To test these hypotheses, the daily prices of each stock in the Dow-Jones Industrial Average were used. The time periods were usually from the end of 1957 to September 26, 1962. For each of the 30 stocks in the Industrial Average, there were between 1,200 and 1,700 observations. The price changes were found to be distributed in a frequency distribution, which was similar to that based on chance, but had a long tail because there were more scattered large increases in price than small ones. This data thus supported the random walk hypothesis[5] since this is the shape of frequency distributions of most economic series which are not causally related to each other.

Dow Theory

Nevertheless, some techniques that are used to forecast the security markets have met with some degree of success. The best known of these is the Dow theory. The Dow theory was named after Charles H. Dow, who was the founder of Dow-Jones & Company and the original editor of *The Wall Street Journal*, the first of the financial publications of his concern. Dow wrote a series of articles in *The Wall Street Journal* in which he analyzed and attempted to explain past actions in the stock market. William P. Hamilton, who was an assistant to Dow and succeeded him as editor, continued these studies in his column in *The Wall Street Journal*, "The Stock Market Barometer." Various individuals have elaborated on the writings of Dow and Hamilton and have stressed different phases of their work or have added their own interpretations so that there is really no one Dow theory.

From a study of stock market averages developed by the Dow-Jones Publishing Company beginning in 1885, Dow recognized that there were three major movements in the security markets: the primary movement, which has varied from less than a year to several years in duration; the secondary reaction, which has lasted from three weeks to three months or more and has retraced from one third to two thirds of the preceding primary swing; and the day-to-day fluctuations. This observation was based upon an average of railroad stocks and one of industrial stocks. Today practically all Dow theorists still work with the Dow Jones Industrial Average and the Dow-Jones Railroad Average.

Forecasting by the Dow theory is based upon the study of the primary fluctuations and the secondary reactions. Usually a primary upward movement has had two or more secondary reactions, and a primary downward movement has had two or three upward reactions. According to the Dow theory, stocks should be bought on a primary upswing when the high point of the last secondary reaction has been exceeded. Since it is impossible to forecast accurately the

---

[5]Eugene F. Fama, "The Behavior of Stock Market Prices," *The Journal of Business*, Vol. XXXVIII (January, 1965), pp. 34–105.

low point of the cycle, the best policy is to wait for a secondary reaction to run its course so as to establish clearly that the primary trend is up. When the market, after a secondary reaction, passes the high point from which this reaction began, it is an indication to Dow theorists that the primary movement is upward and that a new bull market is in progress. For a positive signal to buy, it is necessary for this to happen in both the rail and the industrial averages. Chart 19-2 shows such buy signals and also sell signals.

To sell at the high point of the cycle is also impossible, since the peak cannot be forecast. Therefore, under the Dow theory the investor takes no action on the first downturn in prices when the primary trend is reversed because he is not sure that this may not be another secondary reaction on the upswing. When the market has moved downhill substantially for a period of three or more weeks and then has revived and moved upward from one third to two thirds of its previous drop and then again turned downward, indications are that a secondary reaction on the downswing is in progress. When the market on the downturn exceeds the low point from which the last secondary revival began, a sell signal is given. The determination of the point of such a sell signal is shown in Chart 19-2. It is again necessary for the two averages to corroborate each other for a positive signal.

Chart 19-2

Dow Theory—Major Buy and Sell Signals

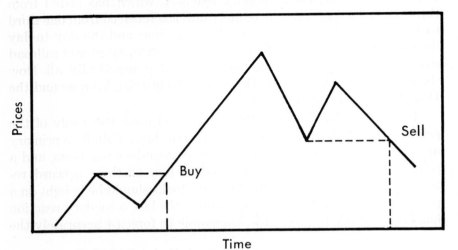

Source: *Hypothetical data.*

This technique, when followed in major market swings, has often been used quite successfully. The Dow system, however, has given many false signals, especially in more recent years. In a market in which wide swings occur, it provides a method for an individual to buy stocks at relatively low prices and to sell them at relatively high prices without trying to forecast the exact tops or bottoms of the market. It cannot work, however, when the market is not subject to large up-and-down movements, since it is easily possible in such a case to have a buy signal at a higher point than a subsequent sell signal. The system has also in part defeated itself, since it has had many adherents and their actions have influenced the course of the market at times.

Since the Dow theory has given false signals, Dows theorists have also used other market factors in conjunction with it. For example, some of them are on the alert for a line being formed in the market. This occurs when for a period of several weeks both the rail and the industrial averages fluctuate within narrow limits of about 5 percent. If both of the averages break out above the line, there is an indication of higher prices, according to Dow theorists. If they break out below the line, the indication is for lower prices. There does not appear to be much logical basis for this phase of the Dow theory, and it has given many false signals.

More recently, stress has been placed on the relationship of volume to price movements. For example, according to this theory a market that has been overbought becomes dull on rallies and develops activity on declines; and bull markets tend to terminate with excess activity after beginning with a comparatively low volume. There is undoubtedly something to the relationship between volume and price, since these factors are important in determining the total demand for stocks, but little of true forecasting value has been developed to date.

Other Techniques

In recent years a large number of other services that attempt to forecast prices in the security markets have appeared. One service has attempted to develop a major change indicator on a logical basis by studying the relationship to security prices of such related factors as the money supply; measures of general economic activity, including leading series; and stock market data on volume, price, and customers' free balances with brokers. These are factors that should logically have some influence on the major movement of stock prices, and it may be possible to develop some type of forecasting technique from them. So far, however, there has been too little experience to determine whether this technique will work.

Another service is based on the principle that in a strong market there will not only be an increase in the averages but also a large number of individual stocks advancing in price. When the number of stocks advancing declines while the market averages are continuing upward, there is an indication of a reversal in movement.

Other services have tried to use odd lot data, that is, data on sales of less than a round lot, as a basis for forecasting. When odd lot sales are moving in a direction different from that of the general market, bullish or bearish signals are given. When in a market upswing or downswing the odd lot traders significantly change their behavior and switch from buying to selling or vice versa, this is a signal to do the opposite. The main difficulty with this system is not only that it has given wrong signals, but it has also given no signal when a signal has been called for. It will, as a rule, give a dependable signal to sell in those speculative markets in which the general public has done a large amount of speculative buying, but such markets have not existed often in recent years.

Attempts to forecast stock price changes will no doubt go on. These prices are, however, among the most difficult to forecast because psychological factors influence them to a large extent. From time to time, also, the uninitiated enter the market and accentuate price swings. The average investor would do well to base his purchases of common stocks on an analysis of the worth of individual stock based on forecasts of the future prospects of particular companies rather than on price forecasts of the stock market in general. In this way he is assured of a reasonable return and relative safety, irrespective of market movements.

QUESTIONS

1. Discuss the factors that lead to price changes in the long run.
2. Describe a procedure for projecting price trends.
3. What effect do costs have on price trends?
4. How does short-run price forecasting differ from long-run forecasting?
5. Describe and evaluate several procedures for forecasting wholesale prices.
6. Describe the procedures used to forecast prices of agricultural commodities.
7. How may monthly price forecasts for such commodities as cotton be developed from annual price forecasts?
8. How can prices of manufactured goods be forecast?
9. Describe the chartist and the random walk theories of stock price movements. What are the implications for the investor of the random walk theory as the correct one?
10. Describe the workings of the Dow theory for forecasting stock prices.
11. Under what conditions would the Dow theory work reasonably well?
12. Discuss several other methods for forecasting stock price changes.

SUGGESTED READINGS

Chase, Richard H. Jr., William C. Gifford Jr., Richard S. Bower, and Peter J. Williamson. *Computer Applications in Investment Analysis.* Hanover: The Amos Tuck School of Business Administration, 1966.

Eiteman, Wilford J., Charles A. Dice, and David N. Eiteman. *The Stock Market.* New York: McGraw-Hill Book Company, 1966, Chapter 27.

Fama, Eugene F. "The Behavior of Stock Market Prices," *The Journal of Business.* Vol. XXXVIII (January, 1965), pp. 34–105.

Lynip, B. F., Jr. *Factors Affecting the Wholesale Price Level.* San Francisco: California and Hawaiian Sugar Refining Corporation, Ltd., 1950.

Rhea, Robert. *Dow's Theory Applied to Business and Banking.* New York: Simon and Schuster, Inc., 1938.

Waugh, Frederick V. *Demand and Price Analysis.* Washington: U.S. Department of Agriculture, 1964.

United States Department of Agriculture. *Handbook of Agricultural Charts* (Annually). Washington: U.S. Department of Agriculture.

CHAPTER 20

Agencies Providing
Forecasting Services

In recent years a number of organizations and individuals have established forecasting services. Some attempt to forecast general economic activity, others only certain phases of business. Many market research organizations also make forecasts as part of their marketing service to business. Much information that is helpful in making forecasts is also developed by agencies of the United States government.

It is impossible to analyze the activities of all or even a substantial part of these services. Some have been in business too short a time for their success to be judged from their records. The businessman must choose among them on the basis of the techniques they use and their success to date. To indicate the range of services offered, the activities of a representative group of companies will be described. The methods used in forecasting will be discussed for those organizations that make such information a matter of public record. The information supplied by the federal government that is of aid in forecasting will also be considered briefly, as well as some of the forecasts published by the government.

THE UNITED STATES ECONOMICS CORPORATION

United States Economics Corporation was founded in 1944 by Arthur O. Dahlberg and Victor von Szeliski, both of whom had done extensive research and writing in national income analysis and demand determination. In 1961 the United States Economics Corporation absorbed the Econometric Institute, which was founded in 1937 by Dr. Charles F. Roos, who died in 1958. The United States Economics Corporation is a wholly owned, but autonomously operated, subsidiary of United Research, Inc., Cambridge, Massachusetts, an organization that developed from a Harvard University consulting group formed during World War II.

One of the services offered by the United States Economics Corporation is periodic written forecasts. Every month updated tables of forecasts are sent out on the following:

(a) GNP and 27 of its component series. These include business, consumer, and government spending, and also personal income, disposable income, and corporate profits.
(b) The Federal Reserve Board Index of Industrial Production and its major components.
(c) Retail trade.

Quarterly data are presented five quarters ahead by quarters and monthly data five months ahead by months. Twelve or more times a year reports deal with some important or timely aspect of the economy, such as capital spending, inventories, consumer spending, prices, wages, and monetary developments. Twice a year a comprehensive report is issued on the economic outlook. The March issue analyzes the most likely impact of the President's "State of the Union" message and his "Budget Message," while the September issue covers forecasts for the next year at a time when many corporate budgets are prepared. The United States Economics Corporation uses many of the techniques discussed in Chapters 17 and 18 in making its forecasts.

The United States Economics Corporation provides a series of consulting services to its clients. They will formulate market guides or "predictors" after making a basic study of the economic forces that affect a company's products or markets. They also make "outlook" presentations to management in which developments likely to affect a business are discussed in some detail. They develop long-range studies that can serve as a guide for capital expansion programs, labor requirements, mergers, and the like. Many of the largest corporations make use of some or all of these services, and some have done so for many years.

STATISTICAL INDICATOR ASSOCIATES

Statistical Indicator Associates publish a weekly bulletin called *Statistical Indicator Reports* that gives data on the statistical indicators selected by the National Bureau of Economic Research as the best indicators of changes in economic activity. Each bulletin presents a chart that shows changes in each of the 26 series during a period of several years, which covers the current cycle. Monthly figures are also presented for each series for the past 12 months. These figures are all seasonally adjusted, except common stock prices, industrial raw material prices, and interest rates on bank loans. There is also an analysis of the data and the charts and some indication of the most likely direction of economic activity in the period ahead. Prospects for future business are often expressed in probabilities, such as a statement that there are 3.5 to 4 chances in 10 that the directions of economic activity will change.

Other information is also presented on a regular basis. Once a month there is an analysis of the duration in months of the expansion or contraction that has been taking place in each series and on the average in the leading, coincident, and lagging series. Composite indexes are presented monthly for the leading, coincident, and lagging series. There is also monthly information on the percentage of series in each group that is expanding.

Statistical Indicator Associates also offer a forecasting service for individual companies. They will prepare annual forecasts of sales on a monthly basis and five-year projections. They make critiques of forecasts made by the staff of a company, which cover such items as forecasting techniques, analysis of the data, and effectiveness of charts.

NATIONAL INDUSTRIAL CONFERENCE BOARD

The National Industrial Conference Board is a nonprofit research organization that is supported by business firms and other organizations which hold memberships in it. It does no specific forecasting as such, but it has several services that aid in forecasting. It publishes a monthly journal, *The Conference Board Record*, that analyzes developments in the economy in such areas as plant and equipment expenditures, government spending, and inventory levels. A sheet of selected business indicators gives past data and current figures on various sectors of production, trade, and distribution; on commodity and security prices; and on financial series, such as bank debits.

The most important of these indicators are brought up to date in a weekly desk sheet of current business trends. The most important qualitative factors of the week are also discussed on this sheet. At the end of each year leading economists from business, government, labor, banking, and the universities discuss the business outlook for the next year. This is a full-scale forum in which many phases of business are covered. Special attention is given to doubtful areas, and in areas in which there are likely to be differing viewpoints several analysts are asked to develop their views. For those members who cannot attend, the proceedings are published late in the year as *The Business Outlook 19--*. This is especially worthwhile as a cross-check on any forecast, since many shades of opinion are represented and thus various viewpoints are obtained on developments in doubtful areas of future business activity.

The Conference Board also makes the surveys of capital appropriations and of consumer buying plans that have been discussed previously, which are published regularly in *Business Record*.

STANDARD AND POOR'S CORPORATION

Standard and Poor's Corporation is one of several services providing data of all types needed for security analysis. It publishes financial information on corporations, up-to-date dividend information, data on bond issue calls and stock rights, detailed descriptions of new issues, a register of directors and executives, and the like. These services are primarily of interest to investors.

One of these services, however, is of special value to a forecaster. That is the *Industry Survey* which covers all major industries. At least once a year each industry is analyzed carefully and factors affecting its future outlook are considered. Supplemental sheets keep this analysis up to date.

As part of this service a monthly bulletin, called *Trends and Projections*, is issued. In it annual forecasts are made of gross national product and its major components and of the Federal Reserve Index of Industrial Production. Monthly forecasts are also made for a quarter ahead for a large group of industries.

Standard and Poor's Corporation does not publish information on all of the analysis done to make its forecasts. It does point out, however, that not only does it do research and analysis on economic data and company data but it also uses a large field staff to check constantly every important company in every industry. This procedure enables the corporation to judge qualitative factors from firsthand contact. The most important of these factors are passed on to subscribers in the *Industry Survey*.

ROY WENZLICK RESEARCH CORPORATION

Roy Wenzlick Research Corporation has been engaged in real estate research and forecasting since the late twenties and has been publishing reports on trends and current developments in real estate since 1932. It is an organization of economists specializing in real estate; of appraisers; and of consultants on real estate problems to banks, insurance companies, real estate firms, manufacturers of building materials, and the like.

Some of its publications are of interest in the field of general forecasting. Several series of bulletins are published on a regular basis under the general heading of the *Real Estate Analyst*, which has several issues per month. The general issues of the *Real Estate Analyst* include a discussion of such items as real estate activity, mortgage activity, residential construction, bank debits, employment, wages, and department store sales. Total construction expenditures in the United States, types of building, construction costs, financing, and the like, are covered from time to time. Articles also analyze trends and current developments in the component parts of building costs, such as materials, labor, and overhead.

Real Estate Trends is issued monthly and provides data on real estate transfers, residential construction, construction costs, trends in the selling price of real estate, and the like. Also issued monthly is the bulletin *As I See*, or *As We See*. It analyzes general economic, monetary, business, and political factors and shows their probable effect on real estate. The January issue contains a forecast of all phases of real estate activity for the coming year, including housing construction, selling prices, total construction, and financing.

The Construction Bulletin, which is published twice a year, is a detailed report on the volume of construction in 206 metropolitan areas. Data are shown for new family accomodations being built for each city. The Spring issue shows the change in the number of new dwelling units for the past year and the previous year. The Fall issue gives the same information for the first half of the year. Summary data are presented on a national basis and for various regions of the country. National averages on the rate of residential construction are also given for cities in various population size groups.

The Wenzlick forecasts are made on the basis of an analysis of all of the factors likely to affect real estate, such as population trends, population shifts, income, and costs. Some use is made of the real estate cycle, which Wenzlick currently holds is just over 18 years in length, but forecasts are not made mechanically by means of projecting such a cycle.

F. W. DODGE COMPANY

The F. W. Dodge Company, which is a division of McGraw-Hill, has a wide variety of services designed to provide information in marketing that is helpful to the construction and related industries. For example, *Dodge Reports* provide management and salesmen with a day-by-day record of what is going to be built and who is going to build it. A series of reports are issued starting with information on contemplated building and running through the planning, contract bidding, and general contract awarding and subcontracting stages. One service of primary interest in the forecasting and sales analysis field is *Dodge Construction Statistics*, which furnish data on the value of construction contracts awarded. The use of such data in forecasting building and general economic activity was described in Chapters 17 and 18, and forecasting sales for an industrial concern will be discussed in Chapter 22.

Dodge Construction Statistics cover all construction on which measurable data are available. This includes all construction except the following: work on farms; work done by the construction forces of public utilities, industrial companies, and the government; and residential alterations and additions. The statistics cover the 48 states in the continental United States. Data are presented for the true dollar value of construction as accurately as these can be developed.

The data are available for some 267 different project types of construction and state and county locations of the project are given. These data are committed to a computer memory unit and from this reservoir of statistical data specific computer runs are made for the project groupings and geographic requirements of specific clients. Such runs can be made for current month figures, for 12-month moving totals, and cumulatively for the year to date. The data can also be compared with the related sales of a client.

The Economics Department provides long-term forecasts for specific types of construction on a retainer basis. An annual forecast of total construction for the coming year is published each October and updated in the middle of the year. This forecast provides estimated dollar figures for various types of nonresidential and residential building and also for major types of nonbuilding construction, such as streets, highways and bridges, and utilities. It also contains a forecast of the Dodge Index of Construction Activity for the coming year.

The data for the *Dodge Reports* and the *Dodge Construction Statistics* are gathered by a field force of over 1,400 men. Most of the data are provided by architects, owners, and general contractors, from an analysis of permits and other records of buildings to be started and from checking in the field. All processing of data and tabulation is handled by the central data processing departments in New York. *Dodge Reports* are issued daily through 18 regional issuing offices, and over 250,000 projects are covered annually by these reports.

PREDICASTS, INC.

Predicasts, Inc., is an organization that provides a whole series of long-run and short-run forecasting and market research services. It has a unique quarterly service called *Predicasts*, which summarizes practically all forecasts that appear in print. One section contains composite forecasts of 160 series such as GNP and its major components in current and in constant dollars, the FRB Index of Industrial Production and its subcategories, new construction, housing, employment, and the like. The composite forecasts are developed by taking the medians of published forecasts and adjusting them as needed to form a consistent pattern for the series being presented, such as the major components of GNP. Forecasts are published for the next year and for several selected future years. The issue of January 15, 1967, for example, presented historical data for 1960 and 1963 through 1966, and forecasts for 1967, 1970, 1975, and 1980. Another section provides data on individual published forecasts of the general economy and the major components and determinants of economic activity. There is also a section of growth products that lists products whose volume is expected to double during the next five years. Another section on key world forecasts lists summary forecasts from articles on major world markets. A major section of each issue contains forecasts on all major industries and thousands of specific products. This section summarizes all forecasts made in articles and published speeches by organizations and individuals. The statements are also coded as to whether they are given as fact, as probable, or as possible.

Predicasts offers the forecaster a great saving in time since all published forecasts are summarized. They are available in one place for ready reference along with recent historical data. This information, is of course, only as valid as the published forecasts that it summarizes.

NATIONAL PLANNING ASSOCIATION

The National Planning Association is an independent nonprofit organization set up in 1934 to bring together leaders from business, labor, agriculture, and the professions to develop workable plans for the future of the nation. Under the sponsorship of a board of trustees and various standing and special committees, it has studied a wide range of problems and issued reports on them.

Some of its studies, such as those on industry in the South, are of interest in the field of business fluctuations, especially in regard to regional trends. Most useful, however, are several studies on trends in economic activity, such as the *American Economy in 1960*, published in 1952, and the *American Economy in 1970*, published in 1959. The latter study analyzes trends in all phases of economic development and projects the level of gross national product on the basis of such analysis. Detailed consideration is then given to various ways in which gross national product could be divided and still provide full employment. The most likely way in which such balance could be achieved is outlined. These studies are valuable as a guide to a long-run economic development, which must be considered first in any long-run forecasting of sales for a particular product.

The National Planning Association Center for Economic Projections makes regular national economic projections based on an analysis of past trends. These are available to subscribers and full-service members in the *National Economic Projections Series*, which provides regularly revised 5- and 10-year projections and also some 20-year projections. These projections cover employment and output by major industrial groupings, detailed components of government expenditures and finance, private construction, and investment and consumer expenditures. They also include figures

on GNP and on the Federal Reserve Board Index of Industrial
Production. A helpful feature is that of providing GNP data on
three bases: the level assuming the continuation of current policies,
the projected level at maximum employment, and at the level based
on the best judgment of the staff. The Center for Economic Projection also publishes annual forecasts of GNP and its major components. These are given as figures for the year and for the first
half and second half.

They also publish a *Regional Economic Projections Series,* which
contains projections of detailed demographic data and various
economic indicators of growth on a state and metropolitan area
basis. Much emphasis is placed on future patterns of migration
on an interstate basis and on the probable relocation of industrial
activity. This is especially useful in making decisions on the location
of plants, warehouses, offices, and the like. These reports are issued
in nontechnical language, but supplemental reports provide extensive
technical discussion.

FORTUNE MAGAZINE

Fortune magazine presents information on the economy and on
the economic outlook in a monthly feature called the "Business
Roundup." In this section of the magazine, staff economists
analyze various factors affecting the economy and devote considerable attention to such areas as spending on capital goods
and consumer spending of various types. Forecasts, which are
presented annually for the coming 18 months, include GNP and
its major components and the Federal Reserve Board Index of
Industrial Production.

Fortune also publishes a semiannual survey of the business mood.
This is based on reports from about 400 executives on their ex-
pectations for sales in their own business in the coming 12 months.
They are asked to report their forecasts in the following categories:

> Down
> Steady
> Up 0 — 5 percent
> Up more than 5 percent

Summary results are presented for the latest survey and they are
compared with earlier surveys.

BUSINESS WEEK

The magazine, *Business Week,* publishes a regular feature called "Business Outlook," which analyzes a wide range of factors affecting the future course of business and of the total economy. An early issue in January is a "forecast" number and contains a forecast for the year of GNP and of its major components. Spring and fall issues contain reports on the capital spending surveys made by the McGraw-Hill Economics Department. These surveys on plans for expenditures on new plant and equipment make comparisons with earlier surveys and also analyze the factors that have led to changes in plans. Articles are frequently published on developments in various sectors of the economy and on significant research on economic problems and trends. The forecast made from the econometric model developed by the Research Seminar on Quantitative Economics at the University of Michigan is published annually in *Business Week.*

UNITED STATES GOVERNMENT

Several agencies of the United States government publish information which is of aid in developing forecasts and some agencies make forecasts for various sectors of the economy. The major ones are the Department of Commerce, Office of Business Economics; the Department of Commerce, Business and Defense Services Administration; the Department of Commerce, Bureau of the Census; Bureau of Labor Statistics; the Department of Agriculture; and the Council of Economic Advisers.

The Department of Commerce, Office of Business Economics, publishes the *Survey of Current Business* on a monthly basis. Each issue contains articles on the general business situation and on developments in several sectors of the economy. It also contains a wealth of statistical information on almost all of the series discussed in this book. The February issue is the Annual Review Number that analyzes the economy during the past year, and the July issue is the National Income Number that analyzes developments in national income data during the past year and trends over several years.

The *Survey of Current Business* also has reports quarterly on plans for expenditures on plant and equipment and on inventory and sales expectations, which were discussed in Chapter 18. A progress report on the econometric model developed by the Department of

Commerce also appeared in the *Survey of Current Business* in May, 1966, and additional reports will be forthcoming as work on the model progresses. Every four or five years a supplement is published called *National Income and Product Accounts of the United States* which provides national income and product account data for the period since 1929.

The Business and Defense Services Administration in the Department of Commerce publishes annual Outlook Studies on a large number of selected industries. They are published in book form under the title, *The U. S. Industrial Outlook for 19—*. This volume contains a summary of the prospects for the total economy and an analysis of past trends and the outlook for each of the industries covered. In most cases specific forecasts are made of the volume of business expected in the field.

The Business and Defense Services Administration also publishes the *Construction Review*. It analyzes past trends in construction and factors affecting this industry. One issue early in the year reviews developments in the previous year, another late in the year analyzes prospects and makes forecasts for the following year. Statistics are published on a monthly and an annual basis on construction activity, mortgage activity, housing starts, building permit activity, contracts awarded, construction costs, materials output, and employment in the construction field.

The Bureau of the Census publishes data on population, the labor force, and characteristics of the labor force that are useful in developing data for a forecast. They also publish projections of population by age and sex for periods of 20 years in the future at five-year intervals and yearly for shorter periods. Estimates are made also of population by states. Projections of the labor force and its composition are made for each five-year interval for 20 years in the future and yearly for several years ahead. The Bureau of the Census also conducts the quarterly survey of consumer buying intentions discussed in Chapter 17.

The Bureau of the Census publishes one of the most significant publications in this field, the monthly *Business Cycle Developments*. This report covers current data in table and chart form on about 90 principal economic indicators. The classification of the series and business cycle dates are those used by the National Bureau of Economic Research. The data are arranged according to their usual timing relationships as leading, coincident, or lagging series and there are also historical comparisons for many series showing the current cycle and previous postwar cycles. A series of leading and coincident diffusion indexes are also presented. The data are available by about the twenty-second of the month following the month of the data.

The Bureau of the Census also publishes *Long-Term Economic Growth* which gives data on economic fluctuations over a long span of years, that is, back to 1860 or to the first year when data are available. Almost 400 aggregate economic time series are covered and almost 800 component series. These include various measures of output such as gross national product, industrial production, and personal consumption expenditures and measures of input such as the amount and types of labor and capital available for producing the economy's output. Also included are measures of the productive efficiency of labor and capital and the processes related to growth such as utilization of productive capacity, education, research and development, profits, monetary series, and the like. Another section provides data on regional and industry trends. Practically all of the data is presented in both chart and table form. The first volume in this series covered the period 1860–1965. Annual publication is planned for several years, as users experiment with the data and suggest changes to improve this publication.

The Bureau of Labor Statistics publishes the *Monthly Labor Review* that contains statistics on the labor force, employment and unemployment, hours worked per week and wage rates, and wholesale prices and consumer prices. It also has articles discussing trends in the labor field and in the economy as they affect labor.

The Department of Agriculture publishes a wealth of data useful in forecasting agricultural income and production through its Statistical Reporting Service. It publishes the *Agricultural Situation* which contains analyses of trends and prospects for agriculture and for various crops. The December issue includes the outlook for crops, prices, costs, income, exports, and the like. Each year a book of *Agricultural Charts* is published for the following year. This publication gives charts and data on agricultural income, prices and costs, and on the situation in each major crop area.

The Council of Economic Advisers publishes one of the most helpful of all publications, its monthly *Economic Indicators*. This book gives charts and data for several years on all major economic variables, including especially the subcategories of GNP. Data are also provided on production, employment, hours of work, exports and imports, prices, and monetary factors. Early in the year the Council publishes its annual report along with the *Economic Report of the President*. This reviews the economy during the past year and relates events in this year to those during the last several years. Current and prospective developments are analyzed in detail. In recent years specific forecasts have been made for the year for GNP and its major components and for the monetary and fiscal areas.

QUESTIONS

1. Discuss the forecasting services of the following organizations:
   United States Economics Corporation
   Statistical Indicator Associates
   National Industrial Conference Board
   Standard and Poor's Corporation
   Roy Wenzlick Research Corporation
   F. W. Dodge Company
   Predicasts, Inc.
   National Planning Association
   Fortune magazine
   Business Week
2. Describe the information published by the United States government that is helpful to a business in its forecasting program.
3. How can forecasting services be used in the forecasting program of an individual business?

SUGGESTED READINGS

See current issues of:
Business Week, "Business Outlook."
Dodge, F. W., Company, *Dodge Construction Statistics*.
Fortune magazine, "Business Roundup."
National Industrial Conference Board, *The Conference Board Record* and *The Business Outlook*.
National Planning Association, *National Economic Projections Series*.
Predicasts, Inc., *Predicasts*.
Roy Wenzlick Research Corporation, *Real Estate Analyst*.
Standard and Poor's Corporation, *Industry Survey*.
Statistical Indicator Associates, *Statistical Indicator Reports*.
United States Department of Commerce, *Survey of Current Business*.
———, Bureau of the Census, *Business Cycle Developments*.
———, Business and Defense Services Administration, *The U.S. Industrial Outlook*.

PROBLEMS ON PART VI

1. Project GNP ten years into the future by:
    (a) Projecting past trends
    (b) Projecting the number of employees and output per employee

2. Using the formulas in Table 16-3, calculate expenditures on services based on past relationships when real disposable personal income expressed in 1957 dollars is $500 billion.

3. From data on regional trends in the economy put out by the Department of Commerce and in the *Survey of Current Business*, study the trend of population, income, and retail sales in your section of the country. What effect are such trends likely to have on the growth of gross private product in your area in the period to 1975?

4. Study the following factors in the current business situation:

    The segment of the typical cycle in which business is at the present time.

    An analysis of the leading, coincident, and lagging series.

    Consumer buying intentions as developed in Federal Reserve surveys.

    Business plans for expenditures on plant and equipment.

    Analysis of new orders, inventories, and sales.

    Analysis of businessmen's expectations.

    Analysis of the monetary and fiscal situation.

5. Prepare a forecast of GNP for each of the next four quarters following the procedures for forecasting each sector of the economy described in Chapter 18. Cross-check the forecasts and prepare a final forecast for each sector and for GNP.

6. Plot the Bureau of Labor Statistics Wholesale Price Index for each year from 1950 to the present. Account for the changes that have taken place.

PART VII

FORECASTING SALES

This part shows how forecasting is used in business to forecast sales. Many factors must be forecast in business, including costs, capital requirements, and labor requirements, as well as sales. The starting point in all of these forecasts is, however, a forecast of sales. Such forecasts need to be stated in dollars and also in units to provide a basis for business planning.

Sales forecasts should not be made entirely from an analysis of the situation in an individual business or in the industry of which it is a part. All business is affected to some degree by general economic activity. Therefore, before a forecast for an industry or an individual business is made, it is desirable to have a forecast of overall economic activity. This background is used to help develop a forecast for an industry, and an industry forecast is generally useful in developing a forecast for an individual business. The steps in developing a sales forecast are usually to forecast general economic activity, then the level of sales in the industry, and lastly the sales of an individual business.

The first chapter in this part discusses methods used to forecast for an industry, the second for an individual business.

CHAPTER 21   *Forecasting Sales for an Industry*

In addition to a forecast of general economic activity, it is desirable to have forecasts of the volume of business in major industries. Such forecasts can help cross-check forecasts of total activity. They also are valuable in helping to determine if unemployment is likely to occur in an industry, to decide if additional workers must be recruited, to estimate the amount of new capital that will be required, and the like. The managers of a business will find a forecast of industry sales helpful in forecasting sales of their business and in planning operations for the next several quarters.

STEPS IN FORECASTING INDUSTRY SALES

In forecasting cyclical movements in an industry, it is necessary to study the factors that have been responsible for changes in sales in the past. The first step in this process is the careful selection of the specific sales items that are to be analyzed. It is necessary to decide whether the sales should be analyzed as a whole or divided into subcategories for study. The latter should be done if different factors affect different classes of sales. For example, in analyzing the factors that have affected sales in the clothing field, better results are obtained by studying separately women's clothing, men's clothing, and children's clothing, since trends are different in each field and the large postwar birth rates affect the last category materially.

The second step is to select the measure of aggregative economic activity that is most closely related to changes in sales of the products being studied. In some cases in which a good is sold to consumers, producers, and the government, the most important factor to study is the relationship to gross national product. In other cases in which a product is sold primarily to consumers, it is probably the relationship to disposable personal income, or in rural areas to cash farm income. In still other fields, such as building hardware, the volume of construction activity may be the most important factor.

515

In order to use such general measures of economic activity as a basis for forecasting industry sales, it is, of course, necessary to have a forecast of such series. This approach of basing a forecast on such general measures is feasible for a business because private organizations and government agencies have spent millions of dollars in developing such forecasts. Many of these are available at little or no cost, and even those bought from research organizations cost far less than it would cost to develop forecasts by other methods. Another reason for using relationships to aggregative measures is that they are often easier to develop than sales forecasts for industries made by other methods.

In addition to relationships to general measures of economic activity, other factors affecting the demand for the product must be considered. Any businessman can easily make a list of fifteen or twenty factors that affect sales in his field. It is seldom practicable, however, to work with more than three or four of the most important variables on a quantitative basis. It is extremely important in selecting these variables to work only with those that are logically related to the series being studied and as nearly as possible directly related causally. These include such factors as changes in the level of income from the past year, changes in price, changes in the expected life of the product, changes in population, and the like.

After having selected the most important variables, it is necessary to consider the nature of the relationships that have occurred in the past. This can be done by charting these relationships or by the techniques of correlation analysis. The correlation approach has the advantage of being definite since, once the general formula is decided upon, any analyst will arrive at the same specific formula. The graphic approach, however, is simpler and is easier for most businessmen to comprehend.

A fourth step is to analyze all of the qualitative factors in the past, present, and future to determine if past relationships will continue. In general, consumer buying habits do not deviate radically from the pattern of the past in the short run, nor do methods of business operation change rapidly in the absence of marked technological innovations. Changes do take place, however, and it is necessary to study the effects of changes in governmental policies, technological innovations, and the like before deciding that past relationships will continue into the immediate future.

A fifth step, or in some cases an alternative to steps two, three, and four, is to develop a forecast by end-use analysis. This technique starts with a grouping of products or services by differing end uses, such as for direct personal consumption, as a material or part for further manufacture in a specific industry, or as a product or service sold to the federal government. It is necessary to determine the relationship of activity in the end-use industries to sales in the industry being forecast. A next step is to forecast the level of sales in each of the end-use industries and then develop an industry forecast from such forecasts and past relationships.

This method is only practicable if the end use is distributed over only a few major industries. It is utilized, for example, in the industrial chemical industry in which most of the sales go to a limited group of users. Detailed information on the end use of industry sales is available in input-output tables, which are discussed in the last section of this chapter. In cases in which it is practicable, industry forecasts may be developed both by end-use analysis and by relationships to aggregate measures of economic activity and the two forecasts used as a cross-check on each other. If the two methods have given similar results in the past and now give significantly different results, it is an indication that all factors need to be studied carefully since chances are good that some significant factors have been overlooked or that past relationships are changing.

The last step is to develop an awareness of the error that will be involved in any forecast which is made. No relationship based on the past can be expected to work perfectly in the future, since there are scores of factors other than the variables used that affect sales, and since new factors also come into play. The effects of these other factors may tend to balance out in most years, but at times there may be an unusual number of them working in the same direction so that the error may be greater than the average.

FORECASTING DEMAND IN THE CONSUMERS' NONDURABLE GOODS AND SERVICES INDUSTRIES

The demand for consumers' nondurable goods is usually easier to forecast than that for consumers' durable goods because the former are usually purchased more frequently and also because they do not last for long periods of time; therefore, the demand for them cannot be transferred to the future to any great extent.

The Department of Commerce has developed the relationship between disposable personal income and personal consumption expenditures for detailed categories of nondurable goods and services. The sensitivity of personal consumption expenditures to disposable personal income is expressed by a figure showing the average change in expenditures in relationship to changes in income. For example, the figure for gasoline and oil for the post-World War II period is 1.6, indicating that expenditures on gas and oil have changed on the average 1.6 times as fast as changes in income. Such figures for the prewar and postwar period for the major categories of consumer expenditures are shown in Table 21-1. This table also shows the sensitivity of a group of expenditures in real terms based on 1957 dollars, thus eliminating the effect of price changes.

During the pre-World War II period the changes in sales of most nondurable goods were determined largely by changes in disposable personal income. The high degree of correlation between sales of nondurable goods stores and disposable personal income was disturbed somewhat during World War II because of shortages, especially of gasoline. In the early postwar period, sales of nondurables were somewhat above the level indicated by prewar relationships but many have about returned to levels indicated by past experience. For example, food sales in constant dollars have shown about the same relationship to income over the years since 1930, except during World War II and the early postwar years. Expenditures on housing and household operation, however, have shown a marked upward shift from the prewar to the postwar period. It is necessary, therefore, to study changes field by field when forecasting most likely sales levels. The relationships for food and housing and household operation are shown in Chart 21-1 and Chart 21-2.

It may also be helpful to correlate per capita sales deflated either by the Consumers' Price Index of the Bureau of Labor Statistics or by the appropriate subcategory of the Bureau of Labor Statistics Wholesale Price Index, such as textiles or shoes and leather goods, with per capita disposable income deflated by means of the Consumers' Price Index. If possible, it is also desirable to correlate the unit sales in a field with an index of the volume of production, such as the Federal Reserve Board Index of Industrial Production. Greater accuracy can be obtained by using the index for nondurable manufactures or subdivisions of this index, such as leather and products, manufactured food products, textiles and products, or

Table 21-1

Sensitivity* of Personal Consumption Expenditures to Changes in Disposable Personal Income

Group	Prewar	Postwar▲	Group	Prewar	Postwar▲
Based on Constant (1957) Dollars					
Total personal consumption expenditures.........	0.8	1.0	Clothing and shoes.........................	‡0.9	....
Durable goods................................	2.1	1.2	Food and alcoholic beverages...............	§ .8	....
Nondurable goods............................	.7	.9	Gasoline and oil...........................	‡ .6	....
Services....................................	.5	1.0			
			Household operation.........................	.9	1.5
Automobiles and parts........................	2.8	1.1	Housing....................................	.2	1.3
Furniture and household equipment..............	1.6	1.0	Transportation.............................	1.0	.3
Based on Current Dollars					
Total personal consumption expenditures.........	0.9	1.0	Household operation......	0.6	1.4
Durable goods............................	1.6	1.1	Electricity..........................	.2	1.8
Nondurable goods............................	.9	1.0	Gas.................................	.2	1.8
Services....................................	.7	.9	Water...............................	.2	1.3
			Telephone, telegraph, cable, and wireless.......	.5	1.6
Automobiles and parts........................	1.9	1.0	Domestic service..................	1.3	.6
New cars and net purchases of used cars.......	2.1	1.2	Other.............................	.6	1.1
Tires, tubes, accessories and parts..............	1.3	.7			
			Housing................................	.5	1.4
Furniture and household equipment..............	1.5	.8			
Furniture.................................	1.6	1.0	Personal services........................	1.0	.6
Kitchen and other household appliances.........	1.3	.8	Cleaning, dyeing, pressing, alteration, storage, and		
China, glassware, tableware, and utensils.......	.7	.7	repair of garments (in shops) n.e.c...........	1.2	.6
Other durable house furnishings..............	1.4	.4	Laundering in establishments..............	.9	.1
Radio and television receivers, records and musical			Barber shops, beauty salons, and baths.......	.8	1.5
instruments......................	2.5	1.0			
			Recreation..............................	.8	.9
Other durable goods.........................	1.4	1.2	Radio and television repair....................	1.1	2.2
Jewelry and watches........................	1.8	.8	Admissions to specified spectator amusements....	.8	‖
Ophthalmic products and orthopedic appliances..	.8	1.3			
Books and maps............................	1.2	1.2	Transportation..........................	.9	.9
Wheel goods, durable toys, sport equipment, boats,			Automobile repair, greasing, parking, storage, and		
and pleasure aircraft......................	1.5	1.5	rental.................................	1.1	1.3
			Automobile insurance premiums less claims paid..	.6	1.0
Clothing and shoes.........................	1.0	.5	Street and electric railway and local bus........	.5	#
Shoes and other footwear.....................	.8	.4	Railway and sleeping and parlor cars.........	1.4	#
Women's and children's clothing and accessories..	1.1	.5	Intercity bus..........................	.7	#
Men's and boys' clothing and accessories........	1.1	.6	Airline................................	n.a.	3.0
Food and alcoholic beverages..................	1.0	.8	Other services..........................	.7	1.5
Food (excluding alcoholic beverages)............	1.0	.8	Physicians............................	.8	1.1
			Dentists..............................	.9	1.4
Gasoline and oil............................	.5	1.6	Other professional services..............	.8	1.1
			Privately controlled hospitals and sanitariums....	.3	1.7
Tobacco products...........................	.5	.8	Funeral and burial expenses.................	.7	.7
Other nondurable goods......................	.7	1.0	Personal business..........................	.8	1.7
Toilet articles and preparations................	.8	1.0			
Stationery and writing supplies...............	1.4	1.2	Private education and research..................	.6	1.3
Fuel and ice...............................	.6	.3			
Drug preparations and sundries..............	.6	1.4	Religious and welfare activities..................	.4	1.0
Magazines, newspapers, and sheet music........	.5	.9			
Nondurable toys and sport supplies.............	1.0	1.3			
Flowers, seeds, and potted plants..............	1.6	1.0			

*Based on least squares using equation $C = aI^a(1+r)^t$ for the period 1929–1940 and $C = aI^a$ for the postwar period where $C =$ personal consumption expenditures, $I =$ disposable personal income, and $t =$ time. The exponent a derived from the data is an approximate measure of the income sensitivity of the expenditure items.
▲In the case of total goods and services, durable goods, nondurable goods, and services, the sensitivity coefficients in this column were based on the twenties and the postwar period.

‡Based on period 1929–1940 and postwar years including income and time as factors. The postwar relations using income alone give a coefficient of 0.5 for clothing and 2.0 for gasoline.
§Based on period 1933–1941 and postwar years.
‖The relation to income was negative from 1947–1953. Since then, these expenditures have tended to stabilize.
#The postwar relation to income has been negative. In the case of intercity bus transportation, there has been some tendency for the relation to be moderately positive in the most recent years.

Source: *Survey of Current Business* (March, 1959), p. 25.

Chart 21-1

Food Expenditures Related to Income in Constant Dollars
1929–1958

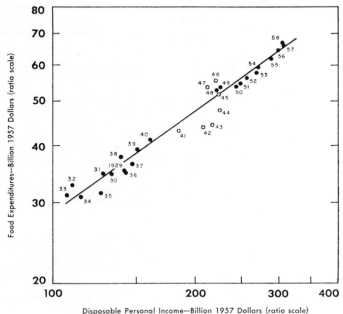

Disposable Personal Income—Billion 1957 Dollars (ratio scale)

Excluding alcoholic beverages

Source: *Survey of Current Business* (March, 1959), p. 24.

tobacco products. It is probably best to make calculations by all
three of these methods before deciding on the sales to be expected
in a particular field from a forecast of disposable personal income.

FORECASTING DEMAND IN THE
CONSUMERS' DURABLE GOODS INDUSTRIES

Forecasting the demand for consumers' durable goods is usually
somewhat more complex than projecting the demand for nondurables, since sales change more rapidly and to a greater degree;
and more factors must be taken into consideration because buying
decisions are more complex. The most important influence upon
the demand for durable goods, just as in the case of nondurable
goods, is disposable personal income. Since the purchase of a consumer durable good usually involves a larger expenditure than does
the purchase of a nondurable good, the direction of change in income

Chart 21-2

Housing and Household Operation Expenditures in
Constant Dollars Related to Income
1929–1958

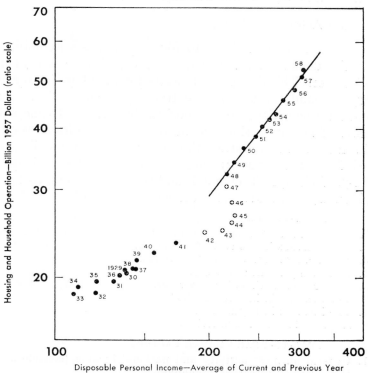

Source: *Survey of Current Business* (March, 1959), p. 28.

from the preceding year is also important. Purchases from any given income tend to be greater when income has been rising from the level of the year previous than when it has been falling. This is probably due in part to the optimism associated with rising income and to the pessimism associated with falling income, and to a lag that probably exists in adjusting expenditures for major items when income is changed.

Also important in determining the demand for many durables is the rate of population growth and the growth in the number of families. Demand is likewise affected by the relative price of the durable good in relationship to the general price level. Changes in the length of life of the good, such as the increasing length of life of automobiles, also influence current demand significantly. The factors involved in determining the demand for automobiles and for furniture will be used as illustrations.

Forecasting Automobile Sales

The most significant item to forecast in the automobile sales field is the demand for new passenger cars by consumers in the United States. This demand is a derived demand arising out of the primary demand for automotive transportation service. Such a demand may be satisfied for a considerable period of time without purchases of new cars, since the automobile is a durable good.

The factors that influence the demand for automobiles can be divided into three groups: long-term factors, factors influencing year-to-year changes in demand, and seasonal factors, as listed by S. L. Horner, of the General Motors Corporation:[1]

LONG-TERM FACTORS

1. The improvement in the product and the lowering of real price.
2. The decrease in the cost of operation.
3. The increased mileage of good roads.
4. Increasing length of car life.
5. The greater availability of service.
6. The increase in installment buying.
7. The increase in population.
8. Improved standards of living.

YEAR-TO-YEAR CHANGE FACTORS

1. General business activity and national income (considering both the level and direction of change).
2. The distribution of national income.
3. The cost of living.
4. The psychological atmosphere — whether optimistic or pessimistic.
5. The extent and character of model changes.
6. The age of cars in the hands of new car buyers.
7. The number of cars scrapped.
8. The used car stocks in dealers' hands and the dealers' working capital position.
9. Financing terms — both the required down payment and the length of time over which monthly installments may be spread.
10. Used car prices and trade-in allowances.

SEASONAL FACTORS

1. Seasonal variation.
2. The dates of new model announcements and new model stimulus.

---

[1] C. F. Roos, et. al., *The Dynamics of Automobile Demand* (New York: General Motors Corporation, 1939), pp. 6, 7.

3. The trend of general business activity and national income.
4. New car stocks.
5. Used car stocks and deliveries.
6. Price change anticipation.
7. Weather conditions.
8. Abnormal interruptions in production.
9. Sales campaigns for both new and used cars.
10. The relative prosperity of different geographical regions and different sections of the population.

Only a few of the most important of these factors can be utilized specifically in studying past sales relationships as a basis for forecasting, but the effect of all of them must be analyzed constantly.

A very careful and detailed study of automobile demand was made in the late 1930's by C. F. Roos and Victor von Szeliski. Later the Office of Business Economics of the Department of Commerce worked on a study of demand in this field. In their study of automobile demand, Roos and von Szeliski developed a system that is based upon the maximum ownership level of automobiles, which is changing continually in response to all of the factors that affect the demand for cars. They have outlined their basic idea in the following five steps:[2]

1. The central point is that the demand for new automobiles is a derived demand, since the primary demand is for transportation service. This is furnished by the total car population, only a part of which consists of cars sold during any given year. New car demand may thus be considered as dependent upon consumers' decisions regarding the number and quality of the cars to be maintained in operation.

2. Consumers are thought of as continuously adjusting the number of cars in operation toward some particular car population called "the maximum ownership level." This concept of a maximum ownership level appears to be of major importance in durable goods studies.

3. The maximum ownership level is regarded as changing continually in response to the economic status of consumers and such other factors as car durability and price.

4. Consumers are likewise continuously adjusting the quality of the car population toward an optimum level by replacements.

5. The rate at which consumers adjust the car population toward the maximum ownership level and the optimum quality level depends upon both general and specific economic conditions.

---

[2]*Ibid.*, p. 22.

The results of the research by Roos and von Szeliski have shown that the most important factors affecting the maximum ownership level are the number of families in the United States, the real discretionary income per capita, and the replacement cost of new automobiles.[3] The use of replacement cost as a factor indirectly takes into consideration also the effect of operating costs, since automobile prices have closely paralleled the prices of automobile parts, tires, and gasoline. Replacement cost also considers durability, since it is derived from an index of the price of new cars divided by the average life of cars.

On the basis of past relationships between these items, a series of formulas have been developed to express the maximum ownership level as inferred from such relationships. The difference between the maximum ownership level at any time in the future and the current number of automobiles in use gives the potential demand for new automobiles. The number of families in the United States changes slowly and thus can be forecast quite accurately. Indexes on the prices of automobiles are available, and the manufacturers set new car prices when announcing new models. The average life of an automobile changes slowly. The major item to forecast is, therefore, real discretionary income per capita, and this can be derived from a forecast of disposable personal income. Thus, all of the data to forecast automobile demand by this method are available.

The Department of Commerce has used a somewhat different basis for determining the demand for new cars. They have developed the relationship between new private passenger car registrations per 1,000 households and a combination of real disposable income per household in terms of 1939 dollars, the percentage of the real disposable income per household of the current year to that of the preceding year in 1939 dollars, and the relationship of the average retail price of cars to consumers' prices. A downward trend has also been introduced into the equation because of the substantial rise in the average useful life of automobiles.

According to the Department of Commerce formula, a 1 percent increase in real disposable income was associated with a rise of 2.5 percent in automobile sales, and each increase of 1 percent in the ratio of the current to the preceding year's income was associated with a rise in sales of 2 percent. The effect of the other

---

[3] *Ibid.*, pp. 87, 88.

factors was smaller but nevertheless significant, since a rise of 1 percent in the ratio of automobile prices to the level of general consumer prices was associated with an average decline in the number of cars sold of 1.3 percent. The trend correction for the increase in the average usable life of automobiles showed that there would have been a gradual decline of about 1.5 percent a year in the sale of automobiles per 1,000 households had there been no change in income per household or in relative prices.[4]

These two methods of determining the demand for automobiles are basically similar. The Department of Commerce method is based upon real disposable income and changes in that income, while the Roos method uses real discretionary income. It is probably more logical to use discretionary income, and that figure can be arrived at fairly accurately from budget studies. Both methods take account of changes in population, since the one is based on the number of households and the other on the number of individuals in the United States. Both formulas introduce the cost element, one as a basic factor standing alone and the other by relating automobile costs to the general price level.

The increasing life of automobiles has also been taken into consideration in both cases. The Department of Commerce has a declining time factor due in large part to this change. Roos determines the maximum ownership level from his formula and then subtracts cars currently in use; this automatically adjusts for the increased life of automobiles, since more cars from past production will be in use as their life increases.

Such past relationships can be used as a starting point to determine demand factors, but they cannot be used alone as a basis for a forecast. This involves a careful analysis of all qualitative factors in the current and prospective situation and a forecast based on judgment concerning the effect of these factors. This has been especially true in the post-World War II period. In 1950 automobile sales increased much faster than demand factors would have indicated, but this increased buying was due to a fear of shortages and higher prices arising out of the Korean War. In 1955 sales increased faster than demand factors would have indicated due to new styling that consumers liked and to easier credit terms. When sales are

---

[4] L. J. Atkinson, "The Demand for Consumer Durable Goods," *Survey of Current Business* (June, 1950), p. 6.

above long-run demand factors for a year, there will be compensatory downward adjustments in the following years. In 1957–1958 sales dropped somewhat faster than demand factors would indicate. Consumers were shifting expenditure patterns as real per capita income first ceased growing and then declined, and they also reacted against the trend toward bigger and more expensive cars. Thus, any forecast can start with demand factors, but it must be based on a careful analysis of all factors in the field.

Forecasting Furniture Sales

The demand for furniture differs in some respects from the demand for automobiles. The response to changes in income is pronounced, and recession years are somewhat lower in relationship to income than prosperous years. There has been a tendency for sales to grow more slowly in relationship to income in recent years than was the case until 1950. These relationships can be seen in Chart 21-3 shown on page 527.

Demand is also affected by changes in the number of families, by the rate of construction of new homes, and by price changes in furniture in relationship to changes in the general level of consumer goods prices. The Department of Commerce has developed formulas that explain the demand for furniture based upon the relationship between these items. In making its estimates, the Department of Commerce developed the multiple correlation relationship between expenditures for furniture in dollars per household and disposable personal income per household, the value per household of private residential construction, and the ratio of the price index for furniture to the index of prices for all goods. These past relationships held up well in describing changes in demand in the postwar period before the Korean War began. Restrictions during this war altered past relationships somewhat. Since the end of the Korean War, there has been a tendency for sales to grow more slowly in relationship to increases in disposable income than in the earlier period.

It must be remembered that various factors affecting the demand for furniture which have not been included in the formula have changed and may therefore lead to somewhat different relationships in the future. One of these is the large increase in the liquid assets of individuals, which makes it somewhat easier for them to buy furniture than when it was necessary to save the purchase price over a longer period of time or to use credit.

Chart 21-3

The Relationship of Furniture Sales to Disposable Personal Income
1933–1957

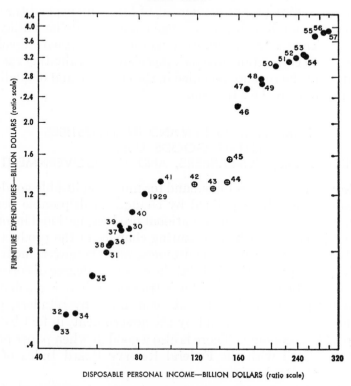

Source: *Survey of Current Business* (November, 1957), p. 19.

The unusually high marriage rates in the postwar period have
been represented in the formula to a large extent by putting it on a
per household basis and by including the value of residential construction; but the relationships may be somewhat different from
those in a period of a much lower marriage rate. The increasing
average age of the population may also gradually affect the demand
for furniture, although it is not clear at present just what the change
will be. The growth of consumer credit also has some effect on
furniture sales, and so does any possible restriction of such credit
by the Federal Reserve System. A forecast of furniture sales must
consider these and other qualitative factors in the present and future
situations as well as demand factors based on past relationships.

The survey of consumer finances made by the Bureau of the Census includes information on intentions to buy furniture. Up to the present time, at least, it appears as if such surveys are useful in indicating the direction of movement of furniture expenditures, but it is too early to tell if they can gauge changes in dollar outlays. As more experience is obtained, this method may prove a valuable supplement to correlation analysis, especially in evaluating the effect of quantitative factors not included in the equation and of qualitative factors inherent in the situation.

FORECASTING DEMAND IN INDUSTRIES SELLING GOODS USED BY PRODUCERS, CONSUMERS, AND THE GOVERNMENT

Although the changes in demand for most nondurable goods used by consumers can be explained by changes in disposable personal income, it is better to use gross national product, national income, or industrial production when measuring changes in the production of products used by producers, consumers, and the government. For example, paper production in total shows a high degree of correlation with gross national product. This is true since there is a substantial demand for paper by the ultimate consumer, by retailers, wholesalers, and manufacturers, and by the government, in fact by every segment of the economy. There is also a good fit when paper production is correlated with the Federal Reserve Board Index of Nondurable Goods Production.

On the basis of a forecast of gross national product, it is thus possible to forecast paper production by using past relationships and by studying the current situation. Such a forecast can be cross-checked by means of a forecast of the Federal Reserve Board Index of Nondurable Goods Production and the past relationships of paper production to it.

Such forecasts of total paper production are of value to the producers of basic paper raw materials and of a diversified line of paper products. Many individual producers, however, will have to study the demand for a particular type of paper, such as book paper, wrapping paper, tissue paper, container board, and various papers used by the building trades. In each sector of the industry it is necessary to find that component of gross national product or industrial production which most closely explains changes in sales in

Chart 21-4

Relationship of Growth of Paper and Products in
Relationship to Industrial Production
1955–1965

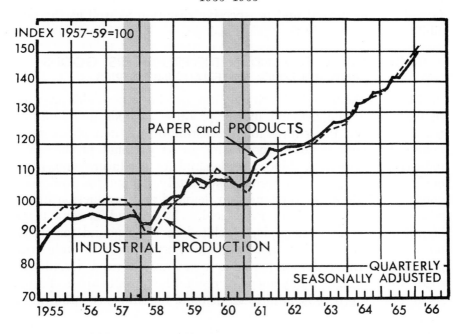

Source: Adapted from "Recent Trends in the Paper Industry," *Economic Review — Federal Reserve Bank of Cleveland* (July, 1966), p. 23.

the past. It may also be necessary to study technological changes that have led to the substitution of one type of paper for another and price changes which may have led to shifts in paper usage.

Chart 21-4 shows the relative growth of demand for paper and paper products in relationship to industrial production during the 1955–1965 period.

The demand for paperboard fluctuates in relationship to economic activity just as the demand for paper does. Since paperboard is used primarily for packing manufactured products it correlates best with industrial production. Until the middle fifties paperboard production was growing more rapidly than industrial production since packing was shifting from the use of wooden containers to paperboard containers. Since 1955 the growth has been only very slightly in excess of that in industrial production, which grew

48.3 percent between 1955 and 1965 while paperboard production grew 50.6 percent.[5]

A forecast of paperboard consumption can start with an analysis of such past relationships. It is also necessary to study carefully all factors in the current and prospective situation as well as the possibility of a change in past relationships.

FORECASTING DEMAND IN THE PRODUCERS' GOODS AND BUILDING MATERIALS INDUSTRIES

Many of the techniques already discussed in other fields are used in forecasting the demand in the producers' goods and building materials field. Procedures for forecasting overall demand in these fields were considered in forecasting gross national product and industrial production. Since the demand for producers' goods is a derived demand, a basic approach is to study demand for producers' goods in relationship to changes in demand and production in the related consumer goods or service field. The demand for some types of railroad cars, for example, is related to the demand for transportation of freight by railroads, and correlates with industrial production. In a recession period new cars are not needed, and railroads are reluctant to buy ahead of needs when profits are declining. As an upturn proceeds, additional demand for cars exists and funds are available to finance these purchases. Past patterns of freight-car demand in relationship to industrial production and a forecast of such production can be used as a basis for developing a forecast of demand for such freight cars.

In some producers' goods fields, pressure indexes may be utilized to indicate increases or decreases in the demand for a particular product. A pressure index shows the relationship between the rate of production or output in a field and the amount of capital equipment used to produce such output. For example, the present rate of use of existing electric power-generating equipment gives some indication of demand for it at a future time; and the ratio of seasonally corrected carloadings to the number of cars owned by railroads gives a reasonable indication of the number of cars railroads will order six months to a year in the future. Such pressure indexes based upon present usage give an indication of the demand in the near future for many types of durable producers' goods.

---

[5]"Recent Trends in the Paper Industry," *Economic Review — Federal Reserve Bank of Cleveland* (July, 1966), p. 23.

In many individual industries it is desirable to employ relationships between new orders, production, and inventory series in a manner similar to that used in forecasting various sectors of overall economic activity. The Department of Commerce has series of this kind available for an increasing number of fields. Trade associations in increasing numbers also gather these figures for their fields.

In some industries it may be possible to arrive at reasonably accurate timing of the changes in demand from lead-lag relationships. This is true in most of the fields that produce construction materials. For example, the sales of manufacturers of plumbing supplies have usually followed by three or four months the F. W. Dodge Company series on residential contracts awarded. The sales of many of the items used in the construction of homes have followed this index in a pattern that follows the use of these materials in building, since supplies are not stocked to any great extent. In looking for lead-lag relationships, only those with a logical basis should be considered since spurious relationships may hold for a period of time. Continuous study is needed even in the case of logically related series, since past relationships may change.

As in all cases of forecasting, it is necessary to study qualitative factors in the industry before arriving at a definite forecast of the volume of business. Such factors as the trend of past sales, the relationship of costs to price, the labor situation, and the general state of confidence must be carefully checked. In addition, an analysis should be made of competing products to see what effect they will have upon demand and also of potential new products that may affect the industry.

USE OF INPUT-OUTPUT DATA IN INDUSTRY FORECASTING

The Office of Business Economics of the Department of Commerce is working on a major new program that involves the periodic preparation of interindustry tables that can serve as a basis for industry forecasts. These tables provide a comprehensive picture of the interaction between the various industries and the final market demand in the economy. The input-output tables show final product flows and value added just as is the case with the National Income and Product Accounts. The final product flows are shown as sales by each industry to consumers, investors, government, and foreigners; and the value added is shown by the industry in which it originates. The input-output accounts also cover the flow of raw materials, semifinished products, and services among industries. The tracing of these flows is the major contribution of input-output accounts.

The tables that are currently available are based on data for 1958. The economy is broken down into 82 industries and functional economic sectors. Work is underway on a much more comprehensive set of tables based on the census of manufactures made in 1963. This set of tables will divide the economy into over 500 sectors and should, therefore, provide much more detailed information than the 1958 data. The OBE plans to develop input-output data as a regular part of an integrated system of national accounts.

Input-output data are usually presented in a table in which each industry is represented by a row and a column, each final market by a column, and value added by one or more rows. The row for an industry shows the distribution of its output to itself and to other industries and to final markets. These final markets are the familiar personal consumption expenditures, gross private domestic investment, net inventory change, gross exports, federal government purchases, and state and local government purchases. The column for an industry shows its consumption of goods and services from the various industries and the value it has added.

Three types of tables have been prepared as part of the input-output accounts. The basic table shows the percent distribution of gross output of each industry to other industries and to final demand. This table and other input-output tables are developed in terms of producers' prices. A second table is in dollar terms and shows the direct requirements from each of the various industries for each dollar of gross output of an industry. It shows, for example, that the household furniture industry purchased $0.01488 from itself for each dollar of final demand. If, for example, it produced $1,000,000 of goods for sale to consumers it would require slightly under $15,000 from its own industry ($1,000,000 × .01488). It would, for example, also require almost $58,000 of fabrics and about $125,000 of wood products. But if the fabrics industry is to produce $58,000 of fabrics, it, in turn, will require about $20,000 from its own industry, $7,000 of man-made fibers, and so on. These demands would in turn lead to still other demands.

A third table shows the total of all such indirect as well as direct requirements. A portion of such a table is reproduced as Table 21-2.

The example of household furniture can again be used since this industry is shown in Column 22 of Table 21-2. To provide for the final demand from an additional $1,000,000 expenditures on household furniture requires $1,016,000 from the industry ($1,000,000 × 1.01602 [from Line 22]). Almost $99,000 is required from the Fabrics industry shown in Line 16 ($1,000,000 × .09888) and almost $183,000 from the Lumber and Wood Products Industry shown in Line 20 ($1,000,000 × .18274).

The rows in Table 21-2 can be used to determine the requirements for the product of an industry due to final demand from other industries. Line 37, Primary Iron & Steel Manufacturing, can be used as an example to show the demand for steel arising out of a $1 increase in demand for the products of some of the industries in Columns 17 to 30. A $1 increase in demand for household furniture leads to a 6 cent increase in demand for steel, a $1 increase in demand for other furniture and fixtures to a 15 cent increase in demand for steel, and a $1 increase in demand for chemical products to a 3 cent increase in demand for steel.

These tables can be used to get a first approximation to the change in demand for the products of an industry resulting from changes in demand in other sectors of the economy. If the demand for household furniture is expected to go up by $1,000,000 the demand for lumber and wood products would go up by $183,000 if all factors remain constant as they were in 1958. Adjustments must, however, be made for various factors which have changed in the years since 1958. The relative prices of household furniture and wood products may have changed and adjustments must be made for such factors. Adjustments must also be made for changes in the relationships between the two industries. Such adjustments will become easier when input-output data are developed regularly on a current basis.

The Office of Business Economics has also prepared a table showing the output attributed to final demand by major sectors of GNP for each industry. Household furniture, for example, has a demand pattern as shown on page 536.[6] It can be seen that 78.1 percent of the demand for household furniture can be attributed to personal consumption expenditures, 13.3 percent to gross private fixed capital investment and so on. This information can be used,

---

[6]*Survey of Current Business* (November, 1964), p. 14.

Table 21-2

Total Requirements (Direct and Indirect) per Dollar of Delivery to Final Demand, 1958.
(Producers' Prices)

	17. Miscellaneous textile goods & floor coverings	18. Apparel	19. Miscellaneous fabricated textile products	20. Lumber & wood products, except containers	21. Wooden containers	22. Household furniture	23. Other furniture & fixtures	24. Paper & allied products, except containers	25. Paperboard containers & boxes	26. Printing & publishing	27. Chemicals & selected chemical products	28. Plastics & synthetic materials	29. Drugs, cleaning, & toilet preparations	30. Paints & allied products
1. Livestock & Livestock Products	0.04274	0.01849	0.02628	0.01915	0.00989	0.01255	0.00628	0.00806	0.00572	0.00744	0.01075	0.00762	0.01832	0.01920
2. Other Agricultural Products	.05467	.07038	.09780	.06407	.02592	.02521	.00994	.01146	.00746	.00883	.01022	.00778	.01314	.01330
3. Forestry & Fishery Products	.00090	.01258	.00146	.13236	.05126	.01743	.00925	.01090	.00523	.00254	.00263	.00170	.00133	.00147
4. Agricultural, Forestry & Fishery Services	.00302	.00328	.00437	.00568	.00244	.00172	.00085	.00094	.00063	.00062	.00073	.00056	.00096	.00102
5. Iron & Ferroalloy Ores Mining	.00116	.00066	.00116	.00086	.00385	.00378	.00905	.00105	.00093	.00063	.00793	.00319	.00225	.00452
6. Nonferrous Metal Ores Mining	.00134	.00087	.00116	.00107	.00108	.00299	.00421	.00135	.00094	.00097	.01069	.00420	.00222	.00368
7. Coal Mining	.00534	.00323	.00460	.00245	.00383	.00502	.00689	.01351	.00735	.00392	.01140	.01249	.00468	.00691
8. Crude Petroleum & Natural Gas	.01326	.00395	.01235	.01618	.01372	.00990	.00880	.01774	.01500	.00816	.04998	.02951	.01757	.02449
9. Stone & Clay Mining & Quarrying	.00109	.00074	.00110	.00124	.00108	.00142	.00192	.00547	.00276	.00146	.00387	.00214	.00215	.00287
10. Chemical & Fertilizer Mineral Mining	.00366	.00184	.00249	.00114	.00064	.00123	.00094	.00417	.00218	.00164	.03924	.01443	.00578	.01116
11. New Construction	0	0	0	0	0	0	0	0	0	0	0	0	0	0
12. Maintenance & Repair Construction	.01287	.01154	.01407	.01496	.01298	.01193	.01094	.01575	.01625	.01675	.01318	.01712	.01072	.01306
13. Ordnance & Accessories	.00036	.00022	.00042	.00018	.00018	.00027	.00061	.00027	.00059	.00084	.00083	.00106	.00045	.00045
14. Food & Kindred Products	.01737	.01253	.01587	.01345	.01112	.02227	.01121	.01823	.01296	.01703	.02923	.02021	.05107	.05688
15. Tobacco Manufactures	.00035	.00043	.00049	.00043	.00049	.00049	.00052	.00043	.00045	.00088	.00071	.00040	.00050	.00066
16. Broad & Narrow Fabrics, Yarn & Thread Mills	.28761	.52484	.75908	.00396	.00301	.00988	.01525	.01637	.00899	.00499	.00498	.00588	.00381	.00366
17. Miscellaneous Textile Goods & Floor Coverings	1.10143	.12340	.10813	.00324	.00190	.02174	.02198	.00493	.00325	.00337	.00205	.00290	.00204	.00161
18. Apparel	.00491	1.21004	.01370	.00257	.00130	.00173	.00232	.00168	.00209	.00065	.00119	.00130	.00112	.00124
19. Miscellaneous Fabricated Textile Products	.00751	.01871	1.07147	.00094	.00065	.00248	.00186	.00369	.00198	.00115		.00173	.00174	.00148
20. Lumber & Wood Products, except Containers	.00628	.00408	.00745	1.40234	.54239	.18274	.09636	.11334	.05368	.02470	.00910	.01054	.00880	.00751

Industry														
21. Wooden Containers	.00053	.00054	.00063	.00065	.00041	.00129	.00125	.00095	.00114	1.03956	.00405	.00075	.00055	.00057
22. Household Furniture	.00011	.00017	.00013	.00013	.00017	.00023	.00039	.02986	1.01602	.00788	.00328	.00372	.00021	.00293
23. Other Furniture & Fixtures	.00008	.00012	.00010	.00009	.00058	.00018	.00032	.02098	.02069	.00152	.00063	.00302	.00013	.00012
24. Paper & Allied Products, except Containers	.03948	.05251	.07744	.03082	.26224	.57308	1.26423	.02298	.03006	.01807	.02612	.04485	.02202	.04131
25. Paperboard Containers & Boxes	.01897	.04083	.01341	.01161	.01516	.05856	.03789	.02832	.02690	.00767	.01011	.02290	.01610	.01458
26. Printing & Publishing	.01869	.05773	.01554	.01683	1.17580	.02478	.02609	.01341	.01551	.01509	.01806	.01609	.01404	.01276
27. Chemicals & Selected Chemical Products	.35590	.18182	1.45777	1.26952	.03939	.03880	.06710	.02369	.03254	.01616	.03036	.06964	.05213	.11084
28. Plastics & Synthetic Materials	.13731	1.07036	.04431	.03065	.00617	.01484	.02005	.01398	.02589	.00729	.01499	.09350	.06625	.21311
29. Drugs, Cleaning & Toilet Preparations	.01933	.01113	1.01906	.01854	.00262	.00454	.00483	.00226	.00265	.00255	.00317	.00571	.00374	.00598
30. Paints & Allied Products	1.00569	.00422	.00953	.00604	.00153	.00189	.00242	.01942	.02323	.00492	.00802	.00270	.00186	.00348
31. Petroleum Refining & Related Industries	.04164	.02989	.05000	.08402	.01288	.02502	.02888	.01374	.01585	.02306	.02804	.01978	.01423	.02156
32. Rubber & Miscellaneous Plastics Products	.01284	.01663	.02645	.01391	.00819	.02133	.02267	.01754	.04963	.00945	.01458	.04440	.01039	.02575
33. Leather Tanning & Industrial Leather Products	.00014	.00015	.00013	.00015	.00016	.00018	.00016	.00192	.00170	.00013	.00015	.00130	.00435	.00052
34. Footwear & Other Leather Products	.00021	.00023	.00018	.00023	.00032	.00039	.00031	.00034	.00064	.00021	.00027	.00351	.00142	.00069
35. Glass & Glass Products	.00214	.02386	.00228	.00323	.00091	.00308	.00132	.04169	.01712	.00180	.00282	.00208	.00183	.00273
36. Stone & Clay Products	.01542	.00859	.00484	.00739	.00333	.00548	.00967	.00939	.00830	.00714	.00842	.00286	.00195	.00345
37. Primary Iron & Steel Manufacturing	.04716	.02278	.01514	.02692	.00697	.01222	.01167	.15406	.06164	.06531	.01154	.01012	.00663	.00835
38. Primary Nonferrous Metals Manufacturing	.01383	.01017	.00611	.00736	.00736	.00685	.00930	.03760	.02688	.00802	.00813	.00737	.00550	.00673
39. Metal Containers	.05193	.02058	.01514	.03275	.00514	.00514	.00157	.08760	.00229	.00229	.00205	.00152	.00112	.00197
40. Heating, Plumbing & Structural Metal Products	.00217	.00132	.00180	.00171	.00129	.00147	.00154	.00165	.00549	.00229	.00205	.00139	.00102	.00119
41. Stampings, Screw Machine Products & Bolts	.00344	.00598	.00517	.00339	.00196	.00354	.00388	.01336	.00985	.00563	.00235	.00140	.00181	.00179
42. Other Fabricated Metal Products	.00740	.01422	.01512	.00697	.00713	.01188	.01765	.04928	.07113	.01596	.00749	.00479	.00041	.00538
43. Engines & Turbines	.00072	.00130	.00084	.00092	.00066	.00058	.00065	.00083	.00078	.00072	.00060	.00047	.00091	.00058
44. Farm Machinery & Equipment	.00068	.00134	.00092	.00123	.00057	.00035	.00043	.00145	.00077	.00063	.00092	.00123	.00035	.00118
45. Construction, Mining & Oil Field Machinery	.00127	.00106	.00073	.00061	.00271	.00061	.00130	.00165	.00104	.00072	.00065	.00047	.00098	.00068
46. Materials Handling Machinery & Equipment	.00045	.00030	.00022	.00087	.00018	.00027	.00039	.00043	.00102	.00047	.00087	.00015	.00023	.00023
47. Metalworking Machinery & Equipment	.00261	.00213	.00169	.00154	.00133	.00236	.00249	.00698	.00475	.00218	.00154	.00098	.00169	.00156
48. Special Industry Machinery & Equipment	.00439	.00418	.00614	.00307	.00490	.00662	.00509	.00198	.00516	.00589	.00307	.00422	.00614	.00435
49. General Industrial Machinery & Equipment	.00213	.00161	.00194	.00301	.00122	.00219	.00218	.00471	.00280	.00248	.00301	.00095	.00194	.00131
50. Machine Shop Products	.00146	.00100	.00091	.00127	.00069	.00117	.00116	.00264	.00104	.00072	.00127	.00061	.00091	.00071
51. Office, Computing & Accounting Machines	.00126	.00433	.00112	.00089	.00219	.00085	.00112	.00325	.00107	.00076	.00089	.00112	.00123	.00090
52. Service Industry Machines	.00040	.00116	.00041	.00036	.00046	.00034	.00038	.01072	.00040	.00037	.00036	.00041	.00040	.00030
53. Electric Industrial Equipment & Apparatus	.00221	.00195	.00167	.00151	.00185	.00177	.00211	.00458	.00248	.00174	.00151	.00167	.00309	.00148
54. Household Appliances	.00051	.00060	.00041	.00035	.00048	.00041	.00033	.00202	.00173	.00038	.00035	.00041	.00044	.00032
55. Electric Lighting & Wiring Equipment	.00096	.00078	.00098	.00111	.00096	.00177	.00229	.00242	.00270	.00228	.00235	.00096	.00078	.00092
56. Radio, Television & Communication Equipment	.00089	.00106	.00090	.00066	.00117	.00067	.00068	.00252	.00119	.00069	.00066	.00090	.00133	.00076
57. Electronic Components & Accessories	.00065	.00088	.00077	.00055	.00090	.00053	.00055	.00151	.00110	.00059	.00055	.00077	.00082	.00054
58. Misc. Electrical Machinery & Equipment & Supplies	.00061	.00055	.00063	.00044	.00073	.00048	.00060	.00085	.00077	.00101	.00044	.00063	.00058	.00056
59. Motor Vehicles & Equipment	.00281	.00257	.00249	.00298	.00298	.00220	.00255	.00784	.00392	.00515	.00485	.00279	.00058	.00283
60. Aircraft & Parts	.00160	.00123	.00257	.00166	.00281	.00078	.00127	.00270	.00123	.00102	.00111	.00166	.00160	.00158

Source: *Survey of Current Business* (November, 1964), p. 27.

	Total	Percent Direct	Indirect
Personal consumption expenditures	78.1	73.2	4.9
Gross private fixed capital investment	13.3	3.8	9.5
Net inventory change	−.3	−.2	−.1
Gross exports	.9	.5	.4
Federal government purchases	3.7	.8	2.9
State and local government purchases	4.3	1.7	2.6

along with a forecast of changes in major sectors of GNP, to get an approximation of changes in the household furniture industry arising from changes in GNP. A final forecast must, of course, be made only after an analysis of changes that may have occurred in relationships which held in 1958 and after a study of all factors that may affect demand.

It is also possible to develop a table showing the demand for each industry in dollar terms that would correspond to a given set of forecast figures for each major category of GNP. This is of doubtful value so long as current input-output data are not available. However, when current data are available, this should prove to be a most valuable tool for forecasting for an industry. This will be especially true when tables for over 500 industries are available.

As was pointed out earlier, all figures in the input-output accounts are in terms of producers' prices, whereas figures used in the national income accounts are in terms of final purchasers' prices. The differences are shown in input-output accounts primarily under two industry groupings, the transportation and warehousing industry and the wholesale and retail trade industry, and in some cases also under the finance and insurance industry. Household furniture may again be used as an example. In 1958 expenditures on household furniture by consumers totaled $4,214 million. This represented $2,417 million at producers' prices, $83 million in transportation charges, and $1,714 million in gross margins in wholesale and retail trade. Such relationships between producers' prices and consumers' prices are available in the October, 1965, issue of the *Survey of Current Business*. These relationships are helpful in shifting from figures for final purchases to output figures at the producers' level and vice versa.

QUESTIONS

1. Discuss the steps in forecasting cyclical movements in an industry.
2. What is end-use analysis? How may it be used to make an industry forecast?
3. Describe the possible procedures for forecasting the demand for nondurable consumer goods and services.
4. (a) Which factors are involved in a forecast of demand for consumers' durable goods?
   (b) Why are some of these different from those used to forecast nondurable goods demand?
5. Show how these factors have been used to forecast sales of such durables as automobiles and furniture.
6. Discuss the problems encountered in forecasting demand for paper.
7. Describe a procedure for forecasting demand for paperboard.
8. How can the demand for freight cars be forecast?
9. What is a pressure index? How can it be used in forecasting demand for producers' goods?
10. How can the demand in the building materials field be forecast?
11. Discuss the role of qualitative factors in forecasting for an industry.
12. Describe input-output accounts and tables. How can they be used to forecast industry sales?

SUGGESTED READINGS

General Motors Corporation. *The Dynamics of Automobile Demand.* New York: General Motors Corporation, 1939. Part 1, Statement of the Problem; Part 2, Factors Governing Changes in Domestic Automobile Demand, Sections 4 and 5.

Goldman, Morris R., Morten L. Marimont, and Beatrice N. Vaccaro. "The Interindustry Structure of the United States," *Survey of Current Business* (November, 1964), pp. 10–29.

Jacobs, Walter, and Winston Clement. "The Postwar Furniture Market and the Factors Determining Demand," *Survey of Current Business* (May, 1950), pp. 8–11, 24.

Leontief, Wassily W. "The Structure of the U. S. Economy," *Scientific American* (April, 1965), pp. 25–35.

Paradiso, Louis J. "Consumer and Business Income and Spending Patterns in the Postwar Period," *Survey of Current Business* (March, 1963), pp. 12–17.

——————, and Mabel A. Smith. "Consumer Purchasing and Income Patterns," *Survey of Current Business* (March, 1959), pp. 18–28.

Forecasting Sales
for an Individual Business

Forecasts of total economic activity and of sales in an industry are useful in determining the general business climate and the direction of sales. For setting sales quotas, scheduling production, ordering raw materials, and the like, however, it is necessary to have a sales forecast for an individual business and for each of its major lines of products if it is a multiproduct firm. General business and industry forecasts constitute a basis for making such a forecast, but other important items must also be considered.

PRODUCT CLASSIFICATION

The first step in forecasting sales for an individual business is a classification of the products sold by that concern. This classification should be made so as to group together those products that have the same factors affecting the level of sales. If a system of product classification is utilized for inventory and production control, many of the same classes can probably be used. Additional classifications needed for forecasting purposes can often be added to such a system, or some of the classes in that system can be combined.

One of the first classifications required is the division between basic products and by-products since the planned level of production of the basic product determines the prospective supply of the by-products that will have to be sold. If the demand for the by-products is elastic, adjustments can be made in price so as to move all of them. If the demand is not elastic, it is necessary to try to develop a market for the projected volume of by-products.

The basic products should be divided into groups for which the factors determining demand are about the same. Differences in demand may be due to the degree of development of products from raw materials to finished goods since changes in consumer demand will affect the various stages in the production and selling process at different times. Therefore, different classifications should be set up for raw materials, products utilized in further manufacture, and finished consumer goods.

Differences in demand may also occur because different types of consumers buy the products or because a different set of factors motivates their purchase. For example, a manufacturer of a general line of shoes will find differences in the demand for dress shoes and play shoes. A manufacturer of electrical controls found that the basic divisions for his products were heating controls and air-conditioning controls. Heating controls were further subdivided into controls for industrial and residential users. Each of these controls was further broken down into controls for gas, oil, and coal units. Significant variations, especially in the field of gas heating, were found between controls for conversion burners and those for new units.

Whenever a study of past sales experience shows appreciable differences in demand determinants, it is necessary to set up a separate category for forecasting purposes. Other factors also affect the production and the sales of a product, and these should be noted and checked in grouping products for sales forecast purposes. A factor that is especially important when business is in a downturn is the degree to which demand may be deferred. For example, the demand for furnace controls for the repair and replacement market may not be deferred for any period of time, but the demand for those for new installations may be put off as disposable personal income decreases.

It is also desirable to make separate lists of those products for which production is based to a significant extent upon contracts received in advance and those products that are sold from current stock. If firm contracts are received well in advance, it may not be necessary to forecast external factors. Even if contracts are received shortly before shipment is expected or if trade practices permit cancellations or postponement of shipment, contracts can still be useful in developing a forecast.

The forecasting department should also have available information on the average size of sale for each of its basic product categories. This information is necessary because sales will tend to be more uneven if made to a few large accounts. The effect on sales of losing one or more of these accounts will be large.

Products should also be analyzed according to the basic raw materials which are used in them so that different influences affecting the price and the availability of raw materials may be taken into consideration in the forecasting program.

ANALYSIS OF THE TREND OF SALES

After the products that are sold by the business have been grouped into categories that have about the same demand determinants, the trend of sales of these products for the last 10 to 15 years should be studied. This trend can then be compared with trends in gross national product, in disposable personal income, or in industrial production to see in a general way how sales have been growing in relationship to the growth in total economic activity.

The trend in sales should also be compared with that in the industry of which this product group is a part. This may be difficult if the industry is not homogeneous. For example, each major chemical company produces a different product mix, and the trends in sales of different products have been quite different. The demand for some plastics has been growing much faster than that for heavy chemicals, and some companies have divisions which are producing the new drugs, which have rapidly increasing sales. However, in such cases it is usually possible to obtain sales figures for major products or groups of products from trade association or governmental sources and to compare company sales of these products in the past with sales nationally.

After the trend for the product group has been established and compared with trends in the economy and in the industry, the results must be analyzed. A thorough study should be made to determine the relationship between company policies and the trend of sales. Changes in price policies, sales policies, production policies, and the like may have caused company sales to grow slower or faster than industry sales.

ANALYSIS OF CYCLICAL VARIATIONS IN SALES

In forecasting sales, it is desirable to study past cyclical fluctuations in sales of each group of products. One of the first steps is to find the relationship between such sales and general business activity.

Relationship to General Business Activity

The basic procedure for finding the relationship between the sales of a company and a logically related measure of general economic activity is the same as it is for an industry. The relationship may at times not be as clear, however, since many factors affect the sales of an individual company to a much greater extent than they do those of the industry. This is true of such factors as strikes in individual plants, local shortages of materials or labor, changed business policies, and the like. It is still worthwhile, however, to see what past relationships have been and to study any deviations from typical patterns in the past.

The following are some of the most frequently used relationships with general economic activity or some major segment of it:

PRODUCT GROUP	RELATED SERIES
Service	Disposable personal income
Nondurable consumer good	Disposable personal income
Consumer good or service sold largely to farmers	Cash farm income
Durable consumer good	Discretionary income or disposable personal income
Producer good	Gross national product or gross private product
Raw material or parts	Federal Reserve Board Index of Industrial Production or a related subindex
Construction material	F. W. Dodge Company Index of Construction Contracts Awarded or a related subindex

In studying past relationships, the trend of sales of the company in relationship to the trend in the related variable must be considered carefully. A company in a growing industry, such as chemicals, may find that its sales are related to changes in gross private product; but the rate of growth is much faster. For example, since 1940 sales of some plastic products have been growing at a rate which is several times the growth rate of gross private product.

In some cases the most accurate relationships may be found by making the correlations after deflating both the sales of the product in question and the measure of aggregative income by appropriate price indexes to obtain the relationship in real terms.

Even if it is not necessary to deflate the series to obtain patterns of past relationships, it may be necessary to deflate the forecast of the dollar volume of sales to put it on a per unit basis. If a concern has an index showing the changes in price of the product being forecast, this is, of course, the best index to use for deflation. If it does not have such an index, the appropriate subdivision of the consumer price index or the wholesale price index may be used.

In some situations best results may be achieved by means of correlation with the Federal Reserve Board Index of Industrial Production, or its durable or nondurable goods component, or one of the subdivisions of these. For most accurate forecasting it may be worthwhile to make such a correlation, even if a close relationship has been found with disposable personal income or one of the other dollar measures of aggregative economic activity. In this way a comparison can be made between the value forecast and the quantity forecast to see if they yield similar results. If such forecasts disagree, it is necessary to study again all of the factors in the situation carefully, for indications are either that past relationships have changed or that factors which were of minor significance in the past are currently of much greater importance.

Regional Factors

If a group of products for which a forecast is being developed is not sold nationally, then it is also necessary to consider the different trends of sales in different regions. This factor may be taken into consideration in several ways. It may be possible to obtain data on past relationships of sales to a related variable, such as disposable personal income, for that section of the country in which a company does business. For example, shoe sales for a concern doing business in Missouri, Illinois, and Arkansas could be related to past disposable personal income in those states. To forecast company shoe sales, it is then necessary to forecast disposable personal income in those states. This can be done from a forecast of national disposable personal income, the trend of income in each of the states in relationship to national trends, and all qualitative factors that affect those states differently from the nation as a whole. This method of finding past relationships can also be used to set up regional or state sales quotas for products sold nationally.

An alternate method is to find the relationship of company sales to disposable personal income for the nation and to adjust for any changes expected from past relationships. The comparison of the trend of sales of the product with the trend of disposable personal income is helpful in making such adjustments. If the reasons for past relationships have been analyzed fully and if the present situation is studied carefully, it should be possible to make a reasonable forecast of sales for the coming year using such past patterns. This method will probably take somewhat less time than a state-by-state or regional analysis, but it is somewhat less useful because it provides no basis for setting sales quotas.

Relationship to Industry Sales

A study should also be made of the relationship of the sales of the concern or of its major product groups to those of the industry in the past. It may be possible to find a regular relationship between sales in the business in question and those in the industry and so devise a forecast from an industry forecast. This method is probably satisfactory if the industry consists of fairly homogeneous units, all producing an essentially similar line of products. This is true, for example, of large segments of the shoe industry in which factories produce a complete line of family shoes. A manufacturer of women's shoes alone will probably find, however, that the relationship of his sales to those of the industry is not regular.

The relationship of the sales of the firm or of one of its product groups to those of the industry may follow one of several patterns. The firm may do a more or less constant percentage of the total business in the field. In other cases the firm may be getting a gradually increasing share of the business, or a gradually decreasing share. If there is such a trend in this relationship, it can usually be found by plotting the percentage of business the concern does in the field. In some cases there may be cyclical divergences in the amount of business done; that is, the percentage of business in the field may be higher when business in general is rising and lower when business is in recession.

Other Factors

The individual businessman may also develop reference-cycle patterns and specific cycle patterns of past sales as an aid to forecasting, following the technique of the National Bureau of Economic Research. Any constant reference-cycle leads or lags will aid in fore-

casting. Information thus obtained about the average duration of
the cycle, amplitude of the cycle, and conformity to the reference-
cycle pattern will also prove valuable. It may be possible to develop
such patterns for major cycles and minor cycles independently and
thus increase their usefulness as a forecasting device.

An analysis should also be made of cyclical variations in sales in
relationship to the cycle in general economic activity or in a related
segment of the economy. This should be done to see if there is any
tendency for cyclical variations in sales of the company to become
more or less severe than those in the industry or in general economic
activity.

Another factor that should be checked is the relationship of the
trend of prices in the field being studied to the general trend of consumer prices. In many consumer goods fields sales will be higher
when prices in a field are relatively more favorable than consumer
prices in general and lower when the reverse is true. The effect of
such divergent price trends may be studied as part of the correlation
pattern and expressed on a numerical basis, or treated as a qualitative factor that is used to modify statistical calculations based on
past relationships.

FORECASTING SALES

The factors affecting sales in the past, both over the long term
and during past cycles, and an analysis and forecast of industry sales
and of total economic activity serve as a basis for making a company
forecast of sales. The first step is to forecast sales on the basis of
economic factors. This should be modified by special information
on sales, if any, that may be available to the sales department. Then
top management should review the forecast and alter it if they feel
that policies should and will be followed which will change the forecast. These three stages, called the first approximation, the second
approximation, and the forecast will be considered in turn.

The First Approximation

In developing the first approximation, the starting point is a
forecast of total economic activity and of industry sales. Past
relationships can be used to develop a tentative forecast from industry and general economic forecasts. This should be done for each
group of products into which the company's products have been
grouped for forecasting purposes.

A complete survey must be made of all qualitative factors in the situation. Economic variables are continually changing, and such changes must be considered in developing a forecast from past relationships. A survey of this kind should include an analysis of the company's marketing activities and any changes in such activities. It should also contain marketing programs of competitors and the effects of any other actions or potential actions of competitors. Also included should be any changes in the competitive picture and any possibility of development of substitute products.

In checking a forecast, it is usually worthwhile also to study trends of costs and profits in the field and in the business in question. If profit margins are being squeezed, the possibility of price increases to the ultimate consumer and their effects on sales should be considered. Low profit margins are likely to affect the expansion of existing businesses and the introduction of new concerns into the field, and so affect future supply.

Before any forecast for a company selling its products to other businesses is complete, a careful check must be made of the trends in each one of the major fields using the product. Some concerns have found it desirable in forecasting their sales to make forecasts of sales in several of the major fields using their products.

The conditions in each of the fields supplying raw materials to the company must also be studied to see if there will be shortages of raw materials or any changes in their prices that will change the prices of finished goods and thus lead to a change in demand and sales.

The Second Approximation

A forecast of sales based upon a study of past patterns of relationship and upon an analysis of all qualitative factors must be adjusted to take special factors affecting the sales of the company into consideration. A major sales drive may be planned early in the year, which from past experience will raise sales 10 percent through June. It may be planned to eliminate a product, to change it materially, or to cut prices to move old stock quickly. All such programs must be considered, and forecasts of specific product sales changed to meet the results expected from them.

It is usually desirable to obtain an estimate of expected sales from the sales force once or twice a year. For such a survey to be most valuable, it must be carefully planned. The sales force should have had time to study all plans for sales promotion during the time of the forecast. Figures should be supplied for sales for the comparable period last year for all regions and for all customers for whom forecasts are desired. A separate forecast is usually desirable for any region in a salesman's territory in which sales experience has varied materially from the rest of the area, and also a separate forecast for each major customer. In cases where sales are expected to be different from those of the preceding year, the salesmen should be asked to give their reasons.

Such information, if carefully developed, is extremely useful. The salesman knows whether customers are moving into his area or out of it. He also knows whether he is likely to get major new accounts or to lose some he has. He may also know whether inventory is piling up in the hands of some of his customers.

Some companies make a more formal users' survey in determining the sales expectations of customers. Customers may be surveyed by mail, by telephone, or by personal interviews. To get a reasonable response, companies usually assure the respondents that their information will be kept confidential and that the results of the overall survey will be made available to them. Some companies have attempted to improve the accuracy of a users' survey by asking for responses from more than one official in the company as, for example, the production manager as well as the purchasing agent. Experience has proved that it is generally better to ask how much of a product the customer plans to buy in total rather than just from the company making the survey. Past experience can then be used to estimate the company's share of the total.

The forecast made from a study of past relationships should be adjusted to bring it into line with any changes that are required by the sales or users' survey. Such a revised forecast becomes the second approximation, which is ready for analysis by top management.

The Forecast

The second approximation should be reviewed by a committee from top management, including representatives from each of the major functional areas. If they feel that it is a proper basis for planning next year's business, they may accept it. If they feel it calls for unattainable levels, they may reduce it. If they feel it is too low to meet their objectives for profit and other factors, such as market position in the next year, they may develop promotion plans to raise the sales level and adjust the forecast in line with such programs.

After the level of sales has been projected for a year ahead, it is necessary to put it on a quarterly basis and a month-by-month basis for at least one or two quarters ahead. This projection requires the calculation of a typical seasonal pattern showing the percentage of the year's business normally done in each month. Before any past seasonal pattern is projected, a study should be made to determine if anything has occurred that might change past patterns. With this information at hand, it is possible to break down an annual sales forecast into monthly and quarterly forecasts.

Review and Revision

Since the economic climate can change quickly at times, the forecasting section should study the situation continually and recommend changes in the forecast if that becomes desirable. Except in unusual situations, such as the buying sprees during the first year of the Korean War, it is sufficient to revise a forecast quarterly in most businesses. Before any major change is made, the sales force should be consulted. In all cases the revised forecast should be approved by the committee of top management that approved the original forecast.

The last step in any forecasting procedure is to study the record of all past forecasts. When a forecast is off, every attempt should be made to ascertain the reason. Such a procedure will increase the analysts' awareness of unusual factors that affect sales from time to time. It will also readily show up changing or new relationships.

SUMMARY OF FORECASTING PROCEDURES

The steps in forecasting for an individual concern may be summarized as follows:

A. Preparation

1. Group the products into classes with about the same demand characteristics.

2. Study the trend of sales of each forecasting group. Account for this trend.

3. Compare trends with those of gross national product or disposable personal income or industrial production and with the industry trend. Account for these relationships.

4. Find a relationship to a logically related general economic variable, nationally if sales are on a national scale, or by states or regions in which sales are made. Explain all deviations from the general pattern of relationship.

5. Find the relationship of sales to industry sales. Account for the general pattern and for any deviations from it.

B. First Approximation

6. Using past relationships, general business and industry forecasts, and a knowledge of all qualitative factors in the present situation, project company sales for a year ahead by product groups.

C. Second Approximation

7. Study all plans for sales promotions and the like and determine their probable effect on sales.

8. Obtain estimates of sales from salesmen by territories and from customers and revise the forecast, if need be, in the light of this information.

D. Forecast

9. Have a committee of top management review the forecast and adjust it if they see fit.

10. Calculate the seasonal pattern. Check to see if there are any factors that might cause it to change. Put the annual forecasts on a monthly and a quarterly basis.

E. Review and Revision

11. Review the forecast at least quarterly. Continually study factors that might make it advisable to change the forecast.

12. Review all past forecasts and determine, if possible, the reasons for errors.

ORGANIZATION AND OPERATION
OF THE FORECASTING PROGRAM

If any managerial function is to be carried on successfully, it must be organized properly. Data on the organization of the forecasting department of a business and on its relationship to other departments have been made available in a study by the American Management Association. Of the 56 firms[1] in the study it was

---

[1]American Management Association, *Company Organization for Economic Forecasting* (New York: American Management Association, Inc., 1957).

found that 24 companies had set up their own forecasting staffs and 32 relied on external sources for their forecasting. Of the 24 only 17 reported on the organization of the forecasting department. Of these 17, seven forecasting staffs reported to the company president, three to the executive vice-president or general manager, and two to the controller. The other five reported to a group of officers or to officers other than those listed previously. A majority stated that they separated economic forecasting from specialized sales forecasting done in the marketing department.

Forecasting, then, is organized differently in many of these corporations, but a few generalizations can be drawn that will serve as a guide to sound practice. Most of the forecasting organizations reported to top management or top financial management. A few reported to the chief sales official. It is usually sound to have the forecasting section report to top management so as to give it independence from influence by sales, production, or budgeting.

A market research section making studies of consumer product acceptance and consumer preferences properly belongs in the sales department. If possible, this section should be kept separate from the forecasting department. In a small business, however, the two may have to be combined because of cost considerations. Such a combined section may be placed in the sales department if proper recognition is given to the possibility of bias.

USING THE FORECASTING PROGRAM IN BUSINESS MANAGEMENT

The forecasts that have been developed of sales in the next year and over a longer period of time are the basis for planning the operations of a business. The long-range forecast is used to plan capital expenditures and long-run financing. The forecasts for a year ahead and for the next quarter are used for top management planning to develop the budget, for sales planning and promotion, for production scheduling and purchasing, and for short-run financing.

Top Management Planning

The forecast is used by top management as a basis for planning for the next year. The projected sales figure may be too low to utilize all facilities of the company and the decision may, therefore, be made to introduce new or expanded programs of promotion. In other situations the decision may be made to introduce new products during the coming year. The forecast may, on the other hand, call for a sales volume that cannot be met from production facilities currently in use. A decision will have to be made to expand facilities, add another shift, or to try to buy parts or even finished goods from others. In some situations the decision may be to raise prices in order to improve profit margins.

Top management also uses a forecast as a basis for review of operations after the period of the forecast is over. Sales are compared with the forecast and the reasons for deviations are studied. The forecast may have been a poor one, and an analysis of the reasons for being inaccurate should help improve the results in the future. But sales in the total economy and in the industry in general may have developed about as forecast, but sales of the company may have been below expectations. This could be due to such factors as the inability to meet orders, a poor promotion program, new sales personnel too, restrictive a credit program, and the like. An analysis of such factors can determine the cause of the problem and provide the information needed to correct it. In some situations the general forecast may have been accurate, but sales for the company may have exceeded the forecast level. The causal factors again need careful study since increased sales may have been due to temporary factors in the programs of one or more competitors. In short, top management can use a forecast as a basis for overall planning and control of the operations of a business.

The expenditures on a forecasting program must be watched carefully to make certain that they are contributing to the overall profitability of a company. A forecasting program can in most cases be made more accurate or more useful in planning and control if enough money is spent on it. But such expenditures must be compared with the benefits to be derived from them in the form of greater income or lower expenses. Increased expenditures are only justified so long as the benefits are greater than the costs.

Budgeting

The data from the forecast are used by the accounting department to develop the budget. The budget includes estimates of sales income by departments that can be obtained from the forecasts of sales by products. Expenses are also estimated by departments for all major subcategories of labor, materials, and overhead. These estimates are derived from a knowledge of the quantities to be produced and the amounts of each factor required to produce various products and cost estimates for each factor. Such cost estimates usually are based on data on future costs supplied by the forecasting department. When significant seasonal variations exist, such figures are usually developed for each month of the year and they may even be developed week by week.

The estimated figures are usually organized into projected income statements for the year, and by months for at least a quarter ahead. These show expected profit from operations and, after allowance for financial expenses and income taxes, show projected net profit.

The budget is usually presented to top management for approval and revision if they feel it is in need of changes. After the budget has been approved by top management, it serves to control expenditures since they must be kept in line with the budget.

Some concerns use a flexible budget program based upon the range of the forecast. If past experience shows that a range of 10 percent above and below the estimated sales figure is usually wide enough to include the actual sales figure, the budget may be based on the most likely sales estimate and on 90 percent, 95 percent, 105 percent, and 110 percent of it. Such a procedure is expensive, but it provides cost control regardless of the level of business. In other concerns the same results are obtained by means of an annual budget of income and expenses and a detailed budget for the next quarter revised quarterly as the latest quarterly forecast is available. Another possibility is to always have an up-to-date budget for a quarter ahead by revising the budget each month for the next three months based on the latest forecast.

Sales Planning

The sales department, which should have had a voice in setting the sales figure used in the forecast, makes use of the budget in planning its operations. On the basis of estimated sales, it sets sales quotas by products and by territories, and in many cases for individual salesmen. These quotas may be set somewhat above the budget so as to provide an incentive to do better than economic factors indicate will be done.

Sales quotas by products can usually be derived directly from the forecast, since a complete forecast is broken down into product categories. Additional work is required, however, to set realistic quotas by territories because the sales of all products do not grow or decline at the same rate in all parts of the United States nor are they equally sensitive to changes in income in all regions. Therefore, in setting sales quotas by territories, the trend of sales of the product in each territory must be studied. It is even more important to study the relationship between changes in sales and changes in income in each territory. In some regions sales may be much more responsive to changes in income than in others. Only by taking these factors into consideration can realistic sales quotas be developed by territories.

Sales Promotion

The sales department must also integrate its sales promotion program with the sales forecast. Special promotional projects must be considered in developing the product-by-product sales forecast. Consideration must be given to pushing those products the potential of which is rising if it is desired to hold or increase the share of the market for such products. Campaigns may also be initiated to change consumer preferences in favor of a product for which the potential is decreasing.

General advertising outlays designed to keep the company name, product name, or trademark before the public are often geared to sales by being set as a percentage of sales. Since such advertising has long-run value, it is generally felt that it should be done when it can best be afforded. The most logical way to accomplish this is to set such expenditures as a percentage of the forecasted sales, not last year's sales.

The sales department can use the sales forecast and its advertising budget as a basis for determining its need for personnel for the year. In this way an adequate force can be provided and trained for the job when it is needed.

Scheduling Production, Personnel, and Purchasing

The production department must develop a production schedule from the sales forecast. If no significant seasonal pattern exists, the forecast can be used directly as the basis for a production schedule. Adjustments must be made if current inventory is either too high or too low for the expected sales level. Schedules must also be geared to practicable levels of operation based upon assembly line time and machine time needed, and other technical factors in the plant.

When a pronounced seasonal pattern in sales exists, it is usually desirable, if it is at all practicable, to smooth out production and to let changes in inventory absorb a large part of the fluctuation. Under present-day conditions with unemployment compensation taxes based to a large degree on the employment record of a concern and with the high cost of training new employees, it is usually cheaper to carry sizable inventories during part of the year to make it possible to regularize production.

Such regularization of production can be done safely only if a good forecasting program exists, which implies a continuous revision of forecasts in the light of changing conditions. The forecast of sales by months is the basis for the production schedule. Total production needed during the year is then planned on a regular basis. It may not be exactly one twelfth of projected sales each month or one fifty-secondth each week, since the various products of the company may have different seasonal patterns and the goal is to regularize overall production. The difference between planned production and forecasted sales shows the projected inventory.

Constant study of present and future sales is needed to make such a program work. At least quarterly, or better yet monthly, the sales forecasts and production schedules should be reviewed and needed changes made. If this is done, changes can be planned carefully since they can be made over a period of several weeks or months.

The production schedule provides the basis for calculating manpower requirements. When calculated in a general way a year ahead and in detail at least a quarter ahead, there is time to recruit personnel carefully and to train new employees adequately. Schedules of machine time required are also developed from production schedules. Machines can be utilized most effectively when requirements are known for a period of time in the future.

The production schedule is also the basis for placing orders for raw materials and parts. Since it takes time to obtain many of the items needed, efficient planning can be done only when a sales forecast exists. Data on probable future price movements supplied by the forecasting staff also enable the purchasing department to buy at the most advantageous time.

A production schedule based on a sound forecast also improves the shipment of finished products. Sufficient quantities of standard items should be on hand at all times to meet the demand. This should make it possible to develop a shipping schedule providing for more or less regular work in that department. It should also be possible to give accurate shipping dates for any orders accepted for special products, since production is planned at least a quarter ahead.

Financing

The finance department can use the forecast, budget, production schedules, and shipping schedules to plan the financing of the business. The shipping schedule, based on the sales forecast and a knowledge of credit terms and experience in collecting accounts, can be used to develop estimates of the flow of cash receipts. Production schedules and cost estimates provide the basis for calculating expenditures month by month. It is also possible to estimate the amount of funds that will be tied up in inventory.

From these estimates the adequacy of the cash position at any time can be determined. It is also possible to determine when short-term borrowing will be necessary and how much is needed and for what period, and thus to plan the financing program in advance.

EXAMPLES OF FORECASTING PROCEDURES

Several examples will show how forecasting programs are developed and used in business. The first example is a steel company that uses many of the techniques described in this chapter. The second is a plumbing supplies manufacturer that has successfully developed a less elaborate procedure. The third is an electric light and power company that forecasts on the basis of the trend, since it is not materially affected by the cycle, and the last is a chemical processing company.

A Steel Company

A large company engaged in producing steel and steel products uses many of the techniques described in this chapter. A staff group consisting of economists, a market analyst, and a statistician is responsible for economic forecasting and sales forecasting. This group is headed by an economist who is under the supervision of the manager of a business research division.

An economic forecast is prepared each year for the economy and for the company. A forecast is made of GNP and such underlying trend factors as population growth, trends in labor conditions, and in productivity. The level of activity in the steel industry is forecast for the next year. On the basis of these forecasts and of the past relationships, company sales are forecast for the next year. A forecast is also developed for each quarter of the year and for each of the company's products.

A long-range forecast is also developed, but in less detail. Forecasts are always available for each year of a five-year period beyond the current year's forecast. The whole series of forecasts are reviewed annually when a forecast for the next year is made in detail. To aid in making long-range forecasts, trends in various sectors of GNP are studied, especially as they relate to the demand for steel.

A Plumbing Supplies Manufacturer

A company manufacturing plumbing supplies uses a less elaborate procedure, since it has found a reliable indicator of sales. It found that its sales lagged four months behind the F. W. Dodge Company figures on the value of residential construction contracts. The first step in its forecasting procedure is to find the relationship between its sales in each of its sales territories and the F. W. Dodge contract figures for that territory. Since contracts show a four-month lead, the relationship is studied with sales lagged four months behind contracts. The ratio is then found between company sales and F. W. Dodge residential contracts in the area. Some territories show a more or less constant ratio, and some a trend up or down for which allowance must be made in forecasting. This ratio of sales to contracts is applied to contracts for the past twelve months. This gives an estimate of sales for the twelve months ending four months in the future. By subtracting sales for the past eight months, a forecast for the next four months is obtained.

The sales managers review all forecasts and make any adjustments they feel are needed before the forecasts become official. Forecasts are compared with actual performance, and the reasons for all deviations are analyzed carefully.

An Electric Light and Power Company

The forecasting procedure of an electric light and power company is based primarily on a projection of long-run trends. Since the building of a large steam or hydroelectric generating plant takes three or four years or more, it is necessary to plan almost entirely on the basis of the trend rather than on cyclical variations in demand. The first step is to estimate residential revenues. This is done from a projection of the trend in the number of users and the trend in the number of kilowatt hours of electricity per user.

To estimate the number of users, it is necessary to make careful estimates of the trend of population in the area being served. Plans for new residential building must also be studied carefully. The forecast of the use of electricity per user can be made by extending the trend line of such use. The forecast of kilowatt hours is converted into revenues on the basis of present and prospective rate structures. A similar procedure is used to forecast sales to and revenue from industrial and commercial users. The trend in this case is checked carefully by an analysis of the pattern of industrial development in the area to find any probable changes in the past rate of growth. Large users are asked to provide information on expansion plans and needs for the next several years.

The effect of changes in general business on the industrial and commercial use of electricity in the area served by the company is taken into consideration in making an annual forecast of industrial sales and revenue. The effect is not considered for residential users because, for all practical purposes, it is nonexistent. The seasonal pattern is used to put annual forecasts on a monthly basis.

A Chemical Processing Company

A chemical processing company that is engaged in the manufacture of specialized cleaning compounds for industrial use makes use of several economic indicators as a basis for developing forecasts. This company has five major sales divisions including a metal industrial division, a food producers' division, a railroad division, a petrochemical producers' division, and a general industries group. This company found that total sales correlated well with gross national product in current dollars, with total manufacturing sales, and with the Federal Reserve Board Index of Industrial Production. Since increased production leads to an increased demand for cleaning compounds and this demand only exists after production has been increased, the FRB Index has a short lead over sales of the company.

The company purchases forecasts of the three series from an economic consulting service. Forecasts are made using all three of the series, and any differences are reconciled by an analysis of all qualitative factors. Such differences as do exist are usually readily explainable as, for example, an increase in the price level which gives the GNP figures a higher value than those developed from the FRB Index. The company pays special attention to shifting patterns in the major sectors of industrial production and uses these factors along with forecasts of total sales to develop sales forecasts for the five divisions.

FORECASTING THE MARKET FOR A NEW PRODUCT

Economic analysis cannot be used as the basic tool for forecasting the demand for a new product. It can help, however, by indicating what general business conditions will be and by showing how similar products have developed in the past. Such forecasting is primarily a project in market research and will therefore not be treated fully here. However, the general methods by which it may be done will be considered.

Sometimes a new product replaces an old product in whole or in part, and forecasting can be done on the basis of the old product. For example, color television will gradually replace black and white. Some idea of the demand pattern can be gained from the black and white television market in the past and at the time the forecast is made for color. Field surveys of buyers' intentions will help gauge the speed of the shift.

Even when a product does not replace another, a field survey will often help establish the demand for it. This may be done in the case of industrial products by showing a sample of prospective users' drawings and specifications, but actual samples are needed for most consumer products. In fact, it is usually best to offer a consumer product for sale in sample markets and then to estimate demand from such sales experience.

In some cases growth curves of similar products may be used as a general guide for sales. For example, the growth in sales of washing machines can be used to help estimate the growth curve for automatic washers, and this in turn the curve for automatic dryers.

All sales forecasting is based on a series of estimates and projections and therefore cannot be completely accurate. The margin of error can be kept within reasonable limits for established products so that forecasts can be used as a basis for production planning if revised quarterly. Forecasts of the demand for new products are less reliable, but even so they are better than basing production on hunches or guesses. Additional study of the factors affecting consumers' expenditure patterns should help in time to improve such forecasts.

FORECASTING IN A WAR ECONOMY

In an all-out defense or war economy the forecaster's job in some fields may be changed materially. He may find that demand is large enough to absorb all of the goods that can be produced, especially under controlled prices. In such a situation the immediate forecasting program becomes one of obtaining information on the volume of raw materials that will be available. It may also be necessary to estimate the amount of labor that can be employed if this is a scarce factor in the area and to look for bottlenecks that may develop in the flow of materials. Under conditions of a Controlled Materials Plan the most important job of the forecaster may well become one of keeping up with changing government allocations and regulations.

During the time that the forecaster is checking available materials and looking for bottlenecks as a guide to future production, he should be continuing his regular studies of demand. In this way he can develop data on the backlog of demand for the product that will occur when more normal conditions return. In doing this, he should study carefully the life of the product, since some deferred demand for short-lived articles may never be made up. In those fields in which materials and labor are more easily available, the basic demand factors may still hold.

The forecaster should carefully consider changes in demand that may arise because of the changing composition of the labor force. More women probably will be employed than formerly and, as a result, the demand for women's clothing will rise. There are also likely to be more old people in the labor force. This will undoubtedly change the composition of the demand for consumers' goods. Demand in various nondurable goods fields may also increase more than would be indicated by past relationships because of the shortages of various types of durable goods. This is especially pronounced in such fields as costume jewelry and liquor.

QUESTIONS

1. Why is product classification important in developing a forecast?
2. Which factors must be considered in classifying products?
3. Why is the trend of sales important in a short-run forecast?
4. How may sales be studied in relationship to some measure of aggregative economic activity?
5. What use is made of regional trends in forecasting sales?
6. How can the relationship of the sales of a particular business to industry sales be used in forecasting?
7. What effect do sales promotions, actions of competitors, and the like have on sales forecasts?
8. How can users' surveys be used in a forecasting program?
9. Summarize the steps involved in forecasting sales for a particular business.
10. Describe the various methods used to organize the forecasting department. Outline the preferred organization for effective business planning.
11. Describe the uses of the forecasting program in the following areas: top management, budgeting, sales planning, sales promotion, production scheduling, and financing.
12. Discuss several examples of forecasting procedures currently in use.
13. What is involved in forecasting the demand for a new product?
14. How does an all-out defense or war economy change the work of the forecaster?

SUGGESTED READINGS

Controllership Foundation. *Business Forecasting.* New York: Controllership Foundation, Inc., 1950. Part IV.

Crawford, C. M. *Sales Forecasting; Methods of Selected Firms.* Urbana: University of Illinois Press, Bureau of Economic and Business Research, 1955.

Goodman, Oscar R. *Sales Forecasting.* Madison: University of Wisconsin Press, Bureau of Business Research and Service, 1954.

National Industrial Conference Board. *Forecasting Sales.* New York: National Industrial Conference Board, 1964.

PROBLEMS ON PART VII

1. A. For the same business used in Problem 5 in Part III, page 276, plot the following:

   Annual sales.

   Annual sales in real terms. (Deflate the sales figures by using a subindex of the Bureau of Labor Statistics Wholesale Price Index or Consumer Price Index.)

   Sales as a percentage of industry sales since 1954.

   B. Prepare a scatter diagram showing the relationship of industry sales to disposable personal income, a subindex of the Federal Reserve Board Index of Industrial Production, or other appropriate index.

   C. Analyze past changes in sales in the industry and in your business accounting, insofar as possible, for all past changes. Forecast sales for the industry and for your company for the next year basing your forecast upon your analysis of past relationships and of the causal factors at work and the present and prospective status of these factors.

2. A. Plot automobile sales for each year since 1955.

   B. On the basis of the factors that affect automobile sales and of the economic factors at work during the period account for the yearly changes in sales insofar as possible.

3. A. From data in *Business Statistics, Supplement to the Survey of Current Business*, and the *Survey of Current Business*, plot the following on ratio paper:

   (a) Paper and paperboard production for each year from 1955 to the present.

   (b) Gross national product for the same period.

   (c) Federal Reserve Board Index of Industrial Production.

   B. Discuss the relationships between these series.

   C. Using past trends and relationships project paper and paperboard production to 1980.

PART VIII

PROPOSALS FOR ACHIEVING ECONOMIC GROWTH AND STABILITY

Major fluctuations in the level of economic activity and in price levels create some of our most serious economic, social, and political problems. In the present state of world affairs, a serious depression or a major period of inflation in the United States would have serious repercussions not only in this country but also in most of the other nations of the world. A growing humanitarian concern for the plight of those afflicted by economic reversals, an awareness of the international as well as domestic political impact of fluctuations, and a faith in the efficacy of policy to cure economic ills have all combined to bring about increased attention toward devising means to stabilize economic activity.

Programs to stabilize economic activity affect all sectors of the economy, both in the short run and in the long run. In the long run the goal of stability must be balanced with the goal of assuring a rising trend of real income. Both long-run and short-run programs must be politically and socially acceptable to our society to be put into effect. To achieve stability but to lose a significant measure of our freedom at the same time is to lose the "cold war" by default. Thus programs to achieve stability involve political decisions that are as important or perhaps more important than economic decisions.

The first chapter in this part will consider policies that can be followed by business and labor for promoting a rising trend of real income, smoothing out seasonal fluctuations, and reducing cyclical fluctuations. This chapter will also consider the goals of a government program to help promote stability and social, political, and economic factors that must be considered in such a program.

Chapter 24 in this part will be devoted to the role of monetary programs in achieving short-run stability and long-run growth. Present monetary policies will be analyzed, and proposals for changes in present policies will be considered. The last chapter will analyze fiscal and other government programs for achieving stability and long-run progress.

CHAPTER 23 *Problems in Economic Policy for Growth and Stability*

Intelligent discussion of economic policy is possible only among those who have an understanding of how an economy functions. This is the reason our chapters on policy come at the end of the book rather than at the beginning, after a theoretical framework for understanding has been constructed and some insights from the historical record have been gained. In this chapter we consider some of the major problems in developing government programs to promote growth and stability and the role of the private sector in that endeavor. Chapters 24 and 25 are devoted specifically to the primary tools of aggregate economic policy — monetary and fiscal policy.

THE NATURE OF ECONOMIC GROWTH AND STABILITY

Economic growth may be judged from the growth in total output of the economy as measured by annual increases in gross national product in constant dollars. Such a measure tells us how much bigger the total economy is becoming over a period of time, but it tells us nothing about changes in the standard of living of the people in the economy. The more significant measure is the growth in real output per capita as measured by increases in real gross national product per capita.

The Nature of Economic Growth

A rising level of real output per capita can be achieved in several different ways. It may be done by using a larger quantity of the factors of production in proper combination or by improving these factors so that more output results from using the same quantity. The factors of production may also be combined more effectively so that a larger output results from their use. The role of each of the factors of production in achieving real growth per capita will be considered first, then attention will be directed to the gains from a better combination of these factors. In the case of labor, growth can be

563

achieved by using more labor so long as the amount of capital per unit of labor is not reduced in doing so. More labor may be used because a larger percentage of the population of active working age is engaged in gainful employment. This may be achieved by having fewer people idle either voluntarily or involuntarily because of unemployment, sickness, or accident. It may also be achieved by lengthening the number of years an individual works during his life span. More labor may also be used by working more hours per week. This has limited possibilities because as hours of work increase much beyond the present work week, output per hour drops rapidly in many fields.

Growth is also fostered by improving the skills of the labor force. This is done through formal education during school years and on-and-off-the-job training after a person begins to work. To get maximum growth, it is necessary also to use the skills of all workers to the maximum. This requires the proper motivation to achieve the optimum output per worker. It also calls for proper job placement, including programs to promote labor mobility. It means no discrimination because of race, color, or creed, which prevents using all available skills to the fullest.

Growth also requires an adequate and balanced supply of labor to meet the needs of the expanding economy. The need for various types of skilled labor must be projected, and a program must be developed to assure the training of the needed workers.

One of the major factors leading to growth is the use of more capital equipment since machines provide many times the power of man and beast. Most significant is the use of better and better machines that turn out more and more goods in relationship to the economic resources used to build and run the machines. This requires research and development to produce the machines and trained scientists and engineers to do such work.

The use of more and more machinery and equipment is possible only if sufficient capital is available for investment. This may necessitate programs to stimulate saving in order to make the capital available.

Significant, too, is the better utilization of natural resources. This may be done in such ways as getting more usable ore from a mine, finding ways to use low-grade ores, using materials that are more plentiful for those which are scarce, and using less material to do the same job. Growth requires an adequate source of raw materials to meet expanding needs. These needs are met through better exploration for materials, the conservation and replacement of present supplies where this is possible, and the development of substitute materials for those that are scarce.

Growth also requires an adequate supply of trained managerial talent. It is furthered by better management methods and by the more effective use of such methods by present and prospective managers. Management is responsible for combining the factors of production so as to achieve the greatest possible output. This is done when more and better capital is made available to labor trained to use this capital. Growth is achieved when labor and capital are used to the optimum. Also desirable is flexibility in plant layout, equipment, and the work force so that labor and capital can be used effectively to meet changing conditions. Mobility of labor and capital helps achieve the optimum combination.

The optimum combination may be achieved when procedures are developed to reduce material handling, expedite the flow of goods in a plant, and the like. These factors are as important in the field of distribution as they are in production. Of equal importance are more efficient procedures for handling work in planning, engineering, accounting, and other white-collar fields.

Stability

In order to achieve the maximum practicable rate of growth, it is necessary to have stability. This does not mean a perfectly smooth rate of growth, but one that is not interrupted by recessions and depressions. In other words, the optimum in stability means the end of the business cycle as we have known it in the past. There would still be some changes in the rate of growth but no periods of cumulative contraction in economic activity.

Many feel that this is an impossibility since they believe that the business cycle is an integral part of the growth process in a free enterprise economy. This has been true in the past, and some fluctuations in the rate of growth no doubt will always occur in a free economy. But the cumulative nature of the cycle is based on the reactions of individuals and groups to real changes and is therefore subject to modification.

The nature of economic development has also lessened the impact of individual changes. Innovations such as the canal, the steamboat, the railroad, and the automobile had a very great effect on the overall economy in their day, but today so many areas exist in which industry and the consumer use machinery and equipment that an innovation is likely to affect a smaller part of the economy. Research has led to so many new things that their impact is more regular than in the past. Therefore, it may be possible to achieve a large measure of stability without hampering growth.

THE GOALS OF POLICY

The habit of assuming that we are all in agreement on the goals of policy or that the goals are obvious is at the root of much of the debate on the wisdom of particular proposals. Economists are in agreement that a policy that leads to the result of more goods and services for everyone is preferred to one that results in fewer goods and services for everyone. Even here we recognize a degree of arbitrariness since such policies may bring about a change in the relative welfare of the individuals of the society. Being the richest poor man may be preferable to being the poorest rich man.

Rigorously, the economist as an economist limits himself to the value judgments implicit in the concept called "Pareto optimality," named for the great Italian sociologist-economist, Vilfredo Pareto. *Pareto optimum* exists when it is not possible to make anyone better off without someone else being made worse off. Consensus is readily achieved in those instances where a particular policy leads to this optimal position. These present no problem. But major problems, in particular the kind considered under the heading of stabilization and growth policy, cannot lay claim to this solution. Still, we can use this criterion to make choices among alternative policies, not in any precise sense, but in some acceptable or workable sense.

Evaluation of any policy involves the evaluation of all the effects of that policy. Most actions have elements which will be judged beneficial, but there will also be results that are undesirable. The question then becomes one of deciding on the basis of the total impact, the relative merits and demerits associated with the proposal or program.

Economic policy always involves technical problems that the economist is trained to answer, and questions of value judgments that the economist is trained to discover, but not to answer. Suppose for example, that economic analysis concludes that a particular tax reduction policy will reduce unemployment by one million men, but that it will also result in a 5 percent increase in the price level. Would this policy be superior to the continuation of a constant level of unemployment and prices? A conscientious answer demands that one be aware of the costs of unemployment to the families of the unemployed as well as to the rest of society. Are there any benefits to society? Surely, everyone will agree that the costs far exceed the benefits. But it is also necessary to analyze the impact of inflation. What difference does it make if we have a 5 percent growth in the price level? Who is hurt? Who benefits? Do these cancel out? Are there ramifications of price level changes on production?

It is too simple to say that unemployment is bad, and inflation is evil. We must sometimes choose between the two evils. This is too heavy a burden to put on economists. It must be left to the public at large. Hopefully, the economist will be helpful in educating the public to the nature of the choices it must make.

GOALS OF A GOVERNMENTAL PROGRAM
FOR PROMOTING ECONOMIC GROWTH AND STABILITY

The pressure to attain economic stability in our economy is so strong that measures to promote stability have been established by law as a goal of national policy.

At the end of World War II, after a debate of about a year, Congress recognized the relationship of the government to fluctuations in the economy by passing the Employment Act of 1946. In this Act Congress declared that it was the continuing policy and responsibility of the federal government with the assistance of industry, agriculture, labor, and state and local governments to use all practicable means consistent with national policy and the free enterprise system to promote maximum employment, production, and purchasing power. This Act provides that the President shall submit to Congress at the beginning of each regular session a report on the current levels of economic activity and the levels needed to carry out the full employment policy. He should also present information on current trends and on the present economic program of the federal government and its effects. In the light of such data, he is to present a program for carrying out the objectives of the full employment policy whenever indications are that they will not be achieved otherwise.

A Council of Economic Advisers, comprised of three members, was set up to aid the President in developing such a report, and a Joint Congressional Committee on the Economic Report has been established to provide economic information and analysis for Congress, especially for the use of other committees. Since the passage of this bill, serious unemployment has not been a problem even though it appeared as if it might be for brief periods in 1949, 1957–1958, and in 1960–1961. Most of the recommendations have dealt with methods of avoiding inflation since that has been the major problem in the postwar period. Up to the present time, however, neither the Council of Economic Advisers nor the Joint Committee on the Economic Report has instituted any plans for coordinating government activities affecting the economy.

Growth and stability are so closely related that the economic policy of the government should include both of them. It is desirable to develop goals to guide government policies in the economic sphere. This should be done democratically by a discussion of the basic issues carried on from the grass roots level to the halls of Congress. Such a definition of goals is always desirable, but it has become essential in our position of economic as well as political leadership in the struggle against communism. Business and labor can plan on a long-run basis much more effectively if they know what to expect from government. Consumers can make long-run decisions, such as buying a home or planning a savings program more effectively, if they know what to expect in the way of economic policies. The development of a set of goals for government economic policy would in itself help promote growth and stability.

In his 1955 Economic Report President Eisenhower stated the goals of our national economic policy as follows:[1] "Our economic goal is an increasing national income, shared equitably among those who contribute to its growth, and achieved in dollars of stable buying power." Such a goal has several important elements. One is a rising trend of real income, a second is full employment, a third is stable prices, and a fourth is the equitable sharing of a growing national income among those who have contributed to producing it. Most Americans will agree readily with these goals in a general way. There is some difference of opinion, however, as to the exact meaning of each goal and the degree to which it is desirable to achieve it.

---

[1]*Economic Report of the President*, transmitted to the Congress January 20, 1955. (Washington: U. S. Government Printing Office, 1955), p. 2.

Problems in Promoting Economic Growth

Let us examine the goal of a rising trend of real income first. There is some question about the rate of growth that should be achieved. Some feel that an annual rate of growth of about 3 percent in gross national product is adequate because this is in line with the trend since the turn of the century and has produced our present high standard of living. Others feel that it is not only possible to grow at a rate of around 5 percent per year but also essential in the present world situation. They argue that the growth of 5 percent per year that was achieved in several of the post-World War II years shows that such a goal is attainable. They also feel it is essential if we are to meet our world-wide military and economic commitments and stay ahead of the Russians in domestic economic development.

There is some disagreement about the possibility of achieving a rate of growth of 5 percent a year and at the same time achieving a stable price level. Some economists believe that such a rate of growth would make it all but impossible to keep prices stable because demand would probably be constantly at or somewhat in excess of current supply.

The biggest disagreement exists about the role of the government in **stimulating** a high rate of growth. Some feel that its role should be restricted to providing a favorable climate for growth and providing incentives through such steps as rapid amortization of new plant and equipment or other tax benefits. Others feel that government should increase its investment expenditures to a level needed to insure a high rate of growth. There is still considerable disagreement about government investment programs in many areas, such as public housing and federal funds for school construction.

At this point we might pause to ask the question that may come as a shock to some readers: Is growth, in fact, a desirable goal, at all? Of course we can't answer the question since it would be necessary to be able to answer such other questions, as whether the people of the United States in 1800 were happier or better off than those of today. We obviously don't know, though most of us might be willing to make a judgment.

Growth of per capita income requires capital expansion — improvements in the quality or in the quantity of capital goods, or in the quality or quantity of "natural" resources, or in the quality of the contribution of the human factor. None of these can be achieved without cost.   The cost is emphasized in the classical expression for saving, namely waiting. In other words, we can have more goods and services in the future only if we give up goods and services in the present.   This may not appear to be a very great sacrifice to an American student of the 1960's, but in many countries of the world a significant increase in saving could be accomplished only with a serious shortening of the average life span as current consumption declined.

The key question for a well-developed society as well as for the underdeveloped is: Who should make the decision as to what the rate of growth of the economy should be? Should this be a collective decision, or should each individual determine his own rate of personal assets growth and thus, in the aggregate, determine the rate of growth of national income?   Should industries engaged in growth-promoting activities be given special encouragement or subsidies, and should industries producing less urgent or even frivolous commodities be penalized in some way?

As a general proposition, most economists would argue in favor of allowing the free market system to determine the rate of growth. If interference with the freedom of the individual to make choices is to be abridged, some quite powerful arguments must be marshalled. Are there such arguments?

There would appear to be two major justifications for attempting to induce a rate of growth faster than might be natural without a specific growth policy. First is the requirement that growth be sufficient to absorb into meaningful employment the additions to the labor force out of a growing population and to reemploy those who would otherwise be replaced by capital. The other justification is the political one of growing at a rate fast enough to continously maintain the nation's military and political strength relative to any potential enemy nations.

The most profound question in growth policy is what society's attitude toward population growth should be. Is a larger human population an absolute good? If not, is there a rate of population growth that is optimum? We know that serious problems arise if population grows at a faster rate than the rate of expansion of economic output. Many nations of the world, particularly in Asia and Africa, can attest to this side of the problem. On the other hand, the governments of many of our most mature economies have felt that the source of some of their most fundamental problems is that population has not grown at a fast enough rate. Probably the safest attitude for an economist to take on this subject is to accept the rate of population growth as given, and to suggest policies that move in the direction of maximizing the per capita income of the actual population.

Full Employment

There is general agreement on the goals of full employment and stable price levels, but disagreement on the exact meaning of such goals. Full employment does not mean that no one is out of work in a free enterprise economy. The demand for labor shifts from field to field, and workers must shift jobs. People may be out of work for a time when they first enter the labor force or when they change jobs voluntarily. A committee of the American Economic Association has developed the following workable definition of full employment[2]:

> Full employment means that qualified people who seek jobs at prevailing wage rates can find them in productive activities without considerable delay. It means full-time jobs for people who want to work full time. It does not mean that people like housewives and students are under pressure to take jobs when they do not want jobs, or that workers are under pressure to put in undesired overtime. It does not mean that unemployment is ever zero.

The amount of unemployment that is consistent with this definition of full employment is generally considered to be around 3 to 4 percent of the labor force, or somewhere between $2\frac{1}{2}$ and $3\frac{1}{2}$ million workers in the late 1960's. When unemployment drops below $2\frac{1}{2}$ million, many areas of labor shortage develop; when it is much above $3\frac{1}{2}$ million, many workers are out of work for protracted periods. There is some debate about trying to keep unemployment at the lower level of the permissible range or allowing it to rise to 3 million or more. The major disagreement occurs when unemployment is between 3 and 4 million. Some feel that vigorous action is called for to reduce it, others feel that no action is necessary since the growth of the economy will produce enough jobs in a short time to absorb the unemployed without creating inflationary pressures.

There is also disagreement about the type of action the government should take when unemployment becomes a serious problem.

---

[2]Committee of the American Economic Association, "The Problem of Economic Instability," *American Economic Review*, Vol. 40 (September, 1950), p. 506.

Some argue for relying on monetary policy, others for large-scale public works, and still others for tax cuts. The various policies advocated in this area will be considered in Chapters 24 and 25.

Increases in aggregate demand lead to the expansion of the money value of national income, but this will be beneficial to the society only if the real output increases and unemployment is reduced. When unemployment is very large, we expect any growth in national income to be primarily in real output and very little in the price level. It depends a great deal, however, on the nature of those who are unemployed. If all of the unemployed were very mobile geographically and flexible in their occupational skills, inflation would not be likely to occur until employment was nearly 100 percent of the labor force. The other extreme is also conceivable. Even if unemployment were a very large percentage of the labor force, if the unemployed were unable or unwilling to move to new locations or other occupations, expansion of aggregate demand might result only in inflation rather than in the diminution of unemployment.

Another important element in the employment versus the inflation problem is the degree of wage flexibility. If, for example, the legal minimum wage were set at a rate well above the marginal revenue product of a large percentage of the labor force, a considerable amount of inflation of product prices would have to take place before these workers could find employment. Any other institutional rigidities imposed on money wages, such as union contracts or industry custom, would have the same effect.

It would be extremely valuable to us to have knowledge of the true relationship between levels of unemployment and price inflation. We would like to be able to answer such questions as the amount of inflation that would be required to reduce unemployment by a given amount if the rate of unemployment were 8 percent, 6 percent, 3 percent, 2 percent, and so on. Chart 23-1 shown on page 573 shows a rough estimate of such a relationship estimated by Samuelson and Solow from 25 years of American data.[3] Such a curve is usually called a Phillips curve after A. W. Phillips who studied the inflation-unemployment relationship for the United Kingdom with such a chart.

---

[3] Paul A. Samuelson and R. M. Solow, "Analytical Aspects of Anti-Inflation Policy," *American Economic Review*, Vol. L (May, 1960), pp. 177–194.

Chart 23-1

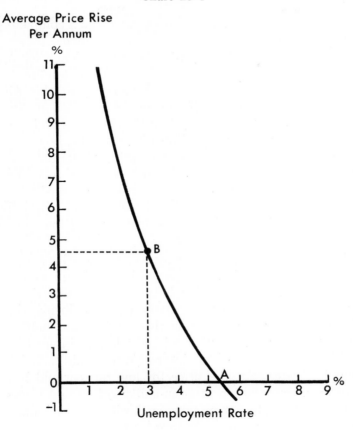

Average Price Rise
Per Annum
%

Unemployment Rate

The Samuelson-Solow estimate is that price stability in the United States could be achieved only at the cost of unemployment of about 5½ percent. This is shown as Point A. Point B can be interpreted as saying that a rate of unemployment of 3 percent would cost about 4½ percent in annual inflation. It would seem that in recent years the record has been a little better than this, but it would appear to be possible to make some significant improvements in the situation. Improvement would be defined as a shifting of the function to the left such that at any given level of unemployment a lower rate of inflation would be experienced. Such gains can be achieved by increasing the mobility of labor through education and training, improved information on employment sources, and other methods by labor and management as well as government.

Stable Price Level

The goal of a stable price level does not mean a completely fixed price level. Prices in general can move up and down somewhat from year to year so long as there is no long-run tendency for prices to increase or decrease. Such fluctuations must be within fairly narrow limits, probably not more than 2 or 3 percent in either direction. Individual prices, of course, will and should fluctuate in response to changes in supply and demand both in the short run and in the long run. Not all are agreed on a goal of price stability, however. Some favor a gradually rising price level with prices rising not over 2 or 3 percent a year in boom years and about stable in recession years. They feel that a gradually rising price level makes it easier to achieve full employment and an acceptable rate of growth, especially in an economy of strong labor unions, imperfect competition among large concerns, and administered prices.

We have just seen that there may be a conflict between the two desirable goals of relative price stability and full employment. There is also, at times, a conflict between stable prices and stable interest rates. This was particularly evident during the latter half of 1966 when the pressure on rising prices was held in check somewhat by monetary policy which allowed interest rates to rise significantly. At that time, interest rates could have been held steady at low rates, but the price for low rates would have been considerably more inflation of commodity prices and wages. The actual response of the monetary authority was a compromise: some inflation and some increase in interest rates.

During World War II and up to 1951, when aggregate demand was increasing more rapidly than the ability to produce, interest rates were kept at stable and low levels, and inflation was allowed to progress. There is no final answer to the question of which route is superior. Inflation and high interest rates both are harmful to some people and helpful to other people. If real output is the same in the two cases, the choice between high prices and high interest rates is a matter of the distribution of income and wealth and the equity thereof.

Equitable Sharing of National Income

The last goal, an equitable sharing of a growing national income among those who helped to produce it, is open to more debate.

Opinions differ widely on what is equitable and, of course, self-interest and group interest become involved. The extremes range from advocates of a return to more or less unregulated free enterprise such as we had it in the 1920's, to government programs of welfare economics to assure a "good life" for all groups. Most individuals are agreed that in developing a program to share the fruits of production equitably, the basic political freedoms must be preserved. This is also generally true of such economic freedoms as the choice of goods to be purchased, the field of labor to be entered, and the type of business to be established. Differences in this field are largely based on differing social and political views and are only, in a small part, based on differences in the analyses of the economic effects of various programs affecting the economy.

Almost any important economic policy has some effect on the distribution of income and wealth. Some attempt to determine this effect should be made even if it is true that as economists we cannot say that one distribution is better or worse than another. There are extreme cases where virtual unanimity would exist. Almost all economists agree that there are extreme distributions of income that are unacceptable both from the standpoint of equity and from the standpoint of viability of the economic and the political systems.

POLITICAL AND ECONOMIC FACTORS THAT AFFECT THE CHOICE OF STABILIZATION POLICIES

Policies designed to stabilize economic activity are affected by the political, economic, and to some degree social patterns that exist in a society. If stability were the overriding goal, it could easily be achieved. But our society has many privileges, obligations, and goals it values above some measure of instability.

Democratic Institutions

We will only follow policies adopted through democratic processes even though, at times, stability might be easier to achieve if someone had autocratic power to change policies. In a period of recession debate may continue in Congress beyond the point at which action is called for to achieve stability because it has been impossible to agree on a shift in policy and enact it into law.

Individual Freedoms

Part of this democratic tradition, or at least closely allied to it, are the rights and freedoms of the individual. This includes not only political freedom as guaranteed in the "Bill of Rights" but also such economic freedoms as the right to own property, to engage in any business not contrary to the public health, safety, and morals, to go into or out of business at will, to choose freely one's field of employment, to work where one chooses, and to bargain freely for a job with any employer.

These economic rights and freedoms have led to a general insistence, at least in peacetime, that government measures to promote stability must operate to affect total spending in an indirect impersonal way, not by detailed regulation of individual economic decisions. For example, restricting housing demand by requiring permits to build houses that are issued on the basis of need for a new house has been rejected, whereas making it impossible for many to build a home because financing is made more difficult is considered appropriate. The one involves a decision based on individual circumstances, the other applies generally.

International Freedom

Several policies in the international sphere have also become so important that they affect policies designed to promote stability. One is the heavy load of expenditures for defense and foreign aid. This must go on under present world conditions in boom years as well as in recession. Part of this commitment to help maintain a strong bulwark against communism is the need to help other countries of the free world to remain strong. This means that our policies must be so designed that we avoid any action that would make it difficult for other countries to maintain stability. This involves such actions as not selling surplus commodites at a time when prices would drop drastically and would materially affect the income of one or more foreign countries.

BUSINESS AND LABOR POLICIES TO PROMOTE GROWTH AND STABILITY

In an economy of small business units and individual bargaining on the part of workers, management and labor have little responsibility for consciously promoting growth and stability. The great contribution of Adam Smith was to demonstrate that in such an economy, if competition existed, the market mechanism would promote the general welfare. The individual entrepreneur under perfectly competitive conditions has no material influence on price or on the total volume of output and can therefore set his level of output to maximize short-run profits without affecting the general economy to a significant degree. But in an economy of large business units, this is not the case. In many fields of production a small group of firms account for most of the output. They are free to set prices within a wide range in the short run, and their actions affect total output in their field materially.

This does not mean that they can set policies at will. The market is still controlling, especially in the long run. Few products have no substitutes, and consumers will shift purchases from relatively high-priced items to lower-priced items. A business is successful in the long run if it produces the goods and services consumers demand at prices that enable the producer to cover all costs of production and to make a profit which attracts the needed capital to the business. Progressive businesses are devoting more and more time and money to research in order to develop new products to meet consumer wants and to find ways to lower the costs of producing them. In such businesses actions cannot be judged on the basis of short-run profit maximization as is possible under competition between small units. It is necessary to take a long-run point of view in making decisions on the share of the market to set as a goal and on prices and the level of output, if the business is to be successful.

The role of labor has also changed from that under conditions of individual bargaining. Contracts negotiated on an industry-wide basis in major industries affect costs and prices and long-run levels of employment. Thus labor must take a long-run point of view to insure its best interest.

An economy of large business and labor units can be organized in different ways for planning what to produce and for setting prices. Decisions on the pattern of goods to produce and on prices may be made by a central planning group, as is done in Russia; or an industry may be allowed to plan output and price policies under government supervision, as is done in many British industries. America is developing another answer: market-oriented research capitalism in which major business units study the wants and needs of consumers and, on the basis of this research, decide on the specific products and services they will produce. Research and development are carried on to produce products at the lowest cost in the long run.

Business and labor have a major responsibility in such an economy for promoting a rising trend of real income and developing policies that will help maintain full employment and a stable price level. This is the only policy consistent with a long-run, market-oriented point of view. In an economy of large units, if business and labor fail in this responsibility, more government intervention will be demanded in a democracy in order to plan for growth and stability.

Policies that are sound in the long run may not be followed in many cases because they are in conflict with short-run self-interest. For example, in a boom period a business may be able to gain a short-run advantage by cutting the quality of its products and so increase profits since demand is high enough to sell goods of any quality. This leads to short-run imbalance because it alters spending and saving patterns. In the long run, however, it is also likely to prove harmful to the business enterprise since consumers do not buy from a concern selling goods of low quality when other alternatives are open to them.

Labor may get a wage increase in prosperity not justified by increases in productivity. Thus, workers gain in the short run. In the long run they may lose in several ways. As others get wage increases to compensate for increased prices, most of the benefits disappear. If wages in a field stay out of line with prices, the incentive toward cost cutting is strong and labor-saving devices will be installed as rapidly as possible. Thus unemployment becomes a problem for some of the workers in this field. Those who remain at work have gained at the expense of those who have lost their jobs.

The policies of labor and management that affect growth and stability will be considered under three topics. First, consideration will be given to policies to promote a rising trend of real income. Next, policies for evening out seasonal variations will be described and discussed. Finally, policies for promoting cyclical stability will be analyzed.

Promoting a Rising Trend of Real Income and a Stable Price Level

One of the outstanding achievements of the free enterprise system has been the high and rising standard of living that it has provided for the population of our country. In fact, one of the basic goals of business and labor in a free enterprise economy must be the provision of goods and services demanded by consumers at the lowest possible prices in the long run. This long-run goal is in harmony with the goal of labor in achieving the highest possible real income in the long run. The goals are the same because only by producing more goods at lower prices can real income increase. It is also in harmony with the goals of progressive individual businesses that are trying to maximize long-run profits by continually lowering the costs of production and distribution. As these growing companies build additional capacity to turn out goods at lower costs, profits are maximized at a lower level of prices. This forces less progressive firms to cut costs or lose out in the competitive struggle.

One of the basic means of achieving this goal is through a program of market research. If the business structure is to provide the goods and services desired by consumers and also by other businesses and governmental units, it is necessary to know in some detail what the demands of each group are. Such research must be carried on continuously since demand patterns change. Gradual change is always going on, and rapid changes take place at times.

It is not sufficient to study consumer and other demands continually. It is also necessary to forecast future demands as accurately as possible. Only in this way can the needed plant be built to meet such demands, especially in an industry where long-range planning is required to design, to construct, and to equip a new plant.

These long-run market studies and forecasts of demand, when made with a reasonable degree of accuracy, help business produce the goods consumers and other groups want. They also help achieve the maximum output from capital and labor. Capital is not used efficiently when sizable amounts of unused capacity exist or when labor in a specialized field is only partially employed. Nor is efficiency promoted when production is increased rapidly to meet shortages. Building plants hastily leads to inefficiencies as does employing a labor force without adequate selection and training.

In order to encourage growth, plans to promote the sale of new products should also be developed on a long-run basis as effectively as possible. When goods that consumers will want in the long run are promoted effectively, demand is built up fast enough to construct plants large enough to turn out goods at low unit costs and to utilize such plants fully. This also helps utilize capital and labor efficiently.

Product research also helps achieve desirable long-run growth. It provides new products to satisfy consumer wants more effectively than old products, and it also provides products that satisfy wants more easily or conveniently or at a lower cost than presently existing products. Product diversification can be used to help promote long-run growth and stability. If a large company makes a series of products that meet different wants, its total demand is likely to be more stable than the demand for individual products. If diversification is well planned, a more regular utilization of full-plant capacity and a more regular employment of labor are made possible. It will also provide for more regular growth since demand for a group of products is likely to grow more steadily than demand for many individual products.

Various steps can be taken to provide goods to consumers at the lowest possible prices. Research to find new ways to cut costs is essential. Such research has been done primarily in production, but it is needed just as much in marketing, personnel relations, financing, and in other areas of management.

Furthermore, research determines the kinds and amounts of labor needed to produce the pattern of goods that will be demanded by consumers, by other businesses, and by the government. Thus, adequate training for workers will be made possible. It will also provide the basis for retraining labor in fields in which demand has declined permanently.

Management and labor should also cooperate to provide mobility for workers from fields in which there is a surplus of labor in general or a specialized kind of labor to fields needing such labor. They should not only provide facilities for retraining when needed but also help in finding areas where labor is needed, and help workers in relocating home and family. This is being done to an increasing degree by companies having plants in various sections of the country. National labor unions can make a significant contribution in this field and thus broaden their service to their members.

The further development of incentives to increase production should be promoted. This requires study to devise the best incentives from the standpoint of the worker and of the company. It also requires cooperation of labor and management to plan, introduce, and use such incentives as effectively as possible.

Long-run growth and stability can also be aided by research in the field of management. The more effectively management plans and carries out long-run and short-run policies the better off the economy will be. Management may not be a science, nevertheless, it has a field of knowledge and techniques that can be learned not only by doing but also by formal training programs through the study of principles from such underlying sciences as economics, mathematics, sociology, and psychology. The application of research in these sciences to management and management training will help to promote growth and stability in the economy.

Proper financial policies can also help attain growth and stability. A business should be financed so as to balance the cost of financing, the safety of financing, and the flexibility for future financing. For example, a concern may be able to sell bonds in a period of low interest rates and get the lowest cost of financing in the short run. However, it may have a good opportunity to expand and need financing in a period in which common stock cannot be sold on a favorable basis. The company may have such a large proportion of bonds in its capital structure that additional bonds cannot be sold without first raising more equity capital. As a result, expansion must be deferred or higher cost financing must be used.

Frequently, business and labor can aid long-run stability by following policies that will steady prices rather than by pursuing policies that will lead to inflation. Inflation has developed in major industries in which there are powerful unions and a few dominant concerns with a large measure of price discretion. Such inflation is referred to as *administrative inflation*.

Both labor and management blame each other for administrative inflation. Management insists that wage increases ahead of productivity lead to price increases; labor, that prices subject to administrative discretion are raised more than need be to cover increased costs. The increased prices raise other wages due to escalator clauses in many contracts and pressure of other groups to keep up with rising prices and thus force prices up in a ratchet fashion.

To help prevent long-run inflation due to management and labor policies, costs should be constantly watched and not allowed to get out of line. This is especially a problem during a boom period. Preventing inefficiencies is a joint responsibility of labor and management. They also have a joint responsibility to prevent average wage increases ahead of average increases in productivity in general. Increasing wages in line with productivity in an individual field in which such increases are above the average can only lead to inflation as other fields try to catch up with the fields getting the larger wage increases. Labor and management should plan jointly to increase overall productivity as rapidly as possible. Only in this way can real wages be increased.

The trend toward negotiating wage contracts running for several years should also be reconsidered. Agreement on working conditions for a period of years helps promote orderly growth, but agreeing on wage increases for each year of a three- or five-year contract promotes administrative inflation. Wages may be increased by an amount agreed upon in the contract when general economic conditions call for smaller or larger increases to promote stability. Serious consideration should be given to wage negotiations on an annual basis.

Escalator clauses that raise wages automatically as the general price level increases also need to be restudied. They have a tendency to promote some degree of inflation. Price increases in the early stages of recovery are the procedure by which the market mechanism allocates goods that are temporarily scarce in relationship to increasing demand. Escalator clauses nullify the operation of the market mechanism. The higher wage rates also raise costs, and this has a tendency to make the higher prices more or less permanent.

The solution to price rises in an upswing is not in the form of escalator clauses that benefit only a few and have little real effect if almost all labor receives wage increases based on minor increases in the cost of living. The real way to offset increased prices that occur early in the cycle is through better forecasting and planning. If long-run demand has been forecast accurately and long-run planning done on the basis of this demand, there will be adequate capacity to meet the increased demand. Then there will be little pressure for price increases due to an increase in demand as prosperity develops.

Evening Out Seasonal Fluctuations

It is desirable from the standpoint of labor, management, and the total economy to smooth out seasonal fluctuations in production and employment. A method of evening out seasonal fluctuations that can be used in some industries is to push sales of the company's product in dull seasons. This can be done effectively by some companies by means of advertising. For example, advertising campaigns by the manufacturers of Aunt Jemima pancake flour succeeded in increasing sales during the summer months, whereas previously they had been concentrated in the winter. The Ruud Manufacturing Company, maker of hot water heaters, was faced with a slump in business during July and August. However, by means of an advertising campaign and summer sales contests it succeeded in eliminating this slump. In fact, July and August became two of its best months for water heater sales. Some of the large chains selling direct to consumers have combated the summer slump by temporary price cuts during this slow season. Manufacturers of consumer durable goods have increased sales during their dull seasons by introducing new models during these periods. The Campbell Soup Company has carried on an extensive campaign stressing the advantages of having one hot dish with each meal even during the summer in order to increase the summer use of soups.[4]

Some companies have evened out seasonal fluctuations by changing the nature of their product somewhat so as to create a demand for it in off-seasons. Manufacturers of ice cream have succeeded in doing this by putting out ice cream with patterns in it appropriate to the Christmas, Valentine, and Easter seasons. The Borden Company, which manufactures Non-Such Mincemeat, has sold its product minus its suet content for ice cream flavoring in the summer.

Still another possibility for evening out seasonal variations is to diversify the market for a product. In such fields as the manufacture of agricultural machinery, this may be done by selling to the South American market at the height of their season, which is at the time of the off-season in the North American market. The manufacturers of metal barrels, who have a large demand for their product for shipping beer during the spring and summer peak in sales of that beverage, have diversified their business by manufacturing barrels to transport alcohol, oil, and various industrial chemicals during the rest of the year.

Another possibility is to induce early ordering for a commodity with a seasonal variation in demand. This may be done by concerted sales campaigns in the off-season. It may also be done by building up a high reputation for the product and then attempting to get

---

[4]For other examples of methods of reducing seasonal unemployment than those given, see Edwin S. Smith, *Reducing Seasonal Unemployment* (New York: McGraw-Hill Book Company, 1931).

orders for the full season in advance. Another aid to early ordering is seasonal billing, under which goods are shipped early but the bill does not come due until 30 or 60 days after the date at which the goods would normally have been shipped. In addition, early ordering with payment in the regular manner may also be encouraged by substantial discounts for goods bought well in advance of regular seasonal needs.

Some concerns have smoothed out seasonal operations by dovetailing the production of items with different seasonal fluctuations. This has been done, for example, by the Hood Rubber Company, manufacturer of rubber footwear for use in bad weather, by adding to its line sports footwear that is used primarily in the summer. The Campbell Soup Company has found it possible to produce soup the year round by developing a complete line of soups, the raw materials for which are available at different times throughout the year. One of the most frequently quoted examples of seasonal dovetailing is that of S. L. Allen & Co., Inc., of Pennsylvania, which began business with a small line of farm and garden tools. After the company had been in business 18 years, it was able to regularize its operations to a large extent by manufacturing the Flexible Flyer sled during the months of the year when it was not active in the farm and garden tool work. Other concerns have solved this problem by manufacturing heating equipment and also air-conditioning and cooling equipment so as to keep business more stable throughout the year.

In some lines of activity it is possible to eliminate seasonal variations in production by building up stocks of goods by producing at a regular rate throughout the year and meeting changing sales from such inventories. This has been done successfully by the paint industry, in which some of the manufacturers have constructed large warehouses that have made it possible to manufacture paint at a more or less regular rate throughout the year even though sales are subject to a definite seasonal. The Eastman Kodak Company has done the same thing with some of its photographic products. This concern, which has also been a leader in the field of business forecasting, has probably carried planning to regularize production as far as any company has.[5]

---

[5] For a description of the method that it uses, see National Industrial Conference Board, *Forecasting Sales* (New York: National Industrial Conference Board, 1947), pp. 39–43.

Policies to Promote Cyclical Stability

Business and labor can follow policies that will help promote cyclical stability. Such policies will be considered in the areas of sales promotion, pricing, production, inventory management, capital budgeting, and research and development.

The first step required to develop a program for promoting cyclical stability is a good program for forecasting demand for a company's products and the most likely sales volume, the demand for capital and labor, and the cost levels. A forecasting program which produces fairly accurate results will help avoid overproduction and shortages that are characteristic of business cycles. Such a program by itself can help materially to stabilize economic activity. It also provides the basis for programs in the pricing, production, capital budgeting, and other areas that can help promote stability.

Sales Promotion Policies. The proper budgeting of sales promotion programs promotes stability. Some businesses have cut advertising and sales promotion programs in periods of recession in an effort to maintain profits. By cutting discretionary expenditures in a downturn, they have helped intensify the recession. Of course, some concerns in a poor financial position may have to cut all possible expenses to prevent a financial debacle; but most concerns are not in such a financial position, especially not in a minor recession. If all expenditures are constantly kept under close scrutiny in good times and bad, cost cutting to eliminate general inefficiencies in a recession should not be necessary. Such cost cutting is not sound management; it not only promotes instability, but it is a sign that management has been inefficient in prosperity.

Sound sales promotion expenditures are an especially poor area for cost cutting in a recession. Such cuts may reduce sales further and will certainly have an adverse effect when business again picks up. In some fields of business additional expenditures on sales promotion are desirable in a recession. Many families have money available for current spending, even in severe recessions. If advertising can overcome temporary psychological restraints on desirable purchases, it is helping to promote stability. Businessmen should study the effect of sales promotion on sales during periods of different economic situations in order to develop sound sales programs in slack periods for the purpose of increasing sales, which contributes to economic stability.

Pricing Policies. Pricing policies can be used along with sales promotion policies to achieve stability. These are not alternatives, but related parts of the "marketing mix." A flexible price policy, if properly worked out, will promote stability more than a policy of rigid prices. To the extent that price changes are used to maximize demand at profitable levels, stability is furthered. The best policy is to study demand at various prices and costs at various levels of output and to use such analysis to set prices and output levels. This must be done on a continuing basis since demand and cost patterns change over the cycle. If a dynamic price policy based on demand and cost analysis is followed, the largest possible sales at profitable levels can be achieved at all stages of the cycle.

Pricing of a new product can also be used to help advance stability. When demand is high, an introductory price can be set high enough to recover a large part of developmental costs early in the life of a product. This is sound when a new product is introduced in a period of prosperity. In a period of recession a lower price that is designed to build up a large volume of sales rapidly will do more for stability than a higher price with a small volume of sales, even though development costs are recovered over a longer period of time. If a product fails, the increased risk of loss should not be serious in the long run for a company regularly producing new products, provided that the market research on consumer acceptance is being done well.

Production Policies. Production policies can be geared to promote stability. Lax efforts to increase productivity in a boom followed by vigorous campaigns in a recession lead to instability. Cooperation of management and labor to keep productivity constantly as high as possible not only lead to long-run growth in real income but provide short-run stability.

Stability is also furthered by business policies and procedures that make possible rapid and smooth changes in production due to shifts in demand. This prevents losses from producing goods that are no longer generally demanded and have to be sold at sacrifice prices. It also makes continued adaptation to changing demand patterns possible and so prevents major maladjustments that can lead to production slowdowns on a large scale. Such planning should help prevent inventory buildups in excess of sales requirements and the succeeding periods of liquidation.

Inventory Policies. If business can succeed in keeping inventories balanced with sales, a major factor in minor recessions will have been eliminated. To do this requires inventory planning that is based on forecasts of future sales. If inventory levels are based on past sales, inventories are bound to be too small in an upswing and too large when sales reach sustainable levels. If they are based on forecasts of sales, they can be built up or depleted at a fairly even rate over a period of several quarters when sales forecasts show they should be changed. Such a policy will help offset the effects of the accelerator principle in the inventory field. If inventories are based on sales forecasts that are reasonably accurate, inventory shortages and surpluses will be largely eliminated.

A cyclical policy of inventory purchases that is based on need and not on speculation, moreover, is necessary for stabilizing inventories. If an individual businessman knows better than the market what will happen to prices in a recovery period, he can buy goods when prices are low and profit from sales when prices rise. But when businessmen generally attempt to follow such a policy, prices rise when all are buying goods. When all have sufficient supplies, prices fall and there is no profit on price rises. Not only is such a policy self-defeating but it creates inventory cycles and instability. Inventory policies based on forecasts are much sounder in most cases. When electronic computers are used to plan and keep records of inventory needs, the savings are frequently great enough to more than offset potential profits on price rises even for companies with unusually able purchasing agents.

Capital Budgeting. Stability can be promoted in the capital budgeting areas. Capital expenditures should properly be planned on the basis of the average rate of return to be earned over their life. If this is done, a company in sound financial position with an expanding demand for its products can justify expenditures in good years and bad, and so help to promote stability. If expansion is based on the ability to recoup a capital investment in a set number of years, such as three or five, many projects will have to be postponed in recession. Regularizing investment based on long-run demand for a product helps a company meet demand in years of recovery. It also enables the firm to build in good years and bad, and thus get the cost saving from careful planning and from a sizable amount of building in years of slow demand and better building prices.

Research and Development Programs. Research and development programs can be planned to aid stability. Long-run programs carried on in good years and bad help regularize income. They also provide new products, some of which should be ready in recession, and so boost sales. Strong companies may follow a counter cyclical policy by increased spending on research, especially on development work, in a recession period in order to bring new products on the market when a sales increase is needed most. All of these policies can be coordinated into a policy of dynamic business planning, at times referred to as profit planning. Sales are forecast and budgets are developed on the basis of such forecasts. If the levels are not satisfactory from the standpoint of the utilization of men and capital equipment and of profit levels, programs are developed in the areas of promotion, pricing, product development, and labor incentives in order to achieve desirable levels of employment and profits. Such a coordinated program becomes the business plan for the year. Dynamic business planning on a regular basis can make a major contribution to stability.

QUESTIONS

1. What do you conceive to be the role of the economist in determining national economic goals and policies?
2. Compare the real costs in achieving economic growth of a relatively affluent society, such as the United States, with the costs to a society in which the majority of the population is at or near a subsistence level of income.
3. Explain how you would go about deciding for yourself what your "trade-off" rate would be regarding the conflict between increased employment and inflation. Relate your discussion to the Phillips curve on page 573.
4. If policy makers must choose between inflation and higher interest rates, what would be the nature of the considerations that should be made?
5. Discuss the following policy issues with reference to "Pareto optimality."
   (a) Tariff reductions.
   (b) Highway construction during periods of full employment.
   (c) Highway construction during periods of serious unemployment.
6. How do you react to the observation that the hurt caused some people by inflation is perfectly offset by benefits derived by others?
7. Explain the most important methods of promoting economic growth.

8. Can you construct a definition of optimum population or optimum growth of population? What would be the important elements in evolving such a definition?

9. This chapter and the following two chapters stress policies of aggregate demand expansion to reduce unemployment. What other approach seems promising?

10. Many government policies to promote economic growth and stability have an impact on the distribution of wealth and income. Can you formulate criterion by which you can determine that one distribution is better than another? Is it possible to argue that change in the distribution is either good or bad?

11. Describe various programs to even out seasonal fluctuations in business activity.

12. Outline and discuss business policies to promote stability in the areas of:
    (a) Marketing.
    (b) Pricing.
    (c) Production.
    (d) Capital budgeting.
    (e) Research and development programs.

13. Describe the purpose and basic provisions of the Employment Act of 1946.

SUGGESTED READINGS

Culbertson, J. M. *Full Employment or Stagnation.* New York: McGraw-Hill Book Company, 1964.

The Economic Report of the President. Washington: U. S. Government Printing Office, annually.

Knorr, Klaus, and William J. Baumol (eds.). *What Price Economic Growth?* Englewood Cliffs, New Jersey: Prentice-Hall, Inc., 1961.

Novack, David E., and Robert Lekachman (eds.). *Development and Society: The Dynamics of Economic Change.* New York: St. Martin's Press, 1964.

Rowland, F. H., and W. H. Harr. *Budgeting for Management Control.* New York: Harper & Row, Publishers, 1945.

Samuels, Warren J. *The Classical Theory of Economic Policy.* Cleveland, Ohio: The World Publishing Company, 1966.

Turner, R. C. "Problems of Forecasting for Economic Stabilization," *American Economic Review,* 45 (March, 1955).

Growth and Stability

This chapter is devoted to an analysis of monetary policies that are designed to promote economic growth and stability. Present programs and policies will be analyzed, and proposals for revisions or for new policies will be considered. The last section of this chapter will consider the problem of a long-run inflationary bias that many believe has been built into our economy.

Chapter 25 deals with fiscal policy, so the question arises as to whether a clear-cut distinction can be made between policies which are to be termed "monetary" and those which are to be called "fiscal." The truth is that considerable ambiguity about these terms exists, and this ambiguity often leads to useless debate and confusion. No difficulty would arise if policies were purely monetary — those which have their impact directly on the quantity or cost of money — or purely fiscal — government spending and taxing programs. But any federal budget has some implications for the money supply. A budgetary deficit requires a decision about its financing, and this will have an impact on the supply or cost of money. A surplus requires a decision concerning its disposition — again, what is done with the surplus will influence the supply or cost of money.

The point is not that we need rigorous definitions of monetary versus fiscal, but that we should recognize the interrelations between the policies called by those names. We should also be aware that many users of these words use them differently.

An approach that is often used is to arbitrarily declare that actions by the central bank (the Federal Reserve System) are monetary policies, and actions by the Treasury are fiscal actions. This works fairly well for the United States, but it is hardly useful in those countries where the Treasury and the central bank are under the control of the same officers.

Our organization of the discussion will be based on the proposition that Federal Reserve policy is mainly monetary policy and so will be taken up in this chapter, and the Treasury policy is mainly fiscal and will be covered in Chapter 25. We, of course, will try to keep the interrelationships in proper perspective.

THE NATURE OF MONETARY POLICIES

The nature of our monetary system and the tools of monetary policy were described briefly in Chapter 3.

The theoretical framework was discussed in Part II. It should be clear that any policy proposal must be based on some theory. There is no alternative. The hope is that the theory we choose is the most accurate picture available of the economy the policy will affect.

The money supply theory presented in Chapter 3 concerned the relationship between the variables which can be directly determined by the monetary authority, the monetary base (B), which is mainly member bank reserves and currency, and the money supply. We used the expression $M = KB$, where K is the relationship called the money multiplier. Recall that K involved the behavior of the public and the commercial banks. It also incorporated the significance of reserve requirements that are controlled by the Board of Governors.

Having a theory which explains how the money supply is affected by monetary policy, we then need a theory which explains how changes in the money supply influence the economy. We considered two basic approaches to this problem. The classical quantity theory approach concludes that changes in money directly influence the level of absolute prices and, when unemployment exists, directly affects the level of real national income. The Keynesian approach concludes that the direct effect of changes in the money supply is on interest rates, which, in turn, affects the rate of investment and thereby, through the multiplier process, national income.

We should emphasize that the analytical apparatus used — classical or Keynesian — is not the source of differences of opinion on the effectiveness of monetary policy. Rather, conclusions differ primarily because of differences in judgment about what the real world is like — the degree of flexibility of wages and prices, the degree to which interest rate changes influence the level of investment, or saving, the degree to which money supply changes will change interest rates and so on.

FEDERAL RESERVE POLICY

Robert V. Roosa divides the responsibilities of the Federal Reserve System into what he calls the defensive and the dynamic responsibilities.[1] Defensive actions are taken by the Federal Reserve System in response to changes in the reserve position of commercial banks caused by others. Defensive actions simply offset such reserve status changes. Dynamic policy aims at either increasing or decreasing the ability of commercial banks to expand the money supply and credit.

The major factors, not involving Federal Reserve action, affecting member bank reserves are gold flows and foreign transactions, currency in circulation, Treasury balances in the Federal Reserve Banks, and float. In addition to these, the volume of required reserves changes as deposits shift among banks with different reserve requirements, between member and nonmember banks, and between time deposits and demand deposits.

If all of these factors were to behave in such a way that the excess reserves in the banking system were to increase by, say, $2 billion, the Federal Open-Market Committee in its defensive posture would sell $2 billion worth of securities. Selling less than that amount would amount to a dynamic action of promoting monetary ease and expansion. Selling more than $2 billion worth of securities would be a dynamic action of curtailing the ability of banks to expand or forcing them to contract money and credit.

In an economy where money was left to manage itself, serious instability would be generated by virtue of these changes in the reserve position of commercial banks. Indeed, in Chapter 5 we looked at the purely monetary theory of the business cycle where the basic cause of the cycle was the flow of reserves into and out of the banks in the form of currency movements and gold flows. Much of the instability experienced in this country during the time of the independent treasury system, from 1846 until the Federal Reserve System took over the fiscal agency function, was due to the flow of funds between the Treasury and commercial banks as the Treasury collected taxes in cash and paid for its expenditures.

Very little controversy surrounds the defensive actions of the Federal Reserve System. A serious snowstorm that would slow the

---

[1]Robert V. Roosa, *Federal Reserve Operations in the Money and Government Securities Markets* (New York: Federal Reserve Bank of New York, 1956).

mails and increase the amount of float shouldn't be allowed to disrupt the money market and the economy. Similarly, just because the public uses more currency in the month or two before Christmas is not justification for a large contraction of the money supply.

The important question at any time is whether it is appropriate to increase or to decrease the money supply to counter the cyclical movement of the economy or to promote growth in real output. If something should be done, there are the further questions of how much and what particular policies should be used.

USING THE INSTRUMENTS OF MONETARY POLICY

The Federal Reserve System uses the various instruments of monetary policy at its disposal to help smooth out seasonal and cyclical fluctuations in economic activity and to meet the needs of the economy for growth. Seasonal variations in the reserves of member banks are principally offset by open-market operations. Some banks may offset seasonal pressures by borrowing from their Federal Reserve Banks, but this happens primarily when pressures on a bank or a group of banks are due to special or unusual seasonal fluctuations.

The provision of bank reserves to meet the needs of a growing economy is partly through open-market operations, partly through changing reserve requirements, and partly through lending to member banks. Reserve requirements are frequently lowered during a period of recession when long-run growth indicates the need for additional reserves. This is done to help provide the stimulus for expansion. Reserve requirements also may be changed when large international movements of gold need to be offset in order to keep reserves in line with the demands of the economy.

The role of the Federal Reserve in helping stabilize cyclical fluctuations is carried on primarily through the use of open-market operations and by altering the ability or the willingness of commercial bank borrowing through the discount window. When economic activity is expanding rapidly and inflationary pressures develop, restraint on monetary expansion is called for to promote stability. The Federal Reserve under such circumstances resorts to open-market operations to provide banks with a smaller amount of reserves than that needed to meet all of the demands for credit. The first reaction is for individual banks that are short of reserves to sell government bonds in order to obtain the needed funds. Such sales provide funds for the individual bank, but they do not increase the overall supply of reserves since other banks lose them as checks are drawn against deposits to pay for the bonds.

As the monetary authorities continue the policy of restraint, more and more banks become short of reserves. This leads an increasing number of banks to borrow from their Federal Reserve Banks to meet shortages in required reserves. As loans are retired and not renewed and funds are used to repay the loans from the Federal Reserve Banks, other banks experience a shortage of reserves. Thus, an increase in borrowing from the Federal Reserve Banks is a normal reaction to a restrictive monetary policy. This borrowing provides an offset to the reduction in reserves brought about by open-market operations, but it does not nullify the effects of monetary restraint. The borrowing will be offset by open-market operations to keep total reserves at the level desired by Reserve authorities.

The cost of borrowing or the discount rate will also be raised to help discourage borrowing. Furthermore, banks in debt to their Reserve Bank use any reserves that they acquire to repay their loan and thus restrict credit expansion. Their lending policies also become more stringent since they are under pressure to repay their indebtedness. The actions of an individual bank to free itself of indebtedness to the Federal Reserve, however, cannot get banks as a group out of debt, because whatever reserves one bank gains are lost by others. Thus as long as the Federal Reserve maintains pressure on bank reserve positions, member banks will remain conservative and even become cautious in their lending policies.

This process is just reversed when economic conditions call for a policy of monetary ease. Reserves are supplied through open-market operations and at times through lowering reserve requirements when long-run expansion requires a larger volume of reserves. The first action of member banks is to reduce their debt to the Federal Reserve Banks. When this phase has come to an end, excess reserves become available for bank loans and investments.

EFFECT OF MONETARY POLICY ON THE ECONOMY

When bank reserve positions are under pressure, banks sell government securities and so reduce their supply of secondary reserves. As their reserves are reduced and they are forced to borrow from their Reserve bank, they become more conservative in their lending policies. The loan requests of marginal borrowers are refused or are reduced in amount. This forces them to spend less to increase inventory or plant and equipment. Banks are less willing to make loans on residential real estate and to consumers for purchasing durable goods. Banks are also less willing to lend to other financial institutions, such as sales finance companies, consumer finance companies, and mortgage loan companies. The lessened availability of credit puts a brake on increased spending. This is reinforced by the increase in interest rates that results when the supply of loanable funds is restricted while demand continues to increase.

The actions of banks also affect other credit markets. As banks try to increase reserves, they sell securities. This takes funds from the money markets at the very time when demand for funds is high. This also helps raise interest rates. Rising interest rates make borrowing less attractive, and marginal projects are canceled or at least postponed.

Rising interest rates also lower the market price of outstanding securities. This makes investors less willing to sell these securities and thus has a tendency to reduce investment that was planned from the proceeds of the sale of securities. Even if a security holder sells his securities, he has fewer dollars to spend.

In periods of credit ease, the effect is largely the reverse. Banks have an adequate supply of funds and are willing to make funds available to other financial institutions. Lower interest rates also encourage investment and raise the price of existing securities, and in this way make their sale more advantageous.

When the new money comes into existence the public will have more money than it had before so adjustment to a new equilibrium position with respect to cash balances is necessary. As we have seen, this adjustment involves the attempts by money holders to shift into other things, securities or real goods. Through this process the prices of goods will rise and interest rates will fall unless unemployment is serious, in which case output will increase instead of the prices of securities, goods, and services.

Reduction of the money supply would be expected to have the opposite effect of money expansion, although there is the general belief that prices are less flexible downward. If this is true, the impact will be more heavily on output and employment rather than on prices.

Monetary policy has an indirect effect through its effect on the expectations of consumers and businessmen. If consumers feel prices are likely to rise, they will speed up purchases of durables; if they expect prices to decline, they will defer them. Businessmen react in a similar fashion to expectations of price changes, to difficulties in financing expansion projects, and to other changes in the economic outlook.

SELECTIVE VERSUS GENERAL MONETARY CONTROLS

The discussion of monetary policies up to this point has been in terms of general controls over the amount of credit available. Selective controls of various types also have been used from time to time, and several of them are still in use. The only selective credit control at present in the hands of the Federal Reserve is that over stock market credit. By changing margin requirements on stock purchases, the Federal Reserve is able to influence directly the amount of credit used in the stock market. This is a highly volatile type of credit affected by speculative activity in the market. Selective controls in this area moderate the degree of general credit action that is necessary to offset speculation and the use of credit in the stock market.

The Federal Reserve had power to control consumer credit during World War II, and again briefly in the postwar period, and for a time also had control over real estate credit; but these powers have not been renewed. Selective credit controls of a limited type are in operation, however, in other credit markets. When the Housing and Home Finance Agency makes it easier to buy houses on credit because it wants to encourage building or, more difficult because it wants to discourage building, it is engaging in selective credit controls. This has also been done, to some degree, when the Small Business Administration has made it easier to obtain loans in a period of recession than in a boom period.

There is a basic difference of opinion about the role of selective credit controls as a permanent instrument for influencing economic growth and restraining inflationary pressures. Those who argue against selective credit controls do so largely on the basis of the efficiency of the market mechanism. They believe that competitive markets can best determine interest rates and the allocation of resources to various lenders. Any government interference can at best produce results that are less desirable in the long run than those established in the market.

Another argument against selective controls arises out of the administration of such controls. They are difficult to enforce in many cases, especially in the field of consumer credit. This is, in part, due to the large number of merchants and dealers involved in selling consumer durables on credit and to the difficulty of establishing true prices and down payments due to the widespread practice of giving inflated allowances for trade-ins as a means of cutting list prices.

One of the major arguments against selective credit controls is that they are not effective. Margin requirements in the stock market do not appear to have any significant influence on stock prices, the volume of stock trading, or even on the amount of credit used in the stock market. To the degree, if any, that selective controls are effective in the segment of the economy in which they are imposed, they only shift the inflationary problem rather than solve it. The funds made idle in one segment of the economy are transferred to other segments, and price pressure develops there.

The proponents of such controls argue that any monetary policy involves discrimination and that there is no real choice between general monetary controls and selective monetary controls from a free economy point of view. They feel that selective controls can prevent maladjustments that lead to instability more easily than general controls. For example, if housing is in a boom while unemployment exists in other areas, these advocates feel that control of housing credit can prevent undue expansion and later collapse; whereas general credit controls are powerless unless the whole economy is to be restrained at a time when such a policy is not required.

There has also been some advocacy of selective controls as a means of stimulating or retarding long-run growth in a sector of the economy so as to establish balanced patterns of growth. Under such a proposal, consumer credit could be used to increase or decrease automobile demand, for example, if it were out of line with what seemed to the regulatory authorities to be balanced growth with the rest of the economy. Such a use of selective controls would, of course, intensify the argument over control by regulation or by market forces.

ANALYSIS AND EVALUATION OF MONETARY POLICY

There is considerable disagreement about the efficiency of monetary policy in helping to promote full employment and a stable price level. Since economic forces are extremely complex and are based on many interrelated factors, it is difficult, if not impossible, to determine the real effect of any policy in isolation. Therefore, we cannot determine exactly what would have happened if monetary policies of a different type had been followed or if the timing of changes in monetary policy had been different.

Favorable Effects of Monetary Policy

Several advantages are claimed for monetary controls over other policies for stability. One important advantage is that monetary controls are impersonal; the monetary authorities determine the total volume of bank reserves, and banks ration the available credit. Such controls do directly affect various groups, however. Since monetary controls affect the volume of and interest rates on bank loans and investments, bank profits are directly affected. Changes in interest rates also redistribute income between those who pay interest and those who receive it. Many individuals and organizations, of course, are in a position to determine in which group they will be; whether lender or borrower. This is, however, not universally true nor is it true at all times even for those for whom it is generally true.

Monetary policy can be very flexible. A powerful and immediate impact need not be instituted. This is particularly true of open-market operations where the impact can be spread out over time in any desired amounts without any change in laws or announcements. Indeed, very few are likely to even know what is going on. Reversal of the direction of policy can very easily be accomplished if it is discovered that the initial action was in error.

It takes some time for monetary policy to influence the economy, but the time lag is probably shorter than for most other policy actions, particularly those which require action by Congress and the executive branch of government.

Many economists believe that monetary policy is more effective in combating inflation than it is in stimulating recovery from depressed conditions. The statement defending this opinion is that during inflationary periods the banks usually have negligible amounts of excess reserves and, therefore, they will be forced to

contract earning assets and demand deposits following any contractionary actions by the Federal Reserve. On the other hand,
during depressions, since banks usually hold significant amounts
of excess reserves, any expansionary Federal Reserve policy will
simply permit but not force the banks to expand.

In addition, as was pointed out in our earlier discussion, Keynesians feel that the liquidity preference function is so elastic that
any increase in the money supply during depressed periods will
have virtually no effect on interest rates. Since the Keynesian
analysis makes interest rates important only to the extent that
they influence investment demand, if interest rates are not lowered
significantly, the impact on investment and national income will
be negligible. The other string to the Keynesian bow is the judgment
that at the low interest rates which prevail during depressions,
investment demand is not responsive to further rate reductions.

Since the people responsible for monetary policy seem to have
accepted this line of argument, they have had little faith in the
power of their tools to bring the economy out of depressions. Consequently, expansionary monetary policy has been somewhat
halfhearted during such periods. At least, so argue the defenders
of monetary policy.

The negative side of the argument is countered point by point
by those who do believe in the effectiveness of monetary policy.
First, on the question as to whether banks with large excess reserves
will increase earning assets and hence the money supply, these
economists contend that under the prevailing economic and banking
conditions, equilibrium for banks requires a large volume of excess
reserves, but if they are provided with additional amounts, they
will seek profitable outlets for them. In particular, when large
volumes of risk-free government securities can be purchased and if
the monetary authorities act aggressively to promote expansion, it
is felt that banks will not continuously allow nonearning cash to
build up.

Rebuttal to the interest rate and investment argument is that
Keynesians have excessively stressed interest as a cost to investors.
They have neglected to observe that at low interest rates, even a
minute reduction in the rate has a very large impact on capital
values, and for that reason an increase in the money supply would
be very expansionary even if the interest rate effect were small.
Ultimately, of course, the answers to these questions are not to be

found in a priori speculation but must be found from empirical tests. Perhaps we have never adequately tested the power of monetary policy in bringing about expansion from a serious depression.

Unfavorable Effects of Monetary Policy

Major criticism of monetary policy lies in the area of timing. The tendency is not to act until it is clear that action is needed. This means that action is usually too late to do the most good. For example, in the beginnings of a recovery period there is a hesitancy to restrict credit for fear of stopping and reversing the recovery. When action is finally taken inflationary pressures are already built up.

Another criticism of monetary policy is that it tends to slow down the rate of growth. In a period of tight money, financing of new projects is more difficult than is the case in a period of monetary ease. New businesses based on new ideas and growing small businesses find it harder to get funds. The forced saving arising in the early stages of a cycle may lead to short-run inequities, but promotes growth by increasing investment faster than voluntary savings.

The argument is frequently made that the high interest rates resulting from monetary restraint slow down investment. This, of course, is true, and this is what they are designed to do. Price stability can only exist when investment takes place from voluntary saving, not from forced saving. Lower interest rates will in the long run stimulate investment if they arise because the supply of funds for investment has been increased through saving. When interest rates are kept abnormally low, prices will rise and thus offset a good part of the real effect on investment.

Monetary policy is also criticised at times because it works a hardship on various groups in society. In a period of monetary ease, it reduces the income of those trying to live on the income from bond investments. It also increases the cost of insurance and pensions. Problems are created for financial institutions since their income from interest is cut. In a period of monetary restraint, other problems arise. The cost of financing a home increases, and the burden falls primarily on young people buying their first home. Small business finds it harder to get funds and therefore feels it is being put at a disadvantage. Financing costs of state and local governments and private institutions, such as hospitals, go up. Those who have to finance at the period of greatest monetary pressure are hardest hit. Such policy is, of course, designed to postpone projects, but some plans cannot be postponed without serious consequences.

Evaluation of Recent Monetary Policy

These conflicts in the use of monetary policy are apparent in monetary action in the post-World War II period. During World War II and for several years thereafter monetary policy was largely geared to government financing needs. After the Federal Reserve-Treasury Accord in 1951, it was again free to be used to promote stability. To date it has been used in four postwar booms, 1951–1953, 1955–1957, 1958–1960, and 1961–1967; and three postwar recessions, 1953–1954, 1957–1958, and 1960–1961.

Postwar Booms. The first boom after the Accord showed satisfactory growth and little inflation. Gross national product increased about 4 percent per year in real terms, and unemployment was below 3 percent per year. Prices of consumer goods rose mildly during the early part of the boom and then leveled off.

During most of this period the System followed a policy of neutrality, that is, it kept credit in line with the needs of the economy, rather than restricting it to any great degree. It did allow member bank borrowing and interest rates to rise slowly.

Some argue that the downturn was due to the tightening of credit in the spring of 1953. This was intensified when the Treasury indicated it intended to sell a long-term bond issue that would reduce funds available for capital investment. The downturn was due primarily to a reduction in federal defense purchases and a reduction in business inventories caused in part by lower defense expenditures. These would probably have led to a contraction even in the absence of credit tightening. Actions in the credit markets may have affected the timing of the downturn, however. It is, of course, impossible to determine if the resulting recession would have been more severe if the boom had gone on longer.

The second boom after the Accord, that of 1955–1957, had many characteristics which were at variance with those of the first boom. Gross national product in real terms increased significantly in 1955, but then it rose little in 1956 and 1957. Unemployment was almost one million workers higher on the average than in the earlier boom.

Prices rose gradually during most of the boom, wholesale prices from early summer of 1955 on, consumer prices from early 1956 on.

In 1955 the Federal Reserve could not exercise active restraint because of the large reserves created to curb the recession. In 1956 and 1957 severe restraint on credit was exercised and credit became very tight. Interest rates rose to the highest levels since the 1920's. This credit policy failed to halt price increases. Whether it kept real gross national product from rising is difficult to determine and not agreed upon. Some ascribe the end of the boom to credit stringency. It is likely that it would have occurred in any event since a capital goods boom resulted in excess capacity and capital goods spending had to be reduced.

In the 1958–1960 prosperity period the Federal Reserve acted early and vigorously to restrict the money supply. In early 1959 there were some signs that the economy would develop an out-and-out boom. This was due in part to the building up of inventories in anticipation of a steel strike. To prevent sharp price increases the Federal Reserve further increased its pressure on bank reserves. The steel strike which began in July stopped the advance in economic activity. Despite active monetary restraint during this prosperity period the cost of living continued to edge upward.

The long expansionary period starting in 1961 was characterized by continuous growth in virtually all segments of the economy. Real per capita income grew, and the percentage of unemployment fell. The price index rose only slightly during the early years, but by 1966 inflation appeared as a problem, though not yet a very serious one. Monetary policy, in these years, was influenced by a concern over the drain of gold that was taking place as overseas spending by the federal government continued large, and investment in foreign countries by Americans grew. The goal of the Federal Reserve was to allow short-term rates to rise to discourage the outflow of funds, but to keep long-term rates relatively low so as not to seriously hinder domestic investment. In line with this the discount rate was raised in 1963, 1964, and again in December of 1965. Open-market operations were used on occasions to slow the rate of growth in the money supply, but over the whole period open-market buying permitted expansion at what was considered an acceptable rate.

Postwar Recessions. The downturn in 1953–1954 was unusually mild. GNP dropped little, and personal income kept on rising while prices remained about stable. The Federal Reserve acted quickly and decisively to ease credit through open-market operations and a reduction in reserve requirements. Assisted by a tax cut, this action helped bring about recovery in the second half of 1954, but it has been criticized as too drastic for future stability. By flooding the banks with reserves in 1954, it made it more difficult to exercise restraint in 1955 when a new boom was in progress.

The recession of 1957–1958 was shorter than that of 1953–1954, but more severe. It resulted primarily from a contraction of inventories and a reduction in capital goods expenditures. Prices continued to rise during that recession. The Federal Reserve did not relax its credit policies until recession was underway and did not increase reserves to anything like the degree it did in 1953–1954. Its actions were motivated as much by the fear of inflation as by the need to stimulate recovery.

The Federal Reserve initiated a policy of lessening of monetary restraint early in 1960 when there were indications that the economy had leveled off. This may have helped to keep the decline in economic activity in the 1960–1961 recession unusually mild. However, the Federal Reserve encountered serious problems in this recession. As they moved to a policy of monetary ease, short-term interest rates dropped and there was a large outflow of short-term capital that enlarged our balance of payments deficit and increased gold losses. This prevented the reduction of interest rates to the low levels reached in earlier recessions since further reductions would have led to increased flights of short-term capital. Therefore sectors of the economy, such as construction which responds to interest rate changes could not be stimulated as effectively as in earlier recessions. To help lower long-term interest rates the Federal Reserve initiated a program of buying longer-term securities. This was done to affect intermediate and long-term interest rates more directly than is the case when short-term funds only are increased by direct action, and banks and other lenders then shift funds to the long-term markets in a search for more attractive investment opportunities.

Federal Reserve policies were reasonably successful in the first post-Accord boom and recession. After that, however, problems were encountered. Inflation was a problem in boom and recession and so was the loss of gold. Policies to stop inflation prevented action to speed up growth. Many feel that a new long-run inflation problem has developed that creates new problems for maintaining growth and stability. This will be discussed in the last section of this chapter in more detail.

PROPOSALS FOR CHANGES IN MONETARY INSTRUMENTS OF CONTROL

Various proposals have been made for changing the monetary instruments used for control of the economy. Some would make relatively minor changes, others more drastic changes. Several such proposals will be considered briefly.

Reserves in Government Bonds

One proposal for a minor change in monetary controls is to require banks to keep reserves in government bonds over and above required reserves. This would prevent banks from converting bonds into cash early in a boom. This would help slow down expansion. It also would make credit control easier for the Federal Reserve. The same end, of course, could be accomplished by raising general reserve requirements. This proposal has the merit of allowing banks to earn interest on the bonds held as reserves, however. The proposal calls for but a minor modification of present procedures. It would make somewhat easier not only the work of the Federal Reserve but also that of the Treasury since an assured market would exist for a significant volume of government bonds. Experience of the last few years has shown that the Federal Reserve can achieve credit tightness and even stringency without such additional power. With it, it might be possible to do so and still keep interest rates on the federal debt lower and make the problems of the Treasury in refunding large maturing issues of bonds somewhat easier.

Automatic Monetary Control

A much more drastic proposal calls for an end to discretionary monetary policy. Several reasons are offered for this change. First, it is felt that the Federal Reserve's record in preventing the extremes of business cycle swings has been worse than what would have happened in the absence of any action. Second, and as a partial explanation of the first statement, the lags in monetary policy are believed to be so long that by the time the action takes effect the economy may already have reversed direction and would need the opposite prescription. Advocates of automatic monetary policy further argue that discretionary monetary policy depends upon a degree of accuracy in forecasting which is beyond our present capabilities.

The proposal itself involves the rule that the money supply should be allowed to grow at approximately the same rate as the long-run rate of growth in productivity. The reason for choosing this rate of growth, of course, is to maintain relatively constant prices over the long term, though it is said that the particular growth rate chosen is not of critical importance to the proposal.

The basic reasoning behind the plan is that a constant rate of growth in the money supply will act as an automatic stabilizer. During an expansionary period when aggregate demand is increasing at a more rapid rate than is aggregate output, interest rates would rise, discouraging investment demand and, to some extent, consumption. It is felt that depressions could not become very severe or last very long if the money supply were to increase continuously, that aggregate demand would have to turn up when the money supply gets large enough. In the depression the interest rate would fall to promote increased investment and consumption demand.

Some proponents of this type of plan advocate congressional establishment of the required rate of monetary growth making elected officials responsible for the policy. Others would advise the Board of Governors of the Federal Reserve System to establish the rate as a guide to policy leaving some flexibility for unusual circumstances. Having such a clear-cut rule of policy would eliminate one important source of uncertainty in the economy. Whereas discretionary policy requires planners to forecast what the monetary authorities will do, a rule requires planners to forecast only the more fundamental variables of the economy.

There are, of course, objections raised to this proposal. Advocates of flexible monetary policy feel it is needed to adapt to different growth conditions and changes in the world economic scene. They also argue that discretionary monetary policy has functioned well when given a chance to work. They feel that a fixed growth rate subject to change by Congress would become a political "football." It would not achieve the advantages claimed for it, but would create new uncertainty in trying to figure out what Congress would do.

The implication that stable growth in the money supply would lead to a more even rate of growth is also open to question. As was seen in Part II on causal factors in the cycle, real changes take place in supply and demand, and these lead to changes in economic activity. The cycle would be different if the money supply were set at a fixed rate of growth, but it would not be eliminated.

The 100 Percent Reserve Plan

An earlier proposal has some of the same features as the proposal for automatic monetary control. It is the proposal for required bank reserves of 100 percent against demand deposits, advocated first by the late Professor Irving Fisher, of Yale. It would abolish the present fractional reserve requirements for commercial banks by forcing them to keep a 100 percent reserve against all demand deposits and to separate completely the deposit and checking function from the investment function. This scheme would remove the power to create credit from the banking system. Any additional funds needed would have to be supplied by the Federal Reserve banks, the Treasury, or some new monetary authority.

There is little question but that the elimination of the ability of the banking system to create credit would lead to some changes in the economy. One effect would be to speed up the velocity of money. This has happened during periods of monetary restraint in recent years. If such restraint became a regular condition in periods of full employment, this development would be intensified. This would be especially true in boom periods in which the demand for funds was unusually high. It could lead to such steps as further vertical integration in industry to eliminate the need for funds to pay for goods in the process of production, and the financing of wholesalers and retailers by manufacturers until goods were sold to the consumer. It is possible that cycles would develop in velocity that would lead to a continuation of the business cycle in a form similar to its present one.

New problems would be likely to develop that would intensify cyclical problems rather than help solve them. There would be continual pressure on the monetary authority for additional monetary supplies during an upswing. This could well add monetary uncertainty, which would be more disturbing to business than the present fluctuations. It is also possible that other problems would be created. Credit creation may make it easier for new businesses to obtain funds and thus employ capital and labor than it would be under a system in which the money supply remained stable and funds for new concerns had to come from other sectors of the economy. The 100 percent reserve plan, instead of working out as its sponsors hope, could create additional problems for growing businesses and add new political problems to the economic sphere.

It is, nevertheless, easy to understand the appeal of the 100 percent reserve plan to so many early economists. In the years before the development of the theory and practice of central banking, the money supply was controlled by private profit oriented businesses, commercial banks. When it was profitable for banks to increase the money supply, they did so. When it was good bank business practice to decrease the money supply, they did so. Usually, when the health of the economy would require increases in the money supply, bank policy dictated reductions in the money supply, and vice versa. Banks were accused of "booming the boom" and "busting the bust."

With the current faith in the ability of the central bank to control the money supply, interest in and advocacy of 100 percent banking have diminished. Even those who favor the plan in principle concede that the gains achieved by its adoption might be more than offset by the disruption of the institutional structure of banking in the United States.

Plans to Keep Money Circulating

Another group of monetary proposals revolves around the maintenance of the level of consumer expenditures. Such schemes as those of Townsend for giving large sums to old people provided they spend them during the same month and those of Major Douglas for handing out dividends to consumers have little to commend them since, if the money is raised by taxes, they would be unjustified transfer payments and, if it is raised by credit creation, the result can only be disastrous inflation. Others following the German economist, Gesell, have advocated taxes on idle funds so as to keep money moving. For example, it has been suggested that a stamp worth two cents be placed on a dollar each week to provide an incentive to keep it moving. To make a tax on money effective, taxes on bank deposits would also be required. There have also been advocates of taxes on depreciation reserves not expended during the year and suggestions that uninvested income be taxed at a higher rate than invested income.

All such schemes would create new difficulties for consumers and businessmen in planning expenditure and investment programs and in all events do not get at the heart of the problem, for the economy always produces sufficient purchasing power to buy all goods produced. Such schemes would also increase inflationary pressures during periods of full employment since they put a premium on the rapid spending of funds. The bias of the underconsumptionist is evident in this approach to policy. While it appears to be true that insufficiency of aggregate demand is frequently an important problem, at other times excessive demand turns out to be the evil to combat.

The Commodity Dollar

A more far-reaching proposal has been made by Benjamin Graham, who has suggested a monetary system under which a group of commodities would be exchangeable for a fixed sum of money. These commodities would be only those dealt in on organized exchanges and those which are nonperishable enough so that they can be stored. Graham has suggested using such commodities as barley, cocoa, coffee, copper, cotton, flaxseed, gold, hides, lead, rye, tobacco, sugar, wheat, and zinc. The government would stand ready to exchange a composite unit of these commodities for a $1,000 certificate at any time. The composition of the commodity unit would be determined by the consumption of the various commodities in the previous decade. Therefore, prices could still fluctuate in response to supply and demand, but the whole package would be stabilized since it could be exchanged for a set sum of money.

Since the government would stand ready to exchange commodity units and dollar units, it is the hope of the sponsor that inflation and deflation would both be avoided because supplies would be built up in periods of subnormal demand and reduced in periods of above normal demand. Such a plan would give support to some of the markets that are most demoralized in a depression period.

Such advantages as this scheme may have, however, would probably be overbalanced by some serious problems that it would occasion. Serious problems of a political nature would have to be faced whenever it became necessary to change the composition of the group of commodities because of long-run changes in the demand for some of them. It would likewise be difficult to keep a fixed price for such a group of commodities, many of which are the products of agriculture, if powerful labor unions were demanding and receiving wage increases that were greater than increases in productivity and thus raising the prices of the manufactured goods farmers had to buy.

Commodity Reserve Plan

Frank Graham has suggested that this multiple commodity reserve plan should be extended to all standard storable goods instead of including only raw materials. He would have an affiliate corporation of the Federal Reserve System purchase liens on any accruing inventory in an amount sufficient to cover a businessman's out-of-pocket costs. Graham maintains that this plan would ensure high production levels since the producer would be better off by producing at his normal level than by cutting production. This scheme adds difficulties to those that would be experienced under Benjamin Graham's plan. A large bureaucracy would be needed to set the amount of out-of-pocket costs. With an assured market, prices might not be lowered as far as they should be to bring long-run supply and demand into balance, and thus additional rigidities would result. Business expansion might also easily be carried to unprofitable lengths since the penalty for mistakes would not be as immediate or as great as it is now.

THE PROBLEM OF A LONG-RUN INFLATIONARY BIAS

The review of the effectiveness of monetary policy since the Accord showed that in the recent booms and recession price pressures and inflation existed despite stringent policies of credit restraint. The Federal Reserve was hampered in promoting growth and also in fighting the recession because of the need to restrain price rises. The reaction of prices during this period and other economic developments have led many to feel that the economy has developed a long-run inflationary bias.

The following factors are used to varying degrees to substantiate the case for such a bias. Prices and wages tend to rise during periods of boom as is to be expected in a competitive economy. This tendency is reinforced by wage contracts that provide escalator clauses to keep wages in line with prices and by wage increases, which are at times greater than increases in productivity. During recessions prices tend to remain stable rather than to decrease as they formerly did. This is due to the power of major unions not only to resist pay cuts in depressions, but also to get pay increases in recession years, through long-run contracts calling for annual wage increases irrespective of economic conditions at the time. It is also helped along by the tendency of large corporations to rely on nonprice competition rather than cut prices. Furthermore, if prices do decline drastically in a field, government programs are likely to be used to help take excess supplies off the market.

There is little doubt that prices would decline in a severe and prolonged depression. Government takes action to restore employment, however, before such a depression is reached, and the downward price pressure of a depression has been lost. As stated in Chapter 23, the inflation resulting from these factors has been referred to as administrative inflation. This is to distinguish it from the type of inflation that results from demand exceeding the available supply of goods, either because demand is increasing more rapidly than supply in the early stages of a recovery period, or because demand from monetary expansion by the banking system or the government exceeds available supply.

Traditional monetary policy is not wholly effective to combat administrative inflation. If money supplies are restricted enough, prices can be kept in line; but this will lead to chronic unemployment and slow growth. It also makes it difficult for new firms and small growing firms to get credit since lending policies are likely to be conservative.

Administrative inflation calls for new tools of governmental policy if it is to be dealt with effectively. Several courses of action have been proposed, but none has gained general acceptance. One proposal is to outlaw industry-wide bargaining so as to cut the power of unions to obtain wage increases of an inflationary type. Another is to outlaw escalator clauses. A related proposal is to return to one-year contracts in order to provide greater flexibility in adapting wage policies to economic conditions.

Another series of proposals would have a present or new federal agency hold public hearings on any price or wage increase that threatened price stability. After a waiting period, industry and labor would still be free to set prices and wages. It is hoped that publicity would forestall or moderate inflationary increases. Some proposals go further, calling for the board to decide on the prices and wages needed to maintain stability, but still leaving management and labor free to take final action. More drastic proposals call for price and wage controls, some in general and some only in basic industries. Another proposal is to use the tax program to discourage profits from administrative inflation. Profits above a predetermined level would be taxed at steeply progressive rates.

There is no one solution to the problem of administrative inflation, and it is not likely to be solved easily or soon. It will probably
be one of the major economic problems to face our nation in the near
future.

QUESTIONS

1. Distinguish between Roosa's defensive and dynamic policies of the
   Federal Reserve.
2. Outline the connection between the monetary authority, the
   monetary base, the money supply, and real income, price levels,
   interest rates, and employment.
3. Contrast the flexibility of prices and wages, upward and downward.
4. What kind of time lags exist between the time the need for monetary
   policy occurs and the time the effect of monetary policy on the
   economy takes place?
5. Evaluate the several tools of monetary policy.
6. Describe the factors that affect bank reserves. Which of these does
   the Federal Reserve control?
7. Describe the use of the instruments of monetary policy to affect
   the trend of economic activity and cyclical and seasonal fluctuations.
8. Describe and evaluate monetary policy in the post-World War II
   period.
9. Evaluate arguments for and against the use of selective credit
   controls to combat inflation and influence growth.
10. Which factors are used to support the case for a long-run infla-
    tionary bias?

SUGGESTED READINGS

The American Assembly. *United States Monetary Policy.* New York: Columbia University Press, 1959.

American Bankers Association. *Proceedings of a Symposium on Money, Interest Rates, and Economic Activity.* New York: The American Bankers Association, 1967.

American Economic Association, Subcommittee of. "The Problem of Economic Instability," *American Economic Review*, XL (September, 1950), 505–38.

Anderson, Clay J. *A Half Century of Federal Reserve Policymaking, 1914– 1964.* Philadelphia: Federal Reserve Bank of Philadelphia, 1965.

Commission on Money and Credit. *Money and Credit: Their Influence on Jobs, Prices, and Growth.* Englewood Cliffs, New Jersey: Prentice-Hall, Inc., 1961. Parts I–III.

Friedman, Milton. *A Program for Monetary Stability.* New York: Fordham University Press, 1959.

Goldenweiser, E. A. *Monetary Management.* New York: McGraw-Hill Book Company, 1949.

Means, Gardiner C. *Administrative Inflation and Public Policy.* Washington: Anderson Kramer Associates, 1959.

Ohlin, Bertil. *The Problem of Employment Stabilization.* New York: Columbia University Press, 1949.

Ritter, Lawrence S. (ed.). *Money and Economic Activity, Readings in Money and Banking*, 3rd ed. Boston: Houghton Mifflin Co., 1967.

Roosa, Robert V. *Federal Reserve Operations in the Money and Government Securities Markets.* New York: Federal Reserve Bank of New York, 1956.

Walker, Pinkney C. (ed.). *Essays in Monetary Policy.* Columbia, Missouri: University of Missouri Press, 1965.

CHAPTER 25 · *Fiscal Policy and Other Programs for Economic Growth and Stability*

In this chapter attention will be directed to fiscal and other governmental programs designed to promote economic growth and stability. These include measures designed to help stabilize disposable income, to influence the propensity to consume out of a given level of income, and to influence the level of investment of all types. This may be done indirectly by means of fiscal policy or by more direct controls, such as price and wage controls. Government policies can also be used to stabilize the level of economic activity arising out of international transactions. A large part of this chapter will consider the overall role of government fiscal policy in promoting long-run growth and stability.

AUTOMATIC STABILIZERS

The workings of a free frictionless economic system are characterized by a multitude of automatically stabilizing forces. When unemployment occurs, wages fall to restore full employment. Excesses or deficiencies of aggregate demand are self-correcting by rising or falling price levels. Imbalances in international transactions are automatically adjusted by gold flows or exchange rate fluctuations. Such equilibrating mechanisms are at the core of most of the great body of economic theory. If these adjustment variables are fully operative the need for economic policy by government is lessened considerably.

However, to the extent that rigidities in prices, wages, interest rates, and so on, exist, and to the extent that factors of production are not completely mobile, the automatic stabilizers of the economy fail to produce the precise results of competitive theory. One view of the role of government in the economy is to break down the frictions that arise and restore, as much as possible, the self-adjusting economy. Others are pessimistic about the ability of government to bring about this result and call for more direct action to cure the resulting evils.

Still another approach is to design the federal government's receipts and outlays in such a way as to provide automatic stabilizers for the economy. In order to accomplish this function, receipts must fall and outlays rise when the economy is moving downward; and receipts must rise and outlays fall when the economy is expanding. We demand somewhat more than this of our fiscal policy since our goal is not simply stability, but stability at a high (near full employment) level of activity.

Our "pay-as-you-go" progressive income tax structure provides us with our most important automatic stabilizer in the sense that as income increases, the withdrawal of purchasing power from the private sector gets progressively greater; and, conversely, during periods of declining income, the withdrawals or taxes decrease more than proportionally. With the progressive income tax then, disposable income will increase and decrease as the GNP increases and decreases but the variation in the former will be much less than in the GNP. For this reason, consumption demand is less volatile than it would be expected to be if taxes were less progressive; and if consumption expenditures are relatively stable, this will have a stabilizing influence on investment expenditures.

The best example of an automatic stabilizer in the complete sense is the unemployment insurance program because it is tied directly to the social goal of full employment. As long as people are out of work, payments from the unemployment compensation fund will continue. Such payments are injections into the flow of national income — large when unemployment is great, small but still positive even when unemployment is small. Contributions into the fund are withdrawals from the income stream and vary as income varies. Thus the entire program acts to stabilize disposable income and serves as a depressant to national income when full employment exists and inflation threatens, but is a stimulant to national income whenever the economy is operating at less than full employment.

The corporate income tax also is an automatic stabilization force even though the rates are not progressive in any very significant way. The reason is that corporate profits themselves tend to increase more than proportionally when national income increases, and decrease more than proportionally when national income decreases. In this way government withdraws spending power from the private economy progressively as income increases.

Other government programs contribute stability to the economy automatically, such as the agricultural price support programs and the social security programs, but none are as important as those we have already mentioned.

The Full Employment Surplus Concept

The Council of Economic Advisers has developed a very interesting technique by means of which one can evaluate and distinguish clearly those elements of government activity that are called the automatic stabilizers, and those which are not automatic, but discretionary acts. The focus of this tool is on the surplus or deficit in the budget of the federal government under the given set of laws and regulations and various levels of national income.

It was shown in Chapter 7 that a deficit financed by monetary expansion was multiplicatively expansionary to the national income, and that a surplus, together with money contraction, was multiplicatively contractive to the national income. Since, as we have just seen, some government expenditures and some government revenues depend upon national income, the size of the deficit or surplus cannot be known unless the size of national income is known. This is shown in Chart 25-1 shown on page 616.

The chart shows that under Fiscal Program A, a surplus of 1 percent of GNP will occur in the event that GNP is at its full potential, and a balanced budget will take place if GNP is 95 percent of potential GNP. At lower levels of actual GNP, budget deficits will come about.

Each of the fiscal programs charted reflects the tax and spending plans of a particular set of laws. The lines all have positive slopes because of the assumption that tax revenues and/or expenditures always vary positively with GNP. Since the horizontal axis is GNP as percent of potential GNP, we can compare the degree of "drag" on national income expansion of two budget plans at different times or places, or, most significantly, of any two proposed fiscal programs.

Fiscal programs with steep slopes are powerful in their counter cyclical effects. Falling incomes bring about rapid decreases in surpluses or increases in deficits; and rising incomes precipitate large decreases in deficits or increases in surpluses. On Chart 25-1, Programs A, B and E all have the same slope; Program C is a weak counter cyclical plan; and Program D is the extreme in its strong

Chart 25-1

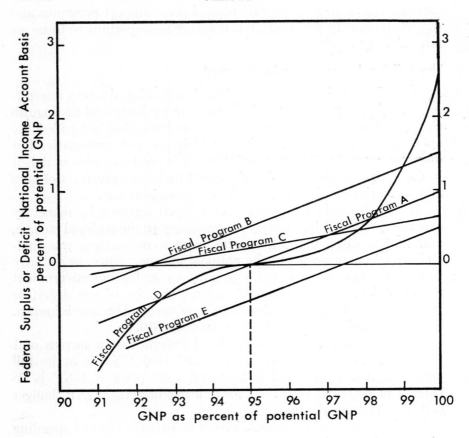

anticyclical impact since surpluses increase at an increasing rate and deficits decrease at an increasing rate.

The line shifts upward whenever an increase in taxes is included in the budget, or when a reduction of spending plans is programmed. Shifting the program lines is called discretionary fiscal policy. If, for example, the economy were operating at about 90 percent of its potential and Fiscal Program *B* were in effect, there would be great pressure to include new spending proposals and/or tax cuts to help stimulate the economy. The function would then shift to Program *A* or, if the action were still more dramatic, to Program *E*.

It is very important to realize that a change in spending or taxes that will produce a given increase in the size of the deficit at the current level of GNP will result in a much smaller deficit, since the action itself would be expected to increase GNP. What that actual deficit would be could only be forecasted, which could be done in the manner of our models in Chapters 6, 7 and 8 supplied with the statistical values of the parameters.

The utilization rate at which the fiscal program line crosses the balanced budget line presumably should be about at that point where it is estimated that further increases in GNP would be largely through inflation.

Balanced versus Unbalanced Budgets

Since the 1930's most economists have struggled to gain acceptance for the idea of planned divergences from the balanced federal budget. Most of the population thought of deficits as immoral or at least as very poor business practice and dangerous. It needed pointing out that deficits could bring about desired expansion of the economy, and it was important to analyze unemotionally the significance of growth in the national debt. As a matter of fact, deficits can be very harmful but so can budget surpluses and even balanced budgets. Under different business conditions each budget situation can be appropriate.

The balanced budget principle does serve the important function of acting as a disciplinary device. At or near full employment any use of resources by the federal government implies the giving up of desired goods or services by the private sectors of the economy. In this condition two basic questions need to be answered. First, does the government's use render a greater "social" utility than the private use? This question has an answer only through the (hopefully democratic) political process. The second question is: Are taxes the best way to induce the private sector to give up the necessary resources? It should be clear that there are alternatives.

The two alternatives to taxation as a means of financing government expenditures are borrowing from the public by issuing interest-bearing bonds or other forms of indebtedness, and borrowing from the public by causing to have issued noninterest-bearing debt, namely, money. How different are they from each other and from taxes?

When government acquires its ability to command resources by taxation of individuals, all evidence indicates that the taxpayer does reduce his own demand for goods and services. The balanced budget multiplier theory indicates that the public does not voluntarily give up quite as much as the government spends so that at full employment an increase in government expenditures matched by increased taxes will have some inflationary effect.

If government acquires its ability to command resources by the sale of bonds, it is not necessarily true that the bond buyers reduce their demand for goods and services at all. The buyers may simply shift from private security holdings to government security holdings, but the result will be for interest rates to rise, which will reduce demand by business for investment and may increase saving (decrease consumption demand) somewhat. If an increase in government spending is matched by an increase in government debt without a change in the money supply, the result on aggregate demand is not greatly different from the increased tax case. There is a difference on the balance sheets of the public in that more government securities are outstanding, and this may influence future consumption behavior.

If increased government spending is made possible by an increase in the money supply, the situation is quite different from the tax and debt expansion method. The money supply will increase if the Treasury borrows from the Federal Reserve System, spends out of its past accumulation of deposits in the Federal Reserve, or issues new gold certificates or new Treasury currency. The money supply may or may not increase if the Treasury borrows from commercial banks, depending upon the reserve position of the banks. When the money supply does increase to allow the additional government spending, the public will give up resources but it must be done by rising prices, the process we referred to earlier as "forced saving."

Inflation redistributes the use of resources from the private to the government sector just as does taxation or borrowing, but it does it in capricious ways. The people who pay may or may not be the ones society's principles would decree ought to pay. In particular, it strikes without reference to economic contribution, equity, ability to pay, or any other criterion.

The situation is considerably different if the economy is experiencing serious unemployment. Then any action that increases aggregate demand can increase output without increasing prices. This is the reason for recommending a deficit, and, if real impetus is needed, to finance it in such a way as to increase the money supply.

In less than full employment conditions government may be able to increase its use of resources without the private sector giving up any because the resources might otherwise be unused.

In order to insure that expenditures, planned or started while the economy was suffering from unemployment, are important enough that the public is willing to pay for them when they must, it is sometimes proposed that tax rates be set to cover the spending at full employment. In terms of Chart 25-1, the fiscal program line would rotate to become steeper but still intersect the balanced budget line at the same point.

We have been speaking here as if the question of balanced versus unbalanced budgets were purely an economic question. In fact, as our news media continuously remind us, the political implications of taxing and spending are often controlling.

THE DUAL BUDGET

Some countries, notably Denmark and Sweden, have adopted a dual budget in which the ordinary operating expenses of government and capital expenditures are separated. Under such a budget system, tax rates are set high enough so that on the average in good years and bad the operating budget is in balance. With fixed tax rates there is, of course, a surplus in prosperity and a deficit in depressions.

Capital expenditures for all types of public construction are planned on a long-term basis and budgeted separately. The funds are raised initially by borrowing, but interest payments and depreciation are added to the operating budget. Only such public construction is carried on as the public is willing to pay for over its life in the operating budget. In short, the same accounting and cost determination practices used in private business are used in government accounting and financial planning. Insofar as possible, capital expenditures are made in years of recession or depression.

A dual budget is not necessarily related to the use of fiscal policy for growth and stability. It is primarily a device to put government operations on a basis of sound planning. Public construction is carried out only if the electorate is willing to assume the full cost of it over its life. It prevents deficits for which no repayment procedure exists. A dual budget, however, facilitates compensatory fiscal planning. It also helps remove many fears of the evil consequences of growing deficits since plans are made to meet the costs of all expenditures over their period of usefulness.

STABILIZATION POLICY

To correct short-run instability, compensatory fiscal policy is being used to an increasing degree. Few advocates of a governmental budget that is balanced year by year remain. To raise governmental revenues or cut expenses in a depression can only help accentuate the downturn.

As has been described, several automatic stabilizers exist in government expenditure and tax programs. To date no use has been made of formulas to guide government action, but some have been proposed. For example, one proposal would automatically cut tax rates when unemployment reached 5 million workers. An alternative formula would set different tax schedules for varying economic conditions, but allow the executive branch of the government to determine when each had been reached.

There are advantages and disadvantages to each course of action. Most economists agree that built-in stabilizers are desirable. Only a few believe they can do the whole job of promoting stability even in relatively minor recessions and certainly not in major recessions. Proponents of built-in stabilizers, and beyond that of special action in each situation, feel economic developments differ enough in each period of prosperity and recession so that each case should be met in the light of its own special features. Unemployment may temporarily top a set level of 5 million workers, for example, but the outlook may be such that inflation is a major hazard and a tax cut, therefore, would be unwise. Some also feel that in a free enterprise economy government should interfere as little as possible and, therefore, oppose intervention approved on a permanent basis under a formula plan.

Proponents of formula plans feel specific action is too slow and too uncertain as to timing. Congress is not always in session and has so many problems that economic action does not always get immediate attention. Furthermore, the business community and consumers are faced with uncertainty since they are not sure that Congress will act or in what way.

When a recession is severe enough so that larger deficits than those resulting from built-in stabilizers or formulas are required to promote recovery, there is seldom complete agreement on the course of action to follow. A decision must be made on changing the level of government spending or the total amount of tax receipts. Increased expenditures or a tax cut of the same amount might involve the same number of dollars initially, but the economic effects would not be the same. If income taxes are cut, disposable income is increased almost immediately under our system of tax withholding. This provides additional income for all sectors of the economy, and an increase in demand for many types of goods. The amount of the increase in relation to the tax cut depends on the proportion of the funds that are spent by the recipients of the tax cut.

If increased expenditures are decided on, the amount of the expenditures determines the initial increase in income for the economy. But the effects of increased expenditures occur more slowly than those of a tax cut since it takes time to get programs started and to complete them. The increased income arises in the first instance in those sectors of the economy in which the money is spent. Thus, the major effect initially will be on specific areas of the economy, not on the economy as a whole.

The secondary effects of spending from a tax cut or from increased government expenditures depend on what the recipients do with the income. To the extent that they spend it on current consumption, total spending is further increased in the short run. The goods for which they spend it determine the sectors of the economy that receive a boost in income. If they invest the added income and it is used for purchasing capital goods, spending is also increased, but with a time lag and in different sectors of the economy. If the money is saved and is added to idle funds available for investment, there is no secondary effect on spending.

The same general types of effects must be considered if economic activity is to be restrained by a decrease in expenditures on the part of the government or by a tax increase. A decrease in expenditures by the government will cut expenditures by at least that amount, and the secondary effects may cut it further. A tax increase may not cut expenditures by the amount of the cut since some taxpayers may keep up their level of spending by reducing saving out of current income or by using past savings. It could, however, cut total expenditures even more if higher taxes discouraged some spending that was currently taking place, such as that on home building or on consumer durable goods bought on credit. This could lead to a cut in spending that was substantially greater than the amount of money taken by the higher taxes.

A decision must not only be made on changing total tax revenues or total expenditures, but also on changing the pattern of taxes or spending. For example, if the durable consumer goods field is depressed and the demand for nondurables has held up well, a cut in excise taxes on durable goods, such as automobiles, may stimulate demand more effectively in this area than a general income tax cut. Cutting income taxes in the middle and upper tax brackets may stimulate demand for durables more effectively than a general tax cut that provides a smaller amount of added disposable income to many people. But in a severe depression, either course of action may be ineffective since the outlook of consumers is so pessimistic that most of them will not make a major expenditure, especially one requiring installment financing. Another example is that of an inflationary economy in which demand for consumer durables is especially strong. An increase in excise taxes on durables would restrain such demand more than an increase in general income taxes producing the same number of dollars of total revenue.

Just as different types of tax changes have different economic effects so do different expenditure programs. If housing is depressed, an increase in public housing expenditures will do more good than an increase in expenditures on conservation; whereas, if rural areas are depressed, the latter may do more good. If steel is depressed, an increase in major public works will provide more stimulus than will a general increase in many categories of government expenditures. If housing demand is inflationary, a decrease in expenditures on public housing will help restrain price pressures; if demand for capital equipment is well ahead of supply, a decrease in government purchases in this area will be beneficial, and so on.

In deciding on a course of action long-run and short-run factors must be considered. In the short run the effect on areas in which unemployment exists is important. Timing is also very important. Major public works, for example, do little to promote stability in a minor recession. By the time work is well underway and the major part of the expenditures is being made, full employment may have been restored and the effect may well be inflationary.

Long-run effects are of major significance and cannot be ignored, especially in a continuing program to promote stability. If demand is stimulated in a field such as agriculture or consumer durables, the effect may be to put off long-run adjustments that are needed for economic balance. There may be too large a proportion of resources in the field to meet current and foreseeable future demands. In a society as dynamically changing as ours, there will always be some industries that will die out and be replaced by new ones. No action should be taken to continue production of goods no longer in demand. In such cases, it would be more effective to promote increased mobility of the resources to other fields or diversification to bring new products into the field to use the excess resources. This also holds true when providing aid to depressed geographical areas of the country. Other long-run effects are also important. For example, when new public parks and buildings are built, continuing expenditures are needed to maintain them. Thus, current expenditures are increased for the long run. Or, if demand is restrained by high tax rates, the propensity to save may be reduced and a shortage of funds for investment may develop. Or, if taxes are cut to stimulate demand, political consideration may make it all but impossible to raise taxes when needed and inflation may be stimulated in the next recovery.

There are many ways in which fiscal policy may be used to promote stability. It can only succeed if it is properly used to achieve the desired effects. This means that the effects of proposed courses of action must be carefully studied both in the short run and in the long run. Integrated programs must be developed to achieve the short-run and long-run goals that have been decided on. To date little progress has been made in this type of planning of government action to promote stability.

LONG-RUN GROWTH POLICY

Until recently the role of the government in promoting short-run stability has received more attention than its role in promoting long-run growth. The analysis of growth in Chapter 23 indicated that growth was dependent upon some factors in the public sector as well as some in the private sector of the economy. If optimum growth is to be achieved, services provided by the government must also grow to meet the needs of the economy. This includes all of the services regularly provided by state and local governments. If some areas cannot afford adequate services, such as education, growth would be aided by having the overall economy provide them. This raises questions about states' rights and government interference in education, but there is little question about it as a means of promoting growth. Services provided by the federal government must also keep pace with the economy. This includes federal highways, waterways, and other major projects called "social capital." It also includes such programs as the United States Employment Service, the activities of the Department of Labor to promote labor peace and help settle strikes, and the work of the Federal Trade Commission.

The need for a growing government program in these areas, growing as the economy grows, is by and large not subject to much disagreement. Some disagreement arises over who will do it — local units, the states, or the federal government — and there is some hesitancy in paying for it. Some hold that the government contribution to growth ends with providing the needed services for an expanding economy. Beyond this, they believe that the greatest contribution government can make is to provide an environment in which private investment can grow. Government programs to stimulate private investment, including aid to research, have been discussed. Some have advocated government investment programs, which are greatly increased in scope and in the volume of funds involved. Such programs have long been advocated by those who feel they are sound in themselves. But recently some have advocated programs of increased government investment as a means of speeding up economic growth. They would increase government investment in such fields as public housing, schools, hospitals, public buildings, and power projects, not only to meet needs in these fields, but primarily to speed up the rate of growth.

Increased government investment programs can, of course, only speed up the rate of growth when it is not at optimum levels. Those who advocate an expanded government investment program on a regular basis feel this is generally true, or true so much of the time that the loss of goods to the private sector would not be material.

GROWTH POLICY FOR UNDERDEVELOPED ECONOMIES

Promotion of long-run growth in underdeveloped societies is usually hamstrung by an insufficiency of saving. It is difficult to ask a people whose standard of living is already far below that of people of well-developed economies to reduce their current consumption even more. Aside from gifts or loans from other countries, more saving is necessary to increase the rate of capital building.

There are steps a government can take to encourage growth in saving aside from the obvious one that so many of such governments seem to favor; that is, they tax the public (a form of saving) or cause inflation (forced saving), and build capital projects with the proceeds. Making the business environment attractive to foreign investors is a relatively painless way to encourage economic development without domestic saving, but this process is frequently hampered by the political popularity of extreme nationalism. Political instability also militates against economic growth by directing resources to the creation of armies and other monuments. It may even lead to the export of the resources saved by the portion of the population that does save.

Financial institutions and instruments fitted to the particular needs of the people can be a significant stimulus to saving and to an efficient direction of saving into the right forms of investment. Actions that lead to smaller families may have the effect of raising per capita income and thus make saving less painful. In fact, anything which results in a larger proportion of productive workers to the total population ought to expand savings. Education and propaganda informing the population of the benefits of thrift and how to accomplish saving may ultimately be a most important policy governments of developing nations must formulate.

GOVERNMENTAL PROGRAMS
TO INFLUENCE SECTOR BEHAVIOR

Up to this point we have dealt with the overall impact on economic activity of the federal budget. Here we shall consider what can be done to influence the spending behavior of the other economic sectors — consumption by households, investment by business, and foreign trade with the rest of the world. Here, the focus is not upon the amount of spending or taxing that may be involved, but upon the particular method or direction the spending or taxing may take. Furthermore, some of the programs require little or no taxing or spending.

Governmental Programs to Influence the Propensity to Consume out of a Given Level of Disposable Income

The government can use its powers to influence the propensity to consume out of a given level of income and has done so to some extent. This has been true primarily in wartime when programs in this area were designed to reduce inflationary pressures, but some programs of this type have been used in peacetime and others have been advocated.

The propensity to consume can be affected by changing the relative relationship between the level of wages and profits. This has been done on a limited basis by laws favorable to union bargaining positions. Since the marginal propensity to consume (MPC) out of wages appears to be greater than the MPC out of profit, such actions are defended by some when the assumption is made that the long-run problem is too low a level of consumer demand. Excess profits taxes also alter the division of the national income, but they have usually been instituted during wartimes on emotional rather than on economic grounds. Direct price, wage, and production controls, along with rationing, also have an important effect on the propensity to consume and have been used in wartime. They are frequently threatened during peacetime inflations, but, thankfully, have not been imposed up to this writing.

Another possibility that has not been used to date is to tax consumption and saving at different rates. In periods of inflation a tax on consumption has been advocated in the form of a federal sales tax.

Excise taxes on particular commodities have been imposed during inflations, and reduced or eliminated during slack periods as counter cyclical acts. In depressions some have advocated taxing saving so as to encourage spending. The proposal to tax spending in an inflationary period has been given serious consideration in the World War II and postwar period, but it has not been used to date.

Another possibility is to stimulate saving so as to reduce the propensity to consume. This has been done through campaigns to buy bonds, especially through payroll savings plans. This worked reasonably well during World War II, but it has had little effect in the postwar period of inflation. Proposals have been made for compulsory savings programs in inflationary periods, but they have received little support except during wartime. Pronouncements by the President and other major government officials to encourage or discourage consumption spending are made at different times. It is not likely that this kind of "jawbone fiscal policy" is very effective.

The social security program probably has had a long-run effect on the propensity to consume. If some of the economic uncertainties of life, due to unemployment, sickness, and old age are lessened, there is less need for current saving. To the extent that a single large-scale insurance type program is more efficient than many individual programs, the propensity to consume is increased. Guaranteed annual incomes and guaranteed financing of education would presumably have the same effect. These programs could not be used countercyclically, but could be used as secular stimulants to consumption.

Government Programs to Influence Investment Expenditures

Government programs also have an influence on investment expenditures, primarily on expenditures for plant and equipment and for housing, but also to a limited degree on expenditures for inventories. Tax incentives have been used to some extent to stimulate investment in plant and equipment. Rapid amortization of facilities needed to meet defense needs stimulated such construction. There have been proposals to use rapid amortization in a period of recession to stimulate capital goods demand, especially in the 1957–1958 downturn. A conscious effort to encourage investment in durable capital goods was the 7 percent tax credit granted to firms making such expenditures. It was instituted in 1962 when it was thought that such stimulation was needed, and it was revoked in 1966 when the fear of an overheated economy prevailed. More powerful variants of this technique are obviously possible up to a 100 percent tax credit on income used for investment purposes.

The effect of corporate income taxes and changes in the corporation tax on investment is different from the effect of the personal income tax and changes therein on consumption. Actually, the important effect of the tax on corporations is likely to be on consumption since it lowers the disposable income of stockholders and/or of the other suppliers of resources.[1] It is true that any tax change which influences expectations of future consumption will have an effect on investment spending, but we shall now proceed to demonstrate that any direct effect on investment by corporate income taxes in likely to be very small.

This, at first surprising, conclusion can be demonstrated with a simple example. Suppose a firm has an investment opportunity under consideration that is expected to yield a net return of 10

---

[1]The incidence of the corporate profits tax is not entirely resolved in the theoretical literature of the subject. For our purpose, identification of the final bearer of the tax is unimportant.

percent. If we can show that the decision to invest or not invest is the same if the corporate tax is 50 percent or if the tax is zero, we should agree that the tax has no effect on investment. For this example, we will assume that the firm borrows the $10,000 needed to buy a machine at 5 percent interest, although the same principles are involved if the project is financed through internal funds or by issuance of additional equity capital.

The pertinent figures are the following:

$10,000 cost of machine

$ 2,500 gross annual return

$ 1,000 annual depreciation

$ 500 annual interest cost

$ 1,000 net annual return if taxes are zero ($2,500 – $1,000 – $500)

$ 500 net annual return if taxes are 50 percent ([$2,500 – $1,000 – $500] × [.50])

This example shows that the firm is better off with no taxes than with taxes, but this is completely irrelevant to the question asked. Will the firm invest in both cases? The answer is yes! It may be objected that the firm is not likely to risk $10,000 in order to earn just $500 annually under these conditions. But that is exactly the point. If the tax rate is 50 percent, the firm risks only 50 percent of the initial capital. This can be seen in two ways. First, if the gross return were zero, instead of $2,500 in our first case, the loss to the firm when no taxes exist is $1,500; but if taxes are 50 percent, the loss to the firm is just $750. Thus, while a firm gains more profit when profits are positive if there are no taxes, it also bears the full loss when there are losses. When the corporate tax rate is 50 percent, the government absorbs 50 percent of all losses.

The second way to see the issue involved is to assume that the machine becomes obsolete or is physically destroyed before operations can start. If there are no taxes, the firm has lost the full $10,000. If the taxes are 50 percent the firm can deduct $5,000 of the loss from its other income so that its actual loss is just $5,000. In other words, the government is a full partner in both gains and losses, and the private firm's decision is unaffected by the proportion of the investment the two partners undertake. Returning to our original example, in both the tax and the no-tax case, the return on risked capital is 10 percent (@ 50% tax: $\frac{\$500}{\$5,000} = 10\%$; @ 0% tax: $\frac{\$1,000}{\$10,000} = 10\%$.).

Relating the simple example to the real world, some qualifications are necessary. For the example to work as presented, it is necessary to assume: (1) that the tax is not progressive, which with only minor qualifications is true of the corporate income tax in the United States; and (2) that either the firm has other income which can be offset by any losses, or that unlimited carry forward and back of profit and loss is permitted, which is also quite close to the case in the United States.

Accelerated depreciation allowances for tax purposes is a stimulant to investment, but not to the extent that is frequently assumed. If, as is typically the case, exactly 100 percent depreciation is permitted, then the only difference between fast and slow "write-offs" is that the taxpayer is permitted to use the tax funds for a longer or shorter period of time. The amount of the tax over the lifetime of the capital is the same in both cases. In order to calculate the advantage of accelerated depreciation to the firm, it is necessary to multiply the difference in after-tax profit by the interest rate for the period of time involved. The most effective way to use this instrument is to create the impression that depreciation schedules will be shortened if increased investment is desired. The best way to create that impression is to shorten them "temporarily." Similarly, if excessive demand pressure seems to be the problem, a lengthening of depreciation schedules may induce some investors to wait until more favorable rules abide.

Capital investment is also encouraged by government programs that make financing more easily available to business firms than would be the case without them. This is done on a long-run basis by such agencies as the Small Business Administration. It is also done on a cyclical basis by making larger amounts of funds available to the SBA in a recession period and by establishing general financing programs as was done when the Reconstruction Finance Corporation was set up during the 1929 depression. Capital investment could be stimulated, and has been to a limited degree, by government programs of research. These have been restricted to the fields of health and of scientific developments related to defense and space age needs. But they could be used more generally not only to develop new products and industries and so create more demand for capital goods, but also to do basic research that is needed to make applied research possible.

During inflationary periods it is generally desirable to depress capital goods construction. This is done primarily through monetary policy. It has been done during wartime by direct controls by requiring special permits to get scarce materials for building. This could, of course, be used in highly inflationary periods in peacetime, but it has not been to date. Demand for housing in our economy is also affected by governmental programs. During the depression of the 1930's steps were taken to stabilize mortgage markets by taking low quality mortgages out of the hands of private investors into government agencies and by setting up government guarantees of new mortgages that met preestablished standards. In more recent years the terms of financing on government guaranteed mortgages have been varied to stimulate or depress housing demand. This is done by changing down payments and repayment periods, as well as interest rates.

Direct government construction of public housing can also be used to stabilize total housing demand. In a general way, it has been used in this way, but some public housing has been built even in years of a housing boom. Government programs of urban redevelopment to replace slums with planned housing projects could also be used to foster stability. The pressure for such programs on a long-run basis, however, has kept their use as a stabilization device minor up to the present time.

Inventory investment is largely unaffected by fiscal policies. Monetary policy has an important effect on inventory investment, however. When credit gets tight in recovery, funds are not available for investment in additional inventory without cutting other uses, and this is difficult because all demand is high. Since inventories are financed to a significant degree by short-term bank credit, monetary policy is especially restrictive. Monetary policy is only partially successful, however, in stabilizing inventory investment. Easy credit in recession encourages inventory build-ups, and stocks usually are being built up at a rate that cannot be sustained by increases in demand before credit becomes tight. This has led to a search for other programs to supplement monetary programs. The government has done little in this area, but it has helped businessmen to control stocks more adequately by making current data available on the level of inventories by basic fields and by stages of manufacture. These data help show when inventories are out of line with past relationships to sales. This has been helpful, but fluctuations in the rate of inventory building have continued to be one of the major factors leading to changes in economic activity in minor cycles.

Government Programs to Influence Foreign Trade and Investment

Governments have been engaged in efforts to influence foreign trade and foreign investments since early modern times and even before. They have had only a very limited measure of success with such programs, however, in promoting growth and stability in foreign trade. In the worldwide depression of the late 1920's and early 1930's foreign trade and investment collapsed almost completely.

In the absence of government restrictions a boom or severe depression in a major industrial country has a tendency to spread to other industrialized countries. For example, if a boom exists in the United States, imports are likely to rise. Since imports from England are substantial, the demand for English goods is increased. This creates increased demand and increased price pressure in England. If these are great enough, they can initiate an upward movement in business after a recession. If a boom already exists, they can add to inflationary pressures. The situation is just the reverse in a depression.

Assume, for example, that England and the United States are both experiencing a period of prosperity and that a severe depression develops in the United States. Imports from England will be cut, and this will cut demand for English goods. It will also cut the means of payment for goods from the United States. To pay for these imports from the United States gold will have to be shipped to the United States. This will reduce the money supply and lead to deflation. The Bank of England will take steps to stop the outflow of gold and this will tend to reduce business further. Thus depression will spread to England, from England to countries with which it trades, and so on.

Further problems arise in a severe depression. Traders in a country experiencing low demand will try to sell goods in foreign markets at a price low enough to move them. This helps demoralize business in the foreign countries.

This spread of business cycles from one country to another led most nations to take steps to insulate their economy from the rest of the world. This was done by means of high tariffs, trade quotas, bilateral trade agreements, barter arrangements, and the like. It was also done by changing the value of domestic currency in relationship to gold to make exports cheaper in world markets and imports more expensive and, therefore, less desirable. The result was a complete breakdown of world trade and investment in the 1930's.

In the postwar world efforts have been made to increase world trade. The United States government has increased exports materially by substantial economic aid to foreign countries. Some of this was short-term emergency aid as, for example, under the Marshall Plan. Some of it is continuing aid to help develop economies resisting communist aggression. The general goal of our aid program in the economic sphere is to help a nation develop to the point of paying for its own imports. In Korea, for example, a very large gap exists between imports needed for economic development and exports. American aid is being used to build up the industries producing goods for export so that trade can be brought into balance.

Stability of trade is also furthered by the International Monetary Fund. The Fund provides for short-term credits to take care of temporary unbalances in foreign trade. It also provides an orderly procedure for changing the value of currencies when this is necessary to promote long-run trade equilibrium. Various steps have been taken to make funds available for foreign investment. The American government has made loans through the Export-Import Bank. The World Bank has financed capital development projects in many countries. It gets its funds by selling bonds that are guaranteed by the member countries. Proposals have been made with increasing frequency for guarantees by the American government of foreign investments. Some call for a general guarantee, others would only guarantee losses due to confiscation of property by foreign governments, confiscatory taxes, and changes in exchange rates.

A related proposal would use tax incentives to stimulate foreign investment. Income from foreign investments could be taxed at a lower rate or not at all. One proposal would not tax any income reinvested in foreign projects.

With the heavy outlays by the federal government in foreign military and economic aid and in prosecuting the conflict in Southeast Asia in recent years, the problem has been of the opposite type.

Gold has been flowing out, and a balance of payments deficit has become significant. In an attempt to mitigate this situation a penalty rate has been imposed upon foreign private investment.

The last series of proposals to be discussed provide for some form of international stockpiling of goods. This could be done by coordinating domestic stockpiling programs. It could also be done by a world agency to buy stocks in periods of surpluses and dispose of them in periods of excess supplies. More extreme proposals call for international quotas for production of basic materials. These have had a poor reception in the United States, except for international agreements to stabilize wheat production and prices. Some propose using international stockpiles as collateral for currency issued by a world bank to be used for settling international balances. Such proposals have received little serious consideration in the United States.

INTERRELATIONSHIP OF FISCAL AND MONETARY POLICY

The discussion in this chapter and in the preceding chapter shows clearly that monetary policy and fiscal policy are operating to meet similar objectives. Since this is true, these policies should be coordinated. If the government is adding to purchasing power by means of a deficit, it makes little sense to have a monetary policy of restraint. Both should usually be working in the same direction. This is just as true in a period of inflation and tight money as in recession. The only reason a question arises at all is because in the American economy these two groups of policies are in the main administered by two separate agencies. Monetary policies are largely the responsibility of the Board of Governors of the Federal Reserve System, a nonpolitical board to which members are appointed for 14-year terms and cannot succeed themselves. Since only one member is appointed every two years, there is at no time a wholesale shift in board membership. Fiscal policy is determined by Congress and by the Treasury Department. Congress and the Treasury usually work in harmony, but may not do so completely when Congress is controlled by one political party and the President is from the other party.

Conflicts have arisen from time to time between fiscal and monetary policy. In recent years the conflict has been largely one over interest rates. Federal Reserve monetary policy has raised interest rates materially, and this has also raised the cost of financing the public debt. Since Congress has by law put a ceiling on interest rates on government bonds, the Treasury has been forced to resort to short-term borrowing. Ceilings on the national debt also regularly force the Treasury to act in ways that are inconsistent with its stabilization goals. In such circumstances the Federal Reserve is forced into being the active agent.

Such conflicts of interest and the possibility of more serious conflicts have led to repeated proposals for a central agency to coordinate monetary and fiscal policy. One proposal calls for a national monetary authority. This agency would have representatives of both the Federal Reserve and Treasury on it and would develop policies that both groups would carry out. Other proposals would put the Federal Reserve Board under the Treasury, or make it a board appointed by the President on a political basis. To date the desire to keep monetary policies out of politics and to keep inflation from becoming a political tool has kept the Federal Reserve Board of Governors an independent nonpolitical agency.

Management of the national debt is another tool that can be used to promote economic stability. There is some question as to whether debt management should be considered monetary policy or fiscal policy since it is the responsibility of the Treasury, but its impact is on the liquidity of the economy.

By debt management we mean the changing of the composition of the debt, mainly in its term structure, but also in the other terms such as marketability, callability, interest rates, ownership restrictions, denominations, redeemability characteristics, and other actual and potential terms. The absolute size of the debt is not viewed as a part of debt management, although when the debt is expanded or a portion is retired important questions of debt management do arise.

There are many considerations the Treasury must keep in mind, such as cost and legality, but we shall restrict our attention to the role debt management can play in a stabilization program. The general proposition is that long-term and less liquid government securities should be increased when inflation is the devil; and when depressed conditions exist, the debt should be shifted to a larger proportion of short-term and more liquid forms of securities. Issues must be tailored to fit the needs of particular classes of potential holders, such as insurance companies, commercial banks, wage earners, and industrial concerns.

With a national debt of over $325 billion, its maturity structure is bound to have an impact on the term structure of interest rates of private borrowers. There are times when it seems desirable to try to increase rates at the short end and decrease long-term rates. Debt management can play a part in such an attempt.

Management of the public debt is so closely related to the activities of the Federal Reserve System, particularly in its open-market operations, that coordination is absolutely essential. Significant gains could undoubtedly be achieved by making the Federal Reserve System completely responsible for debt management.[2]

QUESTIONS

1. Explain the concept of "automatic stabilizers."
2. Explain the full employment surplus concept.
3. Explain the concept of "social capital."
4. Evaluate the principle of annually balanced budgets for the federal government.
5. Do you think that the individual states should engage in counter cyclical fiscal policy to the same extent and with the same techniques as the federal government?
6. Write an essay discussing the merits and any shortcomings you might see in a fiscal program incorporating the following rules:
   (a) The current budget should generally be in balance.
   (b) The capital budget should show a deficit in years when heavy capital building takes place, and should show a surplus in years when capital building is lighter than average, but should be balanced over a long span of time,
   (c) Compensatory fiscal policy should concentrate on reducing disposable income when inflation is taking place by a special tax designed specifically for that task.
7. Evaluate the statement that counter cyclical fiscal policy is necessary only because of the imperfections of the free enterprise system and such rigidities in wages, prices, and immobility of resources as are characteristic of our economy.
8. What considerations are involved in determining whether a particular amount of increased government spending should be handled by additional taxes, by increasing the national debt, or by increasing the money supply? State in each case what major effects would be expected, and then the relative merits or evils of these effects.

---

[2]A. G. Hart and P. B. Kenen. *Money, Debt, and Economic Activity* (3rd. ed.; Englewood Cliffs, N. J.: Prentice-Hall, Inc., 1961), pp. 454–457.

9. Why should Treasury debt management policy operate in the direction of lengthening the maturity structure of the national debt during inflationary periods, and shortening its maturity structure in depressed times?

10. State the major problems in achieving an acceptable rate of economic growth. What role can you suggest for government policy?

SUGGESTED READINGS

American Bankers Association. *Proceedings of a Symposium on Federal Taxation.* New York: The American Bankers Association, 1965.

American Economic Association. *Readings in Business Cycle Theory.* Homewood, Illinois: Richard D. Irwin, Inc. (The Blakiston Co.), 1944. Chapters 13 and 14.

American Economic Association. *Readings in Fiscal Policy.* Homewood, Illinois: Richard D. Irwin, Inc., 1955.

Buchanan, James M. *The Public Finances.* Homewood, Illinois: Richard D. Irwin, Inc., 1960.

Clark, John J., and Morris Cohen (eds.). *Business Fluctuations, Growth and Economic Stabilization,* Part IV. New York: Random House, 1963.

Commission on Money and Credit. *Money and Credit: Their Influence on Jobs, Prices, and Growth.* Englewood Cliffs, New Jersey: Prentice-Hall, Inc., 1961. Parts IV-X.

Committee for Economic Development, Research and Policy Committee. *The Budget and Economic Growth.* New York: Committee for Economic Development, 1959.

Committee for Economic Development. *Defense Against Recession.* New York: Committee for Economic Development, 1954.

Economic Report of the President. Washington: U. S. Government Printing Office, annually.

Hart, A. G., and P. B. Kenen. *Money, Debt, and Economic Activity,* 3rd ed. Englewood Cliffs, New Jersey: Prentice-Hall, Inc., 1961.

Hickman, Bert G. *Growth and Stability of the Postwar Economy.* Washington: The Brookings Institution, 1960.

Jacoby, N. H. *Can Prosperity Be Sustained? Policies for Full Employment and Full Production Without Price Inflation in a Free Economy.* New York: Holt, Rinehart and Winston, 1956.

Musgrave, Richard A. *The Theory of Public Finance.* New York: McGraw-Hill Book Company, 1959.

Poole, N. E. (ed.). *Fiscal Policies and the American Economy.* Englewood Cliffs, New Jersey: Prentice-Hall, Inc., 1951.

Smith, Warren L. and Ronald Teigen. *Readings in Money, National Income and Stabilization Policy.* Homewood, Ill.: Richard D. Irwin, Inc., 1965.

Tobin, James. *National Economic Policy.* New Haven, Connecticut: Yale University Press, 1966.

PROBLEMS ON PART VIII

1. Critically evaluate the following quotation from a Federal Reserve study:

   "In one sense, full employment is a political concept rather than a statistical one. In our economic system, where government has only the residual responsibility for providing full employment and private enterprise has the major responsibility, full employment really means that enough jobs are and will be available to make unnecessary government action to create additional jobs. What number of jobs is considered enough will depend on political attitudes as well as on economic facts. Political attitudes about unemployment and employment will vary with time, location of unemployment, cause of unemployment, and who is affected."

2. Explain in your own words the meaning of the following quotation from a Federal Reserve study:

   "Declining Rate of Growth. A more difficult problem arises if the secular percentage rate of growth declines. If this development is not caused by a shortage of productive capacity, but only by the failure of monetary expenditures to expand at the proper rate, the remedy is still relatively simple (at least in theory): larger expenditures (both public and private) should be made. Failure to do so simply means that the productive powers of the economy go unused, creating unemployed men and resources. But if it is the productive powers that fail to expand at a sufficiently rapid rate, the situation is more serious. It means that technological progress has not been sufficiently rapid to offset the limitations imposed on income growth by a stationary population and existing natural resources. Therefore further additions to our productive equipment increase its capacity at a diminishing rate."

3. Outline a program which you believe business, labor, and the government should follow at the present time to promote economic growth and stability.

4. Suppose you observe the following features exhibited by the economy:

   (a) Prices are rising at a fairly rapid rate (say 6 percent per year).

   (b) Interest rates are near their historical highs (say 7 or 8 percent on public utility bonds).

   (c) Unemployment persists at an uncomfortably high level (say 7 or 8 percent of the labor force).

   How do you diagnose the reasons for this state of affairs, and what policy prescriptions would you suggest? Include in your discussion the role of monetary policy, fiscal policy, and other government policies.

5. Some economists (most notably Professor Friedman) argue that increasing the money supply results in increasing interest rates rather than decreasing interest rates as has been generally argued in this book. We have been assuming "other things remaining constant," but in the real world other things are not constant. What other factors do you think could be introduced into the analysis to bring about the result Friedman says is characteristic of the empirical evidence?